Constitutional Law in Italy

Constitutional Law in Italy

Fifth Edition

Valerio Onida†
Marilisa D'Amico
Costanza Nardocci
Enzo Balboni
Ilaria Carlotto
Paolo Cavaleri†
Matteo Nicolini
Maurizio Pedrazza Gorlero
Giovanni Guiglia
Elisabetta Lamarque
Marta Cartabia
Antonio D'Andrea
Fabrizio D'Addabbo†
Lorenzo Spadacini

This book was originally published as a monograph in the International Encyclopaedia of Laws/Constitutional Law.

Founding Editor: Roger Blanpain†
General Editor: Frank Hendrickx
Volume Editors: André Alen & David Haljan

Wolters Kluwer

Published by:
Kluwer Law International B.V.
PO Box 316
2400 AH Alphen aan den Rijn
The Netherlands
E-mail: lrs-sales@wolterskluwer.com
Website: www.wolterskluwer.com/en/solutions/kluwerlawinternational

Sold and distributed by:
Wolters Kluwer Legal & Regulatory U.S.
920 Links Avenue
Landisville, PA 17538
United States of America
Email: customer.service@wolterskluwer.com

ISBN 978-94-035-5880-6

e-Book: ISBN 978-94-035-5890-5
web-PDF: ISBN 978-94-035-5900-1

Printed in The Netherlands.

The Authors

Valerio Onida† has been Professor of Constitutional Law at the University of Milan, Faculty of Law, since 1983. Previously he has been teaching at the Universities of Verona, Sassari, Pavia and Bologna. He was a Justice of the Italian Constitutional Court from 1996 to 2005 and President of the same Court in the last four months of his term. He was the President of the Italian School for the Judiciary from 2011 to 2015. His research activity covers different branches of Italian Constitutional law, namely the budget process and the spending power, the working of the Italian system of government, the Italian regional system and constitutional adjudication. Among his publications are *Pubblica amministrazione e costituzionalità delle leggi* (Milan, 1967); *Le leggi di spesa nella Costituzione* (Milan, 1969); *L'applicazione della Costituzione fra magistratura e Corte costituzionale*, in *Scritti per Mortati* (Milan, 1977); *'Costituzione italiana' e 'Costituzione provvisoria'*, in *Digesto delle discipline pubblicistiche* (Turin, 1990); *Il giudizio di costituzionalità delle leggi. Materiali di giustizia costituzionale*. I. *Il giudizio in via incidentale* (Turin, 1998); *La Costituzione* (Bologna, 20123, 4th ed. continued by M. Cartabia); *Compendio di diritto costituzionale*, with M. Pedrazza Gorlero (Milan, 2023, 6th ed. continued by M. Pedrazza Gorlero).

Enzo Balboni teaches Constitutional Law at the postgraduate School of Specialization for Legal Professions at the Catholic University of Milan, Faculty of Law, where he has also been Professor of Constitutional Law and where he taught Comparative Constitutional Law. Previously, he was professor at the Universities of Cagliari, Bologna, Trento and Brescia. His fields of research and publications have been on administrative law, regional and local law, comparative constitutional law, constitutional history. Besides other essays and articles, he has published *Le origini dell'organizzazione amministrativa del lavoro* (Giuffrè, 1968); *Il governo locale negli Stati Uniti d'America* (Giuffrè, 1975); *Amministrazione giustiziale* (CEDAM, 1986); *Lezioni di diritto pubblico* (ISU, several editions up to 2012) and *Compendio*

di diritto costituzionale, under the direction of V. Onida and M. Pedrazza Gorlero (Milan, 2023, 6th ed.). He is a member of the board of directors of the legal periodicals *Quaderni Costituzionali* and *Jus*.

Prof. Ilaria Carlotto was awarded a PhD in 'Italian and European Constitutional Law' in 2005. She is Associate Professor of Institutions of Public Law in the Department of Legal Sciences at the University of Verona. She has taught courses in Public Law Institutions, Education Legislation, Tourism Legislation, Protection of Fundamental Rights and Regional and Local Body Law. Her research interests include regional law, constitutional justice, the protection of fundamental rights and the relationship between the ordinary courts and the ECHR. She has authored and edited various publications, including *Il procedimento di formazione degli Statuti delle Regioni ordinarie* (Padua, 2007), *Scritti in ricordo di Paolo Cavaleri* (Naples, 2016) and *La ricerca delle proprie origini nel bilanciamento dei diritti* (Naples, 2020). Along with P. Cavaleri and E. Gianfrancesco she edited the volume *Lineamenti di diritto costituzionale della Regione del Veneto* (Turin, 2013).

Marta Cartabia (PhD, European University Institute, 1993) is Full Professor of Constitutional Law (Bocconi University, Milan), President emerita of the Italian Constitutional Court and has served as Minister of Justice of the Italian Republic in the Draghi Cabinet, 2021–2022. She is currently Vice-President of the Commission for Democracy Through Law (Venice Commission) of the Council of Europe. She has taught at several Italian universities and was a visiting scholar and professor in France, Spain, Germany and US (Michigan, NYU, Notre Dame University, Yale). She is Co-President of the International Society of Public Law; she has also been the President and co-founder of the Italian Chapter of the latter since 2018. She is a member of the Senate of the European Law Institute. She is co-editor-in-chief of the reviews *Italian Journal of Public Law* and *Quaderni costituzionale.* She sits on the scientific and editorial board of a number of academic law journals and is currently a member of the Advisory Board of the *International Journal of Constitutional Law* (*I•CON*). Since 2013, she has been invited to the annual Global Constitutionalism Seminar, part of the Gruber Program for Global Justice and Women's Rights, hosted by the Yale Law School. Among her most recent publications in English, co-authored with Nicola Lupo, *The Constitution of Italy* (Hart, 2022) and V. Barsotti, P. Carozza, A. Simoncini, is *Dialogues on Italian Constitutional Justice: A Comparative Perspective* (Routledge, 2020). She was awarded PhD Honoris Causa by the Scuola Superiore Sant'Anna, Pisa (2020) and by the Complutense University, Madrid (2022).

Paolo Cavaleri† has been Professor of Public Law and Regional Law in the Faculty of Economics at the University of Verona. He is the author of several publications concerning constitutional and regional law, among which are *Iniziativa economica privata e Costituzione 'vivente'* (Padua, 1978); *L'assistenza tra disciplina pubblica e libertà dei privati* (Milan, 1992); *L'evoluzione dello Stato regionale in Italia* (Padua, 1997); and *Diritto regionale* (Padua, 2003).

Dr Fabrizio D'Addabbo† graduated in Law from the University of Pavia. He completed postgraduate studies at the University of Milan, where he received a PhD in Constitutional Law in 1992. In 1993, he received a research grant from the University of Milan. He was a researcher in Public Law in the Department of Law at the University of Brescia, where he also taught Public Law in the Department of Economy and Management and Regional Law in the Department of Law. His major field of research concerned the constitutional organization of the State, in particular the President of the Republic. He was the co-author of *La difficile alternanza. Il sistema parlamentare italiano alla prova, 1985–1987* (Milan 1988); and *Verso l'incerto bipolarismo. Il sistema parlamentare italiano nella transizione (1987–1999)* (A. D'Andrea editor, Milan, 1999). Among his publications are *Sovranità popolare e forma di governo: l'investitura dell'Esecutivo e lo scioglimento delle Camere secondo una concezione rispondente al principio democratico*, in *Alle frontiere del Diritto costituzionale. Scritti in onore di Valerio Onida*, edited by M. D'Amico and B. Randazzo (Milan, 2011); and *Dal sito internet del Quirinale: 'Controcorrente', il discorso di insediamento davanti alle Camere riunite del nuovo Presidente della Repubblica, successore di Giorgio Napolitano (una fantacronaca costituzionale)*, in *Studi in onore di Maurizio Pedrazza Gorlero*, vol. II, *La libertà di informazione e la democrazia costituzionale* (Naples, 2015).

The Authors

Marilisa D'Amico is Professor of Constitutional Law at the University of Milan, Department of Italian and Supranational Public Law; Vice-Rector of the University of Milan for Legality, Transparency and Equality of Rights; and barrister before the Supreme Court(s). She has been Chairholder and Academic Coordinator of the European Fundamental Rights and Women's Rights (EFRiWoR) Jean Monnet Chair until 2023. She teaches 'Constitutional Law' and 'Women's Rights and the Italian Constitution' at the University of Milan. She is Scientific Coordinator of the postgraduate course on the prevention and punishment of violence against women (University of Milan). She is Principal Investigator of the University of Milan's Spoke No. 6, 'Innovation for Sustainable and Inclusive Societies', of the PNRR Project 'MUSA', Multilayered Urban Sustainability Action. She has been Visiting Scholar in 2015, 2016, 2017, 2021 at the School of International and Public Affairs, and at the Law School, Columbia University, in 2023 at Fordham Law School, in 2021, 2022 and 2023 at Berkeley Law. Her scientific research involves all fields of constitutional law and, among these, two main core areas: constitutional justice and fundamental rights protection with a focus on gender studies and women's rights. She is the author of several publications, among which: *Parti e processo nella giustizia costituzionale (1991)*; *Giudizio sulle leggi ed effetti temporali delle decisioni di incostituzionalità (1993)*; *Donna e aborto nella Germania riunificata (1994)*; *I diritti contesi: Problematiche attuali del costituzionalismo* (2016); *Una parità ambigua: Costituzione e diritti delle donne* (2020); *Parole che separano: Linguaggio, Costituzione, Diritti* (2023).

Prof. Antonio D'Andrea has been a student in the Ghislieri College (Pavia) and graduated from the University of Pavia, Faculty of Law. He is Professor of Constitutional Law in the Faculty of Law at the University of Brescia. He also taught Public Law in the Faculty of Economics at the University of Brescia and University of Calabria. His major field of research concerns the State's constitutional organization, focusing in particular on the concrete workings of the system of government in Italy. He has published several essays, among which are *Accordi di governo e regole di coalizione* (Turin, 1991); *Autonomia costituzionale delle Camere e principio di legalità* (Milan, 2004); *Il Governo sopra tutto* (Gussago, 2009); *L'orpello della democrazia* (Gussago, 2015); *L'azzardo costituzionale* (Rome, 2016); *La Costituzione che abbiamo* (Bari, 2017); *L'impatto dell'abrogazione referendaria sulla forma di governo italiana*, in *Quaderni costituzionali*, n. 3/2022; *Il Parlamento e il Governo: le ragioni del rispettivo disallineamento*, in *Diritto costituzionale*, n. 3/2002; in cooperation with others authors, *Verso l'incerto bipolarismo*: *Il sistema parlamentare italiano nella transizione 1987–1999* (Milan, 1999); *Lo sviluppo bipolare della forma di governo italiana* (Milan, 2003); and *La rigidità bipolare del parlamentarismo italiano: Cinque anni di centrodestra (2001–2006)* (Gussago, 2008).

Prof. Giovanni Guiglia graduated in Law from the University of Pavia. He has a postgraduate diploma (Master's) in the Law of Environment and Territory. He has been researching at the Universities of Pavia, Milan, and Verona. He is currently Professor in Public Law at the University of Verona, Department of Law; Member of the Professorial Board of the 'PhD in European and International Law' of the same University; Member of the Italian Association of Constitutionalists; Honorary General Coordinator of the Academic Network on the European Social Charter and Social Rights/Réseau Académique sur la Charte Sociale Européenne et les Droits Sociaux (ANESC/RACSE). He has published several essays, among which are *The Opportunities of the European Social Charter (in Italy)*, in http://www.europeanrights.eu; *The Importance of the European Social Charter in the Italian Legal System: In Pursuit of a Stronger Protection of Social Rights in a Normative and Internationally Integrated System*, in M. D'Amico, G. Guiglia (eds/dir.), *European Social Charter and the Challenges of the XXI Century / La Charte Sociale Européenne et les défis du XXIe siècle*, ESI (Naples, 2014), pp. 51–96; *La Charte sociale européenne et le droit de l'Union européenne: après les conflits, les synergies*, in J. Luther, L. Mola (eds/dir.), *Europe's Social Rights under the 'Turin Process' / Les Droits Sociaux de l'Europe sous le 'Processus de Turin'*, Editoriale Scientifica (Naples, 2016), pp. 123–134; *Le 'socle européen des droits sociaux': une contribution à la synergie entre le droit de l'Union européenne et la Charte sociale européenne*, in 'Droits fondamentaux', n° 15, 2017, pp. 1–18, and *Preambles*, in *The Academic Network on the European Social Charter and Social Rights* (C. Nivard ed.), *The European Social Charter: A Commentary*, Vol. 2, Brill-Nijhoff (Leiden-Boston, 2023), pp. 1–38.

Elisabetta Lamarque is Full Professor of Constitutional Law at the School of Law, University of Milano-Bicocca, where she also teaches Constitutional Justice; a member of the General Council of the Italian Chapter of the International Society of Public Law – ICON•S; and a barrister before the Supreme Courts. She has published over 160 contributions on various topics of constitutional law. Among the other books, articles and book chapters, she authored *Poteri e garanzie (Corte costituzionale)* [*Powers and Guarantees (Constitutional Court)*], in *Enciclopedia del diritto – I tematici*, vol. *Potere e Costituzione* directed by M. Cartabia and M. Ruotolo, Giuffrè, Milan, 2023; *The Italian Constitution: A Personalist Constitution*, in *Italian Journal of Public Law* (*IJPL*), 2022, Issue 2, No. 14; *Corte costituzionale e giudici nell'Italia repubblicana: Nuova stagione, altri episodi* [*Constitutional Court and Ordinary Judges in Italy: New season, other episodes*] (Editoriale Scientifica 2021) and *Prima i bambini: Il principio dei best interests of the child nella prospettiva costituzionale* [*Children First: The Best Interests of the Child Principle in the Constitutional Perspective*] (FrancoAngeli 2016). She also edited, among other works, *Come nasce la Costituzione: I lavori preparatori della Costituzione della Repubblica italiana del 1° gennaio 1948* [*How the Constitution Was Born: The Preparatory Works of the Constitution of the Italian Republic of 1 January 1948*] (Giappichelli 2023), at *comenascelacostituzione.it* and *La richiesta di pareri consultivi alla Corte di Strasburgo da parte delle più alte giurisdizioni nazionali: Prime riflessioni in vista della ratifica del Protocollo 16 alla Convenzione europea dei diritti dell'uomo* [*The Court of Strasbourg and the Advisory Opinions Raised by National Highest Courts and Tribunals: Towards the Ratification of Protocol No. 16 to the ECHR, Preliminary Reflections*] (Giappichelli 2015).

Costanza Nardocci, PhD, is Professor in Constitutional Law, Department of Italian and Supranational Public Law, University of Milan, Italy. She teaches 'Gender Justice', 'Women in Tech: New Frontiers of Gender-Related Rights and Artificial Intelligence', 'Public Constitutional Law', 'Human Rights and Climate Change', and 'Constitutional Rights of Migrants' at the University of Milan, Department of Italian and Supranational Public Law. She is teaching coordinator of the postgraduate course on gender-based violence at the University of Milan. She is a member of the Steering Committee of the HAICU Lab Project within the U7+Alliance. She has been Visiting Scholar in 2015, 2016, 2017, 2021 at the School of International and Public Affairs, and at the Law School, Columbia University, and in 2023 at Fordham Law School. Her scientific research involves constitutional law, national and supranational constitutional justice, and human rights law with a specific focus on: human rights; minority rights; gender studies; multiculturalism; anti-discrimination law; ethnic and racial discrimination; women's rights; indigenous people's rights; constitutional justice; artificial intelligence and discrimination. She is the author of several articles and essays in the field of constitutional law, human rights law and anti-discrimination law and of two monographs on ethnic and racial discrimination and constitutional justice (*Razza e etnia: La discriminazione tra individuo e gruppo nella dimensione costituzionale e sovranazionale*, Naples, 2016 – *Race and Ethnicity: Discrimination Between the Individual and the Group in the Constitutional and Supranational Perspective*; *Il 'diritto' al Giudice costituzionale*, Naples, 2020 – *The 'Right' to the Constitutional Judge*).

Matteo Nicolini holds a PhD in Italian and European Constitutional Law (Verona), where he is Associate Professor of Public Comparative Law. He is also Visiting Lecturer at the Newcastle University Law School (UK) and External Partner at the Centre for the Study of Law in Theory and Practice, Liverpool John Moores University (UK). He has delivered lectures at several Italian universities, as well as at the Universities of Lille, Innsbruck, Tübingen, Barcelona, Madrid, Valladolid, Salamanca, Cork, Stellenbosch (RSA), Alberto Hurtado (Chile), Universidad de las Américas (Ecuador), Newcastle, Birkbeck College, and Liverpool John Moores (UK). His fields of research include comparative method, Italian and European constitutional law, federalism and regionalism, constitutional litigation, law and literature, African law, legal geography, and legal linguistics. He is the author of monographs, essays, and articles in Italian, Spanish and English. Among his recent publications are the monographs (with S. Bagni), *Comparative Constitutional Justice*, Eleven, The Hague, 2021; *Legal Geography: Comparative Law and the Production of Space* (Springer, Cham, 2022); (with Daniele D'Alvia) Global Legal Indicators and Comparative Law: The Factory of Indexes (Routledge, Abingdon and New York, 2025); the edited volumes (with A. Valdesalici), *Local Governance in Multi-Layered Systems: A Comparative Legal Study in the Federal-Local Connection*, Springer, Cham, 2023 and (with R. Mullender, Thomas D.C. Bennett, and Emilia Mickiewicz), *Law and Imagination in Troubled Times: A Legal and Literary Discourse*, Routledge, Adingdon-New York, 2020; *Methodologies of Comparative Constitutional Law: Universalist Approach*, in: *Max Planck Encyclopaedia of Comparative Constitutional Law* [MPECCoL], Oxford, Oxford University Press, 2023, pp. 1–17.

Maurizio Pedrazza Gorlero is Honorary Professor of Constitutional Law in the Department of Law at the University of Verona. He is also Member of the Italian Association of Constitutionalists. He graduated in Law at the University of Milan. He taught Constitutional Law at the Universities of Sassari, Padua, Milan, Catania and Verona, where he also founded and held the *Guido Gonella Chair in Constitutional Law of Journalistic Information.* His scientific interests point to the sources of law, constitutional democracy, constitutional freedoms and social groups, regions and territorial demarcation, journalism and freedom of the press, and fundamental rights. He has published several articles, essays, and books, among which: *Le variazioni territoriali delle Regioni, I* and *II* (Padua, CEDAM, 1979 and 1991); *Giornalismo e Costituzione* (Padua, CEDAM, 1988); *Artt. 131 e 132 Cost.*, in *Commentario della Costituzione*, founded by G. Branca and continued by A. Pizzorusso (Bologna-Roma, Zanichelli-Il Foro italiano, 1990); *Gli atti normativi su intesa: fra modello imperativo e modello contrattuale di prod-zione normativa, I, I procedimenti* (Verona, 1992); (with U. Curi, ed.) *La Repubblica che non c'è* (Milan, FrancoAngeli, 1993); *Le fonti del diritto* (Padua, CEDAM, 1995); *Il potere e il diritto* (Padua, CEDAM, 1999); (with L. Besenyei and G. Erszegi, ed.) *De Bulla aurea Andreae II Regis Hungariae MCCXXII* (Verona, Edizioni Valdonega, 1999); *Breviario delle fonti del diritto* (Milan, Giuffrè, 2005); *Saggi per un corso di diritto della informazione giornalisti-ca* (Padua, CEDAM, 2006); *Il patto costituzionale: Potere e diritto fra protezione ed obbedienza* (Padua, CEDAM, 2009 and 2.a ed. 2012); *L'ordine frattalico delle fonti del diritto* (Padua, CEDAM, 2012); *Congetture costituzionali* (Naples, ESI, 2015); (with S. Catalano) *Le fonti dell'ordinamento repubblicano* (Milan, Giuffrè, 2018); *The Macbeths, Shakespeare e le due maschere del potere* (Pisa, Pacini, 2022); (with V. Onida, ed.) *Compendio di diritto costituzionale*, 6.a ed. (Milan, Giuffrè, 2023); Riti di passaggio. *Cronaca costituzionale della transizione alla 'seconda' Repubblica, 1992–1995* (Verona, Cierre, 2025).

Lorenzo Spadacini received his PhD in Italian and European Constitutional Law from the University of Verona. He is Associate Professor of Constitutional Law in the Department of Law and Institutions at the Universitas Mercatorm, Rome, from academic year 2025/2026, after having served as an Associate Professor in Public Law at the University of Brescia since academic year 2017/2018, and, before that, from 2005, as a Researcher at the same institution. He was a visiting researcher at Cornell Law School during 2011–2012. He has been the Head of the Department for Institutional Reforms of the Presidency of the Council of Ministers in Rome from 2018 to 2022. His specific research fields within the scope of the constitutional law are electoral legislation, Italian regionalism, European integration, separation of powers, and sources of law. He is the author of several publications, among which are *Regole elettorali e integrità numerica delle Camere* (Brescia, 2003); *Separazione dei poteri e funzione giurisdizionale* (Gussago, 2012); *Decreto-legge e alterazione del quadro costituzionale: Distorsioni del bicameralismo, degenerazione del sistema delle fonti e inefficacia dei controlli* (Bari 2022); with Adam Cygan (eds), *Constitutional Implications of the Traghetti Judgment: Italian and European Perspectives* (Gussago, 2012); and with Robert Blackburn & Arianna Carminati (eds), *Parliament as the Cornerstone of Democracy* (London, 2017).

Table of Contents

Table of Contents

Introduction to the Third Edition

Italy is a relatively young State. Under the Savoy dynasty, the Kingdom of Italy was proclaimed on 17 March 1861 as the continuation and transformation of the Kingdom of Piedmont and Sardinia, following the votes (*'plebisciti'*) to annex various territories after the first two 'Wars of Independence'(1848–1849 and 1859). For many years, part of what is now Italian territory remained under the rule of other countries, including the Papal State, and was variously controlled and 'protected' by the great European powers (especially France and the Austro-Hungarian Empire). Only with the 'Third War of Independence' (1866) was Veneto annexed to the Kingdom of Italy, and only in 1870 was the residual territory of the Papal States brought into Italy proper (the Lateran Treaty of 1929 restricting now the Papal State to the very small area of Vatican City) together with Rome which became the new capital. However, the territories to the north-east of the peninsula with Trento and Trieste remained subject to rule by other States; only following the First World War (1914–1918) did they come under Italian sovereignty together with South Tyrol, a land of Austrian nationality and language, and some territories east of Trieste, Slavic nationality and language, which then subsequently passed to the former Yugoslavia (now Slovenia and Croatia) following the Second World War.

The Kingdom of Italy's first Constitution was nothing but the *Statuto Albertino* that had earlier been granted by King Carlo Alberto to the Kingdom of Piedmont and Sardinia in 1848.

The first true Italian Constitution was and is that of the Italian Republic, passed on 22 December 1947 by the Constituent Assembly that had been elected on 2 June 1946 after liberation from fascism, at the same time as the referendum that decided to opt for a republican form of state. The Constitution came into force on 1 January 1948.

This marked a clean break not only with fascist Italy (which, like nazi Germany, never gave itself a written Constitution) but also with the Savoy Monarchy, its Statute and pre-fascist Italy.

The principles of the Constitution are based on those of the Republics that arose in Europe in the late eighteenth and nineteenth centuries after the French Revolution. These then evolved in the twentieth century after the First World War, driven by the democratic and social movements that became established, among others, in Germany with the Weimar Republic of 1919 and in Spain with the Spanish Constitution of 1931. For some years, they were replaced by Francoism in Spain (up to the new monarchist Constitution of 1978) and by the fascist and nazi regimes in Italy and Germany, which were subsequently defeated with the victory of the Allies in the Second World War, the liberation and the rise of democratic republics in Italy (1946) and Germany (1949), as well as with the new French Constitution of 1946.

The Constituent Assembly was dominated by three large parties: Christian Democrats, the Socialist Party and the Communist Party. Despite their very different ultimate aims, they agreed among themselves and with other minor parties on the text of the Constitution, approved by over 85% of votes. It was inspired by the principles of the democratic-social State, in which, in addition to the traditional rights of equality and civil and religious freedoms, there are other rights in recognition of the pre-eminence of the person, bearer of inviolable rights and binding duties of solidarity (Article 2). These included social labour rights (Articles 1 and 4), the affirmation of the Republic's duty to remove the economic and social obstacles that limit in fact the freedom and equality (Article 3), and the rejection of war and the adhesion to an international order of freedom, equality and peace, also with the acceptance of the limitations of national sovereignty necessary for this purpose (Article 11, on the basis of which Italy has also accepted, without changing the Constitution, the prevalence of European law over national law).

The Republic's constitutional system is based on the principles of parliamentary democracy, with a bicameral Parliament almost entirely elected by universal suffrage, and a President of the Republic who represents national unity, and is an institution of coordination and guarantee, elected by Parliament together with a small number of representatives of the Regions. The Government, which must enjoy the confidence of a majority in Parliamentary, is a collegial executive led by a Prime Minister. There is a system of guaranteed regional and local autonomies (Article 5) in which the Regions also exert legislative and executive powers. Judicial power is mostly entrusted to independent professional judges, whose careers are governed by a Council, two-thirds of whose members are elected by the same judges. An important innovation is the provision – first in Europe with the German Fundamental Law of 1949, followed more recently in the majority of European and non-European States – for a Constitutional Court, whose members are elected for a nine-year term by Parliament, the Head of State and the Supreme Courts, and whose role is to check the constitutionality of laws, annulling those which are unconstitutional, and to settle conflicts on allocation of the powers of the State and between the State and the Regions, as well as between the Regions.

The adaptation of the pre-existing legislative, executive, and judicial system to the new principles of the Republican Constitution required a long process of reforms, still in some ways not completed: apart from the partial implementation of the 'programmatic' principles on the subject of social rights and social justice, various fundamental laws dating back to the former systems still survive, although extensively amended.

The political-parliamentary system underwent a major transformation in the early 1990s with the disappearance of some major parties and the radical transformation of others, and the birth of new formations and new unprecedented alliances and coalitions, frequent changes in electoral laws (some declared partly unconstitutional) and profound changes in the distribution of electoral consensus, together with a drastic reduction in electoral participation (from more than 90% until 1979 to less than 75% in 2018). These processes still do not seem to have been settled, as can be seen by the parliamentary political events still in progress.

However, the cornerstones of the constitutional system have so far resisted significant attempts at transformation, and two referendums in 2006 and 2016 rejected proposals for reforms of the Republic's system, although a considerable reform was approved in 2001 regarding regional and local autonomy. Nonetheless, alterations in the functioning of institutions (such as for relations between government and Parliament in the exercise of the legislative function) have been increasing in recent times, exacerbated by political uncertainties.

The Italian constitutional order has not only opened up (without necessitating changes to the Constitution) to the innovations brought by the process of European integration, but the political parties and electorate of Italy have shown – until very recently – broad consent to more extensive economic and political integration in Europe (such as when backing the attempt to approve a European Constitution in 2004, which only failed following the referendums against it in France and the Netherlands in 2005). In any case, European law and jurisprudence of the European Court of Justice in Luxembourg (as well as that of the European Court of Human Rights in Strasbourg) have brought significant innovations in the law and have a large influence on the regulatory system of the Italian Republic.

Valerio Onida
(May 2021)

A special thanks to the co-author Lorenzo Spadacini for his aid in the revision of the text and to my son Marco Onida, an official of the EU Commission, for his aid in organizing the work and keeping contact with the Publisher (VO).

Introduction to the Fourth Edition

After the painful passing of Prof. Valerio Onida (Milan, 14 May 2022), in mutual agreement, the Publisher Kluwer and the family, particularly his son Marco, who had already contributed to the editorial revision of the previous edition, with the consent of the co-authors of the volume, have decided to continue updating the volume dedicated to constitutional law in Italy.

For the strictly necessary parts, the updates concerning the chapters written by Valerio Onida have been taken care of by Antonio D'Andrea and Lorenzo Spadacini with the intention of adhering as closely as possible to the original approach. In particular, the section related to the general introduction, which had only been updated by Valerio Onida until the last months of 2020, has been revised in order to take into account some constitutional changes that had been approved in the meantime during the XVIII and XIX Legislatures, as well as the outcome of the general political elections that occurred on 22 September 2022. These elections concluded with a clear victory for a centre-right coalition, which was able to establish a solid parliamentary majority supporting the current government led by Giorgia Meloni. This government appears to be inclined to place a programme of change in the current parliamentary system at the centre of its action.

The original intent of Prof. Onida to provide, especially to foreign scholars, the necessary information to understand the concrete functioning of the Italian constitutional system without indulging too much in excessively abstract doctrinal reconstructions remains unchanged, although the Italian doctrine, not only in constitutional matters, has always been abundant in such reconstructions, often mixing some peculiarities of the political life with substantive constitutional issues.

Antonio D'Andrea
Lorenzo Spadacini
(March 2024)

This update would not have been possible without the support of all the co-authors, to whom go my warmest thanks. In particular, I wish to thank Professor Antonio D'Andrea and Dr Lorenzo Spadacini who kindly supported coordinating this. My father Valerio would have been happy to see that this joint work has been continued after his death by those who once used to be his students (or students of his students) and who truly share his passion for the Italian Republican Constitution, its eternal values and its teaching to new generations of students.

Marco Onida
(March 2024)

General Introduction

Chapter 1. Historical Outline of the Italian Constitution

by Valerio Onida[†]

§1. The Origins of the State

1. The Kingdom of Italy came into being in 1861 as the result of the transformation of the Kingdom of Piedmont and Sardinia. At the beginning of the nineteenth century, after the Napoleonic wars followed by the restoration of the French Monarchy, the territory of the peninsula was still divided into a number of States. The north-western Kingdom of Piedmont and Sardinia, ruled by the House of Savoy, comprised the present regions of Piedmont, Valle d'Aosta, Liguria and Sardinia. The central-eastern regions of the north of the peninsula, presently occupied by Lombardy, Veneto, Trentino-Alto Adige and the Friuli-Venetia Julia Regions, were still part of the Austrian Empire.

The central part of the country was occupied by the Duchies of Parma and Piacenza and Modena and the Grand Duchy of Tuscany, while the Papal States comprised the area which is presently Emilia-Romagna (with the exception of the area which belonged to the above-mentioned Duchies), the Marches, Umbria and Latium. The Kingdom of the Two Sicilies, whose capital was Naples, stretched across the South under the reign of the Bourbon family.

2. The 1821 and 1848 liberal revolutionary uprisings brought about the creation of provisional governments in different parts of Italy, but it was only in the Kingdom of Piedmont and Sardinia that the *Statuto* promulgated under King Carlo Alberto in 1848 survived the temporary defeat of the liberals. The political aspirations of Italian liberals included unification of the peninsula, although they had very different ideas on how to achieve this goal. The supporters of Giuseppe Mazzini were in favour of a unitary Italian Republic, while other liberals thought they could build a federation of States under the leadership of the Pope as the sovereign of the Papal States.

Towards the middle of the nineteenth century, the political situation in Europe and Italy was such that the plan to unify the peninsula politically could be implemented through the expansion of the Kingdom of Piedmont and Sardinia, with the gradual annexation of the other territories after the so-called wars of independence.

3. Lombardy was annexed after the 1859 war, in which the Kingdom of Piedmont allied itself with France against Austria; at the same time Savoy and the County of Nice were transferred to France. Shortly afterwards, in 1860, the territories of the States in central Italy, including those of the Papal States with the exception of Rome, were annexed to Piedmont after plebiscites. The same happened of the Kingdom of the Two Sicilies, in the aftermath of the expedition of the 'thousand' headed by Giuseppe Garibaldi. The Kingdom of Piedmont, therefore, included almost the entire Italian peninsula (except for Rome and the north-west regions around Venice, still under the rule of the Austrian Empire), and the Piedmontese Parliament proclaimed the Kingdom of Italy (1861).

The political unification of the peninsula was largely completed in the following decade. The 1866 war resulted in the annexation of Venice and the Veneto Region. In 1870, Italian troops conquered Rome and destroyed what remained of the Papal States. The capital of the Kingdom, earlier in Turin and after temporarily in Florence, was moved to Rome.

4. The regions in the north-east of the country (Trentino and Friuli-Venetia Julia) still remained outside the Kingdom's borders and only became part of the Italian State after the First World War (1915–1918) and the end of the Austrian Empire, along with the South Tyrol area, where a large part of the population still speaks German.

Italy took over the territories to the east (Dalmatia) but subsequently lost them after the Second World War (1940–1945) together with a part of Venetia Julia (Trieste returned to Italian rule only in 1954). The Austrian border of Brenner and, except for a few modifications, the French border remained unchanged.

5. It is also worth mentioning that Italy played a role, albeit a minor one, in the history of colonial expansion with the occupation of Somalia (1887–1889), Eritrea (1889) and Ethiopia (1936) in East Africa and Libia (1911–1912) in Northern Africa. After the Second World War, all overseas territories were declared to be no longer under Italian rule, except for the temporary trusteeship on Somalia granted to Italy by the United Nations (UN), which ceased in 1960.

§2. The Constitution of the Kingdom of Italy

6. Even after the capital was transferred to Rome in 1870, the Constitution and laws of the Kingdom of Italy remained largely those of its predecessor, the Kingdom of Piedmont and Sardinia, as enlarged by the annexations. This is understandable in light of the historical process described above.

The legal foundations of the new Kingdom were found in the Savoy monarchy and the *Statuto* promulgated under King Carlo Alberto in 1848. The creation of the Italian State did not, therefore, coincide with any constituent process: the Piedmontese *Statuto* became the first Constitution of the Italian State and continued to govern it, even if only formally, for over eighty years, until 1946.

7. The civil, criminal and administrative laws of the Kingdom of Piedmont were extended to the new territories. Piedmont's strongly centralized administrative structure, based on the French model because of the special ties between the House of Savoy and France, set the standard, with only minor changes, for the whole Kingdom. This explains how a State born from the unification of many different territories and States, each with its own traditions and institutions, managed to become a centralized unitary State with total uniformity as to legislation and administration. Political unity was laid on the deep cultural, social and economic differences existing among the various regions of the country. It must be remembered that although the regions annexed to the new State had very different political and institutional backgrounds, they had never experienced self-government. The new State, therefore, never had to face opposition arising from experiences in self-government prior to the unification. The State was instead perceived, at least by the cultural and political élite, as the historical realization of their aspirations for the freedom and unity of the country. The authorities were nonetheless very careful to prevent the newly gained unity from collapsing. Even very modest plans for administrative decentralization, such as the one proposed by Minghetti in 1862, were rejected for fear that they would jeopardize the newly won unity of the country. A grand project of legislative unification was carried out in 1865.

8. These statutes remained for a long time and sometimes are still considered the basis for the disciplines of the major areas of life, especially administration.

After the adoption of the *Statuto* in 1848, the Piedmontese State and, therefore, the Kingdom of Italy became a 'constitutional' or 'representative' monarchy, modelled on the French Orleans monarchy of 1830 and the Belgian Constitution of 1831. The legislative power was exercised both by the King and by a bicameral Parliament, composed of a *Chamber of Deputies*, elected by a very limited franchise through a single-member constituency majority voting system (except for a short period from 1882 to 1891) and by a *Senate* appointed by the King.

Legislation passed by both Chambers was submitted to the King for assent and promulgation. The executive power, as well as the powers to set the rules for the implementation of the law and those relating to international diplomacy, rested formally with the King, who appointed and removed Ministers. The latter were declared 'responsible', unlike the King, whose person was deemed 'sacred and inviolable'.

9. In practice, a sort of English-style parliamentary government was established from the outset. The office of the Prime Minister was held by a deputy who enjoyed a parliamentary majority and exercised the political leadership of the executive. In case of disagreement between the King (and the government) and the parliamentary majority, the *Chamber of Deputies* could be dissolved.

The government was organized both centrally, through Ministries headed by a Minister, and locally, through prefects, representatives of the government in the Provinces, as well as various decentralized bodies. Initially, only self-governing administrative organs were the municipalities, governed by elected mayors and Councils, but enjoying limited autonomy and strictly controlled by the prefects and the government. Subsequently, also the Provinces, run by elective bodies, became autonomous, albeit with very limited powers.

10. The judicial power was exercised by career magistrates, appointed by the King in accordance with law and not completely independent from the executive.

The *Statuto* recognized the traditional rights of civil freedom (personal freedom, freedom of domicile, of the press, of assembly – though not of association) and economic freedom (property rights), equality before the law without any distinction of 'title or rank', right to admission to civil and military offices.

The definition of rights was left to statutory law, and their effective protection, therefore, depended on the fact that the relevant rules had to be adopted by the Parliament.

11. The system of guarantees was initially based on the power of the judicial to resolve all disputes concerning 'civil or political' rights, though judges were not allowed to annul any administrative act (pursuant to the 1865 Law No. 2248, Attachment E).

In the aftermath of an 1889 reform, the Council of State (modelled on the French *Conseil d'État*) was given jurisdiction over citizens' appeals against administrative acts. This paved the way for a system of 'administrative justice' which is still emblematic of the Italian system.

The difference between civil and administrative justice is based on the case law distinction between 'perfect' rights (whose protection is left to ordinary judges) and 'legitimate interests', namely private rights that the law protects indirectly through the regulation of administrative actions. In practice, since the public administration can frequently and significantly affect the rights of individuals, disputes between the latter and the administration are settled by administrative judges, except when it is clear from the outset that the administration cannot exercise jurisdiction over the supposedly violated rights and except for private-law disputes involving patrimonial rights.

12. Once an Act was passed by Parliament and had received royal assent, it was considered the supreme source of law and its contents could never be limited by any superior provision. Indeed, no institution could review the constitutionality of an Act, except with regard to procedural flaws since judges were not allowed to question legislative intent. This Constitution has therefore been defined as 'flexible' since it could be derogated by an Act of Parliament and because the *Statuto* mentioned no procedure for the amendment of its own provisions (which, in fact, were never expressly or explicitly amended).

13. The *Statuto* declared that the Catholic religion was 'the religion of the State', while other religions were 'tolerated in according to laws'. In fact, the relationship with the Catholic Church was one of the most important constitutional issues that the new State had to face, especially since the conquest of Rome had weakened the temporal powers of the Pope. The 'Roman question' remained open for decades.

The Italian State passed the 'Law of Guarantees' (No. 214/1871). This Act sanctioned the freedom of the Church although it partially subordinated its institutional life to the State. The State supervised the appointment of bishops, but the Church was granted privileged status.

However, for a long time, the Holy See stoutly asserted its claim to temporal power and its independence from the 'usurper' State, by advising the Catholics not to take part in the political life of the Kingdom (this policy became known as the '*non expedit*').

14. A 'conciliation' with the Italian State, prepared for a long time, was finally reached in 1929, during the Fascist regime, with the stipulation of the 'Lateran Pacts' (comprising the Treaty, the Concordat and a financial convention), which put an end to the 'Roman question'.

These agreements provided that the State would yield a small territory which gave rise to the Vatican City State, while the Holy See definitively renounced its claims on the rest of the old Papal States. It also reaffirmed the principle enshrined in the *Statuto* whereby the State recognized the Catholic religion as its official creed (Article 1 of the Treaty), while the Concordat, conceived as a bilateral act similar to international treaties, defined the rights and obligations of the Church towards the Italian State (covering privileges of the clergy, civil recognition of Catholic marriage, Catholic religion education in State schools and recognition of ecclesiastical corporations). The pacts also provided for compensation to the Holy See for the transfer of ecclesiastical property to the State.

15. The post-unification Italian parliamentary system had a very limited franchise (in 1870, those entitled to vote constituted only 2% of the population). A small pool of voters – male citizens with a minimum cultural level or who paid a minimum level of taxes – was shared by 'parties' which were relatively unstable parliamentary groupings, often formed around the most prominent political leaders.

A progressive broadening of the suffrage took place in the last decades of the nineteenth century and the first decades of the twentieth, quite late compared to other European countries. Universal suffrage was granted, but only to men, in 1919.

In the meantime, both as a cause and an effect of the broadening of the suffrage, parties with modern features were founded in Italy. They took the form of stable and well-established organizations all over the country, which formulated political programmes and selected candidates for parliamentary elections, and tried to influence national politics in the Parliament and local politics throughout the country.

The Socialist Party was founded in 1896, and by 1919, it was the largest party of Parliament (in 1921, a split gave birth to the Communist Party). The Popular Party, composed of the democratic Catholics headed by Luigi Sturzo, was founded in 1919 and was largely represented in Parliament in the following period.

The establishment of new mass parties and the decline of the old liberal political class were accompanied by a 1919 change of the system of electing the Chamber of Deputies, which was reformed according to a proportional list method.

§3. The Fascist Regime

16. In Italy, as elsewhere in Europe, the First World War marked the beginning of a new era, including on a constitutional level. As mentioned above, the first Parliament elected after the war, in 1919, was composed of a largely new political class linked to new parties.

Nevertheless, the evolution of constitutionalism between the two wars, which inspired the experiences of the Weimar Republic, Republican Spain and Austria, was missed by Italy, not only because of the persistence of the monarchy but also and most importantly owing to the rise of the Fascist regime in 1922. Like those later established in Germany and Spain, this regime founded its doctrine and procedures on the explicit rejection of the principles espoused by the European liberal constitutionalism.

17. No Constitution was adopted under Fascism (the concept of Constitution being in sharp contrast with the culture of the totalitarian regime), and the country, therefore, continued to be ruled under the *Statuto* adopted by Carlo Alberto. But the legislation and the politics of the regime emptied the *Statuto* of its meaning: liberties were drastically curtailed by repressive laws; political pluralism was abolished with the transformation of the Fascist Party into a State institution and the prohibition of anti-fascist parties; and Parliament was deprived of its powers by a government dominated by its own leader, the '*Duce'* of Fascism in the shape of Benito Mussolini. The ability to elect the Chamber of Deputies was first practically eliminated by providing for elections with a single list of candidates and no guarantee of a secret ballot (1934), and then formally suppressed with the abolition of the Chamber itself and its replacement with a Chamber of Fascist groups and guilds, substantially appointed by the government (1939). The freedom of trade unions was suppressed by the establishment of single government unions, and strikes were prohibited.

Only the monarchy, which saw its influence decreased by the primacy of the '*Duce*', and institutions like the Senate, which were connected to the King, were still alive, although no trace remained of the 'representative monarchical government' mentioned in Article 2 of the *Statuto*.

§4. The Collapse of Fascism and the Constituent Phase

18. During the 1930s, the Fascist regime enjoyed very high levels of passive support in Italy, and its crisis came only with the war and the defeat of the German–Italian alliance.

In 1943, after the Allies landed in Sicily, the King, supported by portions of the Fascist Party, by the Armed Forces and the opposition which had developed within the Fascist Party, dismissed Mussolini and appointed Marshal Badoglio as the Head of Government. The latter shortly thereafter negotiated an armistice with the allied forces. Rome and most of the country were militarily occupied by the Germans, and the King and the government fled to the South, where the occupation troops of the allied forces were advancing. At the same time, armed resistance was beginning to build up in the North.

19. Italy was a theatre of war for two years. An 'Italian Social Republic' headed by Benito Mussolini and proposing a republican version of Fascism was set up in the North, under German occupation.

In the meantime, anti-fascist parties organized and established a *National Liberation Committee* (CNL), which claimed the political leadership of the country and opposed the monarchy's attempt to restore the constitutional order existing before the advent of Fascism. A truce was established between the King and the anti-fascist parties: the 'institutional question', i.e., the choice of the constitutional order, whether monarchic or republican, was deferred until such time as the war was over and the entire country liberated. The King had to transfer his powers to his son, as a 'deputy of the Kingdom', and a provisional government was to be formed by exponents of the parties. At the end of the war a Constituent Assembly, elected by the people, would take any decision regarding the new Constitution. This agreement was put into effect after the liberation of Rome in 1944.

After the liberation of the northern regions (25 April 1945), the supporters of the monarchy maintained that the choice of the form of State be submitted to the people by means of a referendum, which took place the same day when the Constituent Assembly was elected (2 June 1946, with women voting for the first time). The republican choice prevailed with around 12.5 million votes to around 10.5 million in favour of the monarchy, beyond 1.5 million blank or void ballots. King Umberto II – who had in the meantime succeeded his father Vittorio Emanuele III, as the latter had abdicated – left Italy and fled to Portugal, and the transition to the republican regime was assured by the Prime Minister Alcide De Gasperi, until the Assembly elected Enrico De Nicola as provisional Head of State.

20. The Constituent Assembly, three-quarters of which comprised representatives of the three main anti-fascist parties (Christian Democrats, Socialists and Communists), entrusted the drafting of the new Constitution to a seventy-five-member commission, chaired by Meuccio Ruini and made up of many leaders and renowned jurists from all parties. The new Constitution was approved by the Assembly on 22 December 1947, promulgated on 27 December and came into force on 1 January 1948. On 18 April 1948, the first election of the Chamber of Deputies took place (the Christian Democrat party gained almost 50% of votes) and shortly thereafter, the new President of the Republic, Luigi Einaudi, was elected.

Chapter 2. The Features of the Italian Republic

by Lorenzo Spadacini

§1. State Territory, Population and Demographics

21. Italy covers an area of 302,073 km^2. Its territory consists of plains for 23.2%, hills for 41.6% and mountains for 35.2%. The maximum distance from the most northern (Vetta d'Italia) to the most southern point (Capo delle Correnti) is 1,200 km. Italy hosts the entire south side of the Alps mountain range (the highest peak of which, Mont Blanc, 4810 m, is at the border with France) and shares borders with, besides France, Switzerland, Austria and Slovenia. Further borders exist with the two enclaved microstates (San Marino and the Vatican). Due to its well-known 'boot shape', stretching from north to south between the Tyrrhenian, the Adriatic and the Ionian seas, where a large number of islands are located, Italian coasts amount to approximately 8,000 km.

22. The borders between Italy and France derive from those originally existing between the former Kingdom of Sardinia and France based on the Treaty of Turin of 1860 by which Savoy and Nice County were handed over to France in exchange of the French military support to the process of unification of Italy. These borders were partly modified in 1947 (Paris Treaty), following the defeat of Italy in the Second World War, in particular in correspondence to the municipalities of Tende/Tenda and La Brigue/Briga that became part of the French territory.

The border with Switzerland set at the time of the unification of Italy (1861) was extended in 1866 due to the enlargement of the Kingdom of Italy towards east (Veneto) and again in 1919 due to the annexation of South Tyrol at the end of the First World War. The Italian municipality of Campione d'Italia (1,700 inhabitants), on the east coast of the Lugano Lake, is enclaved into Swiss territory.

More complex is the history of the border with Austria, derived initially from the process of unification of Italy, but which evolved significantly as a result of the so-called third Italian war of independence (1866) and related annexation of Veneto; and then at the end of the First World War, when the Italian-speaking region of Trentino was annexed to Italy and with it, based on the Treaty of Saint-Germain-en-Laye (1919), the German-speaking region of South Tirol. Although South Tyrol is located on the south side of the drainage line, linguistically and culturally, the area was part of Austrian Tyrol. Several decades of negotiations with Austria, starting with the De Gasperi-Gruber Agreement of 1946, led to a package of measures for the protection of the German-speaking minority, progressively implemented over the years.

Particularly complex is the history of the east border between Italy and (now) Slovenia. The Treaty of Rapallo of 1920 had assigned Trieste, Gorizia and part of the current territory of Croatia (Istria and part of Dalmatia) to the former Kingdom of Italy. With the end of the Second World War, Istria and Dalmatia (therefore including the parts assigned to Italy by the aforementioned Treaty of Rapallo) became part of Yugoslavia while Trieste became part of a 'Free Territory' (1947) under the Control of the UN Security Council, and including a mix of Italian and Slavic population. This situation persisted until 1954 when zone ‘A’ (urban) of the Free Territory was assigned to Italy and zone ‘B’ (extra-urban towards east) to Yugoslavia. A final border agreement was only signed in 1975 (Treaty of Osimo). Following the dissolution of Yugoslavia, in 1991, Slovenia took over the border with Italy.

23. According to the latest available annual report of ISTAT (Istituto Nazionale di Statistica) , the national institute for statistics, the resident population (including foreign citizens) as of 1 January 2024 was 58,971,230. The number of residents decreased since 2014 (‘demographic winter’) as a result of the sharp decrease of births after 2008, the evolution of mortality (to which the pandemics strongly contributed in recent years) and the balance between immigration and emigration. The presence of foreign citizens as of 1 January 2024 was estimated to amount to 5,253,658, out of which 3,864,018 were non-European Union (EU) citizens.

24. The administrative divisions of Italy, according to Article 114 of the Constitution of the Italian Republic, consist of municipalities, provinces, metropolitan cities, regions, and the state. Regions constitute territorial entities with legislative functions, while metropolitan cities, provinces, and municipalities are local entities with mere administrative functions.

There are twenty Italian regions. According to Article 116 of the Constitution, five of them (Friuli-Venezia Giulia, Sardinia, Sicily, Trentino-Alto Adige/Südtirol, and Valle d’Aosta/Vallé d’Aoste) have special status and, therefore, enjoy particular autonomy for geographical, historical, or linguistic reasons. In particular, the Trentino-Alto Adige/Südtirol region exists only for specific and limited functions. In fact, unlike all other regions, the majority of regional functions in Trentino-Alto Adige/Südtirol region are assigned to the two autonomous provinces of Trento and Bolzano/Bozen, which, for most competencies, are indeed more similar to regions than provinces.

The fifteen regions with ordinary status are then divided into provinces or, in the case of more demographically significant metropolitan areas, into metropolitan cities. As for regions with special status, the Valle d’Aosta/Vallée d’Aoste region does not have a provincial subdivision due to its small extension and population. As mentioned, Trentino-Alto Adige/Südtirol is divided into two provinces with regional competencies. Finally, other special regions (Friuli-Venezia Giulia, Sardinia, and Sicily) have administrative divisions (depending on their statutes) that may have different denominations (in Sicily, for example, the subregional administrative level is represented by so-called free consortia).

The entire territory of the Republic is ultimately divided into municipalities, which constitute the smallest territorial unit mentioned by the Constitution. There are approximately 8,000 municipalities, varying greatly in demographic size: the largest, the municipality of Rome, according to the 2022 census, has 2,755,309 inhabitants, while the smallest have fewer than 40 inhabitants.

25. The Italian Constitution does not expressly provide for the existence of an official language. In linguistic matters, it limits itself to establishing that the Republic protects linguistic minorities with specific norms (for more information on this, including the list of linguistic minorities, refer to Part IV, Chapter 4). For this reason, there are no official data on the number of residents who speak Italian as their first language. Such statistics exist exclusively for the province of Bolzano/Bozen, which is, in fact, the only one where a historically significant linguistic minority exists. According to the latest available official data, from the general population census of the year 2011, in the Province of Bolzano/Bozen, the German-speaking group accounted for 314,604 people, or 69.41%, the Italian-speaking group counted 118,120 people, or 26.06%, and the Ladin-speaking group consisted of 20,548 people, or 4.53%.

Chapter 3. The Features of the Republican Constitution

by Valerio Onida†

§1. Rights and Duties of Citizens

updated by Antonio D'Andrea & Lorenzo Spadacini

26. The Constitution of the Italian Republic, adopted by the Constituent Assembly in 1947, reflects the main trends of the European tradition and embodies many of the principles which took root in continental Europe between the two World Wars.

The classical rights of civil and political freedom are proclaimed and developed in the Constitution. They are also enriched by more specific provisions and more precise guarantees and accompanied by a long list of social rights, peculiar to the 'welfare state' or 'social state', even though this term is not explicitly used in the Constitution, as it is, for instance, in the 1949 German *Grundgesetz.*

27. Freedom of association is expressly guaranteed along with other civil rights (Article 18). Much importance is given to the freedom of religion (Articles 19 and 20), and the choice made by Italy when it entered into the 1929 Concordat, as concerns relations with the Catholic Church, are confirmed (Article 7), even if the Constitutional Court has clarified that the Concordat cannot contradict the 'supreme principles' of the constitutional order and the main substance of the fundamental rights, and if the same Concordat was revised in 1984. The same pattern is followed for relations with other religions, which are regulated by law on the basis of agreements with their respective representatives (Article 8).

The Constitution also places strict limits on criminal law, with the prohibition of the death penalty (Articles 25 and 27).

28. As concerns political rights, a prominent role is played by both the constitutional principle of universal suffrage (Article 48) and the acknowledgement of the role of the parties as a tool for citizens to 'contribute, by democratic means, to national policy' (Article 49).

29. Whereas constitutional provisions in the field of civil and political rights are mainly intended to set precise limits to the exercise of power, thus stressing the inviolability of certain freedoms, economic rights, as they tend to expand even to the detriment of other people's freedom and dignity, are recognized and guaranteed with more caution. Statutes must define the appropriate goals and methods of ensuring that property and freedom of initiative are not exercised at the expense of other rights.

30. In practice, when dealing with personal freedom, freedom of expression or voting rights, the Constitution is concerned with deciding *under which conditions* limits can be set or restrictive measures can be introduced (with formulas such as 'by an explained act of the judicial authority and only in cases provided for by law', Article 13). On the contrary, when it comes to economic rights, the Constitution specifies that these 'cannot be applied in such a manner as to conflict with social utility' and that statutes are to prescribe 'such planning and controls as may be advisable for directing and coordinating public and private economic activities towards social and environmental objectives' (Article 41; the reference to environmental purposes was introduced with Constitutional Law No. 1/2022), as well as to ensure 'the social function' of private ownership and make it 'accessible to all' (Article 42).

31. The proclamation of 'the inviolable rights of the person, both as an individual and as a member of the social groups in which his or her personality finds expression' and the appeal to fulfil the 'unalterable duties of political, economic and social solidarity' correspond to this approach (Article 2). The same can be said for the representation of the classical principle of equality, not only before the law 'without distinction as to sex, race, language, religion, political opinions, and personal or social conditions' (Article 3(1)) but also as 'substantial equality'. It is the responsibility of the Republic to 'remove all obstacles of an economic and social nature which, by limiting the freedom and equality of citizens, prevent the full development of the human person and the effective participation of all workers in the political, economic and social organization of the country' (Article 3(2)).

32. Besides these fundamental liberties, the Constitution grants rights of 'welfare' benefits in the field of work (Article 4), education (Article 34) and social security (Article 38), the provision of which is left to Parliament within the limits of available resources, mostly coming from a tax system based on the citizen's duty to contribute to public expenditures in proportion to their resources, and characterized by progressivity (Article 53), with the purpose of ensuring a redistribution of wealth in furtherance of social justice.

A prominent role is played by the rights of the workers (Articles 35–40), which can be defended and promoted through trade union activities (Article 39) and the right to strike, as defined by legislation (Article 40). Several constitutional principles express particular favour for private saving, widespread small property (Articles 44 and 47), cooperative societies (Article 45).

33. These rights are guaranteed in part by the constitutional requirement that some matters be regulated by legislation, thus limiting the resort to regulations or discretionary decisions passed by administrative bodies. Other guarantees are the full acknowledgement of the right to institute legal proceedings and defend oneself in a court before a judge (Articles 24, 25 and 113) and the creation of a judicial body in order to protect the Constitution, namely the Constitutional Court (Articles 134–137).

34. It is clear that judicial enforcement of welfare rights is only possible if the substance of these rights is defined by Acts of Parliament. However, the constitutional provisions relating to these rights cannot be considered as merely deferring to specific laws or political 'programmes' left to Parliament's goodwill. On the contrary, constitutional provisions outlining aims can prevent conflicting legislative acts (and, in case of violation, justify review by the Constitutional Court) and guide the interpretation of Acts of Parliament.

Moreover, the procedures for reviewing the constitutionality of laws make it possible to integrate and correct the contents of statutory provisions, especially by the frequent appeal to the principle of equality and the connected principle of reasonableness, thus allowing for a broader and more complete implementation of rights.

§2. The Organization of the State

35. The organization of the State, as outlined by the Constitution, is based on the unconditional recognition of the principle of democracy (Article 1, 'Italy is a democratic Republic founded on labour. Sovereignty belongs to the people who exercise it in the manner and within the limits laid down by the Constitution'), with a clear approach aiming at distributing powers and safeguarding individuals against oppressive State actions.

Among the political forces that were particularly involved in the adoption of the Constitution, those leaning towards liberal democratic and social-Christian ideas (especially the Christian Democrats) looked for to make to pass a vision of 'institutional pluralism' which, although in a totally democratic context, could avoid the risks and excesses of parliamentary unlimited 'sovereignty'. Marxist political groups, especially the Communist Party, were more in favour of a system granting as much power as possible to Parliament, which was considered the supreme expression of popular sovereignty, through the mediation of political parties.

36. The 'pluralist' vision prevailed and was largely shared by all the greatest parties. Its fundamental constituent elements are: a 'perfect' bicameral system of government, with two Chambers having the same powers; considerable Head of State's powers; some mechanisms aimed at guaranteeing the stability and authority of the government, which is nonetheless responsible to Parliament; stronger guarantees of independence of the judicial power from the executive; the existence of a body, independent from Parliament, responsible for reviewing the constitutionality of legislation and resolving other constitutional controversies; a regional form of government, with the Regions enjoying legislative and administrative powers, as well as the possibility of influencing national political developments; the possibility of organizing referenda to repeal national laws, on popular or regional initiative, which might oppose Parliament's legislative decisions (Article 75). Another very important characteristic of the 'pluralist' vision is a Constitution which cannot be modified by ordinary legislation but only through a more rigid procedure which, although based on parliamentary deliberations, requires four readings and larger majorities, and eventually a referendum.

37. Not all these elements had, or still have, the same importance, meaning and fate with regard to the evolution of the Italian constitutional experience, as will be shown in the following chapters, especially when dealing with the system of government.

38. The country's political government is based on political representation in Parliament and the principles of the parliamentary system, the application of which will be dealt with in more detail in Part II, Chapter 1. For the time being, we shall only examine its main features.

39. Parliament is composed of two Chambers elected (entirely in the case of the Chamber of Deputies and almost entirely for the Senate, the latter elected on a regional basis) by universal suffrage (Articles 56–58, *see* Part II, Chapter 3). The government is appointed by the President of the Republic (Article 92) and must enjoy the confidence of a majority in the two Chambers and remains in office as long as it retains that confidence (Article 94, *see* Part II, Chapter 6). The Head of State, elected by Parliament which also comprises regional delegates on this occasion (Article 83: *see* Part II, Chapter 2, §1), does not control government but has powers of coordination and guarantee, especially for the resolution of political and parliamentary crises, and can dissolve Parliament before the natural end of the legislature (Article 88, *see* Part II, Chapter 2, §12). Parliament exercises legislative power, and the government exercises executive powers, but the latter may also adopt legislative acts acting on the authority of Parliament and within the limits laid down by it, or in situations characterized by necessity and urgency, but requiring the subsequent ratification of Parliament which has to intervene within sixty days. The representative system is also enriched by institutions of direct democracy, the most important being the referendum, which can be called at the request of a group of voters (almost 500,000) or five Regional Councils, in order to repeal statutes or acts having the force of law (Article 75, *see* Part I, Chapter 5).

40. As far as the territorial distribution of powers is concerned, the Constitution has confirmed the choice of a unitary State (Article 5), made when the Kingdom of Italy was established, although it provides for significant forms of administrative as well as legislative and political devolution, by the creation of twenty Regions (Articles 114–131), governed by elective bodies with legislative and administrative jurisdiction (*see* Part III, Chapter 1). The Republic also has about 8,000 municipalities and over 100 Provinces and Metropolitan Areas (Articles 114 and 118). This part of the Constitution has been deeply reformed by Constitutional Law No. 3/2001 (*see* below, §4).

41. The 'pluralist' spirit of the Constitution appears mainly in its guarantee provisions. In accordance with the continental European tradition, the judicial function (*see* Part II, Chapter 7) is performed by professional magistrates (except for limited cases), usually selected by competitive examinations (Article 106) designed to test their technical skills. Their *status* is guaranteed both by the absence of external restraints (judges are subject only to the laws: Article 101, paragraph 2) and by a centralized system of government that has at its summit a Council composed mainly of representatives elected from among the magistrates themselves, besides other members elected by Parliament (Article 104, *see* Part II, Chapter 7, §2). The independence of 'special' courts (with jurisdiction over administrative, accounting, military and fiscal matters) is instead statutorily guaranteed (Articles 103 and 108): statutes provide for a similar system of partial self-government. Although the judicial function is performed 'in the name of the people' (Article 101, paragraph 1), it cannot be influenced by political decisions taken directly or indirectly by the people in compliance with the democratic principle of majority.

42. Magistrates are not representatives of the people. They are called upon to enforce the law as their knowledge and conscience instruct them: policies are established by parliamentary enactments or executive regulations and decisions, the fair enforcement of which is guaranteed by the judicial bodies and the trial system, culminating in the Court of Cassation's review of the uniform enactment of law (Article 111).

Criminal prosecution is compulsory (Article 112) and hence not dependent on the mere discretionary choices of the prosecutors, which can avail themselves directly of the judicial police force (Article 109). Citizens are protected from possible violations or miscarriages of justice by the trial system (divided into various jurisdictions) and the rules of fair trial, in which everyone can fully exercise their right of defence (Articles 24 and 111).

43. A special feature of the institutional order embodied in the 1947 Constitution is the creation of an organ of constitutional justice. In addition to the classical liberal guarantees of rights (such as the guarantee that certain rights be limited only by statute, the right of judicial protection and the independence of the judiciary), this choice introduced not only a new form of guarantee designed to ensure the observance of constitutional provisions but also a new element in the balance of powers, through the review of the constitutionality of laws and, more generally, the attribution of the power to settle constitutional controversies to the Constitutional Court, a non-representative, judicial body (Article 134). The latter is based on a model first established in Europe with Kelsen's Constitution of Republican Austria, then established in Italy and Germany after the Second World War, and spread more recently to many European and non-European States.

44. The Constitutional Court (*see* Part II, Chapter 9) is composed of legal experts who are in part elected by the judiciary and in part elected or appointed by other constitutional or representative bodies (Parliament and the President of the Republic, Article 135), but all fully independent. This choice reflects the two sides of the constitutional function of the Court: the impartial enactment of constitutional provisions, although often expressing general principles, and the political character of judicial review of legislation, hence entrusted to an independent body, different from the common judiciary. The Court is also called upon to settle constitutional disputes such as controversies between the central and regional powers, or between different State powers, to decide on the impeachment of the President of the Republic and to rule on the admissibility of referenda (Article 134; Article 2 of Constitutional Law No. 1/1953).

§3. The Implementation of the Constitution

45. The implementation of the Constitution was a long and uneven process. Provisions dealing with the relations between Parliament, government and the Head of State, peculiar to the parliamentary system, were implemented from the outset. The ones applying to the Constitutional Court, however, were not implemented until 1955. The system of partial self-government for 'ordinary' magistrates in the form of the High Council of Judges (*Consiglio Superiore della Magistratura*, CSM) was only instituted in 1958. Moreover, most of the Acts of Parliament passed before or during the Fascist regime, including the civil, criminal and procedural codes dating back to the 1930s and early 1940s, remained in force, mainly unchanged, and it was only in 1956 that the Constitutional Court started to repeal, though often in a partial and gradual manner, the provisions openly in conflict with the new Constitution. Only a new criminal procedure code was enacted in 1988.

46. The Referendum Law was only passed in 1970 as a result of a political agreement between the sponsors of the Divorce Law (No. 698/1970) and the Catholic forces who supported a referendum for its repeal. Since the 1974 divorce referendum, in which 59% of the voters opposed the repeal of the law, a high number of referenda have been held, and only in more recent years have voters proved less willing to take part in them. They have been aimed at both contesting new legislation and promoting the modification of old statutes that Parliament hesitated or never bothered to change. The success of referendum petition often encouraged the Parliament to carry out reforms even before the referendum itself could be held.

47. The Constitution's other major innovation, namely the regional system, was not implemented quickly, beginning with only the five 'Special Statute' Regions, set up in the main islands (Sicily and Sardinia) and in some border zones (Valle d'Aosta, Trentino-Alto Adige and Friuli-Venetia Julia, the later in 1963) established from the outset. The other Regions were not set up until 1970 when the State Administration had already been restructured and consolidated according to a centralized pattern. The result was both partial and unsatisfactory, owing to the persistence of centralist legislative and administrative practices, the inadequacy of regional Administrative bodies, as well as the 'national' character and centralization of all political and social forces at least until the 1990s. A stronger devolution programme was enacted by means of ordinary laws in 1997–1998, while in 1999 and 2001, a constitutional reform dramatically enhanced the powers of Regions and local bodies and reduced the State's control over them (but the following years have seen to develop a legislation that extends the interventions of the State, especially in respect of financial matters).

There was also a delay in implementing reforms of the central bodies of government and the administration, as well as in modernizing and adjusting legislation to new problems. The Law dealing with the Prime Minister's Office and government's rule-making power was passed in 1988, and only in 1999–2000 was legislation passed on the reorganization of the central administrative apparatus.

48. Relations between the State and the Church were long 'frozen' by the 1929 Concordat, explicitly cited in the Constitution. It was not until the 1970s that rulings of the Constitutional Court started to call some of its aspects into question. A global revision of the Concordat was carried out in 1984, and only afterwards 'agreements' with minority religious confessions were made in compliance with Article 8 of the Constitution, but as yet there is no general law on non-Catholic denominations, after Law No. 1159/1929.

§4. The Evolution of the Political System and Constitutional Reforms

updated by Antonio D'Andrea & Lorenzo Spadacini

49. Over the course of more than seventy years since its entry into force, the Republican Constitution has been amended on various occasions, and there has been lively debate, in particular since the 1980s, whether there is a need for broader reform.

50. The procedure for amending the Constitution is not particularly complex or difficult to implement: an amendment law, which may be tabled on the initiative either of members of Parliament or of the government, or by a Regional Council, or also by at least 50,000 voters, must be approved by both Houses, each by a dual vote, the second of which must be held at least three months after the first. During the second vote, a majority must be reached (50% plus one of the members) in both Houses. If the two-thirds majority is achieved in both Houses, the constitutional law will be promulgated without further action and will enter into force. If however this majority is not reached, a minority in either House or 500,000 voters or five Regional Councils may ask that it be put to a referendum, in which the law may be approved by a majority of valid votes, irrespective of the turnout (concerning this procedure, *see* further Part I, Chapter 4, §2; and Part II, Chapter 4, §4).

51. Since 1963, a total of twenty-three laws amending the Constitution have been approved (in addition to other constitutional laws to supplement the Constitution), almost all of which have made specific amendments to individual provisions or specific institutes of the Constitution. The most important have concerned: a change to the number of the members of Parliament and a reduction of the term in office of the Senate (1963); a reduction of the term in office of the judges on the Constitutional Court (1967); criminal proceedings against Ministers for offences committed during the course of their functions, which no longer fall under the competence of the Constitutional Court (1989); a prohibition on the early dissolution of the Houses of Parliament during the last six months of the mandate of the President of the Republic (1991); the requirement for a two-thirds majority in order to approve laws granting amnesties or sentence reduction schemes [*indulto*] (1992); a reduction in the prerogatives of members of Parliament (1993); the form of Government of the Regions (1999); the express incorporation into the Constitution of the principles of a 'fair trial' (1999); the right of Italians resident abroad to vote for a portion of the members of the two Houses (2000–2001); the amendment of the title of the Constitution concerning the Regions and the local authorities (2001); the introduction into the Constitution of the principle of equal opportunities between women and men in access to public and elected office (2003); the abolition of the exceptions to the prohibition on the death penalty (2007); the introduction of the principle of balanced budgets into the Constitution (2012); the reduction of about one-third of the number of members in the Chambers (2020) and of the minimum voting age for the Senate (2021); the incorporation in the constitutional text of environmental protection as a principle (2022). Only Constitutional Law No. 3/2001 applied to an entire title (Title V of Part II) of the Constitution on the Regions, Provinces and municipalities, providing for a significant expansion to regional powers.

52. Overall, the constitutional system was not called into discussion, at least as long as the political framework out of which it emerged remained unchanged. As noted above, three-quarters of the seats in the Constituent Assembly (Chapter 1, §4, n. 20) were occupied by representatives of the three great parties (the Christian Democrats, the Socialist Party and the Communist Party), and it was the agreement reached between these three parties – although not without significant contributions from the other minor political groupings, mainly of liberal democratic background – which enabled the Constitution to be approved by 87.9% of the voting members and 81.6% of the members of the Assembly. This is in spite of the collapse of their political alliance in government in mid-1947, which was subsequently headed by the Christian Democrats along with the smaller centrist parties. The Constitution continued to be endorsed both by the governing parties and by the left opposition parties. Reference was often made in this regard to the 'constitutional arch', which excluded only parties representing a limited right-wing opposition (monarchical parties and the neo-Fascist Italian Social Movement).

53. It was only from the 1970s onwards, and more in particular from the 1980s, that tendencies and programmes seeking an overhaul of the constitutional system started to emerge, in particular in relation to the allocation of powers – with a specific focus on enhancing the executive, which according to some was institutionally weak – by amending the system of government, also by introducing a semi-presidential system or a parliamentary system dominated by the premier. At times, even contradictory tendencies emerged (such as first tendencies to the reinforcement of regional autonomy, then followed by tendencies to a reinforcement of the centre). More rarely, although on several occasions, there have also been proposals or suggestions to modify Part I of the Constitution concerning the rights and duties of citizens and the economic and social system.

54. However, at least until today, these 'reformist' tendencies have largely not borne fruit and have not been translated into specific legislation (unless on the occasion of the reform of Regions in 2001), above all as the various political forces have not been able to reach stable agreements between them in this regard.

In 1982–1983, the Houses established two committees, subsequently followed by a bicameral commission, which were charged with proposing constitutional amendments; the proposals made were wide-reaching and detailed, concerning *inter alia* the functions of the two Houses and relations between them, as well as the functioning of the government. However, they were never implemented.

Efforts towards change and the promotion of constitutional reform were stepped up at the start of the 1990s, also as a result of the political changes consequent international events that led to the end of the traditional structure of two opposing blocs dominated respectively by the United States and the Soviet Union.

In 1991, in a message to Parliament which was followed only by a short debate in both Houses, President of the Republic Cossiga even mooted the possibility of the convocation of a new constituent assembly.

55. Two years later, Constitutional Law No. 1/1993 was approved, which laid down a special procedure, as an exception to that provided for under the Constitution, for the adoption of a framework project for constitutional reform – to be submitted to the Houses and subsequently to a mandatory referendum, which would only be valid if approved by a majority of voters – concerning only Part II of the Constitution on the structure of the Republic. The bicameral commission thereby established drew up proposals concerning a modification in the 'structure of the state' (relations between the central State and the local authorities) and the 'system of government' (organization and legislative activity of the government, decree-laws), maintaining the parliamentary system but putting in place instruments to enhance the executive, such as the so-called mechanism of 'constructive no-confidence' (Parliament may only 'dismiss' the premier by proposing another). Also, these proposals were not acted upon.

56. In the meantime, the widespread conviction that it was necessary to establish the tangible possibility of alternating periods in government and opposition, based on the results of elections, by two opposing electoral groupings (right and left) led to the approval by a large majority of two referendums (in 1991 and in 1993) concerning the repeal of certain electoral legislation, which was followed in 1993 by the introduction, in place of the proportional list-based system, of a mixed system providing for three-quarters of elected representatives from single-member constituencies according to the 'first-past-the-post' system, with the remaining quarter on a proportional basis from competing lists, thus constituting a system with a strong majoritarian aspect. This change in turn resulted in effects on the political system.

57. Parallel to this, far-reaching upheaval and changes were affecting the system of parties (also as a result of judicial investigations which uncovered a diffuse system of illegal financing) with the disappearance or transformation of the parties hitherto represented. This radically changed the political settlement that had characterized the country since the start of the republican era.

58. In 1997, a constitutional law provided for the establishment of a new bicameral commission which was charged with examining projects to reform Part II of the Constitution, which was intended ultimately to result in a single overall project to be presented first for approval by the Houses and subsequently to a mandatory referendum, again therefore following a procedure that departed from Article 138 of the Constitution. The Commission's proposals sought to rewrite almost all of Part II of the Constitution, ranging from the structure of the State through the system of government (even departing from the current parliamentary system) to the law governing the judiciary. However, also on this occasion, hopes of a 'major reform' did not bear fruit. It was only in 2001 at the end of the legislature – according to the ordinary procedure pursuant to Article 138 and with the approval only of the centre-left majority of the time, after which it was approved by a referendum, however with a low turnout (only around 34%) – that Constitutional Law No. 3/2001 was approved which, as mentioned above, introduced far-reaching changes only to the title concerning the Regions and the local authorities.

59. In 2005, a constitutional law which provided, *inter alia,* not only for new reforms concerning the Regions but, above all, changes to the bicameral system and rules aimed at ensuring a stronger role and position for the President of the Council of Ministers was approved by a centre-right majority. However, the law was not approved when subjected to a referendum.

The same fate was reserved more recently for the reform approved by Parliament in 2016 (following an unsuccessful attempt to follow once again a special procedure for amending the Constitution) by the majority dominated by the (centre-left) Democratic Party. It sought, among other things, to modify the organization and functioning of the bicameral structure, reserving to the Chamber of Deputies the task of voting confidence in the government as well as the last word on the approval of almost all ordinary legislation while reining in the powers of the Regions and increasing those reserved exclusively to the State.

60. Again in 2005, a new electoral law was enacted which provided for a proportional list system and large constituencies but with a majority premium (on a national basis in the Chamber of Deputies and a regional basis in the Senate), which sought to guarantee control of the Houses to the party or coalition receiving the most votes. However, the Constitutional Court issued a ruling in relation to it in 2014 after the law had been applied in three successive elections (although in the last election no grouping had obtained a national majority in the Senate), which cancelled the provision for a majority premium insofar as it was not associated with a minimum threshold of votes and did not provide for preference votes allowing voters to choose their preferred candidates in the long lists introduced by the parties.

61. In parallel with the new constitutional reform of 2016 (which was not approved in the referendum), in 2015, a new electoral law for the Chamber of Deputies was approved which provided once again for a list-based ballot with a majority premium, although this time associated with a threshold of 40% on national level, or the winning of a second round of the election (run-off), which would be reserved only to the two lists receiving most votes in the first round. This legislation too was also found unconstitutional in 2017 and hence annulled by the Constitutional Court insofar as it provided for a large majority to the list winning the run-off, no matter how many votes it had received in the first round.

It was only in November 2017, shortly before the next elections scheduled for the spring of 2018, that a new electoral law entered into force, which establishes a system for both Houses under which three-eighth of members are elected in single-member constituencies and five-eighth in multi-member constituencies on a proportional basis from the lists presented. However, voters are only able to cast one vote, which is valid both for the candidate in the single-member constituency and the related list or lists.

62. As far as the constitutional reforms are concerned, the author of these pages is convinced that the issue was actually 'mythicized' in Italy as if the roots of evil in this country were to be sought – and remedied – in constitutional rules. The political, social and economic roots of such problems, the likelihood of resolving them by legislation and political procedures, and – most of all – the risks that hazardous reforms could pose to the institutional balance of powers have been underestimated. However, the possibility of carrying out constructive reforms at both the constitutional and other levels aimed at improving the functionality of the system has often been neglected in order to pursue the 'myth' of an overall constitutional reform or of a deep change in the system of government. Only after the parliamentary elections of 2018 did a large majority, comprehensive (at least on the occasion of the last votes) of both centre-right and centre-left parties, approve a new amendment to the Constitution concerning the reduction in the two Chambers to about two-thirds of current membership. The constitutional law was then approved by a referendum in 2020, with a turnout of more than 50% of the voters and a majority of almost 70% of valid votes.

63. The XVIII Legislature once again demonstrates the extreme volatility of the Italian political system, resulting in a change of parliamentary majority three times, each time giving rise to a different government (the most recent of which, a broad coalition, led by Mario Draghi, former governor of ECB). In particular, after the re-election of the incumbent Head of State, a government crisis led to the early dissolution of Parliament and an early political vote. This resulted in a new centre-right majority, led by a party – Fratelli d'Italia (Brothers of Italy) – that had maintained an opposition stance throughout the previous Legislature regarding all of the successive majorities. During that vote, the constitutional reforms that reduced the number of parliamentarians and allowed for the direct election of the Senate by all voters over 18 were also tested for the first time.

64. The stability of the current government, following the favourable numbers in both the Chamber and the Senate for the centre-right coalition (the existing electoral system encourages coalition formation even before the vote), appears to allow the possibility of approving significant constitutional reforms, as envisioned by Prime Minister Giorgia Meloni herself in her inaugural speech before the Chambers. On the one hand, this would involve approving additional autonomy for the Regions, as already allowed by the existing constitutional provisions, and, on the other hand, it would entail overcoming the parliamentary system, which is considered inadequate to govern the Italian democracy due to its alleged complexity. In this regard, the goal apparently is to have a direct election of the executive, somewhat following the French semi-presidential model (or the direct election of Italian Regional Presidents, introduced after the constitutional amendment approved in 1999). Regardless of the merit of these reforms, which seem to be proceeding parallelly, according to the government's and the majority's approach, they unfortunately seem to create a strong division on constitutional matters once again between the governing majority and the opposition forces. Indeed, although considerably weakened by the last political vote, the opposition forces do not appear convinced of the need to implement the aforementioned changes, as is also the case with a substantial portion of constitutional doctrine. Therefore, there remains a significant tension on the constitutional front, which once again exposes the Italian system to the risks of a direct confrontation on constitutional matters.

Part I. Sources of Law

Chapter 1. Introduction

by Maurizio Pedrazza Gorlero & Matteo Nicolini

65. The Italian legal system belongs to the civil law legal tradition and therefore rests on a codified system of rules serving as the primary source of law. As a consequence, the primary source of Italian law is created by national and subnational legislatures in the form of legislation. Although the Italian legal system is mainly codified, custom is a source of law as well. But it cannot run counter to the application of legislation nor originate legal norms conflicting with written provisions (custom *secundum legem*). This means that custom cannot act *contra legem*. To put it another way, customary law can only fill in gaps left by written law, and, where it is found to be legitimate, it may merely integrate written legislation (custom *praeter legem*). If this were the case, custom satisfies the requirements in order to be recognized as a source of law. A typical example of custom *secundum legem* is trade custom, i.e., a practice adopted in business and mercantile transaction that has such regularity of observation in a place as to justify an expectation that it will be observed with respect to the transaction in question. Trade custom complements written legislation, providing that law explicitly refers to it (Article 8, General Provisions of the 1942 Civil Code). Custom is also a source of law at the constitutional level. Although the topic has been debated by scholars, it is possible to recognize room for its existence.

First, the Constitution does not lay down a detailed regulation of all the relevant aspects of the State organization. Thus, custom can integrate the black-letter constitution. Second, the Constitutional Court credited the existence of customs at the constitutional level in the case of constitutional organs' financial records, no-confidence motion towards a single Minister, and parliamentary legislative process.[1]

66. The Constitution does not list all the sources of law. An incomplete list can be found in Articles 1–4 of the General Provisions of the Civil Code enacted in 1942 – i.e., prior to the Constitution – which do not take into account the sources of law subsequently introduced by the same Constitution. Articles 1–4 of the General Provisions of the Civil Code arrange the sources of law on a hierarchical scale, which is based on their legal force. Thus, we find statutes, regulations, corporative norms,

1. *See* Constitutional Court, Judgments Nos 129/1981, 7/1996, and 140/2008 respectively.

and customs. Provisions referring to corporative norms are no longer in force since they were repealed after the defeat of Fascism and the dismantling of its corporative system.[2] Corporative norms should now be replaced by collective labour agreements under Article 39 of the Constitution. This provision, however, has never been implemented (*see* below, Chapter 4, n. 116).

67. As said, the Constitution does not lay down a comprehensive list of the sources of law in the Italian legal system. Indeed, it only refers to primary legislation and constitutional laws. Unlike the *Statuto Albertino*, the 1948 Constitution has experienced a remarkable increase in the number of sources of law. For instance, the Constitution added new sources at the constitutional level, having a force superior to that of the Acts of Parliament, such as constitutional statutes amending the Constitution and constitutional statutes that are not formally incorporated in the body of the Constitution. Moreover, as Italy has a regional framework, the Constitution distributes legislative powers between the national and regional orders of government (Article 117). Furthermore, the Constitution sets ad hoc sources, namely sources that regulate specific subjects, such as the relationships between the State and the Catholic Church (Article 7, II), as well as between the State and other religious denominations (Article 8, III). In other words, Italy has a pluralistic-oriented constitution: there are numerous legal sources, and several entities are entitled to legislate.

68. The sources of law that the Constitution sets forth are mainly constitutional statutes and primary legislation. Parliament is not allowed to introduce any other primary source of law. If it intends to do so, it has to alter the Constitution by resorting to the constitutional amending formula set forth in Article 138 of the Constitution. In addition, the Constitution does not regulate secondary or subordinate legislation that is made by the executive to whom Parliament has delegated part of its lawmaking power. The sole references to subordinate legislation are to be found in Articles 87 and 116, VI, of the Constitution. Whereas Article 87 refers to the enactment of executive regulations by the President of the Republic, Article 116, VI allots subordinate legislation powers among the different tiers of government. Consequently, secondary legislation is 'open' to changes and integrated by subsequent acts of the legislative branch. The subordinate legislative process and all types of regulations can be found in Law No. 400/1988, as amended by Law No. 69/2009. At the regional level, regional basic laws regulate secondary legislation, whereas by-laws are the means through which local authorities can make binding rules under such enabling legislation as Article 7 of Legislative Decree No. 267/2000.

69. Such a high number of sources of law may be classified according to different criteria, which are particularly useful in order to solve antinomies between conflicting norms.

There are three criteria for solving antinomies: the chronological criterion, the hierarchical criterion, and the criterion of competence. The chronological criterion

2. *See* the Royal Decree-Law No. 721/1943 and the Order in Council enacted by the Lieutenant of the Kingdom No. 369/1944.

applies between laws enacted by the same legislative body, or between laws with general or equal competence and rank; between statutes of the National Parliament; between two statutes of the same Regional Legislature; between a statute of Parliament and acts with force of law (legislative decrees, decree-laws, etc.). If there are two inconsistent or conflicting statutes, the latter repeals the earlier to the extent of the inconsistency (*lex posterior derogat priori*).[3]

The hierarchical criterion applies between sources arranged on a hierarchical scale. The source of law with higher rank triggers the invalidity of those with lower rank that are inconsistent with the former. For example, subordinate legislation must be consistent with primary legislation; where there is an inconsistency between primary and subordinate legislation, the former prevails.

The criterion of competence refers to sources of law to which the Constitution confers the regulation of a specific matter to the exclusion of others. For example, the internal organization of the Houses of Parliament is a matter reserved for their own rules (Article 64 of the Constitution). A source without jurisdiction regulating a reserved matter is invalid and can be challenged before the Constitutional Court. In certain cases, it is necessary to apply different criteria in order to solve antinomies between sources of law. For instance, both the criterion of competence and the hierarchical criterion are applied to regulate the relationship between the Acts of Parliament and regional laws.

3. *See* Constitutional Court, Judgments Nos 49/1970 and 63/1970.

Chapter 2. External Sources: International Law

by Maurizio Pedrazza Gorlero & Matteo Nicolini

70. As it draws from itself its own effectiveness, the Italian system is an 'original' one. In this respect, it considers the system of international law – as well as those of foreign countries – as separate. In order to incorporate international law into domestic law, legislative action is required. Consequently, all international sources must be incorporated to produce legal effects in the domestic legal system. The Italian legal system is therefore impermeable to legal rules laid down by external sources unless it allows them to acquire legal relevance within it. This entails a limitation of State sovereignty: such limitation works automatically when the same Constitution upholds such a possibility, such as in the case of international customary law (Article 10, I, of the Constitution). As for international treaties, their incorporation requires legislation, and their ranking depends on the provision incorporating them. Thus, customary norms acquire quasi-constitutional ranking; international treaties enjoy the same ranking as the internal provisions. The Italian legal system has connections with the international, foreign, and the European legal systems. These connections are regulated by procedures and rules and differ from each other in terms of importance and effectiveness.

§1. Incorporation of International Law into Domestic law

71. How international law is incorporated into the Italian legal system depends on the nature of the source. Thus, international customary law and international treaties are incorporated according to different procedures.

§2. Incorporation of Customary International Law

72. 'Customary law' is a source of law. On the one hand, it requires a general and consistent practice of States within the international community ('objective component': *usus* or *diuturnitas*). On the other hand, such practice is followed out of a sense of legal obligation: the international actors consider it to be law and observe it on the grounds of its binding legal effects ('subjective component': *opinio juris ac necessitatis*).

Under Article 10, I, of the Constitution, Italy automatically incorporates 'the generally recognised tenets of international law' (international customary rules) into its legal system. Pursuant to Article 10, I, of the Constitution, incorporation of customary international law is then accomplished through a mechanism of automatic incorporation. It is what Italian jurisprudence calls 'mobile' (or 'formal') reference to the rules produced by international sources at customary level.

It should be argued that 'the generally recognised tenets of international law' also refer to those international treaties and covenants on human rights protection, such as the Universal Declaration of Human Rights, the International Covenant on Civil and Political Rights, the International Covenant on Economic, Social and Cultural

Rights, and the UN Convention on the Rights of the Child. These covenants set a common standard for the protection of human rights and may be considered a universal achievement for all peoples and all nations. However, the Constitutional Court does not uphold the assumption. In the Court's opinion, Article 10, I, of the Constitution only refers to customary international law and, to a lesser extent, those treaties that merely repeat principles and rules whose source can be traced back to customary international law.[4]

Customary international rules (i.e., the domestic provisions which incorporate them) place themselves at an intermediate level between the Constitution and primary legislation. As a consequence, the internal sources incorporating international customary rules can be defined as 'atypical' because they enjoy a special rank as regards ordinary primary legislation (i.e., an intermediate one). If customary rules and subsequent primary legislation are inconsistent, the former repeal the latter to the extent of the inconsistency. On the contrary, primary legislation that infringes customary international law is void and can be challenged before the Constitutional Court.[5]

Consequently, customary international law enjoys a status that is comparable to the Constitution.

The Constitutional Court traditionally distinguished between customs that had come into force prior to the Constitution and those that had come into force after the enactment of the same Constitution. The former usually prevailed over the Constitution according to the *lex specialis rule*. Customary rules enacted after the entry into force of the Constitution could not violate the 'basic principles' of the same constitutional system.[6]

The Constitutional Court recently stated that all customary international law must comply with the 'basic principles' of the constitutional system.[7] To this extent, the Court found that the customary rule of State immunity from foreign jurisdictions could not infringe two fundamental core features of the Constitution: the protection of inviolable human rights (Article 2) and access to justice (Article 24). If it were the case – and this occurred as far as tort claims related to war crimes and crimes against humanity were concerned – the automatic incorporation of customary international law into the Italian legal order would be limited by such fundamental constitutional principles.

§3. Incorporation of International Treaties and Agreements

73. Italy adopts a dualistic approach to international law; i.e., it conceives of international and domestic law as belonging to fundamentally separate legal orders. As a consequence, international treaties are sources of international law but do not have effect in domestic law until they are incorporated by an Act of Parliament.

4. *See* Constitutional Court, Judgments Nos 15/1996, 393/2006 and 102/2020.
5. *See* Constitutional Court, Judgments Nos 278/1992, 172/1999, 131/2001, and 159/2023.
6. *See* Constitutional Court, Judgment No. 48/1979.
7. *See* Constitutional Court, Judgment No. 234/2014.

Hence, international treaties require legislative action for their incorporation into the national legal system. Such incorporation needs either an Act of Parliament, which reproduces the provisions of the treaty (*legge di esecuzione*), or an act to which the treaty is annexed (*ordine di esecuzione* or enforcement clause). While the former directly incorporates the treaty, the latter (enforcement clause) refers to the content of the annexed treaty. The enforcement clause is said to ensure a 'fixed' (or 'material' or 'upon receipt') reference to the specific provisions laid down by the international treaty.

The Act of Parliament incorporating international treaties is an ordinary statute. As a consequence, it is hierarchically inferior only to constitutional sources and may therefore be repealed by subsequent Acts of Parliament, notwithstanding the consequences for the State within the international system as a result of the repeal.[8] However, abrogative referenda cannot be held on acts incorporating international treaties.[9] This last assumption is held on the ground of the constitutional provision prohibiting laws authorizing the ratification of international treaties to be submitted to abrogative referenda (Article 75, II, of the Constitution).

§4. Incorporation of Lateran Pacts

74. According to Article 7, II, of the Constitution, Acts of Parliament incorporating the Lateran Pacts can be amended only by Parliament upon an agreement entered between the State and the Catholic Church. This is due to the mutual recognition of sovereignty of State and Church within their respective jurisdictions. To put it another way, the Constitution regulates State–Church relations according to the so-called concordat principle. Thus, Article 7, II, of the Constitution confers upon the acts incorporating the Lateran Pacts a force of law that is superior to that of the other Acts of Parliament. Moreover, such acts are able to depart from constitutional provisions that do not contain 'the supreme principles of the constitutional system',[10] such as the principle of equal protection of the laws.[11]

In addition, such acts cannot be repealed by constitutional provisions, which do not contain the 'supreme principles of the constitutional legal system'. As mentioned above, the amendment to the pacts is an 'atypical' Act of Parliament, which must be preceded by an agreement between the State and the Catholic Church stipulated in an external legal system common to both. The acts incorporating the Lateran Pacts have a force of law comparable to constitutional laws. In fact, the phenomenon of the 'atypical' sources consists of the separation of the form and the effectiveness of the source. As a consequence, the active force – i.e., the ability of innovation of the legal system – corresponds to a different resistance to abrogation (passive force).

8. *See* Constitutional Court, Judgments Nos 14/1964 and 96/1982.
9. *See* Constitutional Court, Judgments Nos 16/1978 and 26/1982.
10. *See* Constitutional Court, Judgment No. 30/1971.
11. *See* Constitutional Court, Judgment No. 18/1982.

§5. International Treaties Binding Primary Legislation under Article 117, I of the Constitution

75. Article 117, I, of the Constitution, introduced by the Constitutional Act No. 3/2001, states that legislative powers shall be vested in the State and the Regions in compliance with international obligations. Article 117, I, sets up an additional limit to State legislative power since it treats international treaty obligations as hierarchically superior to statutory law.

This limitation appended to primary legislation was originally laid down in the basic laws of the 'Autonomous' Regions.[12] Nevertheless, the Constitutional Court held that all Regions were bound by international treaties and had to respect international obligations.[13]

Scholars have long debated with respect to the question of whether international law binds State legislation under Article 117, I, of the Constitution. On the one hand, it should be argued that this article simply reasserts what Article 10, I, states with regard to international customary law. On the other hand, however, Article 117, I, seems to treat international treaty obligations as hierarchically superior to both national and regional statutory laws. From this, it does not follow, however, that this article incorporates monism into the Italian Constitution. This provision does not automatically incorporate any external source of law, neither domestic nor international, but merely refers to the effects of the incorporation, i.e., to the binding effects of international obligations over the national legal system, as well as the interpretation of these effects by international and supranational tribunals. Article 1, I, of Law No. 131/2003 – which implements Article 117, I, of the Constitution at the legislative level – holds the same assumption, as it expressly refers to both international customary law and international agreements, i.e., to all the external sources of international obligations binding the legislative power and that the Constitution includes in the constitutional bloc.

In the opinion of the Constitutional Court, international treaties that bind primary legislation are only those consistent with the Constitution once they have been incorporated into domestic law. If the treaty matches the above-mentioned criteria, it can be incorporated into the constitutional bloc and used as a parameter for challenging the constitutional validity of primary legislation before the Constitutional Court. As a consequence, a statute held by the Constitutional Court to violate an international treaty under Article 117, I, of the Constitution lacks domestic legal force and is declared unconstitutional. Among the international treaties binding primary legislation, there is the European Convention on Human Rights (ECHR).[14] The Court also attaches binding effects to the interpretation of that treaty that is delivered by the European Court on Human Rights.[15] Furthermore, the Court includes in the constitutional bloc the United Nations Convention on the Rights of

---

12. Article 3, I, basic law for Sardinia; Art. 2, I, basic law for Valle d'Aosta/*Vallée d'Aoste*; Art. 4, I, basic law for Friuli-Venezia Giulia; Art. 4, I, basic law for Trentino-Alto Adige/*Südtirol*.
13. *See* Constitutional Court, Judgment No. 49/1963.
14. Among others, *see* Constitutional Court, Judgments Nos 348 and 349/2007, Nos 39/2008, 331 and 317/2009, 93/2010, 113/2011, 78/2012, and 195/2022.
15. Among others, *see* Constitutional Court, Judgments Nos 348 and 349/2007, 49/2015, 276/2016, 43/2017, 43/2018, 25/2019, and 33/2025.

the Child (CRC or UNCRC);[16] the European Convention on the Exercise of Children's Rights (Strasbourg, 25 January 1996);[17] the United Nations Convention on the Rights of Persons with Disabilities (CRPD);[18] and the European Social Charter.[19]

§6. Conflict of Law Rules

76. The relations between the Italian legal system and the legal systems of foreign countries are regulated by conflicts of law rules and private international law rules. These are procedural rules set forth by Law No. 218/1995, which determines the legal system and the jurisdiction applicable to a specific dispute with a foreign element (e.g., a contract to be enforced in another country). According to the conflicts of law rules, Italy governs the scope of its jurisdiction[20] and determines which law is applicable for resolving the dispute.[21] Moreover, it sets the proper regulation for the recognition and enforcement of foreign judgments.

16. Constitutional Court, Judgments Nos 7/2013, 239/2014, 92/2018, and 102/2020.
17. Constitutional Court, Judgment No. 7/2013.
18. Constitutional Court, Judgment No. 2/2016.
19. Constitutional Court, Judgments Nos 120 and 194/2018.
20. Articles 3–5 of Law No. 218/1995.
21. Articles 20–63 of Law No. 218/1995.

Chapter 3. European Sources

by Maurizio Pedrazza Gorlero & Matteo Nicolini

77. European sources of law are neither external nor domestic ones. In fact, they cannot be properly considered external sources as European law may be regarded as a sui generis legal system. Although European law belongs to a legal system that is external to the Italian one, it may have a direct effect on Italian domestic law according to the principles of direct applicability and direct effect. In addition, European law prevails upon internal sources, according to a principle similar to that of competence. In other words, European law is supreme over national law, and anything contained in the European Union (EU) treaties supersedes domestic legal provisions.[22]

This peculiar relationship between European and domestic laws is due to the Italian dualist position which conceives EU and domestic law as belonging to separate legal orders, although coordinated as they share personal and territorial features.[23] According to the supremacy of EU law over domestic law, the parameters of the competence of the same EU are set by the treaties upon which it is based.

Article 1.2.b of the Treaty of Lisbon (2007) states that the Union shall be founded on the Treaty on European Union (TEU) and on the Treaty on the Functioning of the European Union (TFEU) and that 'The Union shall replace and succeed the European Community.'

§1. The Incorporation of the TEU and of the TFEU (Former EEC Treaty)

78. Upon Italy joining the then European Community, the treaties establishing the European Communities (now the TFEU) and their subsequent amendments[24] were incorporated into Italian law by the national legislation.[25]

Such acts do not follow the principles that apply to the laws incorporating 'ordinary' international treaties. In fact, they cannot be repealed by an ordinary Act of Parliament. Moreover, EU treaties establish their own sources of law, which have to be subsequently enforced into the Italian legal system.

The provisions of the treaties, which establish European sources of law, have a legal force that is comparable to that of the Constitution. This is due to Article 11 of the Constitution: under conditions of equality with other states, this article allows Italy to limit its sovereignty to the extent of the creation of a legal system that

22. Constitutional Court, Judgment No. 183/1973.
23. Constitutional Court, Judgment No. 170/1984.
24. The Merger Treaty 1965, Acts of Accession, budgetary Treaties, the Single European Act 1986, the Treaty on European Union 1992, the Treaty of Amsterdam 1997, the Treaty of Nice 2000 and the Treaty of Lisbon 2007.
25. Law No. 766/1952, No. 1203/1957, No. 454/1992, No. 209/1998, No. 102/2002, No. 130/2008.

ensures peace and justice among nations.[26] Furthermore, Article 117, I, of the Constitution[27] states that Legislative powers shall be vested in the State and the Regions in compliance with constraints deriving from EU legislation, thus explicitly acknowledging the supremacy of EU law.

However, EU treaties must comply with the 'basic principles' of the constitutional system, which cannot be infringed by EU sources of law.[28]

Under the EU Treaty, the Charter of Fundamental Rights of the EU of 7 December 2000 (as amended on 12 December 2007) has the same legal value as the Treaties and therefore the same supremacy EU law enjoys within the Member States. The Constitutional Court has held so as well.[29] Consequently, the Charter implements the constitutional bloc and acts as a benchmark when it comes to reviewing primary legislation.[30]

§2. The Reception of European Law

79. EU primary legislation comprises the treaties incorporated by Parliament. European secondary legislation is passed by EU institutions under Article 161 of EURATOM Treaty and Article 288 of EU Treaty.

Secondary legislation comprises 'regulations', 'directives' and 'decisions'. Article 288 of the TFEU defines these terms as follows:

> 'A regulation shall have general application. It shall be binding in its entirety and directly applicable in all Member States.'
> 'A directive shall be binding, as to the result to be achieved, upon each Member State to which it is addressed, but shall leave to the national authorities the choice of form and methods.'
> 'A decision shall be binding in its entirety. A decision which specifies those to whom it is addressed shall be binding only on them.'

§3. EU Regulations

80. Article 11 of the Constitution has created a 'legislative automatism', which allows European regulations to supersede internal sources. This means that immediately upon its enactment, a regulation operates within Italian law as if its own legislature had produced the measure and to the exclusion of domestic law. They are

26. *See* Constitutional Court, Judgment No. 227/2010.
27. As amended by Constitutional Act No. 3/2001. *See* also Constitutional Court, Judgment No. 67/2022.
28. *See* Constitutional Court, Judgments Nos 183/1973 and 170/1984. *See also* ECJ 05-12-2015. Constitutional Court, Judgment No. 42/17.
29. *See* Constitutional Court, Judgments Nos 80/2011, 236/2016, 269/2017, 119/2019, and 15/2021.
30. *See*, e.g., Constitutional Court, Judgments Nos 20/2019, 112/2019, and 7/2025.

enforceable from the time of their creation, and States do not have to pass any further legislation. This 'legislative automatism' inhibits the decisional power of the domestic source; as a consequence, domestic rules inconsistent with EU regulations become legally irrelevant.

The relations between EU regulations and domestic statutes do not follow the criteria that govern antinomies between internal sources. The Constitutional Court played a pivotal role in shaping the relations between domestic law and European sources. The Italian Constitutional Court originally applied the chronological criterion, privileging the *lex posterior*.[31] However, this thwarted the supremacy of European law. In a subsequent judgment, the Constitutional Court held that it was necessary to challenge the constitutional validity of Italian legislative provisions inconsistent with European regulations.[32] In doing so, the Constitutional Court was able to take under its control a source of legislation of an external system. The European Court of Justice (ECJ) harshly criticized this case law. Finally, the Constitutional Court configured the conflict between domestic laws and regulations as a 'direct violation' of European law.[33] The Constitutional Court has eventually stated that regulations take precedence over previous and subsequent domestic legislation. The Constitutional Court has recently confirmed this rule of construction. National courts must set aside domestic legislation inconsistent with European regulations and must apply the latter in their entirety. Parliament and regional legislatures are also bound to repeal legislation to the extent of the inconsistency.[34] The Constitutional Court has the possibility to set aside national and regional legislation challenged in accordance with Article 127 of the Constitution, which sets the jurisdiction of the Constitutional Court over legislative disputes between State and Regions.[35] This is also due to Article 117, I, of the Constitution. As already noted, it treats EU sources of law as hierarchically superior to both national and regional legislation law. This has caused the 'Europeanization' of regional competences. EU legislation does not have to respect the distribution of powers set forth in the Constitution. The EU is free to allocate its powers between State and Regions according to the criteria enunciated in the EU Treaties. In cases of conflict between regional law and EU law, the latter prevails.[36]

§4. EU Directives

81. EU directives bind only Member States, leaving no discretion as to their objectives. They state general goals and leave the precise implementation in the appropriate form to the individual Member States. As a consequence, some domestic legislative action is required for their implementation; legislation enacted in

31. *See* Constitutional Court, Judgment No. 14/1964.
32. *See* Constitutional Court, Judgment No. 232/1975.
33. *See* Constitutional Court, Judgment No. 170/1984.
34. *See* Constitutional Court, Judgment No. 67/2022.
35. *See* Constitutional Court, Judgments Nos 384/1994, 94/1995, 102/2008, 66/2013, 171/2013, 269/2014, and 38/2015.
36. *See* Constitutional Court, Judgments Nos 384/1994, 94/1995, 102/2008, 66/2013, 171/2013, 269/2014, 38/2015, 161/2019, and 75/2023.

order to implement directives has a legal force that is superior to that of the ordinary Acts of Parliament since it can repeal previous laws and determine the invalidity of subsequent ones. It is then an 'atypical' source, which is not even subject to abrogative referenda. This is due to Article 117, I, of the Constitution, which binds State and regional legislation to respect EU constraints and calls for compliance with EU law.[37]

Some directives lay down obligations which are sufficiently clear and complete so that they are not subject to any exception and condition and do not require intervention on the part of Member States. These directives have a direct effect: individuals may rely on EU law in any action against the government without the need for their particular State to have passed the law within its own legal system. Therefore, they confer enforceable individual rights and impose obligations upon individuals. Both the ECJ and the Italian Constitutional Court have expressly acknowledged this[38] and held that directives could have a direct effect only between State and individuals.[39] In a recent ruling, the Italian Constitutional Court held that in case of conflict between Italian legislation and EU legislation that has a direct effect, national courts have two possibilities. They can either set aside domestic legislation (and apply EU law) or lodge a complaint before the Constitutional Court. The latter possibility must be preferred in case of inconsistency between domestic criminal law and EU law.[40]

§5. THE ANNUAL ACTS OF PARLIAMENT SETTING THE PROPER MEASURES FOR ENSURING THE FULFILMENT OF EU OBLIGATIONS

82. Law No. 234/2012 provides the legislative action required at the national level for implementing EU law. The statute provides us with two forms of legislative action for the precise implementation of EU law. These are the so-called *legge europea* and the so-called *legge di delegazione europea*, i.e., annual Acts of Parliament, which set forth the proper measures for ensuring the fulfilment of EU obligations.[41] Under this act, Parliament directly incorporates and implements directives and ECJ judgments and repeals primary legislation inconsistent therewith. In addition, Parliament can have recourse to both primary and subordinate delegated legislation.[42]

Moreover, Law No. 234/2012 implements Article 117, V, of the Constitution on the participation of Regions in the European decision-making process. Regions are enabled to incorporate EU directives in their fields of legislation in observance of procedures set forth by State law.[43] In addition, an Act of Parliament sets the proper measures for the State to act in substitution of the regions if the latter do not fulfil

37. Among others, *see* Constitutional Court, Judgments Nos 406/2005, 126/2006, 28/2010, and 18/2012.
38. ECJ 5-2-1963 C No. 26/1962; Constitutional Court, Judgment No. 182/1976.
39. Horizontal effect of EU law: ECJ 26-2-1986 C No. 152/1984.
40. *See* Constitutional Court, Judgment No. 7/2025.
41. Articles 29 ff of Law No. 234/2012.
42. Article 35 of Law No. 234/2012.
43. Article 40 of Law No. 234/2012.

EU obligations. Like the State, several Regions approve an annual act, which establishes the proper measures for ensuring the fulfilment of EU obligations.[44]

The State and regional acts setting proper measures for ensuring the fulfilment of EU law have the same force and effect as the single act implementing EU directives.[45]

44. *See* Constitutional Court, Judgment No. 63/2012.
45. Article 34 of Law No. 234/2012.

Chapter 4. Domestic Sources

by Maurizio Pedrazza Gorlero & Matteo Nicolini

§1. The Constitution

83. The Constitution is the fundamental law of Italy and provides the Republic with a comprehensive legal framework. It is hierarchically superior to all the domestic sources, the validity and force of which depend on whether they are enacted according to the same Constitution. Furthermore, the Italian Constitution is 'entrenched' or 'rigid': it sets forth the rules presiding the legislative process that has to be followed when it comes to amending its provisions. It also prevents the same provisions from being amended without respecting the constitutional amending formula enshrined in Article 138 of the Constitution. Procedures for constitutional amendments are thus more burdensome than those envisaged for ordinary laws.

Some constitutional provisions cannot be amended or replaced: for example, Article 139 states that 'The form of Republic shall not be a matter for constitutional amendment.' The 'form of the Republic' refers not only to the periodical election of the Head of State[46] but also to the pluralism which underpins the concept of constitutional democracy. Thus, it encompasses popular sovereignty, local and regional autonomy, the election of political representatives, freedom of thought, association, vote and so on.[47] Moreover, the rigidity of the Constitution puts constraints on both the constitutional and the ordinary legislators and presupposes the judicial review of legislation.[48] The Constitutional Court has adhered to the doctrine of unconstitutional constitutional amendments: these are deemed to be unconstitutional if they infringe the basic features of the Constitution, such as 'inviolable rights' and 'supreme principles of the constitutional system'.[49]

Constitutional core principles are hierarchically superior to any other source of law. It is called the 'super' or 'nuclear' Constitution, which comprises those constitutional provisions, which set the procedural and substantive limitation – explicit or implied – to constitutional amendments.

§2. Constitutional Laws

84. Article 138 of the Constitution sets forth a unitary legislative process for passing constitutional amendments and constitutional laws. Whereas constitutional amendments alter the text of the Constitution, the latter have a constitutional status but are not formally incorporated into the same Constitution. It is not easy to draw

46. Articles 83 and 85 of the Constitution.
47. Articles 1, 5, 56, 57, 21, 18 and 48 of the Constitution.
48. *Ibid.*
49. *See* Constitutional Court, Judgment No. 1146/1988.

a divide between constitutional amendments and constitutional laws: they share common features, and their fields of competence frequently overlap.

Constitutional laws are set at the apex of the legal system. They can amend every constitutional provision with the exception of the 'fundamental features' of the Constitution. Constitutional laws cannot be submitted to abrogative referenda since their amendment and repeal are envisaged provided it is set forth in Article 138 of the Constitution.

There are also atypical Acts at the constitutional level. These are: (a) the constitutional laws that alter the territory of the Regions and (b) the constitutional laws which adopt the basic laws of the 'special' Regions.

I. Constitutional Laws Providing the Territorial Alteration of the Regions

85. Article 132, I, of the Constitution requires a constitutional act in order to create new Regions, merge existing ones, and incorporate one Region into another one. The provision requires that new Regions must be 'vital' since they must have a minimum of one million inhabitants.[50]

The procedure laid down in the provision is extremely complex: (a) the request for territorial alteration must be called for by a number of Municipal Councils representing not less than one-third of the populations concerned in the territorial regrouping; (b) the population must consent to the alteration through referendum; (c) Parliament approves the constitutional law; (d) existing regions may express their views on the proposed territorial alteration.

Thus, the Constitution provides a legislative process for creating constituent units. The process has recourse to a *referendum*, through which the regional population decides its own 'self-identification' as a regional community. As a consequence, alterations cannot be unilaterally approved by Parliament: it can only ascertain, *upon a political basis*, whether the criteria enabling territorial alteration are consistent with Article 5 of the Constitution. If it were the case, Parliament may trigger the proposed alteration and therefore demarcate the self-determined new Region.

II. Constitutional Laws Adopting the Basic Laws of 'Autonomous' Regions

86. Article 131 of the Constitution establishes twenty Regions, five of which (Trentino-Alto Adige/*Südtirol*, Friuli-Venezia Giulia, Aosta Valley/*Vallée d'Aoste*, Sicily and Sardinia) are denominated 'Autonomous Regions'.[51] Autonomous Regions enjoy a higher degree of self-regulation, and their competences are enumerated in their own 'basic laws' (*statuti*), which are approved by Parliament as acts at the constitutional level. As the institution of Autonomous Regions corresponds to ethnic and geographical reasons, this type of constitutional law has a specific object, a specific *nomen juris*: they are indeed denominated *statuti speciali*, i.e., special

---

50. *See* Constitutional Court, Judgment No. 278/2011.
51. Article 116, I, of the Constitution.

basic laws. Furthermore, they have a limited territorial jurisdiction: their territorial scope coincides with the regional territory. Although they are constitutional laws, they are not incorporated into the constitutional text. However, they complement constitutional provisions in order to provide the Autonomous Regions with 'special forms and conditions of autonomy'. They have, then, a special status since they cannot amend all the constitutional provisions but only those falling within their specific field of competence, i.e., the regulation of special regional autonomy.

Constitutional laws adopting the basic laws of Autonomous Regions are usually amended by subsequent constitutional acts. In some cases, however, they can be altered by regional laws. The Constitutional Amendment Act No. 2/2001 grants Autonomous Regions the ability to set their own form of government and electoral system: the act is approved by absolute majority of the members of the regional legislature. The Constitutional Court holds that such an Act is an expression of regional constitutional autonomy.[52] According to Constitutional Amendment Act No. 2/2001, the constitutional laws adopting the basic laws of Autonomous Regions cannot be submitted to confirmative *referendum* under Article 138, II, of the Constitution.

Moreover, the provisions concerning intergovernmental fiscal relations set forth in the special basic laws can be amended by passing either a constitutional Act or an ordinary law of the State, provided that the latter is preceded by an agreement between the State and the Region concerned.[53] The Acts of Parliament based on a State–Region agreement count as constitutional amendments.[54] The same procedure applies when it comes to amending the governmental system of the 'Autonomous' Regions by introducing, for example, the direct election of the regional Presidents or the speaker of the regional legislature.

Finally, Article 10 of Constitutional Amendment Act No. 3/2001 provides a transitional provision: as long as Parliament does not amend the basic law of the special regions, it is possible to extend to them the broader forms of legislative and administrative autonomy that Ordinary Regions enjoy under Title V of the Constitution.[55]

§3. Primary Legislation

I. Acts of Parliament ('Formal' Laws)

87. Parliament passes primary legislation according to Articles 70 ff. of the Constitution. The pieces of primary legislation are also called 'formal' laws: the phenomenon of the 'typical' sources indeed consists of the connection of the form (primary legislation) and the effectiveness of the source (i.e., the force of law).

52. *See* Constitutional Court, Judgment No. 370/2006.
53. Article 54, IV, basic law for Sardinia; Art. 50, V, basic law for Valle d'Aosta/*Vallée d'Aoste*; Art. 63, V, basic law for Friuli-Venezia Giulia; Art. 104, I, basic law for Trentino-Alto Adige/*Südtirol*.
54. *See* Constitutional Court, Judgments Nos 99/2014, 46, 77, 82/2015 and 28/2016.
55. *See* Constitutional Court, Judgments Nos 377/2002 and 408/2002; Constitutional Court, Judgment No. 255/2014.

II. Laws Granting Amnesty and Pardon

88. 'Amnesty' and 'pardon' are acts of collective mercy whereby crimes are wiped out and sentences commutated, remitted or reduced. Pursuant to Article 79, II, of the Constitution, they are granted by an Act of Parliament, which has to be passed by two-thirds of the members of both Houses voting on each single article and on the statute as a whole. The Act therefore requires the approval of both the 'majority' and the 'opposition', that is to say, the two subjects of parliamentary democracy.

Due to the entrenched legislative process required for their approval, laws granting amnesty and pardon have a force of law which is superior to that required by the nature of the effect it produces, i.e., the 'temporary suspension' of the effectiveness of criminal law. Moreover, they cannot be repealed by an ordinary Act of Parliament. If Parliament repealed an Act granting pardon and amnesty, it would infringe the Constitution. Laws granting pardon and amnesty cannot be submitted to abrogative referenda.[56]

III. 'Atypical Laws'

89. We have already examined 'atypical' legislation. Atypical Acts of Parliament are usually the outcome of a legislative process which incorporates additional procedural stages within the parliamentary procedure. Such variation in the parliamentary procedure entrenches atypical laws: their force sets them in an intermediate position between the Constitution and ordinary legislation. As a consequence, they cannot be amended nor repealed by 'ordinary' primary legislation.

The Constitution lays down several 'atypical' laws.

First, there are the laws incorporating the Lateran Pacts and their subsequent amendments, which we have examined above.[57]

Second, an Act of Parliament may separate Provinces and municipalities from a Region and aggregate them into another one.[58] A referendum must be held in order to acquire the consent of the population of the sole municipalities and Provinces concerned.[59] Once the population of the Provinces and municipalities concerned has approved the referendum, the Parliament can pass the Act for territorial readjustment.[60] As far as special Regions are concerned, changes in their territorial identity – even the minor ones – require a constitutional amendment.[61] This is because their basic laws, which were passed as acts at the constitutional level, have undoubtedly

56. Article 75, II, of the Constitution.
57. Article 7, II, of the Constitution. *See* Part I, Ch. 2, §4.
58. Article 132, II, of the Constitution.
59. *See* Constitutional Court, Judgment No. 334/2004.
60. *See* Art. 132, II, of the Constitution. *See* e.g., Law No. 117/2009, which separated the municipalities of the Vamarecchia Valley (Casteldelci, Maiolo, Novafeltria, Pennabilli, San Leo, Sant'Agata Feltria e Talamello) from the Marche Region and aggregated them to the Emilia-Romagna Region; Law No. 84/2021, which separated the municipalities of Montecopiolo and Sassofeltrio from the Marche Region and aggregated them to the Emilia-Romagna Region.
61. *See* Constitutional Court, Judgment No. 66/2007.

entrenched their territory.[62] Despite this, in 2017, Parliament separated the municipality of Sappada/*Plödn* from the Veneto Region and aggregated it to the Friuli-Venezia Giulia Region by passing a piece of ordinary legislation.[63]

Third, Parliament approves the laws incorporating the agreements between the State and non-Catholic religious denominations.[64] Parliament, however, is not compelled to incorporate the agreement, but if it decides to do so, it cannot amend the text of the agreement.[65]

Fourth, Article 116, III, of the Constitution[66] regulates another 'atypical' law. The constitutional provision establishes a legislative process whereby additional forms and conditions of autonomy are granted to Ordinary Regions upon their initiative. The State and the Region concerned must enter into an agreement, which is subsequently passed by both Houses with an absolute majority of their members. The proposed additional special forms and conditions of autonomy are only those indicated in a specific list of concurrent and State exclusive legislative powers. The act must comply with the principles on State–Regions financial relations set forth in Article 119 of the Constitution, after consultation with local authorities. While implementing the constitutional provision, Italian Parliament expressly made Article 116, III applicable also to Autonomous Regions.[67] The Constitutional Court struck down this possibility; as far as additional forms and conditions of autonomy are concerned, Article 116, III, clearly refers only to Ordinary Regions.[68]

Fifth, an Act of Parliament may alter provincial boundaries and create new Provinces within a Region.[69] In the opinion of the Constitutional Court, the act does not require a referendum to be held but only the advice of the Councils of the municipalities concerned.[70]

Finally, the Constitutional Amendment Act No. 1/2012 amended Article 81 of the Constitution and introduced a new atypical law, in accordance with the Treaty on Stability, Coordination and Governance (TSCG) in the Economic and Monetary Union (TSCG), signed in Brussels on 2 February 2010, and incorporated into the Italian legal system.[71] The atypical law on budgetary parliamentary procedure is an Act of Parliament passed by both Houses with an absolute majority.[72] The Act must comply with the principles related to the balance between revenues and expenditures which are set forth in Article 5 of the Constitutional Amendment Act No. 1/2012.[73]

62. The regional territory is expressly demarcated by Art. 1, basic law for Sardinia; Art. 1, basic law for Sicily; Art. 1, II, basic law for Valle d'Aosta/*Vallée d'Aoste*; Art. 1, I basic law for Friuli-Venezia Giulia (amended by Constitutional Law No. 17/2016); Art. 3, basic law for Trentino-Alto Adige/*Südtirol*.
63. *See* Law No. 182/2017.
64. Article 8, III, of the Constitution.
65. *See* Constitutional Court, Judgment No. 52/2016.
66. Introduced by the constitutional (amendment) act No. 3/2001.
67. *See* Art. 11, II, of Law No. 86/2024.
68. *See* Constitutional Court, Judgment No. 192/2024.
69. Article 133, I, of the Constitution.
70. *See* Constitutional Court, Judgment No. 230/2001.
71. *See* Law No. 114/2012.
72. *See* Law No. 243/2012, as amended by Law No. 164/2016.
73. Article 81, VI, of the Constitution. *See* Constitutional Court, Judgment No. 235/2017.

§4. Executive Orders at Legislative Level

I. Decree-Laws

90. Pursuant to Article 77 of the Constitution, decree-laws are provisional measures with force of law. The Cabinet[74] is allowed to enact them in extraordinary cases of necessity and urgency; upon the same day of their enactment, the Cabinet must table them before the Houses of Parliament for their ratification. Decree-laws must be ratified (i.e., turned into an Act of Parliament) within sixty days of their publication in the Official Gazette. Otherwise, the decrees lose effect from their inception. The Houses of Parliament, even if dissolved, shall be specially summoned and shall assemble within five days of the presentation of the decree. Both Houses can either ratify or reject the turning into law of the decree. However, Parliament may regulate rights and obligations arising out of non-ratified decree-laws by passing an ad hoc piece of legislation.[75]

91. Decree-laws may regulate all the fields reserved for primary legislation. Limitations to the enactment of the emergency decrees of the government can be inferred from the Constitution. First, decree-laws may not be used where a field of legislation implies ministerial responsibility: these fields are reserved for parliamentary legislation. We can mention primary-delegated legislation, approval of budgets, Acts authorizing the President of the Republic to ratify international treaties. Second, decree-laws may not be enacted for regulating and sanctioning rights and obligations arising out of non-confirmed decree-laws. Third, they cannot reproduce the content of a non-confirmed decree-law. Finally, the content of the decree-law does not have to be different from that which appears in the title.

Article 15 of Law No. 400/1988 contemplates all these hypotheses and therefore implements the constitutional provisions. In addition, the article states that decree-laws cannot restore the effectiveness of provisions set aside by the Constitutional Court. This provision applies to ordinary laws and regional laws as well.[76] It then introduces additional restrictions to the enactment of decree-laws, which cannot be traced back to constitutional provisions. For example, a decree-law cannot be enacted as far as electoral matters are concerned. Nevertheless, the Constitutional Court acknowledged the possibility of enacting a decree-law in the electoral field.[77]

The Cabinet ought to have recourse to decree-laws provided that there are extraordinary cases of 'necessity' and 'urgency'.[78] These are referred to the current legislative situation and not to the legislative situation that will occur in the future.[79] The effectiveness of decree-laws is limited in time and is destined to fail if the decree is not confirmed within sixty days of their publication. In order to avoid

74. That is the Council of Ministers: *see* Art. 92, I, of the Constitution.
75. *See* Part II, Ch. 4.
76. *See* Constitutional Court, Judgment No. 350/2010.
77. *See* Constitutional Court, Judgment No. 161/1995.
78. *See* Constitutional Court, Judgment No. 29/1995.
79. Article 15.3 of Law No. 400/1988. On the practice concerning the application of these constitutional rules, *see* Part II, Ch. 4.

the loss of effect of the decree, the government has fostered the practice of 'reiterating' the decree-laws. This practice may be considered legitimate as long as the necessity and the urgency – which are the rationale of the enactment of such decree – still continue. On the contrary, the Constitutional Court holds that the reiteration of decree-laws is inconsistent with the Constitution. In fact, decree-laws can be reiterated providing that they are based on 'new' extraordinary cases of necessity and urgency, which justify their adoption.[80]

92. Parliament ratifies decrees-law by enacting a particular piece of legislation, i.e., the so-called *legge di conversione*. The Standing Orders of both Houses[81] and Article 15, V, of Law No. 400/1988 also allow a partial ratification of the decree, as well as the possibility of amending its provisions. After ratification, the Act of Parliament becomes the source of the rules that were previously set forth by the decree. According to the Constitutional Court, the ratification of the decree-law cannot validate substantial and procedural flaws of the decree-law. This means that if the decree is inconsistent with the constitutional requirements upholding its enactment (extraordinary cases of 'necessity' and 'urgency'), the decree-law is unconstitutional and must be set aside.[82] In several judgments, the Constitutional Court held that Parliament cannot amend the decree-law by inserting into it provisions which are not 'homogeneous' to those contained in the decree-law as enacted by the government.[83]

Finally, the government cannot resort to decree-laws when passing broad changes in the legal system. When the government tried to change the territorial reconfiguration of provincial boundaries by decree-law, the Constitutional Court held that such reform was unconstitutional.[84]

II. Legislative Decrees

93. The Houses of Parliament may delegate the exercise of legislative powers to the Cabinet.[85] The Parliament, however, must specify principles and criteria of guidance and delegate the legislative power only for limited time and well-specified subjects.

The legislative decree concurs with the ordinary Acts of Parliament. Antinomies between Acts of Parliament and decree-laws are solved in accordance with the chronological criterion.

94. The Act that delegates legislative powers to the Cabinet ('enabling Act') is a statute enacted by Parliament.[86] Legislative delegation can deal with any field of legislation. Limitations to the enactment of Legislative Decrees can be inferred from

80. Constitutional Court, Judgment No. 360/1996.
81. Article 78 Senate Rule of Orders; Art. 96*bis* Chamber of Deputies Rules of Orders.
82. *See* Constitutional Court, Judgments Nos 171/2007, 128/2008 and 146/2024.
83. *See*, e.g., Constitutional Court, Judgments Nos 22/2012, 113/2023 and 215/2023.
84. *See* Constitutional Court, Judgment No. 220/2013.
85. Articles 76 and 77, I, of the Constitution.
86. Article 72, IV, of the Constitution.

the Constitution. A decree may not be used where a field of legislation implies ministerial responsibility. We can mention the approval of budgets and financial records, the ratification of decree-laws and so on.[87] Fields of legislation reserved for assembly approval are not excluded from delegation, since there is no significant connection between the phenomenon of delegation and that of the assembly reserve.

Delegation is assigned to Cabinet for a limited period of time. The Constitutional Court censured the practice of delaying the publication of the enabling act, in order to draw advantage from a period of time that is longer than that provided in the enabling act.[88] Delegated legislation must comply with the principles and the criteria set forth in the enabling act: these are usually related to the field to which the delegated legislation refers and comprise all the rules that are instrumental to the purposes of the delegation.[89]

95. The validity and the effectiveness of the legislative decree depend on the observance of the limits set forth by the act. The enabling act may contain both constitutional and additional limits.[90] The justification of these additional limits can be traced back to the fact that delegated legislative power is inherently limited.

Legislative decrees, which do not comply with the principles set forth in the enabling act, are inconsistent with the enabling act and therefore indirectly violate the Constitution.[91]

III. Atypical Delegation of Legislative Powers: Legislative Decrees in the Event of War

96. The President of the Republic declares war upon authorization of Parliament,[92] which has the authority to declare a state of war and vests the necessary powers in the Cabinet. It has been disputed whether the conferral of necessary powers to the Cabinet is a type of legislative delegation.[93] It should be argued, however, that the assignment to the Cabinet of the necessary powers implies the assignment of legislative powers and can only be carried out through an Act of Parliament according to the paradigm of legislative delegation. This kind of delegated legislation constitutes an 'atypical delegation', because all the limitations for ordinary delegation (principles, guiding criteria, limited time, specified ends) are lacking.

87. *Ibid.*
88. *See* Constitutional Court, Judgment No. 163/1963.
89. *See* Part II, Ch. 4.
90. *Ibid.*
91. *See* Constitutional Court, Judgments Nos 3/1957 and 104/2017.
92. Article 87 of the Constitution.
93. Article 78 of the Constitution.

IV. Legislative Decrees Implementing the Basic Laws of Autonomous Regions

97. The legislative decrees implementing basic laws of Autonomous Regions are laid down in the constitutional laws adopting the basic laws of the same Autonomous Regions.[94] Through such legislative decrees, the regional basic laws allow the government to transfer the offices and government staff to the Autonomous Regions, and to implement, integrate and specify basic law provisions. Whereas the object, the governing criteria and principles can be implicitly derived from the regional basic laws, there is an indication of a limited time for their enactment. Where appended, the temporal limit has been widely eluded.[95] The temporal limit configures the delegation for the implementation of the special basic laws as a continuous delegation, which can be carried out by several acts. This tends to configure such delegation as an 'atypical' one. Moreover, this type of delegation is also 'atypical' because the delegation itself derives from a provision at the constitutional level to the exclusion of the Acts of Parliament.[96]

The procedure whereby the decrees are enacted provides for an advisory opinion or a proposal on the outline of the decree which is formulated by State–Regions joint committees. The participation of joint committees in the drafting of the decrees set them among the 'atypical' sources.

V. Legislative Decrees Setting Consolidated Legislation

98. Consolidated Acts are legislative decrees. They represent a restatement of primary legislation scattered over several statutes. Consolidated Acts enable previous primary legislation to be repealed. In order to approve Consolidated Acts, the Parliament must delegate the necessary legislative powers to the government. The limits of time, object, guiding criteria and specific limited time can be implicitly derived from the function carried out by consolidated legislation.

In some cases, Consolidated Acts cannot introduce any change in the law: the act is a mere consolidation of all the law on a particular matter within one legislative decree (*testi unici compilativi*).[97] The Cabinet – which normally enacts the Consolidated Act upon parliamentary delegation – cannot amend the legislation in force.[98]

---

94. Article 43, basic law for Sicily; Art. 56, basic law for Sardinia; Art. 107, basic law for Trentino-Alto Adige/*Südtirol*; Art. 65, basic law for Friuli-Venezia Giulia; Art. 48*bis*, basic law for Valle d'Aosta/*Vallée d'Aoste*.
95. Article 108, I, basic law for Trentino-Alto Adige/*Südtirol*.
96. *See* Constitutional Court, Judgment No. 316/2004.
97. *See* Art. 17*bis*, II, of Law No. 400/1988.
98. *See* Constitutional Court, Judgments Nos 80 and 162/2012.

§5. THE OUTCOME OF ABROGATIVE REFERENDA AS A SOURCE OF LAW

99. Pursuant to Article 75, I, of the Constitution, the outcome of an abrogative referendum – i.e., the deliberation of the electoral body that totally or partially repeals a piece of primary legislation – enjoys a status comparable to that of primary legislation.

First, the repeal of a piece of legislation triggers changes in the legal system and therefore renovates the legal system itself. Second, referendum promoters may also call for a partial repeal of legislation through referendum: partial repeals are aimed at carving a new law out of the text of the existing one in order to be submitted to the approval of the electoral body. This gives rise to a kind of *lex rogata* or popular law.

§6. OTHER SOURCES OF LAW AT LEGISLATIVE LEVEL

100. The Standing Orders of Parliament, as well as the regulations and rules of procedure, before the Constitutional Court should be considered primary legislation. Indeed, they are subordinate only to constitutional sources. The criterion applicable to conflicts between such sources of law and primary legislation is that of competence.

I. Parliamentary Standing Orders

101. Article 64, I, of the Constitution establishes that 'Each House adopts its own rules by absolute majority of its members.' Article 72, I, II, III, of the Constitution then states that the Houses of Parliament can set rules establishing shortened procedures for urgent draft legislation. In addition, Standing Orders set the ways in which the workings of committees are made public, the procedures for the consideration of bills.

According to the criterion of competence, matters reserved for parliamentary standing of orders cannot be regulated not only by statutory law but only by sources at the constitutional level. Conflicts between parliamentary Standing Orders and constitutional provisions can arise autonomously or may derive from an Act of Parliament approved in accordance with an invalid Standing Order. In both cases, the Constitutional Court held that Standing Orders are *interna corporis acta* and therefore their constitutional validity is unchallengeable. In this respect, the Constitutional Court ruled that parliamentary Standing Orders could not be subject to judicial review of legislation, since they do not have binding force of law.[99] As regards laws conflicting with invalid Orders, the Act of Parliament approved in accordance with them should be inconsistent with the Constitution as well. However, the Constitutional Court held that the principle that prevents *interna corporis*

99. *See* Constitutional Court, Judgments Nos 154/1985 and 120/2014.

from being challenged before the Constitutional Court is to be set aside only when the Standing Orders directly infringe the Constitution.[100]

II. Regulations and Rules of Procedure Before the Constitutional Court

102. The regulations of the Constitutional Court are provided in Article 14 of Law No. 87/1953, i.e., in an ordinary Act of Parliament, which implements the constitutional provisions concerning the Constitutional Court. These regulations govern the organization and functioning of the Constitutional Court. Additional rules of procedure can be set therein.[101] They are approved by the majority of members of the Court and published in the Official Gazette.

As mentioned above, such regulations are set forth by an ordinary Act of Parliament. However, they can be considered primary legislation. Indeed, the Court enacts them in the exercise of its legislative power, which can be directly traced back to the Constitution. In this respect, the regulations and the rules of procedure can be seen as an expression of the constitutional independence of the constitutional adjudicator. As a consequence, Law No. 87/1953 does not create a new source of law but simply acknowledges a regulatory power directly granted by the Constitution.

In addition, limitations to the principle of constitutional autonomy of the Court operate either directly or through an act of primary legislation. In other words, the organization and functioning of the Court are carried out by an overlapping jurisdiction, in which both primary legislation and regulations concur. Where primary legislation and regulation are inconsistent, it is the Act of Parliament, which prevails. To sum up, the rule that has been adopted is the doctrine of the paramountcy of primary legislation. The Constitutional Court holds that the validity of both the regulations and the rules of procedure are unchallengeable before the Court itself.[102]

§7. Secondary Sources

103. Secondary legislation is hierarchically subordinate to primary legislation. It mainly consists of regulations enacted by the executive, which are listed in Article 17, I and II, of Law No. 400/1988. The list is not exhaustive: the law, which is the foundation of subordinate legislation, allows new types of regulations to be set up. It should be recalled that Article 117, VI, of the Constitution sets the distribution of subordinate legislative powers between the State and Regions. Whereas the State can enact regulations within the fields of its exclusive legislative jurisdiction – insofar as it does not devolve such power to the Regions – the power to issue by-laws is vested in the regions in any other matters.

The current state of the COVID-19 pandemic demonstrates that secondary legislation is open to changes and integrated by subsequent acts of the Legislative

100. *See* Constitutional Court, Judgment No. 9/1959.
101. Article 22, II, of Law No. 87/1953.
102. *See* Constitutional Court, Judgment No. 295/2006.

Branch. The decree-laws enacted in 2020 introduced a two-level pattern through which the COVID-19 pandemic is tackled. On the one hand, the decree-laws directly limited the exercise of fundamental rights affected by the spread of the infection.[103] On the other, they enabled the President of the Council of Ministers to adopt measures in the form of 'presidential conciliar decrees'. The measures implemented the provisions of the decree-laws and adapted them to the changing circumstances caused by the virus outbreak.[104] According to the Constitutional Court, these decrees were not sources of law, but administrative measures.[105]

I. Executive Regulations: Rules and Regulations Supplementing Primary Legislation

104. This type of regulation governs 'the implementation of laws and legislative decrees and EU regulations',[106] as well as 'the implementation and integration of laws and legislative decrees, in which fundamental principles are laid down, with the exclusion of those principles relating to subject matter reserved for regional competence'.[107]

Rules and regulations supplementing primary legislation represent the paradigm of 'subordinate' or 'secondary legislation'. The extension of this concept ranges from supplementing legislation in the strict sense (as a specification of the legislative rules) to the implementation and integration of principles set forth in legislative provisions.

II. 'Independent' Regulations

105. Independent regulations govern 'subject matters where there is no regulation set by acts with force of law at legislative level, provided that they do not refer to subject matters which are in any case reserved for law'.[108]

Independent regulations differ from those regulations which implement and integrate laws. In fact, whereas the ambit of operation of the latter is covered by fundamental principles set by an Act of Parliament, independent regulations provide even in the absence of law. The lack of law must nevertheless be interpreted both as an absence of an explicit legislative regulation assigning statutory power and as a presence of an implicit rule conferring such power.

103. In particular, the right to circulate freely through the country (Art. 16 Const.).
104. Article 3 Decree-Law No. 6/2020 turned into Law No. 16/2020, as replaced by Art. 1 Decree-Law No. 19/2020 turned into Law No. 35/2020.
105. *See* Constitutional Court, Judgment No. 198/2021.
106. Article 17.1.a of Law No. 400/1988.
107. Article 17.1.b of Law No. 400/1988.
108. Article 17.1.c of Law No. 400/1988.

III. Regulations Organizing Public Administration

106. Regulations governing the 'organisation and functioning of public administration according to the provisions dictated by laws'[109] are enacted according to Article 97, I, of the Constitution: 'Public offices are organised according to the provisions of law, so as to ensure the efficiency and impartiality of administration. The regulations of the offices establish the areas of competence, the duties and the responsibilities of the officials.'

The organizational regulations represent a unique model since they implement primary legislation according to constitutional principles. These regulations supplement the provisions of legislative provisions setting fundamental principles.

IV. Authorized Regulations

107. Authorized regulations replace primary legislation under an enabling act such as that of Parliament. In other words, they can deregulate entire legislative ambits by replacing them with statutory ones, provided that the subject matter is not entirely reserved for primary legislation. According to Article 17, II, of Law No. 400/1988, the enabling act repeals the provisions at the legislative level. If the act did not foresee the repeal of legislative provisions, it would be inconsistent with the Constitution since it cannot establish a source in competition with itself. The justifications for 'authorized' regulations can hold good provided that the powers granted are precise and clear, and conferred on an identifiable field. The repeal of legislative provisions will become effective when 'authorized' regulation comes into force. Some objections have been made to the enactment of 'authorized' regulations. However, it is not the 'authorized' regulation which repeals primary legislation but the act conferring the delegated powers. On the contrary, the 'authorized' regulation would repeal an act, which is hierarchically superior to the regulation itself. Moreover, the act repealing legislative norms previously in force also sets forth 'the general rules regulating the subject matter'. As a consequence, the subject matter itself will be regulated both by the ordinary act (which sets forth the fundamental principles) and by the regulation (which sets forth the specific and detailed provisions).

Article 17, IV*bis*, of Law No. 400/1988 explicitly reserves to 'delegated' regulations the possibility to set forth the provisions regarding the organization and functioning of Ministry departments and offices. In addition, the Cabinet must have recourse to 'delegated' regulations for replacing legislative provisions concerning administrative proceedings.[110]

---

109. Article 17.1.d of Law No. 400/1988.

110. *See* Art. 20, II, of Law No. 59/1997, as amended by Art. 1 of Law No. 246/2005 and Art. 4 of Law No. 69/2009.

V. Regulations Implementing European Directives

108. Regulations implementing EU directives are authorized regulations, which replace primary legislation under the authority conferred by annual Acts of Parliament setting the proper measures for ensuring the fulfilment of EU obligations. By withdrawing primary legislation and replacing it with statutory instruments, these regulations deregulate entire ambits which were once regulated by Acts of Parliament. Regulations implementing EU directives cannot be enacted when it comes to either establishing new administrative organs and structures or setting new expenses or levying less revenue. The annual Act of Parliament setting the proper measures for ensuring the fulfilment of EU obligations directly implements EU directives setting new criminal indictments and administrative fines. The act identifies public authorities to which administrative functions related to EU law are to be assigned.[111] The Cabinet can adopt such regulations to act in substitution when Regions do not fulfil EU obligations.[112]

VI. Consolidated Regulations

109. Article 17, IV*ter*, of Law No. 400/1988[113] allows the Cabinet to consolidate subordinate legislation, which is scattered over several acts. 'Consolidated' regulations cannot introduce any change in the law: they are mere consolidation of all the provisions enacted at a level inferior to primary legislation.

VII. Ministerial and Interministerial Regulations

110. Parliament can expressly allow one or more Ministers to enact statutory instruments in the form of rules and regulations for supplementing the provision of an Act of Parliament itself.[114] Through statutory instruments, Ministers are then allowed to introduce regulations that have to be consistent with powers delegated to them by Parliament in enabling legislation. Ministerial and interministerial Regulations must conform both to primary and executive subordinate legislation. As they are hierarchically subordinate to both primary and secondary legislation, they are ranked as third-level sources.

§8. Sources of Territorial Autonomy

111. Italy is characterized by a polyarchy of political decision-making and law-making entities coordinated by the national order of government. This can be considered as a communitarian perspective of the State, useful when it comes to

111. Article 34 of Law No. 234/2012.
112. Article 35 of Law No. 234/2012.
113. Introduced by Art. 5, I, of Law No. 69/2009.
114. Article 17, III, of Law No. 400/1988.

matching the needs of politico-institutional pluralism. The 'State-as-a-community' perspective obliterates the concept of sovereignty and replaces it with a new one, which corresponds to the relationships between nation-state sovereignty (for the purpose of unification and intersubjective coordination) and autonomy (i.e., the power of the subjects of pluralism to self-organize and self-regulate).

Regional and local autonomy impacts on legislative lawmaking. In this respect, autonomy entails the constitutional distribution of legislative power between the national authority and subnational authorities. As a consequence, subnational units have the capability of enacting acts and regulations that are part of the legal system. Sources of territorial autonomy include regional and local sources. It should be recalled that both systems of sources have been profoundly modified by three constitutional amendments, which radically changed the constitutional design as regards intergovernmental relations (between the State, the Regions and, to a lesser extent, the municipalities), regional and local sources of law and the structure of government within the Regions.[115]

I. Sources of Law at Regional Level

112. Legislation at the regional level comprises regional basic laws, regional laws, and regional regulations.[116] Abrogative referenda can be held 'on the laws and administrative measures of the Region' and therefore on regional regulations. Abrogative referenda on regional laws and regulations are set at the primary or subordinate legislation level accordingly.[117]

II. Basic Laws of the Ordinary Regions

113. Ordinary Regions are allowed to enact their own basic laws by passing an act at the legislative level. Basic laws must determine the frame of government and the fundamental principles of organization and functioning of the Region in accordance with the Constitution. In addition, they define how to table bills before regional legislatures and how to hold abrogative referenda on regional laws and administrative decisions. Furthermore, they regulate the forms of publication of regional laws and regulations.[118] Finally, basic laws regulate the 'Council of local government', which is a consultative body between the Region and local authorities.[119]

Basic laws of the Ordinary Regions are passed according to an entrenched procedure, introduced by the Constitutional Amendment Act No. 1/1999. Regional legislatures pass them with an act approved by an absolute majority of their members, with two subsequent deliberations at an interval of not less than two months. This

115. Constitutional Amendment Acts No. 1/1999, No. 2 and No. 3/2001.
116. *See* Art. 123 of the Constitution; Arts 117 and 122, I, of the Constitution; Arts 117, VI and 123, I, of the Constitution, respectively.
117. Article 123, I, of the Constitution.
118. *Ibid.*
119. Article 123, IV, of the Constitution.

act does not require the approval of the Cabinet commissioner. However, the Cabinet can challenge its constitutional validity before the Constitutional Court within thirty days of its publication.

Ordinary Regions enjoy a degree of constitutional autonomy that is higher than that conferred on Autonomous Regions. In this respect, the Autonomous Regions had their own 'basic law' (*statuto*) approved by a constitutional law of the State, without any significant participation or influence of regional Legislatures.[120] Nevertheless, under Constitutional Act No. 2/2001, special regional basic laws can be partially turned into 'regional' basic laws with regard to the form of government and the electoral system. The regional act amending the form of government and the electoral system must be approved by an absolute majority of the members of the regional legislature. This act can be submitted to popular referendum if a certain figure of the regional electors or the members of the Regional Council so request.

III. Relationships Between Regional Basic Laws and the State and Regional Sources

114. The relations between regional basic laws and State law are governed according to the criterion of competence. Furthermore, regional basic laws regulate only those specific fields of legislation which the Constitution confers upon them. We define such fields of legislation as reserved matters: pursuant to Article 123 of the Constitution, the form of government and the basic principles of organization can only be regulated by regional basic laws to the exclusion of State ordinary laws.[121] However, the Constitutional Court holds that regional basic laws have to be consistent with national framework legislation falling under the concurrent legislation; more specifically, the whole range of electoral qualifications (even those for presidential candidates) are reserved to national legislation.[122] Regional basic laws are pieces of primary legislation and must regulate those contents referred to in Article 123 of the Constitution. In fact, they must contain provisions regarding the right to table bills before regional legislatures and promote abrogative referenda on laws and administrative measures of the Region as well as the publication of laws and regional regulations.[123] With regard to its formal effectiveness, Regional Statutes (i.e., the regional statutory act) are hierarchically superior to other regional laws.[124]

120. Article 116, I, of the Constitution, and above § 79.
121. *See* Constitutional Court, Judgments Nos 188/2007, 201/2008, 182/2011 and 188/2011.
122. *See* Constitutional Court, Judgments Nos 35/2014, 178/2019 and 64/2025.
123. Article 123, I, of the Constitution.
124. *See* Constitutional Court, Judgment No. 81/2015.

IV. Regional Laws

115. Regional laws are enacted by regional legislatures in accordance with the Constitution, the basic regional laws and the Standing Orders of Regional Legislatures. Although Regional legislatures enjoy different degrees of legislative powers,[125] regional laws may be considered as a unitary category. In fact, all regional laws have the same *nomen juris* (i.e., the same legal definition: 'regional law') and are passed according to the same legislative process. They share common features as far as their contents and constitutional limits are concerned.

Before the 2001 constitutional reform, ordinary Regions only had a limited legislative power in specific fields listed in the national Constitution. The Constitutional Amendment Act No. 3/2001 led to a reversal in the distribution of legislative powers: the State maintains exclusive legislative power on a limited number of matters,[126] and Regions are vested with implied powers in all subject matters not expressly covered by State legislation.[127]

In this respect, the current distribution of powers between the State and Regions is a reconfiguration of former State–Regions relationships. Whereas former Article 117 allowed regions to make laws providing that there was a constitutional foundation for their legislative powers, now regional legislative powers encounter only those limitations deriving from the existence of a subject matter reserved for State legislative powers.[128] The State, however, has exclusive legislative powers in the subject matters listed in Article 117, II, of the Constitution. This list covers subject matters that traditionally are prerogative of the central State in order to preserve the legal and economic unity of the Republic. Apart from exclusive legislative powers, the State may make laws in relation to the subject matters indicated in the list of specified heads of legislative concurrent powers. Article 117, III, of the Constitution lists the subject matters covered by concurrent legislation: legislative powers are vested in the Regions, except for the determination of the fundamental principles, which are laid down in State legislation. A regional law, which does not comply with such fundamental principles set forth in the State legislation, is deemed to be inconsistent with the State legislation and the Constitution as well.[129]

The Constitutional Court stated that State legislation – which is still in force in those fields that are now devolved to regional legislation – might apply until Regional Legislatures 'cover' the same field with their laws. The legal effects of the 'covering the field' test are those typical of pre-emption.[130] Article 1, III, of Law No. 131/2003 holds the same assumption.

Several important rulings rendered by the Constitutional Court after the 2001 constitutional reform had highly centripetal effects, thus developing an ever more centralistic doctrine. In the opinion of the Court, the principle of subsidiarity (Article 118, I, of the Constitution) allows the State to absorb regional legislative

125. Exclusive legislative powers, concurring legislative powers, residuary legislative powers: *see* Part III, Ch. 1.
126. Article 117, I, of the Constitution.
127. Article 117, IV, of the Constitution.
128. *See* Constitutional Court, Judgment No. 282/2002.
129. *See* Constitutional Court, Judgment No. 161/2012.
130. *See* Constitutional Court, Judgment No. 282/2002.

powers if there is the necessity to comply with the national concern.[131] Furthermore, it must be remembered that the reform only addressed Ordinary Regions but did not have a direct impact on the competences of 'special' Regions, whose powers still derive from their basic laws. Moreover, Article 10 of Constitutional Act No. 3/2001 establishes that as long as the Autonomous Regions do not change their basic laws the broader forms of legislative autonomy set out in Title V of the Constitution apply to them as well. In other words, the legislative powers of 'special' Regions can be considered as the outcome of the intersection of often overlapping and contradicting catalogues set forth in both the Constitution and their own basic laws.

V. Atypical Regional Laws

116. Among atypical regional laws we number those concerning the regrouping of municipalities, which depart from the ordinary legislative procedure. Pursuant to Article 133, II, of the Constitution, Regions may establish new municipality within their own territory and modify their districts and denominations. Laws establishing new municipalities and modifying their districts and denominations are *leggi-provvedimento* (i.e., legislative measures). They are approved by regional legislatures 'after consultation with the populations concerned', which means that a referendum must be summoned.[132] Regional legislatures can either receive or reject the proposed change approved by the electorate.[133] Whatever the legal nature of the referendum may be, it is hard to imagine that the representative body would disregard the will of the people. Although the State can determine the fundamental principles of organization and functioning of municipalities, the Constitutional Court strongly affirmed that the State cannot interfere with the regional exclusive jurisdiction over territorial regrouping.[134]

117. The 2001 constitutional amendments introduced new regional 'atypical' laws as well. Under Article 117, VIII, of the Constitution, regional laws ratify agreements reached by a Region with another Region aimed at the better exercise of their functions. Pursuant to Article 117, IX, of the Constitution, Regions ratify agreements with foreign States and understandings with territorial entities that belong to foreign States in the areas falling within their responsibilities. Finally, the basic laws of 'ordinary' regions introduced entrenched laws, such as financial records and laws adopting regional electoral systems.[135]

131. *See* Constitutional Court, Judgments Nos 303/2003, 6/2004, 383/2005, 278/2010, 79/2011, 232/2011, 163/2011, 7/2016, 61/2018, and 161/2019.
132. *See* Constitutional Court, Judgment No. 50/2015.
133. *See* Constitutional Court, Judgments Nos 2/2018 and 21/2018.
134. Article 117, II, p, of the Constitution and Constitutional Court, Judgment No. 261/2011.
135. *See* Constitutional Court, Judgment No. 2/2004.

VI. Regional Acts with Force of Law

118. Regions cannot enact decree-laws or legislative decrees. An Act with force of law is that stemming from an abrogative referendum. Moreover, regional basic laws introduced new kinds of regional Acts with force of law. Among them, we can mention the consolidated acts, which are approved by regional legislatures. The Standing Orders of regional legislatures are not sources of law.[136]

VII. Regional Regulations

119. Regional regulatory powers have been comprehensively modified by the Constitutional Amendment Acts No. 1/1999 and No. 3/2001. Article 121, II, of the Constitution originally vested regional legislatures with *regulatory powers*. The Constitutional Amendment Act No. 3/2001 replaced Article 121, II, of the Constitution without indicating which organ (either the legislature or the executive) should exercise regulatory powers. The Constitutional Court holds that regional basic laws are free to allot regulatory powers either to the legislature or to the executive.[137]

Moreover, regulatory powers shall be vested in the Regions with respect to the subject matters where they have legislative powers (i.e., exclusive and concurrent legislative powers). Under Article 116, VI, of the Constitution, the State can delegate Regions to enact regulations in fields assigned to the Constitution.

Regional basic laws can set the same regulations envisaged at the State level: rules and regulations supplementing primary legislation; regulations organizing public administration; 'delegated' regulations; regulations implementing European directives. The relationships between regulations and regional laws are governed according to the hierarchical principle. Regulations may be subjected to regional abrogative referenda. The relationships between regional sources and regulations delegated from the State to Regions under Article 116, VI, of the Constitution are governed in accordance with the criterion of competence.

VIII. Local Sources of Law: Municipal, Metropolitan and Provincial Basic Laws

120. Pursuant to Article 114, II, of the Constitution, municipalities, metropolitan cities and Provinces shall enact their own basic laws in accordance with the principles laid down in the Constitution. Municipal, metropolitan, and provincial basic laws set their internal organization in order to fulfil the duties assigned to them. Local basic laws have to be approved by a majority of two-thirds of the Councillors; if such a majority is not achieved, two subsequent deliberations with an absolute majority will be required.[138] Second, the law indicates which subject matters

136. *See* Constitutional Court, Judgment No. 288/1987.
137. *See* Constitutional Court, Judgments Nos 313/2003 and 119/2006.
138. Article 6.2 of the Consolidated Act No. 267/2000 concerning local authorities.

have to be regulated by the basic laws.[139] Furthermore, it indicates the subject matters where the intervention of the basic law is optional.[140] Metropolitan cities enjoy an even broader sphere of autonomy, and their basic laws are enacted in accordance with Law No. 56/2014.

The organization of the local government is a matter reserved for basic laws under the enabling legislation such as the local government acts No. 267/2000 and No. 56/2014. However, primary legislation cannot interfere with the constitutional autonomy of local authorities set forth in Article 114, II, of the Constitution, which expressly protects the self-organization of municipalities and Provinces and the adoption of local basic laws. Furthermore, local basic laws regulate only those specific fields of legislation conferred by the Constitution: to this extent, they are 'limited' sources. Article 6.2 of the Consolidated Act No. 267/2000 states that local basic laws must comply with the principles established by the law.

IX. Municipal and Provincial By-Laws

121. Under Article 117, VI, of the Constitution, local regulations are enacted as by-laws. Indeed, municipalities, Provinces, and Metropolitan Cities are granted regulatory powers for the organization and implementation of the functions attributed to them.

Local regulations are typical examples of subordinate legislation, which implements national and regional primary legislation. The nature of local regulations is twofold. On the one hand, they implement State and regional statutory provisions regarding local organization (so-called organizational by-laws). On the other hand, regulations are hierarchically subordinate to State and regional laws. In addition, they supplement State and regional laws concerning the exercise of local functions in accordance with Articles 7 of the Consolidated Act No. 267/2000 and 4, IV, of Law No. 131/2003 and the principle of competence. Hence, regulations accommodate State and regional legislation to local needs. According to the principle of competence, State and regional regulations cannot interfere in the ambits reserved for local by-laws. To this extent, Article 4, II, of the General Provisions of the Civil Code – according to which regulations of authorities other than the government may not be inconsistent with executive regulations – must be considered repealed.

§9. Labour Agreements

I. Collective Agreements under Article 39 of the Constitution

122. Article 39, IV, of the Constitution provided for collective labour agreements 'having mandatory effects for all workers belonging to the categories referred to in the agreement': these were called collective labour agreements with erga omnes effectiveness. In order to enter into these agreements, the Constitution states

139. Article 6.2 of the Consolidated Act No. 267/2000 and Art. 4, II, of Law No. 131/2003.
140. Articles 8.3 and 11.1 of the Consolidated Act No. 267/2000.

that the contracting trade unions must have been registered at the local or central offices, according to the provisions of the law. The Constitution also sets a condition for their registration: their by-laws must frame their internal organization after democratic character. Moreover, the stipulation of the contract must be entrusted to a single representative body made up in proportion to the number of registered members of the various stipulating unions.[141] In the event of inconsistency between primary legislation and labour agreements, it is the primary legislation which prevails.

II. Private-Law Collective Agreements

123. Article 39 of the Constitution has never been implemented. As a consequence, labour relations are regulated by rules laid down in private-law collective agreements, which bind only workers belonging to the unions that stipulated the agreements.

Nevertheless, private-law collective agreements had their binding force extended beyond the contracting parties, achieving quasi-erga omnes effectiveness. Moreover, primary legislation[142] and the judiciary referred to private-law collective agreements for regulating labour relations, thus extending the guarantees the Constitution grants to workers.[143]

Relationships between statutory law and private-law collective agreements are governed by the same criteria applied for solving antinomies between primary legislation and erga omnes collective agreements. In the event of inconsistency, primary legislation prevails over the agreement.

§10. Trade Customs Referred to in Laws and Regulations

124. Customs directly envisaged by the Italian legal system are the so-called *usi* (trade customs). Under the general provisions of the Civil Code, they apply provided that laws and regulations expressly refer thereto.[144] Trade custom is therefore placed on the last rung of the hierarchical ladder as a third- or fourth-level source: they must be consistent with primary and subordinate legislation, and with ministerial and interministerial regulations as well.

As mentioned above, there is no room for *contra legem* customary sources within the Italian legal system but only for *secundum* and *praeter legem* customary rules.

Trade customs must be collected in a special Official Gazette. Customary rules contained therein are deemed to exist unless it is otherwise proven.[145] The publication in those collections does not guarantee either the existence of the custom or

141. Article 39, IV, of the Constitution.
142. Article 2113 of the Civil Code.
143. Article 36 of the Constitution.
144. Article 8 of the General Provisions of the Civil Code.
145. Article 9 of the General Provisions of the Civil Code.

the correspondence of the collection itself to the customary rules in force. The parties will have to prove the existence of the custom and the custom rule. The judiciary cannot use the *iura novit curia* principle and therefore shall decide on the fact, the law and its source.

Chapter 5. Forms of Direct Democracy and Abrogative Referenda

by Marta Cartabia & Elisabetta Lamarque

§1. Popular Sovereignty, Referenda and Article 75 of the Constitution

125. As in other post-war European democracies, the Italian Constitution provides for instruments of direct democracy alongside those elements of representative democracy which form the backbone of the legal and political system. Article 1 of the Constitution states that '[s]overeignty belongs to the people, who exercise it in the manner, and within the limits, laid down by the Constitution'.

According to the wording of the Constitution, popular sovereignty does not imply an exclusive choice in favour of either direct democracy or representative democracy but instead opens the way to different forms of democracy so that representation may be combined with the direct exercise of the popular will, within the limits set by the Constitution.

The instruments of direct democracy provided for by the Constitution are the consultative referendum (*referendum consultivo*) to modify regional, provincial and communal boundaries (Articles 132–133; *see also*, Part I, Chapter 4), referendum to amend the Constitution (*referendum costituzionale*) (Article 138; *see also*, Part I, Chapter 4; Part II, Chapter 4) and the abrogative referendum (*referendum abrogativo*) to repeal laws or other legally valid acts having the force of law (Article 75). Other instruments of direct democracy provided for under the Constitution include the popular initiative (Article 71) which allows the electorate (with a minimum of 50,000 signatures) to propose a bill to Parliament and the popular petition (Article 50) which allows citizens to petition Parliament directly. Among the instruments of direct democracy, however, it is the abrogative referendum which is the most relevant.

Article 75 of the Constitution establishes that referenda can only be held in order to repeal, totally or in part, laws or other measures having the force of law. This provision was the result of a creative and complex project of direct democracy begun by the Italian academic, Costantino Mortati, in the early 1940s. Mortati's original plan provided for instruments, such as a referendum on the adoption of laws (*referendum approvativo*), to be used when the Head of State returns a bill to Parliament for reconsideration or in order to settle disputes between the Senate and the Camera on the adoption of legislation, a suspensive referendum (*referendum sospensivo*) to suspend the adoption of a law by Parliament, the popular initiative in line with the American or Swiss model so that were Parliament to botch, or dramatically amend, a popular legislative initiative, that law would, for example, be subjected to subsequent popular approval and finally the abrogative referendum to repeal existing legislation, then considered less likely to be used than the other instruments. In the last instance, however, the Constituent Assembly progressively excluded, or made significant cuts to, Mortati's original proposals, partly due to the atmosphere of general mistrust of direct democracy prevailing in Europe at the time and partly because many of the proposals were simply considered too difficult to apply in the representative model of democracy favoured by the Founding Fathers. For this reason, the Assembly only accepted the proposals to introduce abrogative, constitutional and consultative referenda, together with popular legislative initiative and the popular petition, all now contained in the Italian Constitution.

§2. The Implementation and Practice of Constitutional Provisions by Law No. 352/1970

126. The constitutional provisions on referenda were supposed to be implemented, as other key constitutional norms, by means of an ordinary Act of Parliament, but the implementing legislation was only adopted over twenty years later, in 1970. Law No. 352/1970 stipulates the procedural norms to be followed in the case of referenda from the initial proposal through to the popular vote. The passing of the referendum legislation was to some extent facilitated by the political climate prevailing at the time, which favoured the final implementation of the constitutional provisions (the regional system, which had until then been a dead letter, was implemented in the same year), and by two watershed political events in the form of the introduction of two hotly contested pieces of legislation, the 1978 law on abortion (Law No. 194/1978) and 1970 divorce law (Law No. 898/1970). The party of the Christian Democrats tried to have both pieces of legislation repealed by means of referendum, and that led to Italy's first real test of the abrogative referendum procedure, starting with the referendum on divorce in 1974 and followed by the referendum on abortion in 1981.

Since the early 1980s, however, Italy has witnessed a dramatic change in both the number and type of referenda. The succession of referendum campaigns since the 1980s has put a wide range of issues to the popular vote, some quite relevant from a political perspective, others less so. In many cases, it was not even an entire law that was proposed for popular vote, but small parts of it, articles, paragraphs or even single lexical expressions, which thus transformed the referendum from an abrogative to a 'manipulative' instrument which would in effect change the meaning of provisions rather than repeal them. An example of this trend is constituted by the referenda on electoral laws in 1991 and 1993 which, by way of removing some parts of the legislation, in fact transformed the Italian electoral system from a fully proportional model to a mixed electoral regime combining elements of 'first-past-the post' with proportional representation (*see* Part II, Chapter 3). In these cases, the border between 'abrogative' and 'innovative' referendum – which falls out of the scope of Article 75 of the Constitution – is blurred. In any case, the Constitutional Court, which is empowered to judge on the admissibility of referenda, states that the abrogative referenda provided for by the Constitution cannot be used to introduce a new piece of legislation. Therefore, when a referendum concerns the partial repeal of a law, its object must be constituted by a part of the text of the law having an autonomous legal meaning rather than, for example, the abolition of single expressions or single word with no specific legal meaning (*see*, e.g., Constitutional Court, Judgments Nos 36/1997 and 27/2017). Above all, if a referendum request concerns the electoral law of a constitutional body, or one of constitutional relevance, it must in any case ensure that once the law in question has been repealed, a self-applicable law (the so-called resulting legislation) remains in force. Otherwise, the outcome of the referendum could paralyse the normal conduct of the activities of the bodies in question (Constitutional Court, Judgment No. 10/2020).

§3. Referendum Proposals

127. Article 75 of the Constitution states that a popular referendum may be held if called for by a minimum of 500,000 citizens entitled to vote, on the one hand, and five Regional Councils, on the other hand. At the opposite, other constitutional organs, such as the Head of State or the Executive, are not vested with the power of taking a referendum initiative in order to prevent the organs of the State from acting in a populist fashion with regard to referenda.

The initiative has often been taken by the electorate, at times motivated or 'pushed' by a political party which organized the referendum campaign and collection of signatures (Articles 27–28 of Law No. 352/1970).

Since 1993, Regional Councils have also called for referenda on legislation considered as obstacles to regional autonomy, such as those dealing with the regulation of Ministries carrying out functions in which regions have legislative and administrative competence (the referenda about the Ministries of Health, Tourism or Agriculture), or connected with the regional environment (the referendum about oil rigs in the sea of 2016). A regional referendum initiative is valid if voted by at least five Regional Councils with an absolute majority (Articles 29–30 of Law No. 352/1970).

In order to avoid superimposition with other polls, a referendum cannot be called in the twelve months prior to the end of the legislature or in the six months following parliamentary elections (Article 31 of Law No. 352/1970).

A referendum proposal must be submitted to the Central Office for Referenda, appointed annually within the Supreme Court of Cassation (*Corte di Cassazione*) in the period 1 January–30 September. If, after a referendum has been officially called, either the Senate or the House of Deputies is dissolved in advance, the referendum is suspended for 365 days (Article 34 of Law No. 352/1970), thus postponing the vote for a period of time up to two years.

§4. Legality Review by the Central Office for Referenda

128. All referendum proposals are subject to review of legality by the Central Office for Referendum at the Supreme Court of Cassation and a subsequent control of 'admissibility' on the part of the Constitutional Court.

The Central Office has to certify that the proposal is in conformity with Law No. 352/1970. It must verify, for example, that the conditions set out in law have been met, that is, the authenticity and number of the signatures if the referendum has been called by the electorate or the validity of the deliberations of the Regional Councils, and the nature of the measure submitted to referendum, which can be only a law or measure having the force of law, thus excluding secondary legislation or constitutional provisions.

One of the key tasks of the Central Office is to merge referendum questions dealing with very similar issues (Article 32 of Law No. 352/1970) and to block the referendum procedure if Parliament repeals or amends the provisions submitted to referendum prior to the popular vote (Article 39 of Law No. 352/1970). However, the Constitutional Court stipulated that the intervention of Parliament does not imply the interruption of the referendum procedure if the new law leaves the inspiring principle or the basic legal content of the previous provisions largely intact (Constitutional Court, Judgment No. 68/1978). The referendum will still be held, and the issue at stake will be the new law passed by Parliament.

The Central Office also formulates the official wording of referendum questions in consultation with the initiative's promoters so as to help voters if they are required to vote on more than one issue at a time (Law No. 173/1995).

Finally, the legal review of the Central Office must be carried out by 15 December of the year in question, and the documentation must then be submitted to the Constitutional Court for a review of admissibility, to be made by 10 February of the following year.

§5. The Review of Constitutional Admissibility by the Constitutional Court

129. The referendum proposal is submitted to the Constitutional Court for a control of admissibility in order to certify that the referendum is not being held to abrogate laws explicitly exempted under Article 75, i.e., fiscal or budgetary laws, amnesties or pardons or laws authorizing the ratification of international treaties. The Constitutional Court is empowered to adjudicate on the admissibility of referenda on the basis of Constitutional Law No. 1/1953. The Court must certify that the law to be abrogated does not fall into one of the exempted categories under Article 75 and that it is not closely linked to one of them. This is the case, for example, for laws dealing with the implementation of international treaties, which cannot be submitted to referendum as they are closely linked to those for the authorization to ratify international treaties.

Among the category of the laws authorizing ratification of international treaties, an important role is played by those implementing EU regulations (*see*, e.g., Constitutional Court, Judgments Nos 31, 41 and 45/2000). Constitutional case law tends to exclude referenda on such laws because their eventual repeal would cause a breach with regard to EU legislation that could be sanctioned by the Court of Justice of the European Union (CJEU).

Moreover, in a key decision (Constitutional Court, Judgment No. 16/1978), the Constitutional Court established that the review of constitutional admissibility should also be based on other criteria, deriving from the nature of the referenda themselves, as set out by the Italian Constitution. As referenda can only be held to repeal laws or measures having the force of law, the Constitutional Court established that the latter must not concern either constitutional provisions or other provisions of law, 'having a content closely connected to the Constitution': that is, statute laws so closely linked to constitutional laws whose abrogation would affect fundamental constitutional principles.

The Constitutional Court distinguishes between the 'Constitution content connected laws' and the 'essential laws', a category which includes laws dealing with the election of Parliament and other constitutional organs (Constitutional Court, Judgments Nos 17/1997, 42, 49/2000, 45/2005) and also laws that guarantee fundamental values, like the right to life.

In particular, as far as electoral laws are concerned, the Constitutional Court ruled in favour of the admissibility of abrogative referendum on them, despite the fact that this category should be exempt under Article 75, because the final text of the Italian Constitution failed to make this specification due to an error on the part of the drafting committee of the Constitution. Consequently, while the will of the Constituent Assembly was clear, the Constitutional Court chose instead to take the Constitution literally, without considering the original intent of the Framers. Nevertheless, referenda on electoral laws governing constitutional organs are highly sensitive matters insofar as their repeal may have a paralysing effect on the institutions involved. The Constitutional Court (*see*, in particular, Constitutional Court, Judgments Nos 32/1993, 5, 10/1995, 26/1997, 13/1999, 33, 34/2000, 15, 16, 17/2008, 13/2012, 10/2020, 60/2022) considers these effects unacceptable and has therefore ruled that, despite the theoretical admissibility of electoral referenda, the latter must not prevent the institution from functioning effectively. Therefore, an electoral referendum is only admissible where this will not interfere with the effective functioning of the electoral system.

In the same way, referenda cannot be held concerning laws 'with a particular resistance to abrogation', which includes laws dealing with the implementation of the Lateran Treaties (*see*, e.g., Constitutional Court, Judgment No. 16/1978).

The Constitutional Court also adjudicates on the 'homogeneity' of issues subject to referendum. In Judgment No. 16/1978, the Constitutional Court established that a referendum must not consist of a series of questions on heterogeneous issues insofar as this would tend to inhibit the effective and free expression of choice on the part of voters, who can only respond collectively 'yes' or 'no' (Article 48 of the Constitution). The concept of homogeneity has been interpreted as 'internal homogeneity', or that a single referendum cannot include numerous heterogeneous issues, and in terms of the 'homogeneity-completeness' of the questions, according to which the referendum should submit all the provisions concerning the issue to be abrogated to popular vote. In some cases, incomplete questions have been rejected because the exclusion of some provisions strictly linked to those to be abrogated was judged likely to mislead voters. Homogeneity may also simply mean that the aim of the referendum should be clear to voters. Sometimes, homogeneity requirement has been considered as 'teleological clarity': in these cases, the Constitutional Court looked at the clearness of the specific aim of the referendum (e.g., Constitutional Court, Judgment No. 27/2017).

It is also interesting to note that the Constitutional Court has always underlined that, in this specific case, its judgment does not involve the profiles of constitutional legitimacy, neither about the legitimacy of the law submitted to the referendum nor of the legislation resulting from the possible referendum repeal (Constitutional Court, Judgments Nos 46/2005, 47/2005, 48/2005, 27/2017 and 50/2022). Nonetheless, the boundary between the admissibility judgment based on the 'Constitution content connected laws' and the judgment of constitutional legitimacy of the resulting legislation, in some cases, seems very blurry. For instance, declaring inadmissible the manipulative question relating to Article 579 of the Criminal Code, about the crime of consenting murder, the Constitutional Court has stated that the approval of the referendum proposal would have made the murder of anyone, who had validly consented to it, indiscriminately lawful, except in cases of minor age, mental illness and mental deficiency, and would have caused the loss of any protection of human life (both in all other situations of vulnerability and weakness connected to aspects like emotions, family, social or economic, as well as relating to physical health problems), as well as the risk that the right holder could make unconsidered choices (Constitutional Court, Judgment No. 50/2022).

§6. The Vote and the Announcement of the Results

130. After a referenda proposal has been certified for its legality and constitutional admissibility, the referendum proper is held on a Sunday in the period 15 April–15 June, and the result is announced by the Head of State.

The proposal submitted to referendum is approved, as per Article 75, if the majority of those eligible to vote took part in the referendum and if the latter won a majority of valid votes ('white' or null ballots papers are not considered).

If the proposal is approved, it takes legal effect from the day following publication of the decree of the President of the Republic announcing the abrogation in the Official Journal. This decree may, however, postpone the effects of the abrogation for up to sixty days (Article 37 of Law No. 352/1970). On the contrary, if the referendum is not approved, the repeal of the measure in question cannot be proposed for the next five years (Article 38 of Law No. 352/1970).

Part II. Form of Government

Chapter 1. Introduction to the Italian System of Government

by Valerio Onida†

§1. The Italian System of Government: An Outline

131. The Italian system of government embodies many of the classical principles and features of the republican parliamentary system:

a. a Parliament composed of two elective Chambers exercising legislative power and political control over the executive;
b. a collective government which is appointed by the Head of State but is politically responsible only to Parliament and remains in office while retaining its confidence;
c. a President of the Republic, the Head of the State, who is elected by Parliament (joined by a number of representatives of the Regions), although his term is longer than the legislature and not revocable. The President is not politically responsible and participates, at least formally, in many activities of government. He promulgates the laws and issues other important governmental acts. He also exercises the two powers typical of the parliamentary system for Heads of State, namely that of appointing the government and dissolving the Chambers before the end of their normal term.

132. The Constituent Assembly acted in accordance with the principles of the European parliamentary tradition, which Italy had adopted before the advent of Fascism and which were subsequently modified by the passage from the monarchy to the Republic following the referendum on 2 June 1946. Many of the improvements suggested by the experience of the parliamentary republics between the two World Wars were also included in the new Constitution. When the system of government was debated by the committee of the Constituent Assembly responsible for drawing up the new Constitution, a resolution (proposed by Tommaso Perassi) stated, indeed, that the presidential and directorial systems were not suited to the Italian situation and that a parliamentary system tailored to avoid 'the degenerations of parliamentarianism' had to be chosen.

133. As far as the system of central government is concerned, the following points deserve special mention:

a. The bicameral structure of Parliament has not allowed for a substantial distribution of power since both Chambers are elected by direct universal suffrage on the basis of similar electoral systems. Proposals to introduce 'non-political' or professional representatives in the Senate or to make it a Chamber in which the Regions might be, at least partially, represented were not approved. The Constituent Assembly distinguished the Senate from the Chamber of Deputies by setting different ages both for eligible voters and candidates, providing for a 'regional basis' for the election of the Senate, a small number of non-elected life senators and different terms for the two Chambers (five years for the Chamber of Deputies and six for the Senate). It also envisioned (but did not provide in the Constitution) a single-member constituency voting system for the Senate to be implemented, thus distinguishing it from the proportional system of the Chamber. After a reform in 1963, however, the Chambers were both given five-year terms, and the voting system for the Senate, adopted in 1948 and not reformed until 1993, was a fundamentally proportional system, though one still based on regional electoral districts (the election of members in a single-member constituency was adopted only for the case in which a candidate had gotten almost 65% of the votes). The only slight remaining differences between the two Chambers concern the age of eligible voters and candidates and the presence of a few life senators. After the 1993 electoral reform, the voting systems for both Chambers lost their mainly proportional character and became very similar, although not identical. The reform of 2005 (declared partially unconstitutional by Judgment No. 1/2014) adopted a proportional system in large constituencies, with a 'majority prize' in favour of the most voted coalition of parties, on a national basis for the Chamber of Deputies, on a regional one for the Senate. And, even the reform of 2017, still in force, adopted a very similar system for the two Chambers (a single vote to elect one-third of members in single-member constituencies and two-thirds with a proportional system). In respect of their functions and powers, the two Chambers are fundamentally identical: a recent attempt to change the bicameral system profoundly was rejected in the constitutional referendum of 2016. In sum, the Chamber of Deputies and the Senate are very similar from a political point of view. The political groups making up both the assemblies have an essentially national character; the two Chambers sometimes differ in their specific legislative choices (thus lengthening and complicating legislative proceedings while enriching the decision-making process) but normally express the same majority in support of the Government.
b. The Constitution provides for government's decisions to be taken collectively, according to the parliamentary tradition, although the President of the Council of Ministers plays a fundamental leading role, having to 'maintain unity in general political and administrative policy' (Article 95 of the Constitution). So far, however, the practice has shown that coalition governments and divisions within government parties limit the concentration of power in one person in the executive. This tendency is reinforced by the role that each Minister plays in

the formulation and implementation of policies in various fields. One of the main problems faced by the Italian system of government has been therefore to ensure that the executive and the majority which supports it pursues a consistent political and legislative course of action, even if, in recent years, the role of the Prime Minister, in certain circumstances, has become stronger.

c. Relations between government and Parliament are based on parliamentary rules, according to which government depends on the confidence of the parliamentary majority but, at the same time, plays a leading role in the legislative process of that majority. The Constitution requires an explicit vote of confidence when government is sworn in and an explicit no-confidence motion passed by vote in which the Chambers give their reasons to force its resignation (Article 94 of the Constitution). Government can also use its role of 'leading committee' of the majority in order to force the latter to adopt its proposal by moving a vote of confidence. Such a procedure prevents Parliament from assuming exclusive control over all main political and legislative decisions, even if it cannot prevent the so-called extra-parliamentary crisis, when the government spontaneously resigns, due not to a vote of no-confidence but rather to disagreements within the majority or decisions of the parties composing it. The brief duration of Italian governments and the frequent changes in their composition seemed to be for a long time typical of the country's political scene due to the relationships among the different parliamentary forces (no one of them being majoritarian in Parliament) and between the members of the government executive and party leaders. In recent years, deep changes in the political system (*see* below, §2) and the electoral system produced such Parliaments in which political groups are always a large number, but they are less stable, the life of governments becomes longer, but the government more and more frequently 'forces' its majority to support its proposals by moving votes of confidence, or even adopting itself legislation by decree, so that the Chambers often seem to be deprived of a substantial influence on the legislation.

d. The legislative power is exercised both by Parliament and by government. The former can delegate the latter to legislate, adopting an act specifying an object, a time limit and guidelines. In case of need and urgency, government can adopt 'decree-laws' which lose their validity retroactively, unless subsequently validated by both Chambers within sixty days. In recent decades, the use of delegated government legislation and above all of 'decree-laws' has become increasingly more and more frequent. However, these Acts of Parliament converting the 'decree-laws' often change the text of governmental decrees even in a very substantial way. There have been some efforts to provide for certain matters to be regulated by government rather than by Parliament unless they are covered by the 'legal reserve' so as to avoid having to ask for parliamentary approval every time a change in law is necessary: but this result is far away from being reached.

e. The role of the President of the Republic is only partially outlined in the Constitution. In particular, there is no definition of the limits on his ability to influence political decisions, especially in the very frequent cases in which he is called upon to formally enact acts provided for by the Constitution. The only explicit rule is that every act of the President has to be countersigned by a Minister, who assumes political responsibility for the act. The President does not formally have a role as a political leader. He is rather a sort of guarantor of the Constitution, enjoying powers of 'persuasion and influence', that he is able to exercise efficiently on the many occasions in which he is called upon to participate formally in the adoption of acts of other constitutional bodies, especially the government. There are, however, some decisions which are the exclusive competence of the Head of State, namely the appointment of five justices of the Constitutional Court and five life senators. The President's practical influence over major political decisions depends not only on his own personality (he occupies the only constitutional office composed of a single individual) but also on the political and parliamentary situation. If government can count on a strong and stable majority and has an unquestioned leadership, the influence of the Head of State is limited and becomes more discreet. If, on the contrary, the political situation is unsettled, government does not rest on stable foundations, and the political leadership is uncertain (as is often the case in periods of transition when a new balance is still being sought), the Head of State, thanks to his formally dominant position with respect to the government's activities and to the stability afforded by his long term, ends up exercising a wider authority and representing an important point of reference in the country's political developments. Even the most significant powers that the President enjoys, namely choosing the President of the Council with the aim of giving the country a new government, and dissolving the Chambers in advance, allow him to play a more or less important role depending on the political context. Indeed, the choice of the Premier is conditioned by the situation in Parliament, on which government depends for support, whereas the Chambers are generally dissolved only if there is no stable majority and the government is unable to implement its own main policies.

§2. The Political System

updated by Antonio D'Andrea & Lorenzo Spadacini

134. The manner in which the system of government works in practice within a parliamentary democracy is largely dependent upon the configuration of the political system and its dynamics, i.e., on the nature, number, size and attitudes of parties, as well as the relations established between them, in addition to the role performed by social forces.

135. Over the first few decades in the life of the Republic, the party system in Italy was fragmented, although fairly stable. At its heart was the Christian Democracy, established in 1942 drawing also on the inheritance of Luigi Sturzo's Popular Party ('a centrist party looking towards the left', as defined by its leader Alcide De Gasperi), which led governments without interruption from 1946 until 1981, and subsequently also for long periods until 1992. However, it only achieved an absolute majority in the Chamber of Deputies in 1948, thereafter reaching a vote share of between 35% and 40%. The left was occupied by the Socialist Party, the heir of the party founded at the close of the nineteenth century, which after 1948 attracted around 10%–15% of the vote, and the Communist Party, as the successor of that created out of the split with the Socialist Party in 1921, which had the support of between 20% and 30% of the voters. The centre was occupied by the Liberal Party, the Social Democratic Party created in 1947 following a split with the Socialist Party and the Republican Party, which drew on the tradition of the 'historic' Mazzinian republicans of the nineteenth century: except in rare exceptional cases, each of these was voted for by no more than 5% of the electorate. On the right, following the disappearance of the monarchical parties, support for the neo-Fascist Italian Social Movement varied between 5% and 8%.

Until the start of the 1960s, the governmental majorities were based on an alliance between the Christian Democracy and the smaller centre parties, while the largest opposition party remained the Communist Party which, also in view of the international situation characterized by the existence of two blocs and the Cold War, appeared to be destined for eternal opposition, although it was often not without influence on parliamentary decisions.

136. During the course of the 1960s, the Christian Democracy started to work together with the Socialist Party, along with the smaller allied parties from the centre (although not the Liberal Party), giving life to a centre-left majority, which launched economic and social reforms and accelerated the implementation of the Constitution; however, the centre-left settlement soon fell into difficulty. During the 1970s, attempts were made to expand the majority to the Communist Party (which was still however excluded from government) against the backdrop of a country wracked by terrorist attacks, bloodshed and the actions of an 'armed party' (the 'Red Brigades'), culminating in 1978 in the abduction and murder of the Christian Democrat leader Aldo Moro. This was followed by a period in which governments were often built on coalitions, characterized by competition and conflict, between the centre parties and the Socialist Party (known as the '*pentapartito*', i.e., the five-party coalition).

137. The early 1990s saw the rapid and almost unexpected collapse of this political system. On an international level, the fall of the Soviet Union resulted in the removal of one of the premises on which this system was based: the exclusion of the Communist Party from government. On an internal level, there were moves to modify the electoral system towards a majoritarian system (*see* Part I, Chapter 2, paragraph 51) in order to establish the possibility of alternating periods in government by two opposing forces or groupings. In addition, a variety of judicial investigations were launched into a considerable number of politicians of primary standing, which laid bare a widespread system of unlawful party financing alongside political and administrative corruption.

138. Within the space of literally a few months, two of the largest parties, the Christian Democrats and the Socialist Party, were swept away; another party, the

Communist Party, changed its name and composition, losing its left wing. A number of new political forces were created, including parties based on a personal following, and one (the Northern League) with independence or even secessionist tendencies. Even the neo-Fascist party, the Italian Social Movement, changed its name and contributed to the emergence of a broader centre-right grouping (with which many former supporters of the Socialist Party and the Christian Democrats identified) under the personal leadership of a media magnate (Silvio Berlusconi). This force was opposed by a centre-left grouping incorporating members of the former Communist Party and the left wing of the Christian Democrats. The 1994 elections (the first to be held under the new electoral law, which saw the proliferation of an innumerable array of party names and symbols, with sixty-seven standing in the elections) resulted in a totally changed political panorama, which after a period of settlement appears to have resulted in competition between two opposing groupings, with either one or the other destined to prevail in subsequent elections.

139. However, these groupings proved to be anything other than cohesive, with fragmentation within Parliament not falling but rather increasing, often giving life to numerous shifts of Members of Parliament from one grouping to another. More recently, a new group, the 5Star Movement (M5S), has established itself (attracting in the 2018 parliamentary elections a share of almost 33%), which purports to stand outside the classical alternative between left and right, representing a radical challenge to the other political forces and promoting internet-based forms of participation. The centre-right and centre-left groupings have in turn started to splinter, the former into radically nationalist and anti-European groups and more moderate forces and the latter into more moderate and more radical forces. Thus, the Italian political system of today cannot be said to be generally bipartite, or even 'bipolar', as it is split up into at least five or more competing forces or groups of forces. However, starting from the political elections of 2022, a new centre-right coalition emerged, led for the first time by a party, Brothers of Italy, which draws inspiration from previous post-fascist political groupings. While this coalition did not enjoy the support of an absolute majority of voters, it secured the majority of seats in the chambers, thanks to the divisions among the opposition. In fact, the opposition is fragmented into three distinct groupings: a small centrist bloc, a centre-left coalition, and the 5 Star Movement, which, however, saw its previous political support reduced by half.

In the meantime, voter turnout has fallen considerably: whereas until 1979, over 90% of the electorate voted, since then turnout has gradually fallen, reaching a figure of less than 64% in the 2022 general election.

§3. The Social Forces

updated by Antonio D'Andrea & Lorenzo Spadacini

140. The array of social forces has remained relatively more stable than its political equivalent. The organizations of the traditional 'class' trade unions, originally linked in different ways to the historical parties – CGIL (*Confederazione*

Generale Italiana del Lavoro, Italian General Labour Federation), CISL (*Confederazione Italiana Sindacati Lavoratori*, Italian Federation of Trade Unions) and UIL (*Unione Italiana Lavoratori*, Italian Workers' Union) – have always represented most workers, especially those in the private sector. For a long time, they seemed willing to maintain a fundamental unity of action among them, but in recent years, their policies seemed often to split. Other organizations, such as 'autonomous' occupational trade unions with political orientations that differ from those of the historical parties, have also been set up, especially in the public sector.

As far as employers are concerned, industry, especially the large and medium-sized, is represented mainly by Confindustria (*Confederazione Generale Italiana dell'Industria*, Italian General Federation of Industry), whereas other occupational trade unions, sometimes linked to political parties (though less so today), represent the sectors of agriculture, trade and artisan crafts. These organizations, including in particular the three major 'federal' trade unions and the association of businesses (the *Confindustria*), traditionally participated actively in political life and decision-making, including through agreements concluded with the government concerning both employment and salary conditions alongside economic, fiscal and financial policy. In the past, such agreements often constituted a central aspect of national policy, even though they did not at any stage lead to the promotion and empowerment of the role of the body (the National Council for the Economy and Employment) envisaged by the Constitution precisely for this purpose, which many now wish to abolish. More recently, perhaps as a result of the process of the internationalization and increasing financialization of the economy, such practices of concerted action with the social partners have become increasingly rare.

141. Political parties were traditionally powerful in Italy. Their huge financial resources were often connected to unlawful funding systems, unveiled by the judicial investigations that have brought change to the Italian political world. These parties deeply influenced the choice of elected and appointed officials, as well as the main decisions on the country's political life. They also deeply affected both the choice of public leaders at all the levels in which powers of nomination were exercised by political bodies (sometimes even in the business sector, through State-owned companies) and the political and legislative decisions taken by government and Parliament.

This situation was usually referred to as 'government by political parties' and has been the target of much criticism that contributed, among other things, to the weakening of the traditional political system. Currents of public opinion sometimes seem to go so far as to challenge the legitimacy of parties as tools for citizens to 'contribute to national policy' (Article 49 of the Constitution). This has paved the way for open demonstrations of disaffection with regard to politics and dangerous trends towards forms of 'plebiscitary' democracy such as calls for the direct election not only of regional and local leaders (as already provided by law) but also of the President of the Republic or the Prime Minister. Another trend has been the heavy recourse to referendum not as a 'corrective' measure but rather as a tool for citizens to express their open opposition to the party system.

As has been noted above, the Italian political system has undergone profound change over the last three decades. Many or almost all parties today have weak ideological and policy foundations and tend to operate increasingly as simple support organizations for their leaders within a climate of personalized politics.

Changes in the role and manner of operation of means of mass communication have also played a role (television, the internet and social media, which have acquired greater weight also in view of the fall in newspaper circulation) as have new instruments in the quest for electoral support (the growing importance of opinion polls and once again the use of social media).

Also for these reasons, it is difficult to imagine how the Italian political system will appear even in the near future.

The parties that are major players today are largely new creations (the oldest is the 'League' [*la Lega*], which has removed the term 'North' from its name, although still attracts votes predominantly in the north), and thus have a recent tradition and a less well-established ideological depth. The traditional division itself between left and right (along with intermediate centrist positions) has been called into question. Some even assert that it is now a thing of the past. However, this is not strictly speaking true if one considers, for example, the major political questions concerning the role of the state within the economy, the tax system, employment legislation, migration. However, in many cases, the dividing lines are not so stark and various groupings and political forces appear to adopt different positions, depending upon the specific issues. For example, as regards Italy's approach to the process of European integration, there is a dividing line between 'pro-Europeans' and more nationalist forces. The political dynamics have thus become more complex.

Since the general election held on 4 March 2018, Italy has had three different Governments, each supported by different majorities, all with the Five Star Movement, and headed by Premiers chosen outside the Parliament: once with the League (which detached itself from the centre-right coalition, even though the coalition still holds within local elections), headed by Giuseppe Conte; then with the centre-left parties, also headed by Giuseppe Conte, and lastly with almost all the parties, both centre-left and centre-right, supporting a partially 'technical' Government headed by the former President of the European Central Bank, Mario Draghi. After the dissolution of the majority supporting Prime Minister Draghi's government, the chambers were dissolved a few months ahead of schedule. In the September 2022 elections, a centre-right coalition led by the leader of Brothers of Italy, Giorgia Meloni, emerged, and she was appointed as the Prime Minister, securing the expected confidence of the chambers.

In any case, the Italian political panorama has become much more uncertain and volatile within a general climate that is characterized by major conflicts and reciprocal controversies.

Chapter 2. The President of the Republic

by Fabrizio D'Addabbo† & Lorenzo Spadacini

142. Title II (Articles 83–91), Part II of the Constitution (Organization of the Republic) is devoted to the President of the Republic. Provisions concerning the Head of State can be found in other sections of the Constitution as well (i.e., Articles 59, 62 second paragraph, 73 first and second paragraph, 74, 92 second paragraph, 93, 104 second paragraph, 126 first paragraph, 134 paragraph 3, 135 first and seventh paragraph). Furthermore, a number of laws and regulations refer to the Head of State (the most important will be mentioned in the following pages).

§1. The Election: The Electoral College

143. The two Houses of Parliament in joint session are responsible for the election of the President of the Republic. Three delegates from every Region (except for the Valle d'Aosta Region which is represented by only one delegate), elected by the Regional Council in such a manner as to ensure that minorities are represented, take part in the election (Article 83, first and second paragraph, of the Constitution). The rules of this electoral college are the same applying to Parliament in joint session. One of these is Article 63, second paragraph, of the Constitution, which sets out that the President of the Chamber of Deputies and its President's office will preside whenever Parliament meets in joint session.

Owing to the parliamentary nature of this college, the choice of the person who represents the unity of the Nation (*see* Article 87, first paragraph, of the Constitution) depends mainly on political parties, represented by their respective groups in Parliament.

Regional delegates taking part in the election are chosen from among the members of Regional Councils, even though the Constitution does not exclude the possibility of electing other people. Election within the Councils usually by a vote limited to two names is a guarantee of the protection of minorities provided for by the Constitution.

The presence of regional delegates was meant by the Constituent Assembly as a way to increase the President's powers of representation. In practice, however, the political membership of the delegates prevails over their regional origin, as well as the need for an equilibrium among the various national political forces prevails over the autonomous representation of the Regions.

§2. The Electoral Procedure

144. Thirty days before the seven-year presidential term lapses, the President of the Chamber of Deputies summons Parliament in joint session together with the regional delegates to elect the new President of the Republic (Article 85, second paragraph, of the Constitution). According to most of the academic commentators and in practice, the day set out by the Constitution is not the one on which the college should meet, but rather that on which the President is to set a date when Parliament will meet and he is to issue the order summoning the assembly (the termination of the presidential term is calculated starting from the day on which the Head of State was sworn in). This provision is aimed at ensuring that a new President has already been elected upon termination of the period of office of the outgoing one. Since the election might sometimes require a high number of votes (the maximum so far was twenty-three ballots in sixteen days for the election of Giovanni Leone in 1971), someone believes that the electoral college should meet on the day set out in Article 85, second paragraph, rather than on a subsequent date, set at the discretion of the President of the Chamber.

145. If Parliament has been dissolved or is to be dissolved within three months, the election is held within fifteen days from the first meeting of the new Chambers. In the interval, the powers of the existing President are prolonged (Article 85, third paragraph). The reason for such a short term is the need to reduce the *prorogatio* of the outgoing President to the bare minimum. With respect to this subject in the past, the dissolution of the Chambers could be only at the end of their five-year term, given that Parliament could not be dissolved in advance during the last six months of the President's term of office. Presently, however, the President of the Republic can order an early dissolution also in case of coincidence, even partial, between the last six months of his term and the last six months of Parliament (Article 88, second paragraph, of the Constitution, as amended by Article 1 of Constitutional Law No. 1/1991).

In case of 'permanent incapacity' or death or resignation of the President of the Republic, the President of the Chamber of Deputies provides for the election of a new President within fifteen days, unless a longer period be foreseen because the Chambers are dissolved or because their term has less than three months to expire (Article 86, second paragraph, of the Constitution).

146. Submitting specific programmes to mark an official candidacy for the office of President is prohibited in practice. The names of candidates can be put forward only informally by the political groups or during the voting. Debates over such 'unofficial' nominations are not allowed during the election.

Indeed, when meeting in a joint session, pursuant to Article 83 of the Constitution, Parliament acts as an 'imperfect' electoral college, which is not allowed to debate but only to vote. Only remarks about the procedure and reference to the Standing Orders are allowed (the Standing Orders applied are those of the Chamber of Deputies since there is still no special provision on joint sessions: *see* Article 35, second paragraph, of the Standing Orders of the Chamber and Article 65 of those of the Senate).

If official names of candidates were put forward during the assemblies, the choice of the President of the Republic might be seen as the expression of particular political and ideological tendencies. The Head of State, on the contrary, is a representative of the whole Nation, and he is supposed to guarantee the observance of the Constitution rather than play a political role.

147. Members of the electoral college vote by secret ballot. The purpose is always to ensure the independence of the President elected from any political influence that might arise during an open vote. Voters write the name of their favourite candidate on the ballot paper and put it into the ballot box. Those who do not wish to indicate any name can cast a blank ballot.

Passing before the box without inserting any ballot paper, thus expressing the intention to abstain from voting, is behaviour tolerated in practice but criticized. This visible expression of a 'non-vote' has often been imposed by some parliamentary groups on their members to prevent them from voting for unwelcome candidates, thus influencing the decisions of the groups and the result of the following votes. This behaviour allows political groups to exert their influence on voters, somehow violating the principle of secret voting. However, when Members of Parliament (MPs) and regional delegates do indicate a specific name on the ballot paper, their autonomy is fully guaranteed because their parties cannot verify if their instructions about the candidate to be voted were actually followed. Voters have often disregarded these instructions, and votes have therefore gone on fruitlessly or resulted in the election of candidates different from those who had been supported from the beginning by the most important political groups.

148. Pursuant to Article 83, third paragraph, presidential elections need a majority of two-thirds of the assembly during the first three ballots. After the third ballot, an absolute majority is sufficient. The person who is supposed to represent national unity must, therefore, enjoy wider parliamentary support than the government (the confidence in the executive can be expressed by a simple plurality of votes).

So far, owing to the very fragmented composition of the Chambers, the lack of an absolute majority party and the little unity shown by the political groups, the election has often been a compromise between both majority and opposition groups. The election of the Head of State has been 'the moment of maximum dislocation and separation of political parties' (L. Elia) since the choice has seldom been the result of party convergence corresponding to the government coalition. Since run-off elections are not allowed in this case, there is no limit to the number of votes necessary to reach a majority, which in practice has often been very high. Since the Constitution came into force, only two Presidents were elected during the first ballot: Francesco Cossiga in 1985 and Carlo Azeglio Ciampi in 1999; large majorities, sometimes more than two-thirds, were reached other times as well, but almost always after long series of votes. The current President, Sergio Mattarella, was elected for the first time on 31 January 2015 on the fourth ballot, receiving 665 votes out of the 1,009 electors. Mattarella was reconfirmed as the President of the Italian Republic for a second term, receiving 759 votes out of 1,009 electors in the eighth ballot (which is 75.2% of the assembly). He took the oath of office on February 3, thus commencing his second term.

In spite of all the rules aimed at ensuring that the elected President is independent, authoritative and supported by most parliamentary groups, the election of the Head of State inevitably takes on a strong political meaning, thus ending up being very divisive. The fact that parties strive to elect one of their members or at least someone whose political tendencies are not incompatible with their policy should not be surprising if we consider that the elected President is at the centre of institutional and political life for seven years, usually without the possibility of revocation, although he does not become the political leader of the country. Recently, moreover, his influence has increased, especially due to the uncertain political situation. Difficulties in reaching an agreement that satisfies most of the groups explain why the votes are quite often protracted, besides being criticized by the press and public opinion. Hence the proposals to change the present electoral procedure.

§3. Qualification for Election

149. Pursuant to Article 84, first paragraph, of the Constitution, 'any citizen of fifty years of age enjoying civil and political rights is eligible for election as President of the Republic'. The fact that the Head of State should be a 'citizen' (male or female) seems to exclude not only foreigners and Stateless people but also 'Italians who do not belong to the Republic' whom 'the law may place on a par with resident citizens in the matter of admission to public office and elective positions' (Article 51, second paragraph, of the Constitution). As far as the rules on citizenship and civil and political rights are concerned (without prejudice, of course, to the constitutional rules on the matter: for instance, Articles 22 and 48), Article 84, first paragraph, implicitly refers to laws in force, except for the special cases of incapacity.

The minimum age requirement is aimed at ensuring that only a mature, experienced and authoritative person be elected as President, on account of both his previous *cursus honorum* and his merits, even outside the political spectrum.

Although every citizen with the above characteristics can run for election and there have been recent cases of the candidacy of famous people having no connection with the political and parliamentary classes, so far, the office of President has been held by renowned politicians and, almost always, former members of Parliament. The first Head of State to be elected by the Republican Parliament, Luigi Einaudi, President from 1948 to 1955, and Carlo Azeglio Ciampi, President from 1999 to 2006, do not represent exceptions to the rule. The former, a famous economist and former governor of the Bank of Italy, was also a member of the Constituent Assembly and subsequently Minister of the Budget. The latter was also a former governor of the Bank of Italy; he was never an MP, but he became President of the Council of Ministers and subsequently Treasury Minister.

§4. The Oath, the Term of Office and Cases of 'Prorogatio'

150. Before taking office, the President of the Republic swears an oath of loyalty to the Republic and observance of the Constitution before Parliament in joint session, which is no longer made up of the regional delegates (Article 91 of the Constitution). By this solemn act, the elected President also expresses his will to accept the charge. After reciting the ritual formula, the Head of State gives his inaugural address to the Chambers and, indirectly, to the whole Nation. In doing so, he exercises his power of *esternazione*.

The seven-year presidential term (*see* Article 85, first paragraph, of the Constitution) elapses from the day of the oath, by which the President is empowered to exercise his functions. The Constituent Assembly distinguished the length of the presidential term from that of the two Chambers, which was previously five years for the Chamber of Deputies and six for the Senate (subsequently shortened to five years by Constitutional Law No. 2/1963: *see* the present version of Article 60, first paragraph, of the Constitution). The Constituent Assembly decided that the presidential term should be longer than the one of the Chambers especially in order to ensure the President's independence of the majority electing him. Moreover, the President is not supposed to exercise any political functions, and there is therefore no need for his term to be short. His role as 'guarantor' rather requires a certain stability allowing him to stay away from political disputes and party influence.

As stated above, if the election of the President's successor is postponed because Parliament has been dissolved or is to be dissolved within three months, the President's powers are prolonged beyond the seven-year term. This is the only case of *prorogatio* of the Head of State explicitly provided for by the Constitution (Article 85, third paragraph). Moreover, in spite of some authoritative contrary opinions, academic commentators usually admit the *prorogatio* whenever Parliament does not manage to elect the new President pursuant to Article 85, second paragraph, before the term of his predecessor comes to an end. The 'prolonged' President of the Republic is allowed to perform acts of extraordinary management only if they cannot be deferred under the Constitution or the law, while he can issue decrees submitted by the government without any particular restriction.

§5. The Status of the President: Cases of Incompatibility

151. Pursuant to Article 84, second paragraph, of the Constitution, 'the office of President of the Republic is incompatible with any other office'. This provision covers all the cases of incompatibility, much more than the rules on the other constitutional organs. Its interpretation is usually very broad, even broader than its text suggests. The office of President is therefore incompatible not only with elective or non-elective, political, administrative and public positions but also with private ones, both as an employer and as an employee. The President, moreover, is not allowed to perform trade and professional activities. Such a high number of cases of incompatibility are justified by the need to preserve the President's independence and impartiality, which would no doubt be jeopardized if he enjoyed the political and economic power deriving from the offices listed above.

The office of President, of course, is also incompatible with party activities. He should not be allowed to remain or become a member of political groups or movements, even though he renounces to any sort of charge or responsibility. He could join instead cultural and scientific associations as a simple member with no managing function, on condition that these associations are not linked to any political party.

§6. Temporary and Permanent Incapacity and Other Cases of Early Conclusion of the Presidential Term

152. Pursuant to Article 86, first paragraph, of the Constitution, if the President of the Republic proves to be unable to fulfil his duties, they are carried out by the President of the Senate. The Italian constitutional system does not provide for a 'Vice-President of the Republic', with the special institutional role of replacing the President whenever he proves to be unable to fulfil his duties or delegates part of them. In the exercise of presidential powers, which is necessarily personal and direct, no solution of continuity can be allowed; therefore, the Head of State, in case of need, must be replaced by a person holding a different office, such as the President of the Senate.

The President of the Republic could never be replaced at his own choosing, given that his powers cannot be delegated at will. He can be replaced only if specific circumstances prevent him from fulfilling his duties. Should the incapacity be temporary, the President remains in office and, once the incapacity is over, he regains the powers he had transferred (the so-called *sede plena* replacement). Should the incapacity, on the contrary, be such as to prevent the President from ever holding his office again, his duties are fulfilled by the President of the Senate until a new Head of State takes his oath of loyalty (the so-called *sede vacante* replacement). Article 86, second paragraph, lists the various cases of early conclusion of the presidential term: permanent incapacity, death or resignation. In all these cases, the procedure to elect a successor must be started rapidly. Two other cases should be added to the list, as will be seen later on: loss of office and removal from office.

In truth, the Constitution deals with this subject in an inadequate and incomplete manner. Cases of both permanent and temporary incapacity can be supposed, but the Constitution does not explain how to distinguish the former from the latter, nor, more in general, how to recognize a case of incapacity:

a. The first case that deserves mention is physical or mental illness. For the President to be declared incapable, however, the disease should seriously jeopardize the 'quality' of his working activities, so much so that he is no longer able to fulfil his duties. Incapacity is considered as permanent not only when, according to the medical reports, his illness seems irreversible but also when, although it is likely to be cured in the end, it could last for quite a long and indefinite time, maybe beyond the end of the term. Replacement by the President of the Senate is considered indeed as exceptional and temporary and should never extend over many months or even years. In practice, verifying if the incapacity of the President of the Republic is caused by a disease and if such incapacity is temporary or permanent can be a very hard task. In any case, if the Head of State is able to do it, he can declare himself incapable of fulfilling his duties. If he declares himself temporarily incapable, his declaration must be countersigned by the President of the Council of Ministers. If, on the contrary, he declares himself permanently incapable, most academic commentators reckon that there is no need for a countersignature since the declaration is considered a resignation act, which is a *personal* act. The declaration of permanent incapacity is indeed identical to 'a resignation act, which should explain the reasons that justify or impose the resignation itself' (L. Paladin).

If, on the contrary, the President cannot or is not willing to recognize that he suffers from a disease that makes him unfit for work, it becomes very difficult to deal with his case since the Italian Constitution does not specify who should establish the President's incapacity. However, the mere statement of incapacity gives rise to the consequent legal effects, especially to the replacement procedure.

Verifying the President's physical or mental incapacity to fulfil his duties implies two different evaluations: the first is of medical nature, therefore technical, while the second is political and is also aimed at establishing if the incapacity is temporary or permanent. The ensuing decision is expressed in the document by which the Head of State is officially declared incapable. This case occurred only once, in August 1964, when President Antonio Segni was affected by cerebral thrombosis. According to a notice issued by the Prime Minister's Office, the medical bulletin on the Head of State's conditions was transmitted by the Secretary General of the Presidency of the Republic to the Presidents of the two Houses of Parliament and the President of the Council of Ministers. The latter reported it to the Council of Ministers, which *recognized* the impossibility for the President of the Republic to fulfil his duties.

The President of the Senate then convened the President of the Chamber of Deputies and the President of the Council for the 'appropriate evaluations', and the three *agreed* on the need to enforce Article 86, first paragraph, of the Constitution. The President of the Senate was therefore appointed as temporary substitute of the Head of State. Although, at first, President Segni's incapacity to fulfil his duties was carefully deemed temporary, the serious disability he suffered as a result of the disease soon turned out to be irreversible. A few months later, he decided to resign, thus preventing a very likely official procedure to declare him permanently incapable.

Although this procedure was criticized, it had the merit of establishing that the incapacity should be ascertained jointly and on an equal footing by the President of the Senate, in his capacity as the President substitute, by the President of the Chamber, who, in case of permanent incapacity of the Head of State, should provide for the election of his successor and preside over the electoral college, and by the President of the Council, as a representative of the executive responsible to Parliament.

b. If the Head of State goes abroad on an official visit and his absence from Italy is likely to be rather long and should he be very far from the country, all the presidential duties that do not concern the mission abroad are carried out by the President of the Senate, pursuant to Article 86, first paragraph, of the Constitution.

The replacement in this case is aimed at preventing the difficulties that might arise owing to the long distance and impossibility for the President to come back immediately in case of need, with serious drawbacks on the country's constitutional life. This is, however, an anomalous case of 'partial' replacement: the activities carried out abroad by the Head of State pertain to his role of representative of Italy in international relationships while, as long as he is away, the rest of his duties are fulfilled by the President of the Senate. The President of the Republic himself takes the initiative of drawing up the related act, which is countersigned by the President of the Council.

However, the last instance of such a substitution occurred in 2010. In subsequent state visits, in fact, the substitution was not activated.

c. Pursuant to Article 12, fourth paragraph, of Constitutional Law No. 1/1953 (as amended by Article 3 of Constitutional Law No. 1/1989), the Head of State can be suspended from office by the Constitutional Court in case of impeachment for high treason or attempt on the Constitution, as provided for by Article 90 of the Constitution. It is worth mentioning that the impeachment procedure does not necessarily imply suspending the President from office, a measure which can be taken by the Constitutional Court only if it really deems it necessary (which, given the circumstances, should happen in most cases).

d. As stated above, the presidential term may end before the natural date not only for permanent incapacity but also in case of death, resignation, loss of office or removal from office in case of conviction following an impeachment procedure, pursuant to Article 134 of the Constitution, paragraph 3.

As the fifteen-day period within which the election of the successor must be provided for runs from the moment the President resigns (*see* Article 86, second paragraph, of the Constitution), the resignation takes effect immediately and is irrevocable, without the need for other constitutional organs to accept it. Once it is signed, the resignation act replacement starts automatically. According to most academic commentators, the act being *personal*, i.e., performed by the President not in the exercise of his functions but rather as a private citizen, should not be countersigned.

Seven of the eleven Presidents elected so far by the Republican Chambers decided, for various reasons, to resign before the end of their term. Antonio Segni, as we said before, was obliged to resign owing to a serious illness; Giovanni Leone, the target of violent attacks from journalists aimed at disclosing his alleged business and finance offences, decided to resign in 1978 since (in his own words) the 'defamatory campaign' seemed to have 'damaged the political groups' trust' in him; Sandro Pertini resigned in 1985, Oscar Luigi Scalfaro resigned in 1999 and Carlo Azeglio Ciampi resigned in 2006, respectively nine, thirteen and three days before the end of their seven-year term, so as to allow their already elected successor to take up the office of Head of State without delay; Francesco Cossiga, whose institutional behaviour during the last part of his term gave rise to fierce criticism, resigned in 1992, a few months before the end of his term, for the reasons that he explained in his address to the Nation, broadcast by the most important television channels (regarding himself as a President with no more authority and credibility, in order to overcome the severe political and institutional crises of that period, he affirmed the necessity to elect a new Head of State); Giorgio Napolitano, who was elected President in 2006 and re-elected for a second term in 2013, resigned at the start of 2015 (as he explained in his end-of-year television message to the Italian people made on 31 December 2014) both due to his advanced age and also because procedures leading to a far-reaching reform of the republican institutions had already been launched, which had been a precondition set by him for his willingness to accept re-election.

Cossiga's and Napolitano's resignation acts, as well as Leone's (he too had addressed the citizens from the cameras to announce his resignation and give reasons for it), did not contain any explanation, unlike the acts signed by Presidents Segni, Pertini and Scalfaro. In the act signed by Ciampi on 15 May 2006, there was only a reference to the fact that the resignation would have taken effect on the same day that the newly elected President, Giorgio Napolitano, would be sworn in before Parliament in joint session.

e. Save for the case of impeachment, the possibility that the Head of State might lose office owing to the loss of one of the conditions to be elected President (Italian citizenship, enjoyment of civil and political rights) is purely theoretical. Should this highly improbable event occur, the President would be automatically prevented from continuing his term and immediately replaced.

f. About consequences of conviction following an impeachment procedure, such as removal and sanctions, *see* Part II, Chapter 9, §10.

§7. Replacement

153. The President of the Senate may take up the office of Head of State pro tempore as long as the President is unable to fulfil his duties or, should the President retire, until the oath of his successor. The President of the Senate, of course, is allowed to replace the Head of State as long as he retains his office of President of the Senate.

As explicitly stated in some decrees issued in order to provide for the replacement of the President while abroad, when the President of the Senate replaces the Head of State, he is called 'substitute President of the Republic'. In case of both temporary and permanent replacements, the substitute takes office without taking any oath which, as a matter of fact, is not provided for by the Constitution. In order to fulfil his duties correctly, the substitute is subject to the same restrictions as the President of the Republic as regards cases of incompatibility. As long as he replaces the Head of State, the substitute is suspended not only from his duties as President of the Senate but also from any other office or activity incompatible with the office of President of the Republic. Like the President of the Republic, his substitute cannot be held responsible for acts carried out in the exercise of his duties, pursuant to Article 90 of the Constitution. He also enjoys the same legal protection of his person and honour (*see* Article 290*bis* of the Criminal Code).

Some academic commentators do not agree with the fact that the substitute enjoys exactly the same powers as the Head of State. In any case, the substitute must unquestionably perform all the acts that cannot be delayed pursuant to the Constitution or by law, and he is empowered to issue all the decrees that are formally presidential but actually moved by the government. He is also empowered to perform duties implying a control on decisions taken by other authorities (such as returning a bill to the Houses of Parliament for renewed consideration). Generally speaking, although the Constitution does not explicitly limit his powers in any way whatsoever, the substitute should follow conventional rules of behaviour that change according to the circumstances and the necessity to ensure the efficiency of the institutions. If the replacement is *sede vacante*, the substitute cannot exercise his power to dissolve the Chambers since the election of the new President of the Republic must be provided for within the short period set out in Article 86, second paragraph, of the Constitution.

§8. Re-election and Assignment of the Office of Life Senator to Former Heads of State

154. Re-election of the President of the Republic for another seven years (and for other successive terms) is not forbidden by the Constitution. However, until 2013, no President had ever been re-elected, although there was no conventional rule prohibiting re-election, which had been considered by political groupings on various occasions. During the electoral procedure conducted in April 2013, the first five ballots saw the surprise rejection, one after the other, of two candidates who had seemingly been able to secure the votes necessary for election. The prospect of serious political and institutional paralysis led almost all of the main parties to ask the outgoing President Giorgio Napolitano to accept his re-election (a scenario which he had previously rejected) in order to enable Parliament to express unity and national cohesion concerning his appointment. Napolitano accepted, declaring that he could not shirk back from such a responsibility towards the Nation, and was re-elected by a very broad majority of much more than two-thirds of the electoral college. Aside from the events of 2013, according to some academic commentators, excluding the possibility of a re-election by a constitutional amendment would preserve the President's independence and impartiality, which could be jeopardized during the last period of his term if he tried to win the favour of most of the political groups. A similar scenario then arose for Napolitano's successor, Mattarella. He, too, despite initially declaring his unavailability for a new term because re-election seemed at odds with the exercise of presidential functions in an independent position, eventually accepted a new election. This happened after the political forces faced difficulties in reaching a sufficient agreement to identify a different personality in the initial votes for the selection of his successor.

Pursuant to Article 59, first paragraph, of the Constitution, any person who has held office as President of the Republic is by right a senator-for-life, unless he refuses to accept the nomination. When senators by right and for life enter the Senate, the President just informs the assembly, without the need to verify the validity of their admission.

§9. Allowances and Endowments: The General Secretariat of the Presidency of the Republic

155. Pursuant to Article 84, third paragraph, of the Constitution, the allowances and endowments of the President, which allow him to provide for the needs of his private life and family (*assegno*), are established by law. The office of the President must be remunerative, especially because it is incompatible with any other office. According to Article 84, third paragraph, the allowances and endowments, as well as the inalienable movables and immovables (such as the Quirinale Palace in Rome) allocated to the President for the fulfilment of his institutional duties (*dotazione*), are established by law too.

The Head of State is assisted by the General Secretariat of the Presidency of the Republic, set up by Law No. 1077/1948, which implemented Article 84, third paragraph. The Secretary General is the highest authority of the Secretariat. He is appointed by means of a decree of the President of the Republic, countersigned by the President of the Council, after consultation with the Council of Ministers. This advice being obligatory but not binding, the choice of the Secretary General depends almost entirely on the President of the Republic. Should the Secretary General no longer enjoy the confidence of the Head of State, he can be removed from office following a procedure similar to his appointment.

By virtue of the power of self-organization guaranteed to each constitutional organ, the President may organize the Secretariat offices and services, determine the legal and economic status of its staff and manage the financial resources allocated to the Presidency.

§10. Responsibility and Guarantees

156. Whereas the King could not be held responsible for his actions, his person being 'sacred and inviolable' (as it was solemnly set out in Article 4 of the *Statuto Albertino*), under the Republican Constitution, the Head of State is only partially exempt from answering for his illegal actions.

Pursuant to Article 90, first paragraph, the President of the Republic cannot be held responsible 'for acts carried out in the exercise of his duties' save 'in cases of high treason or attempt on the Constitution'. The President must answer for such serious crimes within the framework of the so-called political justice (*see* Part II, Chapter 9, §10). The Head of State, on the contrary, enjoys no immunity from civil and criminal jurisdiction either for acts unrelated to the fulfilment of his presidential duties or for activities carried out before taking office, for which he must answer like any other citizen.

The President can, therefore, be subject to judicial proceedings or measures restricting his personal freedom or even be sentenced to prison terms (in the last two hypotheses – if he does not resolve to resign – the President is no longer capable of fulfilling his duties and his incapacity can be temporary or permanent depending on the circumstances). Some academic commentators, however, reckon that the President should be accused but not prosecuted as long as he stays in office for crimes not covered by Article 90. This would prevent any unjustified or hasty judicial action against the President, who should be fully protected during his seven-year term. Although this opinion was applied in the past by the investigating judicial authorities in a case concerning President Oscar Luigi Scalfaro, it is not laid down in any constitutional rule or law. In fact, in 2003 and 2008, Parliament had approved two ordinary laws aimed at excluding the 'high offices of the State' from undergoing criminal proceedings up until the end of their term. Both these laws – which, for the President of the Republic, related to crimes unconnected with activities pertaining to his office – were, however, declared constitutionally illegitimate by the Constitutional Court (*see*, respectively, Judgments Nos 24/2004 and 262/2009).

However, it is essential for the Head of State to be able to rely on the fact that his communications will remain absolutely confidential. The Constitutional Court thus held that investigating magistrates were not entitled within criminal proceedings to assess the relevance of the intercepted telephone conversations of the President of the Republic for calls made by a person other than the President (*see* Judgment No. 1/2013). The documentation relating to such interceptions must be destroyed immediately in order to guarantee the secrecy of the content of the intercepted conversations. The judicial authorities would only be entitled by law to act differently under extreme circumstances, where necessary in order to protect interests pertaining to overriding constitutional principles, such as the protection of life and personal freedom and the integrity of the institutions of the Republic. According to the Constitutional Court, the confidential status of communications with the President of the Republic is an attendant feature of the President's role as a guarantor of the constitutional equilibrium and as an 'umpire exerting influence'. The efficacy and very practicability of his functions of moderation, initiative and persuasion would be undermined if the contents of individual communications were to be made public in an uncontrolled and indiscriminate manner. Their absolute confidentiality is thus necessary not with regard to any specific presidential function but in order to ensure the effective exercise of all functions, and is unequivocally rooted in the constitutional system, even though it is not formally and expressly asserted.

Finally, the Constitutional Court clarified that the declarations made by the Head of State during his seven-year presidency (so-called *esternazioni* or expressions) are only eligible for immunity pursuant to Article 90 of the Constitution if they are made in relation to the conduct of his functions or are otherwise essential for or attendant to a presidential function (*see* Judgment No. 154/2004). It falls to the judicial authority apprised of a dispute concerning the responsibility of the President of the Republic for the defamation of another person to establish whether there is any such functional link between the declarations and his official tasks, in the absence of which the ordinary provisions will apply.

As stated above, although he cannot be held responsible for acts carried out in the exercise of his duties, the President can be prosecuted for the crimes of high treason and attempt on the Constitution by the two Houses of Parliament in joint session and judged by the Constitutional Court (*see* Part II, Chapter 9, §10).

According to an academic theory, attempt on the Constitution and high treason are not provided for by criminal legislation but rather by the Constitution in a very concise manner. Providing for presidential crimes would mean protecting the values that the President himself is supposed to defend: unity and integrity of the Republic and respect of the Constitution. 'High treason' would therefore consist of behaviour aimed at jeopardizing the security or interests of the Nation, or even at damaging the integrity of the State and its institutions (especially if committed with the assistance of foreign authorities), whereas a serious and malicious violation of constitutional fundamental principles, and of the constitutional provisions concerning the President's powers, could be considered an 'attempt on the Constitution'. Doubts have been raised over the conformity of this theory with the fundamental principle of legality of crimes and punishment. In any case, although this and other theories may seem plausible, the Head of State's responsibility should be established case by case by the impeaching and judging authorities. The distinction between criminal and political liability may thus be rather vague.

It should be noted, however, that the President's behaviour can never be judged in terms of political convenience. The Head of State, indeed, is supposed to guarantee constitutional rules and sometimes admonish or encourage institutional authorities and political parties but never play an active political role.

Nevertheless, the President is exposed to the criticism of political groups, the media or ordinary citizens which, however, can only be aimed at influencing the Head of State's behaviour indirectly. Political censure, furthermore, must never take the form of defamation of the Head of State, which can be prosecuted under Article 278 of the Criminal Code.

§11. Countersignature of the Acts of the President of the Republic

157. Article 90 of the Constitution is closely linked to Article 89, which sets out that 'no act of the President of the Republic is legal unless it is countersigned by the Ministers who have submitted it and accept its responsibility' (first paragraph); 'measures having the value of law and such others as are laid down by law shall also be countersigned by the President of the Council of Ministers' (second paragraph). Pursuant to Article 5, first paragraph, letter d) of Law No. 400/1988, the *Premier* endorses every act of the Head of State that was subject to a resolution by the Council of Ministers.

Given that the President cannot be held responsible for acts carried out in the exercise of his duties, the legal and political responsibilities (the former before courts of criminal, civil and accounting jurisdiction; the latter before Parliament) must be taken up by members of the government; the countersignature is, therefore, essential for the acts of the President to be considered as valid. The expression 'Ministers who have submitted the act' contained in Article 89, first paragraph, is, however, rather misleading (it was apparently a mistake during the elaboration of the Constitution) since not all the acts of the President are submitted by members of the government. Most presidential decrees are the form taken by acts containing normative, political or administrative provisions entirely defined by the executive. One or more Ministers and, if required, the President of the Council submit and countersign the act and accept its responsibility as a result of government decision-making power. Before issuing these acts, the Head of State verifies their legality and sometimes, according to part of the academic commentators, also their merits.

Some presidential acts, on the contrary, can be adopted by the President of the Republic on his own initiative. These acts are countersigned by the Ministers having jurisdiction over such matters. The most important acts must be endorsed by the President of the Council in accordance with law or constitutional practices. In this case, the responsibility of the members of the executive consists in controlling the act by countersigning it, not its authorship, resting solely with the Head of State. The control concerns mainly the legality of the act, although it is also aimed at protecting the governmental political trend.

According to some authoritative sources, there is a third category of presidential acts, termed 'complex', which must be approved by both the Head of State and the Prime Minister. The decrees by which the President of the Council of Ministers is nominated and the two Houses of Parliament are dissolved could be considered as such, although it is probably more plausible to consider them as an expression of autonomous powers of the President of the Republic (*see* below, §12).

158. Not all the acts that formally belong to the President are promoted by the executive or the Head of State himself (or by both). Some of these acts are substantially defined by other authorities: the decrees by which criminal and civil judges are appointed are issued in compliance with the resolutions of the CSM. Those concerning the commissioners of the *Autorità per le garanzie nelle comunicazioni* (which supervises the activities carried out in the field of communications) formally approve the appointments made by the Chamber of Deputies and the Senate, etc. In all these cases, endorsement by the Minister having jurisdiction or the President of the Council is just aimed at verifying that the act comes from the President of the Republic, a mere certification of the authenticity of his signature.

Finally, exceptions to the rule set out in Article 89 of the Constitution are some presidential acts which need not be countersigned. They include *personal* acts, such as the resignation act, which are not performed by the President in the exercise of his functions but rather as a private citizen, regulations and other acts concerning the organization and the staff of the Presidency of the Republic, performed by the President by virtue of the autonomy to which every constitutional organ is entitled. The same applies to measures undertaken by the Head of State as the President of the *Consiglio supremo di difesa* and the CSM. The verbal *esternazioni* by which the President expresses his opinion about the various political and institutional current events, of course, are not susceptible of being countersigned.

§12. Powers Concerning the Parliamentary System

159. The President of the Republic plays a major role in the formation of the government. When a Cabinet resigns, it must do it before the President who, after an often long and complicated procedure, accepts the resignation and appoints the new President of the Council and the Ministers who are proposed by him (Article 92, second paragraph, of the Constitution).

The decree by which the President accepts the resignation of the government must be considered an expression of the presidential autonomous power, although it is influenced by the parliamentary situation. The Head of State can, in fact, reject the resignation (unless it was the result of a no-confidence vote) and invite the executive to formally ascertain the orientation of the Chambers. The act in question, issued without the need of a formal proposal, is countersigned by the new President of the Council, pursuant to Article 1, second paragraph, of Law No. 400/1988.

The decree of nomination of the President of the Council of Ministers can be considered an expression of the President's autonomous powers as well. This act should also meet the requirement of choosing a person who will be able to obtain the confidence of the Chambers. Sometimes, however, governments were appointed in spite of the lack of a parliamentary majority support and, hence, of the fact that they were unlikely to obtain the confidence (in view of a following dissolution of Parliament). The decree of nomination, which is made in the event that the invitation to form a new executive is successfully acted upon, is countersigned by the President of the Council of Ministers himself, and it is by virtue of this that he is vested with that office (*see* again Article 1, second paragraph, of Law No. 400/1988). Thus, signature amounts more to an act of acceptance rather than the usual countersignature. Since the President of the Republic's task is to identify a subject for the appointment as Prime Minister who can secure a vote of confidence in the Chambers, essentially, his or her degree of discretion depends heavily on the political circumstances. When there is a parliamentary majority that solidly expresses a leader for the Government, the President of the Republic has no choice but to appoint him or her. Conversely, there may be cases where the construction of a parliamentary majority is so complicated that only an autonomous initiative by the President can unlock the situation. In more recent times, this has led to the formation of Governments led by individuals, mostly outside the party system, autonomously identified by the President of the Republic and later supported by parliamentary majorities. This was the case with the Ciampi Government (1993–1994), a former President of the Bank of Italy, the Monti Government (2011–2013), a former European Commissioner, and the Draghi Government (2021–2022), a former Governor of the European Central Bank. These were the result of the Presidents' autonomous initiatives, in the face of severe economic and financial crises that, despite the apparent lack of a parliamentary majority, dissuaded the President from dissolving the Chambers. The presidential selection of such individuals resolved the political situation, allowing the formation of politically less cohesive but still effective parliamentary majorities to carry out the legislative term, even though some scholars consider these initiatives to be in tension with the requirement that the President be independent and impartial.

Unlike the previous ones, the decree of nomination of Ministers is not an expression of the President's autonomous powers since the choice of the Ministers who will join the government is up to the President of the Council. In practice, however, the Head of State has sometimes interfered with this choice. Usually, interferences of this form have been admitted and covered by the reserve of the other interested subjects, treating the matter with discretion.

On 27 May 2018, in the midst of an extended and at times dramatic political crisis, the Head of State for the first tame made it publicly known that he had refused to appoint one of the Ministers proposed to him (the Minister for the Economy and Finance), which he did in a statement to the media at the Quirinale Palace. The person vetoed was Prof. Paolo Savona, a renowned economist with considerable experience, who had already been a Minister in the past. However, according to President Mattarella, he was seen as a 'supporter of a policy … that could provoke … Italy's exit from the euro'. The unwavering decision made by the President of the Republic resulted in the failure of the first attempt to form a government by Prof.

Giuseppe Conte, giving rise to heated clashes with the two parties that were in the process of forming a majority in Parliament and risking a new general election in Italy only a few months after the March election.

A few days after the political-institutional 'crisis' discussed above emerged, President Mattarella and the two majority parties abruptly and surprisingly arrived at an agreement that allowed for the formation of a government headed by Prof. Conte in which Prof. Savona was appointed as Minister without Portfolio for European Affairs (an Italian paradox!), while Prof. Giovanni Tria, a leading economist, was appointed as Minister for the Economy and Finance.

The decree of nomination of Ministers, countersigned by the President of the Council who is entitled to propose the Ministers pursuant to Article 92, second paragraph, of the Constitution, is issued at the same time as the two other presidential acts examined above, at the end of the new government formation.

160. One of the most important acts among those expressing the President's autonomous powers is the one decreeing an early dissolution of Parliament. Pursuant to Article 88 of the Constitution, the President of the Republic may dissolve one or both Chambers after consultation with their 'Presidents'; this power, however, cannot be exercised 'during the last six months of his term of office, unless they coincide, partially or entirely, with the last six months of Parliament'. This is the only provision on early dissolution: the Constitution does not specify when the Chambers could or should be dissolved. However, according to the principles on which the form of parliamentary government is founded, it is inevitable that there will be an early dissolution of Parliament when the political factions in the Chambers are unable to form a majority sufficient to confidently support an executive representing that majority. Furthermore, there are no alternatives to dissolution if, for the two Chambers, it proves impossible to regularly perform the parliamentary functions (for instance, where irreconcilable political differences between one and the other end up by paralysing the legislative activity). A discussion has been launched concerning various scenarios, including those that have actually arisen as well as those conceivable only in theory, among both political and institutional actors as well as scholars of constitutional law.

The Presidents of the Chambers to be dissolved, who must be consulted before issuing the related decree, give a non-binding advice that the President of the Republic is free to disregard. The act in question, although it is countersigned by the President of the Council, does not imply a government proposal nor, even less, a resolution of the Council of Ministers on the matter. This confirms that the act of dissolution is 'entirely presidential' and that the Prime Minister does not share in the decision but is only supposed to control its legality. In any case, this control may prove to be far-reaching both due to the major political and institutional significance of the act as well as the fact that the Constitution is silent regarding the cases in which the power may be exercised. The grounds for the dissolution are never specified in the decree. Sometimes, they have been given by the Presidency of the Republic or the Council.

During the last six months of his term (the so-called white semester), the Head of State is not allowed to dissolve the Chambers. This rule is aimed at preventing him from encouraging the formation of an electoral college which might support his reinstatement if the Parliament in office does not seem to favour his re-election. Some academic commentators rather believe that the reason why the President should not perform this duty is that his powers are 'weakened' during the last part of the seven-year term. Just under thirty years ago, the President of the Republic was entitled to dissolve the Chambers even in the last six months of his term if this period coincides, even partially, with the last six months of Parliament. This exception was introduced by Constitutional Law No. 1/1991 in order to avoid the inconveniences that the almost contemporaneous end of the tenth Republican Parliament and seven-year term of President Francesco Cossiga in 1992 would have caused on an institutional level.

In the more than seventy-five years since the Constitution came into force, the early dissolution of one or both Houses of Parliament was all but rare: only once, during the fourth Parliament (1963–1968), both Chambers lasted until the end of their term. The Senate alone, which at that time had a term of office of six years, was dissolved twelve months in advance in 1953, 1958 and 1963, always in order to combine its re-election with that of the Chamber of Deputies. The Senate term was finally reduced to five years by Constitutional Law No. 2/1963, which amended Article 60, first paragraph, of the Constitution.

Since the beginning of the 1970s, no Parliament has ever come to the natural end of its term: both Chambers have been dissolved early thirteen times. Eight of these (in 1972, 1976, 1979, 1983, 1987, 1996, 2008 and 2022) were the result of government crisis brought about by the impossibility of forming a majority and hence a Cabinet supported by Parliament. In February 1992, according to the debatable opinion of President Cossiga, the Chambers were dissolved some months before the natural end of their term owing to their incapacity to legislate and adopt the necessary institutional reforms and for fear that the citizens would associate the 'delegitimization' of the Parliament in office and the political class with that of parliamentary institutions and politics as a whole. President Scalfaro, instead, stated that he dissolved the Chambers in January 1994 for three different reasons. The first was the result of the 1993 referendum, by which the Italians voted in favour of turning the voting system of Parliament from a proportional into first-past-the-post one and the ensuing need to elect new MPs by respecting the citizens' will. The second was the remarkable gap between the numerical composition of parliamentary political groups and the result of two important local government elections held in June and November 1993. The third reason was the discovery by the judiciary of generalized corruption in the management of public funds. This scandal involved many MPs still in office, as well as former Ministers, local authorities and people working in the economic and financial sectors. Afterwards, President Ciampi dissolved the Chambers in March 2001, two months before the natural end of their term, in order to avoid holding the Parliament election during the period of summer vacation, as expected if the constitutional term had been respected. For the same reason, and particularly for the purpose of preventing a 'constitutional blockage' which would have been created due to the end of the fourteenth Republican Parliament in quick succession with the end of his seven-year term as President of the Republic, Ciampi dissolved the legislative Chambers in February 2006 just under four months early. In December 2012, President Napolitano ordered the dissolution of the Houses of Parliament around four months in advance of the natural expiry of the legislature following the resignation of the government in office as a result of the withdrawal of confidence by the main party within the parliamentary majority. Finally, in December 2017, President Mattarella decided to dissolve Parliament around two and a half months before the end of the seventeenth Legislature, concluding that, according to the 'physiological rhythm of democratic life', it was now time to hold a general election.

§13. Other Powers Concerning the Electorate and the Chambers

161. The President of the Republic provides for the election of a new Parliament (Article 87, third paragraph, of the Constitution) within seventy days from the dissolution of the preceding Parliament (Article 61, first paragraph, of the Constitution). By the same decree, he sets the date of the first meeting of the new Chambers, which must be held not later than twenty days after the elections (*see* again Articles 87, third paragraph, and 61, first paragraph, respectively). The decree is issued after a resolution of the Council of Ministers on proposal of the President of the Council and the Minister of the Interior, who also countersign the decree. The same happens when the Head of State provides for a referendum in all the cases laid down by the Constitution (Article 87, sixth paragraph). These acts are an expression of the government's powers, though limited, which can be exercised only by means of a presidential decree. Indeed, the only discretionary element in providing for the elections and referenda and setting the date of the first meeting of the Chambers, i.e., choosing the dates within the limits allowed by the Constitution and by law, is left to a decision of the Council of Ministers.

162. Pursuant to Article 59, second paragraph, of the Constitution, the Head of State may nominate, as senators-for-life, five citizens who have brought honour to the Nation through their exceptional merits in social, scientific, artistic and literary fields. These nominations are the expression of the President's autonomous initiatives and decisions, and the related acts, therefore, do not suppose any government motion. The only grounds given in the act are the field in which the person who was nominated has had exceptional merits. The act is countersigned by the President of the Council of Ministers.

In the first decades of the Constitution being in force, the maximum number of senators-for-life was believed by most academic commentators to be five (excluding former Heads of State, who become senators-for-life ex officio) and this was the practice. In 1984, instead, with the consent of the then President of the Senate, Cossiga, and the Senate Committee on the Elections, President Pertini decided to follow a different interpretation, according to which each Head of State could nominate up to five senators, regardless of the total number of those already in office. This innovative interpretation was also followed by the successor of Pertini, Cossiga. It was very debatable since it considered the nominations more a prerogative of the President of the Republic rather than an institute aimed at ensuring a limited integration of the Senate with particularly illustrious personalities. However, the successors to Cossiga have aimed to restore the previous practice and, as a consequence, today, the persons who have become senators-for-life, thanks to a

President, are only five. More recently, Constitutional Law No. 1/2020 has now modified Article 59 of the Constitution to expressly state now that in any case the number of senators-for-life appointed by the President should not exceed the number five.

163. The Head of State may take the initiative of convening each Chamber in extraordinary session (Article 62, second paragraph, of the Constitution); this is a presidential power in the very strict sense of the word, and it is exercised quite rarely in practice. The related act must be countersigned by the President of the Council of Ministers.

164. Pursuant to Article 87, second paragraph, of the Constitution, the President of the Republic may send messages to Parliament in order to draw the MPs' attention to what he considers to be particularly important issues. These are formal, written acts coming exclusively from the Head of State who freely determines their contents. These acts do not imply a ministerial motion and are countersigned by the President of the Council or by a Minister. Given that the message is strictly presidential, the countersignature does not mean that the government agrees with its contents but only that the legality of the act is thus certified. This power has been rarely exercised so far. The President who has sent the most messages to Parliament so far is Francesco Cossiga. On 26 June 1991, for instance, he sent a very broad and debated message on institutional reforms which was later discussed in both Chambers. The latter, however, usually did not carry out presidential messages and sometimes did not even discuss them.

These messages must be distinguished from the informal written communications from the Head of State to other authorities (the President of the Council of Ministers, the Presidents of the two Houses of Parliament, etc.) and from the speeches he sometimes delivers in Parliament (such as his inaugural address) or, more often, elsewhere (during public ceremonies, official visits abroad or from the TV screen). The messages should also be distinguished from the interviews and impromptu declarations to journalists. In all the above cases, the President does not exercise his constitutional power to send messages but rather the general *facoltà di esternazione* he is entitled with. Therefore, the countersignature is not required (verbal declarations, of course, are not susceptible of being countersigned), while the government is often informed about the text of the speeches before they are delivered. Presidents have made broad use of this power for a long time; in fact, while it may have been positively abused by Francesco Cossiga during the final years of his term in office, even his successors have proved to be highly 'loquacious', albeit adopting a different style and tone. In particular, during the Presidency of Giorgio Napolitano (2006–2015), there was a massive increase in statements of all types, resulting in a continuous and unlimited flow of commentary. The President of the Republic stated his position on every and any significant event within politics of the day, engaging in a heightened form of 'interventionism' which not only jeopardized his neutrality but also highlighted his substantive involvement in the political direction of the State, performing a role that was extraneous to the constitutional design of the system of government. By contrast, the current incumbent, President Sergio Mattarella, appears to have used his power of commentary with caution and a sense of measure that is commensurate with his role as the representative of national unity and guarantor of the Constitution, which the Head of State is called upon to perform.

165. The President of the Republic promulgates the laws (Articles 73, first paragraph and 87, fifth paragraph, of the Constitution) with a different formula for ordinary and constitutional laws laid down in Articles 1 and 2 of Decree of the President of the Republic No. 1092 of 28 December 1985 (*see* Part II, Chapter 4, §3). Although the promulgation is formally a presidential measure, it is part of a process in which the resolving power is basically in the hands of Parliament. Its function is, therefore, to express the 'rule-making will' resulting from the approval of the bill by the two Chambers. The promulgation need not be moved by the government and is countersigned by the President of the Council and the Minister or Ministers having jurisdiction on the matter of the bill. Ordinary laws must be promulgated within one month from their final approval. In cases of urgency, this term can be shortened by means of a resolution of each Chamber passed with an absolute majority (Article 73, first and second paragraph).

Nevertheless, pursuant to Article 74, first paragraph, of the Constitution, before promulgating a law, the President may request a new consideration (the so-called power of 'suspension veto'). If the Chambers vote the bill once more, however, the law must be promulgated (Article 74, second paragraph). This is the result of an autonomous decision on the part of the Head of State, and therefore the relevant act is not moved by the government, which has other means to influence the course of laws and could never oppose the passing of a law approved by Parliament. Bills are returned by means of a written message in which the President gives reasons for the new consideration. Since Article 74 does not specify any particular reason for returning the bills, these reasons can be related not only to formal or substantial constitutionality but also to merits. Given his *super partes* role, however, the Head of State must be very cautious in returning a bill, basing his decision on political grounds. In practice, mainly in the past, bills have been returned so far for breach of the constitutional rule providing for means for covering new expenditures (*see* Article 81, third paragraph, letter f, of the Constitution).

During the last period of Cossiga's presidential term, doubts were raised on the possibility for the Chambers, after having been dissolved, to re-examine and pass once more a law for which the Head of State asked for a new consideration. Cossiga's negative opinion, besides having been opposed by most academic commentators, was contradicted by the activities of the Parliament which, in 1992, after having been dissolved, approved a bill which had been returned (thus obliging the President to promulgate it) and started re-examining another one.

In the seven years of Carlo Azeglio Ciampi's presidency, during the parliamentary procedure of important bills, the President of the Republic felt it appropriate, with observations made beforehand, to point out to the government and to the government ranks the elements of constitutional illegitimacy present – in his opinion – in the legislative bills being examined: approving the laws without deleting the reasons for unconstitutionality would inevitably have caused their return to the Chambers by the President. This practice resulted in puzzlement because the Constitution does not allow for interventions by the Head of State, albeit informal, aimed at changing the content of laws while they are being formed, and furthermore, if the Chambers accept the points made by him and thus approval becomes 'rubber-stamped', in practice the President of the Republic is prevented from exercising his power to send back the bill for reasons other than those already proposed.

Ciampi's successor, Giorgio Napolitano, implemented another contentious line of conduct. In some cases, while consenting to promulgate the legislative bills deliberated by the Chambers and then allowing them to come into force, the Head of State sought to publicly illustrate reasons for dissent or doubt about the provisions submitted for his examination, usually by letters sent to the Presidents of the two Chambers and to the President of the Council. However, the Constitution does not provide for a promulgation that is 'dissenting' or 'with reservations'; strictly speaking, if a law appears to him to be seriously flawed, the President may and perhaps should send it back to the Chambers and then be held to promulgate it if it is approved again even without any modifications being made. However, President Mattarella, Napolitano's successor, has resorted to this practice numerous times, while he has referred a law to the chambers only once during his first term.

§14. Powers of Participation in the Activities of the Government

166. Pursuant to Article 87, fourth paragraph, of the Constitution, the President of the Republic authorizes the submission to Parliament of bills moved by the government upon a resolution of the Council of Ministers. In truth, this power is above all a historical vestige of the time in which the executive power and the power to promote bills rested formally with the King. As the Republican Constitution explicitly entrusts this power to the government, the latter should not need any authorization whatsoever to exercise it. Anyway, the presidential act just fulfils a control function within the process of legislative initiative in which the resolving power is in the hands of the Council of Ministers. Hence, the President of the Republic cannot deny his consent but only return the bill to the government for renewed consideration, giving reasons for it by means of a note, usually not made public, to the President of the Council. This informal process is similar to the one by which the Head of State returns a bill to Parliament for a new consideration before promulgation. The relationships between the President and the government, two distinguished and independent constitutional organs, are marked, however, by a more permanent and discreet cooperation in which the former can exercise his powers of persuasion and influence on the latter.

167. The Head of State can exercise the same powers before issuing decrees having the value of laws (decree-laws and legislative decrees) and regulations (Article 87, fifth paragraph, second part, of the Constitution). The President's function in this case is to manifest the rule-making that will be expressed by the government.

Issuing decrees having the value of laws and regulations approved by the Council of Ministers is parallel to promulgating the laws voted by Parliament; pursuant to Article 5, first paragraph, letter c), of Law No. 400/1988, these decrees and regulations are moved by the President of the Council, who countersigns them together with the Ministers having jurisdiction over the matters of the acts. Regarding the acts having value of law, the President of the Republic has a similar function of control to that entrusted to him for laws. However, regarding decree-laws and legislative decrees, the Constitution does not make express provision for a power of 'suspension veto'. The President may only put forward reservations and objections, of constitutionality or merit, on the bills submitted for his signature and ask the Council of Ministers to revise the controversial aspects. In practice, there have been sent back to government both decree-laws due to a lack of the requisites of necessity and urgency required by Article 77 of the Constitution or for violation of other constitutional regulations and, more rarely, legislative decrees due to non-compliance with the constraints established by the delegating law. Nevertheless, the issuance of decree-laws without the constitutional prerequisites remains a widespread phenomenon in the Italian legal system, where the majority of primary legislation takes the form of decree-laws.

168. Pursuant to Article 87, seventh paragraph, of the Constitution, the President of the Republic appoints, in the cases laid down by the law, the officials of the State. The related acts, although they formally come from the President, are defined by the government, which is responsible for administrative matters and therefore charged with taking decisions concerning the appointment of State officials. A number of other administrative measures taken by the government, and in particular all the ones approved by the Council of Ministers, take the final form of decrees of the President of the Republic. These acts are all listed in Article 1 of Law No. 13/1991. The proposal and countersignature are up to the President of the Council (always when the measure is approved by the Council of Ministers) or, according to cases, to the Ministers having jurisdiction.

§15. Powers Concerning International Relationships

169. The President of the Republic, in his capacity as the 'Head of State' (*see* Article 87, first paragraph, of the Constitution), represents Italy in relationships with other nations, though not exclusively. Pursuant to Article 87, eighth paragraph, he accredits and receives diplomatic representatives. The accrediting concerns Italian representatives and consists in an official request addressed to the foreign Heads of State (or the highest authority of the international organization) to welcome the diplomat representing Italy. The related credential letter, drawn up according to a fixed formula, is proposed and countersigned by the Minister of Foreign Affairs, who is empowered to select the diplomats and to assign them specific functions. Likewise, the President of the Republic receives the credential letters of foreign diplomats who officially are introduced to him.

In his capacity as representative of the Nation in international relationships, the Head of State also ratifies the international treaties signed by the government, i.e., issues the acts by which the Republic complies with international agreements and becomes responsible to the other signatories (Article 87, eighth paragraph, of the Constitution). This does not exclude, in practice, that some agreements be reached 'in a simplified manner' that do not require the President's ratification. The latter is substantially decided by the government, and the related act is countersigned by the Minister of Foreign Affairs. Pursuant to Article 80 of the Constitution, ratification of international treaties of a political nature, or providing for arbitration of judicial settlements, or implying variations of the Nation's territory or financial burdens, or modifications to laws, must be authorized by the Chambers by means of a law.

Finally, owing to his representative role towards the rest of the international community, the President declares a state of war when it has been decided by Parliament (Article 87, ninth paragraph, last part, of the Constitution). The decision is therefore left to Parliament (*see* Article 78 of the Constitution), while the President's duty is to officially manifest the will of the State.

§16. Powers Concerning the Armed Forces

170. Pursuant to Article 87, ninth paragraph, of the Constitution, the President of the Republic commands the Armed Forces.

Employment of the Armed Forces' members depends on the government but since they have to remain politically neutral, their non-political and 'non-operational' leader must be an authority such as the Head of State, the representative of national unity (*see* Part V, Chapter 4). The President can exercise this 'high command' by sending messages, taking part in ceremonies, receiving Armed Forces' members. As we shall see later on, the President also presides over the *Consiglio Supremo di Difesa* (supreme defence council).

Usually, however, the President does not take formal measures, which might give rise to the question of the relationship between the President's and the government's will. It is worth remembering that the question of the Armed Forces' command in cases of emergency was explicitly raised by President Cossiga in 1986–1987 by means of letters to the Presidents of the Council of Ministers of that time. The government set up a commission of experts charged with studying the constitutional side of the issue. The commission drafted a report outlining, among other things, that the 'non-operational command' given to the Head of State is not merely formal and symbolical but should be considered as a way for the President to exercise his typical function of protection of constitutional values (from the condemnation of war to the need to keep the Armed Forces apolitical).

The Head of State also presides over the *Consiglio Supremo di Difesa* (Article 87, ninth paragraph, second part, of the Constitution; *see also* Part V, Chapter 4). This body has the task of examining general political and technical problems relating to national defence and establishing criteria and directions to govern the organization and coordination of activities in any way related to it (*see* Article 2 of Legislative Decree No. 662010). In truth, the latter task would appear to be difficult to reconcile with constitutional law as political oversight over military issues – as is the case for all other matters – falls to the government and Parliament. However, already during the Ciampi presidency but above all on the initiative of President Napolitano, the Supreme Council was transformed from a merely consultative body into an active player in security and defence policy, in particular with regard to overseas missions of the Italian Armed Forces. The Council meets at least twice each year and may be called whenever necessary by the President of the Republic or following a proposal by the President of the Council of Ministers, who serves as Vice-Chairman. The other members are the Foreign Affairs, Interior, Economy and Finance, Defence and Economic Development Ministers along with the Chief of the Defence Staff. The Head of State's duties are those normally fulfilled by the President of a collegiate body: summoning the meetings and deciding the agenda, as well as directing the debates. The related acts need not be moved nor countersigned by a Minister.

§17. Powers Concerning Guarantee Organs

171. Pursuant to Article 135, first paragraph, of the Constitution, the President of the Republic nominates a third of the fifteen judges of the Constitutional Court. These nominations are the result of autonomous initiatives and decisions by the Head of State. Hence, the related decrees need not be moved by the government but are countersigned by the President of the Council of Ministers.

172. The President of the Republic presides over the CSM (Higher Council of the Judiciary) (Articles 87, tenth paragraph, and 104, second paragraph, of the Constitution; *see* Part II, Chapter 7, §2). This is aimed at preventing both the dependence of the criminal and civil judiciary on the government and its complete separation from the other State powers. The Head of State's duties within the *Consiglio* are those normally fulfilled by the President of a collegiate body (summoning the meetings and deciding the agenda, as well as directing the debates). These acts need not be moved nor countersigned by a Minister. In fact, however, the President seldom attends the meetings, and the chair is usually taken by the Vice-President of the *Consiglio* (during Cossiga's presidency, however, tensions were high between the Head of State and the *Consiglio*, especially over the agenda of the meetings). Some of the most important acts approved by the *Consiglio* concerning the magistrates' careers take the form of decrees of the President of the Republic (not in his capacity as President of the CSM) countersigned by the Minister of Justice. The form of these acts is set out in Article 17, first paragraph, of Law No. 195/1958 (*see* now Article 1, first paragraph letter f, of Law No. 13/1991).

173. Law No. 195/1958 also provides that the CSM can be dissolved before the end of its four-year term by a decree of the President of the Republic, having consulted the Presidents of the two Houses of Parliament and Presidency committee of the *Consiglio* itself (Article 31, first paragraph), should it not be able to carry out its activities. This power is not provided for by any constitutional rule that the Head of State has never exercised. The dissolution act should probably be countersigned by the President of the Council of Ministers.

§18. The Other Nomination Powers

174. The Head of State appoints the President and the other members of the *Consiglio Nazionale dell'Economia e del Lavoro* CNEL (National Council of Economy and Labour). This Council is composed of experts, representatives of production categories and representatives of the social promotion associations and the voluntary organizations, and it is an advisory body to Parliament and the government. It has the power to promote legislation and can contribute to the drafting of economic and social laws according to the principles and within the limits allowed by the law (Article 99 of the Constitution). It is composed of sixty-four members, plus the President, who is designated by the government (his name is proposed by the President of the Council, after a resolution by the Council of Ministers) and appointed by means of a decree of the President of the Republic.

The Head of State autonomously chooses eight of the ten 'qualified representatives of economic, social and legal culture' making up the Council, according to the current text of Article 2, first paragraph letter a), of Law No. 936/1986. The related nomination acts must not be moved by the government and are countersigned by the President of the Council of Ministers. The other members of the CNEL are, instead, appointed by means of a decree of the President of the Republic, moved by the President of the Council after a resolution of the Council of Ministers.

175. The Head of State also issues various acts concerning the composition of judicial and auxiliary bodies and the legal status of their members. These measures are not substantially presidential since the related decisions are taken by other bodies, such as the CSM, self-governing bodies of special judges or, on various occasions, the government.

176. Pursuant to Article 1, third paragraph, of Law No. 249/1997, the President of the Republic appoints, by means of a decree, the President and the eight commissioners of the *Autorità per le Garanzie nelle Comunicazioni* (Independent Authority for Publishing and Telecommunications), an agency which does not depend on the executive and carries out important activities in the telecommunications and radio-television sectors. In order to enforce the rules and make sure that the limits laid down by law are respected, the *Autorità* has a wide range of powers, such as advisory, motion and control powers, but also the powers to take resolutions, issue regulations and levy sanctions. The President is nominated by the Head of State after a proposal of the President of the Council of Ministers, having agreed with the Minister of Economic Development and having consulted the parliamentary commissions having jurisdiction. The commissioners are elected half by the Senate and half by the Chamber of Deputies. Hence, these nominations are only formally made by the President of the Republic.

§19. The Remaining Powers

177. Pursuant to Article 87, eleventh paragraph, of the Constitution, the President of the Republic may grant pardons and commute sentences. The power to remit the whole or part of the criminal punishment inflicted on single convicts or commuting their sentences has always been attributed to the Head of State. Nowadays, however, the authority charged with receiving the applications, examining them and making the related proposals is the government, in the person of the Minister of Justice. Applications addressed directly to the President of the Republic are also transmitted to the Ministry for preliminary examination. The pardon takes the form of a presidential decree, moved and countersigned by the Minister.

However, the Head of State can also reject the Minister's suggestions or, vice versa, he can take the initiative for granting pardon and adopt the corresponding decree even if the Minister is opposed; in this case, the countersignature of the Minister is limited to affirming the completeness and regularity of the investigation and of the procedure followed. This is the situation of this issue after the Constitutional Court, by Judgment No. 200/2006, resolved a conflict of attribution between powers of the State promoted by President Ciampi against the Minister of Justice, the subject matter of which was their respective roles in the procedure for granting pardons. According to the Court, it must be considered an 'exceptional instrument used for meeting extraordinary needs of humanitarian nature' which, in the end, has the function of implementing the constitutional values asserted by Article 27, third paragraph, of the Constitution. There is, therefore, to be recognized a substantial power of decision by the President of the Republic 'as the *super partes* office, "representative of national unity" … who is called upon to impartially assess the actual existence of the humanitarian requirements' able to justify 'the adopting of the measure for leniency'.

It should, however, be pointed out that pardons are not always granted on humanitarian grounds and may in some cases result from political considerations, as is clearly shown by recent practice. It would thus appear to be illogical and inconsistent with the systemic principles for the Head of State, as an impartial operator without political responsibility on an institutional level, to be empowered to adopt such measures even without the agreement (and potentially in the face of the explicit opposition) of the Minister of Justice, as the member of the government answerable to Parliament.

178. According to the former version of Article 79 of the Constitution, even the amnesty and extinguishment of criminal punishments were granted by the President of the Republic on the basis of laws approved by the Chambers delegating such powers. Constitutional Law No. 1/1992, however, introduced new provisions preventing the Head of State from exercising this power. Today, extinguishing crimes or punishments is the duty of the two Houses of Parliament by means of laws passed with a majority of two-thirds section-by-section and in the final vote.

179. The Head of State, after consulting a commission on regional affairs composed of members of the two Houses of Parliament and formed according to the laws of the Republic, may dissolve each Regional Council and remove the President of the regional Junta by means of a decree, giving reasons for it. He may do so when the Council and the President of the Junta perform acts contrary to the Constitution or commit serious violations of the laws, or even for reasons of national security (Article 126, first paragraph, of the Constitution, as amended by Article 4 of Constitutional Law No. 1/1999; *see also* similar provisions contained in the statutes of special Regions). Moreover, the approval of a motion of no-confidence against the President of the Junta elected through direct universal suffrage, the removal, permanent incapacity, death or voluntary resignation of the President himself and, finally, the concurrent resignation of the majority of its members cause an early dissolution of the Regional Council (*see* the present version of Article 126, third paragraph, of the Constitution).

The dissolution act, as confirmed by the Constitutional Court, is only formally presidential. The Head of State, however, protects the fundamental guarantees of the Regions by controlling the dissolution act decided by the government before it is enacted. Pursuant to Article 2, third paragraph letter o, of Law No. 400/1988, this presidential decree is issued after a resolution of the Council of Ministers and is proposed and countersigned by the President of the Council (*see also* Part III, Chapter 1, §10).

180. Pursuant to Article 87, twelfth paragraph, of the Constitution, the Head of State confers the honours of the Republic. Today, decisions in this field are taken mainly by the government, although, by virtue of the traditional prerogatives of the King in chivalry matters, the initiative may sometimes be taken by the President of the Republic himself. The presidential decree is therefore issued *motu proprio* or is moved by the Minister having jurisdiction, who is also supposed to countersign it.

Chapter 3. The Structure of Parliament

by Antonio D'Andrea & Lorenzo Spadacini

§1. The Bicameral System: An Introduction

181. The Italian Parliament consists of two Houses, the Chamber of Deputies and the Senate of the Republic (Article 55, first paragraph of the Constitution), both elected by voters.

The members of both Houses are elected for a period of five years, which may not be extended save by a legislative Act of Parliament and only in the event of war (Article 60 of the Constitution). One or both Houses can be dissolved by the President of the Republic before the natural end of Parliament (Article 88 of the Constitution). Article 61 provides that the election of the new Houses should take place within seventy days from the dissolution of the preceding Parliament, and the powers of the latter are extended until the newly elected Parliament meets.

182. The Chamber of Deputies and the Senate exercise almost identical functions (perfect bicameral system). Pursuant to the Constitution, each Chamber drafts its own Standing Orders (by virtue of the autonomy to issue internal regulations), which include important parliamentary rules, as we shall see later on. Some of these rules are simply drawn from constitutional provisions, and others are entirely and freely introduced by the Houses.

The autonomy to issue regulations mitigates the effects of the perfect bicameral system since it remarkably distinguishes the activities of the two Houses, as well as the use by the government of some essential tools (such as the confidence vote) in order to reach its political aims.

The two Houses also enjoy accounting autonomy, which allows them to draw up and approve their own budget without being submitted to the audit of external bodies, such as the Court of Accounts (*see* Constitutional Court, Judgment No. 129/1981).

Each House, by providing for special procedures and by appointing 'internal' judges chosen among the MPs, can also act as a judge on appeals concerning the status and the legal and economic career of its public officers (home jurisdiction).

Mention should also be made to the Houses' privileges, which prevent security forces from entering their seats unless the respective Presidents expressly order it. Defamation of the Chambers (Article 290 of the Criminal Code) and actions preventing the exercise of their functions (Article 289 of Criminal Penal Code) constitute an offence too.

183. The Constitution also provides for some exceptional cases in which Parliament should meet and take decisions in a joint session of both Chambers, i.e.:

a. during the secret ballot election of the President of the Republic (delegates from every region also participate in the election, according to Article 83 of the Constitution) and when the Head of State swears an oath of loyalty before taking office (Article 91);
b. in the case of proceedings against the President of the Republic for high treason or breaches of the Constitution (this decision should be taken by secret ballot with a majority of the entire membership: Article 90);
c. in order to elect one-third of the members of the Consiglio superiore della magistratura (Article 104) and one-third of the Constitutional Court's members (Article 135);
d. in order to draw up, every nine years, a list of persons from which sixteen judges are selected by drawing lots to support the fifteen judges (usually making up the Constitutional Court) in the case of proceedings against the President of the Republic (Article 135, last paragraph).

Article 63, second paragraph, of the Constitution states that the President and the Presidents' bureau of Parliament in joint session are those of the Chamber of Deputies. As provided for by Article 35 of the Standing Orders of the Chamber of Deputies and Article 65 of those of the Senate, when Parliament meets in joint session the applicable Standing Orders are those of the Chamber of Deputies. The Senate's provision, however, recognizes the right of Parliament to issue its own internal regulations when meeting in joint session.

§2. The Electoral System of the Chambers in the History of the Republic

184. Since specific provisions on the electoral system of the two Chambers are not included in the Italian Constitution, their definition is left to Parliament.

For over forty years, the two electoral laws in force in Italy (Decree of the President of the Republic No. 361 of 30 March 1957, which included most of Law No. 6/1948, for the Chamber of Deputies, and Law No. 29/1948, for the Senate) have provided for proportional voting systems, especially for the Chamber of Deputies. These laws were modelled on legislation relating to the election of the Constituent Assembly (Legislative Decree of the Lieutenant of the King No. 74 of 10 March 1946). Furthermore, Decree No. 361/1957, despite the changes about the mechanisms for the allocation of seats, is still in force and regulates the entire electoral procedure for the Chamber of Deputies (and, for what not specifically regulated in its electoral law, for the Senate as well), from the preparation stages to the voting and counting operations.

This legislation has probably encouraged the remarkable fragmentation of the Italian political system, thus allowing medium or even small parties to play an important political role, often disproportionate to their election results. Also, for this reason, specific requests for an abrogative referendum on proportional electoral legislation had already been put forward towards the end of the 1980s by political groups 'alternative' to the traditional ones, whose aim was to overcome the idleness of legislative bodies by introducing a first-past-the-post system. This aim was not reached immediately. In 1991, the Constitutional Court ruled the application for a referendum on the Senate electoral law inadmissible, while it authorized a partial referendum on the preferential vote for the Chamber of Deputies election. In the Court's opinion, electoral laws can be put to a referendum (which has to be just abrogative according to Article 75 of Const.) only if the (partial) repeal does not concern 'fundamental rules' provisions. Otherwise, the risk of a legislative vacuum preventing the election of the Chambers would determine the inadmissibility of the request of such a referendum.

In 1993, during the eleventh Parliament (1992–1994), which was characterized by a general crisis of legitimacy of Italian parties, another application for a partial abrogative referendum on the Senate electoral law was ruled admissible and approved with a large majority of the voters, paving the way for reforms. In August 1993, Parliament (which had just changed the electoral law for municipalities and Provinces by introducing the direct election of Mayors and Presidents of Provinces: Law No. 81/1993) passed the new electoral laws for the Chamber of Deputies (Law No. 277/1993) and the Senate (Law No. 276/1993), both based on the mechanism introduced by the referendum.

They provided that three-quarters of Deputies and of senators were elected in single-member constituencies, by a simple majority single-round vote (the candidate who had obtained the highest number of votes cast was elected: first-past-the-post voting system). The remaining quarter of the seats were distributed by a proportional representation system, each law having different features. As for the Chamber of Deputies, Law No. 277/1993 divided the national territory into twenty-six electoral districts (Article 1) and implied that every candidate standing in single-member constituencies had to be linked to special lists of candidates standing in each of those districts. Only the lists that had obtained at least 4% of the votes cast on a national level would have participated in the distribution of this portion of seats. As for the Senate, Law No. 276 provided for the formation of groups of candidates standing in the various districts of each Region and connecting each other on the basis of the political affinity. Lists and groups, therefore, participated in the share of the remaining quarter of the seats to be allocated proportionally. This was aimed at softening the effects of the first-past-the-post system and at favouring the smallest political groups, whose candidates' election in the single-member constituencies would have been more difficult. The latter, in particular, could benefit from a mechanism devised to the detriment of the biggest groups. As for the Chamber of Deputies (where voters could cast two distinct votes on two different ballot papers, one for the election of the candidate in the single-member constituency, the other for the list, although they could not express preference votes as for the grading of the candidates of the list), the law provided for a deduction from the election result of each list of part of the votes obtained by the candidates linked to those lists and elected in single-member constituencies. As for the Senate, the votes obtained by candidates elected in the regional single-member constituencies were subtracted from the global election result of each group of candidates.

Between April 1999 and May 2000, two requests for a partial abrogative referendum on the electoral legislation of 1993, ruled admissible by the Constitutional

Court, were aimed at strengthening the first-past-the-post system, through the repeal, at least for the Chamber of Deputies, of the proportional distribution of seats among lists.

However, the two referenda, that were not supported by any of the biggest political forces, did not achieve the promoters' objectives because in both cases the quorum established by Article 75 of the Constitution was not reached (namely, the majority of those eligible to vote did not take part in the referendum). Therefore, there was not a consolidation of the first-past-the-post, which had contributed to changing the Italian political system in the 1990s.

As a matter of fact, the use of the new electoral system in three political elections (March 1994, April 1996 and May 2001) had progressively produced an increasing bipolarization of Italian politics, allowing the making up of two coalitions, the centre-left and the centre-right, which alternated in the government of the country. These coalitions, particularly in the thirteenth Parliament (dominated by the centre-left) and in the fourteenth Parliament (dominated by the centre-right), although with some problems, managed to stay united for the entire five-year period.

Lastly, mention should be made of Constitutional Law No. 1/2000, which has modified Article 48 of the Constitution, to ensure the effectiveness of the right of vote to Italian citizens living abroad. Thanks to that modification, the latter have been given the right of electing a small number – fixed by a constitutional provision – of Deputies and senators, in a so-called Foreign District, according to rules stated by ordinary law.

The Constitutional Law No. 1/2001 provided for the election, within the Foreign District, of twelve Deputies and six senators reduced to eight deputies and four senators by Constitutional Law No. 1/2020 that reduced the size of the Chambers. The first election of these MPs took place in 2006.

The electoral law for Italian citizens living abroad is provided for by Law No. 459/2001 (and subsequent Regulations). It distinguishes, within the Foreign District, four areas: Europe (including the Asian territories of Russia and Turkey); South America; North and Central America; and Africa, Asia, Oceania and Antarctica. For each area, a list of the Italians living therein is drawn up and updated periodically so that they can vote by postal ballot unless they choose to vote in Italy.

Law No. 459/2001 states that one Deputy and one senator must be elected in each of the areas mentioned above, while the remaining seats are distributed among those territories depending on the number of Italian citizens who live in the States belonging to them (after the reduction in the number of MPs, there will be no remaining seats regarding the Senate).

Seats are allocated among the lists standing in each territorial division according to the Hare quota and the largest remainder method. Since the lists are open, the individual electoral results of each candidate determine the elected persons within each list.

The official count is made at the Central Office for the Foreign District contextually to that relating to the votes cast in the national territory.

This set of rules, despite the continuous changing of the other electoral provisions, has been stable for the subsequent years.

185. Law No. 270/2005, passed by the Chambers at the end of the fourteenth Parliament (just before the elections) over the opposition's objections, changed the first-past-the-post system of 1993, based, as mentioned, on single-member constituencies aimed at inducing parties to join in only two coalitions in order to have reasonable expectations of success.

For the Senate, under Law No. 270/2005, with provisions in force until Law No. 165/2017, the allocation of seats within each Region was made under proportional representation among lists above 8% and among coalitions of lists meeting two requirements: (1) having achieved, at regional level, more than 20% of votes cast and (2) including at least one list attaining more than 3% support.

However, under Law No. 270/2005 (with a provision cancelled by Judgment No. 1/2014 of the Constitutional Court), if the Regional Electoral Office verified that no list or coalition obtained at least 55% of the seats to be allocated within the Region, it directly provided a further addition of seats (the so-called majority bonus) in favour of the list or coalition having achieved the highest number of votes cast, so that the mentioned threshold was reached.

On the basis of the seats allocated to each list, under Law No. 270/2005, the candidates were proclaimed senators following the order of presentation within that list, which could not be changed by voters (the 'closed lists' system).

For the Chamber of Deputies, according to the mechanisms settled by Law No. 270/2005, the distribution of seats for the Chamber of Deputies was made among lists of candidates standing in twenty-six different electoral districts. Voters, as noted above regarding the Senate, could only cast one vote for one of the lists but could not express preference votes for a specific candidate within the list (the 'closed lists' system).

The closed lists, provided for by Law No. 52/2015 for both the Chambers, have been adjudged unconstitutional by Judgment No. 1/2014 of the Constitutional Court.

Furthermore, pursuant to the 2005 provisions, the political groups, in presenting their election papers, could associate with each other in a coalition. The allocation of seats among the lists, alone or in coalition, was carried out at a centralized level, by using the proportional method of the Hare quota with a possible 'majority bonus' (consisting in allocating 55% of the seats to the list or coalition having achieved the most votes cast), if neither the one nor the other had obtained at least this percentage of seats. This means that in the Chamber of Deputies, the electoral mechanism forced the emergence of a parliamentary majority in any electoral event.

As a matter of fact, in the 2006 election (when the new electoral law was applied for the first time), the competition involved the two alternative coalitions that had characterized the country and political landscape for about twelve years. However, the small advantage of the centre-left majority (especially in the Senate) and the accentuation of quarrelsomeness within the government coalition (including many, even small, political forces) had come to challenge the new electoral mechanisms (as well as the strategy of that coalition and its leadership). In fact, three different requests for an abrogative referendum on some provisions of Law No. 270/2005 were immediately put forward, with the aim to allow a competition only among single lists rather than between opposing coalitions.

However, these initiatives (at first suspended because of the early interruption of the fifteenth Parliament) did not produce any result, since in the 2009 referendum the quorum was not reached. Actually, the elections of April 2008 were preceded by a profound change in the 'alliance strategy' on the part of the biggest political forces and by the emergence, both in the centre-right (which won the election) and in the centre-left, of new formations made up of the 'old' parties, previously only allied. This resulted in a significant reduction of the political forces represented in the Chambers in the sixteenth Parliament; the two biggest parties opposing each other (*Popolo delle Libertà* and *Partito Democratico*) got about 70% of the votes cast and 76% of the available seats.

Therefore, despite the electoral system introduced in 2005 being immediately criticized for having further increased the political fragmentation and for the mechanism chosen to allocate the 'majority bonus' in the Senate (within each Region and not at national level), after the 2008 elections (namely after its second utilization, and also thanks to the 'self-reform' of the biggest parties), it allowed the emergence of a clear majority in both Houses of Parliament.

However, the low resistance of parliamentary groups in the sixteenth Parliament led, in November 2011, to the crisis of the fourth Berlusconi Government and the formation of a new Cabinet, presided over by Mario Monti, a former European Commissioner, and supported by a 'grand coalition' formed by centre-left and centre-right parties.

Under this system, in the 2013 election, in the Lower House, the centre-left coalition was granted the majority bonus of 55% of the seats with 29.6% of the vote, compared to 20% of the seats based on 29.2% support for the centre-right coalition and 17% of the seats for 25.6% supporting the Five Stars Movement (whose leader is the well-known showman Beppe Grillo), demonstrating a very odd allocation of seats under a national proportional system. But in the Senate, the centre-left coalition could not command a majority; therefore, a post-electoral grand coalition was negotiated to instal first the Letta Government, then the Renzi Government and lastly the Gentiloni Government.

In these last ten years, under the new electoral law, there have been six governments with six different Prime Ministers. Above all, the process of simplification of the political landscape suddenly stopped; the main parties of centre-right and centre-left split, and a strong anti-system party, the so-called Five Stars Movement, emerged.

As mentioned above, with Judgment No. 1/2014, of the Constitutional Court, the most characteristic features of the provision of Law No. 270/2005 have been held unconstitutional. First of all, the majority bonuses for the Chamber of Deputies and for the Senate have been sentenced unconstitutional since such a majority bonus is tolerable only if it springs when a reasonable threshold of votes has been reached. Otherwise, if the majority bonus is allocated regardless of the achievement of a threshold by a list or a coalition, the principle of equality of votes is violated as the representative nature of the Parliament. Second, the other most controversial aspect of the described electoral mechanism, the so-called closed lists, has been sentenced unconstitutional. The Constitutional Court stated that such a system is compatible with the Constitution only as long as the lists are short, so that the voter is able to understand which candidate he or she is going to elect. Indeed, if the lists have many candidates, the elector cannot be aware which one of the candidates he or she is likely to support, by merely voting for a list.

After the mentioned judgment, as noted above, a new electoral law was enacted in 2015 with Law No. 52/2015. This new system was again a scheme of proportional representation under which the party list attracting most votes (coalitions having been removed) was granted 55% of seats of the Chamber, as long as it would have reached at least 40% of the ballot. If no list reached 40%, a second national ballot between the two most popular lists would have been held two weeks later and the winner would have taken 55% of the seats of the Chamber. The other seats were to be allocated proportionally among all the losers over the national threshold of 3%. Again, under this new system, the Italian Parliament would always have had a list allowing an allocation of 55% of the seats, i.e., more of the absolute majority of the Chamber. Furthermore, according to the constitutional reform proposals in discussion when the electoral law was passed by Parliament, the Senate would not have been directly elected and would be radically weakened in comparison with the Senate for the time being, which is directly elected and is on exactly the same footing as the Lower Chamber. In particular, under the constitutional reform, the government would have no longer needed the confidence of the new Senate.

This electoral reform, however, would not have been implemented, basically for two reasons. First, the constitutional reform proposals were rejected by a popular referendum held on 4 December 2016, so that the Constitution has not been modified, namely where it requires the government to find a majority in both the Houses and where a direct election by the people of the Senate is provided for. Second, the electoral reform itself has been once again rejected in substantial parts by the Constitutional Court.

After the referendum and this second judgment of the Constitutional Court, the two Chambers would have been irrationally elected through different mechanisms. In 2017, a new electoral law for both the Chambers, Law No. 165/2017, has been approved by the Parliament.

The new law enacted has introduced a mixed system: first-past-the-post for three-eighths of the seats of each House and proportional for the remaining seats.

186. Under this new system, the general elections of 2018 gave birth to two Houses in which no party or coalition gained the majority. As a result, a new government was formed only three months after the elections and a difficult negotiation among different parties. In particular, one party of the centre-right abandoned its coalition to join the so-called Five Stars Movement in order to form a coalition government; the President of the Council of Ministers, Prof. Conte, has been chosen outside of the Parliament, and the leaders of the two parties of the coalition have been appointed as Vice-Presidents of the Council. The Conte Government collapsed in August 2019 after bitter disagreements between the two parties of the coalition. A new coalition was negotiated between the Five Stars Movement and the centre-left parties instead of the centre-right party (Lega), and a second Conte Government was then installed. This second Conte Government itself collapsed in January 2021 after the defection of a small centrist party from the coalition. In order to avoid new elections during the pandemic, the President of the Republic was appointed as President of the Council Mario Draghi, the former European Central Bank President. By a large majority, the two Houses passed the confidence vote installing a Government with ministers from all the parties from the centre-right and the centre-left, including the Five Stars Movement – except one party from the right. A few months before the end of the legislative term, the Draghi Government faced a crisis, and the Parliament was consequently dissolved prematurely by the President of the Republic. In the September 2022 elections, due to the division among political forces outside the centre-right, the latter, despite receiving less than 45% of the votes, managed to secure a majority of approximately 60% of the seats in both Houses, making the most of the single-member majority constituencies provided by the electoral law.

§3. The Election of the Senate at Present

187. Under Article 58 of the Constitution, voters over 40 years of age are eligible for the Senate. Before Constitutional Law No. 1/2021, senators were elected only by voters over 25. According to the mentioned Law, which will be put in operation from the next elections, even for the Senate Article 48 will be applied, which enfranchises every citizen over 18.

Article 57 of the Constitution has been recently changed by Constitutional Law No. 1/2020, approved in 2019 by the two Chambers by a large majority and by the people in a referendum held on 20–21 September 2020. In that referendum, 70% of the voters agreed to reduce the size of the Chambers from 630 to 400 Deputies and from 315 to 200 Senators. The Constitutional Law has been implemented in the September 2022 general election. After the constitutional amendment, Article 57 states the following:

- Elected senators' number 200, 4 of which are elected in the 'Foreign District' (6 prior to the above-mentioned reform).
- The Senate is elected on a regional basis, except for the seats reserved for the 'Foreign District'.
- No region or Autonomous Province (i.e., Trento and Bolzano, with a specification introduced by the above-mentioned reform) may have less than 3 senators (before the reform the minimum number was 7), with the exception of Molise and Valle d'Aosta, having two and one senators respectively (these numbers are not changed by the reform).
- Distribution of seats among the regions is made according to the proportion of their population on the basis of the terms specified above.

Any person who has held office as President of the Republic is by right a senator-for-life, unless he or she refuses to accept the nomination. The President of the Republic may nominate, as senators-for-life, five citizens for their services to the country (Article 59 of the Constitution). Can each Head of State nominate five senators or is this the maximum number of senators nominated by Presidents of the

Republic who can sit in the Senate? This question has been much debated by academic commentators (for further details, *see* Part II, Chapter 2, §13). The abovementioned Constitutional Law No. 1/2020 clearly established that the number of senators-for-life can never exceed five.

188. The election of the Senate is regulated by Legislative Decree No. 533 of 20 December 1993, as modified at last by Law No. 165/2017. Subsequently, Law No. 51/2019 adjusted the system to the new numbers of the two Chambers following the reduction in the size of Parliament by Constitutional Law No. 1/2020.

The allocation of seats within each Region is made by a mixed system.

The seats allocated to each Region are divided into two quotas: three-eighths of the seats are allocated in one-member constituencies by a plurality system; the remaining five-eighths of the seats are allocated by proportional representation among lists of candidates. In order to enact this system, the territory of each Region is divided into a number of one-member constituencies which *grosso modo* amounts to three-eighths of the seats allocated within the Region. The remaining seats are allocated in larger constituencies composed by grouping contiguous one-member constituencies. In these larger constituencies, lists of candidates dispute the seats. Every candidate in a one-member constituency could be supported by a single list in the larger constituency or by a coalition of lists within the latter. The voter, anyway, cannot split the vote: he or she can only vote for a list, and the vote is valuable for the list in the larger constituency and the candidate supported by the list within the one-member constituency. In case he or she votes just for the candidate within the one-member constituency, his vote is divided among the lists supporting him or her, according to the proportion they have one each other on the basis of the votes expressed by the other electors.

In the one-member constituency, the candidate obtaining the most of the votes is elected. For the larger constituencies, the allocation of seats within each Region is made only among lists above 3% at national level or 20% at regional level and among coalitions of lists matching two requirements: having achieved, at national level, more than 10% of votes and including at least one list receiving more than 3% of votes cast. The sum of votes obtained by these lists and coalitions (the votes for the lists below 1% are not counted in order to determine the sum of votes of coalitions) is then divided by the number of seats assigned to the Region in order to obtain the district quota; the global number of votes of each list or coalition is eventually divided by this quota.

The result of these divisions, which could produce fractional remainders, determines the number of seats to be allocated to the mentioned lists or coalitions, while the remaining seats are allocated to the lists or coalitions with the highest remainders. The seats allocated to coalitions are then distributed among the 'internal' lists above 3% on the basis of the coalition quota, calculated by dividing the global number of votes of these lists by the number of seats to be allocated to the coalition.

On the basis of the seats allocated to each list, the candidates are proclaimed senators following the order of presentation within that list.

§4. The Election of the Chamber of Deputies at Present

189. The Chamber of Deputies is elected by citizens of age, i.e., who have reached the age of 18 (Article 48 of the Constitution); those who have reached the age of 25 are eligible for membership (Article 56, third paragraph, of the Constitution).

Pursuant to Article 56, as modified by the above-mentioned Constitutional Law No. 1/2020, after the September 2022 elections, the Chamber of Deputies is composed of 400 members (previously there were 630 Deputies), and the distribution of seats among the electoral districts, the number of which is not specified, must reflect the proportion of the population of each district except for the 8 seats reserved for the 'Foreign District' (there were 12 before the above-mentioned constitutional reform).

190. The election of the Chamber of Deputies is regulated by the Decree of the President of the Republic No. 361/1957, as modified at last by Law No. 165/2017 and thereafter by Law No. 51/2019 which adjusted the system to the new numbers of the house determined by Constitutional Law No. 1/2020.

According to the provisions in force, the distribution of the Chamber of Deputies' seats is made by a mixed system.

The seats are divided into two quotas: three-eighths of the seats are allocated in one-member constituencies by a plurality system; the remaining five-eighths of the seats are allocated by proportional representation among lists of candidates. These proportional seats are allocated in larger constituencies composed by grouping contiguous one-member constituencies. In these larger constituencies, lists of candidates dispute the seats. Every candidate in a one-member constituency could be supported by a single list in the larger constituency or by a coalition of lists within the latter. The voter, anyway, cannot split the vote: he or she can only vote for a list, and the vote is valuable for the list in the larger constituency and the candidate supported by the list within the one-member constituency. In case he or she votes just for the candidate within the one-member constituency, his vote is divided among the lists supporting him or her, according to the proportion they have one each other on the basis of the votes expressed by the other electors.

191. Voters, as already said about the Senate, can only cast a vote for one of the lists whose symbol appears on the ballot paper but cannot express preference votes for one candidate within the list.

Pursuant to the provisions in force, each political force, in presenting its symbol, must also file an electoral manifesto and formally indicate the 'head of the political force'; as already mentioned above, the lists, through mutual formal declarations, can connect to each other in a coalition but each partner of the coalition files an electoral manifesto and indicates a 'head of the political force'.

In the one-member constituency, the candidate obtaining the most of the votes is elected.

The allocation of seats among the lists which, alone or in coalition, compete in the larger constituencies is carried out at a centralized level, by using the proportional method of the Hare quota.

192. The allocation of seats is made only among the single lists that have obtained 3% of the votes cast at national level, and among the coalitions of lists that have achieved, at national level, 10% of votes and that include at least one list having obtained 3% of votes or a list representing a linguistic minority having elected at least two deputies in the one-member constituencies or achieved 20% of votes in a district belonging to a special Region that protects that minority. Once identified the lists that have overcome the above-mentioned thresholds, the Central Office distributes the seats among them after having calculated the national electoral quota (by dividing the global number of votes of the coalitions and lists beyond this threshold by the number of seats to be allocated) and divided the national votes of each list or coalition by this quota. The results of these divisions determine, for the integer part, the number of seats to be allocated to each list, while the remaining seats are allocated, until exhausted, to the lists or coalitions having obtained the highest remainders.

Consequently, the Office also proceeds to determine the subsequent allocation of seats at the larger constituencies' level.

Only after the conclusion of the allocation of all seats among the lists within the larger constituencies, the elected persons can be proclaimed on the basis of the number of seats to which each list has right and following the order of presentation of candidates within the lists. Since some candidates will propose their candidacy in more than one constituency, they could result elected in different districts.

Before Judgment No. 35/2017, they could choose ex post the district of one's election, this having clear effects also on the election of other candidates. Judgment No. 35/2017, on the contrary, has ruled that system unconstitutional. Therefore, Law No. 165/2017 provides for a legislative mechanism which determines automatically the constituency for which the candidate is proclaimed elected.

§5. Election Campaign Laws

193. Law No. 515/1993 contains provisions which have undergone a number of amendments that should ensure equal treatment and access to State Radio and Television Services (RAI), as well as regulate ways and forms of electoral propaganda through other means of communication by parties and candidates involved in election campaigns. These provisions apply both to State Radio and Television Services and to private mass media, starting from the date of the decree calling the election to the end of election day, namely in the period of the election campaign for the national parliamentary elections (there are also provisions aimed at guaranteeing equal opportunity to the access to mass media relating to European, regional, provincial and municipal elections).

194. As for the access to State Radio and Television Services, Law No. 515/1993 provides that, according to the directives of a special Parliamentary Committee (the Committee on Radio and Television Services), equal treatment, completeness and impartiality of information should be ensured for all parties involved in the election campaign. The latter should be granted enough room for their general propaganda activities and election programmes, according to rules set by the Committee itself. As far as national parliamentary elections are concerned, legislative provisions state that, in the above-mentioned period, candidates and members of political parties, as well as members of government, regional executives, Regional Councils and local authorities cannot participate in radio and television programmes of either State or private networks, save for programmes specifically intended for electoral propaganda and for news which give complete and objective information (Article 1, paragraph 5, Law No. 515/1993, as modified by Law No. 28/2000).

Further provisions aimed at granting equal treatment and conditions of access to information and election programmes to all parties and candidates during electoral and *referendum* campaigns are now provided for by Law No. 28/2000, which regulates the 'political communication', and Law No. 313/2003, which includes specific provisions for local television and radio broadcasting.

In particular, Article 5 of Law No. 28/2000 states that, in the election period, the Parliamentary Committee on Radio and Television Services and the AGCOM (i.e., the Authority for Communication Guarantees, an administrative and Independent Authority which is charged with enforcing the administrative rules by levying, if necessary, a series of sanctions, ranging from warnings to pecuniary penalties as well as to revoking the television franchise) must, each for its own competence and after consulting each other, fix the criteria that the information programmes of both State and private national mass media have to comply with. More specifically, it is forbidden to give, even indirectly, hints or voting preferences in any programme which is not expressly intended for electoral propaganda, and television operators are required to manage their programmes 'correctly' and 'impartially' so that voters are not surreptitiously steered.

Moreover, all Public Administrations are forbidden to carry out any propaganda activities, unless they are made in an impersonal way and are strictly connected with their institutional activities. It is finally forbidden to broadcast the result of opinion polls on the elections and voters' political tendencies during the fifteen days preceding the election day.

It should be noted, however, that until now the existing complex set of sanctions (previously levied by the 'Commissioner for Broadcasting and Publishing', then substituted by the AGCOM) has not been enough to achieve the initial aims of the law itself, namely ensuring equal conditions of access to mass media to all the protagonists of the elections. This should have helped public opinion to form free and conscious beliefs, trying to avoid the political bias brought about by the electoral propaganda of the owners of mass media.

195. The above-mentioned Law No. 515/1993 also provides rules about the maximum amount, type and form of expenses of candidates, parties and political groups for election campaigns. These rules are intended to guarantee equal chance of propaganda activities to candidates who have different financial capacities.

In particular, each candidate should appoint an electoral agent, who acts as the only intermediary through whom he or she can raise the funds for the campaign (Article 7(3)). This provision is aimed at ensuring a certain degree of transparency of the sources available to each candidate.

At the end of the election campaign, the electoral agent has to present a report on funding and expenses to a Committee on Elections (Article 13) composed of magistrates and experts. The committee approves the report and, in case of irregularities, can levy sanctions (usually pecuniary), which can go so far as, in case of election of the candidate, to draft a report for the Chamber he or she belongs to with the aim of convincing it to vote upon a resolution disqualifying the candidate from holding the office. Actually, the introduction of the 'closed lists' by virtue of Law No. 270/2005 has drastically reduced the need for propaganda activities on the part of individual candidates, as well as their financial commitment (which is rather directed to their party).

If the two Chambers and a special panel set up by the Court of Accounts find out instead that these limits were exceeded by parties or political groups running for elections, they can levy pecuniary penalties which can even affect the allocations provided for by Article 9 of Law No. 515 for the refund of election expenses borne by candidates and parties that obtained a minimum election result.

§6. Verifying Credentials to Become an MP

196. Article 66 of the Constitution provides that the Chambers (but not the judges) decide as to the validity of the admission of their own members, with the aim of protecting their autonomy and avoiding interference between the judiciary and elected bodies.

Verifying the credentials to become an MP is aimed at ensuring, on the one hand, that the various electoral offices operate correctly and, on the other, that there is no cause of ineligibility which might make the candidates' election invalid, or any cause of incompatibility. The office of MP being incompatible with any other office, the MP would be forced to choose between the two.

The Law establishes both causes of ineligibility (*see* Decree of the President of the Republic No. 361 of 30 March 1957) and causes of incompatibility (*see* Law No. 60/1953), although the Constitution itself lists the following: incompatibility between senator and deputy (Article 65), between MP and member of the CSM (Article 104) or member of the Constitutional Court (Article 135). Ineligibility causes are usually justified as a way to protect freedom of vote since the presence in the election of candidates holding particular offices (such as prefects, Armed Forces' senior officers and magistrates in the districts falling under their jurisdiction) or other governing offices (such as majors of towns with a population of over 20,000 inhabitants, regional councillors) would unfairly influence the election itself.

Incompatibility causes, on the contrary, are more justified as a need to prevent MPs from simultaneously holding managerial offices in agencies directly or indirectly controlled by the State, which could give rise to conflicts of interest.

Ineligibility causes (which include, of course, the loss of the power to vote and be elected) and incompatibility causes may appear after the MP's election. This would produce the effects described above: disqualification from holding the office in the former case and need to opt either for the new office or for the parliamentary one in the latter.

197. According to the Standing Orders of both branches of Parliament, a fundamental role verifying the credentials to become an MP is played by two small committees: the Committee on Elections within the Chamber of Deputies and the Committee on Elections and Parliamentary Privileges within the Senate. The former is composed of thirty members and is regulated by provisions adopted by the Chamber on 6 October 1998. The latter is made up of nineteen senators working in accordance with the special rules approved on 23 January 1992.

Pursuant to parliamentary Standing Orders, appointment of the two committees' members (which cannot be replaced during the term of office of a Legislature) is left to the Presidents of the Chambers who, although they are not required to do so, keep the size of parliamentary groups in mind when taking this decision. This enhances the political nature of bodies entrusted with basically judicial tasks, although the Presidency of these committees is conventionally left to a member of the opposition. Indeed, whenever the competent committee challenges an MP's election, the proceeding set in motion within the Chambers has a judicial nature. The challenge might be due to an appeal by candidates who declare themselves damaged, for various reasons, by a supposedly illegitimate election. The parties are admitted before the committee and allowed to file written briefs. The committee's decision is taken in Chambers.

This kind of decision actually takes the form of recommendations made by the committee to both Houses, which can either accept or challenge them.

Decisions on the validation or annulment of elections, as well as those by which an MP who did not opt for the electoral mandate when a cause of incompatibility was established is disqualified from holding the office, are taken by the full House. In practice, however, the latter hardly ever reject the committee's recommendations, always furnished with findings of enquiries illustrated in the attached written report.

Doubts can be raised, however, on the effective impartiality of the decisions of the two Chambers, given the essentially political nature of their activities, even when they deal with individual legal positions and interests having nothing to do with politics.

§7. Parliamentary Privileges

198. Under the *Statuto* promulgated by King Carlo Alberto in 1848, the Italian legal system already enshrined the right of MPs to exercise the functions connected with their office freely and without the interference of judges. The latter, during the liberal era, were institutionally linked to the King, head of the executive power (as provided for by Article 68 of the *Statuto*, 'justice is derived from the King and is administered in his name by the judges he appoints').

The 1948 Constitution (the same which declares that magistrates are autonomous and independent of any other State power and only subject to the law) provides for parliamentary privileges as well (Article 68), after having stated, in Article 67, that each MP represents the Nation and carries out his/her duties without a binding mandate.

In its first version, the first paragraph of Article 68 mentioned the so-called unchallengeability of opinions expressed or votes given by MPs in the exercise of their duties; the second and third paragraphs, on the contrary, provided for the so-called criminal immunity of MPs who could not be subjected to criminal proceedings or otherwise deprived of personal liberty during their parliamentary mandate, pursuant to the ordinary rules of criminal procedure.

On the one hand, judicial authorities were prevented at any time from prosecuting MPs for opinions expressed in the exercise of their duties and for the reasons that had induced them to give certain votes within their respective Chambers. On the other, the same authorities, especially investigating magistrates, could not subject MPs to criminal proceedings or otherwise deprive them of their personal liberty, even in order to enforce a judgment which can no longer be appealed, without being previously authorized by the Chamber to which the MP belonged (the authorization was therefore meant as a condition for proceeding).

The arrest of an MP was allowed in only one case, namely when he or she was caught in the act of committing a crime for which law provided the arrest as a compulsory measure. The judge in charge of the case was therefore obliged to ask the relevant Chamber's consent to keep the MP in a state of detention.

199. Constitutional Law No. 3/1993 has subsequently modified Article 68 of the Constitution by introducing less favourable provisions for MPs.

Following the amendment of the above rule, especially of its second and third paragraphs, the Italian system no longer forces the judicial authorities to ask the Chamber to which an MP belongs for leave to prosecute him or her. Judges should no longer inform the interested Chamber about any criminal proceedings regarding one of its members. Moreover, no permission must be asked in order to enforce a sentence passed on an MP.

The consent of the Chamber to which an MP belongs is still necessary, instead, for the MP to be subject to restrictions on his or her freedom, such as the arrest (except for the case of *flagrante delicto* described above) or search warrants on his or her person or domicile. Distraint of MPs' correspondence and interception of their conversations or communications in any way whatsoever is also forbidden by the Constitution unless previously authorized (Article 68, second and third paragraphs).

In any case, the Constitutional Court, in Judgment No. 225/2001, recognized to prosecuted MPs a 'legitimate impediment' to participate in the hearing before the judicial authority if they have to take part in a concurrent parliamentary activity. The criminal hearing is consequently postponed.

200. Pursuant to Article 68 of the Constitution, first paragraph, MPs still may not be proceeded against for opinions expressed or votes given in the exercise of their duties (total and permanent immunity). This immunity covers not only criminal but also civil liability, as well as any other form of responsibility different from the one to which they are bound under the Standing Orders of the Chamber they belong to.

Doubts have been raised on the scope of the constitutional provision protecting MPs for 'opinions expressed in the exercise of their duties'. The Constitutional Court (according to a settled case law starting from Judgments Nos 10 and 11/2000) has ruled that this provision covers activities carried out by MPs not only within but also outside their Houses, provided that such activities are connected with their electoral mandate and that there is a link between this 'external' activity and the parliamentary one.

As concerns decisions on the impossibility to challenge MPs' opinions considered by other citizens as detrimental to their honour and other rights protected by law, opinions expressed by the Chamber to which the MPs subjected to judicial proceedings belong (and in some cases, the MPs themselves) and by judicial authorities called upon to pass the judgment often differ. Law No. 140/2003 contains provisions just on the relationships between Parliament and judicial authorities. In particular, it states that if the judicial authority considers Article 68, first paragraph, not to be applied in the proceedings during which the question is raised, it must stay the proceedings and transmit the documents to the Chamber involved for a decision on the case in issue. The Chamber's decision may also be directly stimulated by the interested MP; in this case, the Chamber itself can ask for suspension of the judicial proceedings (Article 3, paragraph 7, of Law No. 140/2003).

If the Chamber, which must decide within ninety days from receipt of documents, reckons that the immunity should be applied in the case in issue, a judge in disagreement cannot disregard that decision directly. Judges can challenge parliamentary decisions interfering in their jurisdiction by raising a conflict of power before the Constitutional Court, which, in short, must ensure the correct exercise of the powers of the Houses to declare their members' opinions unimpeachable.

201. The competence of the Constitutional Court to assess the parliamentary decisions about Article 68, first paragraph, by means of the conflicts of power was for the first time affirmed in Judgment No. 1150/1988. Since then, the Constitutional Court has been frequently asked by judicial authorities to declare parliamentary decisions based on arbitrary assumptions null and void.

Although these mechanisms provided for by Law No. 140/2003 may seem questionable, the Constitutional Court stated, also recently (*see* Judgment No. 46/2008), that there is no constitutional illegitimacy. Therefore, in the Italian legal system, the only remedy for judicial authorities to challenge parliamentary decisions is to raise a conflict of power before the Constitutional Court.

Actually, this remedy was deemed insufficient by the European Court of Human Rights, which has repeatedly condemned Italy for 'denial of justice' towards those who assume having been injured by MPs' defamatory opinions. The Constitutional Court, in fact, does not always come to a decision about these immunities, so that, in that case, they are exempt from any judicial control.

In addition, during the settlement of a specific conflict of power raised by the Chamber of Deputies against a penal judge, the Constitutional Court affirmed (Judgment No. 379/1996) that judicial authorities cannot investigate cases of MPs' conduct if the object of the enquiry is their status as member of the Chambers. This conduct may fall outside the categories protected by immunity and have negative repercussions on other MPs' functions, thus jeopardizing the correct operation of parliamentary activities (as in the case of false certification of identity and replacing absent MPs during a vote).

202. The Italian system no longer provides for the need to ask the Houses leave to subject one of their members to criminal proceedings. The Chambers' consent, on the contrary, is still necessary for penal judges to deprive MPs of their personal liberty, in the broadest sense of the word, or their freedom of domicile.

The existence of provisions preventing MPs from being prosecuted during and only until the end of their mandate is understandable, from a historical and logical point of view, in light of the need to allow the Houses to judge any persecutory intent (the so-called *fumus persecutionis)*, arising from judicial initiatives damaging their members and representatives of the Nation.

However, the above-mentioned constitutional provisions do not mention, unfortunately, which parameters should be used by the Houses when evaluating judicial authorities' requests for leave to deprive MPs of their personal liberties. This gives high discretionary powers to the Houses which can, in fact, deny their consent without even giving reasons for that.

Presently, given the low number of warrants of arrest of MPs (whose arrest was sometimes, also recently, authorized) and the fact that the Houses can deny their consent only for the above-mentioned measures restricting personal liberty (and not for subjecting their members to criminal proceedings), these powers no longer appear as a dangerous tool that Parliament can use to replace or interfere with judicial authorities, especially investigating ones.

203. As regards the proceeding set in motion by the Houses when asked by judicial authorities for leave to deprive one MP of his personal liberties, it is worth underlying the fundamental role of parliamentary committees. The Chamber of Deputies has its own Committee on Privileges (composed of twenty-one members of the Chamber appointed by the President, theoretically without the need to reflect the size of the political groups but practically respecting their proportionality). The committee within the Senate, as stated above, is called the Committee on Elections and Parliamentary Privileges.

The committees collect the evidence after consulting the MP concerned if necessary (or after going through his briefs) and draw up a proposal of consent or denial of the request to deprive one MP of his personal liberties, accompanied by a written report. Both documents are laid before the full House, which can even contradict the proposal (even when Parliament takes decisions on MPs' immunity, the relationship between the committee and the full House is always the same as that existing between a promoting and a legislative body).

The vote on the leave is open in both Houses, according to a questionable interpretation of the Standing Orders, adopted shortly before the amendment of Article 68 when voting by secret ballot was abandoned to reduce the risk that MPs might prevent criminal proceedings against themselves from being initiated. However, voting by secret ballot is still possible if a number of MPs explicitly request it and in compliance with general voting rules of the Houses.

§8. STANDING ORDERS

204. Pursuant to Article 64, first paragraph, of the Constitution, each House drafts its own Standing Orders by an absolute majority of its members. This is an expression of the autonomy enjoyed by the two Houses of Parliament and of their independence from the other constitutional organs.

Standing Orders are not subordinate to Acts of Parliament (*see* Part I, Chapter 4, §6) but should in any case observe the principles relating to the workings of the Chambers set out in constitutional legislation.

The Constitutional Court has so far excluded, owing to formal reasons, that the Standing Orders might be subjected to the review of constitutionality (*see* Constitutional Court, Judgment No. 154/1985, widely criticized by some academic commentators).

Standing Orders regulate the organization and workings of the Houses and their internal sections, as well as the procedures they follow to exercise their functions, including those which are bound to influence the relationship of confidence between the Houses and the government (including confidence or no-confidence votes and the 'question of confidence').

205. Although Standing Orders contain provisions which are supposed to regulate permanently the Houses' organization and workings, they are frequently modified to adapt them to the changing political and institutional requirements.

A global review of the Standing Orders was undertaken by the Houses in 1971, resulting in the adoption of completely new rules. Subsequently, both Houses repeatedly modified many provisions, also by introducing, after bitter debates within the Houses, organic sets of rules (such as in 1981, 1987, between the end of 1988 and the first months of 1989 and, most recently, in 1997 and in 1999 for the Chamber of Deputies and between February and July 1999 and December 2017 for the Senate; in addition, the Senate has also amended certain provisions of its own rules following the reduction in the number of Senators that occurred starting from 2022, while the Chamber did not deem it necessary to proceed with such an update) aimed most of all at strengthening the position of the government and main political groups and therefore often contested by the opposition and minor groups.

The amendment procedure aroused lively discussion and controversy involving the presidencies, especially the president of the Chamber of Deputies.

Since the Constitution does not contain specific provisions on the matter (except for the rule which implicitly imposes an absolute majority vote for amending existing rules), the Houses follow quite different procedures. The Senate's method is very similar to the legislative process. The Chamber has a very different method (especially with regard to the discussion and voting of amendments), centred around the proposing and drafting role of the Committee on Standing Orders (chaired by the president of the Chamber), charged with the drafting of the final text to be laid, along with the amendments, before the full House for approval.

§9. THE SECTIONS OF THE CHAMBERS

206. Within each House, there are a number of internal bodies, such as the President, the parliamentary groups, the Conference of the Presidents of parliamentary groups, the Standing Committees and other permanent bodies.

In compliance with Article 63 of the Constitution, each House elects its President following different procedures (as provided by their Standing Orders), both by secret ballot voting and qualified majorities.

The President's task is to represent the House and supervise the progress of its works. Pursuant to Article 86 of the Constitution, moreover, the President of the Senate carries out the President of the Republic's duties any time the latter proves to be unable to fulfil them.

With reference to the Presidents of the two Houses, as well as to the President of the Republic and the President of the Council of Ministers, both Law No. 140/2003 (Article 1) and Law No. 124/2008, though with different mechanisms, had provided for the suspension of possible criminal proceedings towards them during the entire period they remained in office. These disputable rules, however, have been declared unconstitutional by the Constitutional Court first with Judgment No. 24/2004 and then with the Judgment No. 262/2009. The Court stated that those rules disregarded the principle of equality and introduced a significant departure from the rule of law without the approval of a constitutional law.

Both Presidents have their own bureau supervising all the activities carried out within the respective Houses. The bureau is also composed of four Vice-Presidents, three Sergeant-at-arms and eight Secretaries, so as to reflect the composition of all the groups sitting in the House.

Until 1976, the Presidents of the two Houses of Parliament had always been members of the majority. From 1976 to 1994, on the contrary, the Presidents of the Chamber of Deputies were members of the main opposition party (the Communists, followed by the *Partito Democratico della Sinistra,* Democratic Party of the Left). From 1994 to date there was another reversal of trend. In the 2018–2022 legislative term, however, due to the absence of a predictable majority to support the Government at the time of the President of the Senate election, the latter was elected from a party that would later be in opposition to the first two Governments of the legislature, those led by Prof. Conte. Nevertheless, the party to which the President of the Senate belonged later joined the majority that supported the subsequent Draghi Government.

According to the Standing Orders, the Presidents' most important tasks include scheduling the activities of the Houses following the suggestions of the government and parliamentary groups. Both Houses, indeed, regularly convene a Conference of the Presidents of parliamentary groups, always informing the government, which might send one of its representatives. The Conference takes formal decisions on the scheduling of the activities of the Chambers and can be convened by the Chamber's President in order to analyse the general progress of parliamentary works. In practice, the importance of this body (whose sittings are not open to the public) has considerably increased. Anyway, the majority sustaining the government is able to direct the progress of parliamentary works on the basis of its convenience.

207. Standing Orders provide that parliamentary groups are essential bodies of the Chambers and must be composed of at least twenty MPs for the Chamber of Deputies and seven for the Senate (before the reduction of the number of the senators, the minimum number was ten; no change has been made for the Chamber of Deputies). However, the bureau of both Chambers' Presidents can allow for the creation of groups with a lower number of MPs in order to favour smaller parties, provided that these groups represent a party which was organized inside the country and had a certain election result on a national level.

Members of Parliament whose number is not high enough to form a group or who do not wish to join any parliamentary group can form one mixed group within their own Chamber (the mixed group of the Chamber of Deputies can be further divided into political entities, also in order to represent the linguistic minorities protected by the Constitution).

Each parliamentary group elects its own President. The groups and their Presidents enjoy specific procedural powers.

208. Provision was made for other important permanent bodies as well. Although they only enjoy the power to make suggestions to the full House that takes the final decision, these bodies are involved in the delicate judicial proceedings falling under the jurisdiction of Parliament. As stated above, matters such as parliamentary immunity and procedures to verify election results are dealt with by the Committee on Elections and the Committee on Privileges (there is only one committee in the Senate, the Committee on Elections and Parliamentary Privileges). These committees jointly make up the Committee on Impeachment, charged with presenting a report to Parliament in joint session before the deliberation on impeachment of the Head of State (Article 90 of the Constitution. *See also* Part II, Chapter 2, §10).

As regards the amendment of the Standing Orders of the Chamber of Deputies, mention has also been made to the Committee on Standing Orders, a body provided for by the rules of the Senate as well, where it is chaired by the President of the Chamber. The task of these committees (composed of ten members in both Chambers) is to settle disputes arising over the interpretation of the Standing Orders.

Pursuant to the Standing Orders, the Presidents of the Chambers must nominate the MPs who will make up the committees, without any obligation to reflect the proportions among the political groups or the number of their members, given the special 'technical' functions of the committees. However, as stated above, the balance among the various groups is always taken into account, which basically confirms the political role played by these committees.

209. Article 72 of the Constitution, which provides a general description of the legislative process (*see* Part II, Chapter 4), states that every bill laid before either Chambers must be examined by a committee which can also be a standing one. Indeed, there are Standing Committees dealing with specific matters, partly coinciding with those dealt with by the Ministers.

There are presently fourteen Standing Committees within the Chamber of Deputies (among the most important, the Constitutional Affairs Committee, the Justice Committee, the Budget Committee and the EU Policies Committee). The Senate had the same number of such a Committee as the Chamber before the reduction in the number of parliamentarians, even though the subjects assigned to each of the fourteen Committees did not exactly match those of the Chamber's Committees. Following the reduction in the number of Senators, the Senate Committees are now reduced to ten. However, the different number of committees in the Chamber and the Senate has not posed coordination problems between the Houses until now. Unlike the other ones, their nature is merely political. They are therefore set up by the Chambers' Presidents at the beginning of Parliament, and they have to reflect the number of members of the groups, as well as the appointments proposed by the groups themselves. These committees are re-elected every two years.

Members of the committees who join the government are replaced by other MPs belonging to the same group.

Each committee elects its own President (and a President's office) charged, among other things, with organizing the works of the committee in coordination with the activities of the Chamber. Committees enjoy general powers over the matters they are entrusted with, not only with regard to legislative process. They also exercise general direction and supervision functions on governmental activities and can order parliamentary hearings.

It is also open for the Chambers to set up ad hoc committees for single legislative processes or other duties. Special committees can also be set up with the aim of carrying out parliamentary enquiries (*see* Part II, Chapter 4, §10).

§10. Bicameral Committees

210. Bicameral committees, made up of an equal number of members of the two Houses, are sometimes set up in order to solve the problems of the 'perfect' bicameral system. The Parliamentary Committee for Regional Matters is the only bicameral committee provided for by constitutional provisions (Article 126 of the Constitution). Article 11 of Constitutional Law No. 3/2001, which has modified Title V of the second part of the Constitution related to Regions and Provinces, provided that the bicameral committee for regional matters could also include representatives of Regions and other Local Bodies, according to the Standing Orders of the Chambers, at least until the present bicameral organization of the Italian Republic – which actually does not have a Chamber directly representative of Regions and Local Bodies – is not changed.

When acting in such composition, the bicameral committee for regional matters is charged with the task to express opinions and evaluations on ordinary laws stating the fundamental principles of matters included in shared legislative powers of State and Regions or on laws providing rules about matters reserved for the State legislative power but involving the financial autonomy of Regions. Either the Chamber of Deputies or the Senate could disregard these evaluations only by voting with a qualified majority. This integration, however, has never occurred, although the constitutional organization of the Italian Parliament has not been changed yet.

Various Acts of Parliament regulate the setting up of bicameral bodies exercising general political control and supervision functions (such as the Committee on Radio and Television Services) or advisory functions.

In particular, bicameral committees on constitutional reforms have been recently set up (*see* Part II, Chapter 4, §4).

§11. General Provisions on Resolutions Taken by the Chambers

211. Article 64 of the Constitution sets out that sittings are open to the public, although the Chambers may decide to assemble in private. Government's members, even though they are not members of the Houses, are entitled to attend meetings and are obliged to be present if called upon.

Ministers, moreover, have a right to be heard whenever they request this right. Each House is usually convened by its President that announces the agenda and time of the following sitting. According to the text of the Constitution, the Chambers must meet twice a year and may be convened in extraordinary sessions on the initiative of their President or of one-third of their members or of the President of the Republic. When one Chamber is called upon to meet in extraordinary session, the other Chamber is also convened ipso jure. Actually, except for a brief summer break, the workings of the two Houses are scheduled all the year long.

212. Article 64, second paragraph, sets out that the decisions of the Chambers are not valid unless the majority of their members are present, and unless they are voted upon by a majority of those present, save when the Constitution provides for a special majority (such as, in case of adoption of the Standing Orders or passing of laws amending the Constitution). When it comes to election procedures (such as the election of the Presidents of the Houses), even the Standing Orders (and Acts of Parliament) sometimes provide for special majorities. This does not conflict with the above constitutional provision, which refers to decision-making phases.

The Chamber of Deputies and the Senate have different ways of considering abstentions. According to Article 48 of the Standing Orders of the Chamber of Deputies, members abstaining from voting are considered as absent and therefore cannot make up the majority. Pursuant to Article 107 of the Standing Orders of the Senate, on the contrary, senators abstaining from voting (who are therefore counted among those voting against a decision) can be considered as part of the quorum. As a result, if a senator does not wish to affect the result of a voting, he or she, unlike their counterparts in the Chamber of Deputies, should not participate in the voting itself (this obviously results in a decrease of participants to the votings).

213. Article 94 of the Constitution provides for voting procedures concerning the relationship of confidence between the Chambers and the government, including a nominal vote, which is a form of open vote by which every single MP is personally asked to say yes or no.

As regards the other decisions taken by the Chambers, the various forms of expression of the vote are set out in the Standing Orders.

The 1988 review of the Standing Orders also included the secret ballot as the most common way of voting in Parliament. Changing in favour of open voting was an important reform, aimed at making MPs more responsible to their voters but, most of all, at strengthening the position of the executive within the Chambers. The government, indeed, was often exposed to *francs tireurs*, i.e., MPs of the majority who, by profiting of secret ballot voting, expressed a negative vote on governmental measures without giving any reason for their dissent.

Presently, both the Chamber (Article 49 of its Standing Orders) and the Senate (Article 113) usually vote by an open vote, while secret voting is provided only for votes concerning the election of persons. Secret ballot can be asked by a number of members of the Chamber (thirty) and of the Senate (twenty) with respect to some legislative decisions having neither financial consequence nor affecting principles and freedoms granted by the Constitution (Article 49 of the Standing Orders of the Chamber of Deputies contemplates this request also in other cases, such as passing of electoral laws and setting up Committees of Enquiry).

In both Chambers, voting within the committees is always open, except for votes by which people are elected.

Chapter 4. Parliament: Its Activities

by Antonio D'Andrea & Lorenzo Spadacini

§1. The Passing of Laws: The Equal Role of the Chambers and the Government's Supremacy in Promoting Bills

214. Pursuant to Article 70 of the Constitution, 'legislative duties are carried out jointly by the two Chambers'. This means that a law is considered as formed only when an identical bill is adopted by both Chambers.

The Chamber going through a bill in second reading may, according to its Standing Orders, follow a different procedure than the one adopted by the other in the first reading and modify the text approved by the first Chamber. Should this happen, the bill is passed from one Chamber to the other through the so-called *navetta* (the bill is re-examined only with regard to changes made by the other Chamber and amendments proposed with regard to these changes) until both Chambers adopt an identical text. The law is therefore promulgated by the President of the Republic and enters into force after being published in the Official Gazette.

The Constitution, therefore, does not give one of the two Chambers more powers with regard to the legislative process.

Legislative initiative pertains to the government (which must be formally authorized by the President of the Republic), to each member of the two Chambers, each Regional Council, the *Consiglio nazionale dell'economia e del lavoro* – National Council of Economy and Labour, a body assisting the Chambers and the government in the economic and social sectors – and not less than 50,000 voters. Legislative initiative can also be conferred to other authorities and bodies by means of a constitutional law (Article 71 of the Constitution).

MPs are obliged to introduce their bill into the Chamber they belong to, from which the passing of the bill formally starts. The others are free to introduce it into the Chamber of their choice, thus determining the order of priority between the two Chambers.

215. Legislative initiative coming from the government is doubtless the most important form of initiative, especially in a parliamentary system in which the executive is the expression of the majority of the two Chambers. The government can also avail itself of technical and logistical support when drafting its bills. In some cases, moreover, the Constitution explicitly or implicitly sets out that the government has exclusive initiative on some laws (*see* laws regulating relationships between the State and religious groups, Article 8; acts by which decrees are passed into laws, Article 77; laws authorizing the ratification of international treaties, Article 80; budget laws, Article 81).

The government's role in legislative procedures is actually very different from the one of the other people or bodies having legislative initiative, although the Constitution does not grant special powers to the executive, except for the possibility (set out in Article 72 of the Constitution) of demanding that a bill adopted directly by a committee be discussed and voted on by the relative Chamber.

The government's leading position in the legislative field is rather determined by parliamentary Standing Orders and sometimes by Acts of Parliament: *see* act No. 196 of 31 December 2009 that has strengthened the government's legislative initiative in the financial sector by granting the executive a role of technical support of Parliament with regard to the financial effects of bills and amendments proposed by other bodies.

The government was therefore given the possibility of 'orienting' both the legislative courses within the Chambers and parliamentary decisions and debates. Some examples are the power of the executive to propose amendments departing from what is allowed to other bodies or to draw up special technical reports on the quality and enforceability of provisions contained in the laws, the power to place time limits on debates, in order to 'crush' filibustering by the opposition and, in order to control majority groups, the recourse to open voting and, most of all, to confidence motions.

§2. The Different Procedures for Considering Bills

216. Once introduced into the Chambers, the bill is handed over to the competent Committee, which is chosen on the basis of the specific matter of the bill. The powers of the committee towards the Chamber vary according to the procedure. Article 72 of the Constitution provides for two different procedures: the normal procedure, in which the committee examines the bill in a reporting capacity, the passing of the bill being left to the full House, and the decentralized procedure, in which the committees meet in a legislative capacity, by examining and adopting the bill directly. The Standing Orders also provide for a third kind of procedure, in which the bill is examined by the committee in a drafting capacity, on different conditions in each Chamber. In case the full House of one of two Chambers (as to the Chamber of Deputies, this decision can also be taken by the majority of the members of the Conference of the Presidents of parliamentary groups) states that a bill is urgent (often on the government's request), times provided for by the Standing Orders are reduced by half (the so-called abbreviated procedure which, in the Chamber of Deputies, can be adopted only for a limited number of bills, depending on the length of the works).

Pursuant to Article 72, fourth paragraph, the normal procedure for debating and voting bills by the Chambers is always applied in the case of bills of a constitutional and electoral nature and for those delegating legislative powers, for authorization to ratify international treaties, and for voting on budgets and rectified budgets. The normal procedure is provided for by both Standing Orders in the case of bills converting decree-laws too.

Furthermore, an important role with regard to the choice of legislative procedures and relevant committees is played by the President of each Chamber, although the Standing Orders of the Senate are the only ones fully recognizing this power.

217. When the bill is handed over to a committee meeting in a reporting capacity, the latter first examines the text and, if advisable, amends it. Other committees can (and sometimes must) be called upon to give their advice. After the last reform of its Standing Orders, carried out in 1999, the Chamber of Deputies, if requested by one-fifth of the members of the relevant committee (regardless of the capacity in which it meets), can ask the Committee on legislation, consisting of ten members of the Chamber appointed by the President so as to represent equally both majority and opposition, to give its advice on a specific bill. The committee should say if the bill is homogeneous and simple and if it is properly worded.

The committee finally draws up a written report on the bill (which will be illustrated to the full House by a referee chosen from among the members of the committee), including the text of the bill as amended by the committee itself. This text is the basis for the debate and vote by the full House. The Standing Orders of both Chambers also provide for the presentation of reports by referees belonging to dissenting groups.

The bill is debated by the full House in general and, subsequently, pursuant to Article 72, examined section-by-section and put to the final vote. When each section is examined, the relative amendments are debated and voted upon.

After the changes to the Standing Orders of both Chambers, the final vote on bills is open, save for the above exceptions (*see* Part II, Chapter 3, §11) and is usually made by an electronic procedure.

218. If bills are examined by committees meeting in a legislative capacity, their final text must be approved by the committee itself, without any involvement of the full House. Although, pursuant to the Standing Orders of the Chamber of Deputies, this procedure can be followed only for bills not relating to 'particularly important matters of a general nature' (Article 92), in practice it is used (despite, to date, overall, very rarely) without any distinction between more or less important bills of a general nature, save for bills for which examination by committees meeting in a legislative capacity is forbidden by constitutional rules or the Standing Orders.

Even though the above procedure is followed, MPs who are not members of the committee can propose amendments by illustrating them before the committee itself. General rules on the debate and passing of bills by the full House are applied.

Mention should finally be made to the constitutional rule (Article 72, third paragraph) providing that a bill, until it is finally voted upon, is introduced into the Chamber if the government or one-tenth of the members of the Chamber or one-fifth of the committee demand that it be debated and voted on by the Chamber itself or laid before the latter for its final approval. Moreover, the Standing Orders of both Chambers provide for the automatic referral to the full House of the bills for which the Committee meeting in a legislative capacity is obliged to ask to the 'Filter Committees' (in both Chambers, they are the Constitutional Affairs Committee and the Budget Committee) to give their advice, in the case it does not intend to follow that advice.

219. The third kind of legislative procedure, set out in the Standing Orders and little used in practice because of its complexity, provides for examination of bills by a committee meeting in a drafting capacity. As far as the Senate is concerned, the relevant committee approves each section of the bill and just leaves the final vote on the whole text to the full House. As regards the Chamber of Deputies, on the contrary, the full House votes on each section drafted by the committee before the final vote without debating or proposing amendments.

The Standing Orders of both Chambers, moreover, provide that the full House should set the standards and principles that the committee should comply with when drafting the sections. Article 72, third paragraph, can also be applied to this case. As mentioned before, this rule provides that the government or one-tenth of the members of the Chamber or one-fifth of the committee could demand that the bill, until it is finally voted upon, be debated and voted on before the full House, according to the ordinary Standing Orders.

§3. The Promulgation and Publication of Laws

220. Once the bill has been finally voted upon by the Chambers, the House that last examined it sends it to the government (Article 70 of the Standing Orders of the Chamber of Deputies and Article 75 of those of the Senate). The law is then passed on to the President of the Republic for promulgation.

Pursuant to Article 74, first paragraph, of the Constitution, the Head of State may, however, before promulgating a law, request a new consideration by means of 'a message to both Chambers in which the reasons for such action are set forth' (*see* Part II, Chapter 2, §13). According to the Constitution, it is at the discretion of the President of the Republic to assess the conditions that justify this request. The Head of State may therefore return the law for both legitimacy and substantive reasons. This presidential power has been little used in practice.

If the Chambers are asked for a new consideration, Standing Orders provide that the House of Parliament that was first in voting the bill should re-examine it with the ordinary procedure. If the Chambers vote on the bill once more (no special majority is provided for), the President of the Republic is obliged to promulgate the law: the President, as a matter of fact, can exercise the power to return the law only once (Article 74, second paragraph, of the Constitution).

Laws are promulgated by the President of the Republic within thirty days of their having been voted upon unless a shorter period of time is laid down in laws themselves (adopted by an absolute majority vote of the two Chambers). However, this has never occurred in practice.

Article 1 of Decree No. 1092 of the President of the Republic, dated 28 December 1985, contains the text of the form of the promulgation of ordinary laws, including the statement announcing that the Chambers have passed the bill, the writs of publication and execution, the endorsement and the signature of the *Guardasigilli* (Minister of Justice).

Laws are published both in the Official Gazette (within thirty days of their promulgation) and in the Official Collection of the Legislation of the Italian Republic.

Laws come into force after the so-called *vacatio legis*, i.e., on the fifteenth day after their publication in the Official Gazette, unless the laws themselves provide otherwise (Article 73, third paragraph, of the Constitution).

§4. THE LEGISLATIVE PROCESS OF CONSTITUTIONAL LAWS

221. The process for amending constitutional provisions and passing constitutional laws is set out in Article 138 of the Constitution and is defined as a 'special' process since it is more complicated than ordinary legislative procedure.

In fact, constitutional bills (that, according to the Constitution, can be introduced into the Chambers by all those who have legislative initiative for ordinary laws) are passed by the Chamber of Deputies and the Senate, following the normal procedure for debating and voting bills, in two successive sessions at an interval of not less than three months. Pursuant to the Standing Orders of both branches of Parliament, constitutional bills are handed over to the First Standing Committee on Constitutional Affairs in a reporting capacity, and they must be approved for the second time by an absolute majority of the members of each Chamber.

The Standing Orders provide that whenever the Chambers examine a constitutional bill during a second reading, each of them, after the general debate, immediately proceeds to the final vote of the bill without discussing its sections since no amendment or removal of one or more provisions is permitted (Article 99 of the Standing Orders of the Chamber of Deputies and Article 123 of the Standing Orders of the Senate).

Once they have been passed by both Chambers during a second reading, constitutional laws are published in the Official Gazette (in this case, the publication is just for information and is not aimed, as usual, at starting the so-called *vacatio legis*) and are put to popular referendum when, within three months of their publication, 500,000 electors or five Regional Councils or one-fifth of the members of either Chamber demand it. This referendum is not subject to any validity condition related to the number of those participating in the voting.

The President of the Republic may, therefore, promulgate constitutional laws in two different cases: if none of the authorized persons or bodies demands the referendum within three months or if, once the referendum has been demanded, the law is approved by the majority of the voters participating in the referendum. The promulgation is followed by the publication of the constitutional law and its entry into force. Obviously, the promulgation does not occur in case of negative result of the constitutional referendum.

In order to favour a large agreement among parliamentary groups, the Constitution states that the referendum is not held if the law has been approved in both Chambers, during the second reading, by a majority of two-thirds of the members of each Chamber (Article 138, third paragraph, of the Constitution). In this case, the law is immediately promulgated and comes into force after the usual publication.

222. Does the procedure set out in Article 138 make it too difficult to carry out constitutional reforms? This question has been much debated recently.

Since the Constitution has come into force, this procedure has been followed on a number of occasions, not only to pass important constitutional laws but also to adopt specific reforms of the text of the Constitution itself. In 1963, for instance, the provisions on the composition and term of office of the Chambers were modified; in 1967, there was an amendment to the rules providing for the term of office of the judges of the Constitutional Court; in 1989, jurisdiction to adjudicate on offences committed by Ministers was eliminated among the competences of the Constitutional Court; in 1991–1992, the procedure for the granting of amnesty and indult was modified and the provision on the early dissolution of the Chambers was changed as well; in 1993, there was an amendment to the provisions on MPs' privileges; in 1999, a constitutional reform has introduced the principles of 'fair trial' (Article 111) and has modified some constitutional provisions concerning the organizational structure of the Regions; in 2000 there was the creation of the 'Foreign District' for the election of members of either Chamber (Article 48) and, in 2001, the number of Deputies and senators elected in that District was fixed; again in 2001, Title V of the second part of the Constitution concerning Regions and other Local Bodies was modified; in 2002, the effects of the transitory provision which prevented the members of the House of Savoy from accessing and sojourning in the national territory were eliminated; in 2003, the principle of equal opportunities between women and men for the purposes of access to public offices and elected positions was introduced; in 2007, the constitutional ban to the death penalty has been extended also with reference to war laws; in 2012, the principle of the balanced budget has been introduced; in 2020, the number of senators and deputies have been reduced; in 2021, the voting age for the Senate was reduced; in 2022, the principle of environmental protection was introduced into the Constitution; finally, in 2023, two reforms were approved: the principle of protecting the specific characteristics of islands, on the one hand, and the protection of sport, on the other.

223. Special mention should be made to bicameral committees on institutional reforms. These committees (which are not Standing Committees) are set up in order to make deep changes to the present constitutional rules, so as to find a solution to the problems occurring in practice, especially with regard to the workings of political decision-making organs.

The first bicameral committee was set up by the Chambers during the ninth Parliament (1983–1987) by a motion passed separately on the same day (12 October 1983) and was made up of twenty members of the Chamber of Deputies and twenty members of the Senate, so as to reflect the proportions among the various parliamentary groups. It was chaired by Mr Aldo Bozzi, a prominent member of the small Liberal Party who had also been a member of the Constituent Assembly. The committee was charged with putting forward proposals of amendments to the Constitution in order to 'strengthen political and republican democracy' to be passed into legislation.

The 'Bozzi Committee' remained in office for fourteen months (from December 1983 to January 1985) and, in a climate of strong clashes of opinions among parliamentary groups, presented to the President of the Chamber of Deputies a majority report (signed by the President himself) and as much as six minority reports on 29 January 1985.

The results of the work carried out by the 'Bozzi' Committee had no practical application.

224. The Chambers decided to set up a second bicameral committee at the beginning of the eleventh Parliament (1992–1994).

In the meantime, the debate over reforms and the ways to get as early as possible to their approval had been speeded up after the then Head of State, Francesco Cossiga, had sent a message on the matter to the Chambers (26 June 1991). Also, the newly elected President of the Republic, Oscar Luigi Scalfaro, in his address to Parliament in joint session before taking office (25 May 1992), had confirmed the need for institutions to undergo deep changes and for a new ad hoc parliamentary body to be set up.

The committee was set up following two distinct resolutions taken by the Chambers on 23 July 1992 and was composed of thirty members of the Chamber of Deputies and thirty senators so as to reflect the proportions among parliamentary groups. In the beginning, it was chaired by Ciriaco De Mita (previously Head of Government and Secretary of the Christian Democrats, i.e., the relative majority party until 1994) and, when the latter resigned, by Mrs Nilde Iotti (a communist member of the Constituent Assembly, formerly President of the Chamber of Deputies).

Following the setting up of the so-called De Mita-Iotti Committee, the Chambers increased its role, as well as its capacity of making proposals to the Chambers, by Constitutional Law No. 1/1993, which empowered the committee to present a unique and organic project of amendment of the second part of the Constitution (the one dealing with the organization of the Republic, with the exception of the section concerning the amendment of the Constitution itself) and gave it, to this end, special reporting powers towards the two Chambers of Parliament. Such a task had to be accomplished within six months of the coming into force of the law itself (i.e., one day after its publication in the Official Gazette, on 10 August 1993).

Article 3 of Constitutional Law No. 1/1993, moreover, provided for a departure from the procedure to amend the Constitution set out in Article 138 of the Constitution, in that it established that the project drafted during the six months by the committee and approved by each Chamber, according to normal procedures (two resolutions and qualified majorities), had to be put to popular referendum within three months.

The referendum, however, was not held and, owing to the early dissolution of Parliament in 1994, the Chambers could not even start to examine the text of the project drafted by the committee just a few days before the dissolution.

225. At the beginning of the thirteenth Parliament (April 1996), Constitutional Law No. 1/1997 set up a third Parliamentary Committee on Constitutional Reforms, composed of thirty-five members of the Chamber of Deputies and thirty-five senators, charged with putting forward proposals of review of the second part of the Constitution with regard to the system of government and the bicameral system. Such Committee has been chaired by Massimo D'Alema. At the time he was the political Secretary on the majority party, which supported the government led by Romano Prodi. Later, in the course of the same legislature, Massimo D'Alema himself became President of the Council of the Ministers.

The 'D'Alema Committee' too was granted special legislative tasks by the Constitutional Law by which it was set up (Articles 2 and 3). With a further departure from the procedure to amend the Constitution, that law provided that the Chambers should approve an organic project of constitutional amendment and, in case of two successive votes in favour of it, hold a popular referendum within three months as a definitive vote on the constitutional reform (Article 4). At the end of the first phase of its works (30 June 1997) and within the specified time limits, the committee drew up a draft, rather innovative, project of reform. Examination of this project, however, was suspended in March 1998 – in the period of office of the XIII legislature, which represented the time limit for the activity of the Committee – with the consent of all parliamentary groups because of strong conflicts among the political groups about the passing of legislation relating to the powers of the President of the Republic, for which the committee had proposed the direct election.

With regard to Constitutional Laws No. 1/1993 and No. 1/1997, it should be remembered that academic commentators criticized the decision of legislators of modifying the procedure for amending the Constitution set out in Article 138 of the Constitution. These provisions, in their opinion, must be considered as the expression of a supreme principle of the legal system, which cannot be altered in any way whatsoever.

At the end of the thirteenth Parliament (February–March 2001), despite the failure of the 'D'Alema Committee' and of the 'method' used to approve constitutional reforms, the then centre-left majority, by a narrow margin of votes (only four votes in the Chamber of Deputies and nine in the Senate) and after bitter debates with the opposition, passed the reform of Title V of the second part of the Constitution, relating to Regions, Provinces and municipalities, with the aim of completing the 1999 constitutional reform (which had strengthened the statutory autonomy of Regions and introduced, although provisionally, the direct election of their Presidents).

Therefore, after the victory of the centre-right in the elections of May 2001, at the beginning of the fourteenth Parliament (2001–2006), the first constitutional referendum in the history of the Republic was held. Curiously enough, the referendum was promoted also by the parties which had approved the reform, with the purpose of favouring a direct involvement of the electoral body in the reform itself. Anyway, the constitutional reform passed by the centre-left was directly approved by voters in the referendum held on 7 October 2001, with a poll turnout of just 34.1%; it was approved by 64.2% of valid votes.

Again during the fourteenth Parliament, the centre-right governments, with the full support of the parliamentary majority (which, though being large, did not reach the two-thirds of the Chambers), promoted a global reform of the second part of the Constitution, which was approved by the two branches of Parliament in November 2005, just few months before the new elections and with the firm aversion of the opposition, that won the 2006 elections, thus creating a centre-left executive. Also, this constitutional reform was put to a referendum, which was held on 25 and 26 June 2006. In a climate of greater popular involvement (with a turnout of 52.3%), the electorate clearly rejected, with 63.2% of 'no', the rewriting of the second part of the Constitution. In this case, therefore, the attempt to amend the Italian Constitution with only the votes of the parliamentary majority was avoided and given the extent of that reform, it was possible to speak of a 'popular re-legitimization' of the 1948 Constitution.

During the XVII Legislature, the issue of the great institutional reforms – including constitutional reforms – that cyclically have infused Italy for over thirty years, almost never bringing to completion the 'great' changes designed, has been forcefully reopened. The proposed reform, which affects substantial parts of the second part of the Constitution, would have produced, among other things, significant changes – if not formal, definitely substantial – to the established parliamentary system of government welcomed in our legal order. On 4 December 2016, the constitutional reform proposals to the parliamentary bicameral system, nevertheless, were rejected in a popular referendum by a large majority of the people – 19,419,507 against (13,432,208 for), constituting 59.1% of those voting on a turnout of 65.5%.

§5. Laws Delegating Legislative Powers and Legislative Decrees

226. Pursuant to Article 76 of the Constitution, the government can be delegated by the Chambers to exercise legislative functions by issuing decrees having the value of ordinary laws (the so-called legislative decrees).

The delegation must take the form of an Act of Parliament (called 'delegating law'), having the contents set out in Article 76 and adopted according to the ordinary procedure.

In principle, it is impossible to delegate legislation over matters that, according to the Constitution, must absolutely be regulated by ordinary laws (*see* Part I, Chapter 4).

The fact that the government is obliged to exercise delegated legislative powers is still debated by academic commentators. The executive, in practice, has not often exercised this power within the specified time limits.

Pursuant to Article 87, fifth paragraph, of the Constitution, once issued by the Council of Ministers delegated decrees are promulgated by the President of the Republic under the name of 'legislative decrees', as explicitly provided for by Article 14 of Law No. 400/1988. They enter into force after being published in the Official Gazette, after the ordinary fifteen-day period of *vacatio* provided for ordinary laws, unless they specify a different period.

The exercise of legislative functions may be delegated to the government only within the limits allowed by the Constitution, which also sets out the contents of delegating laws. Such laws must clearly specify the object of delegation (i.e., definite matters and not matters to be determined by Parliament or other organs); main principles and criteria which the government has to follow when exercising delegated legislative functions; the period of time within which the government can exercise the power.

In practice, however, legislation delegated to the government has sometimes more than one object (such as in the case of the implementation of a plurality of EU directives) and rather vague and uncertain criteria and principles. Sometimes, on the contrary, the latter are so detailed that they almost look like the final text of the legislative decrees to be passed by the executive. In order to limit the praxis of delegating laws containing vague and uncertain criteria and principles, Article 16*bis*, paragraph 6*bis* of the Standing Order of the Chamber of deputies, provides that the Committee for legislation is bound to express its own evaluation about delegated laws passed by the government, as concerns their homogeneity, clearness and simplicity.

Article 14, second paragraph, of Law No. 400/1988 provides that the government should transmit the text of legislative decrees to the President of the Republic for promulgation at least twenty days before the end of the delegation period.

In practice, delegating laws have often imposed other obligations (not mentioned by Article 76 of the Constitution) that the government was to fulfil before being able to issue delegated decrees. One of these was the need to ask for the advice of the competent parliamentary committees or other, even ad hoc, bodies on the text of the decree, before the final decision of the Council of Ministers. As a general rule, anyway, whenever legislative delegation lasts over two years, the government is obliged to ask for advice on the text of delegated decrees to the relevant parliamentary committees (Article 14, fourth paragraph, of Law No. 400/1988).

In principle, the legislative decree is only one expression of the instantaneous character of the legislative function delegated to the government. The rule may, however, be deviated from by the delegation law, which can legitimize the repeated use of legislative decrees under the same delegation bill. The law on government activity also states that 'if the legislative delegation refers to a plurality of distinct objects subject to separate regulation, the Government may exercise it through several subsequent bills for one or more of the aforesaid objects' (Article 14.3 of the said Law No. 400). With the introduction of Article 96*ter* of the Standing Order of the Chamber of Deputies, on request of one-fifth of the members of the Committee which has to express its evaluation about drafts of legislative decrees by the government, these drafts are transmitted to the Committee for legislation so that it can express its evaluation concerning the above-mentioned criteria.

§6. Decree-Laws in the Constitution and in Practice

227. Article 77, second paragraph, of the Constitution provides that the government must issue, on its own responsibility and in exceptional cases of necessity and urgency, 'provisional measures having force of law' (i.e., *decreti legge*, decree-laws). Pursuant to Article 87, fourth paragraph, the latter must be promulgated by the President of the Republic with the name 'of decree-laws and the description, in their preamble, of the circumstances … explaining the reasons why they were issued and stating when the Council of Ministers took the decision' (Article 15(1) Law No. 400/1988).

After being promulgated, decree-laws are immediately published in the Official Gazette and usually come into force on the same or the following day.

Decree-laws lose effect 'as of the date of issue' (*ex tunc*) if they are not passed into law within sixty days of their publication. This is why the government, the very day that the decree is issued, is obliged to lay it before Parliament which, even if it is in recess, must meet within five days to consider the decree.

If the decree is converted into law within sixty days of its publication, the law converting the decree is promulgated and published and enters into force on the same day of its publication, as the law itself usually provides for. If, on the contrary, the decree-law is not converted into law by the Chambers or not within the fixed time limits, it loses its effect.

In the first case, the negative decision of the Chambers, taken before the end of the sixty days, is immediately reported by the President of the Chamber which took the decision to the Minister of Justice, who 'immediately' (the day after the voting) publishes it in the Official Gazette. The decree-law thus loses any effect. In the second case, immediate notice that the decree has lost its effect because the time limit has elapsed is given anyway in the Official Gazette by the Minister of Justice (Article 15, sixth paragraph, of Law No. 400/1988).

If the decree is not passed into law, as stated above, it loses its effects retroactively, namely also those produced during the period in which it was provisionally in force.

Article 77, third paragraph, of the Constitution, however, provides that the Chambers may adopt laws to regulate legal questions arising out of decrees not yet passed into law, even validating the effects already produced by governmental measures (the so-called curative laws of the effects of non-converted decree-laws).

By Law No. 400/1988, Article 15, Parliament explicitly defined and thus confirmed the limits that decree-law are met with within the Italian legal system (*see also* Part I, Chapter 4, §4).

228. The use of decree-laws by the government has become very frequent from the fourth Parliament (1963–1968) and, gradually, their number has so increased that we can say today that there is no matter within the Italian legal system which has not been regulated, at least once, by means of a decree-law. Indeed, to date, the vast majority of primary legislation (meaning laws, regardless of the various legal forms, with the force of the law approved by Parliament) is introduced into the Italian legal system through decree-laws. A significant portion of these, moreover, is converted into law by the Parliament following the Government's submission of so-called maxi-amendments along with a vote of confidence. Essentially, when Parliament is tasked with converting in law a decree-law, at a certain point in the process, the Government prepares an amendment that completely rewrites the text of the decree (which can consolidate hundreds of provisions into a single article) and places a vote of confidence on it. This way, the decree-law is converted with a single vote of confidence. Despite interventions by the Constitutional Court to counter abusive practices related to emergency legislation, as reported below, for example, the use of such practices remains widespread in the Italian legal system, where legislative production appears to have substantially shifted to the Government, to the detriment of the Parliament's position.

In practice, the government has often issued decree-laws without meeting the constitutional requirements of necessity and urgency. As a consequence, Parliament has had to examine an increasing number of converting laws, and it was often unable, partly due to the high number of proposed amendments to the decrees, to approve them within the fixed time limits.

When a decree-law was not ratified by Parliament, the government, at least until the Constitutional Court declared it illegal in its Judgment No. 360/1996, used to issue a new decree-law having an identical text or a text modified according to the amendments proposed or approved by the Chambers when the decree is passed into law. The reiteration of decrees not passed into law has often occurred for over ten times, thus subtracting the Chambers, for a long time, part of their legislative powers.

With Judgment No. 360/1996, the Constitutional Court has stopped this practice by declaring null and void a decree introduced more than once into Parliament, stating in no uncertain terms that 'if there is no new and extraordinary assumption of necessity and urgency, a decree-law having the same contents as another that previously lost its effect because it was not passed into law' is unconstitutional for breach of Article 77. Only on some occasions has the President of the Republic, in his turn, refused to promulgate decree-laws that, in his opinion, were neither extraordinary nor urgent.

§7. Conversion of Decree-Laws

229. Converting laws are made up of only one section and must be examined by the Chambers according to their Standing Orders which provide that these bills be included in the Chambers' schedule under particular conditions and actually establish easier examination procedures. For this reason, the government often makes use of decrees to take advantage of the 'fast track' reserved for them and to obtain a quick parliamentary approval of the proposals for reform supposedly more contrasted and controversial.

The attempt to curb the government's tendency to issue a high number of decrees was based on the Standing Orders too. Since 1981 (as regards the Chamber of Deputies) and 1982 (as regards the Senate), before starting to examine a converting bill on its merit, the Chambers were obliged to pronounce their opinions on the existence of the constitutional requirements of necessity and urgency of the bill separately.

In practice, however, these measures did not stop the government from issuing decree-laws since the standards used by the Chambers when considering the bills were mainly political, thus aimed at supporting or opposing the government, depending on the occasion.

230. The Chamber of Deputies, after amendment of Article 96*bis* of its Standing Orders in September 1997, no longer requires the examination by the Committee on Constitutional Affairs and the decision as to the existence of constitutional requirements for the decrees is only left to the full House. The same has been decided for the Senate in 2017, amending Article 78 of the Standing Orders.

The Chamber of Deputies, anyway, always entrusts the examination of converting bills to the Committee on legislation for an opinion on the matter of the decree, as well as on the respect of the limits set out in Article 15 of Law No. 400/1988. The same has been decided for the Senate in 2017.

231. During the examination of the converting bill, the government itself and the groups forming the majority frequently propose amendments to the text of the decree. Parliament, as a consequence, has often passed converting laws having very different contents with respect to the document initially submitted by the government. In this case as well, but once again unsuccessfully, the Standing Orders were used to try to discourage MPs from proposing amendments, especially if unconnected with the object of the decree.

Doubts were raised as to the effects of amendments made to decrees during their conversion: Article 15, fifth paragraph, of Law No. 400/1988 provides that amendments to the text of the decree start to be effective when converting law comes into force (*ex nunc*), unless the converting law itself provides differently. In any case, the amendment to the decree-law cannot be retroactive if such retroactivity is unreasonable.

§8. Political Orientation and Control of Government Activities by Parliament: Non-legislative Acts of Political Orientation

232. The Chambers contribute, as well as the government, to the determination of the country's political orientation, first of all by passing laws, especially those through which Parliament performs its functions in compliance with the Constitution, such as amnesty and indult laws (Article 79), laws authorizing the ratification of international treaties (Article 80) and laws by which the budgets are approved (Article 81).

The Chambers, however, also adopt non-legislative acts of political orientation, aimed at influencing the decisions. The most important acts of this kind are motions, resolutions and other 'political guidelines' called '*ordini del giorno*' (literally: 'orders of the day').

Motions can be voted upon only by the full House. By means of these motions, each Chamber expresses its opinions about the government's political orientation and obliges the latter to comply with them or carry out specific activities.

Resolutions, unlike motions, can be voted upon by both the full House and the committees. They can be submitted by every single MP and are usually voted upon by the full House after the debate that follows 'communications to the Chambers by the President of the Council', i.e., every time the executive is asked or is willing to illustrate its plans and future developments of its political actions (*see* Part II, Chapter 5, §5).

Resolutions aimed at promoting governmental initiatives can also be adopted by the relevant committees, even upon presentation to the Chambers of popular petitions, and after the examination of the decisions of the Constitutional Court, which are always transmitted to the two branches of Parliament.

Pursuant to parliamentary Standing Orders, the Chambers or the committees can also express their opinions or suggestions to the executive by means of 'political guidelines'. These requests anticipate or are subsidiary to the contents of various decisions (such as motions and sections of a bill). 'Political guidelines' make it possible to understand the criteria of enforcement of the main resolution to which they are connected. 'Political guidelines' can be voted upon or simply accepted by the government, sometimes with a low degree of political engagement if considered as 'recommendations'.

§9. Parliamentary Control on the Government's Political Activities

233. The ways for Parliament to control government activities include questions (the easiest and most commonly used). Questions are addressed in writing to Ministers having jurisdiction over a certain matter in order to learn which measures the executive intends to take in relation to a specific event. The Presidents of the Chambers must verify if the question can be addressed. The government reply (in the person of a Minister or a deputy Minister) can be given in writing or orally and, if the second form is chosen, before the full House or the relevant committee, depending on what was specified by the MP who put the question. In the case of oral reply, the MP can say whether he or she is satisfied or not with the reply. The government can refuse to reply to a specific question or ask that the reply be postponed, giving reasons for it.

Pursuant to parliamentary Standing Orders, some of the meetings of the full House and of the committees of the Chamber of Deputies must be dedicated to questions with immediate reply (question time) made by MPs belonging to the different groups, by turns, on general subjects that are particularly urgent or topical from a political point of view. When these meetings take place at the Chamber of Deputies, the Standing Orders provide for television broadcasting and the intervention of the President or Vice-President of the Council of Ministers and, in any case, of the Ministers having jurisdiction. After the illustration of the questions, the government's representative is given a few minutes to reply to each question, and the persons who put the question can briefly reply in their turn.

234. The *interpellanza* consists, on the contrary, in a question by an MP to the government asking the latter to explain the reasons or intentions of its political action on particularly important or general questions.

The *interpellanza* is different from the other questions because of its political-institutional nature since it urges the government to account for its actions in fields in which its political orientation finds expression.

The difference between the *interpellanza* and the other questions seems very obvious in the Standing Orders but is not so clear in practice. Both methods are often used contemporaneously to enquire about specific issues.

The *interpellanze* are first of all illustrated by the MPs who submit them. After the reply of the government's representative, the MPs may say whether they are satisfied with it or not. Pursuant to Article 138 of the Standing Orders of the Chamber of Deputies, if the MPs are not satisfied with the government's reply, they can file a 'motion', thus fostering further debate on the question so as to get the Chamber to take an official decision.

The Standing Orders of the Chamber of Deputies allow government's members not only to postpone the reply but also to not give any reply at all to the *interpellanze* giving reasons for it. Provision was made in the Chamber of Deputies, as well as in the Senate for a number of MPs to submit urgent *interpellanze*, which are rapidly placed on the agenda.

235. Pursuant to Law No. 14/1978, the government should ask for the Chamber's advice before providing for appointment or recommendations of the designation of Presidents and Vice-Presidents of public bodies and agencies, even operating in the economic sector. Parliamentary advice, which is not binding for the government, is given in the two Chambers by the relevant committee and must be motivated. The government shall notify the Chambers of the nominations or recommendations, giving reasons for them.

§10. PARLIAMENTARY ENQUIRIES

236. Article 82 of the Constitution provides that each Chamber may order enquiries 'into matters of public interest'. To this end, it appoints special committees of enquiry so composed as to reflect the proportions among the various political groups.

Each Chamber may, therefore, order enquiries autonomously, by voting special motions. In practice, however, the Chambers have frequently passed special laws setting up Bicameral Committees of Enquiry. Once set up, these Committees may autonomously raise (or resist in) a conflict of power before the Constitutional Court.

Enquiries may serve the purpose of investigating the behaviour of State agencies more thoroughly and giving a political evaluation of the matter but also gathering information that the Chambers deem useful to carry out their legislative activity or other kinds of activities.

It must be noted, however, that proposals to set up committees of enquiry follow the same rules governing the formation of laws in both Chambers. Decisions concerning these committees, therefore, are always taken by the majority, although the government, according to the Standing Orders, cannot raise the 'question of confidence' on them.

237. Article 82, second paragraph, provides that the committees of enquiry carry out their investigating activities with the same powers and the same limitations as judicial authorities. This may result in interference between the committee of enquiry and criminal judges if they both investigate the same facts, though with different objectives. Some committees of enquiry, for instance, investigated and still investigate, sometimes permanently, since they are changed with every new Parliament, the terrorist bombings that occurred in the past or organized crime (they are called Anti-Mafia Committees). Sometimes, the committees of enquiry enjoy even more investigating powers than judicial authorities.

Academic commentators are divided on the constitutionality of such provisions. The Constitutional Court stated that the committees are obliged to transmit all the documents in their possession to the judicial authorities if these documents regard facts that the latter are investigating (*see* Judgment No. 231/1975). In order to prevent such interference prejudicing the achievement of the different objectives of the criminal enquiry and the parliamentary one, the Constitutional Court, in solving a conflict of powers, has imposed the two powers to act in accordance with the principle of loyal cooperation (*see* Judgment No. 26/2008).

Neither the Constitution nor the Standing Orders provide for a procedure of examination of the conclusions reached by the committees of enquiry. Their activity, therefore, ends when they submit a report and, if necessary, one or more minority reports to the Chambers. These reports do not necessarily entail a parliamentary debate.

§11. Parliamentary Hearings

238. The two Houses have more general powers of collecting information. Pursuant to their Standing Orders, the Chambers, and the committees in particular, may order hearings aimed at gathering all the necessary information to fulfil their institutional tasks. Parliamentary hearings, unlike enquiries, are exclusively aimed at gathering information. Therefore, the committees charged with these hearings cannot exercise coercive powers on anybody but only invite them to cooperate spontaneously with Parliament.

In order to gather useful information for parliamentary activities, the committees and the full Houses can ask the advice of specialized bodies such as the National Council of Economy and Labour and the Court of Accounts on the matters lying within their jurisdiction.

239. Parliamentary Standing Orders also allow Standing Committees to order the convening and hearing of Ministers, officials and directors of the agencies subject to government's control. Members of the executive must provide the committees with the information required and can also be invited to account for, even in writing, the enforcement of laws, 'political guidelines', motions, resolutions voted upon by the Chambers or accepted by the government. The same applies to state officials and managers.

§12. Links Between the Chambers, the EU and Other International Organizations

240. Provision was made in both Chambers for committees charged with giving advice and promoting debates on the EU activities and measures and on the implementation of the latter (*see* Law No. 234/2012) and of international agreements in general.

This allows Parliament to participate in the taking and implementation of the decisions of the EU, also by directing and controlling the European policies adopted by the government. At present, both in the Senate and in the Chamber of Deputies, there is a Standing Committee on EU Policy.

Both committees examine, in a reporting capacity, the European Delegations Bill (*Legge di delegazione europea*) which the government must present to Parliament within 28 of February of every year; they also examine the annual reports drawn up by the government on the Italian participation to EU and write their own reports for the full House.

The European delegation law, pursuant to Article 30 of Law No. 234/2012, contains:

1. provisions granting the Government legislative delegation exclusively for the transposition of European directives and framework decisions into national legislation, excluding any other legislative delegation provisions not directly related to the transposition of European legislative acts;
2. provisions granting the Government legislative delegation, aimed at amending or repealing existing state provisions, limited to what is necessary to ensure the conformity of national legislation with reasoned opinions addressed to Italy by the European Commission pursuant to Article 258 of the Treaty on the Functioning of the European Union or the judgments of non-compliance issued by the Court of Justice of the European Union;
3. provisions authorizing the Government to transpose directives through statutory instruments;
4. legislative delegation to the Government for the enforcement of penalties for violations of European Union legislative acts;
5. legislative delegation to the Government, limited to what is necessary to implement provisions not directly applicable contained in European regulations;
6. provisions that, in matters falling within the legislative competence of regions and autonomous provinces, grant delegation to the Government to issue legislative decrees establishing criminal sanctions for the violation of European Union provisions transposed by regions and autonomous provinces;
7. provisions identifying the fundamental principles within which regions and autonomous provinces exercise their legislative competence to transpose or ensure the implementation of European Union acts in matters referred to in Article 117, paragraph 3, of the Constitution;
8. provisions authorizing the Government to issue consolidated texts for the reorganization and harmonization of sectoral regulations while respecting the competences of regions and autonomous provinces; legislative delegation to the Government for the adoption of supplementary and corrective provisions to legislative decrees. The European Delegations Bill, in summary, authorizes the government to enforce the European laws whose enforcement has to be made by statutory instruments. For the enforcement of the other European laws, the government should present to the Parliament another bill, called 'European Bill'. The European law contains provisions for the direct implementation aimed at ensuring the alignment of national legislation with European regulations, particularly in cases of incorrect transposition of European legislation.

As stipulated in Article 30, paragraph 3 of Law No. 234/2012, the European law bill includes provisions aimed at remedying the incorrect transposition of EU legislation into national law, in cases where the Government has acknowledged the validity of objections raised by the European Commission in the context of infringement procedures or pre-infringement procedures. European law may provide for: (a) amendments to state laws subject to infringement procedures against Italy (or judgments of the European Court of Justice); (b) provisions to ensure the implementation of EU acts; (c) the implementation of international treaties concluded within the framework of the Union's external relations.

European law can also include the repeal and modification of laws conflicting with Italy's obligations stemming from its EU membership. Finally, it outlines the conditions for the exercise of the State's substitution power against the Regions that fail to implement EU legislative acts within their areas of competence and do not carry out the implementation and execution of international agreements and EU acts.

Law No. 234/2012 also provides that the Chambers are regularly informed about judicial proceedings and judgments of the Court of Justice concerning Italy, as well as the financial flows between Italy and EU.

The amendments made by the Lisbon Treaty provided, among other things, that at European level, National Parliaments ensure compliance with the principle of subsidiarity on the part of the Union's institutions in preparing the EU legislation. The procedures will have to be governed through specific amendments of the Houses' Standing Orders. Anyway, pursuant to Law No. 234/2012, the government must give adequate and timely information to the Chambers about European legislative initiatives.

Chapter 5. The Executive

by Giovanni Guiglia

§1. The Government: Introduction

241. The term 'Government' has different meanings in Italian legal literature; it indicates *stricto sensu* the supreme body of the executive power.

Part II, Title III, of the Italian Constitution in force, specifically concerns the government. Section I regards the Council of Ministers and starts with Article 92, paragraph 1, which provides that 'the Government of the Republic consists of the Prime Minister and of the Ministers, jointly constituting the Council of Ministers'. Thus, the Constitution defines the basic structure of the government framework, which is essentially identified with the Council of Ministers.

242. In addition to Section I ('Council of Ministers': Articles 92–96), Title III includes two other sections: Section II (Articles 97–98), that deals with the 'Public Administration', and Section III (Articles 99–100), that regards the 'Auxiliary Bodies', even if none of these are part of the constitutional structure of the government. It is this latest feature that confirms the variety of meanings attributable to the term 'Government' in the Italian legal language. Indeed, the Government is often identified with another term – 'the Cabinet', a synonym not to be confused with the recently established Cabinet Council, which consists of the Prime Minister and a limited number of Ministers and cooperates with the Council of Ministers, even if it has a distinct nature (as afterwards explained).

243. This chapter focuses on those government bodies explicitly defined in the Constitution and consequently essential, and on the bodies not entrenched in the Constitution but established on the grounds of praxis and custom or by law, and referred to as additional, contingent or optional.

The *essential government bodies* are:

- the Prime Minister;
- the Ministers;
- the Council of Ministers.

The *additional bodies of government* are:

- the Vice-Presidents of the Council of Ministers;
- the Ministers without Portfolio;
- the Undersecretaries of State, some of whom can be vested with the competences of Vice Ministers;
- the High Commissioners;
- the Special Government Commissioners;
- the Ministerial Committees and the Interdepartmental Committees;
- the Cabinet Council.

The principle of *government self-organization* has long played an important role in the Italian constitutional system, allowing a remarkable degree of structural flexibility.

This is mainly because for forty years, from 1948 to 1988, the last paragraph of Article 95 of the Constitution, which states that 'the law contemplates regulations concerning the Presidency of the Council of Ministers and establishes the number, the responsibilities and the organization of the various Ministries', was not implemented. Law No. 400/1998 entitled 'Rules on government activity and organization of the Presidency' has partly dissipated the doubts about power-sharing among government bodies and, more notably, has regulated their structure, thus contributing to the rationalization of praxis, convention and customs. Many bills dealt with the number of Ministries and their attributions and organization, starting in the previous decades; for example, *see*: Legislative Decree No. 300/1999; Decree-Law No. 217/2001, converted to Law No. 317/2001; Decree-Law No. 181/2006, converted to Law No. 233/2006; Law No. 244/2007; Law No. 172/2009; Decree-Law No. 195/2009, converted to Law No. 26/2010; Law No. 71/2013; Law No. 125/2014; Decree-Law No. 86/2018, converted to Law No. 97/2018; Decree-Law No. 104/2019, converted to Law No. 132/2019; Decree-Law No. 1/2020, converted to Law No. 12/2020 Decree-Law No. 22/2021, converted to Law No. 55/2021; Decree-Law No. 173/2022, converted to Law No. 204/2022.

§2. Structure

I. Essential Organs: The Council of Ministers

244. The analysis of the essential organs of the government starts with the *collegiate body* of government that consists of the President of the Council of Ministers and Ministers, including Ministers without Portfolio. According to the abovementioned design, its composition is strictly delivered by the Constitution. Other public officials may attend or participate in the meetings of the Council but are not eligible to vote. On the contrary, the Presidents of the Special Regions (Sicily, Sardinia, Valle d'Aosta, Trentino-Alto Adige and Friuli-Venezia Giulia) *must* be invited to participate in the meetings of the Council of Ministers whenever an issue regarding a regional specific interest is discussed. Similarly, pursuant to the provisions of the Statute of Trentino-Alto Adige, the Presidents of the Special Provinces of Trento and Bolzano are admitted to the sittings of the Council too. The statutes of these Special Provinces or Regions, adopted by a constitutional law, legitimize the participation of these representatives in the meetings of the Council of Ministers.

A particular role is played by the Undersecretary of State of the Presidency of the Council of Ministers whose main responsibility is to act as Secretary of the Council of Ministers and therefore attends all meetings of the Council. Law No. 400/1988 and the internal regulation of the Council of Ministers (Decree of the President of the Council of Ministers of 10 November 1993) laid down the long-existing procedure, which dated back to the Albertine Statute (*Statuto Albertino*). This procedure has been established over time, although in contrast with Royal Decree No. 466/1901 which delivers that the youngest Minister should act as Secretary.

Other authorities may also attend the meetings of the Council, although no regulation is provided in this respect. These concern, for example, Secretaries of State, High Commissioners, Special Government Commissioners, who are invited to intervene on grounds of their specialist knowledge of a given subject matter on the Council's agenda. Law No. 81/2001 allows the position of Vice Minister for up to a maximum of ten Undersecretaries of State. Vice Ministers can attend the Council of Ministers in order to refer to issues to which they are delegated when invited to do so by the Premier in agreement of the Minister in question. It is clear, however, that attendance of persons other than Ministers cannot alter the structure of the Council since they are not eligible to vote.

245. Law No. 400/1988 provides for the *competence of the Council of Ministers*, in particular in Article 2. The first paragraph of this article states that the Council of Ministers fixes the *general line of government policy* and the *administrative policy* necessary to implement it.

The Council is also called upon to deliberate on 'any matter concerning the general policy of government for which the Chambers have expressed their confidence'. The last section of this paragraph provides a definitive solution to the old-time debate on the body in charge for settling 'conflicts of powers among Ministers', namely the Council. In so doing, the competence of this collegiate body has also been confirmed. Indeed, although entrenched in Royal Decree No. 466/1901, during the fascist period Law No. 2263/1925 has relocated this power to the Prime Minister.

Article 2(2), which should be read in conjunction with Article 2(3)(*a*) and Article 5(1)(*b*), dealing with the responsibilities of the President of the Council of Ministers, provides for the competence of the Council of Ministers with regard to a *confidence vote*'s proposal and the relating procedure (*see* Part II, Chapter 6). The Council of Ministers should approve the proposal of the President of the Council. The announcements to be delivered in Parliament concerning the matter for which a vote of confidence is requested must also be agreed upon by the President of the Council.

Article 3(2) provides a list of subject matters on which the Council is called upon to deliberate. It is submitted that the Council of Ministers deliberates on all statements concerning the political agenda, the programmes and the matters for which the government requires the confidence of Parliament, as explained above (Article 2(3)(*a-q*)). This list also includes:

- draft legislation and proposals for the withdrawal of legislation already submitted to Parliament;
- decrees having the force of law and regulations to be issued as Decree of the President of the Republic;
- measures providing for orientation and coordination of the administrative activity resulting from Article 127 of the Constitution and the special status of Regions and of the Provinces of Trento and Bolzano, except for the Special Regions Sicily and Valle d'Aosta (*see* Constitutional Court, Judgment No. 408/1998);
- guidelines provided by government commissioners, in carrying out administrative duties as delegated to Regions;

- proposals made by the Minister concerned to fulfil the duties falling within the competence of regional governments whenever they need to be replaced due to persistent inactivity in the exercise of delegated functions to be performed within mandatory time limits or whenever rendered necessary by the nature of the interventions;
- proposals to raise conflicts of powers between government and Special Regions and Provinces of Trento and Bolzano/Bozen;
- guidelines concerning international policy and the EU law, draft treaties and draft international agreements irrespective of their political or military nature;
- measures regulating relations between the State and the Catholic Church (Article 7 of the Constitution), which are in turn regulated by the Lateran Pacts;
- measures concerning the relations between the State and religious faiths other than Catholicism (Article 8 of the Constitution);
- measures to be adopted as decree issued by the President of the Republic, subject to the advice of the Council of State, whenever the Minister concerned refuses to conform to such advice;
- reasoned requests for filing of decrees by the *Corte dei conti* (Court of Auditors) pursuant to Article 25 of Royal Decree No. 1214/1934;
- proposals for the dissolution of Regional Councils;
- all measures for which the President of the Council of Ministers considers necessary a Council's decision.

It should be pointed out that the list of measures on which the Council of Ministers should decide is to be considered a definite, and, by no means, an exemplifying list (Article 2(4), Law No. 400/1988).

Article 3 of Law No. 400/1988 provides that the Council of Ministers is also responsible for appointing the chairmen of national bodies, institutions or companies falling within the competence of the Public Administration, with the exception of public lending institutions.

246. The President of the Council of Ministers convenes the Council, determines the meeting agenda and superintends work. Recently, the Council Standing Orders, adopted by the Decree of the President of the Council of Ministers of 10 November 1993, grant the Prime Minister broad discretionary powers on such matters. No mention is made of the structural quorum, i.e., the number of members officially necessary to make a meeting legally valid, and the functional quorum, i.e., the number of votes necessary to take decisions during a meeting. Consequently, the role of the Premier is visibly enhanced both at political and constitutional levels. In determining the voting procedure, the Prime Minister can indeed decide that for some decisions the Council must deliberate unanimously, thus subordinating the existence of government to this prerequisite.

In practice, however, resolutions are rarely subjected to vote, and the Council usually decides unanimously, putting off controversial decisions. This emphasizes the strong collegial nature of the Italian government system.

Starting from the XIV Legislature, it is showing an increasing adoption of voting procedures in the Council of Ministers, consisting in the use of majority, and generating divergences among the Ministers and the political forces of the parliamentary majority.

247. It is worth noting that the Standing Order requires that matters and proposals concerning draft legislation, legal provisions and general administrative measures are examined in preparatory meetings of the Council of Ministers. This is a sine qua non for including the issues in the agenda of the Council of Ministers' meeting. The preparatory meetings are usually coordinated by the Undersecretary/ Secretary of the Council and are attended by senior ministerial officials and by the Presidency of the Council.

II. The President of the Council of Ministers

248. For a better understanding of the role of the second essential body of government, i.e., the President of the Council of Ministers or the Prime Minister, we need to take a brief look at the pre-fascist experience of the constitutional monarchy in Italy when a parliamentary monarchy was in place. At this time, the role of Prime Minister was not constitutionally autonomous; he chaired the Council but was substantially like any other Minister and had no special powers. This is indicated by the fact that he was also often responsible for the Ministry of the Interior. His degree of authority depended essentially on his political weight. Royal Decree No. 466/1901 regulated the responsibilities of the Prime Minister, while those of the Ministers were stipulated in the laws establishing the Ministries or in other acts subsequently adopted on this matter.

249. During the fascist period, the role of the Premier was visibly strengthened. He was renamed 'Head of Government', enjoyed significant key powers in terms of the workings of Parliament and was also the *Duce del fascismo* (Duce of the Fascism) and supreme head of the Fascist Party (subsequently a State institution).

250. The Republican Constitution restored the parliamentary model, while still acknowledging a greater political and institutional role to the Prime Minister as compared to the other Ministers. According to the Constitution, the Prime Minister conducts and is responsible for the general policy of government for which he is therefore accountable. The Prime Minister also promotes and coordinates the activities of the Ministers so as to maintain unity in their general political and administrative activities (Article 95).

As to the structure of government, the Constitution provides for the *monocratic principle* whereby the Prime Minister conducts the general government policy and proposes the appointment of Ministers; the *collegiate principle* whereby government is jointly accountable and responsible for the most important political decisions such as the adoption of government bills and decrees; and the *principle of ministerial autonomy* where Ministers are responsible for any acts adopted in the exercise of their respective Ministries. Due to the decade-long lack of specific legislation dealing with the Presidency of the Council (Article 95 of the Constitution), and in particular, the number, responsibilities and organization of the Ministries, and given the influence of coalition governments and the de facto power of the political parties, governance practice has favoured the consolidation of the autonomy of the single Ministries, whereas the role of the Prime Minister, often caught between contrasting political needs and interests, has lacked a clear and autonomous role. The Presidency of the Council retained some specific administrative functions, while other cross-departmental functions were assigned to Ministers without Portfolio, i.e., responsible for Ministries not explicitly provided by law. Furthermore, the Constitution has not explicitly resolved the question of whether the Head of State has the power to withdraw the authority of a Minister on the proposal of the Prime Minister; and indeed, this is still a matter of today's debates, together with the question concerning the revocation of the same Prime Minister.

251. A reorganization of the government system only took place in the last twenty years when Law No. 400/1988 and Legislative Decree No. 303/1999 regulated and reformed the organization of the Presidency of the Council and the competences of the Council of Ministers, as well as the rule-making activity of government. Similarly, Legislative Decree No. 300/1999, carrying out the legislative proxy provided for by Article 11 Law No. 59/1997, and Decree No. 217/2001 (converted into Law No. 317/2001) have reorganized the remaining government structure, reducing the number of the Ministries from eighteen to twelve, then up to fourteen. The Law by Decree No. 181/2006, now Law No. 233/2006, brought the number of Ministries again to eighteen. Finally, Article 1, paragraph 376, of Law No. 244/2007 (Financial Act 2008) establishes that from the first Government of the XVI Legislature (i.e., after the II Prodi Government, that is, the IV Berlusconi Government), Ministries should be reduced to twelve. During the IV Government of Berlusconi, Law No. 172/2009 brought Ministries to thirteen. By Decree-Law No. 1/2020, converted to Law No. 12/2020, the number of Ministries has been elevated to fourteen, until Draghi's Government, by Decree-Law No. 22/2021, converted to Law No. 55/2021, increased the number to fifteen, transforming the Ministry for the Environment into the Ministry for the Ecological Transition and establishing a special Ministry for Tourism, whose area of concern previously belonged to the Ministry for Culture. In the Meloni Government, the number of Ministries remains unchanged, although with Decree-Law No. 173/2022, converted to Law No. 204/2023, the attributions of some of them have been rearranged, and some of their denominations have been changed, therefore amending Legislative Decree No. 300/1999.

252. The responsibilities of the Prime Minister are strictly linked to the government's general policy activity and to the need to maintain unity in overall political and administrative activities so that 'the Prime Minister is responsible for providing political and administrative guidelines to the Ministers for the implementation of the decisions of the Council of Ministers, as well as those guidelines concerning the responsibility of the Prime Minister for conducting general government policy'. It should be noted, however, that there are no provisions regulating either the duties of Ministers in their relations with the Prime Minister or the precise mandatory nature of the presidential guidelines. Instead, Article 5(2)(*a*) of Law No. 400/1988 states that the Prime Minister provides political and administrative guidelines to Ministers but does not imply that they are obliged to follow them. First, because the relations between the Prime Minister and Ministers are not hierarchical. Second, because the infringement of the Prime Minister's guidelines does not entail special sanctions. Third, because guidelines are merely an instrument to achieve the objectives set by the coalition partners, at the time they entered into a government agreement.

This means that a Minister may not conform to a guideline on grounds of its political interpretation, i.e., insofar as it is not conducive to unity in general political activities, as established in the coalition agreement. It is evident that the effectiveness of the guidelines depends on the judgment of single Ministers. In contrast to the past, when Ministers were real 'delegates' of their respective government parties, they are now keen political representatives who will try to steer government action as near as possible to their own political line, so as to make their party more visible within the coalition and, even more important, before the electorate.

Ministers usually work in accordance with their own political party objectives rather than with the Cabinet as a whole or the President of the Council even when the coalition in power is composed of a relatively small number of parties. This trend is strengthened when party leaders are part of the Cabinet.

253. However, possible contrasts between the Prime Minister and the Minister may need an 'out-of-government settlement', namely during ad hoc meetings with the leaders of the coalition parties, despite the tenor of Article 5(2) of Law No. 400/1988 states that the Prime Minister has the following competences:

– the promotion and coordination of the activities of Ministers with respect to measures of general government policy;
– the suspension of the adoption of measures by the Ministers based on political and administrative grounds which are on the agenda of the meeting of the Council of Ministers;
– in cases of disagreement among government bodies responsible, albeit in different ways, for adopting measures, the Prime Minister can submit the controversial issue to the Council of Ministers for a comprehensive evaluation and a harmonization of the public interests involved and entrust the Council with a decision (Article 12(2), Legislative Decree No. 303/1999); and
– agreement with Ministers on their official statements whenever the latter are likely to affect general government policy because they exceed their ordinary jurisdiction.

Equally important are the responsibilities of the Prime Minister in the name of the government (Article 5(1), Law No. 400/1988):

– the notification of the composition of government as well as any possible reform of the Chambers;

- requesting a vote of confidence – either personally or by delegating a Minister – on proposals concerning the implementation of the general government policy;
- the submission of laws to the President of the Republic for promulgation;
- the submission of draft legislation to the President of the Republic before presenting them to Parliament, as well as decrees having the force of law and government regulations for promulgation;
- countersigning decrees by which laws are promulgated as well as any measure put to the vote of the Council of Ministers, acts having the force of law and, together with the proposing Minister, any other act as explicitly provided for by law;
- presenting draft government legislation to Parliament, also through the delegated Minister, and exercises the powers of government with regard to the legislative procedure to be followed (*see* Article 72 Constitution);
- exercising the powers granted by the legislation in force, with regard to the relations with the Constitutional Court and adjudication of questions of constitutionality as well as of conflicts of powers set by the Court itself (questions of constitutional legitimacy and conflicts of powers; *see* Part II, Chapter 9);
- taking the necessary steps to ensure that government complies with the rulings of the Constitutional Court;
- informing Parliament of controversies pending before the Constitutional Court;
- indicating, either personally or on the proposal of the Ministers concerned, fields where government may legislate with regard to the outstanding cases of constitutional legality.

The following functions are equally relevant, also pursuant to Article 5(2) of Law No. 400/1988:

- guaranteeing the impartiality, the efficiency of Public Administration Offices and carrying out the necessary controls;
- the promotion of the action of Ministers to ensure that public institutions and corporations work according to the objectives set by the laws regulating their autonomy and in line with the general political and administrative policy of government;
- exercising the powers provided by law with regard to national security and State secrecy;
- establishing ad hoc Committees of Ministers which conduct a preliminary examination of issues of shared competence and give their own opinion about the guidelines of government activity as well as on relevant issues to be submitted to the Council of Ministers, possibly involving experts who are not part of the Administration;
- establishing working and study groups in such a way as to represent all the fields of competence of Ministries concerned and possibly involving the opinion of external experts.

Finally, in compliance with Article 5(3) of Law No. 400/1988, the Prime Minister either directly or indirectly via the delegated Minister is responsible for:

- the promotion and coordination of government action with regard to EU policies and ensures a consistent and timely government and public administration action with respect to policy implementation, on which the Prime Minister periodically reports to Parliament (*see also* Article 8 and ff. ones of Law No. 11/2005);
- taking the necessary steps to ensure that government complies with the rulings of the CJEU, through the opportune communication to the Chambers of the above-mentioned rulings in order to allow permanent parliamentary commissions to analyse them; submitting the Parliament an annual relation concerning the steps taken to execute the above-mentioned rulings (Article 1 of Law No. 12/2006);
- the promotion of the enforcement of the judgments of the European Court of Human Rights towards Italy; he shall promptly notify the Chambers of the same decisions for the review by the Permanent Parliamentary Committees and shall submit annually to the Parliament a report on the state of implementation of the above-mentioned judgments;
- providing prompt and precise information to Parliament concerning EU legislative activity as well as the position of government with regard to the same subjects (*see* Article 3 of Law No. 11/2005 too);
- the promotion and coordination of government action concerning the technological innovation, the implementation of the Italian and European digital agenda, the Italian strategy for ultra-broadband, the digitalization of public administrations and businesses, as well as the transformation, growth and digital transition of the country, in the public and private sphere;
- the promotion and coordination of government action concerning the relations with the Autonomous Regions and the Provinces of Trento and Bolzano while supervising the work of government Commissioners.

254. In order to carry out its own duties as well as its initiative, promotion and coordination activities as provided by the Constitution, the Prime Minister can avail himself of the Secretariat General of the Presidency of the Council of Ministers, reorganized in 1999 (Legislative Decree No. 303/1999), and of numerous Departments, Offices and Services. These Departments, Offices and Services can be in the employ of the Secretariat General himself or a Minister without portfolio or a Sub-secretary of State of the Presidency of the Council of Ministers, or they can be retained by the Prime Minister. These organizational decisions can be taken from time to time under the form of decrees of the President of the Council (*see* above paragraph 96), on the basis of his organizational power and in the light of the government programme (*see*, in particular, the Decree of the President of the Council of Ministers 1 October 2012, with its several integrations and modifications, until the recent Decree of the President of the Council of Ministers 3 March 2023).

255. Departments are general management structures comprising various Offices, which may share the same functions and sometimes enjoy almost as much functional autonomy as the Departments (*see*, e.g., the Secretariat Office of the Council of Ministers) and are subdivided into Services, i.e., internal bodies supporting the Departments and the Offices without having general management structures.

The Secretary General is appointed to the General Secretariat of the Presidency of the Council; he has his own Office (*see* Article 32 of the Decree of the President of the Council of Ministers of 1 October 2012) and is assisted by one or more Deputy General Secretaries. The Secretary General is responsible for the operation of the Secretariat, the organization and management of human and instrumental resources of the Presidency of the Council (*see* Decree of the President of the Republic No. 520/1997; Article 7(1) and (3) of Legislative Decree No. 303/1999; Legislative Decree No. 343/2003; Decree of the President of the Council of Ministers 1 October 2012 and its subsequent amendments and additions).

The Prime Minister determines the organization of the Secretariat General whose activity benefits the Ministers delegated by him (Ministers without Portfolio, as subsequently described) and the Undersecretaries of the Presidency of the Council of Ministers.

Therefore, the Prime Minister appoints both the heads of the Offices which cooperate directly with him and those which work with Ministers without portfolio and Undersecretaries of the Presidency of the Council on the basis of their proposal. These appointees stay in charge until the President of the Council or the members of Government with whom they cooperate are in office. As to those bodies for which Ministers or delegated Secretaries of State are responsible, management functions are carried out by government officials and not by the Secretary General of the Presidency. Articles 4 and 14 of Legislative Decree No. 165 of 30 March 2001 govern the relations between the political body and the managerial powers of the government. When a Minister without Portfolio does not manage a Department, the Secretary General of the Presidency coordinates the Head of the same Department (Article 21, Law No. 400/1988).

Furthermore, the Prime Minister determines which offices will cooperate directly with him, which offices will be linked to the Ministers without Portfolio or to the Undersecretaries of the Presidency and determines their composition accordingly. This composition can be modified under proposal of the same Ministers and Undersecretaries interested. In particular, when a Minister without Portfolio manages a Department of the Presidency of the Council of Ministers, the Head of the Department is appointed through a Decree of the Prime Minister in accordance with the proposal of the Minister concerned.

For the performance of specific tasks, for the achievement of specific results or the implementation of specific programmes, the President of the Council establishes specific *Mission Structure* (*see* Article 2(4) Decree of the President of the Council of Ministers 1 October 2012), whose temporary duration is indicated in the decree. In particular, for the organizational support to the Ministers without Portfolio and to the Undersecretaries of the Presidency whose responsibilities or direct reliance are not entrusted to general structures, such *Mission Structures* may be established, at the head of which a Coordinator is appointed (*see* Article 7(4) of Legislative Decree No. 303/1999).

In case of tasks requiring the cooperation of more Departments or Offices (comparable to Departments), the Prime Minister can establish by decree specific *Units of interdepartmental coordination* (*see* Article 7(4*bis*) of Legislative Decree No. 303/1999). The organization of these Units is regulated by decree of the Secretary

General. In the same way, the resources that they use are identified, and the administrative and accounting measures necessary for their operation are adopted (*see* Article 4(2) by the Decree of the President of the Council of Ministers 1 October 2012).

256. The Prime Minister is supported by the work of the Secretary General of the Presidency of the Council, particularly in the exercise of the following staff and integrated functions (Article 2, Legislative Decree No. 303/1999):

- management and relations with the Council of Ministers;
- relations between government and Parliament and between government and other constitutional organs;
- relations between government and European institutions;
- relations between central and local government (Regions, Provinces and Communes);
- relations between government and religious denominations (Articles 7–8 of the Constitution);
- general policy planning and general political decision-making activity;
- coordination of governmental rule-making activities;
- coordination of governmental administrative activity and internal supervision systems;
- promotion and coordination of equal opportunities policies and of government activities in view of preventing and eliminating discrimination;
- coordination of the institutional communication activities of government;
- promotion and evaluation of innovative measures in the public sector and coordination in the field of public works;
- coordination of key government sector policies; and
- evaluation of the implementation of general and sectoral government general policies.

Overall, Legislative Decree No. 303/1999 has rationalized the previous administrative organization and introduced important innovations to improve the efficiency of the Departments and Offices of the Presidency, mainly in terms of the *flexibility principle*. This has allowed for a more comprehensive implementation of Article 95(3) of the Constitution stating that the law contemplates regulations concerning the structure of the Presidency of the Council. Legislative Decree No. 303/1999 – like Law No. 400/1988 – did not limit itself to rationalization, in accordance with the flexibility principle. Instead, it went further to cover the principles of '*speciality*' and '*exclusiveness*'. In this way, the objective, supported by enlightened academic commentators, of regulating the relations between the different bodies of the Presidency by law (i.e., the *rationalization principle*) has been achieved. Similarly, the need for a special, i.e., 'atypical', body of the Presidency as compared to ordinary governmental bodies has been satisfied, and those functions, which do not fall under the competence of the Prime Minister, have been eliminated among the duties of the Presidency. With regard to this, it is necessary to underline that at least eight structures (i.e., Departments and Offices) have been transferred to specific agencies or the Ministries boasting the most similar competencies. Therefore, from the XIV Legislature (2001), the Presidency of the Council of Ministers started having a simpler structure aimed at dealing with the activities that are more coherent with the institutional role of the Prime Minister (management, impulse, trend and coordination). This process led to Law No. 3/2003, followed by several normative and administrative measures to give the Presidency of the Council of Ministers structures already operating by the Ministries (*see*, e.g., the Law by Decree No. 181/2006, then converted into Law No. 233/2006, and the Decree of the Prime Minister of 22 October 2007); however, these structures made the organization heavy again.

257. Nonetheless, the organization pattern which can be derived from Law No. 400/1988, Legislative Decree No. 303/1999 and Decree of the President of the Council of Ministers 1 October 2012, recently amended and supplemented by Decree of the President of the Council of Ministers 3 March 2023, is not exhaustive (in spite of the above-mentioned measures), since the Secretariat General of the Presidency of the Council does not merely provide instrumental support to the work of the Prime Minister but also supports the activities of the Ministers without Portfolio and the Undersecretaries of the Presidency. The elimination of certain operational and managerial structures within the Presidency of the Council is, however, likely to affect the role of the structures themselves, which will be reduced to the functions delegated to them by the Prime Minister. In this way, they will fit perfectly into the institutional system as defined by the Constitution and by the above-mentioned provisions.

258. To confirm the organizational and functional peculiarities of the Presidency of the Council, finally it could be found the Office of Secretariat of the Council of Ministers, placed under the direct coordination of the Undersecretary to the Presidency of the Council, the Secretary of the Council of Ministers, although the head of the Office has the duty to inform the Secretary General on issues of discussion, on the work of the Council of Ministers and on the deliberations adopted (*see* Article 20 of Law No. 400/1988 and Article 33 of the Decree of the President of the Council of Ministers of 1 October 2012).

III. Ministers

259. Thus, the relations between the Prime Minister and the other essential organs of government – namely the Ministers – have become more complicated. In this section, we examine the role of Ministers with Portfolio, i.e., Ministers heading administrative bodies called *ministeri* or *dicasteri.* Article 95 (last paragraph) of the Constitution stipulates in its second part that 'the law establishes the number, competence and organization of the various Ministries'. Whereas after more than five decades, the legislator reduced the Ministries to thirteen, it has most recently increased to fifteen, as already mentioned:

1. Foreign Affairs and International Cooperation.
2. Interior.

3. Justice (the only Ministry explicitly provided for by the Constitution, Article 107).
4. Defence.
5. Economy and Finance.
6. Enterprises and Made in Italy.
7. Agriculture, Food Sovereignty and Forestry.
8. Environment and Energy Security.
9. Infrastructure and Transport.
10. Labour and Social Policies.
11. Education and Merit.
12. University and Research.
13. Culture.
14. Health.
15. Tourism.

There are two first-level structures among the above-mentioned Ministries: the *General Directorates* that have maintained their traditional internal organization and which mainly reflect the nineteenth-century model of the Kingdom of Piedmont and Sardinia, and the *Departments*. In the Ministries in which the first-level structures include Departments, it is not possible to establish a Secretary General, which must be taken out under previous laws or regulations (Article 1, Legislative Decree No. 287/2002). In other words, each administration has the opportunity to choose its own administrative structure, opting between Departments or General Directorates, and, in this second case, to have or not the Secretary General who is directly managed by the Minister.

Departments are responsible for carrying out tasks concerning comprehensive groups of matters and relevant instrumental tasks, including the orientation and coordination of the units of which Departments are composed, and with the organization and management of instrumental, financial and human resources available to them. A Head of Department will replace the Secretary General for each Ministry, responsible for the coordination, direction and control functions. Whenever the Secretary General is removed from office, his functions are shared among Heads of Departments.

As they are appointed at the head of their respective Ministries, Ministers adopt administrative measures, usually as decree; define goals, priorities, plans and programmes to implement and issue the following general guidelines for administrative management and competence; allocate the resulting financial resources to executives in charge for the Ministry's responsibility centres.

As members of the government, 'even if they are not part of the Chambers', Ministers have the right, and if required, to attend their sessions. They must consult them whenever they ask for it (Article 64(4) of the Constitution).

Some Ministers, as will be stated in this chapter, could be entrusted with the presidium of Committees of Ministers and Interministerial Committees: collegial bodies which consist of several Ministers (but also of officials) mainly addressing tasks and sectoral coordination responsibilities.

260. The reform of the Ministries (Legislative Decree No. 300/1999) has also introduced a new body in the organization of the central government, i.e., the Agency, whose responsibility includes technical and operational tasks of national interest, previously carried out by the Ministries and Public Institutions. Agencies work for the benefit of public government institutions, also at a regional and local level. They enjoy full autonomy, within the limits set by law and are under the supervision of the *Corte dei conti* (Court of Auditors) as well as of Ministers concerned in accordance with their orientation and monitoring powers. They are also autonomous as concerns the balance, within the limits of the funds given under the budget of the competent Ministry. Agencies must achieve the objectives set by Ministers. They are also subject to the adoption of their agenda, of their balances and accounting, as well as to governmental inspections to verify that ministerial guidelines are duly implemented.

The Agencies provided for by Articles 8 and 9 of Legislative Decrees Nos 300/1999 and 303/1999 include for example:

- the Agency for Defence Industries: a public agency with special rights and responsibilities established by law which operates under the aegis of the Ministry of Defence (Articles 20(1)a and 48 of Legislative Decree No. 66/2010), and runs the activities of the productive and industrial units of the Defence (Articles 131–143 of Decree of the President of the Republic No. 90/2010);
- the Information and External Security Agency (IESA), established by Article 6 of Law No. 124/2007, which has the task of seeking and processing all the information useful to defend the independence, integrity and security of the Republic from threats from abroad. In particular, IESA is responsible for the activities of security information that take place outside the national territory to protect the political, military, economic, scientific and industrial interests of Italy; the detection and the punishment of the spy's activities outside of Italy but directed against it, and activities that harm national interests. IESA shall reply to the President of the Council and shall inform the Minister of Defence, the Minister of Foreign Affairs and the Minister of the Interior, in a timely and continuous manner, of matters of their own competence;
- the Information and Internal Security Agency (IISA), established by Article 7 of Law No. 124/2007, which has the task of seeking and processing all the information useful to defend the domestic security of the Republic and the democratic institutions from any threat any subversive activity, and any form of criminal or terrorist aggression. In particular, the IISA, within the national territory, is responsible for the same activities that IESA is required to carry out abroad. IISA also responds to the President of the Council and informs, promptly and continuously, the Minister of the Interior, the Foreign Affairs Minister and the Minister of Defence for matters of their own competence;
- the National Agency for the Administration and the Destination of Goods Seized and Confiscated to Organized Crime, established by Article 1 of Decree-Law No. 4/2010 (converted to Law No. 50/2010) and then confirmed by Legislative Decree No. 159/2011 (*Antimafia Code*), has legal personality under public law and has organizational and accounting autonomy, has its head office in Reggio Calabria and secondary offices in Rome, Palermo, Milan and Naples. It is subject

to the supervision of the Minister of the Interior, and its main task is to provide for the administration and destination of seized and confiscated assets to mafias, following final confiscation. Moreover, it assists the Judicial Administrator, under the direction of the judicial authority, in the seizure phase and up to the confiscation of the first degree, and then takes over the direct management of the goods themselves.

261. In the Italian legal system Ministers are not only appointed as Heads of their relative Ministries. They actively support the activity of the Council of Ministers, which is the collegial body of the government expressly provided for by the Constitution. Their liability, as explained in the following paragraphs, is both individual – as concerns the acts of their Ministries – and collegial, as regards the deliberations of the Council of Ministers.

Besides, pursuant to Article 89 of the Constitution, Ministers countersign the acts issued by the President of the Republics in accordance with their fields of competence and are political (before Parliament) and juridical liable (i.e., at civil, criminal and administrative levels).

262. As members of government and although 'they are not members of the Chambers', Ministers have the right 'and, if requested, the duty' to participate in their sittings. When requested, they have to be heard by the Chambers according to Article 64, last paragraph of the Constitution. As analysed in this chapter, some Ministers can also be appointed as Presidents of Committees of Ministers and Interministerial Committees: i.e., collective bodies including several Ministers (but also officers) with tasks of sectorial line and coordination.

IV. Additional Government Bodies: The Vice-President of the Council of Ministers

263. It is now possible to analyse the numerous range of the so-called additional government bodies, starting with those which are ex officio members of the Council of Ministers, the most important being the Vice-President of the Council of Ministers.

It has been noted that the Vice-President of the Council of Ministers is a common element of many republican governments to a point that some authors have considered it as the result of constitutional custom rather than merely the outcome of practice. It should also be said that, unlike the previous practice where a Minister – either with or without portfolio – was appointed Vice-President by the same decree of appointment of Ministers, Law No. 400/1988 now provides that the assignment of the office of Vice-President to one or more Ministers can be proposed during a meeting of the Council of Ministers. It is evident that this discussion can only take place after the appointment of Ministers, simply because prior to the appointments the Council of Minister does not yet exist. In practice, following the introduction of the law, once the Prime Minister has decided to appoint a Vice-President, he usually submits his proposal during the first meeting of the Council of Ministers. The appointment takes the form of a Decree of the President of the Republic, which subsequently shall be published in the Official Journal. The literal tenor of Article 8 of Law No. 400/1988 may suggest that the appointment is a prerogative of the Prime Minister. However, the Vice-President of the Council of Ministers is substantially a political figure since the appointment is usually subject to specific political agreements whose object is to enhance the participation of one or more parties to government coalition. During the meeting of the Council of Ministers, the Prime Minister usually proposes the appointment to the vice-presidential office of a prominent political leader of a party different from his own; a recent example in this regard is represented by the appointment as Vice-Presidents of the Council Antonio Tajani (FI) and Matteo Salvini (Lega), respectively Minister for Foreign Affairs and International Cooperation and Minister for Infrastructure and Transport, in the government chaired by Giorgia Meloni (FdI), in charge since 22 October 2022.

264. Law No. 400/1988 only refers to the case in which the Prime Minister has to be temporarily replaced, as Article 8 states: 'in case the Prime Minister is temporarily absent or unable to perform his functions'. Using this hypothesis, providing that it is for the Vice-President to deputize for or, if several Vice-Presidents are appointed, the senior one has to be in charge; and also specifying that, when the Vice-President has not been appointed, the deputy is due, in the absence of any other disposition by the President of the Council, to the most senior Minister.

V. Ministers Without Portfolio

265. Ministers without Portfolio constitute the second type of additional organ of government. One of the reasons for their introduction was to combine their role with the functions of the Vice-President of the Council, even if this coalition prevailed in the oldest praxis because of the political impact of the role of Minister without Portfolio. The introduction of Ministers without Portfolio, i.e., Ministers who are not responsible for a Ministry, dates back to 1848 when the *Statuto Albertino* came into force. In the past, Ministers without Portfolio have only been used to allow some coalition parties to enhance their representation within the Council of Ministers, as their vote is equivalent to that of other Ministers.

266. Furthermore, praxis highlights another additional profile of this subject, included in Law No. 400/1988. The Ministers without Portfolio have no sectoral but horizontal functions, which are potentially linked to the general coordination of the activities of the government and assigned to the President of the Council. In fact, Ministers without Portfolio are increasingly described as 'Ministers of the Presidency', i.e., Ministers who directly assist the Premier and are responsible for a number of tasks falling within the jurisdiction of the Prime Minister. In addition, they are often put at the head of the Departments mentioned above, which are part of the Presidency of the Council – thus reinforcing their link with the Prime Minister. This is the case of the Ministers without Portfolio responsible for Public Offices, Regional Affairs, Relations with Parliament and Institutional Reform.

267. Law No. 400/1988 widely considers these Ministers without Portfolio as 'Minister of the Presidency', that is assistant of the President of the Council. In fact, the Law provides for in Article 9 that they are appointed with the same appointing decree of the other Ministers 'by the Presidency of the Council' on the proposal of the President of the Council. They receive a specific appointment by the President of the Council (through this latest's decrees) and can be in charge of Departments and Offices of the Presidency. In particular, the Offices of direct collaboration of the Ministers without portfolio are composed of: (a) Cabinet Office; (b) legislative sector; (c) Special Secretariat; (d) Press Office (*see* Article 6(2) of the Decree of the President of the Council of Ministers of 1 October 2012).

The fact that law has increased the functions of the Ministers of the Presidency has led to the institutionalization of their role. Nonetheless, Article 9 of Law No. 400, recently amended by Decree-Law No. 181/2006 (converted to Law No. 233/2006), provides that 'whenever the law or any other normative instrument assign, even with a proxy, specific functions to a Minister without Portfolio or to specific offices or departments of the Presidency of the Council of Ministers, these functions are intended to be respectively assigned to the President of the Council of Ministers, who can delegate them to a Minister or to a Undersecretary of State, and to the Presidency of the Council of Ministers'.

268. Before examining other additional organs of government, it is worth pointing out that a Minister responsible for a Ministry or the person responsible for governmental functions, such as a Minister without Portfolio may be replaced ad interim by another Minister or by the Prime Minister himself. Although it is not explicitly provided for by the Constitution, in practice, this happens often, but now Law No. 400/1988 (Article 9(4)) regulates this procedure. *Interim* office should not be confused with cases where a Minister heads more than one Ministry or a Member of government has more than one assignment. Ministers ad interim are appointed where there is a vacancy due to the resignation of a Minister or for other causes, whenever the outgoing Minister is not to be replaced permanently, as it happened in the first Conte Government, in which the Ministries of Economic Development and of Labour and Social Policy were entrusted to Luigi Di Maio (M5S). *Interim* office is sometimes used when forming the government for those government offices which are not to be entrusted to a specific person or in case the definitive appointment is to be postponed.

Interim offices are established by Decrees of the President of the Republic, on the proposal of the Prime Minister. Pursuant to Law No. 400/1988, the decrees have to be published in the Official Journal.

VI. Undersecretaries of State and Vice Ministers

269. Undersecretaries of State are also part of the accessory organs of government, although they have existed alongside Ministers since 1888. In the past, they were chosen from among Members of Parliament, which is not always the case today. Although the 1948 Constitution makes no mention of Undersecretaries of State, the number of Undersecretaries has increased radically since the Constitution came into force seventy years ago. Law No. 400/1988 has finally rationalized their role while also introducing some relevant changes (Article 10). They are appointed with a Decree of the President of the Republic, on the proposal of the Prime Minister in agreement with the Minister concerned and after consulting the Prime Minister.

270. Undersecretaries of State have essentially two types of assignments. First, they are entitled to attend sittings in Parliament as well as the meetings of the parliamentary commissions in their capacity as government representatives. They participate in the debates in accordance with the guidelines of their respective Ministers and can be asked to answer questions in Parliament. They are mainly responsible for *political and constitutional representation* as confirmed by Law No. 400/1988, and as stated in Law No. 5195/1888, which established them. Second, they are responsible for carrying out administrative functions, delegated to them by the Minister concerned. Functions are delegated *ad personam*, which means that they are valid only as long as the Minister or government official and the Undersecretary of State remain in office. The handing over of functions is formalized by a ministerial decree – according to the 1888 provisions – which is then registered by the *Corte dei conti* (Court of Auditors) and published in the Official Journal.

Undersecretaries of State do not normally attend the meetings of the Council of Ministers since this is not explicitly provided for by the Constitution. Even when their participation is required, they are not entitled to take part in the decision-making phase and are not eligible to vote. As stated above, the only Undersecretary entitled to attend the meetings of the Council of Ministers is the Undersecretary of State to the Presidency of the Council who acts as Secretary of the Council. He is also the first to be appointed. His appointment is formalized by an ad hoc Decree of the President of the Republic on the proposal of the Prime Minister, and in agreement with the Council of Ministers, and countersigned by the Prime Minister.

In the absence of a specific legal provision, in practice, a procedure akin to that for appointment is required for dismissing an Undersecretary of State, i.e., a Decree of the President of the Republic on the proposal of the Prime Minister and the relevant Minister and in agreement with the Council of Ministries.

As to his responsibilities, the practice of giving the Secretary of State the functions of the Secretary of the Council of Ministers has taken root since the time of the monarchy, thus contravening Article 3 of Royal Decree No. 466/1901 providing that this office was to be held by one of the Ministers. Besides legalizing this practice, Article 4 of Law No. 400/1988 also provides that the Secretary of State concerned is responsible for the minutes of the meetings as well as the filing of the deliberations (*see also* Articles 11–12 of the Standing Orders of the Council of Ministers). The Prime Minister can also decide to delegate a number of functions to this Secretary of State, for example, in the field of national security and State secrecy. Besides, the President of the Council can also delegate him the responsibility for Departments and Offices (Article 20 of Law No. 400/1988). Recently, with the Decree of the President of the Council of Ministers 23 October 2022, the signing of the decrees, acts and measures falling within the competence of the President of the Council in charge was delegated to the Undersecretary/Secretary of the Council of

Ministers, with the exception of those requiring a prior deliberation of the Council of Ministers and those relating to the powers pursuant to Article 5 of Law No. 400/1988.

Politically, the Prime Minister considers the Undersecretary/Secretary of the Council of Ministers as very reliable. In practice, then, he belongs to the same party or political group as the Prime Minister, whereas the other Undersecretaries of State of the Council of Ministers often belong to a different party. In practice, with few recent exceptions, this task has been invariably entrusted to a personality of the same party or political movement of the Prime Minister.

It should also be noted that the other Undersecretaries in the Council's Presidency often belong to parties or political forces other than that of the President of the Council.

271. The Undersecretaries of State are not hierarchically subordinated either to the Prime Minister or to their Minister but simply receive guidelines from the Prime Minister or Minister concerned. They cannot countersign measures of the President of the Republic, which, according to Article 89 of the Constitution, must be countersigned by either Ministers or the Prime Minister. Undersecretaries are legally liable before the ordinary judicial authorities under criminal and civil law.

From a political and institutional point of view, it is worth noting how the number of Undersecretaries of State increased in the past, up to sixty-nine in 1991 during the VII Andreotti Government. However, this number is significantly diminished in the latest decade, mainly due to the duration of the shared system of coalitions. The Law of 1888, which was immediately eluded in practice to a point that, according to the doctrine, constitutional custom tending in the opposite direction became the norm, limited the number of Undersecretaries of State to one per Minister. Law No. 400/1988 has referred the solution of the numerical issue to the law concerning the organization of the various Ministries in accordance with the provisions of Article 95 of the Constitution. Article 1, paragraph 376 of the Financial Act 2008 (Law No. 244/2007) provides that, starting from the subsequent government after the II Prodi Government, that is from the first government of the XVI Legislature (IV Berlusconi Government), 'The total number of the members of the government included Ministers without Portfolio, Vice Ministers and Undersecretaries, cannot exceed sixty subjects.' It was necessary to reduce also the Undersecretaries at the time of formation of the Fourth Government Berlusconi: thirty-eight, increased to thirty-nine little later (by Decree No. 90/2008), and subsequently increased again in order to meet functional and political needs. In particular, the total number of members of the government was raised to sixty-five with Decree-Law No. 195/2009 and in the subsequent governments, from the XVI Legislature onwards, has remained unchanged. Moreover, the composition of the Government must be consistent with the principle of equal gender opportunities enshrined in Article 51 of the Constitution (*see* Article 2(4*bis*) of Legislative Decree No. 300/1999).

272. As already mentioned, Law No. 81/2001 and Decree-Law No. 217/2001, then converted into Law No. 317/2001, maintain the political responsibility and the political policy of the Ministers under Article 95 of the Constitution but also provide that: 'no more than ten Undersecretaries can be appointed Vice Ministers' when they are delegated to manage areas or projects that compete to one or more departmental structures or more general Directions. In this case, they are delegated by the competent Minister through the additional assent of the Council of Ministers and after the proposal of the President of the Council.

As above mentioned, the President of the Council, together with the competent Minister, can invite them to take part in the sittings of the Council of Ministers, without possibility to vote, in order to debate about matters related to their delegated competences.

The reasons fixing limits to the increase of Undersecretaries that are appointed Vice Ministers are evident and exquisitely political. In fact, there is no connection between the range of functions delegated by a Minister to a Undersecretary of State and the relative appointment of Vice Minister because the *de qua* regulations do not avoid a Minister to delegate an Undersecretary of State an entire area of competence of one or more departmental structures or more general Directions, even if there is no appointment of Vice Minister.

Second, the inadequacy of this new disposition regarding Vice Ministers appears evident because there is no organic procedural regulation in case of annulment of the delegating procedure aimed at assigning the title of Vice Minister, but also, generally speaking, in case of annulment of a Vice Minister. Therefore, the juridical configuration of Vice Ministers is *sic et simpliciter* similar to Undersecretaries' one.

Third, the *nomen iuris* adopted by the Legislator for this kind of Undersecretaries of State is not appropriate too. In fact, the expression 'Vice' reminds functions which are generically vicarious and reflect a generalized institutional substitution and that cannot be dealt with by these subjects. In fact, besides considering what Law No. 81/2001 provides for political powers and relative ministerial responsibility, it is necessary to notice that, in case of absence or obstacles of the Ministers concerned, Vice Ministers cannot be assigned functions and powers that the Constitution directly and exclusively assigns Ministers. In particular, it is obvious that Vice Ministers, as the Undersecretaries as well, cannot countersign any act of the President of the Republic under Article 89 of the Constitution. It is also evident that a possible Vice Minister of Justice, in case of absence or impediment of the person in charge for this Minister, cannot take disciplinary measures against magistrates because this is a faculty (*rectius*: a power) that Article 107, paragraph 2, of the Constitution directly and exclusively assign the competent Minister for this specific area and the same Minister, and not the Vice Minister, is politically responsible to Parliament.

Moreover, when carefully analysing the involvement of the Council of Ministers, the legislator's attempt to further organize the government's structure in order to better develop, coordinate and realize sectorial and inter-sectorial policies can cause remarkable difficulties in the relations between Ministers and Vice Ministers. In fact, Vice Ministers can also not necessarily be members of the same party of their Ministries and can attempt to rid themselves of their directives underlying the Council approval of the delegating system. Even in the recent praxis, it has been noticed that the political-administrative relations among Ministers and Vice Ministers in the ministerial structures in which their presence is provided for have become competitive. However, the relations among the same President of the Council and the Ministers risk to get complicated because when the Premier intends to invite a Vice Minister to the sittings of the Council of Ministers, he must now find an agreement with the Minister concerned.

VII. Government High Commissioners

273. High Commissioners are not provided for by the Constitution. They are therefore part of the accessory government organs, although they have played a relevant role, especially in the past. The High Commissioner for Hygiene and Public Health, set up in 1945, which became part of government in 1958, the High Commissioner for Tourism set up in 1947, which became a government Ministry in 1959, are just a few examples. High Commissioners may be compared to *out-of-cabinet* Ministers in the British system. They are not part of the Council of Ministers, although they have the right to attend the meetings any time a matter lying within their province is debated (but are not eligible to vote). They are responsible for specific administrative matters which are not dealt with by any Ministry. In the past, whenever operational flexibility was particularly necessary, the ministerial machinery was streamlined by setting up administrative bodies under the supervision of a High Commissioner which enjoyed a certain degree of autonomy and to which a number of functions were handed over.

If we consider the Italian experience, High Commissioners are completely different from Ministers without Portfolio who, as stated above, belong ex officio to the Council of Ministers. Furthermore, unlike Ministers without Portfolio, High Commissioners are not accountable before Parliament and, indeed, they do not depend on Parliament's confidence. They cannot countersign presidential decrees and are subject to criminal law since they cannot benefit from Article 96 of the Constitution. High Commissioners are accountable before government since their appointment is formalized by a presidential decree on the proposal of the Prime Minister and in agreement with the Council of Ministers.

High Commissioners are thus subject to the general policy of the government expressed by the orientation and coordination powers of the Prime Minister and in close cooperation with the Minister concerned.

For example, Law No. 3/2003 established a High Commissioner in order to prevent and fight corruption and other crimes inside public administration. The President of the Council supervised directly and functionally the High Commissioner. Decree-Law No. 35/2005 (converted to Law No. 80/2005) established in its turn a High Commissioner for the fight against forgery that is appointed by decree of the President of the Council after the proposal of the Minister of Productive Activities (the High Commissioner should operate in this latest Ministry). However, the subsequent Decree-Law No. 112/2008 (converted to Law No. 133/2008) eliminated these two bodies (Articles 68(6)(*a* and *b*)) and transferred their respective functions to the competent Ministers, who can delegate them to an Undersecretary.

VIII. Special Government Commissioners

274. Law No. 400/1988 provides for a general legal framework for the Special Government Commissioners which refers, for some matters, to the discipline of High Commissioners, and differs for others. Some Special Commissioners are provided for by special bills with special prescriptions. They are appointed by a Decree of the President of the Republic, on the proposal of the Prime Minister, subject to a decision of the Council of Ministers. This decree lists the responsibilities of the commissioners as well as the resources available to them. The duration of their office is specified in the appointment decree unless their mandate is extended or annulled. Parliament is immediately informed of the appointments, which are then published in the Official Gazette (Article 11(2) of Law No. 400/1998). Article 11(1) explains the reasons for appointing such commissioners and that, as well as exercising the governmental functions provided for by law, Special Government Commissioners must achieve 'specific objectives in the framework of programs or guidelines adopted either by Parliament or by the Council of Ministers or which are necessary to satisfy the need of temporary operational coordination among public administration departments'. Article 11(3) provides that either the Prime Minister or a delegated Minister shall report to Parliament on the activity of the Special Government Commissioner. The direction and coordination functions of the Prime Minister are once more enhanced by the appointment of such Commissioners and, above all, by the fact that it is the Prime Minister who proposes the appointment – and not the Minister or Ministers concerned.

Recently, for example, an Anti-Usury and Anti-Racketeering Special Government Commissioner has been appointed (Article 1, Decree of the President of the Republic 8 November 2020).

IX. Interministerial Committees and Committees of Ministers

275. The Interministerial Committees and the Committees of Ministers were the first additional government organs established in Italian constitutional history. They are collegiate bodies consisting of a number of Ministers with competences of orientation and coordination and sometimes responsible for special tasks.

For example, with Law No. 234/2012 (Article 2), the Interministerial Committee for European Affairs (ICEA) was established, which operates under the Presidency of the Council of Ministers and whose functioning is governed by D.P.R. No. 118/2015. It is convened and chaired by the President of the Council of Ministers or, in his/her mandate, it is convened and chaired by the President of the Council of Ministers, or, by his delegation, by the Minister for European Affairs or, if necessary, by its Undersecretary, and attended by the Minister of Foreign Affairs, the Minister of Economy and Finance and other Ministers who have competence in the subject matters of the measures and issues' agenda of its meetings. The President of the Conference of the Regions, the National Association of Italian Municipalities and the Union of Italian Provinces may also participate when dealing with matters of their competence. The ICEA aims to coordinate the government's policy lines in the process of forming the Italian position in the process of preparing the acts of the EU.

The guidelines defined by the ICEA are communicated to the Department for European Policies, which sets the unified Italian position to be subsequently represented, in agreement with the Ministry of Foreign Affairs, in the EU.

Recently, under Article 4 of Decree-Law No. 82/2021, converted to Law No. 109/2021, the Interministerial Committee for Cybersecurity (ICC) was established at the Presidency of the Council of Ministers with the functions of advising, proposing and supervising cybersecurity policies. The Committee, chaired by the President of the Council of Ministers, proposes to the same the general guidelines to be pursued in the framework of national cybersecurity policies; it exercises high oversight on the implementation of the national cybersecurity strategy; promotes the adoption of the necessary initiatives to foster effective cooperation at national and international levels between institutional actors and private operators interested in cybersecurity, the sharing of information and the adoption of best practices and measures addressing the objective of cybersecurity and the industrial, technological and scientific development of cybersecurity; gives its opinion on the National Cybersecurity Agency's budget and balance sheet.

Law No. 400/1988 distinguishes the Interministerial Committees and the Committees of Ministers 'established by law' (Article 6(3)) but does not explain the difference between the two. The doctrine, nonetheless, has tried to make a distinction between them, especially in terms of the composition of the Committee and the validity – internal or external – of its measures. The distinctions that generally prevail are that Committees of Ministers are made up exclusively of Ministers, whereas the Interministerial Committees are also extended to other subjects: Undersecretaries of State, directors and executive officers of the public administration, and experts.

In practice, there has been a proliferation of these bodies due to the increased workload of the Public Administration and because coordination among Ministries cannot be achieved solely by the 'agreement' principle so that some sort of improved coordination encouraging for stability was needed. As a result, the number of committees has increased to a point that the general policy line of government adopted by the Prime Minister has been in danger of becoming fragmented.

In an attempt to avoid this, Law No. 400/1988 introduced some coordination rules while making the government responsible for the adoption of measures having the force of law and designed to limit and reorganize the number of committees, including those not established by law together with the Interministerial Committees provided for by the regulations in force, with the exception of the Interministerial Committee for Loans and Savings (*Comitato Interministeriale per il Credito e il Risparmio*, CICR). This has led to the abolition of twelve Committees. Today the Committees include: the Interministerial Committee for Economic Planning (*Comitato Interministeriale per la Programmazione economica*, CIPE) and the Committee for Information and Security (*Comitato Interministeriale per le Informazioni e la Sicurezza*, CIPES), whose composition and functions are partly connected with the activity of the Interministerial Committee for the Security of the Republic (*Comitato interministeriale per la sicurezza della Repubblica*, CISR), established by Article 5 of Law No. 124/2007.

Law No. 400/1988 (Article 5(2)(*h*)) also provides that the Prime Minister can issue a decree establishing special Committees of Ministers whose task is to carry out a preliminary analysis of issues lying within the Province of different Ministries and to issue opinions on directives concerning government activity and on relevant matters to be submitted to the Council of Ministers. An example is given by the Committee for the celebration of the 150th anniversary of the Italian Unity, established with a Decree of the President of the Council of Ministers on 24 April 2007.

There is a clear attempt by the legislator to 'reclaim' the powers of the Prime Minister and the Council of Ministers. In practice, committees have indeed mainly benefited those Ministers invited to take part in them and who consequently find themselves in a position of power and influence, also thanks to the fact that the Prime Minister is not a member of any such committee.

X. The Cabinet Council

276. The Cabinet Council is the last of the accessory government bodies – also chronologically since only recently reinstated in the Italian legal system. Indeed, it was in 1983 that this collegiate body reappeared after a brief appearance during the 'period of transition' before the Constitution came into force. Law No. 400/1988 has regulated and formalized this practice, and Article 6(1) stipulates that: 'The President of the Council of Ministers, in the exercise of his duties in accordance with the provisions of Article 95(1) of the Constitution, can be assisted by a Committee to be named "the Cabinet Council", consisting of the Ministers of his choice, in agreement with the Council of Ministers.'

In the past, the Cabinet Council included, besides the Prime Minister and the Vice-President of the Council of Ministers, seven to eight other Ministers. The composition of the Council of Ministers used to be essentially governed by political criteria in an attempt to ensure the participation of the most prominent members of the coalition parties – the so-called heads of the delegation – on a proportional basis, i.e., as to reflect the various proportions of the parliamentary groups regardless of the actual importance and of the competence of the single Ministries. Ministers could, however, be invited to attend the meetings of the Cabinet Council according to their specific competence. Article 6(2) of Law No. 400/1988 has regulated this practice. The highly political nature of this organ was evident from the start when the Cabinet Council was established under the first Craxi Government (1983) and has indeed been confirmed by the practice following the introduction of Law No. 400/1988. According to law, however, the Cabinet Council, if indeed established (interestingly enough, this has not been the case with recent governments), must limit its work to the competence of the Prime Minister and not of the Council of Ministers, thus preserving, albeit formally, the competence of the Council of Ministers. In practice, the political composition of the Cabinet Council can indeed relieve the Council of Ministers of its responsibility to provide for general government policy. The present absence of a Cabinet Council probably helps reduce the political weight of parties and enhances both the autonomy of the Prime Minister and his relations with the Council of Ministers.

§3. GOVERNMENT FORMATION

277. The procedure for government formation includes a long series of informal actions and formal measures leading to the appointment of the Prime Minister and Ministers before the President of the Republic and ending with the swearing-in procedure (Articles 92–93 of the Constitution). This procedure is only partly regulated by written provisions. The Constitution only provides that the Head of State appoints the Prime Minister and the Ministers (Article 92(2)) who have to be sworn in before him (Article 93). All the preliminary phases are regulated by relatively constant *practice*, *conventions* and *constitutional custom* (*see* Part I, Chapter 4, §10).

278. The first phase concerns the notification to the President of the Republic of the resignation of the government in office. Following this notification, the President of the Republic:

– may simply accept the resignation of government as occurred for the first time in 1998 following a vote of no-confidence on a question put by the I Prodi Government to the vote of the Chamber of Deputies, and as also occurred in 2008, after the unfavourable vote of confidence of the Senate presented by the II Prodi Government. These were unconditional and due acceptances since it is established that a government must resign after a vote of no-confidence (Article 94 Constitution; *see* Part II, Chapter 6). Nonetheless, the acceptance of resignation must be accompanied by the request of the President of the Republic to the resigning government to remain in office 'to deal with current matters';
– may decide to defer his decision while requesting that government remains in office to deal with current affairs, in case the government resigns 'spontaneously', i.e., not on receiving a vote of no-confidence;
– may decide to reject the resignation of a government on the grounds that it was not due to political reasons, but merely to the respect of '*constitutional rules of fairness*' towards the President. For example, when the government in office notifies its resignation to the neo-elected President of the Republic. At this point, the President can request government to provide a political justification for its resignation in a parliamentary debate during which the actions taken by government and the reasons making it impossible for government to remain in office are discussed, as happened several times in practice starting from the Gronchi Presidency, passing through the Pertini and Cossiga Presidencies, and then with particular impetus during the Scalfaro Presidency, up to the Mattarella Presidency and the resignation of the Draghi Government. If the President accepts the resignation of the government, the ensuing decree is not signed until a new one is formed; otherwise, the Nation would be left with no government.

279. In times of government crisis, government activity is limited to ordinary business. However, no written rule restricts its powers. In order to limit the powers of the resigning government, the Presidency of the Council issues ad hoc circulars at the outset of the crisis. In the past, after resigning, some governments preferred to avoid appointing, promoting and transferring officials, or adopting draft legislation, while others did the reverse.

During the ordinary administration, the government is only allowed to carry out strictly necessary activities that reflect the main and permanent interests of our legal system, aimed at protecting the constant functioning of public institutions and at guaranteeing public permanent and irrepressible interests. An outgoing government without the Chambers' confidence, such as the I and the II Prodi Government, cannot carry out activities to achieve the political targets of its programme, on which the parliamentary majority was established because the same majority has disappeared after the parliamentary vote.

In practice, when decisions of particular international relevance (such as for the case of the recognition of Kosovo) or otherwise justified by reasons of emergency (such as for the case of the waste in Campania) were needed, the Government consulted all the political groups before deciding. However, the supervision of the President of the Republic in accordance with his high powers of control and guarantee is still relevant when it concerns the acts of a resigning government (such as bills and acts having binding force). The President of the Republic must ensure that the acts of the actual government are constitutionally correct and conform to the juridical needs of the activities that the government intend to adopt.

280. Following the praxis, after resigning, the President of the Republic, in order to be able to make the decisions more consistent with the situation and to be able to choose the person to be appointed for the formation of a government that can obtain the confidence of the majority of Parliament, can consult any useful person.

Some experts consider these consultations compulsory in accordance with a *constitutional custom*. In fact, since the entry into force of the Constitution, as it was also during the time of the Albertine Statute (*Statuto Albertino*), the consultations' praxis had been constantly followed. However, the modalities and the number of subjects consulted, which are first and foremost political personalities varied in time, representatives of the parties represented in Parliament (the Political Secretaries and also the Presidents) and the Presidents of the respective parliamentary groups, on whom the confidence in the government depends. The former Presidents of the Republic and senior state officials, especially the House Chancellors, are also consulted. Sometimes, representatives of social and economic organizations are also consulted.

Obviously, the agenda of the consultations is also influenced by the personality of the Head of State and by any special requirement which may arise from time to time. However, the intention is to give importance to those with greater political and parliamentary weight, sometimes by resorting to longer consultations and informal telephone interviews.

From 1996 to 2013, praxis has demonstrated that preventive indications given to voters by each political group, regarding the candidate Prime Minister, and the clarity of the election results have contributed to a significant simplification of the consultations of the President of the Republic that lost their centrality.

281. Sometimes, the President of the Republic, before forming the new government and after his own consultations, assigns an 'exploratory mandate' or 'exploratory mission'. As subsequently explained, this is not a real assignment or a 'pre-assignment' because the subject chosen for this mandate is not required to form the government and is not the candidate to perform this task but has only the task to analyse through other consultations and meetings with the representatives of the parties represented in Parliament the possibilities to solve the crisis.

Usually, this kind of mandate is invariably assigned to the President of a branch of the Parliament because he has an institutional *super partes* position that makes his position similar to the one of the President of the Republic.

At the beginning of the XVIII Legislature, however, the President of the Republic modified partially the praxis, entrusting a first exploratory mandate to the President of the Senate, with the task of verifying the existence of a parliamentary majority among the parties of the centre-right coalition and the Five Star Movement, and of a shared indication for the conferral of the office of President of the Council, to form the government. The President gave a second exploratory mandate to the negative outcome of this mandate, entrusting the President of the Chamber with the task of verifying the possibility of an agreement of parliamentary majority between the Five Star Movement and the Democratic Party in order to form the government. This practice has been confirmed after the resignation of the Conte II Government. In this case, the President of the Republic entrusted the President of the Chamber of Deputies with the task of verifying the possibility of reconstituting the outgoing majority. The President of the Republic, when there are uncertainties on the possibility to reach a positive result through the subject to assign, gives before the mandate a '*pre-mandate*' in order to verify if there are the conditions for a possible mandate (after contacting the representatives of the political parties) to confer the same subject who is asked to perform the '*pre-mandate*'.

282. By granting the assignment to the '*President responsible*' – verbally, as has been the case since 1958 – the President of the Republic entrusts a person whom he believes will command the confidence of both parliamentary Chambers to form a Government. The 'President responsible' conducts consultation or talks in order to form the Cabinet, at present mostly on the grounds of the coalition agreements settled before the vote, although it is still possible to extend the agreement to other parties wishing to join the majority. The President of the Republic must bear in mind the ultimate objective of forming a government likely to be granted a vote of confidence in both Chambers of Parliament in accordance with constitutional provisions. For this reason, the assignment is usually given to a prominent figure of the political line-up most likely to command a majority in Parliament. However, the assignment may also go to representatives who are not part of the relative majority party or the main parliamentary parties. Indeed, two times since 1948, the person responsible for forming the government has been neither a political representative nor an MP – namely Presidents Ciampi and Dini – but this was exceptionally due to a period of crisis in the Italian changing political system.

A remarkable innovation compared to previous practice had been noted at the beginning of the XVII Legislature, after the uncertain outcome of the February 2013 elections and during the long procedure for the formation of the new government:

the President of the Republic, trying to unlock an irreconcilable political situation, and after having unsuccessfully made use of a pre-appointment (Mr Pier Luigi Bersani, leader of the DP), had, in fact, decided to ask two small group of personalities (the so-called Saggi, which are different in terms of location and competence) to formulate – on essential themes of institutional and socio-economic and European character – precise programme proposals that could be shared by political forces, and, thus, to create the conditions for the assignment.

From 1996 until 2013, the assignment of the mandate has been influenced by the electoral legislation, and therefore it appears to be easier, thanks to the previous indication given to voters by each political party (the 'coalitions') regarding its own government candidate. However, it is still necessary to form a coalition government and the political parties that intend to take part in government to agree concretely not only about the programme but also about the appointment of the Ministers.

At the beginning of the XVIII Legislature, due to the electoral legislation in force (Law No. 165/2017), characterized by a semi-proportional system, and in consideration of the outcome of the elections of 4 March 2018, it was still necessary to form a coalition government and therefore that the political forces willing to participate in the government would agree concretely not only on the agenda but also on the appointment of Ministers. Moreover, it may happen – and it has happened – that, during a government crisis, it is necessary to ascertain the party's intentions about the original coalition agreements, if they exist.

In any case, the President of the Republic must verify if it is possible to constitute a majority in order to prevent the dissolution of Parliament, as happened actually during the current legislature. In particular, Article 94(1) of the Constitution stipulates that government must enjoy the confidence of the two Chambers, thus making it virtually impossible to form minority governments. A majority can, however, be obtained by the abstention of some of the parliamentary groups since absolute majority in both Chambers is not essential. In fact, the confidence does not require the absolute majority of the Chambers that is the positive vote of more than half of their members.

The subject designated promotes in his turn consultations and meetings in order to verify the concrete possibility of forming a new government.

With the implementation of the previous electoral laws for the Deputies Chamber and the Senate, before the entry into force of the new electoral law, Law No. 165/2017, the so-called Rosatellum, which had allowed the quasi-polarization of our political system, if the person in charge was also the leader of one of the two major coalitions opposed in the electoral campaign, there was a tendency to considerably reduce the time of consultations and meetings, since it was clear enough, in the light of the election results, which were the political forces willing to support the new government.

However, as already mentioned, the real difficulties for the subject designated are the definition, or the simple finishing off, of the previous 'programmatic agreements' with the political partners and the drafting of the list of the Ministers to be proposed to the President of the Republic.

Afterwards, the designated subject definitely accepts the assignment and presents the list of the Ministers to the President of the Republic. In the presence of a clear majority arising directly from the election results, the designated subject can immediately accept the assignment without reservation, avoiding the just-mentioned steps.

During the formation of his IV Government, Silvio Berlusconi, who was the leader of the political majority that emerged during the elections of 2008, innovated the above-mentioned praxis. Thanks to the electoral results obtained and to the indication of the leader provided for by the current electoral regulations, he promoted consultations and meetings before the assignment of the mandate. These meetings aimed at defining precisely the programmatic profiles and the composition of the new government. Thus, when the President of the Republic assigned him the mandate, he accepted without reservations and contextually presented the list of the Ministers.

In 2018, at the beginning of the XVIII Legislature, during the second appointment conferred to Giuseppe Conte in the same procedure of formation of the first government, which later resulted in the formation of the executive chaired by him, such reserve was not equally placed by the person in charge, but for other reasons. In fact, the agreement on the political majority willing to support the person in charge before the Parliament and that relating to ministerial appointments had already been reached in his first attempt only failed due to the political and institutional conflict on a specific ministerial role, that is the appointment to the Ministry for the Economy and Finance, as better specified below.

The results of the election held on 25 September 2022, giving rise to the XIX legislature, have allowed the leader of the largest party in the winning coalition to accept without reservation the office conferred on her by the President of the Republic and to present to him at the same time the list of Ministers of the new Government. It was therefore the electoral outcome that greatly facilitated the formation of the Government chaired by Giorgia Meloni, leader of the majority party relating to both the Houses of Parliament and the centre-right coalition. In the face of a political majority formed directly as a result of the popular vote, despite the well-known aporias of the electoral law in force, experienced in the previous legislature, our form of parliamentary government has undoubtedly manifested the best of itself, at least at the beginning of the new one: the responsibility of President of the Council of Ministers has been taken on by the leader of the relative majority party, who has managed to secure a sufficient majority to obtain the confidence of Parliament, thereby also facilitating the essential role of the President of the Republic during the process of forming the Government.

283. Moreover, in the experience just mentioned, thanks to the electoral legislation and the practice referred to, it seems that the responsible President of the Council has been able to exercise greater autonomy in the choice of Ministers, compared with the political forces willing to support her, without prejudice, however, to the prerogatives of the President of the Republic.

284. At this stage of the process of formation, the President of the Republic, if he has not accepted the resigning of the Government yet, for the above-mentioned reasons and under a consolidated praxis, cancels all the reservations that arose during the government's resigning and issues a decree of acceptance of the resignation.

This decree is adopted without any proposal and, such as the decree of acceptance of the resignations of the Undersecretaries of State, is currently countersigned by the new President of the Council, in accordance with a quite recent innovation (1983) in praxis that despite some doubts was included in Law No. 400/1988 concerning the government regulation (Article 1(2)).

In accordance with Article 92(2) of the Constitution, the President of the Republic appoints the new Prime Minister and Ministers by issuing two successive decrees. The incoming President of the Council himself countersigns the decree of appointment of the President of the Council, although the Premier has not yet taken office at the time of decree's countersignature. The countersignature of the incoming Premier – and not that of the outgoing Premier as was the case under the monarchy, before the advent of Fascism – at the foot of decrees of acceptance of the resignation of the President of the Council and those by which the same President of the Council is appointed can be explained with the need to avoid the possibility that the endorsement be denied, which would lead to dangerous confrontations or obstacles to the existence of the government.

The President of the Republic appoints the Ministers by a separate decree, on the proposal of the Prime Minister (Article 92 of the Constitution) who also designates the other government bodies. As widely underlined, in practice, however, because of the need to form coalition governments, to ensure a balance of power among the various groups, also within the same party and above all to ensure a governmental parliamentary majority, political leaders have often played a significant role in the designation of Ministers. Notwithstanding, has this trend been partially reversed with the Premier claiming and partly making use of greater autonomy in his choice of Ministers. On the other hand, it has never been excluded some influence, in this choice, of the President of the Republic, which is responsible for signing the nomination decree: both in the form of an informal 'veto' (never however made public, at least until the recent form the I Conte Government during the XVIII Legislature), compared to certain designations, which for objective reasons and difficult to contest, made assume that the nomination could apparently be inappropriate, and in the form of positive influence, increased especially at the appointment of governments that were not a direct and clear expression of parliamentary forces.

At the beginning of the XVIII Legislature, during the repeated attempts to form a government, however, elements of friction on the institutional level and in the political and juridical debate emerged, concerning the prerogatives that the Constitution assigns to the President of the Republic on the appointment of the Ministers.

The designated Prime Minister Conte proposed first to appoint as Minister of Economy and Finance a renowned economist (Paolo Savona), but considered to be a possible supporter of the exit of Italy from Eurozone. The President of the Republic refused to appoint him, and the two allied parties, the League and the M5S, refused to replace him. As a result, President-designated Conte first renounced his mandate, and after a short time, accepted a new mandate indicating as Minister of Economy and Finance another person, while Mr Savona was proposed for a different Ministry. This allowed the second Conte Government to enter office.

285. Regarding the final phase of the procedure aiming to form the government should be highlighted that, pursuant to Article 93 of the Constitution, before assuming office, the Prime Minister and the Ministers must be sworn in before the President of the Republic and take the following oath: 'I swear to be faithful to the Republic, to abide loyally by its Constitution and its laws and to exercise my duties in the exclusive interest of the Nation.' This wording has recently been included in Article 1(3) of Law No. 400/1988 and is substantially the same as the one normally used in republican systems since no mention of it is made in the Constitution. The swearing-in procedure is a sine qua non for the legitimate exercise of governmental functions.

286. The wide range of powers attributed to government which has not yet been granted parliamentary confidence is another matter of discussion, and this situation can be compared to the resigning government's one. Indeed, also in this case government must limit itself to carry out 'current affairs', although the possibility of intervention in case of emergency as well as the accomplishment of previously agreed commitments concerning the presentation of government draft laws are not excluded. As concerns government draft laws, the number of limits that the government waiting for parliamentary confidence meets is lower than the number of limits of the resigning government, because it is supposed that the government will surely be granted the confidence of the Parliament.

287. When the government is formed and during its activity, the substitution of one or more of its Ministers could be necessary. In praxis, this substitution is called *reshuffle*, that is when one or more Ministers are absent or resign for different reasons, which are sometimes political ones. In particular, resignations can be caused by changes regarding the coalition of government (e.g., as happened during the IV Berlusconi Government after the resignations of the members of *Futuro e Libertà per l'Italia* (FLI)), but also by death, personal or health reasons or jobs that are not compatible with the government activity.

In case of reshuffles caused by political reasons, the praxis comprehends parliamentary debates, and after that, government confidence is voted through a business on the agenda or a motion or a resolution.

Moreover, the resignation of Undersecretaries served or not as Deputy Minister, and depending on changes in the majority of government, does not necessarily lead to a *reshuffle*, since those persons are not in a relationship of confidence with Parliament, given their unnecessary government's organs feature according to Article 92 of the Constitution. Therefore, they can be replaced without parliamentary debates or confidence confirmations, which can, however, intervene for choices dictated by political opportunity and requirements of transparency vis-à-vis voters, but not for a legal obligation pursuant to Article 94 of the Constitution.

§4. The Status and Responsibility of Government Members

288. The *status* of government members is not explicitly regulated by the Constitution, which only covers the issue of criminal liability for offences committed in the exercise of governmental duties. If members of the executive are Members of Parliament, then they will be granted the same treatment as Members of Parliament (*see* Part II, Chapter 3, §7). There is no legal provision preventing Members of government from being Members of Parliament. On the contrary, since the Constitution introduced a traditional parliamentary system during the first decades of the Republic, government members were almost exclusively chosen from among Members of Parliament. Since the 1990s, however, Ministers, and more recently Undersecretaries of State, are frequently chosen from outside Parliament. This growing trend resulted in the appointment of three Premiers (in 1993, 1996 and 2021) who were not Members of Parliament (Ciampi, Dini and Draghi), called upon to lead a government on the grounds of their technical expertise. In the framework of a government reorganization, several proposals have been made to modify the Constitution in order to declare the incompatibility of government offices with a parliamentary mandate.

Nonetheless, a debate has been going on for some years on the need to regulate this matter in an attempt to avoid a '*clash of interests*'. A recent legislative regulation (Law No. 215/2004) determines some cases of incompatibility between government offices and parliamentary mandate.

289. According to the *principles of the parliamentary system*, government is politically accountable before both Chambers which grant and refuse a vote of confidence, in accordance with the provisions of Article 94 of the Constitution (*see* Part II, Chapter 6).

Article 95(1) of the Constitution specifies that the President of the Council of Ministers is politically liable for the general political leadership of the government. Article 95(2) of the Constitution speaks about *political liability* (before Parliament) and *juridical liability* (i.e., civil, criminal and administrative liability) of the Ministers. The Ministers are not only appointed Heads of their Ministries because they fully take part in the activities of the Council of Ministers. Therefore, their liability is both individual (as concerns the acts of their Ministries) and collegial (as regards the deliberations of the Council of Ministers). In particular, the political liability of the single Ministers can be asserted through an individual motion of confidence, which is not expressly provided for by the Constitution. The individual motion of confidence is, although in different ways, accepted by both Chambers that regulate it in accordance with the procedural rules of Article 94, latest paragraph, of the Constitution. The Minister who is subject to a motion of confidence is obliged to resign, as confirmed by the same Constitutional Court (*see* Judgment No. 7/1996).

Furthermore, the Ministers, when countersigning the acts issued by the President of the Republic in accordance with their relative competences and under Article 89 of the Constitution assume both a *political and a juridical liability*. Also, the President of the Council, who is liable for the general policy of the government and under Article 89 of the Constitution, countersigns the acts issued by decree of the President of the Republic, i.e., the acts for the promulgation of the laws, the acts having binding force, the regulations of the government and the acts issued by the Council of Ministers (*see* Article 5(1) Law No. 400/1988).

290. The countersignature is typical of parliamentary systems and represents an essential element of presidential acts, whose validity depends just on them. However, the countersignature is not necessary for the swearing-in procedure of the President of the Republic because this latest subject takes non-transferable liabilities through the countersignature (Article 90 of the Constitution), as well as through acts with which he expresses his opposition to the government and through activities that are typical of the home administration of the President of the Republic. Moreover, the various ways through which the President of the Republic expresses his opinion about current political and institutional matters do not require any countersignature (*see* Part II, Chapter 2, §11).

291. Article 96 of the Constitution regulates the criminal liability of government members but was amended by Parliament with Constitutional Law No. 1/1989.

Article 96 reads as follows:

> The President of Council of Ministers and Ministers, even if no longer in office, may be prosecuted for the offences committed in the exercise of their duties, upon authorization by the Senate or the Chamber of Deputies in accordance with the provisions set out in a constitutional law.

The parliamentary procedure for impeaching government as well as the special jurisdiction to which it was subject has been eliminated. In the past, Parliament could indeed decide in a joint session to impeach the Prime Minister and Ministers. Furthermore, they were summoned before the Constitutional Court, which adjudicated with an enlarged composition.

In accordance with the provisions of Law No. 219/1989, however, a specially set up board of ordinary magistrates must make preliminary enquiries. The authorization required in accordance with Article 96 differs from that needed in the past for Deputies and senators in that, while the latter was limited to the duration of the parliamentary mandate, the former can now be extended beyond the expiry of governmental office.

Constitutional Law provides that the Chamber to which they belong, while in the case of Ministers who are not Members of Parliament or in case of legal proceedings against Ministers belonging to different Chambers, the Senate must issue the authorization, may only prosecute Ministers who are also Members of Parliament upon authorization. Parliament can stop criminal proceedings only when it shows by an absolute majority of its members that the defendant has tried to protect a constitutionally relevant interest of the State; in other words, that he tried to pursue a prominent public interest in the exercise of his duties. In accordance with the Standing Orders of the Chambers, before the concerned Chamber decides, the Committee of Privileges must carry out a preliminary examination of the request. If the committees decide to issue the authorization, and if there are no votes against (a minimum of twenty Deputies or twenty senators), the conclusions expressed by the committee are adopted, and a vote of Parliament (either Chamber) is not necessary.

292. With the exception of the provisions of Articles 90 and 96 of the Constitution and after Law No. 140/2003 (usually called '*Lodo Schifani*'), provisions for the suspension of any criminal proceeding against the President of the Council and the highest offices of State, excluded Ministers and members of the Parliament have been introduced; these dispositions cover any kind of violation, even crimes committed before the acceptance of an office and till its suspension. However, sentence No. 24/2004 of the Constitutional Court considered these provisions of the law illegitimate, in particular because they clash with Articles 3 and 24 of the Constitution.

At the beginning of the XVI Legislature, the government presented the Parliament a new bill having the same object and called '*Lodo Alfano*'. This bill became Law in no less than a month (Law No. 124/2008). However, Judgment No. 262/2009 of the Constitutional Court declared its constitutional illegitimacy because it was in contrast with Articles 3 and 138 of the Constitution. The Law, which included '*Provisions concerning the suspension of any criminal proceeding against the high offices of the State*' and provided for the suspension of any criminal proceeding against the President of the Council, of the President of the Republic and of the Chambers' Presidents from their date of appointment to the conclusion of their offices or functions, introduced by ordinary law and not by constitutional law a new and exceptional form of immunity (or privilege) in favour of the four abovementioned offices.

Therefore, the Court stated that new forms of immunity are abstractly possible in order to protect all the interests that reasonably require safeguard – such as the continuity and the normal procedure adopted by the highest offices of State and their quiet activities. However, they can be introduced only with an appropriate normative source.

After the above-quoted Court's judgment, a new constitutional bill was issued on 12 May 2010 (A. S. No. 2180), which proposed again 'Provisions concerning the suspension of criminal proceedings against the high offices of State' which has not been approved by the Parliament during the XVI Legislature.

Pending the approval of this bill, however, Law No. 51/2010, entitled 'Provisions on impediment to appear at the hearing' (so-called legitimate impediment), which had introduced a presumption of legitimate impediment to appear as accused in hearings of criminal prosecution under Article 420*ter* Penal Procedure Code, in favour of the President of the Council and the Ministers.

As it happened for Law No. 124/2008, it was immediately proposed a specific request for the abrogation of Law No. 51/2010 through a popular referendum under Article 75 of the Constitution; this abrogation was obtained after the referendum of June 2011.

In the meantime, the Judgment of the Constitutional Court No. 23/2011 already declared the constitutional illegitimacy of Article 1(3) of the same Law, 'in the part in which it does not provide for that the judge can concretely value the impediment adduced under Article 420*ter*, paragraph 1, Criminal code' and of Article 1(4), because 'it produces the same effects of a temporary suspension of a proceeding connected with the title of the office, that is with a prerogative established in favour of the titular subject'.

293. The *civil and administrative* (*as well as accounting too*) *liability* of the Prime Minister and Ministers is regulated by the common provisions of Article 28 of the Constitution. Since they are compared to officials and employees of the State, they are considered responsible for acts committed in violation of rights. In such cases, civil liability is extended to the State and to public bodies.

§5. Government Competences

294. The analysis of the essential and additional government bodies shows that the Italian Government now plays a greater role as compared to the past, when it was limited to 'executive functions', because its activity aims at performing concretely as per the guidelines promoted by the Parliament in its legislative function. The expression *executive function* is nowadays inadequate because of the several tasks the Italian government has to deal with after the process of government enforcement during the twentieth century. The highest organ of the Executive Power is collocated in the middle of a *form of parliamentary government* which favours the collaboration among powers that are generally, but not exclusively, related to the traditional functions of a State (legislative, executive and jurisdictional powers) and that does not highlight a strict separation among the same powers, as occurred within other forms of government. In fact, while analysing our system, it was specified that the government represents at the same time the 'executive committee' and the 'directive committee' of the parliamentary majority.

Here is a summary of the most relevant activities for which government is responsible, which are introduced and analysed in detail in other chapters of this Digest:

- *general and sectorial policies*: Government presents draft laws to Parliament (*see* Part II, Chapter 4, §1), among which the most important are: the draft law for the adoption of the State Budget (i.e., the estimated, the final and the multi-year budget) of the Finance Act (*Legge di stabilità*) and related acts (*see* Part II, Chapter 11), as well as draft laws authorizing the ratification of international treaties (*see* Part V, Chapter 3), whereas defence policy (also at domestic level) depends largely on Italy's participation in international and supranational organizations and on the preventive or subsequent intervention of Parliament (*see* Part V, Chapter 4);
- *lawmaking activities*: Government issues decree-laws, legislative decrees and regulations (*see* Part I, Chapter 4);
- *administrative orientation and coordination activity* (the historic *legis executio*): It includes administration at the central and local levels and the adoption of measures with regard to the orientation and coordination of the administrative activity of the Regions (under the new Title V, Part II of the Constitution and Law No. 131/2003; *see* Part III, Chapter 1), as well as the coordination of powers which were handed over to regional governments and the possible replacement of regional governments themselves in case of inactivity and non-fulfilment (in accordance with Article 120 Constitution).

§6. Government and Political Parties

295. Obviously, the practical functioning of the Government, a central and decisive institution in a parliamentary system such as the Italian one, is closely linked to the daily attitude of the parties and the evolution of the political system. In the republican experience, because of the proportional system used for many years to elect the Members of Parliament (*see* Part II, Chapter 3), governments were built, more or less, on broad majorities comprising different parties. In the beginning, centre-oriented coalitions prevailed including the Christian Democrats as a simple majority party as well as the Social Democrats and the Liberal Party. From 1963 onwards, centre-left coalitions were formed consisting of the Christian Democrats, the Socialist Party, the Social Democrats and the Republican Party. For a short span (1976–1979), a 'national unity' coalition was formed including centre-left parties and the Communist Party, followed by centre-left coalitions extending to the Liberals. Majority parties were often part of government – with the exception of the Communist Party because of its so-called *conventio ad excludendum* – and sometimes only provided support in Parliament to governments consisting of other parties or even the Christian Democrats alone. For years, the Prime Minister has been a representative of the simple majority party, the Christian Democrats, whereas in the 1980s, senior representatives of the Republican and Socialist parties were also appointed to this office.

As already stated, coalition governments tend to lead to a fragmentation within government, whereby single Ministers, appointed by the respective parties and enjoying a high degree of autonomy, sometimes disagreed so that the Prime Minister had difficulties in carrying out his duty to maintain unity. This has consequently enhanced the autonomy of administrative sectors belonging to the different Ministries.

296. The crisis of the Italian political system, which emerged in 1992 with the dismantling and the reorganization of traditional parties, is still present. In 1993, the electoral system was reformed, assigning three-quarters of the seats to single-member constituency and developing a pure majority system. Following this reform, a centre-left and a centre-right electoral coalition were formed, allowing for a decade the testing of a political system which was basically bipolar and based on the lack of unity inside the coalitions. This lack was in particular caused by the presence in the electoral system of both a majority and a proportional principle that enlarged the need of 'visibility' of the minor parties by their relative voters.

After the electoral reform in 2005 (*see* Law No. 270/2005), which adopted a proportional system with a plurality premium and the abolition of the single-member constituency, the political situation has further changed and from some points of view has become complicated. During the election in 2006, the new Law, which was hardly criticized for the above-mentioned reasons, did not allow the formation of a parliamentary majority of the Senate, and in 2008, the government was forced to resign because of the non-assent of a confidence matter. The crisis that followed determined the breakup of the two previous political coalitions and the early dissolution of Parliament and caused an electoral competition between the two biggest political parties in the meantime (*Partito Democratico* – PD – and *Popolo della Libertà* – PdL). Several minor political groups and electoral lists surrounded these two parties: some groups are united with the two new parties, while others are not united yet. In 2008, the elections resolved the problem of the breaking up of the political system. The electoral result was determined by various factors, among which it is to highlight the political intent of the two principal leaders to present their relative new compositions in their electoral competition almost completely alone; the choice of the citizens to concentrate their votes only to the two new subjects (*rectius*: to the main coalitions) and the *soglie di sbarramento* (blockage threshold) that blocked the majority of the minor political groups to get seats in Parliament.

However, the results of the elections in 2008 overcame only temporarily this political instability and the long period of transition, which started in 1992. The creation of two new big political parties (*Popolo della Libertà* and *Partito Democratico*), which were in competition during the elections, was not sufficient to eliminate the several contradictions of our political system. In fact, our system lacks cohesion inside the two 'poles' and has parties which are scarcely structured in a society which has more and more difficulties both towards electorate and representing general interests. The dissents inside the coalition of centre-right were not eliminated and emerged clearly in 2010 with the resignations of some members of the government and with the formation of a new political group (FLI), deriving from the separation of a relevant number of members of the party *Popolo della Libertà*.

The confusion generated afterwards caused a relevant reduction of the members of the Parliament in favour of the government and their consequent return in the majority coalition (in particular in the Group of Responsible Initiative). This is the typical example of an almost endemic transformism. In fact, the formation of blocked lists of candidates has transformed Parliament into a gathering of appointed subjects at the mercy of the leading groups and in particular of their relative leaders who can easily attract them and get their favour through various promises (some of them even caused the opening of judicial enquiries). Consequently, the leading groups and their leaders get the total control of their actions because they fear not to be proposed again as candidates or to be listed with an uncertain position.

The governability of the country has suffered damages because of the complications of the political system. Besides, governability suffers the worsening of the national and world economic and financial crisis.

This complex reality, however, did not result in the immediate crisis of the government in charge. The Fourth Government Berlusconi was forced to resign only by the end of 2011, following the economic and financial crisis that has particularly affected our country with the noted events related to the rise in the *spread* between the rate of government bonds and the German Bund, and further increase in our public debt. The collapse of the government's credibility on the domestic and international economic and financial levels is behind the crisis, leading to the formation of a so-called *technical government*, chaired by Prof. Mario Monti – nominated just before senator-for-life by the Head of State – and made up of a large number of so-called technical Ministers, i.e., mostly non-parliamentarians. Supported by an extremely large cross-political majority, never achieved before, with the collaboration of almost all parties represented in Parliament, excluding the Northern League and the Italy of Values. The Monti Government, about a year later, in December

2012, however, was forced to resign by the PdL decision on ending such experience. In fact, the resignation of the Monti Government had happened when the legislature was almost finished so that the elections of February 2013 were so early but slightly compared to the natural expiry date.

The elections held in February 2013, following the resignation of the Monti Government and the premature dissolution of the Chambers, did not offer a clear political framework since within Parliament was not present a major political force capable of forming a new government on its own. Attempts by the Democratic Party (PD) leader, the party most represented in Parliament, to create a coalition with the M5S, have been unsuccessful, and the government crisis has continued until the end of April. This impasse was overcome thanks to the decisive intervention of the re-elected Head of State, Giorgio Napolitano, who succeeded in appointing a 'broad-minded government', that is a large agreement on the programmatic points between PD and PdL – parties historically alternatives – and chaired by Mr Enrico Letta (PD), who also joined other minor political forces. But in November 2013, a real political earthquake took place in the centre-right when, before the National People's Liberty Council (PdL) provided for the suspension of activities to converge towards the resumption of *Forza Italia* (FI), a new political force emerged: the NCD, which, unlike FI, continued to support the Letta Government, whose confidence was confirmed, despite a significant reduction in the number of parliamentarians in his support.

The Letta Government, however, remained in office only until February 2014, when the National Democratic Party's leadership, having noted 'the need and the urgency to open a new phase with a new executive', caused the resignation, paving the way for the appointment of Matteo Renzi, new leader of the PD, as President of the Council.

Matteo Renzi remained in office until 7 December 2016, when he decided to resign after the referendum's rejection of constitutional reform on the Second Part of the Constitution, except of Title IV and almost whole Title VI (on December 4), strongly wanted by his government and already approved by Parliament, in accordance with the procedure laid down in Article 138 of the Constitution.

The Government of Renzi immediately succeeded the Government of the Hon. Paolo Gentiloni, supported by the same political forces and almost identical to the previous executive, nevertheless given the difficulties of dissolving Parliament by the President of the Republic, in the absence of homogeneous electoral legislation for both Chambers.

Following the judgment on illegitimacy of the 2005 election law ruled by Constitutional Court (*see* Judgment No. 1/2014), Parliament has adopted a new electoral law only for the House of Deputies, Law No. 52/2015, and partially illegitimate as ruled by the same Constitutional Court (*see* Judgment No. 35/2017), with its explicit call on the legislator, in particular, to guarantee a homogeneous majority in the two branches of Parliament.

The Constitution does not really require the legislator to introduce identical electoral systems for the two Chambers of Parliament but insists that, in order not to compromise the proper functioning of the parliamentary form of government, the adopted systems, although different, do not hinder, at the end of the election, the formation of homogeneous parliamentary majority.

The fact is that also the new electoral law, the so-called *Rosatellum*, that is Law No. 165/2017, approved in the proximity of the natural term of the XVII Legislature, was not able to ensure stability to the political system and to offer immediately a government majority.

Therefore, in the XVIII Legislature, the negotiations to form the Conte I Government have been very complex and difficult. For the same reasons, it was not easy to find a new majority after the crisis of that Government which ended with the formation of a II Conte Government supported by a politically different majority. The crisis of the latter proved to be so complex that, in order to avoid a dissolution of Parliament during the pandemic, the President of the Republic asked all political groups to support a so-called High Profile Government without – as he said – an explicit political formula. So, in February 2021, the President designed the former European Central Bank Governor, Mario Draghi, as Prime Minister. He formed a Government with some non-politicians and some ministers coming from the vast majority of the political groups in Parliament which supported the new Executive.

It was born with a maximum time horizon of just over two years; that is, until the end of the legislature, it has not identified itself in a political formula, according to the will of the President of the Republic. The Draghi Government was in fact supported by a parliamentary majority that did not coincide with the coalitions that had taken place since 2018, that is, in the XVIII Legislature. It was, however, a composite and very heterogeneous political majority, and for this very reason, every government initiative, all the more if extraneous to the programme originally presented to the Houses, has generated political and party destabilizing tensions, in and out of Parliament. In fact, on many occasions, the political forces belonging to the majority have expressed a dissent, in particular through the position taken by the Ministers inside and outside the collegial body of the Government. The implementation of the National Recovery and Resilience Plan (NRRP) has proved to be an occasion of particular friction – above all normative – between the parties of the composite coalition.

In turn, the approaching election of the President of the Republic has led to increasing tensions in the majority due to the consequences of the success of the President of the Council Mario Draghi, who was openly available to hold the highest office of the State. His election as President of the Republic would have made it very difficult to identify a successor and continue the legislature until its natural end. The election of the President of the Republic was therefore held between the possibility of a crisis of government and the dissolution of the Chambers.

The fact is that the re-election of Sergio Mattarella as President of the Republic was not enough to dispel the crisis of the Draghi Government, which in the presidential speech had been openly praised since it was opened by the substantial 'estrangement' of the M5S from the composite majority that supported it. This political force, on 14 July 2022, has in fact left the majority, taking the opportunity of the conversion of a decree-law voted in the Senate and on which the Government had posed the question of trust. Despite its approval and the consequent conversion into law of the decree, the non-participation of the M5S in the vote has led the President of the Council Draghi to resign.

Nothing new, therefore, in the problematic system of Italian parliamentary government.

In addition to the situation described above, which is evidently still marked at the party political level by many factors of instability, the ministerial and Council Presidency apparatus suffered for decades due to frequent structural and functional reforms – as seen here – characterized by constant mutations and upheavals, which have not contributed effectively to the smooth functioning of the Government.

Chapter 6. Government in Parliament: The Relationship of Confidence

by Antonio D'Andrea & Lorenzo Spadacini

§1. The Presentation of the Government to the Chambers

297. Once the President of the Republic has signed the decrees nominating the Head of Government and the government members, the latter are sworn in individually before the Head of State. The form of the oath is provided for by Article 1, third paragraph, of Law No. 400/1988.

From that moment on, the new government takes office and replaces the previous one. Its powers, however, cannot be fully exercised until it is granted the confidence by both Chambers. Pursuant to Article 94, third paragraph, of the Constitution, the government must present 'within ten days of its formation' its programme to Parliament to obtain its vote of confidence (the so-called *voto d'investitura*). Article 94 provides that each Chamber grants its confidence to the executive by a motion voted on by the simple majority of its members, in which it gives its reasons and which is put to a 'nominal vote', expression that reminds a particularly solemn form of vote: all MPs, one by one, go by the President of the Chamber and explicitly state, with a 'Yes', a 'No' or an abstention, their position about the government.

If one of the Chambers does not grant its confidence to the government, the executive must immediately resign. In practice, this has sometimes happened in the past with the so-called minority governments, namely newly appointed governments which could not rely on a pre-constituted parliamentary majority.

298. In compliance with the principle of equality of the two branches of Parliament, the newly appointed government usually presents its programme before a Chamber different from the one chosen by the previous government.

Pursuant to Article 2, third paragraph, of Law No. 400/1988, the Head of Government, speaking for all the Ministers, presents its programme (previously approved by the Council of Ministers) before the first Chamber.

This declaration is not repeated in the second Chamber, the text being rather distributed among the members.

After the debate and the President's reply, each Chamber votes its confidence by a motion usually submitted by the Presidents of majority groups. In compliance with the Constitution, the Chambers' reasons are given in the motion by simply quoting the Prime Minister's declarations.

If there is more than one confidence motion, the Head of Government decides which motion should be put to the confidence vote.

The vote is nominal; that is, each MP grants or refuses his or her confidence to the government by saying 'yes' or 'no' before the bench of the President, thus assuming public responsibility before the group they belong to and the electorate.

§2. A Contrary Vote on Government's Proposal

299. Article 94, fourth paragraph, of the Constitution provides that 'the contrary vote of one or of both Chambers on a government's proposal does not necessitate resignation'.

The Constitution distinguishes the contrary vote expressed by the Chambers towards specific measures proposed by the government, which is unlikely to affect the relationship of confidence, from the case provided for by Article 94, fifth paragraph, of an explicit vote of no-confidence, which must be expressed by means of an ad hoc motion passed by the Chambers (*see* below, §3). The fact that the Constitution does not force the government to resign in case of the contrary vote by the Chambers on government's proposals does not totally exclude this possibility. Presidents of the Council, indeed, have more than once inferred from a series of parliamentary contrary votes that they would not be able to carry out their political programme, owing to the lack of support from their majority. They have consequently resigned, even in the absence of an explicit vote of no-confidence, thus giving rise to 'extra-parliamentary' crises, which were actually caused by some political groups within the Chambers.

§3. A Motion of No-Confidence

300. Each Chamber can withdraw its confidence in the government in office at any time by a motion in which it gives its reasons and which is put to a nominal vote. Pursuant to Article 94, fifth paragraph, this motion must be signed by at least one-tenth of the Chamber's members. The Constitution also provides that the vote of no-confidence be debated only three days after it has been proposed, so as to avoid 'surprise attacks' by the opposition, which could be tempted to take advantage of the momentary absence of majority MPs from the Chamber.

The passing of a no-confidence motion, unlike the simple contrary vote, forces the government to resign.

In practice, however, no government has ever resigned owing to an explicit vote of no-confidence. The various government crises, with the exception of those of the Prodi Government, the first of which occurred during the thirteenth Parliament and the second during the fifteenth Parliament (*see* below, §4), have always been, at least formally, 'extra-parliamentary', i.e., caused by the spontaneous resignation of the government owing to disagreement within the majority.

On some rare occasions, the Chambers have debated no-confidence motions but have always voted against them or have been preceded by the government's resignations.

The majority political groups and the government itself, indeed, generally consider it useless or even dangerous to come to the point of voting, when the reasons or conditions of the relationship of cooperation on which the majority was based cease to exist.

In any case, the constitutional rule providing for the explicit vote of no-confidence allows the government to decide, in the absence of a motion of this kind, whether it is advisable to resign, according to its political evaluation.

301. The Head of State has sometimes rejected the spontaneous resignation of the Head of Government, inviting the government to verify the existence in Parliament of the political conditions necessary to carry out its activities, or rather to investigate more thoroughly the reasons for the crises virtually open by its resignation (the so-called parliamentarization of government crisis). The President of the Council is free to turn down the Head of State's proposal and to confirm his resignation.

302. Both Chambers allow their members to submit 'individual' motions of no-confidence towards single Ministers.

303. In the absence of a constitutional provision on the matter, doubts have been raised about the legality of parliamentary votes aimed at forcing one single government member to resign, thus distinguishing his or her political responsibility from the whole context of the relationship of confidence. In practice, however, motions submitted by opposition groups blaming the attitude of single Ministers and asking for their resignation have been debated and voted on by Parliament. The government has generally replied by asking for a confidence vote (*see* below, §4) on a resolution submitted by the majority expressing support to the Minister in question, thus identifying the single Minister with the whole government.

304. Once, however, a motion of no-confidence was voted on a Minister who disagreed with the government on some points and had not resigned even after an open invitation of the Head of Government. The Minister, who was subsequently replaced by the Head of State as suggested by the President of the Council, raised a conflict of power before the Constitutional Court, which rejected the reference (*see* Judgment No. 7/1996).

305. Provisions on the debate of no-confidence motions about single Ministers in both Chambers are exactly the same as those set out in Article 94 for no-confidence votes towards the whole government:

1. the Chambers must give their reasons for the motion, which must be signed by at least one-tenth of their members;
2. the motion must be put to a nominal vote and can be debated only three days after it has been submitted;
3. the motion must be voted upon by the simple majority of the Chamber's members.

§4. The Question of Confidence in Theory and Practice

306. If the government fears a negative parliamentary vote on a deliberation that it considers as relevant for the fulfilment of its political objectives, it often makes it a 'question of confidence' before the Chambers, thus declaring that, if the Chambers vote against the deliberation, this vote will be meant as a no-confidence vote and will bring about the resignations of the government. This tool is used by the government whenever it wishes to verify the confidence of parliamentary majority towards its actions and to get Parliament to approve its plans quickly.

This tool had already been used even in the absence of a specific constitutional rule providing for it and well before the question of confidence was partially regulated, in 1971, by the adoption of a special provision in the rules of the Chamber of Deputies.

The question of confidence is presently provided for by both Standing Orders, as well as by Law No. 400/1988. Article 2, first paragraph, letter b, provides that the President of the Council of Ministers, directly or in the person of a delegated Minister, is charged with raising the question of confidence before the full House, and not before parliamentary committees, with the consent of the Council of Ministers. Article 161 of the rules of the Senate just provides that the government cannot make proposals to amend the Standing Orders or the general conditions and internal workings of the Senate a question of confidence.

Article 116 of the rules of the Chamber of Deputies is a more complex provision. Not only does it set out restrictions on the use of this tool by the government, such as in case of votes unrelated to its political programme concerning, for instance, the setting up of committees of enquiry, or committees granting leave to prosecute an MP or verifying the result of elections or nominations but also it sets out the procedural effects of the government's initiative.

307. Both branches of Parliament provide for procedures which differ from the ordinary ones when dealing with questions of confidence.

First, the vote must be nominal, just like all the confidence votes set out in Article 94 of the Constitution. During the past, when voting in Parliament was usually by secret ballot, questions of confidence were even used to impose nominal votes, thus preventing the risk of *francs tireurs* within the majority.

Second, since the subject of the confidence vote is chosen by the government, the latter manages to force the Chamber to vote on that subject exclusively, thus preventing votes on any amendments. This is why questions of confidence have been used in order to overcome the problem of filibustering by the opposition through the submission of various amendments to a particular text of law.

308. There is no provision on the effect of a negative vote by Parliament on a question of confidence. In that event, however, the President of the Council of Ministers is supposed to be forced to resign immediately, since Parliament's decision should not be considered as simple dissent, given the meaning that the government itself has attached to the question.

In practice, every time the government, within a legislative procedure, has made a specific matter a question of confidence, the parliamentary majority has always approved its proposals.

309. The 'question of confidence' can also be used outside a legislative procedure, namely when the President of the Council of Ministers, after speaking to the Chambers on behalf of the government, makes the passing of resolutions proposed by the leaders of the majority to their respective Houses a question of confidence, to make sure that his or her government still enjoys the confidence of Parliament.

This generally occurs following a positive control of the political unity of the majority parties, or after the government's crises, started because of disagreement within the majority, are solved by the reunification of the coalition, which prevents the Head of State from forcing the executive to resign. In both cases, the confidence vote towards the executive by the two branches of Parliament has always had the meaning of a 'ratification' of the settlement of the dispute within the majority, which helped the government to resume its political activities.

In two cases, however, the first on 9 October 1998, during the thirteenth Parliament (when the Chamber of Deputies rejected by 312 votes to 313 the resolution on which the Head of Government, Romano Prodi, had raised a question of confidence) and the second on 24 January 2008, during the fifteenth Parliament (when the Senate rejected by 156 votes to 161 a resolution of the second Prodi Government), the Parliament did not approve the government's resolutions, bringing about its immediate resignations and the consequent government crises. The result of these crises, caused by an explicit declaration requested by the government, has been therefore identical to the one that would be produced by a no-confidence motion voted upon by the Chamber towards the executive.

The President of the Council of Ministers' choice to ask the Chamber of Deputies for a confidence vote after the control of the political unity of his majority had failed seemed rather questionable, especially on a political level. Until that moment, nobody had proposed a no-confidence motion towards the government, neither the opposition nor that part of the majority which had started to be rather critical of the government political choices and which finally decided not to confirm its confidence to the government, forcing the President of the Council of Ministers to resign.

Chapter 7. The Judicial Power

by Marilisa D'Amico & Costanza Nardocci

§1. 'Judges Are Only Subject to the Law'

310. By stating that 'justice is administered in the name of the people' and that 'the judges are subject only to the Law', Article 101 of the Constitution sets out a fundamental principle that gives the judiciary a very different role than the one it used to play under the 'Statuto Albertino'. The Statuto stated indeed that justice was administered 'in the name of the King' by judges appointed personally by the monarch himself.

The main characteristic of Italian judges is, therefore, the fact that they are subject only to the Law regardless of any other authority, especially the executive. On the contrary, in the past, on the contrary, judges were officials dependent on the Government and its political power. Hence, the principle of separation of powers, which is far from being applied to the relationship between legislative and executive power, is strictly observed when it comes to the judiciary.

The fact that judges are only subject to the Law, besides guaranteeing their independence, establishes a link between the judiciary – which is neither elected nor carries any political responsibility – and popular sovereignty expressed by-laws passed by bodies elected by the people and responsible for their political actions.

The activities of judges and their relationship with the law have changed dramatically over the last century, especially if compared to the eighteenth-century model of State, where judges (defined as 'the mouth of the law') were only supposed to enforce the law without any discretionary power.

There is a growing awareness that every kind of interpretative activity has intrinsic creativity, especially in a complex and pluralistic legal system producing a wealth of rules like the Italian one.

Nowadays, furthermore, the judiciary (judges of ordinary jurisdiction and, if necessary, the Constitutional Court) is also charged with reviewing the constitutionality of laws, which requires something more than just a literal interpretation of the law.

§2. The 'External' Independence of Judges: Composition and Functions of the *Consiglio Superiore Della Magistratura*

311. The Constitution ensures the independence of judges in two different ways:

1. The external independence of the judiciary as a whole from outside pressures by any other State organ, especially by the government.
2. The internal independence of every single judge within the judicial system, namely from interference by other judicial organs.

The independence of judges is guaranteed both by preventing any sort of influence on their activities and pressures that might derive from decisions on their careers. The external independence of judges is guaranteed by preventing any influence exerted on them by any other organ, also under Article 104 of the Constitution, which states that 'the judiciary is an independent structure and is not subject to any other authority'. To achieve this aim, the Constituent Assembly decided that the Ministry of Justice, as well as any other authority not strictly connected with the judiciary, was not allowed to take decisions on the careers of ordinary judges, such as transfers, promotions, and disciplinary measures. The Assembly reckoned that this might have influenced the autonomy of judges and, as a direct or indirect consequence, their independence and, thus, decided to entrust these functions to a 'governing body of the judiciary', composed mainly of magistrates: the so-called CSM (Higher Council of the Judiciary). The *Consiglio Superiore della Magistratura* is not a judicial body (except for when it delivers disciplinary measures) but mainly carries out administrative functions. Under Article 105 of the Constitution, the *Consiglio* is competent to appoint the judges by competition, assign them to the various offices, confer functions on them, as well as to deal with the promotion and disciplinary aspects.

The *Consiglio* is, thus, enabled to prevent any sort of influence on the judiciary as a whole and on individual judges. As a representative body of magistrates, it often comes to defence, even against the criticisms and threats coming from politicians towards individual judges' actions or decisions.

Chaired by the President of the Republic, until the 2022 Reform (*see* below, Par. No. 5.1.), the *Consiglio* was composed of twenty-seven members. Sixteen were magistrates elected from and among their ranks, while the remaining eight were either full university law professors or advocates, all of whom elected by a joint session of the two Houses of the Parliament.

The President and the General Procurator of the *Corte di Cassazione* are ex officio members of the *Consiglio*.

According to the previous electoral system (for the new regulation, *see* below, Par. No. 5.1.), the sixteen ordinary judges of the *Consiglio* were elected by magistrates among 'those belonging to all categories' (*see* Article 104, paragraph 4, Constitution), by way of a personal, secret and direct vote. Aiming at the implementation of this rule, Law No. 44/2002 provided that two of the sixteen seats were allocated to judges belonging to the *Corte di Cassazione* still in office, four seats to public prosecutors with merit's function and ten seats to judges with merits' function. Candidates were elected in three national electoral colleges for each of the mentioned categories according to the number of votes (Article 23, paragraph 2, Law No. 195/1958 modified by Law No. 44/2002). Every elector votes for a candidate in each category through the sign of his/her name on the voting paper. Candidates are chosen from various lists normally representing the currents in which the National Association of Magistrates is divided.

312. Under Article 22 of Law No. 195/1958, the other members of the *Consiglio* were and continue to be elected by the Parliament in joint session, by secret ballot, and the majority of three-fifths of the members of the two Houses (or the majority of three-fifths of the voters after the second counting). Candidates must be full university law professors and advocates of at least fifteen years of practising experience.

Owing to the numerical superiority of members elected by judges, the Council is defined as a 'self-government body' of the magistracy. However, it is not an entire self-government body, owing to the presence of lay judges, who prevent the judiciary from being detached from the other powers.

Therefore, the composition of the *Consiglio* meets two important requirements or constitutional needs: first, it avoids external interference; second, it prevents the independence of the judiciary from turning into a detached and exclusive guild.

The elected members of the *Consiglio* hold office for four years and are not immediately re-eligible.

Under Article 5 of Law No. 1/1981, they cannot be 'prosecuted for the opinions expressed in the exercise of their functions concerning a specific matter'. The Constitutional Court highlighted that such immunity concerns 'any form of expression of the thought, though not other forms of behaviour for which the members of the *Consiglio* may be criminally prosecuted' (Constitutional Court, Judgment No. 148/1983). The Court also ruled that this provision 'consistent with the design of the Constitution', especially with Article 104 and following constitutional provisions, which set out that the exercise of the functions of the *Consiglio* is a fundamental way for the judiciary to preserve its autonomy and independence (*see* Judgment No. 148/1983).

As stated above, the functions of the *Consiglio* mainly concern the career of judges. It also fulfils, however, auxiliary duties such as advising the Minister of Justice on questions concerning the judicial system.

313. Measures concerning the *status* of the magistrates are undertaken through a decree of the President of the Republic, after a proposal of the Minister of Justice, or by a decree of the Minister himself and always following a resolution of the *Consiglio*. They can be appealed to a Court of administrative jurisdiction. The Constitutional Court highlighted that this form of judicial control, which is necessary for the protection of individual rights and interests under the Constitution, does not conflict with the autonomy of the judiciary (Constitutional Court, Judgment No. 168/1963).

A section of the *Consiglio* is, then, tasked with disciplinary measures towards the judges. It is composed of nine effective and six deputy members. The effective members are the Vice-President of the *Consiglio*, in his capacity as chairman, two members are elected by Parliament, one of whom is the Vice-President of the section, a judge of the *Corte di Cassazione* who adjudicates on points of law, and five magistrates who adjudicate on the merits of the laws.

The disciplinary process can either be set in motion by the Minister of Justice (Article 107 Const.) or by the Procurator General of the *Corte di Cassazione*. More precisely, only the latter has to proceed (Article 14 Legislative Decree No. 109/2006). More broadly, disciplinary actions follow the same rules as trials (Constitutional Court, Judgment No. 12/1971): the judgment, called *sentenza*, must not take the form of a presidential or ministerial decree, unlike all the other acts of the *Consiglio*. Decisions of the disciplinary section can be appealed to the *Corte di Cassazione* on points of law.

Sanctions include reprimands, loss of seniority, and dismissal from office.

In the past, before the reform, the *Consiglio* has often been obliged to work, in the absence of specific provisions, in a self-regulating manner, i.e., by taking general resolutions on the careers of judges. But Law No. 105/2005 and Legislative Decree No. 106/2006 introduced the predetermination of offences and disciplinary conduct relevant and remedied the problem of indeterminacy of the same offences, since the original formulation of the rule on disciplinary offences referred to behaviour likely to injure the prestige of the judiciary. The current framework, specifically stating the disciplinary offences, limits the discretion of the Council by identifying behaviours considered deserving of sanction.

§3. The Powers of the Minister of Justice

314. The Minister of Justice has very little powers compared to the past.

315. Although these powers continue to play a significant role and might be summarized as follows:

- He/she is entrusted with the organization and operation of services concerned with the administration of law (Article 110 of the Constitution).
- He/she may make specific requests to the *Consiglio* concerning the legal status of judges (appointment, assignment to the offices, conferring of functions, transfers and, promotions).
- He/she may ask for and give information on the administration of justice.
- According to Article 107, second paragraph, of the Constitution, he is entitled to undertake disciplinary actions towards the magistrates (a process which has to be set in motion at the same time by the General Procurator of the *Corte di Cassazione* according to Article 14 of Legislative Decree No. 109/2006).
- He/she may advise the *Consiglio* on several issues, including the conferral of executive powers, a question that must be agreed upon by a committee of the *Consiglio* itself and by the Minister. The Constitutional Court ruled that the agreement must be based on a principle of fair cooperation although, if the two do not manage to reach an agreement, the *Consiglio* is empowered to take the last decision (Judgment No. 379/1992; Judgment No. 380/2003).

§4. The 'Internal' Independence of Judges

316. The independence of judges as individuals is set out, as stated above, in Article 101, second paragraph, of the Constitution which, by providing that 'the judges are subject only to the Law', ensures their utmost independence of any sort of influence but their professional skills and devotion.

This aim is also pursued by other constitutional provisions, which concern their appointment by competition, the security of tenure, and the absence of hierarchy within the judiciary.

Entry to the judiciary is by competitive examination (Article 106, first paragraph, of the Constitution), i.e., by an unbiased selection which is usually open to everybody who has taken a degree in Law.

The Constitution itself provides a few exceptions to this rule. First, honorary magistrates can be appointed to perform judicial functions (not by profession). According to Article 106, second paragraph, they may even be elected, although they are not today, and they can perform only the duties attributed to individual judges, as they cannot be part of a collegiate body. These magistrates are presently the *giudici di pace* (Law No. 374/1991).

The second exception is represented by the so-called *giudici popolari*, i.e., ordinary citizens with secondary school qualifications who are selected by drawing lots to sit on the *Corte d'Assise* of the first instance and of appeal. This is the only implementation of citizens' direct participation in the administration of justice provided for by Article 102 of the Constitution.

According to Article 107, first paragraph, of the Constitution, judges cannot be removed from office, nor transferred without their consent. They can be dismissed or suspended from their duties or even transferred to other courts or given other duties only using a decision of the CSM, taken for reasons laid down by regulations.

No other public employee enjoys so extensive guarantees. The aim is to allow magistrates to pass their judgments with the utmost objectiveness. Therefore judges can be, first of all, transferred against their will only if they have committed a disciplinary wrong (Article 13, Legislative Decree No. 196/2006). This kind of transfer is a disciplinary sanction that can be ordered at the end of disciplinary action. Second, under Article 2, second paragraph, of Legislative Decree of the King No. 511 of 31 May, modified by Legislative Decree No. 109/2006, magistrates can be transferred if they cannot, for any objective reason but not their fault (otherwise there a disciplinary sanction), even against their will, 'administer justice under the conditions required by the prestige of the judicial system' (the so-called environmental incompatibility).

The consistency of this rule with Article 107, first paragraph, of the Constitution has always been questioned. If magistrates must be above all suspicion, this could lead to strict control over their private lives to prevent behaviours that might jeopardize their credibility.

Under Article 107, third paragraph, judges differ from one another only on account of their functions. This means, as said, that hierarchies are not allowed within the judicial system: no senior judge could ever give instructions to a junior judge on his way of passing judgments (*see* Constitutional Court, Judgment No. 40/1964). The Constitution provides that the powers of every single justice department should never interfere with the powers of higher departments (*see* Constitutional Court, Judgment No. 143/1973).

There are, however, different degrees of adjudication: decisions taken at first instance can be appealed and be quashed in whole or in part and be further appealed to the *Corte di Cassazione*. This does not mean, however, that courts of the first instance are hierarchically subordinate to courts of appeal and the latter to the *Corte di Cassazione*: judges are completely independent in the exercise of their functions. Moreover, all judgments have the same degree of enforceability, regardless of the judge that passes them. This is why judicial power is defined as *diffuso* (widespread).

Magistrates do have a professional status, however, and the Constitution, therefore, provides for their career and promotion (Article 105). To prevent decisions on the career of magistrates – though exercised by their self-governing body or under its supervision – from influencing their independence, a system of automatic promotion according to seniority or non-discreditable actions was introduced. Seniority is more and more taken into account when assigning judges to specific departments or conferring executive functions on them. This has made the selection of magistrates according to their merit and industriousness harder and harder.

§5. The Organization of Justice in Italy: The Civil and Penal Jurisdiction and the Constitutional Role of the Public Prosecutor[146]

317. The principle of judicial unity implies that all the judicial functions are performed by one judiciary enjoying full independence. Opponents of this principle advocate the existence of various judicial units with jurisdiction over the different types of law.

The Constituent Assembly reached a compromise between these two extremes. Although it proclaimed that the principle of judicial unity was as a fundamental aspect of the Italian legal system and explicitly forbade the appointment of special judges (i.e., outside the ordinary judicial system) and extraordinary judges (i.e., specially appointed to settle previous disputes) (Article 102 of the Constitution), it admitted several exceptions to the appointment of special judges (Article 103).

Provision was also made for the revision of the special jurisdictions existing before (VIth Transitory and Final Provision) and for specialistic sections joined by 'properly qualified citizens who are not members of the judiciary' (Article 102). In the words of the Constitutional Court, these sections are not a '*tertium genus* between special and ordinary courts, but rather a *species* of the latter' (Judgment No. 76/1961).

318. The Italian judicial system is therefore a system in which ordinary courts are supported and supplemented by special courts with significant functions.

A reform introduced remarkable changes in the general organization of civil and penal justice (*see* Legislative Decree No. 51/1998 implementing Law No. 254/1997 – delegation to the government for the implementation of the *giudice unico*).

For the purposes of criminal jurisdiction, the reform provided for the dissolution of the *Preture* and for transferring its powers to the *Tribunale*, which is composed

146. For the details regarding the new regulatory framework which came into effect following Law No. 71/2022, *see*, below, Par. No. 5.1.

of three judges only in particular cases, and is a monocratic court in all the others, even when it acts as a Court of Appeal of decisions taken by the *Giudice di Pace*.

For the purposes of civil jurisdiction, the law provides that the *Tribunale* must be composed of three judges in several cases and be a monocratic court in all the others.

319. Courts of criminal cognizance also include the *Tribunale del riesame* empowered with the review, even on their merits, of measures restricting personal freedom (Article 309 of criminal procedure code). There is a *Tribunale del riesame* in each district of the Court of Appeal. The cognizance depends on the place where the court that originally heard the case is situated.

The *Tribunale* can either allow or reject the appeal (to be made within five days of the judgment being handed down) and uphold or quash the decision of the lower court by an *ordinanza* passed in Chambers.

Investigating departments are staffed by judicial magistrates acting as *pubblico ministero* within the *Procure* (*Procura generale* near the *Corte di Cassazione; Procure generali* near the *Corti di Appello; Procure della Repubblica* near the *Tribunali* and *Tribunali dei minorenni*).

According to Article 112 of the Constitution, 'the *pubblico ministero* is responsible for instituting penal proceedings', although he or she has jurisdiction over some civil and administrative matters as well.

Criminal investigations by the *pubblico ministero* are therefore mandatory. The aim is to ensure the equality of citizens before the law, as well as the impartiality of the *pubblico ministero*, whose autonomy is thus guaranteed.

The Italian justice excludes solutions in force in other systems, such as the plea bargaining, in which the public prosecutor and the defendant can negotiate the sentence and eventually drop some of the charges.

The power to institute penal proceedings is usually denied to private citizens, who can only submit their complaints to the *pubblico ministero*, who will then set the criminal process in motion. There is, therefore, a distinction between crimes prosecuted ex officio by the judiciary and those prosecuted upon a complaint, which is sometimes a necessary condition for instituting penal proceedings.

The *pubblico ministero* is a magistrate of ordinary jurisdiction safeguarded by the guarantees of independence laid down by the law (Article 107, last paragraph, of the Constitution), not necessarily the same enjoyed by the *giudici*.

The *procure* are hierarchical structures in which the Heads of the departments may give instructions to their assistants, who can also be assigned or revoked the causes with a justification.

The system of distribution of the causes is different from that adopted by judicial magistrates.

According to the Constitution, the judicial police are at the direct disposal of the judiciary (Article 109 of the Constitution). This constitutional provision was not implemented by creating a specialistic section of the criminal police, but rather by entrusting specialistic sections especially set up within the ordinary police forces (*Polizia di Stato, Arma dei Carabinieri, Guardia di Finanza*) with the tasks of the criminal police. The double dependence of the criminal police on the judiciary and on the force they belong to the caused inconvenience which the new Code of Criminal Procedure tried to solve by creating specialistic sections of the criminal police under the supervision of the *Tribunale*, the *Giudice,* and the *Pubblico Ministero* and by increasing the functional dependence of criminal police agents on the judiciary as well as, at the same time, by reducing their hierarchical dependence on the force they belong to (Article 55 and ff. sections, Code of Criminal Procedure).

§5.1. The 2022 Reform of the Italian Judicial System

The Italian judicial system recently underwent a significant process of reform following the coming into force of Law No. 71/2022 (*Delega al Governo per la riforma dell'ordinamento giudiziario per l'adeguamento dell'ordinamento militare, nonchè disposizioni in materia ordinamentale, organizzativa e disciplinare, di eleggibilità ricollocamento il ruolo dei magistrati e di costituzione e il funzionamento del Consiglio superiore della magistratura*).

Law No. 71/2022 intervenes on both the normative framework related to the *Consiglio*, amending Law No. 195/1958, and several legal provisions regarding the *status* of the magistrates and the overall organization of judicial offices.

With respect to the *Consiglio*, Law No. 71/2022, the major reform impacts on the electoral system governing the composition of the body with the aim of ensuring the establishment of a truly independent organism. Within this perspective should be interpreted the legal provision that explicitly requires the magistrates to exercise their functions independently.

As for the composition of the *Consiglio*, Law No. 71/2022 mainly impacts on the system of election of the magistrates (so-called *membri togati*). It first increases the number of the magistrates within the *Consiglio* that is now twenty. The twenty magistrates are now elected relying on a mixed electoral system based on binominal constituencies and on a proportional recovery for the allocation of five seats reserved for judges exercising merit's functions.

With respect to the non-judicial component of the *Consiglio*, worth mentioning is the explicit reference provided under Article 30 that indicates that the remaining members should be elected according to the principle of transparency and gender equality.

The other field of intervention of the Reform concerns, instead, the careers of the magistrates.

One of the most interesting aspects deals with the regulation of the separation between adjudicative and investigative functions. The new Law provides on this that the change from adjudicative to investigative functions, and vice versa, may be made only once during the magistrate's career and within a specific time frame, meaning within the nine years since the first assignment of functions.

A second aspect worth mentioning here deals with the magistrates' participation in politics. For the very first time, in fact, the Italian legal system benefits from a comprehensive regulation concerning, on the one hand, the possibility for magistrates to run for political, European and administrative elections and, on the other, the regulation of their willingness to exercise again their previous judicial functions.

§6. Constitutional Provisions Regarding Special Judges

320. As said already, the principle of judicial unity is mitigated by the presence of special judges.

Some of these are explicitly provided for by the Constitution (Article 103): the *Consiglio di Stato* (Council of State), a court having jurisdiction to review administrative decisions, the *Corte dei Conti* (Court of Accounts), and the military courts. Moreover, under Article 125 of the Constitution, 'first degree courts for administrative actions', the *Tribunali amministrativi regionali*, are set up in every Region under Law No. 1034/1971 (on administrative judges *see* Part II, Chapter 8).

Under Article 103, third paragraph, military courts in times of peace have jurisdiction over military offences committed by members of the Armed Forces. Such offences are provided for by the Military Code of Peace: Decree of the King No. 1022/1941 and ff. amendments. The Constitutional Court has declared the special provisions on military offences and severe punishment provided for by the code unconstitutional, thus making them more similar to ordinary offences and punishment.

The decisions of military tribunals of the first instance can be appealed to the *Corte militare di Appello* (Article 57 of the military order code). Both the military courts and the Court of Appeal are composed of military magistrates and officials of the force the defendant belongs to, although the number of military magistrates is always higher. Decisions of the military courts can be appealed to the *Corte di Cassazione* (judging in its normal composition) on the same grounds set out in the Code of Criminal Procedure (*see* Constitutional Court, Judgment No. 1/1983). The prosecutors are instituted by the *Tribunali militari*, the *Corte militare di appello* and the *Corte di Cassazione* (Article 58 of the military order code).

Independence of the military courts is guaranteed by the *Consiglio della magistratura militare* (Council of the military magistracy) (Legislative Decree No. 66/2010, so-called military order code), chaired by the President of *Cassazione* and composed of the General Procurator of the *Cassazione* itself, two members elected by military judges, including at least one military magistrate of the *Corte di Cassazione* and one member having no connection with military justice appointed by the two Presidents of the Houses of Parliament.

§7. The Revision of Special Jurisdictions

321. Although the Constitution, under the VIth Transitory and Final Provision, explicitly stated that a revision of the special courts set up before the promulgation of the Constitution (and not provided under Article 103) was to be carried out within five years of the effective date of the Constitution, the intention of saving these courts prevailed over the wish to repeal them.

The time limit set out in the Constitution was not deemed as mandatory and the term 'revision' was meant as an obligation for Parliament to change the organization of the courts, to ensure their independence under Article 108, second paragraph, of the Constitution (Constitutional Court, Judgment No. 41/1957).

Special courts, therefore, continued to carry out their activities, often with compositions and rules very far from the principles set out in the Constitution about the judiciary. The constitutionality of these instances was raised so often that the Constitutional Court eventually eliminated those which did not comply with the principles of unity and independence of the judiciary (*see* Judgments Nos 133/1963; 93/1965; 55/1966; 30/1967; 49/1968; 60/1969; 121/1970; and 164/1976). Other times, however, the court feared that the activities of some of these courts could not be easily transferred to the ordinary judiciary and preferred to wait for their revision rather than ruling them unconstitutional.

The example of tax courts is emblematic. The Constitutional Court, in its effort not to declare these courts unconstitutional for breach of the principle of independence, initially stated that their nature was 'administrative rather than judicial' (*see* Judgments Nos 6 and 10/1969). Once the revision of these courts was undertaken by Legislative Decree No. 636/1972, the Court affirmed that the judicial nature of these courts had been ascertained by promoters of the decree by a sort of 'authentic interpretation' (*see* Judgments Nos 28/1974 and 215/1976).

Therefore, today there are still other special jurisdictions in addition to those provided for by Article 103. The most important ones, especially for the volume of their caseloads, are tax courts (on this subject, *see* Part II, Chapter 8).

§8. Judicial Activities and Constitutional Rights of Citizens

322. The Constitution provides not only for the organization of the judicial system, the legal status of magistrates, and the exercise of judicial functions but also for the protection of the rights of citizens from the judiciary:

a. Article 25, first paragraph, of the Constitution sets out the fundamental principle of the giudice naturale (natural judge), strictly connected to the prohibition of appointing special judges (Article 102, second paragraph). 'No one may be punished except based on a law already in force before the offence was committed' also means that everybody is entitled to a judge appointed based on a law that has come into force before the offence was committed. Article 25, first paragraph, prohibits not only any chance of competence with retroactive effects but also the appointment of a competent judge by anyone but the legislator. The Constitutional Court, however, ruled that exceptions to Article 25 are allowed if the change is aimed at protecting the independence of judges with objective and general rules (*see* Judgments Nos 50/1963 and 10/1966). The new Code of Criminal Procedure, to exclude any discretionary power when a cause is passed from a court to another, states that the standards for the assignment of causes and replacement of judges are set in advance by the CSM (Article 4 of Decree No. 449 of the President of the Republic of 1988).
b. Article 24 of the Constitution guarantees the right to legal proceedings ('anyone may bring cases before a court of law in order to protect their rights under civil and administrative law') and to defence ('defence is an inviolable right at every stage and instance of legal proceedings'), which means that the parties are free to assert their rights (right to self-defence) and that legal aid is provided to

everybody (Constitutional Court, Judgment No. 59/1959). Article 24, however, was not enforced immediately. For criminal purposes, for instance, it was not enforced until 1988, with the new Code of Criminal Procedure. The Constitutional Court had to make up for this legislative vacuum by a number of judgments. Mention should first of all be made to the enforcement of the right to defence from the act of the defence police (i.e., acts carried out during investigations prior to the trial: gathering information about the person indicted, searches, gathering probative material) (*see* Judgment No. 86/1968), as well as during the phase of investigations in criminal procedure. The court also enforced the principle of equality between prosecution and defence, by ensuring, for instance, the possibility for the defender to participate in the examination of the defendant, which was previously granted to the prosecutor alone (*see* Judgment No. 190/1970). The Constitutional Court enforced the right to institute legal proceedings and to defence in civil proceedings as well, by repealing some rules that hindered its full implementation. It is worth mentioning, for instance, the declaration of unconstitutionality of the so-called solve et repete in fiscal matters, i.e., the principle according to which appeals against decisions of fiscal authorities were allowed only subject to the payment of the tax (Judgment No. 21/1961). Mention should also be made to the various judgments by which the Court ruled that the parties to a trial must be guaranteed the same rights to produce evidence of their innocence, and provision of a legal counsel in proceedings of separation of spouses (Judgment No. 171/1971). The court also wondered if the right to defence implied the right to reject the legal counsel (thus opting for self-defence). It eventually ruled that the legal counsel ensures the full defence of the parties as well as the right progress of the trial (Judgments Nos 125/1979 and 188/1980); therefore it limited the discretionary choice made by the parties to the trial.

c. Article 24, third paragraph, of the Constitution states that 'the indigent are entitled, through special provisions, to proper means for action or defence at all levels of jurisdiction'. This principle has been enforced by Law No. 217/1990 and now by Article 74 and ff. of Legislative Decree No. 115/2002, adding to the old system of legal aid a new provision of free advocacy in court for all those who do not reach a minimum level of income provided for by law.

d. Article 25, second paragraph, states that 'no one may be punished save based on a law which has come into force before the offence has been committed'. The aim of this rule is to prevent any arbitrary action against the freedom of citizens, as well as to acknowledge the definite and exact nature of criminal offences, to be meant as a ban to issue criminal rules which do not state clearly what is lawful and what is not (*see* Judgments Nos 393 and 394/2006).

e. Article 27, first paragraph, states that 'criminal responsibility is personal', i.e., that no one can be held responsible for offences committed by somebody else. According to this principle, people should never be held responsible if there is no relationship of cause and effect between their own will and the offence they committed (*see* Judgment No. 3/1956). This principle also led the Constitutional Court, in its famous Judgment No. 364/1988, to rule Article 5 of the Code of Criminal Procedure, which stated that ignorance of criminal law was irrelevant, partially unconstitutional. The court affirmed that no one can be held responsible if ignorance of criminal law depends on an event independent of one's fault.

f. Article 27, third paragraph, provides that the accused 'are not considered guilty' until the final sentence has been passed upon them. It also entails the obligation to regulate trial proceedings and institutions in such a way as to prevent the accused from suffering any negative effects before their culpability has been definitively established.

g. Another principle concerning the exercise of judicial functions is the obligation to provide valid reasons for all legal proceedings (Article 111, third paragraph, of the Constitution). It has a double function: first, it allows citizens who are parties to a trial to defend themselves against an unfavourable decision in the various degrees of adjudication; second, it allows all citizens and all the other judges to learn the reasons that prompted a judicial decision.

§9. Constitutional Review of Article 111 of the Constitution and Introduction of the 'Fair Trial' Principles

323. On 10 November 1999, the constitutional law on 'the introduction of the fair trial principles in section 111 of the Constitution' was finally adopted, following a long legislative path. This reform was launched also to deal with some practical difficulties and followed a dubious outcome of a judgment passed by the Constitutional Court (No. 361/1998) providing for new rules about evidence production in criminal trials. The reform introduces several innovative elements which have an impact not only on the principles governing the judicial system but also on some other principles – which we have just mentioned – contained in the first part of the Constitution, namely the right to institute legal proceedings and to defence (Article 24) and the principle of the natural judge established by law (Article 25). The reform of Article 111 of the Constitution introduces some important principles in the Constitution which were already contained in Article 6 of the ECHR as well as in Article 14, paragraph 3, of the International Covenant on Civil and Political Rights.

The first part of the law concerns all kinds of trials. It reads: 'Fair trials must be provided for by law' and also adds that 'All trials must be carried out according to the principle of cross-examination, on a fair basis and before an impartial judge.'

Finally, the general rule of the 'reasonable duration' of trials is stated, so introducing the principle already stated by the above-mentioned international treaties.

324. The second part of the reformed text of Article 111 of the Constitution contains principles pertaining only to criminal trials. It establishes that: 'in the criminal trials, everyone who is charged with a criminal offence has the statutory right to be notified promptly and confidentially of the nature and cause of the charges made against him/her; she/he must be given adequate time and conditions to prepare his/her defence; she/he has the statutory right to examine, or have examined, the witnesses testifying against her/him in court, to obtain the attendance and examination of witnesses on her/his behalf under the same conditions as witnesses against her/him and to obtain all other evidence on her/his behalf; she/he must be assisted by an interpreter if she/he cannot understand or speak the language used during the trial'. This shows how detailed this matter is.

The text then contains some rules which were introduced in an attempt to overrule Judgment No. 361/1998 of the Constitutional Court, providing for different principles. The new text reads: 'Criminal trials are regulated by the principle of cross-examination for evidence gathering. The indicted person cannot be declared guilty on grounds of the statements made by a person who has deliberately refused to be examined by the indicted himself/herself or by his/her lawyer.' However, the following paragraph provides that: 'the law regulates those cases in which evidence is not gathered according to the principle of cross-examination following an agreement with the indicted person, or due to practical impossibility or to prove misconduct'.

A very critical aspect of this reform is the impact that it will have on pending trials. It is evident the risk of a long suspension of those trials on the ground of their consequential illegitimacy, declared by the judges or raised by the opposing parties, due to the reform.

Article 2 of the reform text states that a 'law' will regulate the application of the principles contained in the text itself to criminal trials pending on the date of its coming into force. This provisional matter has been considered by Parliament by passing Law No. 265/2001. But the enforcement of this Law provoked mainly new workload for the Courts and incremented the loss of time. Although the presence of Law No. 265/2001 of the European Court of Human Rights often condemns Italy for the breach of Article 6 of the ECHR. The right to a fair trial is also enshrined at the supranational level by the above-mentioned Article 6 of the European Convention. Despite the reform of Article 111 of the Constitution, Italy has been condemned several times because of the length of its judicial proceedings. To overcome the findings of non-compliance with the European Convention, the legislator has thus intervened with Law No. 89/2001, providing compensations for damages following the unreasonable length of national proceedings. The entry into force of Law No. 89/2001 has though not until now significantly reduced the high numbers of applications brought before the European Court of Human Rights, whose response has often been not only the finding of a breach of Article 6 of the Convention but also the choice for the pilot-judgment procedure.

§10. JUDGES CIVIL RESPONSIBILITY

325. As far as judges civil responsibility is concerned and under Article 28 of the Constitution ('[o]fficials of the State or public agencies shall be directly responsible under criminal, civil, and administrative law for acts committed in violation of rights In such cases, civil liability shall extend to the State and such public agency'), at the time of the coming into force of Italian Constitution judges could be responsible only in case of acts committed with fraud or official misconduct (*see* Articles 55 and 56 of the 1940 Criminal Code).

It was only with Law No. 117/1998 that civil responsibility, as an indirect responsibility – the State was the sole institution which bears responsibility – opened up to include cases of serious negligence, as provided under Article 2, §2, of Law No. 117/1988, whereas §3 detailed the specific cases in which State's responsibility, through indirect judges responsibility, might arise.

Following the CJEU's judgments – *Kobler v. Austria* (30 September 2006) and *Traghetti del Mediterraneo v. Italy* (13 June 2006) – and the 2009 EU Commission's infringement proceedings, concluded with the EU Court of Justice's judgment stating Italy's not compliance with EU Law, the legislator approved Law No. 18/2015.

Law No. 18/2015 reformed the previous mechanism of civil responsibility as set out under Law No. 117/1988 by increasing the number of cases of responsibility and by extending cases of civil responsibility to violations of EU Law. Although maintaining the State as the entity bearing responsibility for judges' misconduct, therefore excluding citizen's direct action towards judges, Law No. 18/2015 has softened the procedure mainly through the abolition of the existing admissibility filter on the merit of the application (Law No. 117/1988 provided for an initial admissibility filter before examining the merit of the request).

Chapter 8. Judicial Control of Administrative Action

by Enzo Balboni

§1. INTRODUCTION

326. The subject that we are now briefly confronting constitutes the core of the matter known in the university syllabus as administrative law, even if it has important constitutional implications. In fact, some articles of the Constitution deal directly with this matter: Articles 24, 103, 111, 113 and 125. Moreover, to have or not a constitutional backing and guarantee of one's rights against the Public Administration is, from all points of view, noteworthy and in many instances decisive.

§2. EVOLUTION OF THE PRINCIPLES OF ADMINISTRATIVE JUSTICE IN ITALY

327. The ancient and conservative conception of the State – what is known as the type of State that adopts the 'rule of law', or better: a certain idea of the relationship between the citizens and the State – implies a position of (fundamental) equality between these two subjects.

This means that, when a dispute arises between public powers and citizens concerning the limits of their respective areas of competence and/or power, another subject, extraneous and impartial with regard to the contending parties, must be appointed in order to settle the dispute. The legal system entrusts the jurisdictional function to this 'third subject': the ordinary judge with his distinct status and independent position.

Behind this conception – that we may call purely liberal – there was a strict interpretation of the principle of the separation of powers, according to which it was essential that the administration was completely separated from the jurisdiction in order to place the public and the private interests at the same level before an impartial judge.

The Belgian Constitution of 1831 took this direction. The same position was adopted – some years later – by the members of the Italian Parliament which, under Premier Marco Minghetti's guide, drafted the law, which, promulgated with No. 2248, Annex E, on 20 March 1865, is part of the body of Laws of the Unification and still today is a fundamental piece of public law legislation.

§3. POWERS AND LIMITS OF THE ORDINARY JUDGE OVER THE PUBLIC ADMINISTRATION

328. The above-mentioned Annex E abolished the Tribunals of the *contenzioso amministrativo* (*contentieux administratif*, in the French tradition), which were administrative organs existing in the different States before the Unification.

They were entrusted with the resolution of certain disputes between citizens and public authorities. Meanwhile, the ordinary judges (who until that moment only knew of disputes between private parties) were entrusted with all matters involving a civil or political right.

Within this area of matters there were included all those cases where it was possible to show that – to a certain extent – the Public Administration could be concerned.

However, according to the liberal principles of a strict separation of powers, the ordinary judge was not permitted to revoke or modify the administrative act done by the various authorities.

The ideological assumption was that, in case he would revoke or modify the administrative act, the ordinary judge would actually interfere in the exercise of the administrative power which he was forbidden to take count of.

However, when knowing of an illegitimate administrative act, he simply ought not to apply it, meaning that he should have judged leaving out of consideration of the existence of that act.

All these principles, even if they enlarged the judge's competencies (and consequently, they extended also the protection of the citizen, considering that the acts and behaviour of the administrative authorities which infringed a right were submitted to the judge), simultaneously came to limit, to a high degree, his powers.

These issues determine still today the powers and limits of the ordinary judge's action whenever an administrative act involves a right of a subjective nature (*diritto soggettivo*).

§4. The *Diritto Soggettivo Perfetto* (Full Subjective Right)

329. This can be defined as the legal position of a citizen which is protected in a direct, actual and personal manner.

We refer to a right within a legal relation, in the sense that the subjective right is, in the administrative sphere, the reverse of an obligation which falls on the Administration. For instance, where the Public Administration is part of a relation involving rights of a private nature, its contractual obligations (for instance: the payment of debts in due time) will certainly create a position of right in favour of the citizen who enters into a legal relation with the Administration itself.

Far more complicated is the matter of the so-called public subjective rights. In this regard, over the centuries and even in the nineteenth century (when liberal views coexisted with other still authoritarian ones), an approach has been consolidated according to which the administrative power – as the engine active and responsible for pursuing the public interest – had (and still today has) the power to weaken and – to a certain extent – 'degrade' the position based on a right of a subjective nature, turning it into a different position (and a less protected one) called legitimate interest (*interesse legittimo*).

§5. THE *INTERESSE LEGITTIMO* (LEGITIMATE INTEREST)

330. So the property rights of the individual are not considered absolute and untouchable rights anymore, but they are regarded as rights conditioned on the existence – or, reciprocally, the survival – of a public interest which aims, in case of necessity and always in a legitimate and proper manner, towards a quantitative and, sometimes, qualitative reduction of the rights that can even lead to its elimination.

To give an example, let us consider the compulsory acquisition of a piece of land (*espropriazione per pubblica utilità*), motivated by the need to build a railway or a road. In this case, the owner of the land is entitled to the following expectations protected by law: the right to receive an expropriation indemnity and the legitimate interest that the Administration, when exercising its power to reduce or eliminate his property right, behaves in a legitimate matter, that is to say respecting all the guarantees, that expropriation law provides for, which must be fulfilled by the expropriation order.

Another example of a legitimate interest is that of the person who asks the Mayor to grant him/her a building permit in order to build in a land which he/she owns. In fact, also in this case the so-called *jus aedificandi* is conditional on and limited by the right of all citizens to a rational use of the land, which the Mayor exercises on behalf of the whole community when granting or denying the building permit, stating at the same time the reasons why, so that the unsatisfied part may ask redress.

§6. SIMPLE AND DIFFUSED INTERESTS

331. Placed a step downwards with regard to the position of the 'legitimate interest', there are those types of general interest that everyone of us have in that the Administration must always pursue, in the best way, the public interest: so that it builds roads, hospitals, aqueducts, etc., it approves a town planning scheme or it protects the environment. Furthermore, in the last quarter of the twentieth century, a movement has been started, especially by protectionist associations, with the aim of obtaining the recognition of the subjectivity of the so-called spread interests, also from a legal point of view.

The extension of the *locus standi* eventually reached the statute book (Law No. 241/1990) and now concerns also other qualified associations, with regard to the interests specified in their respective original statutes. As a consequence, the power to challenge the administrative acts deemed illegitimate is now a larger one.

Indeed, associations devoted to the protection of environment and consumers' rights have now the power to impugn administrative decrees and acts concerning their field of activity: so actions, which could not be easily promoted by individual citizens (for lack of a distinctive and personal and actual interest), are brought on by trained and resourceful social formations.

§7. The Historical Evolution of the Administrative Justice System

332. Let us tackle again, briefly, the historical evolution of administrative justice in Italy. After the law of 1865 which protected legal positions of a subjective nature, all those other positions that were defined, at that time, of legitimate interest, as described above, remained unprotected.

Moreover, the law of 1865 was interpreted by ordinary judges in a strict sense. Thus, they would not recognize a right, but only an interest – to which regard citizens could only file a complaint before administrative authorities – each time a provision which granted the power to degrade a right was issued, even if that provision was found, during the subsequent examination of the case, to be illegitimate.

In order to put an end to this harsh situation and to provide for a judge in charge of the interests, and thanks to statists such as Silvio Spaventa and Francesco Crispi, Law No. 5992/ 1888 was approved. This law created the Fourth Section of the Council of State (this organ has existed as a consultative body since the reign of King Carlo Alberto, 1831).

In this manner, the jurisdictional attributions concerning incompetence, excess of power and breach of law against acts – of individual or general quality – issued by the administrative authorities having as their object a legitimate interest, were assigned to the Council of State. The power of the Council of State was limited to the annulment of the contested act. But its competence was extended so that it could require the Administration to fulfil its obligations to comply, with respect to that particular case, the decision taken by the ordinary judge which recognized an infringement of a civil or political right.

The fundamental infrastructure and moreover the mind of administrative justice – and therefore of the judicial control of administrative action – was built in the direction now described and, with minor changes, is still in force today. Also, the recent codification of 2010 has stated a progress without revolution: in other terms a confirmation.

§8. The Principles Enshrined in the Constitution

333. We have dwelt long on the legislative evolution of the principles of administrative justice in Italy because the fundamental reasons of our system can only be understood as a succession of stratifications beginning from 1865, through which the matter has been mould again, but never to such an extent as to deny its fundamental principles.

Specifically, these consist in the creation of a legal position – peculiar to the Italian legal system – called '*legitimate interest*', which is different from that of a subjective nature, and in the establishment of two different systems of protection entrusted to two different judges – the administrative and the ordinary judge, respectively – endowed with different powers.

Eighty years after the original choice was made and in a completely different social environment with respect to the liberal ideology then prevailing, the Italian

Constitution could – as someone maintained – have radically changed the fundamental principles of administrative justice. On the contrary, these principles were confirmed and completed, even renewed by the Constitution.

Therefore, it is possible, for our purposes, to draw the fundamental principles on the matter from the articles of our basic law. These are:

a. solemn confirmation of the fundamental basis of the protection granted: 'Everyone shall have the right to undertake legal proceedings in order to protect his rights and legitimate interests' (Article 24 Const.);
b. confirmation of the creation of a specific judge for the legitimate interests: 'The Council of State and the other organs of the administrative justice' (this reference caused the subsequent creation of the Regional Administrative Tribunals (TARs)) 'have jurisdiction to protect, against the Public Administration, the legitimate interests and also the rights of subjective nature, concerning some specific matters indicated by the law' (Article 103);
c. establishment of an Administrative Tribunal in each Region (together with the possibility of having decentralized sections of it in other cities of the Region) as the first instance of administrative jurisdiction (Article 125). Actually, the TARs were established by Law No. 1034/ 1971 and are nearly thirty all over the country (not counting the internal sections);
d. attribution to the supreme ordinary jurisdictional body – the Court of Cassation – of the power to decide, but only with regard to legal grounds related to the jurisdiction itself, on complaints against decisions issued by the Council of State or the Court of Counts (Article 111);
e. solemn reconfirmation of complete jurisdictional protection, without exceptions, of the legal position related to a right or a legitimate interest harmed by any act of the Public Administration (Article 113, paragraph 1);
f. postponement to the instrument of the general law for the determination of the jurisdictional organs which shall be entrusted with the power to annul any illegitimate or non-expedient administrative act (Article 113, paragraph 2). At present, this power is endowed to the TAR, and the Council of State, on appeal.

Law No. 205/2000 with special regard has deeply changed the pre-existing system of the exclusive jurisdiction of the administrative judge (*see* below, §11). Both subjective rights and legitimate interests in some very wide matters such as public services, town planning and buildings and public contracts were entrusted to the Administrative Tribunals and the Council of State (*see* below, §10) that decide every question about any kind of public and private rights and interests in these fields.

§9. The Jurisdiction of the Ordinary Judges

334. According to the well-known limits laid down by the principle of the separation of powers, which pervades the whole subject and therefore the dualism – which represent an *unicum* in the experience of western European countries – the ordinary judge is normally in a secondary role in our system. However, in recent years, his jurisdiction has been extended to those fields that include only subjective rights.

Examples of these fields are: questions of law concerning public employees with private trade contracts; compulsory health measures affecting the individual; expulsion of foreigners; decisions taken by the Authority for the safeguard of personal data.

§10. Administrative Jurisdiction

I. Organs and Structure

335. From 1 January 1974, in compliance with the previously mentioned Law No. 1034/1971, the TAR started to operate all over the country as first instance organs of the administrative jurisdiction. In all the regional capitals (and also in some separated cities), there is a TAR consisting of a President and at least five judges nominated as a result of an open competition. (For this part the enrolment is similar to that of ordinary judges.) The judging bench is formed by three judges.

The TAR of Lazio – obviously based in Rome – is organized into three sections and several subsections, necessary because of the higher number of petitions (*ricorsi*) converging there. That TAR is competent to know all those acts – starting with the ones issued by the central organs of the State: the Ministries – which have effect beyond a single regional district.

The Council of State, in its turn, is the judge to whom – as we already know – in general, the citizen or the administrative authority, which have lost the case in the first instance, can appeal. Its judgments cannot be the object of further appeal. It is only allowed to appeal to the *Corte di Cassazione*, understood as the Court competent in settling conflicts upon grounds of jurisdiction (Article 111 Const.): that happens, for instance, whenever the Council of State has ruled on a matter which was not in its competence but entrusted, instead, to ordinary jurisdiction.

The Council of State was traditionally organized into three jurisdictional sections, flanked by three other sections with consultative functions, through which the Council of State carries out its parallel duty of high legal-administrative advisor, as we saw before. From 2008, in order to accelerate the judgments and curtain a huge backlog of cases, the President of the Council of State, has been entrusted the power of appointing, at the beginning of every year, the sections thereby.

Each section, when exercising its jurisdictional function, is made up of five judges. From the organizational point of view, the TAR and the Council of State are not considered as part of the judiciary system in the strict sense: they are special jurisdictions, and the Council of State is, as well, an advisor of the government.

At the same time, however, while acting as a jurisdictional body, the Council of State has become more independent, but inevitably its members maintain links and acquaintances with the effective centres of the Government.

II. The Jurisdiction of Administrative Judges

336. First of all, the administrative judges have the important general competence of controlling the legality of the administrative acts which are deemed to be unlawful.

The grounds upon which the administrative act can be declared unlawful are called *vizi* (vices); they are the following:[147]

a. *incompetence*: when it has been issued by an authority which is different from that which has the power of acting in the particular case. The incompetence can be territorial as well as related to the matter concerned or the degree (in the hierarchical scale of the Public Administration) of the issuing Administration;
b. *excess of power*: when the administrative authority has wrongly exercised its discretionary powers. This happens whenever a public authority exercises its power in case and for purposes different from those which it was given by the law. The act can be annulled for excess of power if it is proved before a TAR (or the Council of State on appeal) that it clearly contradicts previous measures, or that it caused an open and evident injustice, or that there was inequality of treatment, or that the motivation for it was lacking or deficient;
c. *breach of law*: when the administrative act that has been issued fails to comply with a provision of law or regulation. This is, for instance, the case in which the law requires the advice or opinion of a technical organ before the act can complete its issuing process. Forgetting to ask such a required opinion could expose the act to the risk of being challenged and subsequently annulled.

There is also a special jurisdiction on the merits of an administrative decision, its concern being not the lawfulness but the expediency or opportunity of the administrative action.

This type of jurisdiction is provided for few and numerated matters. It is sufficient to remember here two of those. The most important one is certainly that regarding the complaints presented with a view to obtaining compliance and fulfilment of the obligations that falls on the administrative authorities to accept, follow and give execution to the judgment of ordinary and administrative judges. A second matter concerns – for instance – the urgent municipal ordinance issued by the Mayor, when exercising his power as a Government official, with regard to construction, public order or urgent health issues.

While exercising this jurisdiction – that is significantly called 'on the merits' – which allows a control wider than that of strict legality the judge has a wider power both to receive and consider the proof proposed and to reform – and not only annul – the administrative act challenged.

Finally, there is an 'exclusive' jurisdictional competence[148] appearing in those situations in which there is an inextricable connection between a right of subjective nature and a legitimate interest. In these cases, the legislation has entrusted, from 1923 onwards, the competence to decide on the issues to the administrative judge

147. Article 21-octies, l. 241/1990.
148. Article 133, d.lgs 104/2010.

with a view to avoid a situation in which the citizen is compelled to start two different legal procedures, and consequently to file two cases.

The principal matter in this type of complaints was the one regarding public employment, until in recent years the labour relations of almost all the employees of the public administrations have been reconducted to the common civil law system and the jurisdiction of the ordinary judges.

§11. Special Administrative Jurisdiction

337. This great achievement was the outcome of a deep doctrinal effort, which was concluded with an important decision of the Court of Cassation (*Corte di Cassazione)* adopted at unified Sections, N. 500/1999. Since then, and especially due to Law No. 205/2000, other very broad matters have been entrusted to 'exclusive' jurisdiction of administrative judges: so public services, town planning and buildings, and public contracts and also against the decisions of the independent administrative authorities. Furthermore, the administrative judge has been given the power to condemn the Administration, which has adopted illegitimate acts, to restore the damages so caused to privates.

In the past, the citizen damaged by an illegitimate act had first to impugn it before the administrative judge, then to ask for restoration before the ordinary judge (and if legitimate interest were damaged, often ordinary judges would deny any kind of restoration). This meant that full restoration was mostly impossible and always extremely slow (it could easily take a decade to end every instance both of ordinary and administrative judgment). Today, both annulment and restoration can be requested before the administrative judge, which also has a broader array of provisional protection and enquiring powers. This – and many special, quicker judicial procedures – has led to a stronger and more effective protection of private and public interests.

Nevertheless, this system seems to many scholars to have gone a long way far from the one underlying Article 103 of the Constitution. To distinguish between ordinary and administrative jurisdiction, the aforementioned disposition referred first and foremost to the distinction between subjective rights and legitimate interests: exceptions were admitted, only if provided for by law. Now, actually, areas of exception, i.e., of exclusive administrative jurisdiction, are provided for by law: but they are so large, that they have become the main criteria of jurisdiction division, not mere exceptions. But the Constitutional Court saved the constitutionality of Law No. 205 with its Judgment No. 204/2004 prompting the legislative body to arrive at a thorough definition of the matter which took effect from Decree No. 104/2010.

In general terms, the approach of our Constitution is contrary to the existence of special jurisdictions of any type (the most peculiar ones are obviously the criminal ones) including the administrative ones. Article 102 of the Constitution establishes an express prohibition to create new special jurisdiction.

Nevertheless, the Sixth *disposizione transitoria e finale* (Provisional and Final Statement) of the Constitution established that the special jurisdictions already existing on 1 January 1948, except the Council of State, the Court of Accounts and the military Tribunals, had to be reviewed within five years (but this has been done far later and in a rather partial and disorganized way).

Meanwhile, many special jurisdictions have been declared contrary to the Constitution by the Constitutional Court on the basis of a lack of independence and impartiality of the judges (this happened, for example, for the Municipal Councils on election matters, Judgment No. 93/1965; for the *Giunte Provinciali Administrative*, Judgment No. 30/1967; and for the *Consigli di Prefettura* regarding accounting matters, Judgment No. 55/1966).

Now we give a short reference to the principal special administrative jurisdictions existing at present.

I. Courts of Tributary Justice

338. After a long delay, there has been a change in the world of the tributary justice with the transformation of the previous branch of administration named Tax Commissions towards a more judicial structure and jurisdictional procedures. In execution of Law No. 130/2022, they are operating from 16 September 2022 and were required in order to obtain the benefits of the European funds generated by NextGeneration UE. Major improvements in this field include an autonomous and professional role of tributary judges and, at the upper level, the institution of a new Tributary Division of the Court of Cassazione. Moreover, the procedures of conciliation were strengthened, and the cases of disputes of moderate value were decided by a monocratic judge.

II. Water Tribunals

339. Concerning a scarce and precious good, the special competence with regard to water has its origin in the particularity of the issues connected with public water regulation. As a matter of principle, water is normally property of the State or other public bodies and can only be conceded to a private for a regulated use. The disputes on this subject are judged by special regional tribunals, which are – actually – specialized sections of the Courts of Appeal existing in each Region's capital. These specialized sections are formed in a manner so as to make good use of the knowledge and experience of technicians (functionaries on the administrative side) together with those of the ordinary magistrates. In Rome, there is the *Tribunale superiore delle acque* (Water Supreme Court) that usually operates as the Judge of Appeals and, concerning some minor matters, as the unique judge.

III. Court of Accounts (*Corte dei Conti*)

340. We will examine in a wider way the Court of Accounts– that could also be translated as Court of Audit, having specially in mind its administrative functions –

when we will analyse the ways and means of the administrative control, whose functions were entrusted to this body of magistrates created a long time ago (*see* Part II, Chapter 10).

Now we will concisely examine its jurisdictional functions established in Article 103 of the Constitution, and which are exercised by the regional sections and, in second instance, by the central sections or sometimes by the united sections of the Court.

The Court of Accounts has competence with regard to:

a. the so-called *giudizi di conto* (account trials) which can be started against accountants, treasurers and whoever handles public money and is therefore obliged to give an account for the use he made of it;
b. the trials regarding the *administrative liability* of functionaries and public managers who, through their conduct – active or by omission, even if not done on purpose but only with negligence (provided that is gross negligence) – have produced damages to the Administration; in this case those persons are bound to indemnify for the damages caused (*see* Article 28 Const.);
c. the trials concerning *pension issues* with regard to public employees, civil and military workers, and war pensions.

IV. Military Justice

341. It has competence for the crimes committed by the members of the Armed Forces according to the military codes for time of peace or war and has a distinct and somehow specific organization different from that of the ordinary judges. There are two levels of jurisdiction: first grade, with three tribunals, and one as an appeal Court. Anyway, its real importance has decreased from the year 2000, when the compulsory military service was suspended with the consequence of a sharp diminution of the cases submitted.

Chapter 9. The Constitutional Court

by Marilisa D'Amico & Costanza Nardocci

§1. Functions

342. As the President of the Republic, the Constitutional Court is considered by the Constitution as separate power compared to the three traditional State powers. Its task is to ensure that these powers are exercised correctly and, more specifically, that the Constitution is observed.

According to Article 134 of the Constitution, the Constitutional Court's most important function is to review the constitutionality of laws or acts having the force of law (i.e., State and regional laws, legislative decrees and decree-laws) and to ensure their conformity with the requirements of the Constitution.

Its second task is to settle questions of jurisdiction between the various organs of the State, the State and the Regions, and between the Regions themselves. The Court must decide which organ has jurisdiction over the contested function or, in case of conflict between the State and the regions, if the State or the Region have respectively interfered with regional or State jurisdiction. The third function, exercised by the Court with a different composition, is to try accusations against the President of the Republic for high treason or breach of the Constitution. The fourth function of the Court, as provided for by Constitutional Law No. 1/1953, is to adjudicate on the admissibility of referenda aimed at repealing State laws (*see* Part I, Chapter 5).

§2. Composition

343. Since it is supposed to guarantee the protection of the whole Constitution, the Court has a mixed composition, and its judges are chosen by three different State powers.

The Court's composition, as well as the requirements for being appointed as a judge, are a guarantee, on the one hand, of the judges' professionalism and technical skills and, on the other, of the fact that they are not the expression of any political force.

The Constitutional Court is composed of fifteen judges. Under Article 135 of the Constitution, one-third is appointed by the President of the Republic; one-third is elected by Parliament in joint session, and the other five are elected by the members of the ordinary and administrative Supreme Courts. The Court, therefore, meets two important requirements: it keeps a close link with the organs reflecting representative democracy and it is supposed to be as independent as the judicial power. To ensure that the Court's judges possess the highest technical skills, the Constitution states that 'the judges of the Constitutional Courts shall be chosen from among members of the Judiciary, including those retired, of the ordinary and administrative higher Courts, university professors of law and lawyers with at least twenty years practice' (Article 135, second paragraph). To grant the stability of the Court and the independence of its judges, as well as a certain degree of replacement, the Constitution provides that judges stay in office for a long period (nine years) and are not eligible for immediate re-election.

In case of proceedings against the President of the Republic, the Court is enlarged with sixteen persons 'chosen by lot from among a list of citizens having the qualification necessary for election to the Senate, which the Parliament prepares every nine years through election using the same modalities as those followed in appointing ordinary judges' (Article 135, paragraph 7).

The procedure for appointing the judges of the court is set out in Law No. 87/1953 and Constitutional Law No. 2/1967 and can be briefly summarized as follows: judges appointed by the President of the Republic are chosen by an act which can be defined as personal (i.e., by which the President decides personally, without the influence of any other authority). Judges appointed by Parliament, as provided by Article 3 of Constitutional Law No. 2/1967, are 'elected by the two Chambers in joint session, by secret ballot and the majority of two-thirds of their members', while a three-fifths majority is enough for the votes following the third one. These judges have always been appointed as a result of agreements between majority and opposition parties (although the agreement must be validated by a majority vote).

Judges nominated by the Supreme Courts are elected by three different constituencies, one made up of all the members of the Court of Cassation, one consisting of all the judges of the Council of State, and one of all the judges of the Court of Accounts. Three judges are elected by the first constituency and the others by each of the remaining constituencies.

344. Under the Constitution, the Court elects from among its members a President who remains in office for three years and may be re-elected. The President of the Constitutional Court plays an important role, especially in organizing the various activities and assigning the cases to each judge. Every single judgment of the Court, however, is discussed and taken by the plenary assembly, following the report of a judge. The judgment and its grounds are read and approved by all the judges who are not allowed to express 'dissenting' or 'concurrent' opinions, like in other countries. The choice of the referee, however, plays an important role, especially for minor issues.

§3. The Origins of Constitutional Reviews

345. Before the Republican Constitution entered into force in 1948, there was no judicial review of legislation in Italy, since the 1848 Statute could be amended by any ordinary law. The question of the review of constitutionality was much debated by the Constituent Assembly. Its members saw it as a valid tool for the protection of liberties and had large expectations of the role of constitutional justice.

Many recommendations were made at the beginning as to the kind of control to be chosen. The choice was between a widespread control by all the judges, consisting in ruling that the challenged rule is unconstitutional but only in the particular hearing in which the constitutionality is raised (North American system) and centralized control by a single body separate from the judicial power, which may declare that the rule is unconstitutional and therefore invalid, with erga omnes effects (the system in force in Austria at that time).

The Constituent Assembly eventually chose the latter solution, which reflected the typical fear of Europeans of giving too much power to the judiciary.

Three proposals were put forward on the ways of raising the constitutionality of norms before the Constitutional Court. The first one was to raise it before a court hearing a particular case (*via incidentale*). In this case, the judgment would have applied only to that particular hearing unless, as proposed by Calamandrei to the second subcommittee, the parties to the hearing during which the constitutionality had been raised would have appealed to the Constitutional Court, which could have declared the norm invalid with erga omnes effects. The second possibility, and maybe the most important for the members of the Assembly, was to allow citizens to raise the constitutionality directly, within a certain limit of time (*giudizio in via principale e astratto*). The third and final possibility was that the constitutionality could be raised by a certain number of citizens, Regional Councils, or qualified organs (*see* Patricolo's project, submitted to the second subcommittee). The question, however, was not solved by the Constituent Assembly, owing to communist opposition to the proposal of the citizens' direct action, for fear that 'any' citizen, for personal interests, might raise the constitutionality of a law of Parliament, thus opposing the will of the representatives of the people.

The judgment was eventually taken by the Constituent Assembly by Constitutional Law No. 1/1948, which states that the constitutionality should be raised during a particular hearing and be therefore limited to the solution of a defined dispute (Article 1, Constitutional Law No. 1/1948). The direct appeal to the Constitutional Court was limited to the disputes between State and regions (*see* Article 127 of the Constitution and Article 2, Constitutional Law No. 1/1948).

This choice limited the potentiality of the review but, at the same time, made judges of ordinary jurisdiction much more aware of the importance of the matter.

Our system, as a matter of fact, entrusts the courts of ordinary jurisdiction with deciding in which cases a question of constitutionality has to be referred to the Constitutional Court.

Adjudication *via incidentale* seemed the best way to guarantee an intervention of constitutional judges in all the branches of our legal system.

§4. Adjudication *In Via Incidentale*

346. The features of our system of judicial review of legislation are largely the result of the above-mentioned judgments.

To be admitted to the review of constitutionality, the question must be raised during a judiciary proceeding (*in via incidentale*), i.e., when the law has to be concretely enforced by ordinary judges. The role of ordinary judges was clear since the first years of existence of the Constitutional Court. There was in the first years the fear of the judges refraining from referring the questions of constitutionality to the Court, thus preventing it from adjudicating upon these cases. This fear partially proved to be groundless and today, judges use this power regularly.

As stated above, the question of constitutionality must be raised during a particular proceeding. The Constitutional Court has interpreted the word 'proceeding' in a very broad manner, to include hearings before courts of special jurisdiction (Constitutional Court, Judgments Nos 6 and 10/1969 and 274/1974), or even before organs that do not have real judicial functions (Constitutional Court, Judgments Nos 12/1971, 226/1976, and 384/1991).

The judgments of the Constitutional Court on the matter have evolved progressively, not always in a consistent manner. To encourage judges to raise the highest possible number of questions, the Court stated that they could be raised both during a proceeding that could be qualified as a hearing according to the principles laid down by the Court itself, even if the case is not heard by judicial organs (*objective principle*), and during a proceeding before a judicial organ, even if it exercises an administrative function (*subjective principle*) (Judgment No. 83/1966).

The Court subsequently reviewed the 'subjective' principle. According to its latest judgments, the matter should only be referred by a judicial body in the exercise of its 'adjudicating' functions (*see* Judgments Nos 17/1980, 376/2001, and 218/2011).

The Court has always recognized the right of bodies such as the disciplinary section of the CSM (Superior Council of Judges) (Judgment No. 12/1971) or the Court of Accounts when it exercises its auditing functions (Judgments Nos 226/1976 and 384/1991) to raise questions of constitutionality. The admissibility of such a referral is substantially due both to the position the CSM and the Court of Accounts have within the legal system and to the type of cases heard by these courts. Therefore, questions that are not usually raised before judicial organs can be referred to the Court for adjudication on their constitutionality. The Court considers the arbitrator is also capable of raising questions of constitutionality.

The constitutionality can be raised by one of the parties, the investigating magistrate, or even by the judge (Article 1, Law No. 1/1948 and Article 23, Law No. 87/1953).

347. The judge of the proceeding during which the question is raised (*giudice a quo*) must, however, verify the existence of two conditions before referring the matter to the Constitutional Court. First, the judge must make sure that the question is essential for the proceeding, i.e., that 'the judgment may not be given independently of having resolved the connected issue of constitutional legitimacy of the law' (Article 23, Law No. 87/1953).

In other words, the enforcement of the rule suspected to not conform with the provisions of the Constitution must be included in the reasoning made by the judge to settle the case (*see*, among many others and the previous Judgments, Ordinance No. 130/1971). If the question is unnecessary to settle the case, however objectively relevant and well grounded it may be, it cannot be raised in any way whatsoever. The close link between the settlement of the proceeding and the solution of the question of constitutionality has often been underlined by the Constitutional Court.

The Court has often rejected the reference for lack of relevance or topicality, or because it was tardy or premature, or even too abstract.

In the scrutiny on the existence of the relevance criteria, the Court has also progressively opened up its interpretation as to avoid areas of lacking control of constitutionality – the so-called zone franche – meaning cases where the challenges on the motivation on the relevance might badly affect the following analysis of the merit of the referred question of constitutional legitimacy. From this perspective, the Constitutional Court had declared admissible questions of constitutional legitimacy concerning the principle of legality in criminal law (*see* Judgment No. 184/1983) and, more recently, the two landmark cases on national electoral laws (*see* Judgments Nos 1/2014, first, and 35/2017, later).

However, it is the judge of the hearing who decides whether or not the question must be considered relevant for the judgment. As a consequence, the Court is requested to verify that the arguments invoked by the judge on the relevance of the raised question of constitutionality are plausible. The other criterion that enables the question of constitutionality to be brought before the Constitutional Court is the so-called non manifestly groundless (*non manifesta infondatezza*). Judges here enjoy a wide margin of discretion in verifying whether this criterion is met in the case at issue, which may often even result in preventing the Court from adjudicating the questions of constitutionality at stake. The scrutiny on the non manifest lack of ground of the question of constitutionality and, eventually, the rejection must always be motivated according to the law (Article 24, Law No. 87/1953), even if no remedy exists before Courts' denial to bring a question of constitutionality before the Constitutional Court.

348. In case the question of constitutionality is judged as relevant and not manifestly groundless, the judge refers it to the Constitutional Court for adjudication through an act called '*ordinanza di rimessione*', which should include explicit references to the rule thought as being unconstitutional, the constitutional provisions that are supposingly violated and, lastly, the arguments on the recurrence of the relevance and on the non manifest lack of ground of the raised question of constitutionality. Following the submission of the question of constitutionality to the Constitutional Court, the judge will have to wait for the Constitutional Court to judge on the question at stake before deciding the case that will remain therefore pending until the definition of the constitutional proceeding.

The act opens the constitutional proceeding before the Constitutional Court, and it is said to define the boundaries of the question of constitutionality, the so-called *thema decidendum*, which should cover the legal provision suspected of unconstitutionality, the constitutional provisions likely to be violated and the reasons of the denounced contrast between the former and the latter. The *thema decidendum* must be clear enough to allow the Constitutional Court to understand the core issue at stake, providing it with all the elements to judge on the merit. In short, the *thema decidendum* cannot be limited to a generic assertion of unconstitutionality. This means that the judge cannot raise questions of constitutionality, proposing two different or alternative interpretations of the same rule, nor the judge is allowed to defer to the Constitutional Court a mere question of interpretation of the legal provision at stake.

Furthermore, it is worth underlining that the judge's reading of the question of constitutionality very often influences the judgment of the Constitutional Court, as the latter should confine its judgment to the approach suggested by the referring judge. However, there might be exceptions. Sometimes, the Constitutional Court may decide to amend the judge's general approach, even raising an additional question of constitutionality, logically related to that originally raised by the judge, before itself through a process called '*autorimessione*'.

The order must be notified to the parties and the investigating magistrate (Article 23, Law No. 87/1953), and it is published on the Official Gazette so that everybody will have knowledge that a question of constitutionality is pending before the Constitutional Court.

Within twenty days, the parties to the hearing before the referring judge have the right to be represented in the proceeding before the Constitutional Court. The prosecutors, instead, are not allowed to appear before the Court because they are not a 'proper part' and have a peculiar role in the criminal proceedings (*see*, among others, Judgment No. 262/2009).

The President of the Council of Ministers, through lawyers appointed by the Government, or the President of the executive of the Regions, the so-called *Giunta* should the question concern a regional law, have the same right within the same time limit.

The constitutional hearing, thus, includes a sort of cross-examination which is not essential to the final judgment as the presence of the party is a possibility (*Zagrebelsky*), but it is not necessary for the purpose of the final judgment.

Until the 2020s Reform of the Rules of the Proceeding before the Constitutional Court, the Court usually did not allow persons (third parties) or social formations (*amici curiae*) other than those who were parties to the original proceeding before the judge *a quo* to join the constitutional process. However, the Constitutional Court's case law witnessed across the years exceptions to this rule, especially with regard to the intervention of third parties.

The 2020 Reform, which concerns both the adjudication '*in via incidentale*' and that '*in via pricipale*' (*see*, below, §5), impacted on two core ambits: the identification of individual and social formations, other than the parties of the judicial proceeding before the judge *a quo*, possessing interests related to the raised question of constitutionality to submit their arguments and observations (*see* Articles 4, 5, 6, 7) and the gathering evidence process (*see* Articles 14, 15, 16, 17).

As of the recognition of the right to submit additional arguments to the Constitutional Court, the Reform brought a more significant innovation concerning the *status* of the so-called *amici curiae* under Article 6 that are now entitled to submit a short document, no more than 25,000 characters, providing the Constitutional Court with additional and different arguments compared to those already presented by the parties. Article 16 specifies that the *amici curiae* will not acquire the *status* of parties in the constitutional proceeding.

The novelties of the Reform, conversely, impacted less on the position of third parties as the rules now governing their statutes within the constitutional process recognized and included into law provisions the established Constitutional Court's case law. Despite the recognition of the right to submit documents supporting – as most likely, it is the case – the thesis of the non-compliance with the Constitution of the legal provision at stake, third parties and *amici curiae* do not take part to the contradictory before the Constitutional Court, which continues therefore to be confined to the parties of the judgment *a quo* and to the representatives of the Government.

The other ambit touched by the Reform dealt with the gathering evidence process.

Before the 2020 Reform and according to Article 14 of the Rules of Proceeding, the Constitutional Court could carry out preliminary investigations to gather evidence, although it seldom adopted this measure, probably because they could not be requested by the parties.

On this last point and as mentioned, the 2020 Reform also aimed to implement the powers of the Constitutional Court to gather data and additional documentation for the purpose of the definition of the raised question of constitutionality by the hearings of experts on the subject at stake. The role of the experts is regulated under Article 17 of the Rules of Proceedings that now provides that where the Constitutional Court deems it necessary to gather data and information on the matters surrounding the raised question of constitutionality, it could opt to hear distinguished experts ('*chiara fama*') in ad hoc meetings in chambers with the presence of the parties. The Constitutional Court may likewise decide to ask the experts to provide documents and written texts that will be provided to the parties to ensure the transparency of the gathering evidence process.

Additional amendments to the Rules of Proceedings have been, later, adopted in 2021.

The Court gives judgment in Chamber if the parties are not represented or the referral seems to be manifestly groundless (Article 26, Law No. 87/1953). In all the other cases, the trial is public.

§5. Adjudication *In Via Principale*

349. Applying directly the Constitutional Court to have the constitutional legitimacy of law or act having the force of the law judged is a prerogative of the State and the regions, which can respectively challenge regional or State laws interfering their constitutionally guaranteed jurisdictions.

A constitutional reform (Const. Law No. 3/2001) has amended the previous system of direct referral to the Court by making the two procedures uniform.

Therefore, the government can refer a question of constitutionality on a regional law within sixty days from its filing on the only ground that the regional law exceeds its competence. Regions have the right to challenge State or other regional laws, if they exceed their competence, within the mandatory time limit of sixty days from the filing of the referred law.

More precisely, the reference to the Court could be made by the government because the law exceeded regional competence in the broadest sense of the word: any breach of the Constitution could justify the challenge. On the contrary, Regions must complain about the violation of the constitutional rules regarding their competencies (Judgment No. 274/2003).

Unlike in proceedings *in via incidentale*, in proceedings *in via principale,* the Constitutional Court is seized directly and is the only court called upon to rule on such disputes. The constitutional process is consequently a party process and ceases if the appellant releases the action with the consent of the other party; second, the Court acts as 'court of last resort' (since there may be no appeal against its judgments). Therefore, the Constitutional Court recognized its standing to make a preliminary request of ruling to the ECJ under Article 19 of the TEU (Judgments Nos 102/2008 and 103/2008).

Finally, in consideration of the nature of party process, Law No. 131/2003 introduced a precautionary power of the Court in the proceeding *in via principale*: it is settled that the Court can suspend the effectiveness of the contested act if its execution may present a 'risk of irreparable harm to the public or to the legal order of the Republic rarely requested by the parties and not yet been admitted by the Court' (Judgment No. 204/2010).

§6. Effects of Different Types of Constitutional Court Judgments

350. If the reference is allowed, the Constitutional Court may decide that the norm is unconstitutional. Only in cases concerning regional laws challenged by the government before those laws are enacted, according to the previous system, the Court's judgment of unconstitutionality forbids the promulgation either of the entire law or of that part of the law that the Court has declared null and void. In the other cases, the Court's judgments concern laws already enacted and promulgated.

In compliance with Article 136 of the Constitution, judgments of unconstitutionality have erga omnes effects.

The possibility of extending the effects of the judgment not only to future cases but also to previous ones (except for final judgments) has been long debated.

The solution came with Law No. 87/1953, which provides that rules declared to be unconstitutional can no longer be enforced, thus admitting that the declaration of unconstitutionality can also be applied to pending trials, even though they were started before the declaration itself. The retroactive effects of the declaration, after all, are a consequence of the subsidiary nature of the constitutional hearing: it would be illogical to oblige the judge who raised the question of constitutionality to enforce that law, consequently declared unconstitutional, simply because the trial was pending when the Constitutional Court decided: in this case the interest in raising (*see* Constitutional Court, Judgment No. 127/1966).

351. Judgments of unconstitutionality, therefore, also apply to cases started before the ruling of unconstitutionality but yet 'unsettled'.

The question of the limits in enforcing the judgments of unconstitutionality, after all, falls under the jurisdiction of ordinary judges, even though the Constitutional Court has sometimes assumed this task (*see* Judgments Nos 266 and 501/1988; 50/1989; 1 and 124/1992, by which the Constitutional Court specified the limits of the retroactive effects of such judgments). There is only one case, provided for by Law No. 87/1953, in which the judgment of unconstitutionality can be applied to previous final judgments, i.e., when it concerns a criminal rule which led to a final criminal sentence. In this case, the judgment and its effects are no longer valid (Article 30, fourth paragraph, of Law No. 87/1953). More recently, in a tax law case, the Constitutional Court chose to limit the temporal effects of one of its judgments (No. 10/2015) confining them to the future and, conversely, neglecting their efficacy retrospectively in the light of the safeguard of paramount constitutional interest. By contrast, in the following judgment (No. 70/2015), in a similar tax law case on a social security issue, the Court departed from the above-mentioned approach, therefore allowing its judgment to be effective retrospectively. These contrasting judgments gave rise to a challenging debate, though tempered by the approach undertaken with Judgment No. 70/2015 in that it resorted to the traditional approach of the Court towards the temporal effects of its judgments.

The Court can also reject the reference, although this type of judgment does not hold that law to be valid; other judges can raise the same question in a different case and the Court itself can allow it. Only the judge of the hearing in which the question was already raised cannot raise the same question again during the same hearing.

The judgment of the Court can also take the form of orders or judgments which do not define the merits of the question but rather settle the proceeding related to the original hearing (the so-called judgments of inadmissibility).

Within adjudications *via incidentale*, these judgments can be due to both the lack of relevancy of the question and the formal defects of the order by which the acts are transferred to the Court, such as, the fact of providing inadequate reasons to support the relevancy of the question or its irrelevancy or a wrong submission of its *thema decidendum*. Within adjudications '*in via principale*', judgments of inadmissibility can be due, for example, to formal defect of the act of reference or to defect of a real interest of the Regions to protect their legislative competencies.

§7. Interpretative and Manipulative Judgments

352. The Constitutional Court has adopted further judgment techniques, going beyond the simple alternative between a ruling that a norm is constitutional or unconstitutional. If a rule can have more than one interpretation, the Court may reject the interpretation given by the act of reference, thus rejecting the reference itself not because the question is irrelevant, but rather because it is based on a wrong interpretation. These judgments are called interpretative.

These judgments, however, are not binding for the judges, who are subject only to the law in compliance with Article 101 of the Constitution. If they decide to raise the question afresh, the Court might reconsider the matter and eventually allow the reference by ruling that the norm is unconstitutional.

If questions are raised based on indisputable interpretations usually given by the judges (*diritto vivente*, 'living law'), the Court always allows them, even though it means taking a judgment of unconstitutionality.

In the absence of a uniform and indisputable interpretation, the Court, of course, is free to give its interpretation of the rule. The Court itself has always repeated that judges have the right and the duty to choose among the various interpretations of the law the one which 'conforms to the requirements of the Constitution'.

The Court may also rule that a norm is unconstitutional only in the part in which it states something or in the part in which it does not state something or even in the part in which it states something instead of something else. These judgments are called manipulative.

This 'something' does not coincide with words already contained in the text of the law, which remains unchanged, but rather with new provisions set out in the judgment of the Court. This technique has been widely criticized for allegedly invading the field of the legislator and judges. In the words of Gustavo Zagrebelsky: 'if the legal system provides for a rule, it is up to judges (all judges) to "draw it from the system"; if such a rule does not exist, it is up to legislator (and nobody else) to introduce one. The Court cannot interfere with the jurisdiction of the courts in the former case, and that of the legislator in the latter'.

Vezio Crisafulli replied that the Court does not create new rules but just takes them as they are from the Constitution or the legislative system. The Court has often adopted judgments as such, especially to avoid legislative vacuums usually created by mere judgments of unconstitutionality, thus solving the problem of adapting the legal system to the constitutional guarantees without waiting for the intervention of the legislator. The Court did so, for instance, to avoid vacuums in the Criminal Code and in that of Criminal Procedure, which both contained rules introduced before the entry into force of the Constitution that has never been modified accordingly.

The Court's recent tendency is to consider norms unconstitutional in the part in which they do not provide for something, without stating explicitly what should be added but just the general principles that the legislator will have to comply with. It might be recalled Judgment No. 170/2014 on the so-called forced divorce following cases of gender reassignment by one of the spouses, where the Constitutional Court declared Articles 2 and 4 of Law No. 164/1982, *Provisions on the correction of the assigned gender*, unconstitutional 'insofar as they do not provide that the order reassigning the gender of one of the spouses, which causes the dissolution of the marriage or the cessation of the civil effects resulting from the transcription of the marriage, must in any case allow the maintenance of a relationship regulated by law, if both spouses so wish, under another form of registered partnership that grants adequate protection to the rights and obligations of the couple, in a manner to be specified by the legislator' or Judgment No. 286/2016, on mother's name attribution to children, in which the Constitutional Court stated the nonconformity with the Constitution of the rule which may be inferred from Articles 237, 262 and 299 of the Civil Code, Article 72 of Royal Decree No. 1238/1939, *Law on Civil Status*, and Articles 33 and 34 of Presidential Decree No. 396/2000, Regulations on the review and simplification of the Law on Civil Status, adopted pursuant to Article 2 of Law No. 127/1997 'insofar as it does not permit the married couple to attribute also the mother's name to the child by mutual agreement at the time of birth'. These judgments might create problems to enforce the norm if the legislative power neglects or takes a long time to re-enact it.

One last observation has to do with cases where, although the Constitutional Court refuses to rule on the constitutional illegitimacy of the provision at issue, it, therefore, reminds the legislator to intervene in the contested matter. This 'warning' reflects the separation of competencies between the Constitutional Court and the legislator. Put differently, when there are several ways to reconcile a legal provision of suspected unconstitutionality with the Constitution and it is only for the legislator to choose how to do it, the Constitutional Court declared the question of constitutionality inadmissible because of the existence of a plurality of solutions asking for the legislator to intervene on the matter at stake. In the field of fundamental rights, the Constitutional Court has frequently adopted this approach, especially in cases of lack of regulation (*see* Judgment No. 61/2006 on mother's name attribution to children; Judgment No. 138/2010 on same-sex marriage).

Sometimes, in cases of prolonged legislative *inertia*, the Constitutional Court might eventually decide to judge on the merit of the raised question of constitutionality to supply the lack of intervention of the legislator and, as a consequence, the persistent violation of constitutional rights. Worth mentioning is that, recently, the Constitutional Court chose to raise before itself a question of constitutionality on (so-called *autorimessione*) the previous question of constitutionality referred by a judge about the transmission of the parents' surnames to their children. In doing so, the Constitutional Court allowed the transmission of the mother's surname and overcame its previous decisions of inadmissibility due to the persistent lack of intervention of the legislator.

Finally, it should be recalled that, more recently, the Constitutional Court inaugurated a new type of decision to react, once again, to the defective relationship with the legislator in cases of persistent denials of adopting laws to solve issues of non-compliance with the Constitution (*see* Judgment No. 131/2022). Reference is made to the option of the Constitutional Court to give the legislator a specific amount of time to adopt a law to ensure the legislative resolution of an ascertained contrast between a legal provision at issue with the Constitution subordinated to a following Constitutional Court's judgment in case of legislative inertia (*see* Judgment No. 207/2018 and the following No. 249/2019; *see also*, Judgment No. 132/2020). This new type of judgment has been called the so-called deferral to a date certain to emphasize, on the one hand, the willingness of the Constitutional Court to establish a concrete collaboration with the legislator, and, on the other, the possibility for the Constitutional Court to timely sanction persistent constitutional rights' violations.

§8. Jurisdictional Disputes Between Branches of State

353. The Court is also charged with deciding on conflicts about the limits of functions between the powers of the State if they break out between organs which are competent to express the will of the power they belong to irrevocably (Article 37 of Law No. 87/1953).

If the dispute involves the government, which has a very hierarchical structure, the executive is represented in the proceeding by the President of the Council of Ministers (*see* Law No. 400/1988 Article 2, No. 3, letter g)). The Court, however, has ruled that the process can be set in motion by Ministers as well, insofar as their responsibilities are concerned (Judgments Nos 379/1992; 7/1996; 200/2006).

As far as the judicial power is concerned, each judge is entitled to set the process in motion, but only 'when exercising their judicial functions' (*see* Judgment No.

87/1978). Investigating magistrates, like the other judges, are denied the same possibility by the Constitutional Court when they do not exercise their judicial functions (Judgment No. 16/1979), but they are recognized as 'powers of the state' when they exercise their non-fungible powers of criminal prosecution (*see* Judgments Nos 263, 264, 265, 462, 464/1993 and, above all, 420/1995; Judgment No. 1/2013).

As far as the legislative power is concerned, the two Chambers are entitled to set the process in motion (Judgments Nos 1150/1988; 406/1989; 339/1996; 132/1997; and 334/2008), while the same power was denied to their internal organs.

In particular, the parliamentary commissions of enquiry set up under Article 82 of the Constitution were considered by the Court constitutional powers as they necessarily replace the plenum of the two Houses and emanate their powers. The Court also recognized that ceased the Commission of Enquiry, for example, because of the expiry of the term, the standing to be a part in the conflict returns to the Chamber (Judgment No. 241/2007).

The President of the Republic (Judgments Nos 150/1980; 154/2004; 200/2006; and 1/2013), the Constitutional Court (Judgment No. 77/1981), and the Court of Accounts when exercising its auditing functions (Judgment No. 406/1989) have the same power because, although they do not belong to the three classical and traditional powers of the State, they enjoy constitutionally guaranteed functions. The process can also be set in motion by committees promoting referenda, as representatives of the 500,000 voters who signed the request of a referendum (*see* Judgments Nos 69/1978; 1 and 2/1979; 30 and 31/1980; 137/2000; 198/2005; 38/2008). The Court, however, has excluded this possibility if the legislation is likely to undergo further changes after the referendum (Judgment No. 9/1997).

The disputed matter must consist in 'the delimitation of the competence of each power of the State under the Constitution' (Article 37 of Law No. 87/1953). This power can either be explicitly set out in constitutional legislation or be inferred from it. It can also be inferred from ordinary laws implementing constitutional legislation.

The proceeding can be initiated not only in cases of alleged abuse of power (*vindicatio potestatis*) but also when the improper use of power by an organ results in interference with the jurisdiction of another organ (Judgment No. 1150/1988 is very clear on this point). This possibility has increased the importance of this legal institution, as the conflicting relationships between the judiciary and the legislative concerning the prerogatives provided under Article 68 are highlighted (*see* Judgments Nos 10 and 11/2000).

The Court adjudicates on the limits of the jurisdiction exercised by the challenged powers and, if a measure was taken in the meantime, the Court declares it invalid (*see* Article 39 of Law No. 87/1953).

§9. Jurisdictional Dispute Between the State and the Regions or Between Regions

354. This type of proceedings between the State and the regions can only concern administrative or judicial measures.

Disputes over legislative measures are dealt with by the Constitutional Court according to the rules set by the procedure *in via principale*.

The State can be represented by the President of the Council of Ministers and the Region by the President of the *Giunta*.

The measure can be challenged within sixty days from its service or publication (Article 39, first paragraph, of Law No. 87/1953).

This remedy often concurs with the one granted by administrative courts, so entailing a problem of coordination between constitutional and ordinary jurisdiction. In fact, on the one hand, no other party than the State and the Region is allowed to be represented in this kind of hearing, on the other, there is uncertainty about the limits of admissibility of this type of constitutional proceeding.

The object of the conflict can also consist of behaviour that interferes with the jurisdiction of another organ (Judgments Nos 11 and 12/1957).

The Court decides which organ is entitled to the challenged power, and if a measure was undertaken in the meantime, it declares it invalid.

§10. The Criminal Jurisdiction of the Constitutional Court

355. The Constitutional Court has jurisdiction over criminal matters as well. It is charged with trying accusations against the President of the Republic for offences committed in the exercise of his State functions: high treason or breach of the Constitution (Article 90 of the Constitution).

The power to try accusations against Ministers for offences committed in the exercise of their functions formerly rested with the Constitutional Court but was transferred to ordinary judges by Constitutional Law No. 1/1989, which sets out special provisions on the matter. This power allowed the Court to pronounce its unique criminal judgment in 1979, in the *Lockheed* case. There has been a long debate over the meaning of presidential offences. Some scholars reckon that they should be treated as ordinary crimes, according to the principle which states that crimes and punishments should be absolutely established by law (Article 25, second paragraph of the Constitution and Article 2 of the Criminal Code).

Others believe that the political meaning of these offences demands a certain degree of flexibility when implementing the relevant constitutional provisions.

The President is impeached by Parliament with a procedure consisting of two different stages: the examination by a bicameral committee (Article 3, Constitutional Law No. 1/1989) followed by the judgment of the assembly.

In case of an indictment, a proceeding starts before the Constitutional Court. According to section 13 of Constitutional Law No. 1/1953, 'one or more commissioners are elected for the prosecution'.

The Court judges with its 'enlarged' composition (*see* above, §2). The proceeding consists of the preliminary investigations and the trial. The final judgment cannot be appealed in any way whatsoever.

In compliance with section 13 of Constitutional Law No. 1/1953, the Court can enforce criminal punishment, within the limits of the maximum penalty allowed by the legislation in force, as well as by other constitutional, administrative and civil penalties, depending on the type of offence court's discretionary power in determining these sanctions is therefore very high.

§11. The Judgment on the Admissibility of Referenda for the Repeal of Legislation

356. Besides exercising the powers provided for by Article 134 of the Constitution, the Court also acts as a judge on requests of repealing referenda, in compliance with Article 2 of Constitutional Law No. 1/1953. As recognized by the Court in its Judgment No. 16/1978, this power is different from all the others, since it consists of a mandatory form of control, an explicit request being absent. Law No. 352/1970 describes this judgment as a fundamental stage of the referendum; it cannot be omitted without affecting the correctness of the procedure and automatically follows the judgment of legitimacy given by the Court of Cassazione. The Court of Cassazione has to judge the referendum to verify its conformity to the provisions of Law No. 352/1970; after this first control, the Constitutional Court is automatically involved in the referendum procedure, to carry out the control of admissibility of the referendum (for more details on this two-folded control, *see* Part I, Chapter 5).

357. About the procedural aspects of the judgment of the Constitutional Court, it could be noticed that following Article 33 of Law No. 352/1970, the Court decides over the admissibility of referenda without a public hearing, but only in Chamber. However, Article 33 of Law No. 352/1970 prescribes that the government and the Committee or the Regional Councils that have promoted the referendum can introduce written acts to defend their reasons. On the contrary, the law neither allows nor forbids oral interventions aimed at illustrating the reasons for the admissibility or the inadmissibility of the referendum. However, the Court has interpreted the silence of the law on this point in the sense that it permits an oral discussion within the Chamber (*see* Judgment No. 33/2000): the subjects who are mentioned in Article 33 can take part in this discussion before the Court, illustrating the reasons for or the reasons against the admissibility of the referendum (*see* Judgment No. 45/2005). As already explained above, these subjects can be the government, the regions, the committees promoting the referendum – as mentioned by Article 33 of Law No. 352/1970 – but the Constitutional case law has extended this opportunity also to other subjects, such as committees against the referendum (*see* Judgment No. 31/2000). In any case, these subjects cannot be qualified 'parties of the process' in the technical sense of the word and have not the right to discuss in Chamber, but they are in some way *amici curiae* (*see* Judgment No. 45/2005).

If the Court rules a judgment of inadmissibility of a referendum, this does not prevent a new referendum concerning the same subject from being proposed again in the future. Because its judgment is an intrinsic part of the referendum procedure, the Constitutional Court is deeply affected by the political problems and the tensions often occasioned by referenda. According to Article 2 of Constitutional Law No. 1/1953, the Constitutional Court should only verify that the legislation submitted to the referendum is not included in the categories for which the referendum is expressly forbidden under the Constitution (Article 75, second paragraph, of the

Constitution), i.e., amnesties or pardons, laws authorizing the ratification of international treaties, fiscal or budget laws. Starting from its Judgment No. 16/1978 on, the Court has provided further reasons for inadmissibility (on this subject *see* Part 1, Chapter 5).

§12. The Constitutional Court and the Supranational System of Rights Protection: The Relationship with the European Court of Human Rights

358. In the last decades, the Constitutional Court's case law has developed and shown another interesting point of view that refers to the relationship established with the European Court of Human Rights and its jurisprudence.

How the Constitutional Court relates to the supranational system of rights protection reflects what is provided under Article 117, § 1, of the Constitution which requires the State and the Regions to act in compliance with EU Law as well as in accordance with international obligations.

From this perspective, and departing from the place reserved for EU's sources of law, as designed by the Constitutional Court in its case law (on this, *see* Part I, Chapter 3), the Constitutional Court has established a mechanism to react to conflicts between national laws and the ECHR, as interpreted by the European Court of Human Rights, beginning with Judgments Nos 348 and 349/2007.

In those judgments, the Constitutional Court stated that, in case of contrast, not amendable by means of interpretation, between national laws and the ECHR, as interpreted by the European Court of Human Rights, domestic Courts and tribunals can neither apply the contrasting national provision nor follow the European Court of Human Rights' judgment, but are instead required to refer the question of constitutional legitimacy raised under Article 117, § 1, of the Constitution before the Constitutional Court. The Constitutional Court, therefore, maintains the role of verifying whether national law is in compliance with the Conventional system of human rights protection, excluding judges' competences on the scrutiny on the existence of a conflict between the two levels of fundamental rights protection.

The above-mentioned approach has been first confirmed by the Constitutional Court in its subsequent case law as demonstrated, among others, by Judgments Nos 311/2009, 317/2009, and 264/2012.

The design of the relationship between the two Courts was sketched even clearer in 2015, especially with respect to the status reserved to the European Court of Human Rights' case law in the domestic legal system. The main question, therefore, revolved around whether and to what extent the European Court of Human Rights' judgments should or should not possess binding effects for domestic jurisdictions.

In the landmark Judgment No. 49/2015, the Constitutional Court, thus, reviewed its previous interpretation by restricting the cases where the European Court of Human Rights' case law needs to be considered binding within the domestic legal system. In doing so, the Constitutional Court stated that 'there is no reason to require the ordinary courts to use the interpretation chosen by the Strasbourg Court to resolve a particular dispute unless it relates to a "pilot judgment", meaning a judgment adopted under Article 61 of the Rule of Procedure of the European Court of Human Rights or in case it relies on existing established case-law on the matter at stake. As a consequence and in light of this interpretation of the effects of the European Court of Human Rights' judgments, Italian Courts, will have to implement the provisions identified at Strasbourg in cases involving "consolidated law" or a "pilot judgment"" (*see* §7 of 'Considerato in Diritto'). Following the Constitutional Court's judgment No. 49/2015, the European Court of Human Rights in the Grand Chamber's *Parrillo v. Italy* case (No. 46470/11, 27 August 2015) severely criticized the Constitutional Court's self-restraint expressing its disappointment on the poor place reserved for the European Court of Human Rights' case law by the domestic legal system.

From this perspective, it is currently under debate what will be the effects and the implications of the relationship between the Constitutional Court and the European Court of human rights as traced by the most recent, and not yet overturned, domestic case law.

Perhaps, an indication of the unwillingness to take seriously the European Court of Human Rights' case law could be associated with the denial expressed by the Italian Parliament to ratify Protocol No. 16 to the European Convention of Human Rights, which introduces the advisory-opinion procedure and which would have conversely introduced an additional mechanism to more strongly interlace the domestic legal system to the conventional system of human rights protection.

§13. The Constitutional Court and the Court of Justice of the European Union

359. Recent Constitutional Court's case law has likewise shown novelties as to the relationship with the CJEU.

A first issue arises out from national judges' obligation to rule in compliance with EU Law, in accordance with the principle of primacy, by disapplying the national provision that violates the European law. In doing so, a special role has been played by the preliminary reference to the CJEU made by national courts in order to defer questions regarding the correct interpretation of EU law.

In this context, after the entry into force of the Lisbon Treaty, the Charter of Fundamental Rights acquired not only binding legal force but also the status of source of primary law of the EU. Thus, in case of violation of the Charter's provisions with direct effect, the national judge has the chance to immediately set aside national laws that are in contrast with the former. In such cases, disapplication replaced the raising of a constitutional legitimacy question for the violation of the 'corresponding' provisions of the Italian Constitution.

Therefore, due to the 'constitutional stamp' of the Nice Charter and the possibility that judicial review may evolve into a non-centralized constitutional review, starting from Judgment No. 269/2017, the Court has attempted to limit – albeit partially – the immediate exercise of disapplication by national judges. In particular, in cases of dual preliminary, that is, when a national law simultaneously conflicts with a provision of the Nice Charter and one of the Italian Constitution, the Court has given the judge the option to also raise the question of constitutionality.

Beyond such a switch in the relationship between the preliminary order to the Court of Justice and the *in via incidentale* adjudication and as a mechanism to avoid contrasts between national and EU law, the Constitutional Court, both in the *via principale* and in the *via incidentale* adjudication, has made use of the preliminary referral to the CJEU (since 2018 the question has been raised four times, *see* Referral Orders No. 117/2019, No. 182/2020, Nos 216–217/2022). In this way, the principle of loyal cooperation among Courts is safeguarded.

For the first time, in 2008, the Constitutional Court referred a preliminary order to the CJEU within the *via principale* adjudication (*see* Judgments Nos 102 and 103/2008, on the interpretation Articles 49 and 87 of the EC Treaty, which was followed by Judgment No. 216/2010, declaring the unconstitutionality of national law because of its non-compliance with EU law; *see also*, Judgment No. 66/2013), recognizing its legitimacy to make use of the preliminary referral as judge of the unique resort (so-called *unica istanza*).

Concerning the *in via incidentale* adjudication, it was with Judgment No. 207/2013 that the Constitutional Court ruled for the first time on the admissibility of a preliminary referral to the CJEU. In Judgment No. 207/2013, the Constitutional Court, stated that 'although the Court of Justice has already handed down various judgments on the matter, it appears necessary to request that Court to give a preliminary ruling on the interpretation of paragraph 5(1) of Directive No. 1999/70/EC about the question of constitutionality referred to this Court since there is a doubt regarding the precise interpretation of that provision of Community law and the resulting compatibility of the national legislation'.

Direct enforcement of EU Law, as interpreted by the CJEU, and its limits have eventually been at the centre of the so-called *Taricco* case. In the '*Taricco* case', the Constitutional Court, referring with Judgment No. 24/2017 a preliminary order to the CJEU on a matter concerning criminal tax law evoked the well-known '*controlimiti*' theory putting forward arguments in favour of a hypothetical non-applicability of EU law in case of its nonconformity with the fundamental principle of legality provided under the Italian Constitution (on the EU's sources of law, *see* Part I, Chapter 3). Following the Court of Justice's judgment (C-42/17, M.A.S. and M.B.), the Constitutional Court (Judgment No. 118/2018) has eventually closed the 'saga', arguing that the question had to be held ill-founded, because of the inapplicability of the so-called Taricco rule to the pending criminal proceedings in that it was not in compliance with the principle that offences and penalties must be defined by the law.

Chapter 10. The Public Administration in the Constitution

by Enzo Balboni

§1. Duties and Powers of the Public Administration

360. The duties entrusted to the State, to its organs as well as to other public bodies have been subject to a continuous expansion especially during the last hundred years. Public duties were once restricted to the national defence, the maintenance of security and public order, the construction of general interest works (roads, bridges, ports and so on) and the regulation or protection of a few economic activities (special manufactures, internal or international commerce, etc.).

Those duties have subsequently been multiplied, extended and developed to include instruments of cultural and civil growth, economic and social welfare for the benefit of the universal population. In constitutional terms, the public duties are the reverse face of the coin where the individual and social rights are imprinted. In a first enumeration, these regard: Education, Transport, Public Health, Social Security, and Assistance of the poor. All these activities and public services were entrusted to public bodies and were – and to a certain extent also nowadays are – carried out by public employees who are part of the Public Administration.

The latter refers not only to the State and its organs (and internal offices) but also to any type of public territorial and/or functional body when it is collectively considered. To those, or better to their activities, it has been granted the distinctive characteristic which makes the difference from the activities of private persons: 'the power to command' that is equivalent to 'power to give peremptory orders'.

This power confers the capability to unilaterally modify the legal position of private persons to whom administrative measures are addressed. This is, of course, the prevailing difference of administrative acts in comparison with contracts which, by definition, requires the mutual consent of two parties placed at the same level.

The main foundation for the Public Administration's power stands on the basic presumption, that is also a general principle, that it acts for the benefit of the people: the public interest. Once the public interest is correctly identified and the power is exercised according to the law, the interest of private persons – physical or legal – must give way and submit.

This is the so-called authoritative side of the public activities (functions) which presents also a social and welfare dimension that is characteristic of contemporary democratic States.

Since 1990, many statutes and mainly Law No. 241/1990 (the general law on administrative procedure) allow the Administration to make contracts with privates, instead of exerting its authoritative and unilateral powers, when this is not in contrast with the public interest. Sometimes, these contracts actually take place of traditional public acts: sometimes, they only establish some points the Administration is bound to respect in the exercise of its powers. This has given great momentum to so-called consensual administration, as an alternative way of public activity. It is actually rather obscure – and therefore disputed – whether these pacts or covenants are ordinary civil contracts or peculiar public law contracts.

§2. The Constitutional Principles Regulating Public Administration Activities

I. The Principle of Legality

361. The powers of the Public Administration as relevant as above-defined could not be justified unless in the frame of the legality principle, that in English legal terms can be squarely defined as the 'rule of law'.

According to this principle, the public activity puts into effect a superior will which has been quite accurately defined in a statute (*legge*) passed by Parliament and through which certain intrusive powers and particular means have been conferred to various public bodies.

According to the fundamental principle of legality, any administrative action must respect the limits established in a general and abstract way by the law. In fact, those limits cannot be exceeded by these administrative acts which are begotten by the law. When this happens, we are in the presence of an illegitimate use of power. Therefore the act can be declared void and annulled.

As we will see later on, the Public Administration must make good use of its power, especially with regard to the remedies which are at citizens' disposal against illegitimate and/or inappropriate administrative acts.

362. The principle of legality is put into effect through many efficacious means: either at the level of the internal controls of the Administration or through the judicial review operated by special Administrative Tribunals (not to be confused with those of the same name operating for instance in Great Britain) or by ordinary courts.

II. The Principle of Reserve of Legislation (*Riserva di Legge*) in Relation to the Organization of Public Offices

363. In order to complete the indications concerning the principle of legality, we should observe that the Constitution (Article 97) requires that the so-called organization of public offices must be regulated by statutes, adopted by the Parliament, and not by the Government within the exercise of its administrative and regulatory function.

We face, therefore, an application of the *riserva di legge* principle. It is common knowledge that this principle refers to the cases in which the Constitution itself requires that a certain question or matter can only be regulated by a parliamentary statute. Consequently, we hold that issue as one *reserved for the domain of the law.* This choice is made because the Parliament's instrument is considered the most appropriate mean, and the one that better protects the rights of the individuals, in order to regulate certain matters which are deemed to be particularly sensitive and important.

With regard to the organization of the public offices, we must make reference to a *riserva di legge* principle although considered in a relative way, according to which only the guidelines and the essential elements of the matter concerned must be regulated by the legislative branch, whereas the executory and more detailed profiles can be established by regulations and other administrative acts which stay in the Government's domain.

In the last few years, statute law has indeed strengthened the normative power of Administration about the organization of the public offices. Nowadays, statute law mostly dictates very broad principles, leaving vast areas of this matter to administrative regulation. Often, in order to do so, statute law abrogates pre-existent statutes, only to make room for administrative regulation to take their place (this is the so-called *delegificazione*). Anyway, many scholars consider this evolution a breach of the *riserva di legge* and a not so appropriate way of enlarging the executive sphere.

III. Democratic Principle

364. We should never forget that our form of State is deeply inspired and modelled by the principle of democracy, according to which the sovereignty belongs to the people and is exercised in its name. This is not without consequences: one thing is to have a Public Administration at the service of a State like a property of an absolute king or of a dictatorial regime, and a different thing is to have a Public Administration at the service of a democratic State, that should mean: at the service of all citizens.

Bringing the Administration nearer to the citizen's needs, and more efficient, is the aim of the administrative reforms which have been initiated in the last decades, concerning, among other issues, the legal regime of civil servants, powers and responsibilities of the leading officers and their relations with political organs, the structure of the different Administrations.

According to the general principle of subsidiarity, some years ago a large reform – known as *Bassanini reform*, from the name of the Minister who promoted it – has transferred or devoluted a great number of powers and functions to the regional and local administrations. This innovation, and the 2001 reform of Title V of the Italian Constitution (*see* Part III, at least Chapter 1), has brought a new administrative system, nearer to the people than ever since Italy exists as a single national entity. These were the intentions. Whether this will bring an actual increase of effectiveness and democracy in public activities, it is still to determine: but such is the ambitious aim of these reforms that have now constitutional coverage and strength.

IV. Impartiality Principle

365. This principle is expressly established in Article 97 of the Constitution, where it is prescribed that 'public offices are established and organized by the law (i.e., a statute) so that the good functioning and the impartiality of the Administration are assured'.

Accordingly, the Administration when carrying out its duties must exclusively pursue the public interest. There should not be room, therefore, for favouritism, arbitrariness or punitive activities against anyone. Everyone must be treated in the same way, on a unique standard, respecting the equality principle.

In case of infringement of this principle, ascertained by the judge, the administrative acts considered to be partial can be annulled.

V. The Good Functioning Principle

366. The Constitution not only places the administrative activity under the law and requires that this activity does not proceed to unjustified discriminations but also establishes a further leading principle: the good functioning principle, in other words: efficiency and good performing. We are actually facing an indefinite concept; yet this encloses the following more specific indications: fairness and correctness during action together with the best use of public means and resources. A particular branch of studies, the science of administration, is the academic field where are monitored the procedures and techniques suited to improve the quality of public action. Efficiency, however, must never be seen as an end in itself, but as the most solid, incisive and economic way to achieve the general interest.

367. The principles of impartiality and good functioning should gain effectiveness in administrative procedure. Law No. 241/1990 has given the general discipline of the administrative procedure, that is the sequence of acts and activities that bring to the final decision of an administrative authority. The procedure is open to private citizen or enterprises who are interested in that decision: they can read and copy administrative documents and express their opinions, that the Administration is bound to consider in its decision. The decision must be motivated, and the beginning of the procedure must be communicated to those who may be interested in it. This allows the Administration to be informed – through the action of interested privates – of all the aspects of the relevant issues and in this way it can reach a more rational and objective decision.

VI. The Principle of Responsibility of the Public Officers

368. Introducing a notable and severe innovation, the Constitution (Article 28) dictates that State and other public bodies officials and employees (i.e., civil servants) are directly responsible, according to criminal, civil and administrative laws, for actions done in breach of a right.

Therefore, a citizen who might be harmed by an administrative act or by an unlawful action which has caused him an 'unjust damage' can start legal actions directly against that official. Moreover, since often the official or the employees are not able to respond with their personal properties and goods of the damages they caused, Article 28 states that, in these cases, the civil responsibility is extended to the State and to the public bodies which employ the official or employee who is liable for the damages. As a consequence, in this case, the State (or other public bodies) and the official are jointly liable for damages.

VII. The Principle of Respect of the Balance of the Budget

369. A new constitutional provision that has modified the pre-existing Article 81 approved in 2012 requires, in general terms and according to EU rules, that all actions of the Public Administration should be carried on respecting the principle of the balance of the budget and the sustainability of the debt. About this important matter we refer to Chapter 11.

VIII. The Access to the Public Offices on the Basis of the Equality Principle

370. Article 51 of the Constitution establishes that: 'All citizens of either sex can have access to public offices, included the elective ones, under equal conditions and according to the requirements established by the Law.' This is a specific application and confirmation of the equality principle contained in Article 3, specially relevant regarding the access to working activities.

In relation to offices subject to election some recent electoral laws, had established, for promotional purposes, that both males and females must be included among candidates both for the municipal, provincial or regional assemblies and for the Parliament. This in accordance with a new rule, added as a new paragraph in Article 51, which provides equal opportunities between women and men as candidates.

371. It may be of interest to underline that the 2001 reform of Title V of the Constitution has specifically bound the regional laws to respect this full equality and to promote equal access to public offices (Article 117, paragraph VII).

IX. The Principle of Open Competition for Access

372. In order to grant access to public offices to the best among the applicant citizens, the admittance to the Public Administration as a civil servant is subject to an open competition. Likewise, all citizens meeting the requirements requested and wishing to apply compete on equal terms and on an equal status and the most competent, able or appropriate should result (hopefully) winners (Article 97).

However, the Constitution, as an exception to the rule above-described, provides the possibility of accessing to public offices without an open competition, in cases provided by statute Law. Unfortunately this is not an unusual case.

Nevertheless, in the last years, it has gained consent the idea that political bodies and offices – and especially the political head of administration at each government level – centrally or locally should be able to freely choose some top-level public bureaucrats (fiduciary officials) on a contract base of some years duration. In this way, the so-called spoils system (an American heritage) has been accepted in recent statutes as an exception, albeit allowed by the Constitution in contrast, to the basic principle of access to public offices by competitive examination (concorso). One must admit that this practice has highlighted various abuses.

X. The Decentralization and Autonomy Principles

373. The Constitution includes, among the 'fundamental principles' enshrined in the first twelve of its articles, those referring to the administrative decentralization, regarding the services which are in the responsibility of the State, and those devoted to promote and bring forward 'the local autonomy' with a general view to foster the institutional pluralism. For a detailed analysis of these principles we refer to Part III, Chapter 1, dedicated to regional, provincial and municipal autonomies.

XI. The Principles Assuring 'Justice' in the Administration

374. As a further implementation of the principle of legality, it is provided that all administrative acts issued by the Public Administration can be submitted for a review by an Administrative Tribunal acting as a first jurisdiction or in appeal by the Council of the State. Furthermore, the administrative bodies are often organized in such a way that their acts can be submitted for an internal re-examination by an administrative authority different from the one that issued them (audit).

With regard to this matter, that is of particular importance, we refer to Part II, Chapter 8.

§3. Administrative Organs with Consultative and Control Functions

375. In addition to the organs of active administration of the State, with the Government and Ministries at the top of the hierarchy, which we examined in General Introduction, Chapter 2, besides the territorial public authorities established or recognized by the Constitution (the regions, the provinces, the municipalities and now the metropolitan cities) entrusted with public duties characterized by the principle of political and administrative autonomy, which will be examined in Part III, Chapter 1, and lastly, in addition to the peripheral bodies of the central State organization, two other peculiar subjects are part of the Public Administration and both combine an administrative and a judicial function.

These two institutions are the Council of State and the Court of Accounts which, first of all, are established and regulated at the constitutional level, which gives to them an undeniable relevance. Both carry out two separate functions: a legal, administrative and consultative function for the benefit of Parliament and Government, on the one side, and that of a special jurisdictional body on the other side (Article 100).

I. The Council of State

376. The Council of State was established in Savoyard Piedmont in 1831, following the Napoleonic model of the French Conseil d'Etat. After two centuries, also in our days the Council of State ranks itself as the top-level legal-administrative advisory institution in Italy.

In addition, it carries out very important functions for the safeguard of justice in the exercise of the administration. In fact, as we saw in a previous chapter dedicated to the administrative justice, it is for the Council of State to issue final decisions with regard to the recourses submitted by private citizen or by public entities against administrative acts deemed to be unlawful or grossly inappropriate.

The Council of State enjoys a remarkable and well-deserved good reputation. Even if its role commands to be careful of the governmental demands and necessities, its advices and its decisions usually show competence, solidity and impartiality and are received with respect and attention by all political actors as well as the citizens.

The Council of State performs its advisory function through three of its six sections; the remaining perform jurisdictional functions. Each section consists of a President and at least seven councillors. In cases of complex or very relevant matters, the Council of State may exercise these functions through the full Assembly (*Adunanza generale*) of all three advisory sections. Recently a new relevant section was instituted to examine governmental normative acts of major importance (*regolamenti*).

Half of the members of the Council of State come – following an internal promotion procedure – from inside: that is from the ranks of TAR and a quarter are chosen through a very selective competition of a double grade.

The last quarter of the councillors are discretionally nominated by the Government among persons who, considering the activities, experiences and studies they carried out, fulfil the suitability and quality requirements. The law guarantees the independence of the members of the Council of State before the Government. Measures concerning the career and specific charges of the councillors are adopted by a body whose head is the President of the Council himself, and most members of which are elected by the magistrates of the Council and of Administrative Tribunals, except for four of them who are appointed by the Chambers of Parliament.

377. The Council of State is asked by the Government to give legal opinions (*pareri*) on administrative matters. This is a general power that can be exercised anytime without any particular provision. However, the most important cases in which the Council of State intervenes are provided for by the law. In this situation, a difference should be made between facultative and mandatory opinions. The latter, if provided for by the law, must always be requested; otherwise the act, adopted without hearing the opinion required, could be annulled on the grounds of infringement of the procedure.

A mandatory opinion is required in the following case concerning:

1. every administrative general regulation adopted by the Council of Ministers or by any single Minister and every *testo unico* (a compact text that collects and coordinates all the existing primary and secondary regulations about a single subject);
2. decrees deciding the extraordinary petitions addressed to the President of the Republic for the annulment of illegitimate public acts;
3. general ministerial guidelines for public contracts.

In the past, the Council opinion was required for a much wider range of acts: nowadays, statute law trend is to reduce preventive controls on public acts and to enforce general management controls, such as the one of the Court of Accounts.

Sometimes, the opinion is considered to be binding or partially binding. When it is binding (e.g., in the very rare cases when the Government decrees about the reacquisition of Italian citizenship, after it has been lost) the opinion must be followed. Again, in the case of extraordinary petitions to the President of the Republic: *ricorso straordinario*, the opinion of the Council must be followed.

The several provisions concerning the administrative functions of the Council of State were included in the *Testo Unico* No. 1024/1924 and its implementing and/or amending regulations. Recently a new legislative decree (No. 104/2010) has fully reorganized and rationalized the matter.

II. The Court of Accounts

378. The Court of Accounts is, like the Council of State, an independent body with a long and solid tradition. Moreover, like the Council of State, it enjoys a remarkable reputation.

Like the *Consiglio di Stato*, this Court carries out two different types of functions: an administrative function in form of control and a jurisdictional one. The latter is exercised on the following matters: public accounting, civil and military pensions and public employees' responsibility towards the Public Administration and was treated in a different chapter when we dealt with the administrative jurisdictions.

379. As a preliminary remark, we should only note that each control function is, essentially, a review of an act issued by an independent and specialized body from the point of view of legitimacy and/or the correct exercise of discretion.

With regard to the moment when the control is exercised, we can distinguish between a preventive and a subsequent control on the performance of the executive power in a wide sense.

Considering the total of fourteen sections of the Court of Accounts – or Court of Auditors, if we especially consider this capacity – only three administrative ones carry out control functions; the other eleven sections exercise jurisdictional functions.

The head of the Court of Accounts is its general President, but each section has its own President assisted by councillors (*consiglieri* and *referendari*); the *procuratore generale* exercises the functions of a public prosecutor (*pubblico ministero*) supported by the vice-*procuratori*.

The members of the Court of Accounts – whose title is magistrates – are generally designated on the basis of an open competition (*concorso*).

Nevertheless, a certain number of councillors (up to half of the members) can be appointed among experts chosen by the Government by a resolution of the Cabinet. One must underline that this is a relevant and unusual power.

380. The Constitution (Article 100) and the law guarantee the independence of this institution and also provide that the members of the Court of Accounts are basically irremovable, enjoying a status equivalent to that of the ordinary judges.

A special independent board – whose Head is the President of the Court himself, and most of which members are elected by all the magistrates of the Court (the '*Procuratore generale*' is a member as well), except for four of them who are appointed by the Presidents of the Chambers of Parliament – deliberates about measures on appointment, specific charges and career of the magistrates of the Court.

381. Article 100 of the Constitution states that the Court of Accounts carries out the control over the legitimacy of governmental acts.

The laws which regulate this matter indicate the acts subject to control. In particular: government decrees deliberated by the Council of Ministers; general regulations; contracts exceeding a certain (large) amount; general instructions upon administrative activity.

Given the preventive nature of such a control, the act subject to it does not come into effect – therefore it cannot be enforceable – unless the Court of Accounts gives its visa (*visto*).

Usually, the acts are submitted to the Court by the various Ministers at an internal office, specially created for that purpose, entrusted to a Court of Accounts member called Councillor. If the Councillor makes remarks, he sends the act to the section with controlling functions for a motivated decision on this point.

In case the decision confirms the remarks raised, the Minister concerned can:

a. accept the remarks and, consequently, modify the act following the indications given by the Court of Accounts;
b. prompt to issue a motivated resolution by the Council of Ministers ordering the Court of Accounts to carry out the act anyway.

In the latter case, the Court proceeds to the registration 'with qualification' – in legal wording – of the act subject to its control. As a consequence, the Court of Accounts will fortnightly transmit to the Parliament the list of the decrees recorded 'with qualification'.

This allows the Parliament – especially the members of the opposition – to ask the Government to answer during Question Time and give justification for its conduct.

However, it is important to underline that the cases of an act being 'registered with qualification' are very few. In any case, the Court of Accounts watchdog function is noteworthy and causes a sound awe.

382. Article 100 of the Constitution specifies that the Court of Accounts carries out a more important subsequent control regarding the State budget. The subsequent control takes place once the administrative acts became effective.

Every year the Court of Accounts is requested to issue a report on the regularity – which is called the *parificazione* of the final balance – and the property accounts of the State.

This is the stage in which the Court of Accounts experiences the most peculiar nature of its power: that of matching cold budget figures and estimations with the point of view of political opportunity, expediency and efficiency. Furthermore, Law No. 20/1994, states that the Court of Accounts carries out a subsequent control on the administration of the budget and of the estates of all Public Administrations, as well as the control on the expenditures of EU's funds. The Court of Accounts, therefore, controls the legitimacy and regularity of the acts of administration as well as the performance of every administration's internal controls. Besides, it assesses the compliance of the administrative activity with the objects established by the law while estimating, from a comparative point of view, costs, means and timing of the performance of the administrative action. The Court of Accounts sets out, every year, the programmes and landmark criteria to which it refers to while exercising its control function and issues a general report for the Parliament. Finally, this Court takes part, in the cases and in the ways which are regulated by the law, in the subsequent control on the financial administration of those bodies to which the State grants ordinary financial contributions (thus, excluding occasional or extraordinary ones).

Also in this case, the main function of the Court of Accounts is to control the good use of public money and to refer about it to the Parliament.

Finally, we must refer again to the constitutional innovation arisen from the review and integration of Article 81 of Const. approved in 2012, which requires the balance of the State budget and has therefore enhanced the role and enforced the powers of the Court of Accounts.

§4. The National Council of the Economy and Labour

383. Given the difficulties to find a better position, we shall follow the order of the Constitution which place in the same section (at Article 99) the basic regulations concerning another auxiliary organ of the State with consultative function for the benefit of Parliament and Government: the National Council of the Economy and Labour (CNEL).

The CNEL was established in Italy in 1957, and its regulation was modified and rationalized by Law No. 936/1986 and Law No. 214/2011.

This body updates an old and, to a certain extent, an unusual and somewhat peculiar idea (that of an organic and never conflicting representation of the productive categories: workers and entrepreneurs) and recalls, obviously in a different scenery, some experiences which took place between the two World Wars in the Weimar Republic, in France and during the Italian Fascism (the corporative experiment of the 1930s).

Its members are: the President, fifty-four representatives of the categories producing goods and services in public and private sectors and ten experts, to be nominated among exponents of economic, social and legal culture.

The appointments are made by a decree of the President of the Republic upon a resolution of the Council of Ministers. Members hold office for five years; there is an incompatibility between the position of CNEL's members and that of members of Parliament.

384. The Government and the Houses of Parliament may ask the CNEL for opinions and advice on the matters which involve guidelines on economic, financial and social policy and, generally, on every issue falling within the field of economy and labour. In August 2023, the Government asked a guideline on the matter of the minimum wage.

On its own initiative, with regard to the same matters, the CNEL can address to Parliament and to the Government its evaluations and suggestions, as well as it can propose legislation, in this way exercising its own legislative initiative, but with effective modest results.

This power is relevant from a constitutional point of view, but it has actually been exercised only on a few occasions. As a matter of fact, the CNEL has never really taken off, because of the little political attention paid to it by the social partners. Effectively, both the trade unions and the organized entrepreneurs have preferred to confront in a direct negotiation and with the Government taking part as a mediator and high guarantor.

After an initial try to abolish it with the Constitutional referendum of 2016, the political and institutional relevance of CNEL is low nowadays, despite its last two Presidents held a ministerial chair.

§5. The Independent Administrative Authorities

385. In order to meet a need that can no longer be disregarded in several market economies, including Italy over the last thirty years, several administrative Commissions following the Anglo-American model have been created. They have been designated with different names and competences but they have in common, at least, the following characteristics: they carry out, independently from the Government and Ministers' activity, a regulatory and surveillance function with regard to important economic sectors with a view to guarantee that those operating in the economic scene behave with loyalty, fairness and honesty in order to maintain a real competition among them, and taking into account the consumers' and users' interests.

It is sufficient to indicate here the essential elements of the main recently established Authorities, taking into account that they are composed of few members chosen from personalities with specific and ascertained professional qualifications and experience and with undisputed morality together with a strong sense of independence.

The members of the Authorities are usually nominated by the President of the Republic following the proposal of the President of the Council of Ministers after a deliberation by the Council.

Sometimes the Parliament also takes part in the nomination through the power of designation held by the Presidents of both Houses.

386. Somehow, the Bank of Italy may be considered a forerunner of such authorities. It enjoys a sound and solid tradition of independence from the Government and Parliament. Its Governor is appointed by the Government for six years renewable only once. Nowadays, after the creation of the European Central Bank, located in Frankfurt, the Bank of Italy has lost the monetary function ('coining') but still performs relevant surveillance functions on the banks and the entire credit function.

Law No. 216/1974 (subsequently amended and updated) created the CONSOB (*Commissione nazionale per la società e la borsa*): a kind of watchdog on Stock Exchange and related markets. The CONSOB is entrusted with the delicate and extremely important mission of surveillance of the best fairness and accuracy of shares, stocks and bonds and of the activity of the companies whose securities are the object of daily quotation at the Stock Exchange. The CONSOB can take all the measures deemed necessary to guarantee the transparency of the information and the fairness of the transactions on the markets. It can do so, urgently if necessary, through a handful of provisional orders. These decisions, as the ones adopted by all the administrative authorities, may be reviewed by the organs of the administrative jurisdiction, as already explained in Chapter 8.

Law No. 516/1987 created the ISVAP (*Istituto per la vigilanza sulle assicurazioni private e di interesse collettivo*). The ISVAP has the objective of controlling those private companies that sell insurance and related financial products.

387. Nowadays, in the political and economic field, the mass media (television, radio, internet, newspapers, periodicals and social media) are of extreme importance in the formation (and manipulation) of the public opinion. The producers of mass communication include public entities (RAI-TV) as well as big private entities.

In the field of the mass communication media, it is necessary to control the concentrations and, in general, to supervise the maintenance of an effective competition within the system in order to assure that different opinions can be expressed and to guarantee the objectivity (at least in a tendential way) of the information. In this field, regulatory and surveillance duties are now entrusted to the *Autorità per le garanzie nelle comunicazioni* provided by Law No. 249/1997.

388. An important role is given to the *Autorità Garante della Concorrenza e del Mercato* – also known as the Anti-trust Commission – created by Law No. 287/1990.

As its name suggests, the main duty of the Commission is to control the enterprises operating in the market in order to prevent any company or economic entity from abusing of monopolistic or dominant positions in the market. To this end, the Commission has the power to prohibit certain conducts and issue regulations and harsh fines as well as offer its professional opinion on questions of concentration.

389. Law No. 675/1996 has instituted the *Garante per la protezione dei dati personali* (a collegiate Authority) that oversees the protection of personal information handled both by private and by public powers. In the past years, almost every organization, private or public, has deeply changed the management of information about physical persons, in order to comply with the strict regulations of the Authority, which has also the power to inflict sanctions on trespassers (up to the full prohibition and block of every data management).

We should also consider the *Autorità per l'energia elettrica, il gas e il sistema idrico,* initially created by Law No. 481/1995, and integrated by Law No. 211/2011 with regard to water use. This important authority regulates and supervises the activities of these sectors, especially about the tariffs, mainly for the protection of users and consumers. Operators are both private and public. This authority has its legal head office in Milan and has recently changed its name in Arera, having regards to the networks of public utilities.

390. Beginning January 2014 a transport agency – Autorità di Regolazione dei Trasporti – became operative. Its main task is promoting and protecting competition in the transport sectors. ART is an administrative independent body headed by a Council composed by a President and two other members. The Council is nominated by the Parliament Commissions on the transport affairs for a non-renewable period of seven years; its headquarters are in Turin.

391. Last but not least we must mention another Authority that was set up in 2014, to fight corruption. Its name is *Autorità nazionale anticorruzione* (ANAC), and it monitors public agencies for transparency compliance and enforces anti-corruption guidelines. It has the power to inspect offices and confiscate documents. The Government has given to ANAC (under pressure of a favourable public opinion) the power to intervene directly in public works contracts (beginning from the selection of the competitors). In case of an investigation for alleged corruption, the Authority may transfer the management to an external expert so that the work can go ahead even during the judicial enquiry. Raffaele Cantone (previously a judge of the higher level) was named as the first Chairman of ANAC, helped by four other Commissioners. The actual President is Giuseppe Busia.

392. In the last decades the importance of de-subjectivized powers within democracies has increased. In this way and along these lines, one tries to build another defence bastion against illiberalism. An important contemporary political scientist (Pierre Rosanvallon) has arrived to say that 'their vitality has become so essential as the other constitutional instruments in the age of the presidentialization of democracies'.

Chapter 11. The Budget Process

by Valerio Onida

§1. The Budget

393. On the subject of the budget and public spending, the Italian Constitution has adopted the basic rules typical of all democratic states (and already existing in the constitutional system prior to the Republic), according to which Parliament is responsible, on the one hand, for basic decisions of a legislative nature in matters regarding taxation (Article 23, 'No personal service or payment may be imposed, save according to law'), and, on the other hand, an annual law is required to pass the State budget, an accounting document which analytically shows all revenues and expenditures forecast during the fiscal year, and states the conditions for the administration's use of the powers of financial management, particularly the spending powers (Article 81).

394. Constitutional Law No. 1/ 2012 *(Introduction of the principle of a balanced budget in the Constitution)* has amended the Constitution's Articles 81 (about the national budget), 97 (on the obligation of public administrations, including non-governmental ones, to ensure balanced budgets and the sustainability of public debt), 117 (on the 'harmonization of public accounts' as a matter of exclusive competence of the State) and 119 (on regional and local finances and the obligation to ensure balanced accounts and to comply with the constraints imposed by EU law). It has introduced in the Constitution the principle of a balanced budget, in accordance with the provisions of the EU TSCG in the Economic and Monetary Union, agreed between the countries in the Euro area and another eight EU Member States, according to which (Article 3, paragraph 2) the 'Contracting Parties' undertake to put into effect the balanced budget rules 'through provisions of binding force and permanent character, preferably constitutional, or otherwise guaranteed to be fully respected and adhered to throughout the national budgetary process'.

395. The new constitutional law provides that 'the State guarantees the balance between revenue and expenditure in its budget, taking into account the adverse and favourable times in the economic cycle', and that 'borrowing is only allowed in consideration of the effects of the economic cycle and, with the approval of the two Chambers by absolute majority of its members, when exceptional events occur' (new text of Article 81, first and second paragraphs). such as serious financial crises or other extraordinary events beyond the control of the State

It also provides (new sixth paragraph in Article 81) that with a law passed by an absolute majority of members of each Chamber, and in accordance with the principles defined by a constitutional law, there will be established 'the content of the budget law, the fundamental rules and the criteria for ensuring the balance between revenues and expenditures in budgets and the sustainability of debt by all the public administrations as a whole' (*see* Article 5 of the Constitutional Law No. 1/2012, and Law No. 243/2012).

396. According to Article 81 of the Constitution, the budget is annual, is prepared and submitted by government and is approved by Parliament which passes a specific law. Article 81 states that such approval must normally occur prior to the beginning of the financial year to which the budget refers, failing which, if the approval is not given in time, a special law has to authorize the so-called provisional budget period, lasting a maximum of four months (since the financial year now coincides with the calendar year, the temporary financial period may not go beyond 30 April).

Until the recent reform, the budgetary laws could only indicate revenues and expenditure resulting from the application of existing legislation. It was on the other hand prohibited to introduce provisions into budgetary laws entailing new revenues or expenditure, in order to avoid confusion between annual budgetary decisions and the statutory provisions governing revenues and expenditure. Amendments to such legislation which the government and Parliament sought to introduce each year had to be contained in an annual law (so-called finance law or stability law), which had to be approved before the budgetary law. The constitutional reform of 2012 has now removed that prohibition; the annual budgetary law now contains, in a first section, the provisions governing revenues and expenditure aimed at achieving policy objectives, while a second section makes provision for revenues and expenditure based on current legislation and, separately, any changes resulting from the provisions laid down in the first section. This occurs both for the relevant financial year and for the three-year period. However, it is not permitted to include in the budgetary law provisions delegating legislative authority to the government, provisions relating to the general legal system or the organization of executive administrations and not to specific activities involving expenditure or revenues, or measures 'of local or micro-sectoral nature': the aim (although this is often contradicted by the facts) is to avoid pressure being exerted to incorporate specific provisions into the annual law in order to benefit from the expedited parliamentary procedure guaranteed for it. In fact, the annual finance law has a privileged course in Parliament, relatively guaranteed as regards its definition times, and regarding which there is a maximum political commitment on the part of the government and the majority, also with recourse to the question of confidence (*see* Part II, Chapter 6). The finance law, and today the budget law, thus becomes a convenient 'convoy' to which 'cars' of legislative and spending provisions can be attached, which would otherwise have had greater difficulty or scarce possibility to pass the parliamentary examination. This, however, is causing the legislative process to become muddled and less transparent.

The parliamentary debate on the annual budget law takes place, as regards both Chambers, in a special budget session and is normally concluded prior to the beginning of the year.

397. The Constitution does not specify how the revenues and expenditures should be broken down in the budget. In traditional accounting systems, the basic unit of the budget is represented by the single 'item' (*capitolo*) of revenue and expenditure: as regards expenditure, the amount shown under the item represents the maximum ceiling not to be exceeded by the administration. Parliamentary approval concerns larger amounts: titles (*titoli*) and types (*tipologie*) for revenues, and projects (*programmi*), which are grouped into 'missions' (*missioni*) indicating the main tasks and the strategic objectives, for expenditure; each programme is entrusted to a single responsible office for management. The units are divided into items by an administrative process entrusted to the government, who can vary them, within each unit, even after the parliamentary approval.

Corresponding to each large division of the administration (Prime Minister's Office and Ministries) there is a table of expenditures, along with a general summary framework with reference to the three-year period.

The revenues and expenditures are today represented both on an 'accrual basis' (i.e., entering to the budget the amounts which are expected to become payable to government during the year, and those in respect of which the administration is authorized to undertake financial commitments during the same year) and on a 'cash basis' (i.e., indicating the amounts which are, respectively, expected to be received and paid out during the year). A dedicated article of the law stipulates the maximum amount of public sector debt instruments that may be issued during the year, both in Italy and abroad, after deducting the amount of debt that is to be redeemed.

398. Each year Parliament is also called on to approve the final report or statement of accounts, showing the revenues and expenditures relating to the last fiscal period and the financial results for such period. Again, this report is drawn up by government, based on data produced by the administration. It is then audited to ensure its credibility and compared to the budget by the accounting supervisory authority, the Court of Auditors (*Corte dei conti*), by means of a jurisdictional procedure (so-called *parificazione,* i.e., equalization), and is then submitted to Parliament for approval by a special law. The approval of the statement of accounts does not, however, condition the work of the administration.

399. Under the Constitution, the laws passing the budgets and final accounts are subject to the ordinary approval procedure on the part of the two parliamentary assemblies (hence they may not be enacted by the committees, Article 72, paragraph 4) and are not subject to repeal by referendum (Article 75, paragraph 2). Clearly, since they are instruments of parliamentary direction and control on the executive authority, the budget laws could never be enacted by government either acting for delegation of Parliament or as an urgent measure by decree-law, even if this is not explicitly stated in the constitutional text.

From 1978, it was provided that the budget process would take place through a coordinated series of instruments of which the annual budget forecast is only the end result.

The government has to present to the Chambers by 10 April each year the Document of Economy and Finance (DEF) in order to conduct non-legislative parliamentary deliberations, and by 30 April it presents to the Council of the European Union and the European Commission the 'Stability Programme' and the 'National Reform Programme'. The DEF contains the schedule of the Stability Programme which sets out the objectives of economic policy, the framework of economic and public finance provisions for the following three years, the policy objectives, the trends predicted according to current legislation, and the schedule of the National Reform Programme which also indicates the state of progress in the reforms started, the priorities of the country and the main reforms to put in place.

By 27 September, the government has to present an 'Update Report' on the DEF to Parliament for its deliberations, and by 20 October the bill for the State Budget.

§2. THE FINANCIAL 'COVER' OF LAWS PROVIDING FOR NEW EXPENDITURE

updated by Antonio D'Andrea & Lorenzo Spadacini

400. Reference is made in the Constitution to all the laws which give rise to a new or additional expenditure with respect to that resulting from previous legislation, stating that they should 'set forth the means' for covering the expenditure in question (Article 81, new text, paragraph 3). This is a constitutional provision intended to avoid Parliament being able, through spending legislation, to negatively impact the balance of budgets without taking on responsibility for the measures needed to reinstate the same. It does not, as such, preclude recourse to public debt, and hence to deficit spending policies, but requires Parliament to explicitly assume responsibility for this when deliberating a new or additional expenditure; and moreover, after the reform of 2012, compliance is required with the criteria and parameters related to balancing the budget, according to the European rules.

This constitutional obligation (breach of which has on several occasions given rise to the remittance of laws to Parliament by the President of the Republic – *see* Part II, Chapter 2 – and to statements concerning the constitutional illegitimacy of laws, especially regional laws, on the part of the Constitutional Court) is necessary both when the new or additional expenditure is intended to be covered by the budget for the period underway at the time of approving the law, or when it is destined be effected (on a mandatory basis) in the following years (not only those considered in the multi-year budget), running the risk of jeopardizing the equilibrium of the budget.

The same obligation is extended to the legislative measures of the Regions (with reference to the expenditures to be covered in their respective budgets), as well as those imposing new or additional expenditures charged to the budgets of other entities of the so-called enlarged public sector; and also to the laws which reduce the revenues.

The indication of means may consist in the utilization of any kind of revenues, or in the reduction of other expenditures, or even of funds already set aside in the budget to cover the new expenditure. But the issue of new public debt is now only permitted under the Constitution, as mentioned above in §1, in order to take account of the effects of the economic cycle or following the occurrence of exceptional events, and in the second case is conditional upon prior approval by both Houses of Parliament granted by an absolute majority of their members (new Article 81(2)).

401. The constitutional obligation to indicate financial cover for the new or additional expenditures is integrated with the parliamentary regulations aiming to make it more difficult for the Chambers to approve legislative provisions without correctly complying with this obligation, through the opinions of the budget committees, which may only be opposed with the vote of the plenary assembly.

The constitutional rules, which have recently been made significantly more stringent, coupled with control by the European institutions, should as a matter of principle be capable of preventing an uncontrolled growth in spending that is not covered by revenue along with an increase in public debt. However, the public debt in Italy still remains very high (in 2022 around 145% of gross domestic product), even though the ratio between revenues and expenditure before debt interest now reports a significant 'primary surplus'. Moreover, there are discussions as to whether it is appropriate during a time of crisis to maintain such restrictive constraints on deficit spending policies.

402. However, as things currently stand it is not so easy to conceive of a scenario in which revenue and public spending policies could be replaced or corrected – leaving aside the obligations under EU law, temporarily suspended during the Covid period until 2023, and potential sanctions imposed by the European institutions – by judicial rulings such as those adopted by the Constitutional Court on the basis of constitutional law, considering the ways in which it may be apprised of such questions (mostly when the law is already in force: *see* Chapter 9, §§4, 5 and 9), and above all the difficulty in translating criteria that depend on economic evaluations (such as 'the effects of the economic cycle') into precise legal rules.

Part III. The State and Its Subdivisions

Chapter 1. Regions and Local Authorities

by Paolo Cavaleri† & Ilaria Carlotto

§1. Regional and Local Self-Governing Authorities in the Italian Constitution

403. The complex system of territorial autonomies described in the Italian Constitution of 1948 undergone a major reform several years ago. Constitutional Law No. 1/1999 makes changes to the governance and statutory autonomy of the Regions, and Constitutional Law No. 3/2001 (confirmed by popular referendum) has radically changed Title V of Part II of the Constitution and redesigned the form of the State, significantly reinforcing the role of regional and local autonomies. As administrative authorities, the Regions, Provinces, Communes and Metropolitan Cities all manage the interests of their communities through representative bodies but have very different historical points of departure. The Regions are relatively young, dating back to the 1948 Republican Constitution, which made legal provision for five regions with Special Statute (Article 116) and fifteen regions with ordinary statute (Article 131). The Provinces are the result of a long institutional evolution which – during the monarchical-liberal period – were initially created as local government bodies and were grafted onto the old administrative districts which demarcated the powers of a large number of local state offices (such as the Prefectures, the Superintendencies of Finance and the Local Education Authorities). However, it must be pointed out at this juncture – in relation to an issue which will be considered in greater depth below (*see* below, §14) – that various attempts have been made in recent years to reorganize and/or abolish the Italian Provinces, which have resulted *inter alia* not only in a reduction in their powers but also their transformation into second-level authorities. The Communes existed long before Italian Unification and were modelled on a pattern of local authorities dating back to the French Revolution and based on two principles: the institution of a municipality for each local community, however scarcely populated, and the introduction of a unique legal status for the Communes, regardless of the differences among them in terms of size, geographical location, economic situation or historical traditions. Regarding the municipality of the capital city of Rome, Article 114, paragraph 3, of the Constitution provides for the adoption of a special status, stated by Article 24 of Law No. 42/2009 and subsequent Legislative Decrees No. 156/2010 and No. 61/2012, as amended by Legislative Decree No. 51/2013. Finally, the Metropolitan Cities, for which provision was first made by Law No. 142/1990, are even more recent but only assumed constitutional significance following the 2001 reform. In particular, Article 23 of Law No. 42/2009 provides that, on proposal from the Communes and Provinces concerned, subject to popular referendum, in each of the areas around the main Italian cities, a Metropolitan City can be instituted, acquiring the functions of the Province and adopt a special regulation. After many struggles, the Metropolitan Cities were specifically regulated by Law No. 56/2014 (known as 'Delrio Law'), as described below (*see* §14).

404. The reform of Title V of Part II of the Constitution appears to place all territorial authorities on the same level. Indeed, the new text of Article 114 asserts that the Republic, apart from the State, is constituted by, rather than 'divided into', Regions, Communes, Provinces and Metropolitan Cities, which are defined as 'autonomous authorities with their own statutes, powers and functions according to principles set out in the Constitution'. This may appear to be a significant innovation with respect to the preceding constitutional framework, where only the autonomy of the Regions was defined directly by the Constitution, at least in its key features, while the autonomy of the other territorial authorities (then Provinces and Communes) was only dealt with indirectly, through the State legislator whose task it was to define this guardianship in more detail. In my opinion, however, the reform of Article 114 must be considered primarily as a declaration of principle, given that other constitutional data reveal that many, and certainly not negligible, differences still exist between the Regions and the smaller territorial authorities. It is the Constitution which specifies the functions of the Regions whereas those of the Communes, Provinces and Metropolitan Cities are still governed by State and regional law. The same applies for statutory autonomy which is only regulated by the Constitution for the Regions. Moreover, only the Regions have legislative jurisdiction (i.e., the power to pass legislation); only the Regions have the power to make recourse to the Constitutional Court to challenge State legislation in the making deemed prejudicial to those constitutional norms which defend the role of the Regions, and only the Regions have the power to challenge the State over conflicts of competence with regard to acts considered detrimental to regional autonomy.

It is not coincidental that Italian regulation is generally defined as 'regional'; the fact that Italy is constituted by Regions means that the body of regulation has a very particular form which must be kept distinct from the 'federal' one, even if the distinction is justified basically in quantitative terms, as argued by Kelsen. Even following the constitutional reform of 2001, the Italian Regions still appear to lack many of the powers traditionally associated with a federal State. In particular, they are excluded from the formulation of State policy (often legislative), insofar as no provision has been made for either of the two Chambers of Parliament to be composed of regional representatives; in specific policy areas, where 'concurrent' jurisdiction has been maintained they are compelled to legislate according to the basic principles established by State legislation; they cannot take part in the process of constitutional review; they have neither the legal power nor the public force to maintain internal order, and their organs are subject to various forms of State control (substitutive interventions, the dissolution of the Regional Councils and removal of the President).

405. On the basis of the Constitution (cf. in particular, the new text of Articles 117 and 118), the territorial authorities now enjoy legal and administrative autonomy, with the difference that in the case of the Regions, legal jurisdiction comprises both legislative and regulatory responsibilities, while the smaller local authorities only enjoy regulatory responsibility in the organization and execution of the administrative functions assigned to them. Thus, the regulation appears to attribute political autonomy to all the territorial authorities, in the sense that the latter can to pursue ends, and to meet needs and make freely selected choices, in the sphere of the powers attributed to them, and of their respective competences.

Prior to the recent reform of Title V, legislative responsibility was only assigned to the Regions in matters expressly indicated by the Constitution and Special Statutes, with the consequence that it was the State which enjoyed wide-ranging powers in all areas *not* explicitly assigned to the Regions. More recently, however, Constitutional Law No. 3/2001 has assumed the stance typical of a federal system of governance and reversed this criterion so that it instead specifies those matters where the State has legislative responsibility while simultaneously affirming the principle that 'the Regions retain legislative responsibility in all matters not explicitly reserved to State legislation' (new text of Article 117, paragraph 4). This same criterion applies, in substance, to the dividing up of regulatory responsibility between the State and the Regions.

With regard to administrative jurisdiction, Constitutional Law No. 3/2001 generally assigns administrative functions to the Communes, except where these are conferred to, 'the Provinces, Metropolitan Cities, Regions and the State in order to guarantee their unitary exercise […] on the basis of the principles of subsidiarity, differentiation and proportionality' (new text of Article 118, paragraph 1).

The constitutional reform thus presented has a clear line of continuity with Law No. 59/1997 which, in order to introduce what is referred to as 'administrative federalism' (Article 1, paragraph 2), prepared the ground for the conferral to the Regions and local authorities of 'all the functions and administrative tasks relating to the treatment of the interests and promotion of the development of the respective communities', and 'all the administrative functions and tasks localizable in the respective territories […] exercised by any organ … of the State … or through … other public subjects'. This conferral excludes only those functions and tasks traceable to policy areas explicitly listed by the law, in particular, foreign affairs, defence and public order, justice, education and monetary policy. This process has been realized through a series of legislative decrees adopted by government on the basis of the delegation in Law No. 59/1997. Of these, Decree No. 112/1998 stands out for making provision for the Regions and local authorities to enjoy a wide range of functions and administrative competences (the other decrees dealt with *specific* sectors).

406. One can say that this is, above all, the result of the progressive consolidation of the principle of subsidiarity in Italian regulation, according to which – without concealing the ambiguities that may emerge – functions and administrative tasks must be distributed among the different levels of government in such a way as to allocate to the higher levels only those competences which cannot be carried out with the necessary levels of efficiency and rigour by the levels of government nearest to the citizens concerned. This principle was introduced by the convention on the 'European Charter for Local Autonomies', and resumed in Italian regulation with Law No. 439/1989, and subsequently by the European Treaties. It has now been included at the constitutional level, not only in the 'vertical' (or 'institutional') sense mentioned above (Article 118, paragraph 1) but also in a 'horizontal' (or 'social') perspective, in order to maximize the role of the private actors in the satisfaction of the needs of the community. It must be stressed that the new Article 118, paragraph 4, commits the State and the autonomous territorial authorities to lend support to, 'autonomous initiatives on the part of citizens, as single individuals and members of associations, in activities of general interest, on the basis of the principle of subsidiarity'.

On the basis of the new text of Article 118, paragraph 2, the classification of the administrative functions falling within the competence of the various territorial authorities is performed on the basis of the principle of subsidiarity, not only by State law but also by regional law. In perspective, the situation which emerges is anything but rigid or homogenous, in the sense that the distribution of the functions among the different tiers of government varies in relation to the characteristics of the different local communities and the organizational resources of each territorial context.

Generally speaking, the smaller territorial authorities (primarily the Communes) are assigned the functions of active administration, while those tasks of wide-ranging coverage, such as coordination and planning, are assigned to the Metropolitan Cities and to the Provinces, leaving the Regions exclusive jurisdiction in the functions of policymaking, planning, coordination and promotion for the entire territory.

407. Before proceeding to an analysis of the various institutes of regional law and the local authorities, although it is not possible to provide any particularly detailed analysis in this study, it is important in any case to take account of the launch in recent years of a new process of constitutional reform which would have significantly scaled back the role of the regions along with that of the local authorities (with the abolition – or at least the 'de-constitutionalization' – of the Provinces) and created a variegated bicameral model under which the Senate would represent the local government bodies. This reform was however rejected by the electorate in the constitutional referendum held on 4 December 2016.

§2. The Origins of the Italian 'Regional' State

408. The historical origins of the Italian Regions must be understood in the light of the scheme for administrative regionalization formulated in 1861, at the dawn of

Unification, by the then Ministers of the Interior, Farini and Minghetti. The project was based on the assumption that the creation of Regions would increase the protection of the cultural, social and economic features of the various local areas, improve the effectiveness of their administrative actions and the selection of their political class. In the last instance, however, the fear that the creation of the Regions would – in addition to being a useless and expensive duplication of public institutions – undermine the newly conquered unity of the State prevailed, and the scheme was rejected by Parliament. Even though they were not implemented on an institutional level, regionalist theories continued to fuel debate well into the interwar period. This was when regions started to be conceived of as genuinely political entities, especially thanks to the People's Party, founded in 1919 by Don Luigi Sturzo, and coincided with the annexation of Trentino-Alto Adige and Venetia Julia (which had always manifested strong separatist trends vis-à-vis the Austro-Hungarian Empire) to Italy.

In Italy, the onset of Fascism in 1922 imposed a totally centralist conception of the State, frustrating autonomist expectations and suffocating any pre-existing provincial and communal authorities. For the next twenty-five years, the prospects of the 'regional' State were effectively blocked by the fascist regime and only began to emerge with its collapse and the onset of the radical reforms of the State by the anti-fascist political forces in the second half of the 1940s. In 1946/1947, the Constituent Assembly was entrusted with drafting the Constitution of the new Republican State following the first post-war elections in June 1946 and was encouraged to grant a strong element of autonomy to regions by the Christian Democrats (successors to the People's Party), the Action Party, the small Republican Party and part of the Liberal Party. However, the other political forces in the Assembly were preoccupied with the protection of the unity and indivisibility of the State. In the last instance, however, the thesis promoted by the Catholic forces, that fundamental human rights must include the right to realize oneself within a plurality of social groups, including local communities, had a catalysing effect on the Assembly and produced the necessary number of votes in favour of a regional structure of government.

This decision was also influenced by the strong autonomist trends which had been previously manifested in parts of the country (in some cases, as in Sicily, even taking the form of separatist attacks). A High Commissioner and an Advisory Committee (representing the various political and social forces) had been established since 1944 in Sardinia and Sicily as extraordinary and provisional bodies of local government. The Council of Sicily had even devised an autonomous system which included wide-ranging legislative powers and led to a plan for a Regional Statute, which was approved in slightly amended form by government with the Royal Legislative Decree No. 455/1946 in order to avoid the risk of armed insurrection. In 1945, the Valle d'Aosta also witnessed the creation of the new 'autonomous district of Valle d'Aosta', which replaced the old Province of Aosta. This was headed by a President, a Junta and an Elective Council, and was immediately allocated administrative functions which were supposed to be followed by legislative autonomy.

409. Finally, the De Gasperi-Gruber agreement between Italy and Austria, signed in Paris in September 1946, provided not only for a series of measures to protect the German-speaking inhabitants of South Tyrol but also, and more importantly, for the exercise of autonomous legislative and executive powers in that territory. These measures anticipated the creation of the Trentino-Alto Adige Region and the Autonomous Provinces of Bolzano and Trento and had a structure and functions that made their institutions very similar to those of the Regions.

In the circumstances, the Constituent Assembly could choose either to set up regions solely in this part of Italy or to extend this structure of government to the entire national territory. After extended debate, the Assembly opted for the latter, a choice which highlighted the existence of differing viewpoints among the political forces. The *plenum*, for instance, decided that the Regions should not enjoy all the legislative powers proposed by 'the Commission of 75', responsible for drafting the Constitution. The provisions dealing with the regional system were finally included in the Constitution and were, in the words of Meuccio Ruini, one of the most authoritative members of the Constituent Assembly, its 'greatest innovation'. This then is the genesis of the constitutional provisions dealing with the regional autonomies and suggests why regional governance has been divided into two distinct levels.

410. The first level concerns those Regions which enjoyed particular forms and conditions of autonomy under the Special Regional Statutes adopted by a State constitutional law (Article 116 of the Constitution). These Regions had already satisfied some of their autonomist expectations prior to the introduction of the Constitution in 1947. In order to abide by Article 116, the Constituent Assembly was reconvened (in compliance with final and transitional provision XVII) to assimilate the Regional Statute already in force in Sicily by means of Constitutional Law No. 2/1948 and to approve the Special Regional Statutes for Sardinia, the Valle d'Aosta and Trentino-Alto Adige (Constitutional Laws No. 3/1948, No. 4/1948 and No. 5/1948). The only Special Regional Statute not approved by the Constituent Assembly was that of Friuli-Venetia Julia, considered a Special Status Region on account of its Slovene minority; its Special Statute was only adopted fifteen years later (by Constitutional Law No. 1/1963) owing to outstanding difficulties, both at the national and international level, which lasted until long after the end of the Second World War.

The second level of autonomy is defined as 'ordinary' and includes the other fifteen Regions (the fourteen Regions initially scheduled were joined in 1963 by Molise, after it separated from the Abruzzi Region). Given the lack of objective criteria on their geographical, administrative and economic identity, these Regions were classified on the basis of outdated statistics used in the Kingdom of Italy to collect demographic and economic data in the previous century. This reveals the inherent weakness of the Ordinary Regions and their lack of common historical roots.

The Constituent Assembly, probably in view of adjusting the original plan, also delivered a provision regarding the fusion of the existing Regions or the creation of new ones by means of a constitutional law (Article 132 of the Constitution), as well as the displacement of Provinces or Communes from one Region to another by means of an ordinary Act of Parliament. And it was precisely in accordance with this constitutional provision, which was not given practical effect for a long period, that in 2009 seven municipalities from Alta Valmarecchia detached from Marche Region and incorporated in Emilia-Romagna Region, or the outcome of one of the numerous other initiatives launched (sometimes also for economic reasons) by municipalities from the Ordinary Regions that intend to transfer to the neighbouring Regions with Special Statute. More specifically, with the approval of Law No. 182/2017, the municipality of Sappada was allowed to detach itself from the Veneto Region in order to join Friuli-Venezia Giulia.

In recent times, to confirm the uniqueness that characterizes certain areas of the territory, and in particular the Special Regions of Sicily and Sardinia, the Legislator has introduced a new paragraph within Article 119 of the Constitution, by virtue of which the Republic recognizes the peculiarities of the islands and promotes the necessary measures to remove the disadvantages deriving from insularity (Article 119, paragraph 6, of the Constitution as implemented by Constitutional Law No. 2/2022). In this way, the principle of insularity is constitutionalized and therefore also acts as a parameter of legitimacy for the consequent regulatory interventions.

§3. The Creation of the Regions

411. The approval of the four Special Regional Statutes in 1948 constituted the first step towards the regionalization of Italy. It did not coincide, however, with the full and practical implementation of regional autonomy, since most of the constitutional rules required special implementing provisions (mainly for the transfer of State administrative functions to each of the Regions), which were passed quite late. But in spite of the difficulties, the Special Regions were not left in the sort of institutional limbo in which the Ordinary Regions remained for so long and which, despite the fact that the Constitution provided that the election of their Councils should be held by 31 December 1948, were only formally instituted twenty years later.

The approval of Law No. 62/1953 on the legal institution and organization of regional bodies did not lead, as was hoped, to the rapid institution of the Ordinary Regions. Governmental political forces clearly feared that the opposition parties might 'highjack' or 'occupy' the regional 'machinery' in areas where they had a majority, with evident repercussions at the national level. These obstacles were only removed when Centre-Left Cabinets, in the 1960s, created a different political and ideological climate and led to the enactment of the most important constitutional provisions concerning the regional system, i.e., those relating to the Ordinary Regions, in 1970.

At the beginning of the fifth legislature, the changed political and institutional situation meant that all the measures necessary to create the Ordinary Regions and render them operative were passed one after another: Law No. 108/1968, on the election of Councils (passed in June 1970); Law No. 281/1970, on regional finance; the May–July 1971 laws on the approval of the Regional Statutes by Regional Councils; the January 1972 decrees on the transfer to the Regions of State administrative functions, followed by three implementing decrees of 24 July 1977, in particular, Law No. 616/1977.

§4. The Organization and Competencies of the Ordinary Regions

412. The Constitution makes provision for the overall organization of the Ordinary Regions, the distribution of tasks among their governing bodies and their relations, in a system of governance based on a Council, Junta and President, and by each Regional Statute. In November 1999, some key amendments were made to the provisions contained in the Constitution which have, among other things, reshaped the system of regional government, particularly with the introduction of the direct election of the President of the Junta; they have modified the drafting procedure for the Regional Statutes and have empowered the Regions to regulate election procedures for the Council (previously regulated by State provisions).

Over the years, various Regions have approved more or less organic regional laws, which are based on a proportional electoral system on district level awarding a variable majority bonus, in order to guarantee a certain stability to the executive body. Thus, it confirms the approach already followed by state Law No. 43/ 1995. These electoral laws also have the requirement to introduce measures to promote gender equality. In this regard, it should be noted that with Decree-Law No. 86/2020 the Government, exercising its substitute power, is intervened by introducing the provision of dual gender preference for the 2020 election of the Regional Council in Puglia Region.

Again with regard to the election of members of the Regional Council, it is also important to recall Decree-Law No. 138/2011 (converted into Law No. 148/2011) which, in order to achieve the objectives laid down in relation to the coordination of public finances, stipulated the maximum number of eligible regional councillors in each Region on a proportional basis in line with the resident population, thereby forcing various regions to modify their legislation (including *in primis* the Regional Statutes) in order to reduce the number of members of regional assemblies. Although the determination of the number of members of the Regional Council is a matter reserved for the Regional Statute – as it is constitutive of the 'system of government' – the State legislation was upheld as constitutional (Constitutional Court, Judgment No. 198/2012).

Finally, in the same delicate link among state and regional sources in electoral matters, the Constitutional Court recently emphasized that the ban on a third consecutive term for the President of the ordinary Regions pursuant to Article 2, paragraph 1, letter f) of Law No. 165/2004, as related to ineligibility, pertains to the fundamental principles within the jurisdiction of the State legislature (Constitutional Court, Judgment No. 64/2025).

The Council only exercises legislative powers according to a procedure (described in the Regional Statute and Council Standing Orders), similar to that adopted for the drafting of State laws with the difference that regional laws are passed by a single Chamber and cannot be voted by a committee. While all statutes contemplate an ordinary procedure under which, as is known, after the bill drafted during the committee stage has been examined, it falls to the Council to approve the text article by article and by a final vote, most of the new statutes have adopted a procedure under which the committee is involved in the drafting stage. Finally, a minority of Regions have also introduced a procedure under which the committee is also involved in the substantive decision-making stage, although not without raising doubts as to the constitutionality of such an approach.

Following the changes introduced by the constitutional reform of 1999, the powers of the Council have been considerably reduced. Not only has it been deprived of the power to issue regulations (i.e., measures belonging to the category of secondary legal sources), but also, even more important, has the President of the Junta – who is elected by direct and universal suffrage – the power to appoint and revoke the members of the Junta (prior to the reform, both the Junta and its President were elected by the Council). The Council, however, can still vote by an absolute majority a motion of no-confidence on the President of the Junta, leading to the resignation of the entire Junta and the dissolution of the Council.

The most significant element of this renewed constitutional framework is the prominent position occupied by the President of the Junta over and above the collegiate executive body, despite the fact that the Constitution states that it is the Junta which is 'the executive branch of regional government'. As well as representing the Region, passing laws and regulations, supervising the administrative functions allocated by the State, the President 'oversees the policy of the Junta for which he is also accountable'. Hence, the previous structure of governance of the Ordinary Regions (mainly of an assembly type), which accorded all functions (above all, that of determining overall regional policy) to the competence of the Council, has been discarded. Since the reform of 1999, a new system of regional governance has been in place; this is based on two bodies elected by direct franchise, namely the President of the Junta who is responsible for conducting general policy and the Council which exercises the powers of supervision and guarantee. The fates of the two bodies are inseparably linked, so much so that the cessation of one of them will also result in the end of the term in office of the other: thus, if the President of the Junta dies, resigns, becomes permanently ineligible, is removed by the President of the Republic or loses a confidence vote in the Council, this will result in not only a requirement for the Junta to resign but also the dissolution of the Regional Council; at the same time, the parallel resignation of a majority of the members of the Council will result in the removal from office of the entire executive body.

This rough pattern will be integrated into the new Ordinary Regional Statutes which will replace the present ones pursuant to the new text of Article 123, subject to the passing of a law by each Regional Council adopted by absolute majority in two successive decisions. Government has the power to submit the question of the legality of this implementing law/Regional Statute – and only that – to the Constitutional Court. The Regional Statute can be subject to a referendum upon request by one-fiftieth of the Region's voters or one-fifth of the Members of the Council. The Constitution explicitly states, however, that the new Regional Statutes can make provision for a system of governance which diverges from the model described above (without prejudice to the basic principles of the Constitution), for example, by not introducing the election of the President by direct and universal franchise, even though in actual fact none of the new Ordinary Statutes has availed itself of this possibility (*see* most recently the Statute of Basilicata Region, which entered into force in 2016, thereby completing the approval stage for a 'second generation' of statutes).

413. In addition to dealing with the regional form of government, the internal organization of the Regions and their basic operational principles, the Regional Statutes also contain rules governing the right of legislative initiative, referenda and the publication of laws and regulations (Article 123). The Regional Councils, however, have unanimously decided to extend the coverage of their Regional Statutes, by introducing a series of general principles to be followed by specific regional activities. However, according to constitutional case law (*see* Constitutional Court, Judgments Nos 372, 378 and 379/2004), assertions of this type do not have any legal effect and perform simply a cultural and political function.

It is also worth mentioning the provisions dealing with forms of popular participation in political life. Pursuant to the Constitution, the regional referenda for which provision is made under the Regional Statutes can, unlike their State counterpart, not only repeal laws but also repeal administrative measures and, in the case of consultative referenda, alter regional, provincial and communal boundaries. Moreover, the statutes of the Ordinary Regions provide for the right of citizens, associations and local authorities to submit opinions or recommendations to the Regional Councils and for the Council Commissions to consult local authorities, citizens and social groups in order to improve the performance of regional tasks. The Regional Statutes also stipulate that citizens should participate in the drafting of general administrative measures. Once again, the new statutes provide for guarantor bodies for the statutes and put in place various liaison mechanisms in order to favour cooperation between the Region and both the State and the local authorities, establishing the Council of Local Government Bodies, as required under the Constitution itself in Article 123, paragraph 4.

§5. The Organization and Competencies of the Special Statute Regions

414. The organizational order of the Special Regions, outlined in their statutes, is based on the allocation of functions among the Council, Junta and President. The fact that, according to Article 116, such statutes are 'adopted with constitutional laws', and therefore discussed by the Italian Parliament, may suggest that such Regions lack the sort of statutory autonomy enjoyed by the Ordinary Regions. Indeed, in the original version of the Special Statutes, only those of Sardinia (Article 54, u.c.) and the Valle d'Aosta (Article 50, u.c.) make explicit provision so that in typically statutory matters (i.e., form of governance, organization of internal regional affairs, the right of legislative initiative, the right of referendum and the publication of laws and regional regulations) the rules of the respective Special Statutes could be changed in the forms for which provision is made under Article 123, paragraphs 2–3, by the respective Regional Councils.

With the recent introduction of Constitutional Law No. 2/2001, however, Italy has now moved on to the partial reform of the Special Statutes, in particular, with the provisions for the direct election of the Presidents of Special Statute Regions and the Autonomous Provinces of Trento and Bolzano and the recognition of the power of domestic self-governance similar to that assigned to the Ordinary Regions and to *all* the Special Statute Regions (and not just Sardinia and the Valle d'Aosta).

Following the reform, each Special Statute assigns the task of determining the form of regional governance, the procedures for the election of the President and members of the Junta, the relations between the organs of the Region, the exercise of the popular legislative initiative and the rules governing regional referenda to a 'reinforced' regional law. This is approved with a process very similar to that provided for under the new text of Article 123 for the approval of the Ordinary Statutes, with the difference that the decision is taken with a single, rather than a double vote, with an absolute majority.

Quite apart from this (partial) alignment of the special regulations with those of the Ordinary Regions, the fact remains that the Special Statutes have a different function from the Ordinary Statutes, insofar as they provide for the principles governing the election of the Councils (implemented by a regional law), regional financing, the supervision of regional organs, and also specify the policy areas assigned to the competence of the Region. In synthesis, they carry out in relation to each special regulation the role exercised by the Constitution in relation to the regulation of the Ordinary Regions as a whole.

To date, the governance of the Special Regions has generally been considered of a basically parliamentary nature. This qualification is supported not only in the textual provisions of the Special Statutes, so much as in consolidated practice (confirmed by Council regulations), from which one can deduce that it has usually been the Junta, elected by the Council, which formulates the political programme requiring a vote of confidence on the part of the Council.

This situation changed following the approval of Constitutional Law No. 2/2001, from the moment that content of the decisions made with regard to the governance of the Ordinary Regions was effectively extended to the Special Statute Regions so that, with the exception of the Valle d'Aosta and the Autonomous Province of Bolzano, the same standard model, based on the popular direct election of the President, has been provisionally introduced for the Special Statute Regions. At the same time, each Special Region can now assert some degree of independence (with the reinforced regional law), in autonomously determining its form of government. It is worth noting that Regional Statutes, like the laws amending the Constitution and other constitutional laws, cannot contrast with the 'supreme principles of the constitutional system' and are therefore subject to constitutional review, as explicitly stated by the Constitutional Court (Judgment No. 1146/1988).

§6. General Aspects of Regional Legislative Autonomy

415. The main function of regional autonomy is the legislative function. Prior to the 2001 reform, we can deduce from the Constitution and the Special Statutes that the Regions could exercise various types of legislative responsibility in those policy areas explicitly assigned to them and which are differentiated on the basis of the limitations to which each was subject.

Following the stance generally adopted in legal theory and practice, in the first place, the so-called primary or full legislative responsibility recognized solely to the Special Statute Regions and the Autonomous Provinces had to be taken into consideration. In addition to being bound by the Constitution, this responsibility was limited, externally, by 'limitations of merit', i.e., the national interest and the interests of other Regions, which it was Parliament's task to safeguard and by limitations of legitimacy, i.e., the basic legal norms of State legislation dealing with economic-social reform, international obligations and general legal principles, monitored by the Constitutional Court.

The second type of legislative responsibility, the so-called concurrent responsibility, was recognized both to the Special Statute Regions and to the Ordinary Regions. In addition to the limits cited above, this is subject to an internal constraint, represented by the basic principles established for each policy area by State legislation.

In addition to the two types of responsibilities described above, there is the so-called activating and integrative-activating regional power to implement and integrate the provisions of State laws which enables the Regions to legally implement State legislation adapting it to specific local conditions.

It was the job of the ordinary State legislator to concretize the constitutionally defined limits of the legislative jurisdiction of the Regions also with respect to the national interest. The 'limitation of merit' has frequently been used (with the guarantee of constitutional jurisprudence) in order to justify State legislation in policy areas assigned to the Regions and which make 'cuts' of competences to the benefit of the State and the detriment of the Regions; in this sense, the 'limitation of merit' is invoked to defend the national interest and not as a criterion to evaluate the legislative discretion of the Regions. In this sense, for example, in the areas denoted as 'fairs and markets', 'public health care and hospitals' and 'mines', the functions concerning national fairs, the classification of key national hospitals and the overall planning of mining activity are reserved for the State.

In addition, the State legislator has also introduced, *praeter Constitutionem*, another limitation, initially designed to circumscribe the administrative autonomy of the Regions, but which ended up being extended to legislative responsibility. This is the limit associated with the performance of the function of policymaking and overall coordination. The objective here is to guarantee the needs of a unitary character, an activity which is consequently reserved for the State. Notwithstanding the fact that it was only provided for by ordinary law, and not explicitly dealt with by the Constitution, the consolidated jurisprudence of the Constitutional Court has accorded the State power of policymaking and overall coordination a certain, albeit implicit, constitutional basis. According to the Court, this limitation had to be applied without exception 'to the entire circle of autonomous authorities', that is to say, not only the Ordinary Regions but also the Special Statute Regions and the Autonomous Provinces.

416. In comparing the reform of Title V to the constitutional order, one has the impression that the latter has generated significant innovative and confirming effects which maintain, in other words, institutions or principles for which provision is already made in the original text of the Constitution and more importantly, the 'constitutionalization' of decisions already codified in ordinary legislation. The most striking innovation introduced by the constitutional reform of 2001 is the inversion of the criterion used to distinguish the spheres of the legislative responsibility assigned respectively to the State and the Regions. Indeed, while in precedence it was the areas of competence of the Regions which were explicitly listed (by the Constitution and the Special Regional Statutes), the reform of Title V instead indicates the policy areas where the State has 'exclusive' legislative responsibility, while simultaneously affirming that 'the legislative responsibility with reference to all areas not expressly reserved for the legislation of the State is due to the Regions' (new text of Article 117, paragraph 4). So that, for example, industry, commerce, public works, insurance and social welfare all fall within the jurisdiction of the Regions, while policy domains such as foreign affairs, defence, the monetary system, public order, civil and criminal regulation remain within the competence of the State.

With this reversal of the perspective adopted by the Constituent Assembly in 1947, the reform reinforces the legislative authority of the Regions and makes provision for the completion, with the indispensable constitutional adaptations, of the operation carried out at the administrative level with the 'Bassanini Law' No. 59/1997, which granted the territorial autonomies all those administrative functions not explicitly reserved for the State.

However, the reform does not constitute a complete break from the past. Even if the activating and integrative-activating responsibilities are abolished, concurrent legislative responsibility is maintained (i.e., between the State and the Regions) with the policy areas specified in paragraph 3 of new Article 117 and constitutes an element of (questionable) continuity with the preceding constitutional order. While it is true that this concerns very different policy areas from those listed in the original text of Article 117, the continuity is, structurally speaking, evident because the determination of the basic principles is still reserved for State legislation, while all the remaining matters are left to the Regions.

However, two significant innovations in this field merit special attention. The first concerns the inclusion of fiscal autonomy as a matter of concurrent competence (*see* paragraph below), thanks to which the Regions can set their own income and regional taxes, in conformity with the basic principles of State legislation (previously the Regions were only empowered to implement existing State legislation). The second is that the power of the Regions in matters within their competence, to directly realize (via legislation where necessary), the normative acts/legal acts of the EU (*see* below, §13 in this chapter) has been explicitly 'constitutionalized', and a similar power is also recognized, *ex novo*, with regard to international agreements (*see* below, §12 in this chapter).

It is beyond the scope of this analysis to evaluate the range of areas assigned to the exclusive competence of the State, and the concurrent competence of the State and Regions, or to analyse whether the remaining matters (the competence of the Regions) are really strategic, in the sense that they finally realize regional autonomy, or whether, on the contrary, the matters (completely or in part) reserved for the State are, in both number and nature, redundant with respect to the sole objective that can justify such a legal reserve, i.e., the protection of the unitary needs and indivisible interests of the Italian State. Although we cannot expand on the thorny problem of the identification of the meaning and content of these matters, we can note that prior to the reform of Title V, the State legislator, starting with Presidential Decree No. 616/1977, sought to adapt the reading of the – frequently obsolete – categories specified in the Constitution to the times and that the Constitutional Court generally concurred with the choices made. Indeed, after a first phase where the 'objective' criterion of interpretation prevailed (linked to the content of the matters understood *stricto sensu*), jurisprudence has successively adopted a more dynamic interpretation, in some cases even to the point of adopting a 'teleological' criterion (which includes the end result, even where the original activity is not strictly covered by the matter in question). In addition, where it is not yet possible to vest legislative authority in one single body, the Court has invoked the criterion of the 'prevalence' of one particular area over another and, where this has also proved to be inadequate, the application of the principle of 'loyal cooperation' between the State and the Region, which must be achieved in particular in the form of agreement within the Conference on the State and Regions. However, although the Constitutional Court has hitherto always asserted that the principle of loyal cooperation does not apply to legislative procedures, it has recently ruled unconstitutional a parent statute insofar as it provided that the implementing legislative decrees should be adopted only after obtaining the opinion of the Conference on the State and Regions, rather than after reaching agreement with it (Constitutional Court, Judgment No. 251/2016).

It is apparent that constitutional case law is particularly important also in this area. This is not only because it has always been through the positive classification of policy areas that the sphere, the competence of the State and (negatively) that of the Regions are identified but because many of the matters reserved for State legislation have been defined in the new Article 117 in such a way as to justify, depending on their interpretation, more or less marked interference (referred to as 'transversal' in practice) in the competences assigned to the Regions, particularly in the areas of education, the environment and civil and social rights. It is sufficient to mention the inclusion among the exclusive powers of the State of the 'protection of competition', 'environmental protection' and the 'determination of essential service levels relating to civil and social rights which must be guaranteed throughout the national territory', which inevitably end up impinging upon many of the powers allocated to the Regions. Moreover, the areas over which competence is shared include the coordination of public finances, a 'cross-cutting' matter in relation to which the State has in recent years introduced various fundamental principles that delineate the legislative powers of the Regions in many sectors. Finally, where necessary due to humanitarian requirements, constitutional case law also allows derogations to be made from the normal division of competences through the 'engagement of subsidiarity' mechanism under which certain administrative functions are shifted due to subsidiarity considerations (pursuant to Article 118 of the Constitution) from regional to State level, the logical corollary being that these will of necessity be organized and regulated by State legislation (*see* Constitutional Court, Judgment No. 303/2003).

The complexity of the division of competences between the State and the Regions has recently emerged during the epidemic crisis, so much so that some scholars have questioned the relevance of regionalism to support – if not even the abolition of – the need for centralization of the health system in search of a sort of uniform model. The Constitutional Court intervened on the exercise of State and Regional competences that inevitably intertwine and overlap, ruling that the management of the pandemic is entrusted to the exclusive State competence in the matter of 'international prophylaxis' and that the Regions are allowed to intervene in limits in which the measures adopted by them are harmoniously inserted in the framework outlined at national level (*see* Constitutional Court, Judgment No. 37/2021).

This concise overview attempts to describe the basic structure of the new legislative autonomy of the Ordinary Regions shaped by the reform law, without going into too much detail. Nevertheless, one specific consideration must be stressed, and that is the introduction, alongside the special autonomy of the five Special Statute Regions, of a new form of 'speciality' which can be described as 'widespread'. The new text of Article 116, paragraph 3, stipulates that the forms and particular conditions of autonomy can also be attributed to other Regions (on the initiative of the Region involved and subject to consultation with the local authorities) with a law approved with an absolute majority by the Chamber of Deputies and Senate, on the basis of an understanding between the State and the Region.

This greater autonomy consists of the participation of the regional legislator in the regulation of some of the matters which fall within the exclusive jurisdiction of the State, in particular, law and order, general rules governing public education, the protection of the environment, the ecosystem, and Italy's cultural heritage and at the same time the simultaneous abolition or attenuation of the constraint imposed by the basic principles established by the State in some areas (to be singled out one at a time) covered by concurrent regional legislation.

It should be noted that, after years of not substantial implementation of the provision, some Regions have recently embraced the path towards the recognition of forms of greater autonomy by the State, starting the negotiations with the government.

More specifically, while Emilia-Romagna has started negotiations directly with the Executive, Veneto and Lombardy have deemed it appropriate to advance all negotiations by an advisory referendum that took place in October 2017 and in which the majority of regional electors voted in favour of further forms and special conditions of autonomy to be grant. This consultative referendum, legally non-binding and, in addition, not necessary because it is not provided for by Article 116, paragraph 3, of the Constitution had purely a political aim. These initiatives were therefore followed by pre-agreements between the involved Regions and the Government that, however, did not lead to anything substantial.

Therefore, the issue of differentiated autonomy was relaunched at the beginning of the current 19th Legislature, through the approval (on government initiative) of a specific ordinary law implementing Article 116, paragraph 3, of the Constitution (Law No. 86/2014), aimed at better specifying the procedural and substantive rules that should then lead to specific individual laws granting more autonomy to the Regions concerned.

The process of approving this law was followed by a heated debate, deeply dividing those who see differentiated regionalism as a potential for improving the efficiency of the entire legal system and those who see it as a harbinger of serious divisions in the country. The intense discussions subsequently resulted in four constitutional legitimacy proceedings initiated by several regions (*see* Puglia, Tuscany, Sardinia, and Campania), as well as a request by the electorate for its repeal by referendum.

With Ruling No. 192/2024, the Constitutional Court partially upheld the issues raised, declaring the unconstitutionality of several provisions of the law in question. It is not possible to fully address the full content of the aforementioned ruling, but it is important to highlight how the Court provided an interpretation of Article 116, paragraph 3, of the Constitution, clarifying that the granting of additional autonomy to ordinary Regions must concern not entire field or areas of matters, but specific legislative and/or administrative functions concerning those matters, where, in light of the principle of subsidiarity and based on appropriate investigation, there is a reasonable justification for performing in this way. The transfer of a function from the State to the Region can occur if there is a justified judgment of greater adequacy at that level, which corresponds to the criteria of effectiveness and efficiency of allocation, fairness of distribution, and political accountability of the interested Region towards the affected population. Article 116, paragraph 3 of the Constitution represents therefore a sort of expression of the flexibility inherent in the principle of subsidiarity, 'which allows each Region to request a derogation from the order of distribution of functions generally deemed optimal by the Constitution' (*see* Constitutional Court, Judgment No. 192/2024).

Following the critical effect of the ruling, the Constitutional Court declared the referendum request inadmissible, deeming the subject matter of the question unclear (Constitutional Court, Judgment No. 10/2025). Now, it is up to Parliament to decide whether and how to revise Law No. 86/2024, which currently has a significantly reduced content.

It is also worth noting that, in its Judgment No. 192/2024, the Constitutional Court confirmed the determination of essential levels of performance (so-called LEP), to be carried out with primary sources, is a prerequisite for the recognition of differentiated autonomy in matters affecting civil and social rights.

§7. The Limits of Regional Legislative Autonomy

417. Apart from the distinction between State legislation which is specialized by policy area, and regional legislation of a more general nature, the other basic feature of the reform is the 'levelling out' between the two responsibilities, both subjected to the same limits, stipulated in the new text of Article 117, paragraph 1 in observance of the Constitution, Community regulation and international obligations. However, the reform did not completely discard the preceding constitutional rule which specified that the content of the limitations of regional legislative responsibility must be determined by State legislation, insofar as concurrent regional responsibility has been maintained, and is not only bound by the limits cited above but must also still comply with the basic principles governing the issues at stake which are established by State legislation.

On the basis of this deeply innovative stance one can conclude that (although legal theory is divided on this point) regional legislative responsibility is not subject to any constraint, other than those explicitly indicated by the Constitution which expresses and defends the value of the unity of the regulation of the Italian Republic consecrated in Article 5. The consequence is that respect for the unitary requirement can *only* be imposed on the legislative responsibility in this form and using this instrument.

In particular, limitations which had been stipulated in the preceding system precisely in order to defend the unitary needs of the Italian State, such as the basic rules governing State legislation on economic or social reform, and general legal principles, no longer apply. For the same reason, following the reform the 'limitations of merit' (in particular, that of the national interest) also appear to have been abolished; there is now no trace of them even in the provision dealing with the supervision of regional laws (cf. the new text of Article 127). This constitutes a considerable step forward for regional autonomy, especially if one considers that the national interest has often been invoked by the Constitutional Court as a justification for State laws intended to limit – but which in fact heavily circumscribe – regional competence. However, as mentioned above, an effective guarantor of unitary requirements has in any case been found by the Court to lie in the principles of subsidiarity, differentiation and adequacy in accordance with the new version of Article 118 of the Constitution (*see* Constitutional Court, Judgment No. 303/2003).

Before moving to an analysis of the legislative powers of the Special Regions, the characteristics of which differ from those of the Ordinary Regions, it must also be recalled that, alongside legislative powers, the Constitution also vests the Regions with regulatory powers over all matters that do not fall under exclusive State competence, moreover providing for the possibility for the State to delegate regulatory powers to the Regions also in areas falling under exclusive State competences (Article 117, paragraph 6 of the Constitution). Furthermore, the regulatory powers of the Regions must be exercised in accordance with the regulatory authority which the Constitution vests in the local authorities 'in relation to the organization and conduct of the functions allocated to them'.

418. It remains applicable to the differentiated autonomy Regions, whose legislative authority is defined by the old Special Statutes still in force. These have retained their original structure and list the matters attributed to the Region they refer to – distinguishing those of primary (or full) authority from those of concurrent authority and those of supplementary-implemental authority – and not the matters for State competence, as instead does the new Article 17 of the Constitution. However, it should be said that Constitutional Law No. 3/2001 is not entirely without effect as regards the Special Regions since it adds a 'clause in greater favour' to their advantage in Article 10, whereby, up to adjustments of their respective statutes, the provisions of the reform do not just apply to the Ordinary Regions but also to the Special Regions in the parts that provide for broader forms of autonomy than those already attributed to the Special Regions (and the Autonomous Provinces).

The effective application of this clause to the legislative authority of the differentiated Regions presumes – evidently – two steps. First, there must be ascertained whether the limits set by the Special Statutes for the old primary (or full) authority were greater than the limits set by the reformed Article 117 of the Constitution on the new general-residual authority of the Ordinary Regions. Subsequently, there has to be identified by what right each Special Region (or Autonomous Province) is competent to legislate in the various matters, by means of comparing the catalogues of the respective statutes and those, partly explicit and partly implicit, that emerge from the new Article 117 of the Constitution.

Considering that some of the limitations originally set by the Special Statutes have not been precisely reprised by the new Title V, and therefore should no longer be applied (this is the case of the fundamental rules of the State laws for economic-social reform and of the general principles of the juridical system), the general-residual authority certainly appears more advantageous. This has been admitted by the Constitutional Court which, for instance, has denied the applicability of the limitation of the State rules of economic-social reform to the legislative authority of a Special Region in a matter which, catalogued in accordance with the statute among those of primary (or full) authority, according to the new Article 117 of the Constitution, forms part of the general-residual authority of the Ordinary Regions (*see* Constitutional Court, Judgment No. 274/2003).

It still needs to be clarified what is the solution to be given to the other cases that may arise. Considering the above legal rulings, it appears that the clause of greater favour should, without doubt, be applicable even in the hypothesis of a matter – of concurrent authority according to the Special Statutes – that can be ascribed to the area of general-residual authority as per Article 117, paragraph 4, of the Constitution.

What does seem hard to resolve, however, is the case of a matter that is of primary regional authority according to the statutes, but of concurrent authority or exclusively pertaining to the State's authority according to the new Article 117: here, perhaps the statutory discipline should be retained (an idea in this respect can be taken from Constitutional Court Judgment No. 48/2003), with the consequent application of the old limitations represented by the fundamental rules of the economic-social reforms and by the general principles of the juridical system.

As it is possible to see, as things stand, the reconstructing of the limitations that the legislative authority of the differentiated Regions (and the Autonomous Provinces) is subject to in the various matters is excessively complex and all falls onto the shoulders of the constitutional judge. It would, therefore, be appropriate to finally proceed with a thorough revising of the Special Statutes, as is already required by the already mentioned Article 10 of Constitutional Law No. 3/2001.

§8. The Administrative Autonomy of the Regions and Local Government Bodies

419. According to the original text of Article 118, paragraph 1, the Regions must carry out administrative functions for all those areas in which they have legislative competence, according to the principle of 'parallelism'. Paragraph 3 of Article 118 added that the Regions should 'as a rule exercise their administrative functions through delegation to the Provinces, Communes, other local authorities or their offices'. The reasoning behind the provision was to limit the functions carried out directly by the Regions to a minimum, thus relieving them of the burden of active administration and leaving them free to carry out the tasks of planning, coordination, policymaking and financing. In this way, the Constituent Assembly wanted to achieve the double objective of reducing the number of regional offices to an indispensable minimum, and of ensuring that administrative action, exercised by the territorial authority closest to the citizens, corresponded as far as possible to the needs of the local collectivities (with a sort of anticipation of the principle of subsidiarity).

However, these constitutional recommendations have generally been overlooked. For a number of reasons (primarily because the smaller territorial authorities were not always deemed capable of operating efficiently or economically), the Regions have preferred to create their own complex administrative apparatus and have moreover set up a series of practical bodies, companies, agencies and joint-stock companies.

The new Article 118 has completely reshaped this situation, with a system of public administration characterized by a move away from all forms of regional and State centralism. In the first place, the reform sets aside the principle of 'parallelism' and delegation to local authorities and establishes a general rule that basically assigns all administrative functions to the Communes, with State or regional laws, except in cases where these are 'conferred on the Provinces, Metropolitan Cities, Regions and State, on the basis of the principles of subsidiarity, differentiation and proportionality' in order to 'guarantee their unitary exercise'. This should result, it is envisaged, in a significant scaling back of the regional administration as it has developed to date since many administrative tasks, including above all directly managed services, will have to be allocated to the smaller local government bodies, with a preference for the municipalities.

In order to give full effect to this complex redistribution of administrative powers in accordance with the principles laid down by the new version of Article 118 of the Constitution, it will thus be necessary to enact dedicated State and regional legislation. The task of State legislation will be – primarily – to identify the fundamental functions of the municipalities, Provinces and Metropolitan Cities pursuant to Article 117 (paragraph 2, letter p) of the Constitution, taking account of the characteristics specific to each type of body and the functions historically performed. Second, the State legislation will also be required to identify the functions currently performed at central level that do not need to be exercised centrally and should thus be allocated to the Regions and the smaller local government bodies in accordance with the principles of subsidiarity, differentiation and adequacy.

In the areas falling within its competence, the regional legislator will rather be required to vest the local authorities with the administrative functions that do not need to be exercised on a unitary basis at regional level, applying the same principles.

It is important to note that the incorporation into the Constitution of the principles of subsidiarity, differentiation and adequacy means that they will henceforth constitute parameters with reference to which the Constitutional Court may be called upon to assess the legitimacy of the choices made by State or regional lawmakers.

According to the new text of the Constitution, the smaller local government bodies will be vested not only with fundamental functions and those vested in them under State and regional legislation in the manner described above, but also with other functions, which are defined as inherent functions (cf. Article 118, paragraph

2, of the Constitution). The literature has offered various interpretative solutions in an attempt to identify the meaning and scope of this concept, including one which identifies inherent functions as being equivalent to fundamental functions. However, the most important aspect is the position taken by the State legislator which, by Law No. 42/2009 authorizing the government to implement Article 119 of the Constitution (regarding which *see* below, §9), 'provisionally' identified the fundamental functions of the municipalities and the Provinces, without however referring to their inherent functions. However, the ultimate designation of the fundamental functions of the municipalities, Provinces and Metropolitan Cities must in any case fall to State legislation enacting Article 117 (paragraph 2, letter p).

In particular, as far as the municipalities are concerned, legislation has been recently enacted by Decree-Law No. 95/2012 (converted into Law No. 135/2012), Article 19 of which specifies by name a full range of fundamental functions and the bodies in which they are vested.

The position of the Provinces regarding this issue appears to be more complex. In fact – in line with the rejected proposal for constitutional reform – Law No. 56/2014 (known as the Delrio Law) provided for the administrative functions of the Provinces to be scaled back significantly, identifying a defined and limited range of fundamental functions (the aims of which largely related to the provision of guidelines and a statement of policies), which will, however, remain vested in the Provinces. Otherwise, the Delrio Law provides according to a complex procedure that all other functions hitherto performed by the Provinces will be reallocated by the State or the Regions in line with their respective areas of competence. On account of the rejection of the proposed constitutional reform, which would have led to the de-constitutionalization of the Provinces, justifying the removal of powers from them also on the administrative level, renders the current framework even more complicated given that Article 118 of the Constitution still acknowledges that the Provinces are vested with their own inherent functions as well as those granted under State or regional law.

As far as the Metropolitan Cities are concerned, Law No. 56/2014 provides that they are to be allocated the fundamental functions identified for the Provinces, those granted as part of the above-mentioned process of reallocating the functions of the Provinces that are not fundamental, those allocated in accordance with Article 118 of the Constitution as well as certain specifically designated fundamental functions.

§9. The Financial Autonomy of the Regions

420. The Constitution also recognizes the financial autonomy of the Regions, evidently considering this an indispensable precondition for other forms of autonomy. This is usually interpreted as comprising both the power of self-determination in matters of expenditure and decision-making capacity in matters of revenues (fiscal autonomy).

The original formulation of Article 119, paragraph 1 states that the Regions, 'have financial autonomy in the forms and modes established by the laws of the Republic, which coordinate it with the financing of the State, Provinces and Communes'. In constitutional praxis and jurisprudence, this has been interpreted as a sort of open deferment to the discretionary power of the ordinary legislator, rather than as a guarantee for the Regions.

From the institution of the Regions until today, the State legislator has followed very different lines of conduct, traceable to two distinct phases in implementing the constitutional provisions. Until 1996, a basically 'derived' or 'transferred' model of regional finance was adopted, in the sense that the Regions enjoyed the financial means specified and quantified (prevalently) by the State, and only in small part determined by them. The Regions received practically all the resources necessary to carry out their normal functions from the sharing out of what is referred to as 'the general fund' and 'special funds'. The first, after having been initially supplied by revenues from Treasury taxes, ended up by being determined discretionally by the State legislator, annually during the drawing up of the State budget. The second, very considerable source of funds, were assigned to the Regions, via the appropriate legislation and earmarked for specific sectors (e.g., agricultural activity, family health clinics, public transport and health). Among the sources of regional income, 'own' regional taxes, generically provided for by Article 119, played a very marginal role. Such taxes (e.g., the tax on regional concessions, the regional car tax and the tax on the State concessions of State property and national patrimony) were not only specified by State law but also precisely regulated in all respects of assessment, collection and liquidation. The Regions only retained the authority to set quotas of State tax revenue, with maximum and minimum values preset by the State legislator.

As of 1996, the policy focus of Italian fiscal legislation has partly changed, concentrating on a marked reduction of the derived character of regional finance on the income side and the removal of the destination constraints on the expenditure side. The reform process (which culminated in Decree No. 56/2000, implementing the delegation of Article 10 of Law No. 133/1999) takes as its guideline the replacement of the greater part of the fiscal transfers, both free and entailed, with other forms of income. The latter take the form of new 'own' regional taxes, i.e., the tax on university study, the special tax on solid waste disposal and, above all, the regional tax on productive activities (IRAP), in addition to Treasury taxes, i.e., the consumption tax on methane gas and personal income tax (IRPEF) and in profit-sharing with Treasury taxes, i.e., the indirect tax on petrol and value added tax (IVA).

This new system of financing, which finally began to take the local tax yield into account, is completed by the institution of a '*fondo perequativo nazionale*' which is, as its name suggests, designed to reduce territorial socio-economic inequalities and allow the Regions to guarantee uniform and minimum levels of performance throughout Italy.

421. The new text of Article 119, as amended by Constitutional Law No. 3/2001, includes much of its original content and thus largely confirms the legislative scenario introduced by the 1999–2000 measures. At the same time, however, the reform makes some premises to give further breath to the financial autonomy of the Regions. As regards confirmation, the provision formally specifies a principle already deemed implicit in the old text and that is regional financial autonomy in terms of both resources and expenditure; moreover, it confirms the emphasis on 'own' regional taxes and profit-sharing (calculated on the basis of the local income from Treasury taxes).

However, having a greater effect are the new features, on which only some very sketchy evaluations can be expressed at this time which, moreover, should be verified on the basis of the indispensable interventions by the national legislator, as will be seen, and the constitutional law. The main observations seem to be the following. The first concerns the constitutional coverage provided to the equalization fund, first provided for simply by ordinary law. Another one of great importance is that Article 119, paragraph 2, of the Constitution, according to which the Regions 'establish' and 'apply' their own taxes and revenues, seems to legitimize the Regions to introduce new taxes without the need for a State law for instituting them and to regulate them entirely. Thought could be given to exercising a 'concurrent' type of legislative authority which, as such (*see* above, §6), is of the Region's competence, except for the determining of fundamental principles, reserved for the State. In support of this conclusion, there is, on one side, the fact that in the list of matters of concurrent legislation (referred to in Article 117, paragraph 3, Constitution) there is a matter called 'coordination of public finance and the tax system'; on the other side, as a corollary, it is possible to invoke the words of Article 119, paragraph 2, of the Constitution, which, after having attributed tax powers to the Regions, then limits the exercising to complying with the 'principles of coordination of public finance and the tax system', which must be evidently established by the State. In my view, this assumption is clearly in tune with the overall reasoning of the reform since the acquiring by Regions of the power to tax is crucial for increasing their overall autonomy.

Also important is the affirming of the principle contained in the new text of Article 119, whereby the resources available to the Regions (as well to the Communes, Provinces and Metropolitan Cities) should allow to 'fully' finance the public functions attributed to them. This indication ensures the economic sustainability of regional activities and, as pointed out in literature, also gives the Regions the possibility to appeal, as regards the State regulations for implementation, for the control of reasonableness from the Constitutional Court.

There are some reservations, however, about the provision in paragraph 5, according to which the State shall set aside 'additional resources' and carries out 'special actions' ad hoc in favour of certain Regions, to enable them to provide for 'purposes other than the normal exercise of their functions', to remove economic and social imbalances and to facilitate the exercise of the individual's rights. Given the wording of the provision, there continues to be a doubt whether, in actual application, this instrument will consolidate the position of the Regions or increase the powers of the State. In any case, the Constitutional Court has provided some criteria for avoiding that these funds become 'an indirect but pervasive means for State interference … and of allowing policies and guidelines governed centrally to overlap those legitimately decided by the Regions' (Constitutional Court, Judgment No. 16/2004).

Notwithstanding all this, in order to implement this new design of regional finance it is also essential, as pointed out by the Constitutional Court, to have prior intervention by the State legislator which 'in order to coordinate all the public finances, should not only establish the principles that Regional legislators should follow' and determine 'the general lines of the entire tax system' but also identify 'the limits' within which the power to tax by the State and by the Regions can take place (Constitutional Court, Judgment No. 37/2004).

For many years, the State legislator has failed to achieve any concrete results, until there was approved Law No. 42/2009 that set forth the 'Mandate to the Government on fiscal federalism, being implemented by Article 110 of the Constitution', which has been recently followed by a series of legislative decrees.

The so-called fiscal federalism, which the above Law No. 42 aims to achieve, should be identified in a system characterized by effective regional self-government and by the accountability of the governing bodies of the Regions to their communities. The key step in this direction consists of overcoming the derived funding, eliminating transfers from the centre and replacing them with the resources available in the territory from taxes imposed by the Regions themselves or by jointly participating in State taxes. For a balanced and sustainable 'fiscal federalism', it is also essential, however, to equalize in favour of territorial areas 'with less fiscal capacity per inhabitant'. This is not to achieve a total uniformity (which would contradict with the very reason for Regionalism to exist) but to ensure throughout the national territory the level essential for the enjoyment of fundamental civil and social rights while respecting the values of unity and of solidarity that are the foundation for the existing constitutional order.

The complex legislative manoeuvre ushered in by Law No. 42/2009 tends to be pursuing these objectives. As regards revenues, its most significant parts relate to identifying the taxes of the Regions, that of joint participation in State taxes and the ways for determining the equalization fund. As regards expenditure, great importance is given to introducing the mechanism of standard costs for covering the most important services of the Regions (for instance, in health, education and social assistance), instead of the criterion of 'historic expenditure' applied up to now since this is considered a source of inefficiency and waste.

422. Nevertheless, it must be pointed out that, over the course of recent years, the implementation of 'tax federalism' has been significantly slowed as the economic and financial crisis that has also affected Italy along with the resulting need to rebalance the public finances has led the State legislator to adopt measures resulting in a new form of tax centralism and replacing once again the preferred model of tax federalism with direct State funding. This demonstrates the expansion of the above-mentioned state principal competence on the coordination of public finances according to which the State, with the adjudication of the Constitutional Court, has significantly reined in the legislative autonomy of the Regions and the powers available under the Regional Statutes. Thus, it would envisage the possibility to endorse the scholarship which argues that the coordination of the public finances has now turned into an end in itself, which is thus capable of impinging upon any regional competence whatsoever.

This is again the logic underlying also Constitutional Law No. 1/2012 (along with the implementation legislation laid down by Law No. 243/2012) which, in introducing the requirement of 'balanced budgets' into Article 81 of the Constitution, made changes also to Articles 117 and 119 of the Constitution. In fact, with effect from financial year 2014, the Constitution provides in the first place that the harmonization of public budgets will no longer be a matter over which competence is shared, as provided for under the 2001 constitutional reform, but will rather become an exclusive competence of the State (Article 117, paragraph 2, letter e, of the Constitution); second, it provides that the financial autonomy of the Regions over revenues and expenditure (in addition to that of the local authorities) must be exercised in accordance with the principle of balanced budgets and expressly imposes a requirement to abide by the economic and financial constraints resulting from EU Law (Article 119, paragraph 1, of the Constitution); finally, it provides that the Regions may use debt in order to finance spending on investment provided that 'repayment plans are defined in parallel and upon condition that … the principle of balanced budgets is respected' (Article 119, paragraph 6, of the Constitution).

If, in the face of an economic-financial emergency, further aggravated by the pandemia, the Government had already taken steps to postpone the implementation of fiscal federalism to 2023 (in this sense: Legislative Decree No. 137/2020), the new budget law for the year 2023 has intervened again on the revenue autonomy of the Ordinary Regions, with a further referral to 2027 (or to the previous year where the conditions exist), and this in coordination with the implementation of the NRRP.

In this regard, the Government's delegation law for tax reform (Law No. 111/2023, as amended by Law No. 120/2025) was recently enacted. Articles 13 and 14 of this law establish new principles and guidelines for regional and local taxes for the implementation of fiscal federalism. These guidelines aim, in particular, to revise some of the provisions of Legislative Decree No. 68/2011, as well as rationalize regional taxes and overhaul the tax system for local authorities. This legislative delegation was then followed by a draft legislative decree, currently in progress by the Government. Its approval deadline is scheduled for the end of August 2026 (with a deadline of August 2028 for any supplementary and corrective decrees).

423. The Special Regions are to be considered separately, as they are vested with special forms and conditions of financial autonomy, which specifically lead to the allocation to each Region of significant shares of the proceeds from taxes collected as specified in the respective Special Statutes, which as is known are contained in constitutional laws.

However, Law No. 42/2009 has also introduced certain changes in relation to the Special Regions. In fact, although this Law applies to the Ordinary Regions, Article 27 provides that also the Special Regions must contribute to the achievement of objectives of revenue equalization and solidarity and the internal stability pact and comply with the obligations laid down by Community law for the purpose of the coordination of the public finances. As a result, the Special Regions have overhauled their financial arrangements on the basis of bilateral agreements concluded between the State and each individual Region, which have subsequently been implemented by ordinary State legislation, as provided for under the respective statutes. Since it is not possible to consider this question any further in this study, we limit ourselves to highlighting that the Constitutional Court itself has confirmed that any financial initiative taken by the State that impinges upon the financial autonomy of the Regions may only be adopted in accordance with the 'consensus' procedure enshrined in the Special Statutes, and thus with the agreement of the Region concerned (*see inter alia* Judgment No. 178/2012). On this point, however, the latest bilateral agreements signed provide that, in the event of exceptional public finance needs and for a limited time, the State can unilaterally modify the contribution requested from the single Region.

§10. The State Supervision of Regional Activities

424. In order to guarantee the limits applied to regional competences, the constitutional regulation makes provision for State mechanisms of supervision of regional acts and organs, which were all affected by the 2001 reform. Starting with the supervision of regional laws, the new text of Article 127, paragraph 1 states that, 'when it considers that a regional law exceeds the competence of the Region, the Government may raise the question of [its] constitutional legitimacy before the Constitutional Court within sixty days of its publication'. This 'successive' supervision is extremely linear, and it is the result of a simplification of the original system in two basic respects. In the first place, through the suppression, as per the original text of Article 127, of the deferral (preceding the promulgation and publication of regional legislation), that government can request in order to generate a new decision by the Regional Council. And second, with the abolition of the 'supervision of merit' (albeit unknown in praxis), provided as a guarantee of respect for the national interest or that of other Regions, and which was entrusted to Parliament. It should be noted that, in continuity with past trends, current legal theory tends to interpret the expression, 'exceeds the competence' in the sense that the violation of *any* constitutional norm, and not only those relative to the sharing out of competences between the State and the Regions, can be lodged with the Constitutional Court. This observation is significant, above all if one takes account of the fact that the Region may in turn challenge State legislation before the Court, although may only do so exclusively in order to protect its own sphere of competence (Article 127, paragraph 2, of the Constitution).

Also among the controls that can be exercised on regional laws, the possibility recognized to the Court of Auditors, in the judgment of equalization of the general report of the Regions, to challenge the invasive regional laws of State legislative competences before the Constitutional Court (*see* Constitutional Court, Judgment No. 196/2018).

It should be noted, however, that the Constitutional Court is also granted the power to suspend the main contested legislative acts as a precaution, where it is believed that their execution may involve the risk of irreparable prejudice to the public interest or to the legal system of the Republic, or the risk of serious and irreparable prejudice to the rights of citizens (Article 35 Law No. 87/1953 as amended by Law No. 131/2003). It is in application of this rule that the Constitutional Court with Ordinance No. 4/2021 has, for the first time, suspended the regional law of the Aosta Valley, which, notwithstanding the State legislation containing measures to combat the COVID-19 pandemic, intervened allowing the carrying out of a series of social and economic activities.

425. Prior to the reform of Title V in order to understand the State control of the administrative acts of the Regions, one needed to refer, in the first place to Article 125, paragraph 1, and to a series of legal provisions that created a general and preventive system of legitimacy control. In cases of important decisions, this supervision was extended to their merit, by referring them back to the Regional Council, with a reasoned request for re-examination. In the last decade, this body of regulation has undergone a series of amendments (introduced by Decrees No. 40/1993 and 479/1993, and subsequently Law No. 127/1997, grafted onto the trunk of Law No. 62/1953) that have progressively reduced the acts subject to control and abolished the 'control of merit'. In a more radical intervention, Constitutional Law No. 3/2001 made explicit provision for the abrogation of Article 125, paragraph 1, from which, according to the interpretation taking root in the praxis, is also derived the abrogation of the ordinary legislation relative to the matter, and thus the abolition of the controls on the relative regional administrative acts.

The only exception is constituted by the survival of the 'management control', which basically consists of the verification of the 'correspondence of the outcomes of administrative activity to the objectives established by law, [making] a comparative evaluation of the costs, modes and time limits [necessary to] carry out administrative action' (introduced by Article 3, paragraph 4, Law No. 20/1994, and entrusted to the Court of Auditors). Indeed, as stressed in the past by the Constitutional Court (*see* Judgment No. 29/1995), this supervision of the functionality and efficiency of the administrative action need not necessarily be traced to the repealed Article 125 (which instead refers, implicitly, to external controls, carried out ex ante, on single acts). Moreover, seeing that the management control consists of an overall and ex post verification, with no impact on the legal efficiency of single acts, one can say that this is a question of a control sui generis, which can only lead to an 'auto-correction' on the part of the authority controlled. Besides, following the 2012 constitutional reform, the constitutional foundation for the controls performed by the Court of Auditors may now be considered to lie in the provisions laying down the principle of balanced budgets (including in particular Article 119, paragraph 1, of the Constitution). Although it is not possible to offer any more detailed commentary regarding this issue, it is nonetheless appropriate to take account of the fact that, in recent years, the controls performed by the Court of Auditors over the Regions have been expanded further as the Court is charged with monitoring compliance with the principle of a balanced budget in relation to the internal stability pact and the obligations resulting from Italy's membership of the EU, as well as verifying the pursuit of the objectives laid down by regional legislation. Thus, it falls in particular to the Regional Control Division of the Court of Auditors to approve the closing statement of accounts of the Regions, which obliges each Region, in the event that any irregularities are ascertained, to adopt within sixty days the measures required to re-establish a balanced budget, failing which it will be prevented from implementing the expenditure programmes affected (*see* Decree-Law No. 174/2012, converted into Law No. 213/2012). However, further measures providing for a control by the Court of Auditors over regional laws concerning the approval of prospective budgets and closing statements of accounts have been ruled unconstitutional on the grounds that they encroached upon the competence of the Constitutional Court and infringed the political and legislative autonomy of the Regions

(Constitutional Court, Judgment No. 39/2014). Moreover, the Constitutional Court has also ruled unconstitutional legislation providing for the ability of the government to carry out checks into the propriety of administrative and accounting management in the event that the Region was affected by an evidential financial imbalance (Constitutional Court, Judgment No. 219/2013).

Finally, we must specify that Article 134 has not been the object of reform, so that the power of government to lodge a complaint with the Constitutional Court for any act committed by the Regions deemed to encroach on the sphere of competence assigned to the State by the Constitution, raising the question of a conflict of competence, still applies. Until recently, it was considered self-evident that this was a question of non-legislative acts, but more recent constitutional jurisprudence has shown signs of a different orientation. According to Articles 39–40 of Law No. 87/1953, an appeal can be lodged with the Court within sixty days from publication of the act, and the latter can, for serious reasons, be suspended pending the Court's decision.

426. The 'substitutive' interventions that the State is authorized to adopt in the event of persistent inactivity on the part of the Regions in the execution of their functions to the potential detriment of the national interest or defaulting on Community obligations can also be considered an expression of a power of control. Prior to the 2001 constitutional reform, this substitutive control has been regulated, over time, by various State legislative provisions. In particular, Article 5 of Decree No. 112/1998 which provided for a procedure whereby the Prime Minister set the defaulting authority a time limit within which to comply, after which the Council of Ministers nominated a Commissioner who intervenes in substitution. In extremely urgent cases, this provision can be adopted directly by the Council of Ministers but must be immediately communicated to the Conference on the State and Regions (*see* below, §11, below), which can request its re-examination within fifteen days.

427. In 2001, with the reform of Title V, the new Article 120, paragraph 2, of the Constitution introduced for the first time a power of reserve control on constitutional level. This is a power which the government may exercise both in relation to regional bodies and those of other local government bodies in the event of the 'failure to comply with international law and treaties or Community legislation or where there is a serious risk for the safety of individuals and the public at large, or where required in order to protect legal unity or economic unity and in particular to protect essential service levels relating to civil and social rights'. As is required under Article 120 of the Constitution, ordinary legislation has been enacted to give effect to the constitutional provisions concerning the reserve power, putting in place 'procedures capable of ensuring that the reserve powers are exercised in accordance with the principle of subsidiarity and the principle of loyal cooperation'. This legislation was contained in Article 8 of Law No. 131/2003 (implementing the constitutional reform of 2001), which replaces the provisions laid down by Article 5 of Legislative Decree No. 112/1998. Aside from the requirement of prior notice to take action within 'a suitable time limit', the new legislation differs from the previous legislation in various respects: it provides in fact, first, that the Council of Ministers may at any time adopt directly the necessary measures, and not only in case of urgency, and need not limit itself to appointing a commissioner *ad acta*, second that the President of the Junta of the Region concerned may attend the meeting of the Council of Ministers and finally that the various action falling to the Council of Ministers may be taken 'also on the initiative of the Regions and local authorities'.

428. Nevertheless, Law No. 131/2003 does not resolve the many unclear aspects present within Article 120, paragraph 2, of the Constitution, considering that this article uses highly generic formulations, including first and foremost the protection of 'legal unity or economic unity', the meaning of which has not been clarified in any way under ordinary legislation.

Indeed, in some way Law No. 131/2003 has enhanced the difficulties for interpreting bodies, in particular with regard to the doubt as to whether Article 120, paragraph 2, of the Constitution envisioned legitimizing interventions by the government on a reserve basis exclusively in the area of administrative activity or whether it could also extend to legislation. In fact, Article 8 of Law No. 131 explicitly vests the government with the power to adopt measures, 'including legislative', on a reserve basis if necessary, without clarifying whether this meant to legitimize simply the adoption of acts with regulatory status or also legislative acts. Finally, all doubts have recently been dissolved by admitting the substitute power through State legislative acts in the face of regional default. With Decree No. 86/2020 (converted to Law No. 98/2020), the Government has, in fact, exercised its substitute power pursuant to Article 120, paragraph 2 of the Constitution against the Puglia Region, which, although warned, had not taken steps to adapt its electoral legislation to the State principle that provides for double gender preference.

429. With regard to other problematic aspects it is however important to note the contribution provided by constitutional case law. It is important in particular to note that, according to the Court, Article 120, paragraph 2, of the Constitution does not constitute the sole basis for the exercise of reserve powers, but rather 'provides only for an *extraordinary* reserve power of the Government … without prejudice to the possibility … of other instances involving the exercise of reserve powers available under sectoral legislation' (Constitutional Court, Judgment No. 43/2004).

430. In the past, the State control of regional organs consisted of the dissolution of a Council which had performed acts contrary to the Constitution or seriously infringed the law, an extraordinary and exceptional measure that has never been applied. The reform realized with Constitutional Law No. 1/1999 also introduced the power to dismiss a President of the Junta again for having performed acts contrary to the Constitution or for having seriously infringed the law. About this, the legislator has moreover enacted legislation identifying certain instances involving a serious breach of the law which will result in the dissolution of the Council and the removal of its President. First of all, Legislative Decree No. 149/2011 stipulated as a serious breach of the law a situation of serious financial distress with reference to the health care deficit; however, this provision was ruled unconstitutional by the Constitutional Court (Judgment No. 219/2013). Other cases have moreover been identified under Decree-Law No. 174/2012 (converted into Law No. 213/2012), insofar as it subjects the Regions the requirement to take action within a specified deadline in order to reduce the costs of the regional political system in various ways (from a reduction in the number of councillors and executive officers to the overhaul of the system of allowances, benefits, etc. paid to councillors). The dissolution and dismissal must be made with a presidential decree, proposed by government, and subject to the opinion of the Interparliamentary Committee on Regional Affairs.

According to the new formulation of Article 126 of the Constitution, the dissolution of the Council and the removal of the President can be ordered for reasons of 'national security' (understood as a general safeguarding clause covering unforeseeable situations).

Contrary to what appeared in the old text of Article 126 of the Constitution, no provision is made for the Council to be dissolved when it does not meet the request from the government to replace a Junta or President that has committed acts contrary to the Constitution or serious infringements of the law, since there has been introduced in these cases the direct removal of the President.

In addition to these cases of 'sanctionary' dissolution, it should be noted that the 1999 reform also introduced a 'functional' dissolution in the case of approval by the Council of a 'no-confidence motion against the President of the Junta elected by universal and direct suffrage'. Hence comes – as seen (cf. above §4, paragraph 411) – not only the obligation for the resignation of the entire executive but also the dissolution of the Council, based on the clause *aut simul stabunt, aut simul cadent.*

Also leading to the dissolution of the Council is 'the removal, the permanent incapacity, the death or the voluntary resignation' of the directly elected President, and the 'simultaneous resignation of the majority of members of the Council' (Article 126, paragraph 3, of the Constitution).

§11. Cooperation Between the State and the Regions

431. This distinction of competences and the complex system of controls do not mean that State–Region relations are exclusively characterized by a logic of clear separation (if not opposition) between the respective spheres of competence. In effect, a coordinated and efficient execution of the legislative and administrative functions cannot ignore the contemporary context and the harmonization of regional interests with national interests, as indicated so synthetically in Article 5 of the Constitution which combines the unity and indivisibility of the Republic with the values of autonomy and decentralization.

Moreover, the fact that the regulation also adopted the criterion of cooperation to describe the relations between the State and the Regions not only emerges from constitutional declarations of principle, such as this, but also from other factors. First, the Constitution regulates in detail the participation of the Regions in many key State functions: for example, the presentation by the Regions of bills and requests for referenda (abrogative and constitutional); the participation of regional delegates in the election of the President of the Republic; and the role of the Regions in the procedures to be followed when altering the territorial boundaries of the Regions, Provinces and Communes. Second, there is the fact that within the framework of the constitutional system, the Constitutional Court has gradually defined the principle of 'fair collaboration', to the point of making it a constant point of reference.

From the body of constitutional jurisprudence one can deduce that such a principle imposes an elastic vision of the distinct competences of the State and the Regions, but that above all it requires, on the one hand, that the instruments of communication created by the State legislator are applied not out of mere formalism, but in order to realize a concrete and efficient collaboration. On the other hand, even without precise legislative provisions, when there is, 'a multiplicity of heterogeneous interests, referable to different subjects of constitutional importance', some sort of linkage must be made (Constitutional Court, Judgment No. 286/1985). The third and final factor is the behaviour of the ordinary State legislator, which has gradually created a vast range of instruments of collaboration between the State and Regions, ranging from the simplest forms, such as the reciprocal obligation of information, to more complex and incisive ones, such as formal agreements requiring the consensus of all the actors involved. Between these two extremes, there are a whole series of proposals, requests for opinions, conventions, consultations, planning agreements and the creation of politically mixed collegial organs.

With regard to the latter, it is important to stress that their role and number have been reorganized following the institution, in 1988, of the Conference on the State and Regions. This is a permanent body composed of the Prime Minister, and the Presidents of the Regions and Autonomous Provinces, with the participation of the Ministers involved and civil servants as required. Following the recent introduction of additional measures, the tasks of the Conference are no longer limited to those of information, consultation and communication, but have been extended (*see* Article 9 of Law No. 59/1997 and Decree No. 281/1997), so as to allow it to promote and ratify understandings and agreements between the State and the Regions. Moreover, it must be obligatorily consulted on the plans for legal State provisions in matters of competence of the Regions, and it should generally take part in all decision-making processes of general interest.

432. Some rather unstructured appeals for State–Region cooperation also surface in the reform of Title V. Starting with the new Article 120, paragraph 2, which makes the first explicit reference to the 'principle of fair collaboration' as a guiding principle (together with that of subsidiarity) to inspire the ordinary legislator in the regulation of the substitutive power of government. Furthermore, Article 118, paragraph 3 stipulates that the legislator must provide forms of coordination and understanding between the State and the Regions in matters of immigration, public order and security and the protection of cultural goods (matters that fall under the exclusive legislation of the State). Finally, Article 11 of Law No. 3/2001, which – until the structure of Parliament is changed to transform one of its branches into a Chamber representing the Regions (and local authorities) – stipulates that 'the regulations of the Chamber of Deputies and the Senate […] can make provision for the participation of representatives of the Regions, the Autonomous Provinces and the local authorities in the Parliamentary Committee for Regional Issues'. This is an evidently interlocutory solution (which has come under criticism from various perspectives of legal theory), and anything but lacking in importance, since in the event that the Committee expresses a contrary opinion on a bill on concurrent legislation or financial coordination it must be voted with an absolute majority by the Assembly. In the meantime, during the conversion of the Legislative Decree No. 91/2017, it was envisaged that the Commission for regional issues could carry out fact-finding activities as well as consult the various regional representatives. In particular, based on the new Commission regulation, it is envisaged that every six months a discussion session is held with the territorial autonomies, which are also granted the power to transmit documents and reports to the Commission.

§12. The Regions and International Relations

433. In political, scientific and legal situations, there has long dominated the opinion that the monopoly of taking on obligations at international level and their execution within the legal system should be attributed to the State. With the result that the regions could be stripped of that part of their competencies as and when affected by the international activities of the State.

Later, however, the evolution of the legal system, characterized by a gradual increase in the role of territorial autonomies, led to the tempering of the rigid notion whereby the so-called power over foreign affairs should be allocated exclusively to the State, and also led to the affirmation of the principle that it is not entirely precluded to the Regions to perform some activities at an international level.

In a first stage, the Regions were authorized to carry out both 'promotional activities abroad' and 'activities of mere international importance' because of some measures by the government going back some time (this specifically relates to Article 4, paragraph 2, D.P.R. No. 616/1977 and D.P.R. 31 March 1994), the effects of which are combined with those of an innovative constitutional jurisprudence (*see* mainly Constitutional Court, Judgment No. 179/1987).

To perform 'promotional activities abroad' it was necessary to obtain prior agreement with the government, which could also be achieved tacitly if the government did not object within forty-five days of learning about the programme of initiatives that the Regions intended to pursue abroad in the following year. As for the 'activities of mere international importance', there had to be distinguished those for which no formalities were required for them to be performed (studies, information, exchange of information, conferences, etc.) from those (such as twinning, statements of principles and intents and formulating of proposals) for which the Regions had to give prior notice to the government to obtain its consent, which would be understood as granted if, within twenty days, the government had not opposed it, with the exception of any contrast with the broader policies of the State or being outside the scope of regional interests.

The reform of Title V marks a second phase, which sees a further advancement of this process. On one side there is included in the concurrent legislative authority the matter of international relations of the Regions (Article 117, paragraph 3) and, on the other, these Regions are enabled – within their sphere of competence – to proceed with international agreements (Article 117, paragraph 5).

But there is more because Constitutional Law No. 3/2001 stipulates that the Regions can enter into agreements with States and with local authorities within another State, even 'in the cases and with the forms governed by State law' (Article 117, paragraph 9, of the Constitution).

This last provision was implemented by Article 6 of Law No. 131/2003. As regards the relations with territorial bodies within another State, it is allowed (Article 6, paragraph 2, of Law No. 131 cit.) that the Regions and Autonomous Provinces of Trento and Bolzano, in matters within their legislative powers, can enter agreements 'designed to foster their economic, social and cultural development and also to perform activities of mere international importance'. Before signing for these activities, they must be notified to the Presidency of the Council of Ministers and the Foreign Affairs Ministry so that they and the relevant Ministries may make any comments, which must be sent within the following thirty days. Only after thirty days have elapsed without comments from these subjects can the Regions sign the agreement.

The most significant profile, however, is the *treaty-making power* which, as a result of the 2001 reform, the Regions can exercise with foreign States. This power is limited by Law No. 131/2003 (Article 6, paragraph 3) to 'executive and application agreements for international agreements that have duly come into force', to 'agreements of a technical-administrative nature' and to 'policy agreements aimed at promoting their economic, social and cultural development', in compliance with the Constitution, with the constraints deriving from international obligations and with the lines and directions of Italian foreign policies, as well as with the fundamental principles dictated by the State laws in matters of concurrent regional competence. Some procedural limitations were also introduced, in the sense that the Autonomous Regions and Provinces are required to promptly notify the Ministry of Foreign Affairs and the Presidency of the Council of Ministers about negotiations, and they in turn notify the relevant Ministries. The Ministry for Foreign Affairs may indicate principles and criteria to be followed in conducting negotiations. If these negotiations take place abroad, the relevant diplomatic representations and the competent Italian consulate departments, in agreement with the Autonomous Regions or Province, shall cooperate with conducting the negotiations. The 'authority to sign' under the rules of general international law and the Vienna Convention of 1969 – by which the international activity of the Regions becomes binding on the State under international law – is granted to the Regions by the Ministry of Foreign Affairs only after this Ministry has ascertained 'the political expediency and legitimacy of the agreement'. In case of disagreement between the Ministry and the Region, the question is referred to the Council of Ministers which decides once having heard the President of the Region concerned. Once this preventive verification process has been implemented, the Ministry of Foreign Affairs is required to give full powers to the regional body responsible for the negotiations and conclusion, and cannot deny them at its own discretion (*see*., in this respect, Constitutional Court, Judgment No. 238/2004).

In any case, the Autonomous Regions and Provinces cannot express opinions about the State's foreign policies, nor can they take on commitments from which derive financial obligations or charges for the State or which damage the interest of Communes, Provinces and Metropolitan Cities.

As already noted, according to Article 117, paragraph 5, of the Constitution, 'the autonomous Regions and Provinces of Trento and Bolzano, in matters within their competence … shall be responsible for opening and implementing international agreements'. Article 6, paragraph 1, of Law No. 131/2003 implements the constitutional requirement stipulating that the Autonomous Regions and Provinces shall 'directly' be responsible for implementing and executing just those international agreements ratified by Italy, notifying the Ministry of Foreign Affairs and the Presidency of the Council of Ministers beforehand, which can formulate criteria and comments over the next thirty days. If failing to do so, without prejudice to the responsibility of the Regions to the State, the provisions relating to the substitutive power of the State will be applied, which the same law (Article 8, paragraph 1, paragraph 4 and paragraph 5) provides for pursuant to Article 120, paragraph 2, of the Constitution.

§13. The Regions and the EU

434. By virtue of Italian membership of the EU and the primacy of Community law over Italian law, European norms can affect regional competences, to the point of departing from the 'normal constitutional distribution of domestic competences' (Constitutional Court, Judgment No. 126/1996). This can only occur on the basis of the organizational requirements of the EU and on the condition that the basic principles of the constitutional regulation and the inalienable rights of the individual are respected. This general stance, which has already been adopted by constitutional jurisprudence, is now echoed by the new text of the Constitution which formally subordinates the legislative jurisdiction of both the State and the Regions, in line with the constraints deriving from Community regulation. Paradoxically, the Constitution had ignored the phenomenon of European integration until the reform of 2001.

Apart from this significant innovation, the reform of Title V arguably provides a constitutional basis for the rather diversified body of regulation governing relations between the Regions and the EU which had already been stipulated by the ordinary State legislator. First of all, there is the inclusion, in the concurrent legislation, of 'relations between the Regions and the European Union' (Article 117, paragraph 3). Indeed, beyond the broader content that can be traced to a sector thus defined, we can conclude that in this way the Regions are constitutionally guaranteed what the legislator has already attributed to them for some time, i.e., the faculty to provide for and to operate regional offices, or other mechanisms of communication and information within Community institutions.

Finally, and above all, Article 117, paragraph 5 which states that, 'The Regions … , in matters within their competence, take part in the decisions to formulate normative Community acts and make provision for the implementation and execution of the acts of the EU, in conformity with the procedural rules set by State legislation that regulates the exercise of the substitutive power in the case of default' can be interpreted as giving a constitutional foundation to Region–EU relations. In particular, all the legislation in force dealing with the drafting and implementation of European law can be traced to Article 117, paragraph 5.

However, it must be stressed at the same time that the role of the Regions within the process of European integration has been enhanced not only thanks to the amended Constitution but also in actual fact as a result of the changes made to the European Treaties by the Treaty of Lisbon (which came into force in 2009).

In fact, while the various European Treaties adopted since Maastricht did not recognize a role of particular significance for the Regions, the new European Treaty by contrast pays greater attention to the internal structure of the States.

Reference may be made in this regard to the new Article 4 of the TEU insofar as it formally recognizes the system of local and regional government and, in particular, Protocol No. 2 (on the application of the principles of subsidiarity and proportionality), which obliges the Commission and the European bodies with power of legislative initiative to take account of the local and regional dimension when proposing and providing reasons for European legislation. The Protocol also provides for the possibility for National Parliaments to consult with the regional Parliaments when assessing the consistency of a proposed European act with the principle of subsidiarity and also recognizes the power of the Committee of the Regions to challenge before the Court of Justice any European act that violates the principle of subsidiarity.

It was also in order to bring the law into line with the new European Treaty that the State legislator approved Law No. 234/2012 which, replacing the previously applicable Law No. 11/2005, regulates the participation of Italy in the process of formulating and implementing the legislation and policies of the EU.

435. As far as the phase involving the formulation of European law is concerned (the so-called ascendant phase), Law No. 234/2012 provides by way of implementation both of the provisions of the Constitution as well as European law for the convocation by the government of the Standing Conference on the State and Regions at least once every four months ‘in order to reconcile the national policy direction concerning the drafting the EU acts with the requirements represented by the Regions’ (Article 22). It also imposes on the government a broad duty to provide information regarding draft European acts to the Regions which, in the areas falling under their competence, may within thirty days submit their observations or ask that a formal agreement be reached with the government within the ambit of the Conference on the State and Regions (Article 24). In addition, again in relation to matters falling under regional competence, the Conference may request the government to state a reservation within the Council of the EU that the matter is subject to examination, following which the Conference may rule within thirty days concerning the contents of the proposed European acts.

Finally, by way of implementation of Protocol No. 2 on subsidiarity, the Regional Councils may submit their observations to the Houses in good time concerning the compatibility of the proposed European acts with the principle of subsidiarity (Article 25).

436. Moving on to an analysis of the role performed by the Regions with a view to the implementation of European law (the so-called descendant phase), Law No. 234/2012 grants the Regions, in line with the requirements laid down in the Constitution (Article 117, paragraph 5, of the Constitution), the power to implement and execute European legislative acts in the areas falling under their competence. However, in parallel, it vests the State with a reserve power in the event that the regional bodies fail to act.

As far as directives are concerned, which as a rule need to be transposed through legislation, it has been provided that the Regions may directly implement European directives within areas falling under their competence. However, if competence is shared, it falls to the Law concerning the implementation of European law to identify the fundamental principles with which the Regions must comply when implementing and applying acts of EU law. The government must inform the Houses of Parliament every six months concerning the status of the implementation of European directives by the Regions.

In the event that a regional legislator fails to act, in order to avoid an outcome under which Italy incurs liability towards the Union for a breach of EU law, the State may provisionally draw up appropriate implementing legislation in order to give effect to the Community obligations. However, in order to protect the autonomy of the Regions, these provisions have subsidiary status, in the sense that they only apply unless and until regional legislation is adopted.

Again with the aim of preventing or putting an end to infringement proceedings against the State, Law No. 234/2012 requires the Regions to take all necessary steps in order to remedy in a timely manner any violations of European obligations that are attributable to them and to implement promptly the judgments of the Court of Justice. In these cases, the State may not only exercise the necessary reserve powers but also has a right of recourse against any Regions in breach.

Finally, as has already been pointed out, it must be recalled that also Article 119 of the Constitution on the financial autonomy of the regions and the local authorities has been amended in the light of the obligations resulting from EU law. In particular, in recognizing the financial autonomy of the Regions and local authorities over revenues and expenditure, Article 119, paragraph 1, of the Constitution, as amended by Constitutional Law No. 1/2012 also provides that the municipalities, Provinces, Metropolitan Cities and Regions 'shall contribute to ensuring compliance with the economic and financial constraints resulting from European Union law'.

§14. The Local Authorities

437. On the basis of the new Article 114, paragraph 2, the Communes, the Provinces and the Metropolitan Cities (together with the Regions) constitute 'autonomous entities with their own statutes, powers and functions according to the principles set down in the Constitution'. However, the very summary description of the autonomy of the smaller territorial authorities at the constitutional level means that we need to examine the ordinary legislation to understand the precise dimensions of this autonomy. In particular, as far as the municipalities are concerned, the principal reference legislation is contained in the Consolidated Text of Laws on the Regulation of the Local Authorities (Legislative Decree No. 267/2000), while, as far as the Provinces and Metropolitan Cities are concerned, the provisions are now laid down by the recently enacted Law No. 56/2014 (known as the 'Delrio Law') which, as mentioned above, significantly overhauled the Provinces and established the Metropolitan Cities.

438. Pursuant to Article 3, paragraph 2, of the Consolidated Text on Local Authorities, the municipality is the local government body that represents the local community, attends to its interests and promotes its development. As noted above, it is the local government body in which administrative functions are vested as a matter of preference, unless they need to be allocated to higher authorities due to requirements of uniform regulation, in accordance with the principle of subsidiarity, differentiation and adequacy (Article 118, paragraph 1). Schematically speaking, the organization of the Communes is based, like that of the Regions, on three key bodies: the Council, Junta and Mayor. In accordance with Law No. 81/1993, it is the electoral college which appoints not only the Council but also the Mayor with direct and universal suffrage for terms lasting five years. Furthermore, with reference to the setting of the maximum number of consecutive mandates of the Mayors, the Constitutional Court has recently ruled that the domestic legislation adopted by the Consolidated Text on Local Authorities for the Municipalities of the Ordinary Regions imposes itself as a principle that must also be respected in the Special Regions (*see* Judgment No. 60/2023). These reforms have certainly reinforced the role of the monocratic organ. Indeed, the power to nominate and revoke membership of the Junta falls within the jurisdiction of the Mayor, legitimated by direct popular election. In Communes with over 15,000 inhabitants, the office of Executive Officer is incompatible with membership of the Council although persons who are not members of the Council may be chosen as executive officers. The Mayor, with the collaboration of the Junta itself, is responsible for the supervision and overall management of the local authority within the framework of the general lines of the political-administrative policy programme presented to the Council. The duration of the Council depends on the Mayor's term of office but the power to pass a vote of no-confidence on the executive with an absolute majority, with not only the consequent removal of the Mayor and Junta but also the dissolution of the Council, and the need to call new elections, is assigned to the Council, as the organ of command and control.

Finally, the Mayor also works as a 'government official' in the sense that he carries out, in his capacity as the head of a State organ, various functions, for example, in matters relating to the public Registrar, public law and order, elections and the collection of statistics. Moreover, he has the power to adopt contingent and urgent provisions in order to 'prevent or eliminate serious dangers threatening the safety of the citizens'.

439. As noted above, in recent years the Provinces have been the focus of considerable scrutiny so much so that, with a view to reducing the 'costs of politics', a reform process was launched with a view to their abolition (or in any case their de-constitutionalization) on the grounds that 'they were pointless'. However, following the rejection of the proposed constitutional amendment – which would have removed any reference to the Provinces from the Constitution – they continue to benefit from a constitutional footing.

Law No. 56/2014 (Delrio Law), approved with a view to the successive entry into force of the constitutional reform, later rejected by the electorate, defines the Provinces as 'large-scale territorial authorities' and as noted above provides for a significant reconfiguration of the competences vested in them. In addition, that Law provides for the transformation of the Provinces into a second-level authority, the governmental organs of which will no longer be elected, as has hitherto been the case, directly by the electorate but rather by the municipal institutions themselves. Provincial organs include in particular: the President of the Province (elected by the Mayors and councillors from the municipalities of the Province among those same Mayors), the Provincial Council (elected by the Mayors and councillors from the municipalities of the Province among those same members) and the Assembly of Mayors (comprised of the Mayors of the municipalities of the Province). It should also be noted that both the President of the Province and the Provincial Councillors continue to maintain the municipal office appointed. Moreover, conversely, the dissolution of the municipal mandate implies the end of the provincial office too. The abolition of the direct election of provincial bodies has been, and continues to be, a matter of lively debate within the scholarship, although the Constitutional Court does not held the provision as unconstitutional (*see* Judgment No. 50/2015).

440. As mentioned above, the Metropolitan Cities initially provided for under Law No. 142/1990 and incorporated into the Constitution by the 2001 reform were in actual fact established and subjected to regulation following a long gestation period only by Law No. 56/2014 (Delrio Law). During an initial stage, Article 23 of Law No. 42/2009 provided that acting on a proposal by the municipalities and the Province concerned, which was to be subject to a popular referendum, a Metropolitan City could be established by Legislative Decree in each of the areas surrounding the major Italian cities and would have taken on the functions of the Province according to a special regulatory framework. Subsequently, by Decree-Law No. 95/2012 (known as the spending review decree), converted into Law No. 135/2012, it was provided that the establishment of the Metropolitan Cities would be mandatory (and not only optional) by 1 January 2014 and that this process would entail the parallel abolition of the Provinces for the respective territory (Article 18). However, by Judgment No. 220/2013, the Constitutional Court ruled that provision unconstitutional on the grounds that it had been introduced by an urgent decree-law. Finally, Law No. 56/2014 was enacted, providing for the establishment and laying down the rules governing, in the Ordinary Regions, ten Metropolitan Cities (Turin, Milan, Venice, Genoa, Bologna, Florence, Bari, Naples, Rome Capital and Reggio Calabria), along with the parallel abolition of the corresponding Provinces, which has moreover passed muster before the Constitutional Court (*see* Judgment No. 50/2015).

According to Article 1, paragraph 2, of the Delrio Law, the Metropolitan Cities are large-scale territorial authorities, the general institutional purposes of which are 'care for the strategic development of the metropolitan territory', the 'promotion and integrated management of services' and 'care for institutional relations pertaining to its level of government'.

As for the Provinces, the Metropolitan Cities also have second-level bodies: the Metropolitan Mayor, which coincides with the Mayor of the capital municipality;

the Metropolitan Council, which is elected by the Mayors and members of the Municipal Councils; and the Metropolitan Conference, which is chaired by the Metropolitan Mayor and comprised of the Mayors of the municipalities belonging to the Metropolitan City. Moreover, in contrast to the provision laid down for the Provinces, the Delrio Law recognizes, although under certain conditions stressed by the law itself (Article 1, paragraph 22), the Statute of the Metropolitan City possibility of providing for direct election of the Mayor and the Metropolitan Council with an electoral system provided by the state law (currently not yet approved).

Regarding Sardinia, Sicily and Friuli-Venezia Giulia, the principles entrenched in the Delrio Law are to be considered principles of great economic and social reform for the regulation of cities and metropolitan areas, in accordance with the respective Special Statutes and on this argument the Constitutional Court was able to confirm that the provisions on the indirect election of the territorial bodies also fall within the principles of great economic and social reform with the consequence that the Regions with a special statute cannot derogate from them (*see* Constitutional Court, Judgment No. 168/2018). Currently, regional laws established the Metropolitan Cities of Palermo, Catania and Messina in Sicily and Cagliari in Sardinia.

It should be outlined that in front of these present circumstances in any case the regulation of Provinces and Metropolitan Cities could be the subject of further reassessment. In fact, a unified bill aimed at restoring the election by universal and direct suffrage of the President of the Province and the Provincial Council is currently discussed in Parliament, as well as the introduction of the same direct election in Metropolitan Cities. In particular, with reference to the latter, the Constitutional Court, in virtue of its own precedent (*rectius* Constitutional Court, Judgment No. 50/2015), has recently requested the intervention of the Legislator in order to review the system of designation of the Metropolitan Mayor since it is deemed not to be consistent with the constitutional provisions (*see* Judgment No. 240/2021).

441. While it is not possible in this study to consider the matter in any further detail, it must finally be pointed out that, again from the perspective of a general review and reduction of the number of local authorities, the Delrio Law was enacted also in order to regulate forms of association between municipalities, reformulating the law governing unions between municipalities (such as local authorities comprised of two or more municipalities allowing for the associated performance of functions and provision of services) and incentivizing mergers between municipalities (namely the establishment of a new municipality by the merger of two or more existing contiguous municipalities).

§15. The Relationship Between the Regions and the Local Authorities

442. In the original text of the Constitution, the relations between the Regions and local authorities were based on two key axes. The first required the Regions to carry out their normal administrative competences via the Provinces and Communes using the instruments of the delegation of functions or use of local authority offices (e.g., Article 118, paragraph 1). The second was the power attributed to a regional organ to carry out general and preventive supervision of the acts of the local authorities (Article 130, paragraph 1).

The reform of Title V provides for more delegation and attributes administrative regional functions directly to the Communes (*see* above, §8), while simultaneously abrogating Article 130, with the effect of eliminating the preventive supervision of the acts of the Provinces and Communes. This may lead us to suspect a serious weakening of the constitutional fabric of the relations between Regions and local authorities, but this is not the case. Constitutional Law No. 3/2001, indeed, demonstrates a desire to place the relations between the Regions and the local authorities on a new footing so as to guarantee their effective and constant collaboration. Although signs of this were already present in the regulation prior to the reform (thanks to provisions stipulated in many statutes of the Ordinary Regions), the Constitution was silent on this point. This gap has now been filled with the new text of Article 123, paragraph 4 which imposes the creation of an ad hoc organ ('in every Region the Statute regulates the Council of the local autonomies, as the organ of consultation between the Region and the local authorities'), which could play an important role, for example, in view of the content of regional legislation in fiscal matters, or those concerning the allocation of administrative functions in the application of the principles of subsidiarity, differentiation and proportionality.

Part IV. Citizenship and Fundamental Rights

Chapter 1. Citizenship

by Marilisa D'Amico & Costanza Nardocci

443. As far as citizenship is concerned, Article 22 of the Italian Constitution states that 'no one can be deprived of his or her citizenship […] for political reasons'. The paragraph is of peculiar importance as only some of the principles enshrined in the Italian Constitution equally apply to each and every individual, whereas other rights and duties explicitly refer to Italian or foreign citizenship (*see* Article 10 and Article 16).

444. First and foremost, it bears to point out that the principle of equality, enshrined in Article 3 of the Italian Constitution, unlike Article 2, where the inviolable rights of the *person* are recognized, explicitly refers only to citizens ('*All citizens* shall have equal social dignity and shall be equal before the law, without distinction of gender, race, language, religion, political opinion, personal and social conditions', emphasis added). However, the Constitutional Court, from its early years of jurisprudence, has clarified that '[i]f it is true that Article 3 explicitly refers to citizens only, it is also certain that the principle of equality applies to foreigners when it comes to respecting […] fundamental rights' (Constitutional Court, Judgment No. 120/1967).

445. The rules currently in force within the Italian legal system are set out under Law No. 91/1992 and Law No. 736/1994.

446. According to Italian legislation, citizenship is acquired in compliance with the so-called *ius sanguinis* criteria.

447. In short, anyone who was born of someone who is already a citizen is a citizen by right, regardless of his or her birthplace. Previously, only those who were born of an Italian male parent could become Italian citizens. The current legislation, in accordance with the principle of equality between the sexes, states instead that the child of a father or mother who is already a citizen is a 'citizen by birth' (Law No. 91/1992, Article 1, and, also, Constitutional Court, Judgment No. 30/1983).

448. The principle of the *jus soli*, meaning the acquisition of the Italian citizenship according to the birthplace, is enforced to avoid cases of statelessness. A person who is born within the Italian territory becomes an Italian citizen by birth if both parents are unknown or Stateless or, according to the law of the parents' State, in case the citizenship of that State is not transmitted by birth (Article 1).

Moreover, according to the provisions of Law No. 91/1992, citizenship might be acquired:

a. by a minor recognized or declared to be the child of an Italian citizen, or even adopted by an Italian citizen (Article 2 or 3), or by a minor living with a parent who has acquired citizenship (Article 14). In this case, the citizenship can be relinquished when the child comes of age if he or she is already a citizen of another country (acquisition by *juris communicatio*);
b. by choice, by the foreign or Stateless person whose father or mother, grandfather or grandmother has a citizen by birth, or does his military service or is a civil servant in Italy, or has been living for at least two years in Italy when he or she comes of age. Foreigners who were born and have always been living in Italy when they come of age can also choose to become Italian citizens. In all these cases, citizenship can be acquired by expressing the wish to become an Italian citizen and by making this request within the specified period (Article 4) (acquisition by choice);
c. by request, accepted through a decree of the Minister of the Interior, by the foreigner or the Stateless person married to an Italian citizen after he or she has been living in Italy for six months or after three years of marriage. This request can be rejected if the person was convicted for particular crimes, or justified reasons related to national security, upon the agreement of the Council of State (subsections 5 and 8) (acquisition by request, that must be accepted by means of a decree of the Home Secretary). A foreign woman who marries an Italian citizen, instead, can no longer obtain the Italian citizenship *ex lege*;
d. by the concession of the President of the Republic, having consulted the Council of State and upon the proposal of the Home Secretary, by the foreigner who has been living in Italy for several years (from three to ten). Under Article 9 of the act, this number can vary according to the fact that the foreigner:
   - is a child or second-degree grandchild of an Italian citizen by birth – an immigrant's child or grandchild – or was born in Italy;
   - was adopted after the age of majority by an Italian citizen;
   - is a citizen of an EU Member State or Stateless;
   - has been a civil servant for at least five years (acquisition by the concession of the President of the Republic, upon the proposal of the Home Secretary. Previously the President must consult the Council of State).

Therefore, the acquisition of Italian citizenship very often depends on residence in Italy (except for the case of foreigners who do their military service or work as civil servants).

On 13 October 2015, the Chamber of Deputies of the Italian Parliament approved a law proposal aimed at challenging Law No. 91/1992 with the purpose of opening up to new cases of citizenship acquisition based on the ius soli principle.

The main novelty dealt with the choice of introducing the ius soli principle as a criterion of citizenship acquisition for children born on the Italian territory (*see* Article 1 of the law proposal).

Together with the ius soli principle, the law proposal brought about another criterion of citizenship acquisition called ius culturae. From this perspective, the law proposal stated that minors born on the Italian territory or who come to Italy within twelve years or who have attended regularly at least five years of a school institution belonging to the national educational system might acquire Italian citizenship.

As for the choice of finally unbinding the link between *ius sanguinis* and citizenship, it can also be added that the law proposal seemed to have acknowledged the Constitutional Court's interpretation of membership to the political community outlined, first, in Judgment No. 172/ 1999 and, later on, recalled in Judgment No. 119/ 2015. In both cases, the Constitutional Court emphasized the role of the duties in the citizenship building process as means of cutting the relationship between ethnicity and citizenship vice versa implied by the *ius sanguinis* principle.

However, the law proposal has never been approved, despite the public debate on the feasibility of the introduction under the law of new forms of citizen acquisition still gaining attention.

449. Beyond the discussion about the criteria of acquisition of citizenship, it is worth underlining that even the most important cause of loss of citizenship is connected to residence.

450. This happens when Italian citizens:

1. are also citizens of a foreign country;
2. acquire for the first time foreign citizenship; or
3. acquire it again.

Also, they may lose Italian citizenship if they reside or take up residence abroad (Article 11).

On the contrary, an Italian who chooses to acquire the citizenship of another country does not lose Italian citizenship automatically: Italian law still provides for double nationality.

The loss of citizenship can also take the form of a sanction towards citizens who have accepted public employment or a public office offered by a foreign state, agency, or international organization of which Italy is not a member. In this case, they must refuse to comply with the request of the government to resign.

The same sanction applies to citizens who, during a war with another State:

a. have accepted or held a public office or public employment in that State;
b. have chosen to do their military service in that State; or
c. have even taken the citizenship of that State.

The loss of citizenship occurs at the end of the state of war (Article 12). Doubts have been raised about the conformity of this provision with Article 22 of the Constitution.

451. Additionally, citizenship may be voluntarily acquired again by all those who have lost it, and particular conditions (i.e., residence in Italy, military service, State employment) occur. The Home Secretary, however, after consulting the Council of State, can forbid the new acquisition 'for serious and justified reasons', within a year from the occurrence of the above conditions (Article 13). The status of a citizen gives entitlement to a series of specific rights and duties, which are not recognized for non-citizens. In particular, the Constitution guarantees some political rights, especially the right to vote, to citizens only. Likewise, only citizens are supposed to accomplish some public duties (such as the duty to defend the homeland or to do their compulsory military service in all the cases provided by law). Anyway, in 2010 the Court confirmed that the rights (apart from political rights) must be recognized 'the individual not as participants in a given political community, but as human beings' (Judgments Nos 105/2001, 249/2010).

Finally, it should also be mentioned that, alongside Italian citizenship, the membership to European Union implies the feasibility of an additional form or type of citizenship, that is the so-called European citizenship, which bears more resemblance to that of Nation States for the importance of the consequences of its possession.

On this, in fact, every citizen of an EU Member State has this kind of citizenship, as it is provided under Article 20 of the TFEU (which replaced Article 17 of TEC). EU citizenship does not replace national citizenship, but rather 'it adds' something to national citizenship.

An EU citizen shall enjoy the rights conferred by the EU Treaties. On this, Article 3 of the TEU provides that EU States shall offer their citizens an area of freedom, security, and justice without internal frontiers. Moreover, Article 21, § 1, of the TFEU recognizes, among others, the right to move and to reside freely within the territory of EU Member States, and Article 22 of the same Treaty provides for the right to vote and to be elected in local elections in light of the place of residence as well as the right to vote in the Country of residence for the European Parliament elections.

More recently, and despite the debate on the 2015 proposed legislative reform of the criteria of citizenship's acquisition, the Italian Parliament ratified the 1961 United Nations Convention on the reduction of statelessness with Law No. 162/2015. According to Article 5 of the Law, a stateless person might apply for naturalization following five years of his/her legal residence in the Italian territory.

It should be highlighted that such a provision is of paramount importance in light of Italy's compliance with international obligations as statelessness is a severe human rights violation as it is the deprivation of citizenship Article 22 of the Italian Constitution made an explicit reference to.

Chapter 2. The General Aspects of Fundamental Rights

by Marta Cartabia & Elisabetta Lamarque

§1. Introduction

452. Part I of the Constitution contains a long and detailed 'Bill of Rights', especially from Article 13 to Article 54 which is divided as follows:

- Title I – Civil Relations,
- Title II – Ethical and Social Relations,
- Title III – Economic Relations, and
- Title IV – Political Relations.

Before this 'Bill of Rights', however, the Constitution deals with some fundamental principles helping the reader to understand the global organization of the relations between State and society. Article 2 of the Constitution States that:

> The Republic recognises and guarantees the inviolable rights of the person, both as an individual and as a member of the social groups in which their personality finds expression, and requires that the fundamental duties of political, economic and social solidarity be fulfilled.

Here we examine the following fundamental principles:

a. the inviolability of fundamental rights;
b. entitlement to fundamental rights; and
c. the acknowledgement of fundamental unwritten rights.

Before analysing these principles, it must be noted that the Italian Constitution never mentions the words 'fundamental rights', but rather 'inviolable rights'. It is not wrong, however, to consider these two expressions as equivalent, except for the legal meaning that the term inviolability sometimes assumes in the Italian legal system.

§2. The Inviolability of Constitutional Rights

453. The proclamation of the inviolability of fundamental rights by Article 2 is not just a way to lend moral weight to the rights subsequently listed in the Constitution. It has a precise legal and cultural meaning.

Affirming that fundamental rights are inviolable is tantamount to a rejection of the public rights theory elaborated by German academic commentators of the nineteenth century (Gerber, Laband and Jellinek) and subsequently taken up in Italy. This theory considers citizens' rights vis-à-vis the State as a consequence of the self-limitation of State powers, which the latter could always change in its favour.

Affirming that fundamental rights are inviolable means, on the contrary, that they must be respected by all public authorities, including legislators and the authorities responsible for amending the Constitution. Inviolability therefore is a sort of implied 'eternity clause' German style (Article 79 of the GG). The State has no control over fundamental rights and cannot breach them, not even following to the complex procedure for amending the Constitution (*see* Part II, Chapter 4). This then is the legal meaning of inviolability as proclaimed by Article 2: inviolable means definitive, mandatory and untouchable. Fundamental rights are therefore not only protected against the executive power – as in the eighteenth century, especially in the liberal era when the main provision with respect to fundamental rights was the fact that they could only be limited by statute – but also constitute a limit for Acts of Parliament as well as for any other legal act, including constitutional laws, laws amending the Constitution and other equivalent sources (EU provisions, international customary laws and Concordat provisions). The Constitutional Court shares this opinion. In one of its leading decisions (Constitutional Court, Judgment No. 1146/1988), it stated that the supreme principles of the Italian Constitution, including the inalienable rights of individuals, 'cannot be either subverted or modified in their essential contents, not even by laws amending the Constitution or other constitutional laws'. In spite of the lack of a constitutional provision explicitly stating that such fundamental rights cannot be the object of a constitutional amendment (such as Article 19, paragraph II, of the German Constitution or Article 53, paragraph I, of the Spanish Constitution), the Constitutional Court has clearly declared their absolute inviolability. The Constitutional Court's judgments, however, have not done away with all the doubts as to the meaning and scope of such inviolability. The only certainty is that the inviolability of personal rights does not mean the absence of limits. No right is absolutely protected by the Constitution, and all rights are subject to limitations, in compliance with the necessary guarantees provided by the Constitution and in compliance with the principle of proportionality.

454. First of all, it is necessary to identify which aspects of constitutional rights are to be considered inviolable. Clearly, inviolability cannot cover every single expression and implication of these rights. This is why the Constitutional Court deems that only the essential content of fundamental rights cannot be the object of constitutional amendment and must therefore be considered inviolable. The different ways of expressing these rights can, and sometimes must, be changed with the passing of time by Parliament, by means of either an ordinary law or an amendment to the Constitution.

The general constitutional provisions protecting fundamental rights can, therefore, be changed. What cannot be changed in any way whatsoever is the basic content of these rights. The laws, including laws amending the Constitution, producing such an effect would certainly be considered in breach of the Constitution by the Constitutional Court (*see* again Constitutional Court, Judgment No. 1146/1988).

Another difficult question is how to identify the inviolable rights from among all those set out in the Constitution. The Constitution is not clear in this respect. Inviolable rights are cited generically in Article 2 and there is no reference to which of the rights subsequently mentioned in Article 13 and the following articles can be considered as such. Later on the Constitution defines as inviolable only some of the rights, namely personal liberty (Article 13), freedom of domicile (Article 14), the liberty and secrecy of correspondence (Article 15), and the right to a judicial defence (Article 24), but this selection is not intended to exclude all other rights. Analysing the text of the Constitution will clearly not provide a solution to this problem. It is self-evident that some rights, such as freedom of expression or association, are inviolable even though this is not explicitly stated in the Constitution. However, other cases are not so clear.

Given the absence of precise indications in the text, the task of identifying inviolable rights and defining their basic contents is largely left to the Constitutional Court.

§3. The Beneficiaries of Fundamental Rights

I. Individuals and Social Groups

455. Article 2 of the Constitution obliges the Republic to recognize and guarantee the inviolable rights of the person, 'both as an individual, and as a member of the social groups in which their personality finds expression', thus protecting, besides the individual, the social groups in which the social dimension of men and women is expressed. This and other constitutional provisions, which develop the contents of Article 2, especially freedom of association (Article 18), together with the rights of the family (Articles 29–34), freedom in the organization of trade unions (Article 39), freedom to freely form political parties (Article 49), freedom of religious affiliation (Article 19), the basic freedoms enjoyed by religious denominations (Articles 7–8) and the protection of linguistic minorities (Article 6), indicate that the Constitution favours pluralism and the autonomy of social groups.

The philosophy of the Italian Constitution, as well as many other constitutions since the Second World War, is in contrast both with the nineteenth-century theory which only acknowledged the relations between the individual and the State and, most of all, under Fascism, when the State tried both to incorporate professional associations into State bodies – the corporate State – and distrusted any other form of private association. This highlights the innovative scope of the Republican Constitution, which contains a set of provisions particularly in favour of social groups, to the extent that it offers them the same fundamental rights as individuals (*see* General Introduction, Chapter 2). What exactly do we mean by social groups (formazioni sociali)? Which forms of associations are entitled to fundamental rights? Even though it is quite difficult to give a precise definition, it can be inferred from the Constitution that it includes both natural groupings, such as the family and linguistic minorities, and voluntary groupings, namely associations (even those not legally recognized), political parties, trade unions and religious denominations.

Public institutions are certainly excluded from the group since they cannot be considered the expression of social pluralism: the distribution and decentralization of public agencies is the expression of another principle, i.e., institutional pluralism, protected and promoted by Article 5 of the Constitution.

A more debated question is the possibility of including companies and economic associations in general under the category of social groups enjoying fundamental rights protected by the pluralistic principle of Article 2. Even those who adopt a broad interpretation of the notion of social group usually tend to distinguish groups having an economic nature from the others by affirming that they cannot enjoy fundamental rights on the same conditions. Thus, even though all social groups, including economic ones, are deemed to enjoy important rights such as freedom of domicile and liberty and secrecy of correspondence, there are doubts as to their entitlement to freedom of expression including, for example, advertising (even because, more convincingly, advertising must be considered a form of economic initiative, protected by Article 41 of the Constitution rather than a form of free speech enshrined by Article 21).

456. Can social groups be considered the direct beneficiaries of fundamental rights? Most academic commentators conclude that social groups are only indirect beneficiaries of such rights and that the latter are solely enjoyed by individuals. Increasing the value of social pluralism would only allow individuals to benefit from those rights that are usually exercised collectively. With this aim in mind, for instance, there should be no right of associations to freely establish themselves, but rather a right of individuals to freely establish associations. This interpretation appears to be confirmed by the Constitution. Article 2 does not touch on the rights of social groups as such, but instead cites, 'the inviolable rights of the person … in the social groups in which his personality finds expression'. However well founded, this specification about the direct or indirect way in which social groups benefit from fundamental rights does not appear to produce significant practical consequences, since providing for the 'rights of individuals to form associations' means in many cases recognizing these same rights to the 'associations of individuals'.

II. Citizens and Non-nationals

457. Article 2 of the Constitution recognizes inviolable rights of every human being and therefore does not distinguish between citizens and foreigners.

On the contrary, Article 3, establishing the principle of equality and equal social dignity, refers only to 'citizens'.

Moreover, in the 1948 Constitution the only explicit reference to the legal status of foreign nationals is contained in Article 10(2), as another of the twelve fundamental principles. However, in stating 'the legal status of foreign nationals shall be determined by law in accordance with international treaties in this area', even that article clearly does not exclude, but actually allows, differences between the treatment foreigners and Italian citizens.

Moreover, the list of the constitutional rights of the individual written in Part I of the Constitution does not contain any reference to foreign nationals or immigrants. In fact, many of the individual fundamental rights listed therein refer in their text only to 'citizens'.

It is therefore due exclusively to the case law of the Constitutional Court, which has sought to reach beyond the literal provision of the Constitution favouring a 'systemic and non-fragmented' interpretation (Constitutional Court, Judgment No. 264/

2012), in the light of the overall spirit underlying it, that today the basket of fundamental rights of immigrants and foreign nationals recognized in Italy may be considered to be very rich.

458. The essential principles which the Constitutional Court still uses are contained in a long-standing judgment in which the Court, interpreting collectively the three constitutional provisions asserting the fundamental principles mentioned above – Article 2, which recognizes the inviolable rights of the individual, along with Article 3, which guarantees equality, and Article 10(2) on the legal status of foreign nationals – started to assert that, even though within the text of the Constitution many articles on human rights, and the very principle of equality, refer to citizens, they must however also apply to foreign nationals where it is necessary to respect fundamental human rights (Constitutional Court, Judgment No. 120/1967).

This assertion would subsequently be developed and nuanced in various cases in which it was applied. However, it may be regarded as the decisive turning point which introduced the issue of immigrants' rights into the case law of the Constitutional Court, rejecting the notion that only citizens benefited from the rights protected under the Italian Constitution. In fact, the current trend within the case law of the Constitutional Court follows precisely in the wake of this first judgment in seeking to extend inviolable rights also to foreigners as far as possible, rights that are granted 'to individuals not just because they belong to a determined political community, but because they are human beings' (Constitutional Court, Judgments Nos 105/2001 and 249/2010). However, as will be seen in the following section, a number of contradictions remain in the very case law of the Constitutional Court, which still need to be resolved.

§4. The Status of Non-nationals

459. In order to address the difficult issue of foreign nationals and their relationship with public authorities – an issue that has over the years turned into something of a hot topic on the Italian political agenda, just as and perhaps even more so than in other European countries – it is important to start from the fact that the text of the 1948 Constitution considers only 'outgoing' migration, i.e., emigration from Italy abroad, thereby engaging with the historical situation of Italy towards the end of the nineteenth century and in the first half of the twentieth century; by contrast, it ignores the opposite phenomenon, which however predominates today, of foreign immigration into Italy.

Article 16(2) indicates that this was the perspective of the Constituent Assembly as it contains a reference to movements into and out of the country but considers only movements by Italian citizens, to which it grants the right to emigrate and to return at a time of their choosing, while remaining silent on the right of entry of non-citizens into Italy. Before considering the constitutional case law in greater detail, which as mentioned above has been the true author of the rules on the legal status of foreign nationals under Italian law, it is important to recall that non-nationals are directly affected by certain constitutional provisions.

As has already been pointed out, Article 10(2) states that 'legal status of foreign nationals shall be determined by [Italian] law in accordance with international treaties'. Consequently, the Italian Parliament is not completely free when enacting rules concerning non-nationals, due to the limitations imposed by international law and treaties that Parliament is constitutionally obliged to follow. Thus, the status of non-nationals is guaranteed by an enhanced 'law' (on the notion a 'reserve of law' and its variants *see* below, §9 in this Chapter).

Second, the Constitution deals with the right to political asylum. Pursuant to Article 10(3) of the Constitution, 'foreign nationals who cannot enjoy the democratic freedoms protected by the Italian Constitution in their own countries shall be entitled to the right of asylum within the territory of the Republic, subject to the conditions established by law'. The conditions governing the granting of political asylum for non-nationals were first established by Law No. 39/1990, which was subsequently followed by further Italian legislation, and above all by numerous acts of EU law. In order to enjoy this right, it is not necessary that non-nationals are persecuted in their own country (in this case the rights of refugees are applied, as per international law). In order for political asylum seeker status to apply, it is sufficient that a country does not guarantee the main fundamental freedoms, even if those freedoms are formally recognized in a bill of rights.

Third, following Article 10(4) of the Italian Constitution, non-nationals cannot be extradited for political reasons, although this limit on extradition cannot be applied to the crime of genocide (Constitutional Court, Judgment No. 7/1967). Another limit on extradition, which is not explicitly written into the Constitution, but has been recognized by the Constitutional Court (Judgments Nos 54/1979 and 223/1996), concerns crimes punishable by the death penalty. Since the Italian Constitution prohibits the death penalty (Article 27), the Constitutional Court has deducted that Italy cannot cooperate with other countries by means of extradition when the country of origin of the non-national is likely to apply penalties prohibited under the Italian Constitution.

Returning to the constitutional case law on the status of foreign nationals, it must be noted that, at the beginning of its activity, the Constitutional Court found differences in the legislative treatment of foreign nationals compared to Italian nationals to be reasonable and proportionate, even in relation to a fundamental right. Also at present it still justifies the evident difference in treatment in the area of political rights, which entirely precludes foreign nationals from the right to vote and the right to stand as a candidate in elections, in accordance with Article 48 of the Constitution.

However, over the years, the Constitutional Court has changed its attitude, recognizing for foreigners, for instance, the right to life (Constitutional Court, Judgment No. 54/1979), the right to a defence (Constitutional Court, Judgment No. 198/2000), the right to health and medical care (Constitutional Court, Judgment No. 252/2001), the right to marriage (Constitutional Court, Judgment No. 245/2011), every constitutional guarantee of personal freedom (Constitutional Court, Judgment No. 275/2017) and so on.

Above all, in recent years, the Constitutional Court has referred in a considerable number of decisions to the general principle that it is manifestly unreasonable to subject the award of social benefits related to the basic fundamental needs of the human person (which presuppose a situation or invalidity or disability) to the holding of entitlement to stay in the country, the issue of which is besides conditional upon receipt of a particular level of income, and noted that any discrimination between Italians and non-nationals in this area – the area of fundamental *social* rights – would breach Article 3 of the Italian Constitution, in addition to Article 14 ECHR (*see*, for instance, Constitutional Court, Judgment No. 40/2013, which ruled Italian legislation unconstitutional insofar as it subjected the award to non-Community nationals staying legally in the country of the carer's allowance and the disability pension to the requirement of possession of a residence card, now the EC long-term residents' permit).

Again in the area of social security, the Constitutional Court has on several occasions intervened in order to avoid evident discrimination between Italians and foreign nationals even in cases that do not concern the primary needs of the individual. A striking case concerned, for example, a regional law guaranteeing the right to travel free of charge on public transport to Italian nationals who were entirely disabled along with a travelling companion. The Constitutional Court held that this measure extended beyond the essential levels of social benefit which the Region was required to guarantee. However, if the Region was to guarantee transport free of charge to the disabled, it was required to do so in accordance with the principle of equality, construed as reasonableness, as there is no factual de facto difference between the position of a disabled Italian national and that of a disabled foreign national that could justify a difference in treatment (Constitutional Court, Judgment No. 432/2005). More recently, the Constitutional Court, when declared unconstitutional the so-called baby bonus (Constitutional Court, Judgment No. 54/2022), in the part in which they excluded certain categories of citizens not belonging to the European Union from the granting of benefits linked to maternity, stated that European legislation provides for equal treatment by Member States of third-country nationals in social security and social benefits.

The Constitutional Court also introduced an aspect of unprecedented reasoning to the issue of immigration in asserting that social integration is not achieved solely through the recognition of greater rights, which turn the immigrant into a passive subject of the legal order benefiting from social security, but also through the conferral of duties, which enable the foreign national to become an active participant in solidarity. To refuse to foreign nationals the ability to participate in an activity of social solidarity thus constitutes an unjustified limitation on the full development of their personality, and for this reason a provision restricting only to Italian nationals the ability to perform voluntary civil service has been ruled unconstitutional (Constitutional Court, Judgment No. 119/2015).

Moreover, the Court also stated that 'whilst the legislator is free to stipulate particular consequences for any factual differences existing between Italian nationals and foreign nationals …, it cannot place foreign nationals ... in a condition of social "subordination" without any appropriate justification [since] ... status as a foreign national cannot be considered in itself "as an admissible reason for different and less favourable treatment"' (Constitutional Court, Judgment No. 186/2020, declaring unconstitutional the law providing that 'a residence permit … shall not constitute grounds for registration in the residents' register' of the relevant municipality of residence for lawfully resident asylum applicants).

The reasoning of the Constitutional Court on the right of entry into residence and free movement within Italy operates on a different level. According to the Court, this is not one of those 'fundamental rights' under Article 2 of the Constitution that are vested in a human being as such, and therefore no constitutional coverage whatsoever is afforded to foreigners.

In addition, the Constitutional Court always repeats that the legislation governing the entry into and residence by foreign nationals within the country is associated with a balancing of various public interests, including, for example, public security and health, obligations under international law and the national policy on immigration. Consequently, the legislator benefits from a very broad discretion in this area, which is only limited in the event that its choices are manifestly unreasonable (*see inter alia* Constitutional Court, Judgments Nos 62/1994 and 353/1997). On the contrary, in a case involving the relationship between a child and a parent, the Court held in Judgment No. 202/2013 that the Italian legislation on the expulsion of foreign nationals who have committed specific offences violated Article 3 of the Constitution and was unreasonably detrimental to family relations, which should receive privileged protection under Articles 29, 30 and 31 of the Constitution and, at the same time and in the same measure, under Article 8 of ECHR.

Therefore, in order to combat the phenomenon of illegal immigration, the legislator may, exercising its broad discretion, also choose to deploy the criminal law (Constitutional Court, Judgment No. 250/2010). However, according to the Constitutional Court while illegal immigration may be regarded per se as an offence, it is still nonetheless unacceptable for the legislator to provide that any given ordinary offences (e.g., theft or murder) be punished less severely if committed by an Italian national than if committed by a foreign national illegally present within the country. In fact, in ruling unconstitutional the so-called aggravating circumstance of irregular immigration status, the Constitutional Court in fact asserted that 'a general and absolute assumption that illegal immigrants are more dangerous, which has implications for the sanctions imposed […], turns into a "stigma", which operates as a premise for different treatment under the criminal law of the individual'. The aggravating circumstance of irregular immigration status was therefore ruled unconstitutional (Constitutional Court, Judgment No. 249/2010).

Ultimately, as has been noted by certain authors, the constitutional case law appears to follow the compensatory logic of 'hard outside/soft inside' since on the one hand it allows the political majorities to stipulate in a practically arbitrary manner the conditions governing the entry of migrants into Italy and their residence there, while on the other hand it asserts universal status for rights. In doing so, it bravely promotes a stance rooted in solidarity offering broad protection to the rights of foreign nationals, even in cases involving social rights that have a considerable impact on the public finances, above all during periods of economic crisis.

§5. 'New Rights'

460. Article 2 of the Italian Constitution generically recognizes the inviolable rights of individuals before the detailed 'Bill of Rights' listed in Articles 13 ff. poses a crucial problem of interpretation. Is it intended as a summary clause of the rights subsequently set out in the same text or an open clause implying the recognition of implicit, unwritten, fundamental rights?

On the one hand, the development of social life generates new human needs that deserve the same protection enjoyed by fundamental rights declared in Article 13 ff. of the 1948 Constitution. Although its aim is not to evoke natural law, Article 2 could stimulate the recognition of new fundamental rights by the courts, going beyond the boundaries of positive written law. On the other hand, the introduction of new fundamental rights could alter the balance of constitutional values and jeopardize the protection of written rights by weakening or suppressing some of them. Indeed, since the rights are kept together by a complex network of relations, introducing new fundamental rights could weaken the original rights written in the Constitution.

In spite of its declarations on the impossibility of founding new inviolable rights on the basis of Article 2, the Constitutional Court's attitude towards 'new rights' is not strict and narrow-minded, since it admits the existence of 'fundamental inviolable rights ... which necessarily derive from those enjoying constitutional protection' (Constitutional Court, Judgment No. 98/1979).

The Court has recognized, for instance, the right of unborn child to life (Constitutional Court, Judgment No. 27/1975; about the similar protection of embryos, *see* Constitutional Court, Judgments Nos 151/2009 and 229/2015) and the right to gender identity as an expression of the right to personal identity (Constitutional Court, Judgments Nos 98/1979, 161/1985, 221/2015 and 180/2017). It has also recognized the rights of decorum, honour, respectability, privacy and reputation as inviolable (Constitutional Court, Judgment No. 38/1973), as well as the right to housing (Constitutional Court, Judgments Nos 217/1988, 404/1988 and 252/1989), the right to privacy (Constitutional Court, Judgment No. 139/1990), the right to leave one's country (Constitutional Court, Judgment No. 278/1992), the fundamental right to keep one's own name as an essential distinguishing mark of personal identity (Constitutional Court, Judgment No. 13/1994, where the Constitutional Court based its judgment solely on Article 2, although the right to a name is explicitly provided for by Article 22 of the Constitution; *see also* Constitutional Court, Judgment, No. 18/2021), the right to marriage (Constitutional Court, Judgment No. 245/2011), the right of an adoptive child to know his or her origins (Constitutional Court, Judgment No. 278/2013); the freedom of sexual self-determination (Constitutional Court, Judgment No. 141/2019).

As far as the right to life is concerned, the Constitutional Court has said that the criminalization of assisting suicide is not, in itself, contrary to the Constitution but is justified by the need to protect the right to life, especially of the weakest and most vulnerable persons (Constitutional Court, Judgment No. 242/2019). In that case, the Constitutional Court declared Article 580 of the Criminal Code unconstitutional insofar it did not exclude the criminal punishment of those who facilitated the fulfilment of the free and informed intent to commit suicide on the part of a person being kept alive by life-support treatment such as hydration and artificial nutrition and who is suffering from an incurable illness that is a source of intolerable physical or psychological suffering but yet remains wholly capable of making free and informed decisions, provided that the assistance to suicide follows an effective offer of palliative care and provided that the existence of the above-mentioned conditions are verified by a public health facility, after consulting the territorially competent Ethics Committee.

In conclusion, the Constitutional Court tends to use Article 2 always as a tool for a broad and dynamic interpretation of other constitutional provision concerning the enumerated fundamental rights, and sometimes considers it as an open clause, i.e., as an autonomous source of rights, in order to protect at a constitutional level 'new rights', different from those listed in Articles 13 ff. of the Constitution, as recognized by the international and European bills of rights and by legal development and changes in the social context.

§6. Fundamental Rights under the Italian Constitution and International Legal Norms

461. The above matter is in some way connected to the problem of introducing 'new' rights into the Italian constitutional system through international legislation. The international protection of human rights has gradually increased, especially thanks to the European Convention on Fundamental Rights and Fundamental Freedoms signed in Rome in 1950 and its judicial remedies. Italy has signed many international treaties and is part of the system introduced by the European Convention.

462. In order to understand the role of these international declarations and their relations with the fundamental rights protected by the national constitutional system, it is necessary to explain the status of international legal norms in the national legal sources.

An important change occurred with the Constitutional revision of 2001 as far as the legal status of international treaties is concerned.

According to the dualist Italian tradition, every international treaty must be ratified by the National Parliament in order to be enacted. Consequently, international legal norms generally assume the force of the source on the basis of which they are transformed into internal provisions. Thus, it is necessary to distinguish between international legal norms of a customary nature and legal norms based on specific international treaties.

The former are assimilated through the 'permanent transformer' of Article 10 of the Constitution (the so-called automatic adjustment), and assume the legal status of constitutional rules, since they are only subordinate to the supreme principles of the constitutional system (*see* Constitutional Court, Judgment No. 238/2014 on State immunity for war crimes).

The regime of international treaties, on the contrary, changed over the years. Before the Constitutional revision of 2001, they usually assumed the force of the law (*see* Part I, Chapter 2, and Part V of Chapter 3). The position of international treaties, including those protecting human rights, was therefore subordinate to the Constitution and basically equivalent to that of ordinary laws (*see* Constitutional Court, Judgments Nos 323/1989 and 15/1996 for more details). The Constitutional revision of 2001 has introduced a new version of Article 117 of the Constitution that reads: 'Legislative powers shall be vested in the State and the Regions in compliance with the Constitution and with the constraints deriving from EU-Legislation and international obligations.'

This provision has been interpreted by the Italian Constitutional Court as granting international treaties an 'intermediate' value between the Constitution and the ordinary legislation enacted by the National Parliament (or by the Italian Executive, if we refer to legislative decrees of decrees-law). Consequently, they are not allowed to derogate the Constitution, but, however, the national legislation is required to conform to them.

As a result, the international treaties are more and more important within the case law of the Constitutional Court. Even before the revision of 2001, the Constitutional Court has frequently quoted these treaties, especially the ECHR, in its judgments. Even though the provisions contained in these treaties were not used directly as parameters of the Court's judgments, they have played a major interpretative role in the Italian system, often allowing the Court to broaden the scope of the rights protected by the Italian Constitution (*see* Constitutional Court, Judgment No. 388/1999). After the revision of 2001, the importance of the international treaties, and in particular the ECHR, has grown, since they have been formally recognized as parameters in the judgments of judicial review of legislation (*see* below, §8).

§7. European Multilevel System for the Protection of Fundamental Rights

463. The Italian constitutional protection of individual rights is part of a multilevel system of fundamental rights protection, where an important role is played by the European Court of Human Rights (ECHR) and the CJEU. Some constitutional provisions (i.e., Articles 11 and 117.1 of the Constitution) have been interpreted, by the Constitutional Court, to incorporate in the Italian system of rights the European Courts' case law.

464. In this chapter, the European systems of protection of fundamental rights will be examined separately. Let us begin with the European Union.

465. At the very beginning of its existence, the protection of fundamental rights was not one of the goals of the European Community (now EU). The first treaties of the 1950s did not contain any catalogue of fundamental rights, and the need to ensure the protection of those rights in the European Community was not even mentioned. The lack of any form of protection of fundamental rights can be explained by the decision to entrust to the national constitutions the task of ensuring respect for fundamental rights in the European area. Before the ECJ ruled the principle of supremacy of EU law, national constitutional provisions were considered prevailing over all the acts of the Community institutions and therefore also the protection of fundamental rights was guaranteed by national constitutions and national courts for what concerned EC competences.

However, once the principle of the supremacy of Community (European) law and its direct effects were established, as a consequence, a free regulation zone was indirectly created, where no protection of fundamental rights was granted. After several requests from national constitutional courts, the ECJ, since the *Stauder* decision (ECJ 12 November 1969 C-29/69), held that the protection of the fundamental rights of citizens against acts of the Community institutions falls within its powers, thus covering a gap in human rights enforcement. Since the proclamation of the Charter of Fundamental Rights of the EU, in 2000, the protection of fundamental rights in the EU has gained a growing importance.

466. Article 6 TEU lists the European guarantees of the fundamental rights reading as follows:

1. The Union recognises the rights, freedoms and principles set out in the Charter of Fundamental Rights of the European Union of 7 December 2000, as adapted at Strasbourg, on 12 December 2007, which shall have the same legal value as the Treaties. […]
2. The Union shall accede to the European Convention for the Protection of Human Rights and Fundamental Freedoms. […]
3. Fundamental rights, as guaranteed by the European Convention for the Protection of Human Rights and Fundamental Freedoms and as they result from the constitutional traditions common to the Member States, shall constitute general principles of the Union's law.

Within the EU, consequently, the protection of fundamental rights is based on three major instruments: the Charter of Fundamental Rights, the ECHR and the Constitutional Traditions Common to the Member States:

a. *The Charter of Fundamental Rights*: it was approved in 2000, but it is only when the Treaty of Lisbon entered into force in 2009 that the Charter was granted legal binding force. The Charter is nowadays recognized as having the same value of the European Treaties.
b. *The European Convention on Human Rights*: the European Convention and the decisions of the Strasbourg ECHR have played an important role in the Court of Luxembourg case law. Although the EU is not as such part of the Convention, the CJEU takes very seriously the case law of the European Court of Human Rights.
c. *The Constitutional Traditions Common to the Member States*: before a written Bill of Rights was adopted, the Court of Justice has elaborated the fundamental rights taking them from the constitutional traditions common to the Member States and by the ECHRs.

This relationship can be described in three major points:

1. *Separation.* The legal relations between the European and national protection of fundamental rights should run along a precise demarcation line: two systems of reference values, two orders of courts, two specific areas of application. More specifically, the fundamental rights are guaranteed by the ECJ against acts of the European institutions, referring, as judicial standards, to the Charter of Fundamental Rights, the principles drawn from national constitutional traditions of the Member States and to the European Convention of Human Right. Different provisions of the European law provide that the protection of fundamental rights of the European institutions shall not extend in any way the competences of the Union as defined in the Treaties (Article 6 of TEU and Article 51 of the Charter of Fundamental Rights). However, national constitutions and Constitutional Courts keep on preserving their effectiveness against all the national acts not involved in European law enforcement.
2. *Incorporation.* The separation doctrine did not resist untouched over time. Very soon, the Court of Justice ruled that although his decisions refer essentially to acts of the European institutions, they also affect, to some extent, the Member States, in cases where government regulations come within the scope of European law (so-called incorporation doctrine). Until recent years, the Court of Justice has been rather cautious in referring to this doctrine. Today, especially after the entry into force of the Charter, whose Article 51 restate the aforementioned doctrine of the incorporation, there is a tendency to expand more and more European protection rights even in areas that should remain within the Member States powers.
3. *Counter-limits.* Following Article 11 of the Constitution, that reads: 'Italy agrees […] to the limitations of sovereignty that may be necessary to a world order ensuring peace and justice among the Nations', the Italian legal order complies with all obligations deriving from the EU legal system, including fundamental rights. However, since Judgment No. 183/1973, the Italian Constitutional Court has reiterated the counter-limits doctrine that implies that the limitation of sovereignty cannot include the basic fundamental principles of the Italian Constitution. Therefore, the Constitutional Court is required to protect those principles from any breach, included those that might derive from the European legislation. The counter-limit doctrine has recently become topical once again due to a referral order to the ECJ by the Italian Constitutional Court itself about the principle of legality in criminal matters after the *Taricco* judgment of the European Court (ECJ, 8 September 2015, C-105/14). In that order, the Italian Court has asked the European Court if its judgment must 'be interpreted as requiring the criminal courts to disregard national legislation concerning limitation periods that precludes, in a significant number of cases, the punishment of serious fraud affecting the financial interests of the EU, or that provides for shorter limitation periods for fraud affecting the financial interests of the EU than those applicable to fraud affecting the financial interests of the Member State, *even when the setting aside such legislation would contrast with the supreme principles of the constitutional order of the Member State or with the inalienable human rights recognised under the Constitution of the Member Stat*e' (Constitutional Court, Judgment No. 24/2017). The

answer of the ECJ, however, was able to avoid the clash between the two legal systems (ECJ 8 September 2015, C-105/14, and Constitutional Court, Judgment No. 115/2018).

§8. THE FUNDAMENTAL RIGHTS AND THE ECHR

467. Chronologically, the relationship between the Italian legal system and the ECHR has to be divided into two stages, the watershed moment being when the Italian Constitutional Court handed down the so-called twin Judgments Nos 348/2007 and 349/2007.

Originally, in dealing with the ECHR, Italy employed the dualistic approach traditionally used in the relationship between the Italian legal system and international law. On the basis of this approach, the ECHR took effect when it was implemented by Law No. 848 in 1955, thereby giving it the efficacy of an ordinary law. As a consequence, from a domestic standpoint the ECHR for many years was pacifically considered a primary source of law that could be derogated by subsequent primary legislation or acts have force of law (such as decree-laws and legislative decrees).

In truth, a part of Italian legal scholarship considered this approach unsatisfactory. Indeed, the protection of fundamental rights is an essential element of all modern constitutions, as clearly demonstrated by Article 16 of the Declaration of the Rights of Man and the Citizen of 1789. On the basis of these considerations, many writers saw the need to provide the ECHR with a kind of 'constitutional entrenchment' that was more in line with the fundamental rights that it contained. For a long time, these interpretations elaborated by Italian legal scholarship remained merely theoretical and speculative until in the 1990s – in coincidence with the entry into effect of Protocol 11 of the ECHR which radically reformed the jurisdictional system of protection from violations of the ECHR by allowing individuals to apply directly to the Court, once all domestic remedies had been exhausted – the Constitutional Court began to test new theories on the basis of proposals put forward by legal scholars. Above all, from then on the Constitutional Court has always appreciated the value of the ECHR and the case law of the Court in Strasbourg at least from an interpretative standpoint. At the end of the last century, a famous statement was made by the Constitutional Court, according to which the Constitution and the international human rights treaties 'integrate and complete each other through interpretation'. In the meantime, many of the ordinary judges and even the Court of Cassation began to enhance the role of the ECHR far beyond that foreseen for ordinary legislation (Constitutional Court, Judgment No. 388/1999).

As underlined above, the real epochal change took place in 2007 when the Constitutional Court handed down Judgments Nos 348 and 349/2007. In truth, a decision by the Constitutional Court had been expected ever since the amendment to Title V of the Italian Constitution in 2001 and, in particular, Article 117, paragraph 1, which affirms that 'legislative power shall be exercised … in accordance … with international obligations'. According to many writers, this provision allowed the ECHR and also other international treaties to be accorded a greater passive force with respect to ordinary laws and therefore be considered interposed parameters in constitutional review without actually being elevated to constitutional rank in terms of their active force. This was indeed the interpretation given by the Constitutional Court in Judgments Nos 348 and 349/2007.

With these two decisions, the Constitutional Court established several fundamental principles with regard to the relationship between the Italian legal system and the ECHR. In particular, in terms of judicial remedies, the Constitutional Court affirmed that all issues concerning the compatibility of domestic laws with the ECHR implicate judicial review of constitutionality which is competence of the Constitutional Court and that conflicts of this nature cannot be resolved by the ordinary judges through disapplication of the national law violating the ECHR. In the two judgments of 2007, the Constitutional Court unequivocally affirmed that issues concerning the contrast between domestic legislation and the ECHR are issues of constitutionality and therefore are not under the jurisdiction of the regular courts. More precisely, in the presence of contrasts between domestic legislation and the ECHR, the ordinary judges may resort to *conform interpretation*, but they cannot resort to *disapplication* of domestic law: 'the ordinary judge has the task of interpreting the domestic provision in conformity with the international provision, within the limits established by the texts of the provisions in question. If this is not possible, then the judge must appeal to the Constitutional Court to address the issue of constitutional legitimacy' (Constitutional Court, Judgment No. 349/2007).

In other words, the *legislator* has the task of *conforming* the Italian legal system to the rights protected by the ECHR, *the ordinary judges* have the task of *interpreting* the law *in conformity* with the ECHR and the Constitutional Court has the task of declaring *unconstitutional* a domestic law that does not offer sufficient safeguards for the rights protected under the ECHR.

It must be noted that some years after its first judgments on the ECHR the Constitutional Court has provided some other complementary clarifications about the obligation on the part of the Italian courts to follow the interpretation of the text of the European Convention made by the Strasbourg Court, stating that the national courts will only be obliged to implement the provision identified at Strasbourg in cases involving 'consolidated law' or a 'pilot judgment' (Constitutional Court, Judgment No. 49/2015).

§9. The Principle of Equality

468. The principle of formal equality proclaimed by Article 3 of the Italian Constitution, which states that 'All citizens are invested with equal social status and are equal before the law' is anything but new, since it dates back to the French Revolution and was adopted during the liberal era by all States governed by the rule of law.

The principle of equality, however, has gradually assumed new meanings. First, the fact that the principle of equality is set out in a rigid constitution such as the Italian one makes it binding for the legislator too. If, in other times, the main guarantee of the principle of equality was the law, the current need is to protect equality even against the law. Therefore, in the present constitutional system, the principle of equality is binding not only for the judiciary (*see also* Article 101 of the Constitution) and public administration (*see also* Article 97 of the Constitution) but also for legislators.

Second, even the content of the principle of equality has become more complex. This principle is designed to prevent both arbitrary discrimination among individuals in identical or similar situations, and arbitrary assimilation among individuals in different situations. In short, the Constitutional Court concludes that, by virtue of the principle of equality, identical situations should enjoy identical legal treatment while different situations should enjoy a different legal treatment. In particular, legislation based on the 'suspect' criteria mentioned by Article 3, paragraph 1, are deemed unconstitutional and are subject to the strict control of the Constitutional Court. We are talking about distinctions based on sex, language, race, religion, political beliefs and personal and social status. Laws causing a discrimination according to these criteria are deemed unconstitutional by the Constitutional Court.

Legislative distinctions based on criteria different from those mentioned above are examined by the Constitutional Court in the light of the principle of reasonableness. In other words, the Constitutional Court judges the consistency of the distinctions and assimilation made by the legislator by comparing them with the treatment used in other de facto situations.

As a consequence, judgments on laws dealing with the principle of equality must take into account not only two elements such as the contested provision and Article 3 of the Constitution but also a third element or *tertium comparationis*, i.e., a third provision which is compared with the original provision subject to constitutional review. The violation or respect of the principle of equality by a specific provision emerges from the comparison with another provision of an ordinary law.

It is no doubt difficult to set general rules on the matter. Nevertheless, the Constitutional Court has defined the following general criteria:

a. the fairness of the classification made by the legislator with respect to the individuals taken into account and considering the reference legislation;
b. the provision of homogeneous treatment that reasonably takes into account the essential features of the classification […] of people to whom such a treatment is reserved; [and]
c. the proportionality of the legal treatment to the classification made by the legislator, taking into account the objective aim of the reference legislation. Such proportionality must be examined in relation to its practical effects (Constitutional Court, Judgment No. 163/1993).

469. Article 3, paragraph 2, of the Italian Constitution completes and develops the principle of formal equality by affirming the principle of *substantial* equality when it states that:

> It is the responsibility of the Republic to remove all economic and social obstacles which, by limiting the freedom and equality of citizens, prevent the full development of the individual and the participation of all workers in the political, economic and social organisation of the country.

The principle of substantial equality justifies and encourages the passing of legislation designed to ensure the equality of treatment and opportunity to the weakest individuals or classes of individuals in unfavourable situations. The Constitutional Court has appealed to the principle of substantial equality in order to justify affirmative actions that guarantee privileged treatment to weak categories. To date, such actions have taken the form of laws in favour of women in the professional field (Constitutional Court, Judgment No. 109/1993). In more recent times, examining legislative measures aimed at curbing public spending in order to face the economic and financial crisis, it has also maintained that the technical instrument of the automatic pension increases conditions the discretionary choices of the legislator because, among other things, it draws up and pursues 'a project of substantive equality, in accordance with the requirements laid down in Article 3(2) of the Constitution, thereby avoiding any differences in treatment to the detriment of certain pensioners' (Constitutional Court, Judgment No. 70/2015). Moreover, the Constitutional Court recognized that 'the personal circumstances that may limit equality undoubtedly include disability', irrespective of the type of legally relevant disability, either physical or mental, and subsequently it struck down the legislation stipulating that Italian citizenship may only be acquired if an oath of allegiance is sworn, on the grounds that it gave rise to a form of marginalization of persons who were, on account of a mental disability, unable to swear the oath (Constitutional Court, Judgment No. 258/2017). The principle of formal equality and the principle of substantial equality do not contradict, but instead complement each other, given that Article 3, paragraph 2, justifies legislation that, although apparently discriminatory towards certain categories or groups of citizens, actually reaffirms the equality of conditions, realizing full legal equality. Article 3, paragraph 2, on the one hand, includes an autonomous principle, i.e., the principle of substantial equality, which justifies interventions in favour of some groups of individuals and, on the other hand, also acts as an interpretative criterion for the principle of formal equality. The latter, in any case, is affirmed by distinguishing the legal provisions applying to the various categories of individuals depending on their actual differences.

§10. Two Instruments for the Protection of Fundamental Rights

470. The Constitution ensures the protection of some rights by providing that they must be regulated by Acts of Parliament and not by regulations passed by the Executive. This limit is frequently applied to fundamental rights, considered a basic element of the life of citizens and the democratic nature of the legal system. It is the body representing the popular will, and not the Executive, that is therefore allowed to pass legislation in this field. This instrument is called 'reserve of law'.

This rule, however, is also a burden for Parliament, which is obliged to pass legislation in this field without being able to defer it to other sub-legislative sources. The Executive, in truth, can issue legislation equivalent to formal laws in the field of fundamental rights, i.e., decree-laws and legislative decrees, not only for formal reasons (because these decrees are equivalent to laws passed with the ordinary procedure) but also for substantial reasons, since the passing of these decrees must always be preceded or followed by an Act of Parliament (*see* Part I, Chapter 4).

Executive, however, cannot issue regulations in this field and the public administration, and to a certain extent, the judiciary itself, cannot be accorded powers that can be used to establish the scope and limits of fundamental rights.

This reserve may be absolute or relative.

If it is absolute, the matter must be entirely regulated by Acts of Parliament, or decree-laws and legislative decrees of the Executive (except for merely technical aspects: *see* Constitutional Court, Judgment No. 171/2023).

If it is relative, the general norms must be issued by a statute law, although it can be subsequently developed and completed by the regulations of the Executive. Since it is not easy to understand when the Constitution provides for the absolute or relative reserve of the rights it enshrines, the choice is partially made according to a literal or formal interpretation. When the Constitution states that restrictions on personal liberty are permitted only in such cases and manner as the law provides (Article 13), the protection is deemed to be absolute. On the contrary, when it states that no personal service or payment may be forced on anyone, save 'according to law' (Article 23), or that public departments are organized 'according to the provisions of the law' (Article 97), the protection is considered to be relative. According to this principle, the protection of fundamental rights is presumed to be absolute: legislation passed in this field can only take the form of laws and acts having the force of law.

According to some academic commentators – an opinion confirmed by the Constitutional Court – what really matters is not the kind of protection (absolute or relative), but its object and scope. The general principle is that only Parliament is allowed to make the essential choices regarding some matters set out in the Constitution. The essential elements of some matters are very broad (as is the case for crimes and punishment), while for other matters the protection is ensured by providing that ordinary laws regulate the essential elements and the necessary rules of implementation be issued by subordinate acts.

When the reserve is relative (e.g., Article 23 of Const., providing that individual duties and taxes, or Article 97 of Const., about public office organization) the law cannot provide for a broad allocation of power: for this reason, for instance, the Constitutional Court has ruled the unconstitutionality of statutory provisions which attributed to city mayors a broad power to take urgent measures in order to prevent and eliminate threats to public safety and urban security (Constitutional Court, Judgment No. 115/2011).

471. The second instrument for the protection of fundamental rights applies above all to the articles of the Constitution dealing with 'civil relations'. Thanks to these instrument restrictions on fundamental rights, especially personal liberty, freedom of domicile, communication and press can be prescribed only by means of an official judicial order or '*mandato*'. The reason for this 'reserve of jurisdiction' is that the judicial authorities are called upon to enforce the law impartially and independently (Article 101) and to guarantee the respect of the limitations imposed by the Constitution and statutes on fundamental rights.

Enforcement of laws placing restrictions on fundamental rights may thus be a prerogative of the judicial authorities. Nevertheless, the police authorities may also carry out provisional measures in urgent cases (except for the freedom of communication). Such measures, however, must be ratified by the judicial authorities within a very short period of time.

§11. Judicial Remedies for the Protection of Fundamental Rights

472. The Italian legal system does not provide citizens with specific judicial remedies for the protection of their fundamental rights. The violation of a fundamental right can be reported, in general, to an ordinary or administrative judge with due jurisdiction. Understanding the judicial remedies for the protection of fundamental rights requires an analysis of the organization and powers of the judiciary (*see* Part II, Chapter 7, Chapter 8).

Thanks to its role of prevention of violations coming from legislators, or the power to amend the Constitution, the Constitutional Court is considered the final and essential element of the judicial protection system of fundamental rights. The Italian system, however, does not allow citizens to appeal directly to the Constitutional Court for the protection of their rights. Such an appeal must take the usual forms, in particular, that of the preliminary ruling (*see* Part II, Chapter 9).

Chapter 3. Key Rights Enshrined in the Constitution

by Marta Cartabia & Elisabetta Lamarque

§1. Introduction

473. All the classical rights deriving from the liberal state, and rights typical of contemporary social democracies are enshrined in the Italian Constitution. The rights set out in Title I of the Constitution have been inherited mainly from the liberal era. These are, for instance, personal liberty and freedom of residence, freedom of expression and religion, the right to judicial protection, as well as the principle of formal equality.

These rights are designed to protect individuals from interference by the State and are referred to as negative freedoms, i.e., those which oblige the State to *refrain* from action.

In harmony with the development of many other contemporary constitutions, the content of the Italian Constitution is much broader compared to the first declaration of rights: in addition to the classical nineteenth-century freedoms, the protection of which has been confirmed and reinforced, the Constitution also recognizes political rights, especially the right to vote and to freely form political parties, which can be considered rights of the citizens to make their contribution to the life of the State. Provision is also made for social rights (right to education, health, health care, etc.) that oblige the State to guarantee certain services by means of positive action. Economic freedoms have lost their inviolable nature, especially the right of ownership and the freedom of contract. These freedoms were considered inviolable and sacred in liberal states, while today they are guaranteed insofar as they have a social function and utility. Let us take a closer look at the most important inviolable rights enshrined in the Italian Constitution.

§2. Personal Liberty

474. Article 13 of the Constitution proclaims the inviolability of personal liberty. Natural persons are thus protected against situations of temporary or lasting subjection resulting from physical coercion. Personal liberty therefore consists of all the faculties possessed by natural persons and its expression is the claim to avoid illicit physical coercion.

The Constitution concentrates on the problem of arbitrary detention and provides for the traditional habeas corpus. Article 13 states that 'no form of personal detention, inspection or search is permitted, nor other restrictions on personal liberty save by order of the judiciary for which the motive must be stated, and then only in such cases and manner as the law provides'.

The cases and manner in which an individual can be subjected to restrictions to freedom can be established by an Act of Parliament only or an act of the Executive having the force of law (absolute reserve of law). Such legislation must be complete and detailed so as to protect the citizen both against the Executive, which cannot issue regulations on the matter (except for regulations which implement legislation), and against the misuse of discretionary powers by the judiciary.

This is why the Constitutional Court does not hesitate to declare unconstitutional those rules prescribing restrictions on personal liberty without determining precisely the cases and manner in which such restrictions can be imposed by the judiciary (*see*, for instance, Constitutional Court, Judgment No. 238/1996 on taking blood samples).

Moreover, restrictions on personal liberty can only be authorized by a motivated act of the judiciary, in compliance with the law. Pursuant to the Constitution, the police authorities may also take provisional measures placing limits on personal liberties, though only in 'exceptional cases of necessity and urgency, strictly defined by law'. It follows that the legislature is obliged to specify the precise circumstances in which the police authorities can impose restrictions on personal liberties so as to prevent the police from acting too freely. In any case, these measures are provisional and must therefore be communicated within forty-eight hours to the judiciary. If the latter do not ratify them within this time, the measures are revoked and declared null and void.

475. Provisional measures that can be taken by the police authorities (on condition that they are ratified by the judiciary) include mandatory and optional arrest in the case of people caught in the act of committing certain crimes (Articles 380–381 of the Code of Criminal Procedure), investigative detention of people seriously indicted of certain crimes, even if they are not caught in the act of committing the crime, when there is a risk of evasion (Article 384 of the Code of Criminal Procedure), as well as compulsory attendance for the examination or confrontation of a defendant (Article 376 of the Code of Criminal Procedure). The Constitutional Court, however, clarified that the measure of the so-called mandatory quarantine ordered by the legislator in times of pandemic for people who tested positive for Covid-19 does not affect personal freedom, and therefore does not require the activation of the reserve of jurisdiction because, as the Constitutional Court stated, 'the verification of the state of positivity is not combined with any moral stigma, and cannot cause mortification of equal social dignity, also because it is a condition shared with millions of individuals, united by nothing more than exposure to an airborne pathogen' (Constitutional Court, Judgment No. 127/2022).

Besides these provisional measures, there are three other forms of restrictions on personal liberty.

First, there are restrictions on personal liberty following conviction to a prison sentence.

Mention should also be made of precautionary measures in criminal proceedings, taken prior to judgment, which are only admissible in compliance with Article 27 of the Constitution, for which a person cannot be considered guilty until final sentence has been passed. According to the Constitutional Court, precautionary measures must never anticipate the punishment and can only be ordered for precautionary reasons or reasons strictly pertaining to the trial (Constitutional Court,

Judgment No. 64/1970). Indeed, Article 274 and the following articles of the Code of Criminal Procedure provide that precautionary measures can only be taken in the three following cases:

1. for investigation purposes, especially in order to preserve the authenticity of evidence;
2. in order to prevent the defendant from escaping; and
3. in order to prevent the defendant from committing other serious crimes.

The need for preventive detention must be established on every single occasion. The legislature therefore cannot provide the preventive detention, instead of another lighter pretrial measure, of all those accused of a particular crime. In a great number of judgments, the Constitutional Court has repeatedly asserted that in the light of the relevant constitutional principle of inviolability of personal freedom (Article 13) and of the presumption of innocence (Article 27), the legislation governing pretrial measures must be based on the criterion of the 'minimum sacrifice necessary' of the personal freedom, so that every criminal court must have the power to choose the measure adequate to the single case, and to order the most severe measure, i.e., the remand in custody, only when all other measures would be inadequate (Constitutional Court, Judgments Nos 265/2010, 164/2011, 231/2011, 331/2011, 110/2012, 213/2013, 232/2013, 48/2015 and 191/2020).

In addition, Article 13 of the Italian Constitution provides that the maximum period of preventive detention should be laid down by law. The Constitutional Court ruled that the calculation of maximum period of preventive detention, provided by the criminal procedure code, must cover the period of imprisonment that the accused suffered abroad waiting for the extradition towards Italy or in execution of European Arrest Warrant (Constitutional Court, Judgments Nos 253/2004 and 143/2008).

Besides detention for conviction and preventive detention, the legislation in force (especially Law No. 1423/1956 amended by Law No. 327/1988) envisages preventive measures that can be applied to suspects, even in the absence of a crime, in order to fight forms of organized crime such as the Mafia.

Such measures can be imposed on vast and heterogeneous categories of people, such as Mafia suspects, those convicted of crimes related to arms trafficking, habitual vagrants, people notoriously and habitually involved in unlawful business, etc. Other categories of people who can be subjected to coercive preventive measures are stipulated in Law Nos 575/1965 and 646/1982, concerning the Mafia and the Camorra. One could also add Law No. 152/1975, enacted in order to combat 'political terrorism' in the 1970s; and Law Nos 401/1989 and 45/1995, to combat violent behaviour in football stadiums and at other sporting events; and Law No. 438/2001, which extends the field of application of preventive measures to those suspected of taking part in acts of international terrorism. These measures can even be taken in the absence of a crime and have consequently been widely criticized, since the cases provided for are too vague and give the competent judicial authorities too broad discretionary powers. The Constitutional Court has generally judged these preventive measures as constitutionally legitimate, although it has specified that they cannot be taken on the basis of mere suspicion, namely on the basis of subjective and uncontrollable assumptions (Constitutional Court, Judgment No. 126/1983). It also stated that preventive measures restrictive of personal freedom and the freedom to communicate confidentially are subordinated to observance of the principle of legality and respect for the reserve of jurisdiction (most recently Constitutional Court, Judgment No. 2/2023, which declared unconstitutional the code of anti-mafia laws and prevention measures, in the part in which it includes mobile phones among the devices that the police commissioner can prohibit, in whole or in part, the possession or use).

The individual is granted special judicial remedies against these measures, including the opportunity to appeal to the *Tribunale del Riesame*, called upon to render very rapid judgments on the merits of measures placing limits on personal liberty taken by the judiciary.

In addition, the Italian Constitution states that appeals to the Supreme Court of Cassation against measures limiting personal liberty are always allowed (Article 111, paragraph 7) and specifies that 'Any act of physical and moral violence against a person subjected to restriction of personal liberty shall be punished' (Article 13, paragraph 4), therefore requesting the legislature to impose a criminal sanction for such acts.

Moreover, it should be remembered that the consistent direction taken by the case law of Italian Constitutional Court is that the constitutional protection of fundamental rights continues to operate even in the case of persons whose personal freedom has been legitimately restricted, albeit within the limitations imposed by the particular conditions involved. The Constitutional Court, indeed, reiterates that people in a state of detention, despite being deprived of most of their freedom, nevertheless always conserve its residue, which is all the more precious because it constitutes the last area in which their individual personality may grow (*see*, lastly, Constitutional Court, Judgment No. 20/2017, on the inspection and stamping of the correspondence of prison inmates). Consequently, prisoners enjoy not only the right to defence, and particularly to confer with counsel during the enforcement of the sentence (Constitutional Court, Judgment No. 212/1997), the right to judicial protection against every administrative act taken by the prison service (Constitutional Court, Judgment No. 26/1999), and the right not to live in conditions contrary to human dignity due to prison overcrowding (Constitutional Court, Judgments Nos 279/2013 and 204/2016, in the implementation of the 'pilot judgment' ECHR, 8 January 2013, *Torreggiani and others v. Italy*) but also, for instance, the right to health (Constitutional Court, Judgment No. 165/2015), the right to vote (ECHR, Grand Chamber, 22 May 2012, *Scoppola v. Italy* No. 3 maintained that 'the legal provisions in Italy defining the circumstances in which individuals may be deprived of the right to vote show the [Italian] legislature's concern to adjust the application of the measure to the particular circumstances of the case in hand, taking into account such factors as the gravity of the offence committed and the conduct of the offender'), the right to information and the right to study (Constitutional Court, Judgment No. 122/2017) and so on.

§3. The Right to a Fair Trial

476. This right has been introduced by a constitutional review in 1999 (on this point *see* Part II, Chapter 7, §9).

§4. Inviolability of Personal Domicile

477. Article 14 of the Constitution states that personal domicile is inviolable, thus protecting the privacy of the activities carried out by citizens in isolated places. Freedom of domicile is protected by *jus prohibendi*, i.e., the right to forbid the admittance of other people into one's own domicile, and *jus admittendi*, i.e., the right to admit other people into one's own domicile.

It is worth stressing that the notion of domicile set out in Article 14 is very broad. In order to receive the protection of the Constitution, domicile should consist of a privately owned dwelling – a definition which includes workplaces, offices, firms, seats of political parties, trade unions and associations, besides, of course, personal dwellings. In a contested judgment of the Constitutional Court, the protection of Article 14 was extended to motor cars (Constitutional Court, Judgment No. 88/1987). The only indispensable condition for a person to enjoy the freedom of domicile is the actual possession, even illicit, of the place in which he or she wishes to enjoy privacy. Possessing by virtue of a lawful title is therefore not necessary in order to exercise freedom of domicile. Any place, provided that it is isolated from outside and actually owned or occupied on a private basis, could therefore be considered as a protected domicile in compliance with Article 14. In this regard, the Constitutional Court stated that the constitutional protection cannot be triggered in case of police shooting on private conducts potentially visible to third parties, such as the one that takes place on a balcony overlooking the public way (Constitutional Court, Judgment No. 149/2008).

As regards provisions on the restrictions on freedom of domicile, Article 14, paragraph 2 refers to Article 13 on personal freedom: no inspection, search or attachment can be carried out save in cases and in the manner laid down by law and by order of the judiciary for which the motive must be stated (absolute reserve of law and reserve of jurisdiction). In exceptional cases of necessity and urgency, the police authorities may carry out provisional measures which must be ratified by the judiciary within the same time limits established by Article 13 for personal freedom.

Article 14, paragraph 3 provides for some exceptions to the general rules on the restrictions of freedom of domicile. Public authorities other than judicial ones can carry out verifications or inspections of personal domicile for reasons of public health and safety or for economic and fiscal purposes. Work inspectors, for instance, can carry out their supervisory activities in workplaces (Constitutional Court, Judgment No. 10/1971), and the police can enter buildings used for commercial or industrial activities in order to carry out inspections and supervision for economic and fiscal purposes (Constitutional Court, Judgment No. 122/1974). Inspections and other measures of Article 14, paragraph 3, It. Const., in fact, cannot be coercive but must be conducted with the cooperation of the individual.

§5. The Freedom of Movement, Residence, Expatriation and Emigration

478. Article 16 of the Constitution provides for freedom of movement and residence in any part of the country.

All citizens have the right to travel freely anywhere in the country (freedom of movement) and to take up residence, abode or work in any part of the national territory (freedom of residence).

Restrictions on the freedoms of movement and residence can be prescribed only by an Act of Parliament (reserve of law). The protection, in this case, is reinforced. Italian scholars call it 'reinforced reserve of law' since the legislature is first of all bound by the Constitution not to impose restrictions on freedom of movement and residence of particular individuals but only general restrictions, i.e., restrictions that can be imposed in the abstract to a general category of individuals. It should be noted that the Regions cannot adopt provisions hindering the free movement of persons and goods in the national territory (Article 120 of the Constitution). Moreover, legislature can impose restrictions on the freedom of movement and residence only for reasons of health and security, namely to protect the physical and mental health of citizens or to guarantee the so-called material public order, safeguarding peaceful cohabitation, and the safety of people and goods.

No restriction may be prescribed for any kind of political reason. In contrast, freedom of movement and freedom of residence can be limited by police and other administrative authorities, as well as by a court, since Article 16 does not contain any 'reserve of jurisdiction'.

479. Freedom of expatriation allows citizens to leave the territory of the Republic and re-enter it freely, save for such limitations as prescribed by law.

Legislation on passports (Law No. 1185/1967) outlines some obligations that can temporarily restrict or impose conditions on the freedom of expatriation. These obligations are connected to parental responsibility, or legal requirements, in the case of persons subject to criminal or financial penalties or security measures. If the restrictions provided for by law do not apply, the relevant authorities are obliged to issue the passport and cannot exercise their discretionary powers.

Freedom of expatriation is also connected to freedom of emigration, protected by Article 35, paragraph 4. The Constitution, however, provides for a particular kind of right to expatriation, distinct from the individual right to emigrate, and that is the collective right of economically disadvantaged social classes to emigrate in order to seek work abroad. This is why, unlike freedom of expatriation, freedom of emigration is not simply a negative freedom (i.e., consisting in the freedom to leave Italian territory), but also a positive freedom, requiring State activities of assistance and control of the phenomenon of emigration for the protection of the emigrants themselves, through the setting up of offices, even abroad, that provide assistance for preparing the documents of expatriation, transport and labour, as well as social welfare services. It is worth mentioning Law No. 205/1985 and its subsequent amendments, setting up the committees of Italians abroad (the so-called *comitati per gli italiani all'estero – COMITES*), which carry out activities connected to social and cultural life, social welfare and school assistance, as well as vocational training of Italian émigrés.

The law, however, can restrict freedom of emigration or impose obligations for reasons of public interest, as it did with Article 9 of the Royal Decree-Law No. 2205/1919, empowering Executive to restrict the emigration towards a certain Region for reasons of public order in case of danger for the emigrants.

§6. Freedom of Assembly

480. Article 17 of the Constitution entitles citizens to 'hold meeting peaceably and without arms'. The wording of Article 17 should not be interpreted strictly as the freedom of assembly also applies to non-nationals.

Meetings are protected by the Constitution on condition that they are held peaceably and do not represent a threat for the safety or security of other citizens (hence the ban on arms).

The right of meeting is not subject to authorization on the part of the authorities. Citizens are free to gather in private places or in places open to the public, where access is free subject to the respect of certain conditions (theatres, universities, cinemas, etc.). On the contrary, notice must be given to the authorities for meetings in public thoroughfares (streets, squares). Specifically, the organizers of this kind of meeting must notify the police headquarters at least three days prior to the meeting. Notice is compulsory for the organizers, who can be fined in the case of non-compliance. The rights of other citizens attending the meeting should not, however, be jeopardized by the organizers' attitude, and the spontaneous meeting posing no real danger for public safety or security should not be forbidden for the simple lack of notice to the authorities (Constitutional Court, Judgments Nos 90/1970 and 11/1979).

Meetings, wherever they are held, can only be forbidden, according to the Constitution, for well-established reasons of security or public safety. Meetings in public thoroughfares must be notified in advance in order to allow the police to prevent those that may pose a risk to public security and safety, depending on the circumstances in which they are held, and also to set the time and location for such meetings. Prior notification also allows the police authorities to supervise the course of the meeting and, if necessary, interrupt it if it degenerates and becomes dangerous for public safety and security

§7. Freedom of Association

I. Associations in General

481. Protecting freedom of association is part of a wider project outlined in different parts of the Constitution. Its aim is to increase the value of social pluralism and groups, defined mainly by Article 2 of the Constitution (*see* above, §2). Article

18, which provides for freedom of association, deals more specifically with voluntary social groups. This provision is coordinated with other constitutional rules providing for some special kinds of associations, such as trade unions, political parties and religious associations.

The freedom of association supports the right to form new associations without public authorization and to join, refrain from joining, or withdraw from existing associations (the so-called negative freedom of association). Furthermore, it is forbidden to make the enjoyment of individual rights conditional on membership of any particular association, except in cases such as membership of professional associations with public interest objectives.

Article 18 protects all kinds of association, regardless of their aims unless the latter are forbidden to individuals by criminal law. The law cannot impose on restrictions on associations which are not already prescribed for individuals. Only the activities forbidden to individuals by criminal law represent a limit for associations. These are, for example, criminal conspiracy or associations connected to the Mafia (Articles 416 and 416*bis* of the Criminal Code). Consequently, if certain behaviour is not (or no longer) qualified as a crime when committed by an individual, the same activity cannot be considered a crime when conducted by an association (*see* Constitutional Court, Judgments Nos 87/1966 and 243/2001 for an interesting application of this principle).

Besides the limits deriving from criminal law, it is also forbidden to set up secret associations and associations which pursue political aims by means of organizations of military character.

The constitutional rules on secret associations were enforced by Law No. 17/1982: it is not possible to consider an association as secret, and therefore to forbid it, because it simply does not reveal its articles of association, the names of its members, or some of its activities. Secret associations can only be forbidden if, by concealing some of their characteristics, their aim is to set up occult centres of power and to pursue covert political aims. The law forbids those associations which, 'by hiding their existence and not revealing their aims and social activities, or not disclosing their members partially, entirely or even reciprocally, carry out activities aimed at interfering with the functions of constitutional organs, public authorities' (Article 1, Law No. 17/1982).

Associations with a military organization are also forbidden if they pursue political aims (Legislative Decree No. 43/1948 and Constitutional Court, Judgment No. 5/2014).

Secret and paramilitary associations are forbidden in order to protect the effective democracy of the political system, by preventing the setting up of organizations whose purpose is to conquer or administer power without respecting the democratic rules set out in the Constitution.

Associations pursuing aims which conflict with the content of Article 18 can be dissolved. Before the administrative authorities can dissolve an association, the judicial authorities must verify the existence of the conditions listed in Article 18. An important exception to this rule was the ban on the Freemasons' Lodge 'P2', dissolved by Law No. 17/1982 without judicial pronouncement.

Except for the limits set out in the Constitution, the Italian legal system provides for complete freedom of association. It must be noted that constitutional protection of social pluralism and groups has been increased by statute, especially by means of various financial measures which benefit associations which work to promote the aims of the Constitution. *See*, for instance, Law No. 266/1991 on voluntary organizations, providing for a broad range of tax allowances and incentives to registered associations carrying out social activities provided for by law and Law No. 383/2000 which recognizes the public function of 'associations of social promotion', i.e., non-profit associations carrying out social functions, at times, on behalf of the public authorities.

II. Political Parties

482. Article 49 of the Constitution protects the freedom to freely form political parties as an expression of the general freedom of association. Civil law defines political parties as simple unrecognized associations subject to the general legal status of this kind of association (Article 36 of the Civil Code). The Constitutional Court ruled that political parties are organizations of the civil society, to whom are attributed constitutional functions (Constitutional Court, Judgment No. 79/2006).

These associations are dealt with in a separate part of the Constitution because political parties are groups of people by which citizens can 'contribute by democratic means to national politics' (Article 49).

The Constitution takes party pluralism as granted when it hints at competition among political parties. Citizens can therefore set up new political groups without authorization.

The only limitation laid down by the Constitution is the democratic nature of the parties' political activities. This limit does not concern the structure and internal party organization, which is not now subject to restriction, but rather the methods of political competition with respect to other political parties. As the Constitutional Court has pointed out, the democratic method is aimed at preventing the 'violent usurpation of powers' and orientating the political action towards the 'respect of popular sovereignty entrusted to legally formed majorities, the protection of minority rights and compliance with freedoms set out in the Constitution' (Constitutional Court, Judgment No. 87/1966).

The Italian Constitution, unlike other constitutions such as the German one, for instance, does not forbid so-called anti-system parties, which do not support the values enshrined in the Constitution but instead tries to oppose them. The reorganization of the former Fascist Party, however, is prohibited, as stated by the XIIth Transitory Provision.

According to Article 98 of the Constitution, the right to join a political party is subject to limitation for those categories of citizens who must guarantee impartiality in the exercise of their public or institutional function, such as members of the judiciary, members of the Armed Forces on active duty, members of the police and diplomatic and consular representatives abroad.

The activities of Italian political parties can be funded through a system which has been the object of a lively political debate and significant reform in the last years. Initially, provision was made for a direct State subsidy as a refund of election expenses for political parties which had presented their lists in a certain number of constituencies and obtained a specified minimum result at the elections (*see* Law No. 195/1974, subsequently amended by Law No. 11/1978, Law No. 659/1981 and Law No. 22/1982). The grants for election expenses were partly allocated in equal measure to all the entitled parties, partly in proportion to the votes obtained during the elections. Provision was also made for a further State subsidy for parliamentary groups' activities and the 'functional activities of their parties'. Given the close links between parliamentary groups and parties, it is self-evident that the second grant was aimed at funding the parties. These grants too were distributed partly in equal measure to all parliamentary groups and partly in proportion to the number of their members.

This system provoked lively discussion, so much so that, when the citizens were called upon to give their opinion on the matter in a referendum held on 18 April 1993, legislation providing for State subsidy to the parties through parliamentary groups was repealed, whereas State grants to help cover election expenses remained in force as provided for by Law No. 515/1993. Subsequently, new legislation (Law No. 2/1997) was issued to allow taxpayers to decide, when paying their income tax, whether to allocate a very small share of their income tax (with a minimum set by law) to funding movements or parties with at least one elected representative in Parliament. A special tax deduction system has also been envisaged for grants in favour of movements or political parties made by both natural persons and corporations or commercial entities. However, the provisions of Law No. 2/1997 were not very successful, because very few citizens opted to support political parties through voluntary contributions.

Later on, the Parliament passed a new law focused on the refund of electoral expenses in proportion to the electoral results of each political party (Law No. 157/1999).

This system of public funding to political parties was subsequently modified (Law No. 156/2002 and No. 517/2006) and then abolished. Decree-Law No. 149/2013 (converted in Law No. 13/2014) now provides again only the possibility for every taxpayer to devote a share (the two per thousand) of his or her income tax to a political party and to fund it directly and on a voluntary basis with a low-tax regime. Not every political party, however, can receive these contributions: only the parties that adopt a statute with certain contents and that are registered in a national register and controlled by a special public commission.

III. Trade Unions

483. Another kind of association explicitly protected by the Constitution are trade unions. Article 39 states that the 'freedom in the organisation of trade unions is affirmed' and provides for the total freedom to set up, organize and become members of employees' or employers' unions. Trade unions that opted for the legal form of unrecognized associations (which give them the greatest freedom of action and organization) are thus granted full freedom and autonomy.

The Constitution does more than just enshrining the freedom and autonomy of trade unions. It gives them a special status, different from that of other associations. This provision, however, is still ineffective, given that no enforcing law has been passed to date.

According to the Constitution, without prejudice to the freedom of trade unions to be set up as simple unrecognized associations, trade unions registered with local or central offices and statutes providing for an internal organization on a democratic basis are entitled to make collective agreements which are generally enforceable (for all the members of the category of workers to which the agreements are addressed), through trade union representatives, who must reflect proportionally the wishes of their members.

Today, however, trade unions are still private associations: their collective labour agreements lack general legal enforceability and are only binding for their signatories, as all other private-law agreements.

However, since the very first years of the Italian Constitution, the Supreme Court of Cassation extended the economic effects of collective agreements to all workers belonging to a particular category because in these matters the collective agreements contain the economic parameter necessary to give practical application to the right to a sufficient wage in proportion to the quantity and quality of the work carried out. This is the so-called direct horizontal effect (in labour proceedings) of Article 36.

§8. Freedom of Religion

484. Religion is dealt with in the Constitution in many provisions: in both articles specifically dedicated to it (Articles 7, 8, 19 and 20 of the Constitution), in the enunciation of the principle of formal equality in Article 3, paragraph 1, of the Constitution, which explicitly prohibits any discrimination based on religious grounds.

Article 19 of the Constitution protects the freedom of each human being to profess and propagate his religion. Each individual is recognized and guaranteed, therefore, not only the freedom to personally adhere to a particular religion but also the freedom to propagate their faith to induce others to join, possibly through the criticism of other people's religious beliefs as long as the criticism is not expired in contempt (as Constitutional Court, Judgment No. 188/1975). Complementary to the freedom to adhere and propagate any religion is the so-called negative freedom of religion, or freedom from religion, that is not to profess any.

The Constitution also protects freedom of worship, both individually and in a group, both in private and in public places: the only limit that meets the freedom of worship is that it can be applied with rites contrary to the *buon costume* (or morality: on interpretation of this common limitation of freedom of expression, cf. below §10). This is without prejudice, however, to the application of the rules governing meetings taking place in a public area. Even if they have a religious nature, they can be prohibited or dissolved, if they might act as a threat to public safety (generally on freedom of assembly, cf. above, §6).

The Italian Constitution explicitly protects freedom of religion even in its collective moment: social groups with religious purposes are protected, whether they are associations or religious denominations, and whether the religious denomination has or not an agreement with the Italian State pursuant to Article 8 of the Italian Constitution (*see* immediately below and, as far as opening places of worship is concerned, which is considered an essential component of freedom of religion, *see also* Constitutional Court, Judgments Nos 63/2016 67/2017). So, public authorities have the duty to make places for worship available; they cannot create obstacles to such access, and they are prohibited from discriminating among religious denominations gaining access to those public spaces (Constitutional Court, Judgment No. 254/2019).

In addition, according to Article 20, 'The ecclesiastical nature and the purpose of religion or worship of an association or institution may not be due to special legal limitations or special taxation with respect to its constitution, its legal status or any form of activity.' It is forbidden, therefore, to impose special burdens on social formations because of religious purposes they may pursue.

Traditionally, in Italy, the majority of the population has always been Catholic. For this historical reason, the Italian legal system has recognized a specific position to Catholicism. The Constitution provides a concordat between the State and the Catholic Church, and an agreement for the religious denominations who wish to formalize their relations with the State (Articles 7 and 8 of the Constitution). In recent years, the main problems related to freedom of religion originated, on the one hand, by the flows of immigrants from outside the EU involving the spread of a wide variety of religions among the population, and, on the other hand, by the spread of secular positions in the public sphere. Thus, the Constitutional Court has repeatedly affirmed the principle of the secularism (*laicità*), understood as not indifference of the State before the religious experience, but the equidistance and impartiality of the law with respect to all religious denominations, as the supreme principle inviolable (Constitutional Court, Judgments Nos 203/1989, 149/1995, 334/1996, 329/1997 and 63/2016). As a result, the Constitutional Court has repeatedly intervened to affirm the equality of treatment of different religions, for example, in the field of blasphemy law (Constitutional Court, Judgments Nos 440/1995, 329/1997, 508/2000, 327/2002, 168/2005), the witness oath (Constitutional Court, Judgment No. 149/1995) and as far as tax incentives and exemptions in favour of religious denominations were concerned (Constitutional Court, Judgment No. 235/1997).

Some years ago many disputes arose regarding the display of religious symbols in public buildings such as polling stations, courtrooms and schools. In particular, the presence of crucifixes in classrooms was the subject of a complex court case, which stemmed from the Veneto Administrative Court, involved the Council of State, the Constitutional Court and even the European Court of Human Rights (ECHR). Some argue that the public display of the symbol of a religion followed by the majority of the population, as is the crucifix, is a violation of freedom of religion of the people who do not recognize this symbol, either because they follow other religious beliefs or because they are atheists. While the Constitutional Court had to dismiss on the merit the controversial question (Constitutional Court, Judgment No. 389/2004), the European Court of Human Rights has finally considered that the presence of the crucifix in Italian schools does not result in any violation of individual rights (ECHR, Grand Chamber, 18 March 2011, No. 30814/2006, *Lautsi v. Italy*). The European Court noted that the presence of a symbol does not exercise any form of compulsion on individuals, and it does not force students to acts of worship or other actions of a religious nature and thus does not violate freedom of religion. In addition, whereas in Italian public schools there is an atmosphere of openness to the presence of other religious expressions, using symbols and teaching marked with pluralism, the European Court stated that the crucifix does not determine any infringement of freedom of education.

§9. Freedom of Communication

485. Article 15 of the Constitution protects the liberty and secrecy of correspondence and all forms of communication. This liberty is different from freedom of thought since it protects the secrecy of interpersonal communications and correspondence addressed to previously determined individuals, for instance, with letters, e-mails or telephone conversations.

The liberty and secrecy of correspondence and interpersonal communications are provided for by Article 15 so that limitations on this freedom can 'only be enforced by decision, for which motives must be given, by the judiciary with the guarantees laid down by law'. This freedom is more heavily guaranteed than others, so much so that nobody, the police itself included, is allowed to interfere with these communications, save by an act of the judiciary.

The Constitutional Court has underlined that the provisions of Article 15 of the Constitution also apply to the interception of telephone calls, which must be made under the direct control of a judge (Constitutional Court, Judgment No. 34/1973). This concerns not only the content of telephone conversations but also the so-called external data, such as the time and date of the conversation, the number dialled and so forth (Constitutional Court, Judgments Nos 81/1993 and 281/1998).

§10. Freedom of Expression and Freedom of the Arts and Science

486. The freedom of speech – to use the very language of the Italian Constitution – or the freedom to express one's thought as set out in Article 21 of the Constitution has always been defined by the Constitutional Court as a fundamental element of democracy and an authentic keystone of the entire system (Constitutional Court, Judgments Nos 9/1965 and 84/1969).

The specific object of the right protected by Article 21 is the expression of thought, i.e., the freedom not only to hold any sort of opinion or conviction but also to make them manifest to other people.

Article 21 includes freedom of opinion, as well as freedom of information: since it is very difficult to distinguish facts from opinions, provision is made without distinction for the freedom to disseminate news, opinions and comments (Constitutional Court, Judgment No. 105/1972), even though the right of information as interpreted by the courts is conditioned by limitations, such as the truth of the facts described, the need to meet an effective social interest by making these facts known and the correctness of declarations (Court of Cassation No. 5259/1984). Moreover, revealing facts concerning the private life of people is subject to limits, given that the right to privacy is considered a fundamental right of the human person guaranteed by Article 2 of the Constitution.

If the exemptions for the exercise of the right to criticize and of the right to report cannot be asserted, a person can be punished with imprisonment for up to one year or with a fine of up to EUR 1,032 (Article 595 of the Criminal Code). However, the aggravated circumstance provided by Article 13 of the Press Law (Law No. 47/1948), which contemplates the mandatory penalty of imprisonment in addition to the financial penalty, has been declared unconstitutional (Constitutional Court, Judgment No. 150/2021). On that occasion, the Constitutional Court has specified that the prison sentence must be applied only in exceptional circumstances, in accordance with the Court of Strasbourg case law.

Article 21 only protects the mere expression of thought and does not cover behaviour which may influence actions. This is why the Constitutional Court considers that behaviour such as criminal incitement should not be protected by Article 21 (Constitutional Court, Judgments Nos 16/1973 and 65/1970).

The only explicit restriction laid down by the Constitution on the freedom to express one's thought is the respect of the *buon costume* (the 'morality'), which was, in the Founding Fathers' view, the respect of sexual decency (Constitutional Court, Judgment No. 1063/1988), but now is to be interpreted in a broader sense as the respect of human dignity (Constitutional Court, Judgment No. 293/2000). This restriction cannot, however, be imposed on the particular expressions of thought in the arts and sciences, given that liberty of the arts and science and the teaching of these subjects is provided for by Article 33.

Although the only explicit restriction is the *buon costume*, the Constitutional Court has identified another (implicit) limitation on the freedom of expression, i.e., public order in a material sense, implying, for instance, the prohibition to 'express one's thought freely in the middle of the night with a loudspeaker at full volume' and the need to make arrangements for public meetings and speeches which can be rescheduled if and where necessary (Constitutional Court, Judgments Nos 168/1971 and 138/1985). In general, freedom of expression must take into account all the other values enshrined in the Constitution, such as personal honour and the right to privacy, as noted before, and respect for secrets designed to protect constitutional values.

This means that freedom of expression should be reasonably balanced with other constitutional rights and values deserving the same kind of protection. In this sense, for instance, the Italian Parliament passed the long-awaited legislation to address cyberbullying, defined as any use of the internet to offend, threaten, abuse, blackmail, denigrate and steal the identity of minors (Law No. 71/2017).

Article 21, paragraph 1, also provides for the means by which thought can be expressed, i.e., 'by word of mouth, in writing and by all other means of communication'. A brief reference should, therefore, be made to the most important *media*: press, radio, television and show business.

The Constitution is only explicit with regard to the press which cannot be subject either to authorization, i.e., discretionary measures taken in advance by the public authorities, or to censorship, that is supervision of the content of documents. The only repressive means allowed is seizure, which can be ordered by the judiciary or the police in case of real urgency and when the immediate intervention of the judiciary is not possibly subject to ratification within the next forty-eight hours. Seizure is allowed only in the case of offences specified in the press law, or in the case of a violation of the provisions prescribed by law in order to render public the name of the editor-in-chief (*see* Law No. 47/1948).

Article 21, paragraph 5, of the Constitution also lays down that the law may prescribe, 'by means of provisions of a general nature, that the financial sources of a periodical publication be made known', with the clear aim of allowing the reader to be informed on the underlying interests of the various newspapers. Besides these transparency requirements, the Constitution does not deal in more detail with publishing. It was only in 1981, with Law No. 416 (and subsequent amendments) that the creation of monopolies, oligopolies and dominant positions was prohibited in the publishing sector, thanks also to the supervision of a special Independent Authority (the AGCOM). The strict restrictions on concentrations in publishing and, as we shall see later on, television companies constitute an essential element for the protection of the fundamental value of pluralism in the field of information (*see* Constitutional Court, Judgments Nos 826/1988 and 155/1990).

487. Radio and television broadcasting is not taken into consideration by the Constitution. The legislation concerning these activities has varied considerably over time. Originally, the radio and television media were a State monopoly. At around the middle of the 1970s, various decisions by the Constitutional Court opened up, although only marginally, the opportunity for private citizens to run local cable television installations (Constitutional Court, Judgment No. 225/1974) and relay stations for foreign broadcasting (Constitutional Court, Judgment No. 226/1974). The issue of concentrations of radio and television companies involved the Constitutional Court for many years, despite the silence of the Constitution about that theme and the absence in the constitutional text of the passive profile of freedom of information, that means the right of citizens to be informed. Because of the scarcity of technical resources in terms of radio frequencies available for the transmission of programmes throughout the national territory and the absolute awareness of the capacity of the television to have a persuasive impact on the will of the citizen-voter, more than other media, the Constitutional Court tried to safeguard the principle of 'external pluralism': at first the Court legitimized the public monopoly regime (Constitutional Court, Judgment No. 59/1960), but then, it took note of some technological improvements and opened up the possibility for private individuals to operate over the television systems in the local areas (Constitutional Court, Judgment No. 202/1976) and repeaters of foreign transmitting stations (Constitutional Court, Judgment No. 226/1974). In the meantime, the Constitutional Court kept promoting legislation which guaranteed a stronger degree of pluralism within the RAI (the Italian Television and Radio Network) – the so-called internal pluralism – as the sole holder of the public concession at that time. The RAI was, therefore, subject to the directives of a parliamentary Commission and the direction of a board whose members were appointed by the Presidents of the two Chambers of Parliament with a view to 'opening it to the various social, cultural and political currents' (Law No. 103/1975).

A few years later, the Constitutional Court also liberalized local television broadcasting by Judgment No. 202/1976, thus paving the way for the erosion of the State monopoly in the television sector, which was implemented also through various links among different local broadcasting stations. In less than ten years, in the absence of legislation on the use of frequencies and the problem of concentrations, Italy witnessed the emergence of some national private TV channels with the presence, which rapidly became dominant, of one single group. At the beginning, Parliament simply legalized the existing situation (Law No. 10/1985, previously Decree No. 807/1984, which the Constitutional Court found in compliance with the Constitution by Judgment No. 826/1988 only due to the provisional nature of the legislation), then, starting from 1990, passed general legislation in the TV sector (Law No. 223/1990).

The system provided for by law was mixed (public and private). The RAI owned three national networks, and private citizens were allowed to run televisions installations, upon authorization, on condition that a dominant position is not established. Most importantly, nobody is allowed to own either more than three networks or more than 25% of the networks provided for by the national plan or to create multimedia concentrations involving the press, radio and television. With regard to these restrictions, the Constitutional Court ruled that some of the provisions of Law No. 223/1990, preventing a single private citizen from possessing up to three television networks, were illegitimate because they were against the principle of 'external' pluralism in the information sector (Constitutional Court, Judgment No. 420/1994).

Later on, Law No. 249/1997 set up the AGCOM, a real independent governing body in this field, having an important control function with regard to the respect of the antitrust legislation, which was amended by the same law. The value of the 'external' pluralism in the national television broadcasting was subsequently affirmed in the Constitutional Court, Judgment No. 466/2002.

Not even the transition from analogic to digital, which radically changed the technological scenario with the multiplication of channels allowed by new technologies, has resolved the many legal issues. Regarding the theme of 'external pluralism', the regulation of audio-visual media services is still laconic about the frequency assignment method. From the point of view of 'internal pluralism', the Executive still exercises strong control over the public service, especially through its power to appoint the board of directors and the CEO of RAI.

The internet in Italy is still waiting for a comprehensive set of rules. Up until now, the ordinary courts extended to the Web the constitutional principles and the existing legislative rules, even if born to regulate other means of information. Sometimes, for instance, in matter of website seizure, the courts apply to the professional online information the same guarantees provided for the press. The European Union, with the recent approval of the Digital Service Act, has made an effort to regulate digital service. This package of rules aims to create a safe digital space in which the fundamental rights of all users of digital services are protected, on the principle according to which 'what is illegal offline is also illegal online'.

§11. Protection of the Family

488. The Constitution deals with the family and family relationships in various articles. Specifically in Article 29, which qualifies the family 'as a natural society founded on marriage'; in Article 30, which governs the relationship between parents and children, 'even if born out of a marriage'; in Article 31, which gives the public authorities responsible for promoting 'economic measures and other provisions the formation of the family and the fulfilment of its duties', and to protect motherhood, childhood and youth, promoting the institutions necessary for that purpose. In addition, the term 'family' is used in other articles: Article 36 of the Constitution, providing that the salary of the employee must provide for himself and his family an existence free and dignified life, or even Article 34, paragraph 4, of the Constitution, evoking families as recipients of checks to ensure the right to education, and Article 37 of the Constitution, providing protection to 'essential role in the family' of the woman worker.

The text of Articles 29 and 30 of the Constitution has an objective character of compromise, due to the harsh contrast between the secular and Catholic cultural trends that characterized the debate in the Constituent Assembly on many issues, such as the indissolubility of marriage and the status of children born out of the marriage. The signs of this compromise between the two parties in the constitutional text are found, for example, in the presence of specific restrictive clauses regarding equality between spouses, which can be established by law 'to ensure the family unit' (Article 29, paragraph 2, of the Constitution) and equality between legitimate children and children born to unmarried parents among them, to which the law must ensure every legal and social protection, as long as 'compatible with the rights of members of the legitimate family' (Article 30, paragraph 3, of the Constitution).

These constitutional provisions have never been the subject of constitutional reform, but over the past seventy-five years, they have been interpreted in very creative ways, which have yielded many away from the letter of the Constitution. These interpretations, on the one hand, take account of the changes in the Italian society while, on the other hand, take the moves by proper systematic interpretation of the rules governing family relations in the light of Articles 2 and 3 of Const.

In particular, the provisions limiting equality between spouses and equality among children have been understood, both by the Constitutional Court that the legislature since the reform of parts of the Civil Code concerning family law (Law No. 151/1975), as having less strength with respect to the proclamation of the equal dignity of all individuals and the general principle of formal equality without distinction of sex and personal and social conditions in Article 3, paragraph 1 of the Constitution. For instance, the Constitutional Court declared unconstitutional the provision of the Civil Code which prohibited incestuous children to act for the judicial declaration of paternity and maternity (Constitutional Court, Judgment No. 494/2002) stated that the general provision recognizing the rights of the family as a natural society founded on marriage (Article 29, paragraph 1, of the Constitution) 'does not justify a conception of the family enemy of the people and their rights', as the provision of Article 2 of the Constitution 'proclaims, in accordance with what has been called the "personalistic" principle, that the value of social formations, including prominently the family, is in the end a way to allow and even encourage the development of the personality of human beings'.

As for the spouses, the reform of family law and some judgments of the Constitutional Court have declared unconstitutional all the numerous rules that differentiated the position of the wife from that of the husband, the first of which proclaimed that the husband 'head of family', up to Judgment No. 286/2016, that declared unconstitutional the traditional legal rule that every child must be attributed its father's surname only at birth, and cannot be attributed also the mother's surname, even if so requested by both parents. In that occasion, the Constitutional Court stroke down the rule on the grounds that it violated both the principle of equality between husband and wife and the child's right to be identified from birth by the surname of both parents.

As for the children, the ruling of the Constitutional Court and legislative reforms, up to Legislative Decree No. 154/2013, have eliminated all the discriminations between legitimate children and illegitimate children in personal and property relations with parents.

Furthermore, the constitutional provision stating that 'it is the duty and right of parents to support and educate their children, even if born out of the marriage' (Article 30, paragraph 1, of the Constitution) has been subject to systematic interpretation in the light of Articles 2 and 3 of the Constitution and has acquired an autonomous meaning from the context in which it is located. Moreover, from the beginning, the matter of filiation has progressively become a base for the construction of a system of constitutional guarantees in favour of minors (the so-called status of the constitutional rights of the child). Again, a coordinated reading of the rules laid down in Articles 2, 3, 30 and 31 of the Constitution has given rise to constitutional rulings in accordance with the instructions from the numerous international conventions to which Italy is a member, the so-called principle of the best interests of the child (from Constitutional Court, Judgment No. 11/1981 up to Constitutional Court, Judgments Nos 7/2013, 272/2017, 102/2020 and 32 and 33/2021).

If these claims are commonly shared, more controversial is the relationship between Article 2 and Article 29 of the Constitution in relation to the issues raised in the constitutional protection of the de facto family and same-sex marriage.

As to the first problem, Article 2 seems also to protect a de facto family characterized by a degree of stability found, although such protection would be difficult to define in its exact content and is still less extended than the legitimate family, to which the Constitution confers a higher rank according to Article 29 of the Constitution (Constitutional Court, Judgment No. 310/1989).

As for the other issue of same-sex marriage, the Constitutional Court has made clear that the idea of family protected by Article 29 of the Italian Constitution is the traditional one, based on the marriage of a man and a woman; however, the concept of 'social group' as protected by Article 2 of the Constitution comprises also homosexual unions, seen as stable coexistence between two people of the same sex. At the same time, the aspiration for such a legal recognition of same-sex couple cannot be obtained by a judicial ruling. It is for Parliament instead, in the exercise of its sole discretion, to determine the forms of assurance and recognition (Constitutional

Court, Judgments Nos 138/2010 and 174/2014, followed by Law No. 76/2016, 'Regulations on civil unions between persons of the same sex and discipline of cohabitation').

§12. HEALTH SAFEGUARDS

489. The Constitution recognizes and guarantees health as a 'fundamental human right' and the protection of both as a right of the individual and as a collective interest (Article 32, paragraph 1, of the Constitution).

The right to health, the prevention of the disease and not to be harmed in his/her own health is, therefore, a real absolute individual right, operated in not only the vertical direction, i.e., towards the public authorities but also horizontally, towards other individuals. Hence, the right to compensation for biological damage in the event that a third party had wrongfully caused damage to the physical and mental health of others is a non-pecuniary damage that can be compensated along with other pecuniary damages (Constitutional Court, Judgment No. 233/2003). Just like every fundamental right, however, even the right to health has to be balanced and limited by other rights. A well-known case of reasonable balance stroke between the right to health (and the derived right to a healthy environment) and the right to work (from which the constitutionally significant interest of maintaining employment along with the duty incumbent upon public institutions to take all efforts to that effect are derived) is the *Ilva* case, regarding a decree-law that authorized to continue an industrial business activity recognized as strategic for the national interest even where the plant has been seized by the judicial authorities, in accordance with requirements laid down in an integrated environmental permit. In that occasion, the Italian Constitutional Court made the following general statement: 'All fundamental rights protected by the Constitution are mutually related to one another and it is thus not possible to identify any one of them in isolation as prevailing absolutely over the others. Protection must at all times be systematic and not fragmented into a series of rules that are uncoordinated and potentially conflict with one another […]. If this were not the case, the result would be an unlimited expansion of one of the rights, which would "tyrannise" other legal interests recognised and protected under constitutional law, which constitute as a whole an expression of human dignity' (Constitutional Court, Judgment No. 85/2013).

The Constitution guarantees free medical care only to the 'poor' (Article 32, paragraph 1, of the Constitution), but the legislature, by establishing the National Health Service (with Law No. 833/1978, as substantially revised by Legislative Decrees No. 502/1992 and No. 517/1993), is committed to ensuring 'maintenance' and 'recovery of physical and mental health of the entire population, regardless of social and individual backgrounds'. In this respect, the right to health is a right which creates a positive burden to public authorities and, as such, is subject to budgetary constraints. Consequently, the scope of the health care provided by the State may, therefore, vary depending on the economic circumstances. However, the level of health care can never fall below a minimum level, which guarantees the essential content of the right to health. In recent years, the economic crisis has dramatically affected the public funds and required to shrink the welfare benefits, included those related to the health care system. Moreover, a number of services that used to be provided by public institutions for free are now subject to the contribution of the citizens. In this regard, the Regions had to undergo a dramatic reduction in their financial budget and on their turns had to reduce the service to the citizens. In fact, the constitutional text, resulting after the reform of Title V of Part II of the Constitution, assigns a prominent role to the Regions in health services, as well as a concurrent legislative power between the State and the Regions in the same matter. Because of the crisis, the State legislator has reduced the funds to be handed to the Region for the health care system. However, the central State was required to guarantee a minimum standard of services, because it still retains the exclusive legislative power in relation to the 'determination of essential levels of services concerning the rights … social entitlements to be guaranteed throughout the national territory' (*see* Article 117, paragraph 2, letter. m) of the Constitution and Constitutional Court, Judgment No. 187/2012).

Health as a collective interest has led to guarantee of a healthy environment, too. A healthy environment is, however, the subject of a real individual right only when the health of the individual comes into play in a direct and timely manner.

The need to protect health as a collective interest may also require people to submit to certain medical treatments such as, for example, mandatory vaccinations (*see*, lastly, the highly controversial Decree-Law No. 73/2017, converted with amendments in Law No. 119/2017, which has added a lot of mandatory vaccinations for school-age children, and the subsequent judgment of the Constitutional Court No. 5/2018). In this regard, however, the Constitution stipulates that health care can only be imposed by the law and that in any case cannot violate 'the limits imposed by the respect for the human person' (Article 32, paragraph 2, of the Constitution). The constitutional case law has also affirmed the right to compensation from the State when, following compulsory vaccination, the individual has suffered personal damages (Constitutional Court, Judgments Nos 307/1990, 28/1998, 423/2000 and others, up to No. 107/2012). Declaring unfunded the doubts about the constitutionality of the rules imposing vaccination obligations against Covid-19, the Constitutional Court confirmed its case law, according to which the legislative measure was proportionate and in compliance with Article 32 of the Constitution, because of the need of 'a reconciliation of the right to freedom of care of the individual with the co-existing and reciprocal right of others and with the interest of the community' (Constitutional Court, Judgments Nos 14/2023, 15/2023 and 16/2023).

Currently, one of the most discussed topics on health care and on their obligation regarding end-of-life problems is the thin line between aggressive treatment and euthanasia. It is believed that Article 32 of the Constitution while protecting the right to health care protects the freedom to refuse medical treatment, even when such a refusal can result in a premature end-of-life. The problem has arisen in particularly dramatic cases where patients, for the clinical conditions in which they are found (e.g., in vegetative state), are unable to express their will. As part of a very complex and discussed case of *Eluana Englaro*, the Supreme Court of Cassation ruled that in the case of patients unable to understand and express their will, if they are in a permanent vegetative state, hydration and artificial feeding, may be interrupted if the following conditions are fulfilled when: (a) after a rigorous clinical appreciation, the vegetative state is irreversible and (b) the choice of interrupting the treatment is expressed on the basis of evidence that is clear, unequivocal and convincing, which means that the patient's voice can also come from her previous statements, her personality and lifestyle. If one of the conditions is missing, the court must deny the discontinuation of medical treatment (Court of Cassation No. 21748/2007). Ten years later, the Parliament, after several attempts, could pass a bill on this issue. Law No. 219/2017, in fact, contains provisions on living wills/advance directives and norms on informed consent to medical treatments for adults and children and on the doctor–patient shared planning of treatments. The Constitutional Court then stated that the criminalization of aiding suicide (Article 580 Criminal code) is not in itself in conflict with the Constitution; however, in extreme circumstances, 'the absolute prohibition of aiding suicide ends up unjustifiably and unreasonably limiting the patient's freedom of self-determination in the choice of therapies, including those aimed at freeing him from suffering'. These extreme circumstances were identified exactly by the Constitutional Court itself when it declared unconstitutional Article 580 Criminal code 'in the part in which it does not exclude the punishment of those who […] facilitate the execution of the suicide intention, independently and freely formed, of a person kept alive by life support treatments and suffering from an irreversible pathology, a source of physical suffering or psychological conditions that he considers intolerable, but fully capable of making free and informed decisions, provided that these conditions and the methods of execution have been verified by a public structure of the national health service, following the opinion of the territorially competent ethics committee' (as Constitutional Court, Judgment No. 242/2019, preceded by Constitutional Court, Judgment No. 207/2018; *see also* Constitutional Court, Judgment No. 50/2022, Chapter 5, paragraph 5).

§13. The Right to Education

490. The right to education is a social right based on the right to educate, including the freedom to teach and freedom to set up and run schools, and the right to education, including the freedom to choose the school and the right to be educated.

The right of instruction, laid down in Article 33, paragraph 1, of the Constitution, is one of the aspects of the freedom of expression and is, therefore, an inviolable right, which can only be limited for the purpose of protecting other interests provided for by the Constitution, through the usual balancing of values. However, since teaching, unlike the other forms of expression, is aimed at protecting the social interest of instruction, provision was made for State controls, as laid down by law, with the aim of verifying both the suitability and preparation of teachers (Constitutional Court, Judgment No. 77/1964) and ensuring that teaching is imparted according to precise programmes in compliance with the constitutional values of cultural, artistic and scientific pluralism.

Parallel and complementary to the freedom of instruction is the freedom to found and run schools by organizations and private citizens. Besides public schools which, according to Article 33, paragraph 2, must cover all types and grades of schooling, organizations and private citizens can set up and run schools not funded by the State (Article 33, paragraph 3). Although it is not subject to discretionary authorizations, the freedom to found and run schools is conditional on the need to ensure that education is correctly given. The Republic, first of all, lays down general rules for education (Article 33, paragraph 2) with the aim of establishing some basic conditions for all kinds of schools. Furthermore, the law ensures the pupils of 'private schools which apply for official recognition' must enjoy conditions equivalent to those of pupils attending public schools (Article 33, paragraph 4).

Regarding the right to education, school pluralism is guaranteed by the freedom of access to the school, which is 'available to everyone' (Article 34, paragraph 1).

In any case, the right and duty to attend compulsory and free elementary education for at least eight years is provided for by the Constitution (Article 34, paragraph 2). To be more precise, teaching services, premises and facilities necessary to the organization of the school are all free while the same does not always apply to books, means of transport, school lunches, etc. At the end of compulsory education, only 'capable and deserving' pupils, even though without financial resource, can attain the highest grades of learning by means of the contributions that the Republic guarantees within the limits allowed by law and special budget appropriation.

§14. Rights of Workers

491. In the section entitled 'Fundamental Principles', the Constitution 'guarantees the right of all citizens to work' and binds the Republic to promote such conditions as will make this right effective (Article 4). The right to work is not intended as a right to find and keep an occupation, since the State does not exert full control over the global economic situation, including places of work, in a system dominated by free-market principles (with the exception of State interventions for social purposes). Article 4, on the contrary, is aimed at affirming a fundamental constitutional value which represents an interpretative principle of all the other economic and social constitutional provisions. Such a value is also a programme and a commitment to be respected by the legislature and the other public authorities in order to implement a policy of full employment, albeit with the inevitable accommodation of other rights and interests laid down in the Constitution.

The above-mentioned instructions and commitments for public authorities must be completed with Article 35 of the Constitution, in which the Republic undertakes to safeguard labour in all its forms and the professional training of workers. In that view, Law No. 92/2012 – the so-called Jobs Act, as subsequently amended and implemented – tends to reform the labour market deterring employers from using fixed-term contracts, changing the rules on lay-offs, renewing the system of social shocks absorbers, strengthening active labour market policies and promoting the employment of women and older workers.

Article 4, however, also contains some other individual rights, such as the freedom to choose an activity or a profession (*see*, among many others, Constitutional Court, Judgments Nos 45/1965 and 248/1986); the freedom from unreasonable obstacles to admission to the chosen field of work (*see*, among many others, Constitutional Court, Judgments Nos 61/1965 and 207/1976), such as corporate-like privileges and discriminations based on sex. Article 4 also enshrines the right to carry out a working activity of one's own choice and according to the professional qualifications for which a person is employed (Constitutional Court, Judgments Nos 3/1957 and 194/1976), the right not to be arbitrarily and unfairly dismissed (*see* Constitutional Court, Judgments Nos 176/1986 and 97/1987 and more recently Constitutional Court, Judgments Nos 194/2018, 59/2021, 125/2022 and 150/2022), and so on.

Employed persons are also entitled to wages in proportion to the quantity and quality of their work and in any case sufficient to provide them and their families with a free and dignified existence (Article 36, paragraph 1, of the Constitution). This right is immediately enforceable before a court. The standards laid down in collective agreements are usually considered by the courts as the basis for judging whether wages are sufficient and proportional. Collective agreements therefore take up de facto general enforceability in the Italian system, at least as far as decisions about the economic rights of workers are concerned. The right to daily and weekly rest and to paid annual holidays (Article 36, paragraph 2) are immediately enforceable and cannot be relinquished.

Working women and children are particularly protected by the Constitution. Women are entitled to equal conditions of work and the same wages for the same work as male labour. It is worth mentioning that the Constitution also provides for the right to equal access to public office, without distinction of sex (Article 51). The only possible exceptions to equality between men and women are those which allow women to 'fulfil their essential family duties and provide for the adequate protection of mothers and children' (Article 37, paragraph 1).

The protection of work also consists in the above-mentioned freedom in the organization of trade unions (Article 39) and freedom of emigration (Article 35). We should instead concentrate on the right to strike which 'is exercised within the sphere of the laws concerning the subject' (Article 40).

Providing for the right to strike in the Constitution consisted in a reversal of the previous legislative situation, in which striking was considered a crime. Today striking is a constitutional right which can directly be enforced before a judge and freely exercised without any civil or criminal punishment. According to the Constitution, the procedures governing the exercise of this right may be set by law. Indeed, a special law provides that workers in the public utilities can strike, provided that the 'essential services' are guaranteed, i.e., without interruption of the public service (Law No. 146/1990, amended by Law No. 83/2000). At the same time, the right to strike can be restricted when it is necessary to guarantee other rights laid down by the Constitution (Constitutional Court, Judgments Nos 124/1962, 31/1969, 220/1975, 290/1974 and 4/1977).

§15. Right to Social Security and Assistance

492. The right to social assistance and the right to social security can be distinguished according to the groups of individuals who are supposed to enjoy them. The right to social assistance is aimed at guaranteeing every citizen unable to work and lacking the resources necessary for existence the basic financial resources allowing them to lead a dignified existence. Article 38 explicitly states that the right to social assistance is guaranteed to citizens unable to work and lacking the resources necessary for existence. This is a fundamental provision. The Constitution, however, also states that the main objective of the assistance for the disabled is to allow them to integrate themselves into the various fields of work. This is why the disabled and persons incapable of employment are entitled to education and vocational training by means of programmes and special facilities provided for by law.

On the contrary, the right to social security is guaranteed to workers, namely individuals who practise a profession or have practised it in the past, and is aimed at giving them adequate insurance for their requirements in case of accident, illness, disability, old age and involuntary unemployment. Both rights are immediately enforceable before a judge and oblige the State to guarantee certain services (*see* Constitutional Court, Judgments Nos 103/1981 and 349/1983). It is therefore up to the State to create a system of social assistance and security allowing individuals to enjoy these fundamental rights. The law must balance out, under the supervision of the Constitutional Court, the requirements of social assistance and security and those connected to the enjoyment of other constitutional rights and the pursuit of other general interests. The precise amount of the services supplied to citizens by virtue of the right to social assistance and security must be set by law, taking into account, of course, available financial resources. Because of the financial constraints that became evident in the years of the economic and financial crisis, the pension system was substantially revised by Decree-Law No. 201/2011, converted with amendments in Law No. 214/2011 (the so-called Fornero pension reform), that, *inter alia*, chose the contributory scheme for every type of state pension and raised the retirement age for both sexes.

The fact that these rights must be first of all guaranteed by the State does not prevent, however, spontaneous displays of solidarity, as laid down by Article 38, last paragraph which states that, ‘the freedom of private assistance is affirmed’.

§16. Economic Freedoms (Cross Reference)

493. In the section dealing with economic relations, the Constitution also guarantees some economic rights and freedoms, including freedom of economic initiative and property. For an analysis of these rights, *see* Part V, Chapter 2.

Chapter 4. The Protection of Linguistic Minorities

by Marta Cartabia

§1. Constitutional Provisions Protecting Linguistic Minorities

494. There are a number of linguistic minorities living in Italy. The largest are the German speakers and Ladin minority of the Trentino-Alto Adige Region; the French speakers of the Valle d'Aosta Region; and the Slovene speakers in parts of Friuli-Venezia Giulia. The other linguistic groups living in Italy are the small Greek, Albanian, Catalan, Provençal and Croatian minorities.

In accordance with the principles of social pluralism enshrined in Article 2, the Italian Constitution explicitly mentions linguistic minorities and guarantees their negative and positive protection.

The negative protection consists in the prohibition of discrimination against linguistic and cultural minorities living in Italy as set out in Article 3 which, after proclaiming the general principle of equality before the law, explicitly forbids any discrimination on the basis of language and race. All forms of discriminatory policies against ethnic, cultural and linguistic minorities are thus prohibited, in stark contrast to the past. In the fascist period, for example, in order to denationalize and forcedly assimilate minorities, the use of languages other than Italian was forbidden, names and surnames were forcibly Italianized, the settlement of Italian speakers in areas inhabited by linguistic minorities was encouraged and, in the case of the German speakers of Tyrol, their emigration was encouraged.

The principle of equality is not exclusively or specifically aimed at protecting minorities but forbids any form of discrimination against cultural or linguistic minorities. Article 3, paragraph 2 and Article 6 of the Constitution also provide for a positive protection of minorities living in Italy in order to preserve their cultural and linguistic identity.

495. Article 6, in particular, states that 'the Republic safeguards linguistic minorities by means of special provisions'. This constitutional rule was implemented by means of few general laws applying to all minorities living in the country, as well as by a greater number of laws protecting specific minorities such as the German and Ladin speakers in Alto Adige, the French speakers in the Valle d'Aosta and the Slovene speakers of Friuli-Venezia Giulia.

496. Recently, the Constitutional Court faced the case of a Veneto regional law classifying the 'Veneto people' as a national minority under the international Framework Convention for the Protection of National Minorities. In that occasion, it held that protection of minorities (including linguistic minorities) is a supreme principle of the pluralistic constitutional system, and that both State-level and regional and provincial lawmakers must be involved in actively ensuring the concrete effectiveness of such protection. However, the identification of national minorities must fall within the exclusive purview of the State legislator and, above all, the Regions may not classify themselves, as such, as 'national minorities', which would undermine the unity of the conglomeration of regions within the Republic (Constitutional Court, Judgment No. 81/2018).

§2. General Laws for the Protection of Minorities

497. As a general application of Article 6 of the Constitution, the Italian Parliament has issued Law No. 482/1999, which provides some guarantees for a specific number of linguistic minorities, namely the Albanian, Catalan, German, Greek, Slovene, Croatian, French, Provençal, Friulan, Ladin, Provençal and Sardinian speaking minorities (Article 2 of Law No. 482/1999). Before this general law, only fragmentary rules could be found in the legal system, such as the first law on the broadcasting system (Law No. 103/1975) which grants ethnic–linguistic minorities the right to produce and broadcast their own programmes and Law No. 935/1966 that abolished the prohibition on foreign names for Italian citizens. Today, these and other guarantees are provided in the general law on the protection of minorities. This law has opted for a system of guarantees based on the territorial settlement of the linguistic and cultural minorities so that it applies only in those municipalities where one or more linguistic minorities reside. However, the application of this law is subject to a decision taken by the Provincial Council, after following a procedure that involves the citizens and municipalities involved.

The guarantees provided by the law comprise the opportunity to use and teach languages other than Italian in preschool, primary and secondary schools, to use the language of the minority in contacts with the public administration, in official documents of local authorities, and public broadcasting. Moreover, the law contains an invitation to the central and regional governments, as well as to universities – to promote courses, research programmes and other cultural activities aimed at fostering the knowledge and diffusion of minority languages and culture throughout the country.

Last, but not least, the general law on the protection of minorities contains a specific provision to compensate for the offence caused to individual identity by the forced Italianization of names under fascist legislation and allows the citizen to keep their present names and surnames or to restore their original form (Article 11 of Law No. 482/1999).

§3. Special Rules Protecting the German and Ladin Speakers in Trentino-Alto Adige

498. Starting from the De Gasperi-Gruber agreement of 5 September 1946, many national and international norms have been enacted in order to ensure special positive protection for the German and Ladin minorities in Trentino-Alto Adige. The nature of these rules depends on the special form of territorial autonomy of the Provinces of Trento and Bolzano, as set out in the 1948 Constitution of Trentino-Alto Adige, subsequently amended in 1971. These two Provinces are entitled to an important role in the protection of the linguistic minorities living in their territories.

For example, each of them is entitled to challenge laws passed by the State, Region or Province before the Constitutional Court, for breach of 'the principle of protection of the German or Ladin minorities' (*see* Part II, Chapter 9 on the Constitutional Court).

Other rules of procedure explicitly protect minorities: for example, according to Article 56 of the Special Regional Statute, when a law is deemed prejudicial to the equality of the rights of linguistic minorities, the majority of the councillors belonging to a particular linguistic group may request that the matter be put to the vote of each linguistic group. If the request is rejected or if the law is adopted even though two-thirds of the linguistic group which made the request vote against it, this group may challenge the law directly before the Constitutional Court within thirty days of its publication. This method has only been used in a few cases, both concerning electoral matters (*see* Constitutional Court, Judgments Nos 261/1995 and 356/1998).

Moreover, regional, provincial and communal councillors of the Province of Bolzano can challenge administrative measures considered prejudicial to the principle of equality of all citizens before the Regional Administrative Court of Bolzano (Article 92 of the Special Regional Statute). The positive protection of minorities is also guaranteed by the principle of 'proportional ethnic allocation' (Article 89), thanks to which civil positions in the public administration, including the judiciary, in the Province of Bolzano, are distributed among citizens of the three linguistic groups according to the size of each group, as reported in the official population census. This method is compatible with Article 6 of the Constitution but seems to contradict other constitutional provisions, such as Article 51, providing that all citizens are eligible for public office on conditions of equality. The 'ethnic proportion' method has raised some doubts, especially concerning the respect of the privacy of the individuals who declare that they do not belong to any of the three linguistic groups. This is why the Constitutional Court ruled that it should only be applied on very special occasions.

There are many rules protecting minorities from a linguistic point of view, thus contributing to a regime of linguistic separatism. In the Trentino-Alto Adige Region, German enjoys the same status as Italian, so much so that many administrative documents are written in both languages (Articles 99–102 of Special Regional Statute). Citizens in this Region may speak either German or Italian without distinction with public officials, including the judiciary.

Education must be in the mother tongue of students, while the other language is always taught as the second language (Article 19).

It must be stressed that these provisions are only applied on a territorial basis – i.e., in Trentino-Alto Adige – and not on a personal basis: they do not protect the individuals belonging to a particular linguistic minority irrespective of where they live (Constitutional Court, Judgment No. 213/1998), but only within Trentino-Alto Adige.

§4. French Speakers in the Valle d'Aosta

499. French speakers in the Valle d'Aosta are protected first of all by the fact that they live in a 'Special Statute Region'.

Many rules protect the use of Italian and French according to a bilingual system which favours exchanges between the two linguistic groups.

According to Article 38, paragraph 1, of the Special Regional Statute of the Valle d'Aosta, French is officially equal to Italian, so that official documents may be written in either of the two languages without distinction, with no obligation to write a bilingual text. Accordingly, the State administration in the Valle d'Aosta is obliged to hire officials born in this Region or speaking French (Article 38 of the Special Regional Statute of the Valle d'Aosta).

As regards education, regional schools must provide for the same number of French and Italian classes, and teaching of some subjects in French is allowed (Article 39 of the Special Statute of the Valle d'Aosta).

§5. Slovene Speakers in Friuli-Venezia Giulia

500. In Friuli-Venezia Giulia, the presence of a linguistic minority justified the institution of a 'Special Statute Region'. However, because of the international problems concerning the area of Trieste, this Region was not created until 1963 (Constitutional Law No. 1/1963).

The protection of Slovene speakers in Friuli-Venezia Giulia is less complex than that of the minorities of Trentino-Alto Adige and the Valle d'Aosta, as recognized by the Constitutional Court, which declared that:

> Article 6 of the State Constitution and Article 3 of the Special Regional Statute – closely linked to Article 3 of the State Constitution – do not imply that the Slovene minority in the Province of Trieste must of necessity be protected by rules similar to those adopted in Trentino-Alto Adige or the Valle d'Aosta. The Italian legislature is allowed to choose manner and form used to guarantee the protection of the Slovene minority (Constitutional Court, Judgment No. 28/1982).

Indeed, with the exception of some organizational rules, the most important provisions in favour of linguistic minorities in Friuli-Venezia Giulia are contained in Article 3 of the Special Regional Statute. They guarantee equality of rights and treatment to all citizens, regardless of their linguistic group, and the protection of all their ethnic and cultural characteristics. Some rules also concern education. The teaching language is Slovene in some regional schools, even though in primary and secondary schools (though not in preschools) teaching the Italian language is compulsory, although it must be done by bilingual Italian–Slovene teachers.

Part V. Specific Issues

Chapter 1. Relations Between the State and Religious Denominations

by Marta Cartabia & Elisabetta Lamarque

§1. Equality of Religious Denominations and Their Different Relations with the State

501. The decisions of the Constituent Assembly dealing with the relations between the State and religious denominations were inspired by the principle of equality of legal treatment. The situation existing under the pre-1945 legal system was heavily conditioned by the Concordat signed in 1929 between the State under Mussolini and the Roman Catholic Church headed by Pope Pius XI. The Lateran Treaties (*Patti Lateranensi*), as they were known, recognized the independent sovereignty of the Vatican and contained a Concordat which established Roman Catholicism as the official religion of the Italian State. This effectively penalized all other religious denominations which were only allowed to operate after the Executive had certified that their basic principles were not in conflict with those of public order (Law No. 1159/1929). By contrast, the Italian Republican Constitution stresses equality of religious denominations (*see* Part IV, Chapter 3, §8, on freedom of religion) even though the Roman Catholic Church enjoys a privileged position as illustrated by Articles 7 and 8, which regulate respectively the relations between the State and the Church, and between the State and other religious denominations.

Although Article 8(1) states that, 'all religious denominations are equally free before the law' the Constitutional Court did not interpret this as meaning that all other religious denominations should enjoy same legal treatment with that afforded the Roman Catholic Church. The consequent legal disparities between the treatment of the Roman Catholic Church and other religions were not considered discriminatory given the 'ancient and uninterrupted tradition of the Italian people' vis-à-vis the Catholic religion (Constitutional Court, Judgments Nos 125/1957, 79/1958, 39/1965 and 86/1985). In recent years, however, considering the secularization of the Italian society and its pluralistic composition, the orientation of the Constitutional Court in such matters has tended to shift towards a more secular interpretation of the State's role as that of an impartial legal guarantor of all religious denominations (Constitutional Court, Judgments Nos 329/1997, 149/1995 and 203/1989; *see also*, Part IV, Chapter 3, §8 on freedom of religion), especially after the Concordat with the Church in 1984, which established that the Catholic religion was no longer the official religion of the Italian State. Indeed, the Constitutional Court has consistently reaffirmed that the principle of the secular State, on the basis of Articles 2, 3, 7, 8, 19, 20 of the Italian Constitution, does not mean that it is indifferent to the existence and operation of religious denominations but that it is instead committed to guaranteeing freedom of religion, within a context of cultural and confessional pluralism (*see* Constitutional Court, Judgments Nos 203/1989 and 63/2016).

However, the fact that the Constitution provides for agreements with all religious denominations – i.e., a Concordat with the Roman Catholic Church and a series of 'agreements' with other religious denominations – does not mean that the theoretical equality enjoyed by all religions will lead to a uniform legal treatment of the relations between the State and different religious denominations but simply implies the adoption of rules which will vary in accordance with every ad hoc bilateral agreements. It must be noted, in addiction, that the decision to start negotiations with a view to concluding an agreement with an organization is a discretionary matter for the Executive, which could be held accountable for it as a political matter before Parliament, but not before the courts: in other words, 'there is no judicially enforceable claim – for any association that so requests, asserting that it is a religious faith – to the opening of negotiations pursuant to Article 8, paragraph 3 of the Constitution' (Constitutional Court, Judgment No. 52/2016, in a case where the Union of Atheists and Rationalist Agnostics – UUAR was involved).

§2. Relations Between the State and the Catholic Church

502. Article 7 of the Constitution declares that the State and the Church are both 'independent' and 'sovereign', each within its own specific sphere of activity: jurisdiction over temporal matters in the first case and spiritual matters in the second, with matters of mutual interest, the so-called mixed matters, governed by Concordats.

Prior to the adoption of the 1948 Constitution, relations between the Italian State and the Roman Catholic Church were already based on Concordats in the form of the Lateran Treaties/1929. The Constitution accepts, and makes explicit reference to, the regulation of relations with the Catholic Church in accordance with the Lateran Treaties which were subsequently amended so that today relations between the State and the Church are regulated by the amended Concordat, or 'Villa Madama agreements' as they are known, in 1984.

Most scholars agree that the regulation of State–Church relations via the Lateran Treaties as stipulated in the Constitution does not mean that these Treaties (or any subsequent amendments to them) are part of the Constitution or enjoy the status of constitutional laws. Nevertheless, the provisions of Concordats do enjoy a special legal regime.

First, as per Article 7 of the Constitution, the Lateran Treaties may be amended by subsequent reciprocally acceptable agreements between the State and the Church implemented by Act of Parliament. If the State decides to make unilateral changes to the provisions by which the Treaties are implemented, it must carry out the procedure of constitutional amendment (*see also*, Part I, Chapter 4).

As far as contents are concerned, besides the matters regulated by the Concordat, which include respect for religious holidays, the legal status of buildings used for religious purposes, the regulation of ecclesiastical bodies and Roman Catholic universities, mention should be made of the special status of religious marriage (Article 8 of the Concordat/18 February 1984) and Roman Catholic religious instruction in State schools (*ibid.*, Article 9).

As regards the former, the Lateran Treaties recognize the civil validity of marriage celebrated according to Roman canon law on condition that the bans of marriage be published, that the priest officiating explain the civil effects of marriage to the married couple by reading them the relevant sections of the Civil Code and that the act be registered in the public register of marriages. Italian law also recognizes the validity of religious decrees annulling marriages issued by ecclesiastical courts after a civil Court of Appeal has certified that this has been done in compliance with Italian civil law.

The second key aspect of the relations between the Italian State and the Church is Roman Catholic religious instruction in State schools. In addition to guaranteeing the Roman Catholic Church, together with other organizations and citizens, the right to establish private non-State schools, subject to private school regulation (*see* Article 33 of the Constitution and Part IV, Chapter 3, §13), and given 'the value of religious culture and the fact that Catholic principles are part of the historical heritage of the Italian people', the Italian Republic provides Catholic religious instruction in all State primary and secondary schools. School students are entitled to choose whether or not to take religious instruction: parents choose for primary and secondary school students and high school students decide for themselves. After the new Concordat came into force in 1984, however, the problem arose as to whether students opting out of religion instruction should be obliged to choose another subject to substitute it. The Constitutional Court eventually ruled that those not wishing to attend Roman Catholic religious instruction to be in a condition of 'non-obligation' and therefore not legally obliged to attend other classes (Constitutional Court, Judgment No. 203/1989).

The financial side of the relations between the State and the Church was reformed by the 1984 Villa Madama agreements, which provide, pursuant to Law No. 222/1985, the assignment of a percentage of personal income tax to the Church. More precisely, taxpayers may allocate the so-called eight per thousand of their tax yield to finance social or humanitarian projects run by the State and for religious purposes such as financial support of the clergy, charity activities directly carried out by the Catholic Church and other religious denominations. Taxpayers must specify their choice in their annual tax return and, if they prefer not to express any preference, the 'eight per thousand' is automatically allocated according to the highest proportion of the total preferences expressed. The law also provides tax relief for those making donations to religious non-profit-making associations or bodies.

§3. Relations Between the State and Other Religious Denominations

503. The main aspects of the legal status of religious denominations in Italy are their freedom of organization (Article 8(2)) and the power to enter into agreement with the State.

Article 8 allows religious denominations to regulate their internal organization by means of legal provisions provided these are in compliance with the fundamental principles of the Italian legal system. In turn, the State is debarred from regulating in matters relating to the operation or existence of religious denominations. This was confirmed by the Constitutional Court, which ruled that a part of the State provisions governing the eligibility requirements for members of the Councils of Jewish Communities were unconstitutional (Constitutional Court, Judgment No. 43/1988).

Relations between the State and religious denominations are regulated by State laws on the basis of agreements with the representatives of those denominations. When the negotiations between a religious denomination and the Executive are successful, an agreement is signed. At this point, if Parliament decides to pass a law, its content must conform to the aforementioned agreement.

Thus, the provisions are included in an atypical law, preceded by an agreement with the religious denomination. It should be noted that Article 8 provides for a system of sources of law similar to the laws implementing agreements with the Catholic Church, even though they cannot depart from constitutional principles, as is the case for the rules of the Concordat with the Roman Catholic Church. Since 1984, the year of the amendment of the Concordat with the Catholic Church, there has been a sharp rise in the number of agreements with other religious denominations. To date, agreements have been signed with the representatives of the Waldensian communities, the Union of Jewish Communities, the Assemblies of God in Italy, the Seventh Day Adventist Church, the Baptist Church, the Lutheran Church, the Orthodox Archdiocese, the Church of Jesus Christ of Saints of Last Days, the Apostolic Church, the Italian Buddhist Union, the Italian Hindu Union and the Italian Buddhist Institute Soka Gakkai.

The content of these agreements, though it varies to some extent in accordance with the specific needs of different religious denominations, is very similar to part of the 1929 Concordat with the Catholic Church.

Such agreements include, for example, rules on spiritual assistance in barracks, hospitals, nursing homes, rest homes and prisons; rules governing religious instruction in schools, marriage, buildings used for religious purposes, religious holidays (especially for Judaism in order to avoid possible conflicts in the workplace) and rules regulating financial relations with the State. With regard to this last point, it should be stressed that most of the religious denominations which signed an agreement with the State are entitled to be allocated the so-called eight per thousand of taxable personal income, as established for the Catholic Church.

Chapter 2. The Economic Constitution

by Marta Cartabia

§1. The Italian Way to a Mixed Economy

504. The choice of an economic model as the basis for the Italian Constitution was a very difficult and controversial choice for the Constituent Assembly. Members of different cultural and political tendencies – i.e., Liberals, Catholics and the Left – were to struggle dramatically on this matter. Their economic models were different: the Liberals were oriented towards a market economy, the Left was inspired by the idea of a collectivist economy and the Catholics were ready to accept free-market economy but only if properly controlled, in order to pursue social justice aims. A compromise was reached also thanks to the fact that, on the one hand, the Liberals were not absolutely firm on a pure form of market economy and were ready to accept some degree of public intervention in private and free competition. On the other hand, the Left did not consider that the means of production could be rendered collective, at least in the short term, and were therefore ready to accept that, for the time being, private individuals would play a prominent role, provided that a different development of the economic system was not to be absolutely excluded in the future. Therefore, in economic matters, the choice of the Constituent Assembly was a compromise accepted by everyone and made possible by the will of all political parties to avoid freezing the economic model on a particular form in order to allow for system change in the future. Therefore, only some fundamental elements of the economic system were set out in the Constitution, so that different possibilities of development were left open for the future. The agreement outlined an economic system based principally on private enterprise, without excluding the idea of an actual State economy and above all without leaving the country's economic life to the whims of the market. On the contrary, the Constitution states that freedom of private enterprise is controlled by the State which is responsible for correcting the market in order to direct free economic activity towards the ends of social justice. In fact, all rights and freedoms accorded to private individuals in the economy are precisely limited and conditioned by social rights and interests, strongly protected by the Italian Constitution. Thus, private economic enterprise 'cannot be in conflict with social utility', and the law prescribes such planning and controls as may be advisable for 'directing and coordinating public and private economic activities towards social aims' (Article 41 of the Constitution). Private property can be limited in order to 'ensure its social function' (Article 42). Collectivization and nationalization are possible in order to pursue 'purposes of general utility' concerning economic activities with 'a character of general interest' (Article 43). Regulation governing the ownership of land must be aimed at 'equitable social relations' (Article 44). Cooperation is recognized and guaranteed for its 'social function' (Article 45).

Employee involvement in company management, set out in Article 46 of the Constitution, is aimed at the 'economic and social progress of labour'. The Constitution constantly reaffirms the importance of social interests in the economic field, thus underlining, on the one hand, the choice of a mixed economy, a social market economy, where public and private actors coexist; on the other, it specifies the kind of mixed economy shaped by the Constitutional Assembly: State intervention in a capitalist economy aims at pursuing social justice. To be more precise, it aims at the social purposes described in other parts of the Constitution, starting from Article 2 which, after stating the inviolability of constitutional rights, underlines the 'unalterable duties of economic, political and social nature', and from Article 3(2), which states that 'it is the responsibility of the Republic to remove all economic and social obstacles which [...] prevent the full development of the individual'. Mention should also be made of social rights, recognized and guaranteed by Title II of Part I of the Constitution: the right to health services, education, social assistance and security and so on. Therefore, the Constituent Assembly, as it included the Italian Republic among the mixed-economy countries, also established precise and peculiar features of the economic and social system, i.e., the inclusion of social aims in the configuration of economic activities.

Therefore, these were the fundamental choices of the Constituent Assembly as far as the economy was concerned. As to the actual relations between State-owned and private companies, and between private enterprise and State intervention in the economic sector, the Constitution left much room for manoeuvre to future legislators, who were allowed to change the shape of the Italian economic system and to transform it over time, always within the limits mentioned above. In fact, social aims for which the legislator can limit and control the free-market economy are stated in the Constitution by means of basic principles which acquire a particular meaning when placed in their historical context. They change in history as they are characterized by a great dynamism: The meanings of social interest, social aims, public interests, social function – all expressions used in the Constitution – cannot be determined previously, and in the abstract, they change according to the concrete historical situation. The Constitution stipulates that various rules should be established by law, thus giving legislators the opportunity to monitor and directing economy towards social aims, according to the needs of society and to the political tendency of the majority in a given historical moment.

Hence, even though they are supposed to respect the limits of a controlled market economy system – which accepts the coexistence of private, public and social factors and excludes collectivism – for example, legislators have had the opportunity to adapt economic and social relations to political transformations. This is why, during the last seventy years, the Italian Republic has gone through different phases in which economic and social relations have changed deeply. It is evident that, from the creation of the Italian Republic to the end of the 1980s, State intervention in economic and social matters has grown continuously, with a peak at the end of the 1980s. In that period, the State became an economic agent or entrepreneur, in a more or less direct form as the main agent of the welfare system with public health services and social security, although financial or other contributions to private companies have not been completely eliminated.

Obviously, this raised public expenditure to very high levels, to a point where it was impossible to control, which, together with other factors, led to a reversal of the trend, starting from the beginning of the 1990s, also due to changes in the European legal system, starting from the Maastricht Treaty.

505. The Italian legal system is currently characterized by a decrease in State intervention in the economic sector, thus favouring the sort of market expansion which needs greater control. This tendency is clearly shown, on the one hand, by the privatization of economic activities previously carried out by the State and, on the other, by the regulation of private competition.

506. As far as privatization is concerned, it must be stressed that it consisted of two different phases, ended in the early 1990s: in the first, State-owned companies become joint-stock companies and in the second, their shares are sold to private companies or individuals.

As to provisions on competition, the first relevant intervention of the legislator was Law No. 287/1990, which was modelled on the corresponding European rules and was based on three main principles: the prohibition of a dominant position of a unique enterprise in its own market; the prohibition of agreements among groups of companies working in the same sector aimed at, or having the effect of, preventing, tightening or heavily distorting competition; and the control of mergers. In the same law an ad hoc Independent Authority (*the Autorità Garante per la Concorrenza e il mercato* – AGCM) was set up in order to monitor compliance with correct market behaviour and competition law. It is modelled on independent administrative authorities, which are increasingly common in the Italian and other European legal systems. This organ is in charge of monitoring the market by carrying out investigations in specific economic sectors aimed at ascertaining and punishing violations of competition law.

Moreover, from the beginning of the 2000s, competition has gained in constitutional significance because Article 117, paragraph 2, of the Constitution, after the constitutional reform of 2001, establishes that the State has the exclusive legislative powers in the matter of 'competition protection'. Consequently, the Constitutional Court, in passing judgments on the constitutional legitimacy of laws issued by the State or the Regions, had to define the notion of competition and draw the consequences from it. The Court affirmed that the concept of competition under national law reflects that adopted under European and international law and includes not only every antitrust measure (for instance: legislative protection measures *stricto sensu* applicable to the decisions and actions of undertakings that have a negative impact on the competitive structure of the markets, and which regulate control procedures including, if applicable, penalties; legislative measures to promote competition which seek to open up a market or to consolidate their opening by eliminating entry barriers, reducing or eliminating restrictions on the free expression of entrepreneurship and competition between companies, and in general the restrictions on the procedures for carrying on economic activity), but even every liberalization action that aims at ensuring and promoting competition 'in the market' and 'for the market' (Constitutional Court, Judgments Nos 401/2007, 430/2007, 160/2009, 45/2010, 270/2010, 200/2012 and so on, up to No. 287/2016).

Finally, in more recent times, the Parliament has passed the first annual 'Law on Market and Competition' (Law No. 124/2017). This regular tool aims at promoting the development of competition, guaranteeing consumer protection pursuant to the EU principles, stimulating innovation and attracting more investment in Italy. The areas covered by this first annual law are insurances, pension funds, communication, postal services, energy, environment, banking, lawyers and notaries, engineers, dentists, pharmacies, transports, tourism.

§2. The Two Fundamental Principles of the Economic Constitution: Freedom of Economic Enterprise and Property

507. In a narrow sense, economic rights, guaranteed by Title II, Part I, of the Constitution, are based on two fundamental principles: freedom of economic enterprise and property. Actually, the Constitution includes a high number of provisions concerning economy: nationalization (Article 43), agricultural ownership (Article 44), cooperation (Article 45), the right of workers to participate in management (Article 46), savings, issuing of credit and purchase of homes (Article 47), to cite the main ones. Nevertheless, they can all be unified under the two elements of economic enterprise and property: all other provisions in this field are only specifications or applications of the same principles. In fact, nationalization, the exclusive presence of the State in some economic activities and worker involvement in management derive from constitutional principles governing the freedom of economic enterprise (Article 41), while laws concerning agricultural ownership, savings and housing policies are a natural effect of the general principles established for property (Article 42). This is why special attention should be paid to Articles 41 and 42 of the Constitution, which set out the basic principles of economic relations applying to the laws of the various sectors.

To be more precise, in the reading of the Constitutional Court, the constitutional provisions on economic activities and those relating to property are strictly intertwined. This is clearly demonstrated by the decisions of the Constitutional Court, which do not distinguish the scope of Articles 41 and 42 of the Constitution, also because regulation of economic activity implies similar laws for property, at least concerning the means of production and products deriving from economic activities. In fact, the Constitution implies the coexistence of public and private economic activities and ownership with strong limitations on the rights of private companies aimed at guaranteeing the social function of the Italian model of mixed economy or social market economy provided for by the Constitution.

As a matter of fact, through the different interpretation of Article 41, the constitutional case law has emphasized in turn, the right of private economic initiative, which valorizes the adoption of measures to protect competition and imposes the abolition of all the restrictions to markets, on the other side opportunity of bolstering interventions that derogate the principle of free markets in order to protect the rules on essential public services, needed in the actual context of financial and economic crisis (Alitalia case, Constitutional Court, Judgment No. 270/2010).

§3. PRIVATE AND PUBLIC AGENTS IN ECONOMIC PRODUCTION

508. The provision which most of all places the Italian 'Economic Constitution' among mixed-economy models is Article 41 which, after stating that 'private economic enterprise is open to all', specifies that 'it cannot be in conflict with social utility or be prejudicial to security, freedom or human dignity' and that 'law establish suitable plans and controls in order to direct and coordinate public and private economic activity towards social aims'.

First of all, this rule implies the existence of economic activities carried out by public agents in addition to private individuals. Article 43 also confirms that the State can participate directly in economic life by stipulating that some economic sectors can be reserved or transferred to the State, public bodies or workers' or consumer communities (Article 43). Reserving or transferring companies to the State (nationalization), the Regions (regionalization), the Communes (municipalization) or workers (socialization) is an extraordinary intervention as it can only involve companies or groups of companies which provide essential public services or monopolies; it must also involve companies with a 'general interest' character. Collectivization must pursue the public utility and if it derives from expropriation, compensation must be paid to private individuals or enterprises formerly carrying out the economic activity. If we consider how the right of collectivization is limited by the Constitution, it is clear that the Italian legal system chose to prevent the State from taking over part, or the majority of, the means of production. As a result, collectivization has always been rare in Italy. Since the Constitution came into force, Article 43 has only been applied twice, when ENI (*Ente Nazionale Idrocarburi*, National Hydrocarbon Agency) was given the sole right to carry out research and produce hydrocarbons in some geographical areas (Law No. 6/1957), and the nationalization of companies producing electricity, which led to the creation of ENEL (*Ente Nazionale dell'Energia Elettrica*, National Electricity Agency) by Law No. 1643/1962.

It must be noted that, in order to respect Article 41, economic activities carried out by the State must comply with profitability rules: were this not the case, State-owned companies would be privileged compared to private companies and would, in the last instance, jeopardize the freedom of private enterprise thus conflicting with Article 41.

State participation in the economy reached extremely high levels, especially with the system of *partecipazioni statali*, based on a network of joint-stock companies operated by a private regime but whose shares were State-owned, mostly by finance holding companies run by government. Starting in the nineties, this system has been reformed by an extensive programme of privatization, in order to reduce the levels of State participation.

§4. FREEDOM OF PRIVATE ECONOMIC ENTERPRISE

509. As stated above, Article 41(2) establishes *limitations* to the freedom of private economic enterprise, by specifying that 'it cannot be in conflict with social utility or prejudicial to security, freedom or human dignity', while Article 41(3) specifies the *means* to condition economic activities officially: 'the law prescribes such planning and controls as may be advisable for directing and coordinating public and private economic activities towards social objectives'.

Article 41 provides for two kinds of State participation in private economic activity: it establishes negative limitations, leaving private entrepreneurs the opportunity to operate freely but with limits which can be resumed in the prohibition of putting profit before human dignity and social objectives (Article 41(2)), and positive limitations by which public authorities can regulate economic activity: economic planning which can be developed by the State and relative advisable controls.

Economic planning, its limits and its being more or less binding caused much debate, maybe more than anything else, both within the Constituent Assembly and, afterwards, in the political world. In fact, while drafting the Constitution, legislators were involved in a controversy because of an amendment which suggested the introduction in the Constitution of a law establishing that: 'in order to guarantee the right to work of all citizens, the State will coordinate and regulate production activities, according to a plan ensuring the best profitability to the community'. This suggestion caused much alarm and the fear that it would legitimize the sort of economic planning, typical of a State-controlled economy, precisely when the Constituent Assembly was heading towards a form of market economy, albeit a controlled one. Therefore, the Assembly decided to avoid any other reference to economic planning by the State, in favour of more neutral interventions aimed simply at directing, without constraining free private activity by introducing too strict rules.

This form of planning is not in conflict with private economic enterprise, as set out in Article 41(1), also because, as asserted by most academic commentators and by some judgments of the Constitutional Court, it is not the economic activity which is free, but the economic enterprise. This means that even though a private individual is free to start and carry out an activity, this does not mean that they be allowed to do so unconditionally. Economic activity is limited by Article 41(1)(2) so that if a private individual does not think it suitable or profitable to carry out an activity on State conditions, they can renounce it, but if the activity is continued, the entrepreneur cannot ignore such limitations.

Public intervention in the economic sector has been of different kinds, such as determining official prices, which limits freedom of contract is one of its most significant aspects. More often, these measures consisted in favouring or discouraging entrepreneurial decisions by making them profitable or disadvantageous. One example was granting tax relief or financial facilities to those who took socially useful decisions, such as investing funds in the disadvantaged *Mezzogiorno* or creating new jobs.

On the contrary, the controversial total economic planning, although included in the Constitution, was never put into practice.

§5. Cooperative Societies, Handicraft and Small Industries

510. Article 45 of the Constitution lists two particular kinds of economic activities: cooperation on a basis of reciprocity and artisan trades. Both are very much encouraged because they allow a greater participation of workers in the economic organization of the country, according to the fundamental principles set out in Article 3(2). The Constitution favours these forms of production by providing that promotion of cooperation on a basis of reciprocity, as well as protection and development of artisan trades guaranteed by law.

The main characteristic of *cooperative societies* is that they are non-profit-making, but instead provide benefits to their members. Usually, these benefits are not financial, but in goods or services, or even jobs or preferential conditions. The Civil Code also distinguishes them from associations and foundations on the one hand, and business societies on the other, because of their special purposes.

Article 45 of the Constitution stipulates that the special features and objectives of these societies must be subjected to proper controls and that they must be recorded in special prefect's registers and submitted for ministerial supervision. In recent years, means of supporting and providing incentives to cooperative societies were established by law, in accordance with the Constitution. Special mention should be made of Law No. 59/1992, generally providing for cooperative societies; Law No. 381/1991 on associations providing educational, social and health care services or carrying out activities to help the disabled find employment; and Law No. 460/97, on the non-profit organizations of social value (Onlus).

Artisan trades, frequently characterized by owner-employees (*see* Law No. 443/1985), are protected and have less administrative and accounting burdens than those usually imposed on other companies.

§6. Worker Participation in Management

511. Article 46 of the Constitution recognizes the right of workers to participate in management, in accordance with Article 3(2), which promotes workers' participation in economic organization. The fundamental purpose of this article is to favour all forms of cooperation between work and capital 'with a view to economic and social progress of labour'. The forms of participation are not defined in the Constitution which leaves the legislators the task to establish their manner and limits. In any case, worker involvement in company management is subject to production requirements.

The most important applications of Article 46 are to be found in the Workers' Statute (Law No. 300/1970, especially Articles 9 and 19), which accords powers of cooperation, control and influence on company management to trade union delegates, rather than to workers directly. There is no provision for forms of joint management such as those found in Germany.

§7. Ownership in the Italian Constitution

512. The Italian Constitution accepts different kinds of ownership: first, Article 42 guarantees both State and private ownership. Second, as private ownership is not regulated directly by Article 42 but by ordinary laws, property regulation varies according to the kind of goods taken into account. This is why there is not a unique set of rules governing ownership, but rather a multiplicity of laws which can vary considerably. Since the social value of a country estate is very different from that of a work of art, a quarry, a car or a building, legislators valued property interests and social requirements differently, so that different kinds of goods are governed by different property regulations. However, albeit within limits, it is the Constitution which allows differential property regulation besides Article 42, other laws explicitly provide for and promote land ownership, especially small or medium-sized holdings (Article 44), and the purchase of homes and holdings directly farmed by the owners (Article 47).

§8. Public Ownership

513. As far as public ownership is concerned, the owners are the State, local public bodies (Regions, Provinces and Communes) and other public bodies. They can all own real estate and land according to rules very similar to provisions on private ownership. From this point of view, public ownership only differs from private property in that the owners are public bodies. Nevertheless, some public bodies, such as the State, Regions, Provinces and Communes can own a special kind of public property, having a particular legal status (Article 822 and ff. sections of the Civil Code). This public property is part of the public domain and the patrimony of the State.

The public domain consists in land ownership and some real estate such as libraries and museums, explicitly listed in the Civil Code. These properties can be natural or artificial. The former are at the service of the community (the seashore, rivers, lakes, etc.), and the property belongs, of necessity, to the State.

The latter are created to satisfy community needs and are part of the public domain only if they belong to one of the above-mentioned public bodies: this is the case for roads and motorways, waterworks, historical interest buildings, etc. The public domain is inalienable; it cannot be subjected to *usucapione* (a means of acquiring ownership by possession of a thing for a given length of time) nor expropriated. It can be transferred from one public body to another (e.g., from the State to a Region).

The properties of the patrimony of the State are listed in the Civil Code (Article 826) and include forests, mines, quarries, public buildings, etc. Their purpose must be public even when they are transferred.

§9. Private Ownership

514. As stated above, the Constitution recognizes private as well as public ownership insofar as, '[O]wnership is public or private'.

The Constitution does not describe private property as an inviolable right, as was the case in the previous legal system. The legislator can limit and regulate its acquisition and enjoyment in order to ensure its social function and render it accessible to all (Article 42). Nevertheless, this does not mean that private property regulation is only a legislator's duty, first because it cannot be abolished by the legislator as the Constitution guarantees the existence of both public and private ownership.

Second, the Constitution states that private ownership should be limited to guaranteeing its social function or to rendering it more accessible. From a legal perspective, the concept of social function is obviously an indefinite one; it is a kind of valve whose meaning is determined mostly by the legislator. Nevertheless, laws which limit private property can be submitted to the review of the Constitutional Court which verifies the legislator's decisions, also in terms of the principle of reasonableness. Lastly, limitations on private ownership must have an objective and general character; i.e., they must establish the general legal regime of the properties or certain category of properties. If this is not the case, i.e., if the limitation concerns a single and particular property, the constitutional principles on expropriation must be applied.

§10. Expropriation and Partial Expropriation

515. The Constitution explicitly provides for expropriation (Article 42, paragraph 3), i.e., actions to deprive an individual of the ownership of a particular property in cases prescribed by law, in the general interest, with provision for compensation.

As stated above, expropriation – provided for by Article 42, paragraph 3 – does not consist only in the total deprivation of property or of another right, but also in the so-called partial expropriation: measures which strongly affect the ownership of a particular property, such as the imposition of military requisition or restraints in the field of town planning to an indefinite time (*see* Constitutional Court, Judgments Nos 6/1966 and 138/1993). This kind of expropriation must comply with Article 43, i.e., be prescribed by law, be of general interest and be compensated. Partial expropriations hence differ to a great extent from the general limitations imposed on private ownership set out in Article 42. According to the Constitutional Court, the fundamental difference between non-compensated limitations and partial expropriations is the fact that the former are general and the latter are particular (*see* Constitutional Court, Judgment No. 328/1990): limitations imposed on an individual must be compensated, while limitations imposed on entire categories of properties are intended to ensure the social function of the property, according to law.

Compensation for expropriation does not necessarily correspond to the property's market value: the Constitutional Court concluded that compensation does not always mean the total refund of the value of the expropriated property. In any case, compensation must be serious: it cannot be purely symbolic, insignificant or apparent, or completely ignore the characteristics of the property. At the moment, according to the Constitutional Court, compensation should correspond to a percentage of the commercial value of the property. Hence, the refund is calculated on the basis of the market value of the property (*see* Constitutional Court, Judgment No. 130/1993). It has to be intended as a 'fair compensation' (the phraseology used by the Court is *serio ristoro*): *see*, for example, Constitutional Court, Judgment No. 148/2008 that, considering the case law of the European Court of Human Rights, declared unconstitutional some provisions regarding housing legislation in the part in which they provided 'still and undifferentiated counting criteria'.

§11. Land Ownership

516. Agriculture is given special attention in the Italian Constitution, both to land ownership and to economic agricultural activities. This is not surprising, given that Italy had an agriculture-based economy at the time in which the Constitution was written.

Article 44 describes the main objectives and instruments to carry out a far-reaching agricultural reform. The objectives of the reform are the 'rational utilization of the land' and the establishment of equitable social relations (i.e., better production efficiency and more social equity), which should be obtained by promoting the purchase of holdings directly farmed by the owners. If we consider these two objectives in the historical context of the Constitution, it is clear that the main target was large landed estates. The possession of land by a few owners was considered one of the main social injustices in an agriculture-based country. Moreover, it was not a productive economic system since it promoted extensive farming without encouraging agricultural transformation. Article 44 clearly opposes large estates when it calls for their transformation, the imposition of limits to private land ownership, the institution of productive units and suggests incentives for small and medium-sized holdings. Likewise, Article 47 states that 'the Republic … encourages … the purchase of … holdings directly farmed by the owners'.

In the 1950s, all legislation on agricultural reform applied in certain regions went in the same direction. At the same time, agricultural contracts were reformed and uncultivated lands were assigned.

§12. Private Savings and the Purchase of Homes

517. Article 47, paragraph 2, favours private savings, especially when allocated for the purchase of homes, of holdings directly farmed by the owners, or invested in large productive national enterprises. Article 47 both commits the legislator to implement the objectives therein and forbids all other provisions in conflict with them. It aims at protecting modest and long-term private savings from inflation. This law has been interpreted as a prohibition for the State from carrying out inflationary monetary policies likely to have negative repercussions on private savings.

Chapter 3. International Relations

by Giovanni Guiglia

§1. Drafting Treaties

518. With regard to international relations, the fundamental provisions are contained in the basic principles of the Constitution of Italy (Articles 10 and 11) and in the constitutional reform of Title V.

This reform has introduced important innovative elements (in particular as regards Articles 117 and 120 Constitution), rationalizing praxis and unsatisfactory legislative dispositions.

Above all, and without analysing the relations between the Italian legal system and the EU in this context, the innovations concern:

- the assertion of the constraints deriving from international obligations for all legislative, national and regional acts (Article 117(1) of the Constitution);
- the subjection to the exclusive national legislation of 'foreign policy', but also of 'the international relations of the State' (Article 117(2) (*a*) of the Constitution);
- the concurrent legislation of the 'international relations with Regions' (Article 117(3) of the Constitution);
- the recognition of Regions' competence to implement international agreements concerning subject matters of regional competence 'in accordance with the procedural rules set out in State law' (Article 117(5) of the Constitution);
- the external power of Regions: 'in the areas falling within their responsibilities, Regions may enter into agreements with foreign States and local authorities of other States in the cases and according to the forms laid down by State legislation' (Article 117(9) of the Constitution);
- the substitutive power of the State, that can act 'for bodies of the regions, […] in case of failure to comply with international rules and treaties or EU legislation' (Article 120(2) of the Constitution).

Article 117(1) of the Constitution states that 'Legislative powers shall be vested in the State and the Regions in compliance with the Constitution and with the constraints deriving from EU legislation and international obligations.'

This article introduces a new disposition, which is innovative for the State but not for the Regions, and that is original as regards obligations based on agreements. In fact, Article 10(1) of the Constitution already provided for the obligations derived by general custom. This disposition represents a principle of juridical civilization aimed at avoiding that the State, while infringing obligations freely accepted towards other States, may commit international crimes – although in a legal way at national level.

At the same time, Article 1(1) of the Law implementing the above-mentioned Title V of the Constitution, No. 131/2003, delivers that the Italian legal system consisting State and Regions conforms to the generally recognized principles of international law (Article 10 of the Constitution), and agrees to the limitations of sovereignty deriving from *international treaties* and other agreements (Article 11 of the Constitution). By using the expression '*international treaties'*, the provision states that the regional legal system must respect the treaties Italy stipulates in simplified form, as afterwards explained.

519. As regards the powers of the constitutional bodies concerning the relations between Italy and other States, the Constitution, on the one hand, only provides for the President of the Republic to ratify international treaties upon authorization of the Parliament, whether required, to accredit and receive diplomatic representatives (Article 87(8) of the Constitution) and to make declarations of war as have been agreed by Parliament (Article 87(9)of the Constitution; *see* Part II, Chapter 2); on the other hand, it states that 'Parliament shall authorise by law the ratification of such international treaties as have a political nature, require arbitration or a legal settlement, entail change of borders, spending or new legislation' (Article 80 of the Constitution; *see* Part II, Chapter 4).

It should be noted that the legislative initiative, in this case, despite the different opinions that can be found in the doctrine, is not reserved for the government: several parliamentary initiative bills, authorizing the ratification of international treaties, have been declared admissible, in particular from the thirteenth legislature onwards.

The last paragraph of Article 72 of the Constitution, also provided the authorization to the ratification, stating that 'the ordinary procedure for consideration and direct approval by the House [of Parliament] is always followed in the case of […] ratification of international treaties […]'. In other words, the possibility for a parliamentary Commission to authorize such treaties is excluded.

Besides, according to the Constitutional Court (Judgment No. 16/1978) and the legislative dispositions for the execution of the treaties, the law to authorize the ratification of the international treaties cannot be submitted to abrogative *referendum* pursuant to Article 75 of the Constitution (*see* Part I, Chapter 5). As well, there is no other form of popular consultation or involvement in the procedure to form treaties.

Therefore, the Italian Constitution granted the ancient principle of the ratification of treaties by the President of the Republic, as the solemn expression of the State's will to bind itself towards other States under the international law, and to regulate the Parliament's role in forming some types of treaties. With reference to the powers and functions of the constitutional bodies, there is no mention at the national level about *the initiative, the negotiation and the signature of international agreements*. Moreover, there was no related mention in the Constitution before the reform of Title V concerning the so-called external power of the Regions.

Now, the new Article 117(3) of the Constitution, refers to the concurring legislation applied to the 'international relations' of the Regions, and Article 117(9) of the Constitution, recognizes this regional role establishing that Regions can stipulate agreements with States, and treaties with local territorial bodies.

520. Except for the above-mentioned limited regional powers, the government, conforming to the *foreign policy* and the *international relations* as exclusive competence of the State (Article 117(2)(*a*) of the Constitution; *see also* Constitutional

Court, Judgment No. 211/2006), undertakes all the necessary measures to form treaties, even when the Constitution is silent in regard to this competence. These measures are obviously different from the dispositions that the Constitution precisely provides for about the President of the Republic (*ratification*) and the Chambers (*authorization to ratification*, whether required). Basically, the government has competence in the *negotiation* and the *signature of the treaties*, as well as the initiative to *undertake the same negotiations*, including the foreign power within the governmental function of political agenda. The Ministers Plenipotentiary have the power to negotiate and sign treaties' drafts: the Head of the State formally conceive their powers after government's proposal, while the President of the Council and the Foreign Minister may sign an agreement without gaining full powers.

Furthermore, the Constitution does not provide any government's formal obligation to inform previously the Parliament, except for the dispositions of Article 80 of the Constitution.

Only with the entry into force of Law No. 839/1984, it has finally been foreseen that the executive must inform the Parliament of all the agreements 'authenticated' by it. In other words, pursuant to Article 4 of this law, once the document containing the original treaty is signed by the plenipotentiary, the Ministry's Legal Affairs Service transmits to both Chambers both the basic information of the agreement and the certified copies of the signed treaty.

However, with regard to relations with the President of the Republic in the sector in question, it is believed that the government has, in general, an obligation to inform him or her in all the upward phase of the formation of international acts.

Nevertheless, there rests a clear democratic deficit in the negotiation cycle: the Chambers, in fact, are informed in a phase in which it is almost impossible to change the text of the agreement, unless new negotiations are reopened, and taking responsibility of the State in international law. These, therefore, will just have to accept or deny the whole content, in particular also during the authorization for ratification phase.

Naturally, the legislator's actions remain valid in the event that the treaty provides, in addition to the order of execution, precise provisions for adapting the internal legal system to the obligations deriving therefrom, as well as the guiding and monitoring powers belonging in general to the Chambers and by virtue of the fiduciary relationship that binds the government to them, according to the principles and rules of the parliamentary system (Article 94 of the Constitution).

The parliamentary guiding function also includes the political debate that takes place annually in relation to the state budget, alongside the typical instruments with which the Parliament takes decisions aimed at directing the government's activity in foreign policy, i.e., agendas, motions and resolutions; the latter, in particular, are increasingly adopted by the competent commissions of the two Chambers.

Besides, an important point to stress is that in the past the government excluded several times the Parliament from the procedure of formation of political treaties, adopting the '*provisional application of the treaties*' formula (*see* Article 25 of the Vienna Convention on the Law of Treaties of 1969) while waiting to obtain the specific authorization to ratification. In particular, this has happened for the execution of agreements concerning the expedition of contingents in Sinai (1982), in Suez (1984) and in Beirut (1982, 1984).

As regards the transposition into national law of those agreements, as well as of any treaty applied provisionally, it should be recalled that this is ensured by the ordinary arrangements used for the treaties in force. In particular, the implementing order shall be adopted following the subsequent ratification of the Treaty and shall have retroactive effect, making express or implicit reference to the date of its provisional application. Consequently, it has been noted that the use of this method of transposition, while not allowing for a timely adaptation of the domestic legal order to the obligations arising from the provisional application of a treaty, allows it to be granted the same status as the treaties in force. Notwithstanding the silence of the Constitution, that seems to consider ratification the only way for the State to undertake international treaty obligations, the republican praxis confirmed the pre-existing possibility to sign simplified treaties and agreements. Pursuant to Article 12 of the Vienna Convention on the Law of Treaties of 1969, these treaties and agreements are international acts that become effective by their signature or by a simple exchange of dispositions without ratification and, in other words, without the possibility to activate formal controls by the President of the Republic. It is obvious that these treaties and agreements cannot include the content of the treaties for which Article 80 of the Constitution requires the previous parliamentary authorization for their ratification.

In fact, in practice, according to the statistical data collected from the XII Legislature, there is a clear predominance in terms of quantity, also in the matters referred to in Article 80 of the Constitution, since the ever more pressing needs of technical skills and confidentiality are part of this phenomenon, as well as the need to promptly obtain immediately operational decisions at international level. Examples include:

- the Memorandum of Understanding with Sudan on Combating Crime, Border Management and Migration Flows, including Return, signed on 3 August 2016. The corresponding agreement has not been published, not even in the 'ATRIO' section of the website of the Ministry of Foreign Affairs and International Cooperation;
- the Memorandum of Understanding with Libya, signed in Rome on 2 February 2017, 'on cooperation in the field of development, combating illegal immigration, trafficking in human beings, smuggling and strengthening of border security between the State of Libya and the Italian Republic', not published in the Official Journal or communicated to the Presidents of the Chambers, as provided for the Articles 13 and 14 of the Memorandum of Understanding.
- annul Articles 1(1)(*f*) and 4 of Law No. 839/1984, which the Italian Government has, however, published on its official website;
- the recent exchange of notes, on 8 and 9 April 2021, between the Italian Government, via its embassy in Paris, and the French Government, on the dispatch of an Italian military contingent to Mali, requested by the President of the Republic of that country and under the French command of the 'Barkhane force', to assist the Malian armed forces in the fight against terrorism, published in the 'ATRIO' section of the website of the Ministry of Foreign Affairs and International Cooperation.

521. As regards the competences and the national procedures of the government, a main aspect that needs emphasizing is that, since the entry into force of Law No. 400/1988, the prevailing competence of the Foreign Minister and the President of the Council (but not of the Council of Ministers) in this matter was admitted. The Council of Ministers was usually excluded from the negotiation and signature of international simplified treaties and agreements. In particular, in case of treaties, the Council of Ministers has only submitted the text of the draft for the authorization of the ratification for its required deliberation but without any previous information during negotiation and stipulation. In case of treaties and agreements in simplified form, the signature of the Foreign Minister or the President of the Council was required; therefore, the Council of Ministers was completely excluded from their formation procedure.

Law No. 400/1988 provided for the essential deliberation of the Council of Ministers on 'the lines of international and EU policy' and on 'the drafts of international treaties and agreements, apart from their denomination, of political or military nature' (Article 2(3)(*h*) of Law No. 400/1988). In this way, the Council of Ministers attains a collective liability for simplified treaties and agreements too.

§2. The Implementation of Treaties in the Italian Legal System

522. In order to become effective in domestic law, international treaties must be implemented by means of internal provisions in compliance with the constitutional principle of legal sources. These provisions may be ordinary laws whenever the matter must be regulated by means of Acts of Parliament or whenever it is necessary to amend legislation in force before the implementation of the treaty. Treaties may also be implemented by means of either hierarchically 'inferior' provisions or regional laws whenever the matter falls within the legislative competence of the Regions pursuant to Article 117(5) of the Constitution (*see* Part III, Chapter 1).

523. Enforcement may be set by directly applying compulsory rules, that is by means of an *ordinary adapting procedure* reshaping international provisions through an internal regulatory act or – whether necessary – implementing rules and adopting reference standards necessary for the application of the Treaty, if it does not contain, in whole or in part, self-executing norms. Incorporation of international treaties into the national legal system can ask therefore an Act of Parliament that reproduces the provisions of the treaty (*legge di esecuzione* in the strict sense). However, more often it is through the so-called *implementation order* or *enforcement clause* (*ordine di esecuzione*), that is by a *special adapting procedure*: the domestic legislative act merely states that 'full and complete execution is given to the treaty [agreement] between the Italian Republic and [...]', the text of which is annexed. In such a case, the content of the implementing rules of the Treaty is indicated *per relationem*. The enforcement clause is said to ensure a 'fixed' (or 'material' or 'upon receipt') reference to the specific provisions laid down by the international treaty.

The provisions of the Treaty (which fall under international law) and the relevant implementing rules (which fall under national law, although their content can be derived from the text of the Treaty) remain logically and legally distinct. The *implementation order* must also be contained in a legislative act suitable for laying down the rules in question according to the constitutional order and may, therefore, be enclosed, as appropriate, in a law or a statute (*see* Part I, Chapter 2).

Experts underlined that the new Article 117(1) of the Constitution can determine the direct implementation of international treaties in our legal system and the impossibility for the national legislator to amend them. Moreover, it was highlighted that the power to adopt the implementation order, even with reference to the agreements stipulated by the State, is now included among the competences of Regions in the implementation of international treaties concerning subject matters they are assigned to pursuant to Article 117(5) of the Constitution.

Generally and in current praxis, the law allows the authorization to ratification of the treaty and the issuing of an order to implement the same treaty. However, these two legislative procedures, that is the authorization to ratification and the implementation of duties deriving from agreements, must be kept separated.

Chapter 4. Constitutional Principles Relating to the Armed Forces

by Valerio Onida

§1. The Italian Constitution and the Deployment of the Armed Forces

524. The Constitution contains provisions dealing with – while not entirely regulating – the organization and activity of the Armed Forces in Italy.

525. The constitutional provisions relating to the participation of the Italian State in supranational organizations designed to establish an international order aimed to 'ensure peace and justice among nations' and the concomitant limitations of sovereignty are inspired by the general principle that 'Italy condemns war as an instrument of aggression against the freedom of other peoples and as a means for settling international controversies' (Article 11). These provisions were primarily formulated with a view to UN membership (reached by Italy in 1955) but were subsequently widely applied to justify 'limitations of sovereignty' with respect to the EU and its organizations. Thus, beyond the national territory, the system of the Armed Forces may be organized and deployed for the sole purposes of external defence or collaboration within the context of supranational institutions, for peacekeeping operations, and for humanitarian duties. In this respect, Italy's membership of North Atlantic Treaty Organization (NATO) in 1949 has led to the strict integration of the Italian Armed Forces within the military system of the Atlantic organization and to the establishment of NATO bases within Italian territory. While this is unlikely to lead to substantial constitutional objections so long as the actions of the NATO military system have the sole objective of defending the Member States, it becomes controversial in cases where NATO forces are engaged in non-defensive operations in foreign territory which have not been decided by the UN.

§2. Military Service

526. From a strictly national perspective, the Constitution's principal concern with respect to the Armed Forces is that – in specifying the 'unalterable duties of political, economic and social solidarity' (Article 2) – 'the defence of the country (*patria*) is sacred duty of citizens' (Article 52, paragraph 1) and that 'military service is compulsory within the limits and in the manner established by law' (Article 52, paragraph 2). Constitutional case law distinguishes between the generic yet universal duty of all citizens to defend – albeit not exclusively by participating with military organization and activities – and the specific obligation to perform military service, which can, and arguably must, be limited by the law: actually it only applies to male citizens deemed fit and not exempt for other reasons. Moreover, the law recognizes that male citizens who qualify for compulsory military service but have a conscientious objection with respect to the use of arms may opt for a substitutive civil service of equal duration. Law No. 64/2001 provided for the institution of a 'national civil service' as a voluntary alternative to compulsory military service.

However, compulsory military service has in fact disappeared insofar as Law No. 331/2000 and Legislative Decree No. 215/2001 provided that it has been 'suspended' by 1 January 2007. Since that date, the Armed Forces are made up of professional or voluntary soldiers, both men and women, and compulsory recruitment will only take place in times of war or international crisis in order to supplement the professional and voluntary forces.

§3. The Organization of the Armed Forces

527. Article 52, paragraph 3, of the Constitution states that the organization of the Armed Forces 'shall be based on the democratic spirit of the Republic'. This statement of principle is designed to avoid any likelihood of the Armed Forces becoming a separate body within the State based on principles which differ from, or are in conflict with, those governing civil society. This does not preclude the need for special rules, based *inter alia* on the demands of military discipline, applicable to the Armed Forces, but it does prevent the military system from remaining outside the application of constitutional principles and from affecting the enjoyment and exercise of basic constitutional rights on the part of its members, other than in the manner and to the extent deemed indispensable to safeguard the specific requirements peculiar to the Armed Forces. One such constitutional limitation prohibits 'professional soldiers in active service' (together with other categories of public officers) from belonging to political parties in order to safeguard the political 'neutrality' of the Armed Forces (Article 98, paragraph 3). These principles are implemented with Law No. 382/1978 which regulates the exercise of freedom rights on the part of soldiers and prohibits membership not only of political parties but also of trade unions, excludes the right to strike, but does provide for special elective representative bodies within the military corps.

528. The Constitution has maintained special military jurisdiction in criminal matters (military tribunals: Article 103, paragraph 3), but limits this legal competence to offences of an exclusively military nature committed by members of the Armed Forces, i.e., by soldiers on active duty (*see* Part II, Chapter 7, §§6 and 7). Thus, the military criminal codes which relate to both wartime and peacetime and the legal military system in force prior to the Constitution of 1948 still apply under the republican system.

However, the large number of cases brought before the Constitutional Court is a clear indication that the original military criminal system was not consistent with constitutional principles and that a separation of the Armed Forces with respect to the general system is no longer justified, with the result that a great many provisions under the military codes not in line with the Constitution have been dropped.

§4. The Command Structure

529. In matters of organization and operation, the Italian Armed Forces are subject to the rule of law and come under political authority. This is implicit in their nature as State bodies, albeit with special duties, and implied by the relevant constitutional rules found in Article 87, paragraph 9, wherein it is stated that the President of the Republic 'commands the Armed Forces' and 'presides over the supreme defence Council'.

There is a consensus that the command referred to in this norm is not the effective command, which – according to the rules of the parliamentary system adopted by the Italian Constitution – falls exclusively on the official organ of executive authority, i.e., government, and in particular the Minister of Defence; nor is it the technical-operational command, which is exercised according to the procedures and hierarchies provided by law, and which come under the authority of the general defence staff and the general staffs of the various Armed Forces: instead, it is merely a high command, expressing the political neutrality of the Armed Forces and their loyalty to the Italian State and its institutions. As the representative of national unity and the guarantor of the Constitution, the President of the Republic is bound to ensure that the Armed Forces are not exploited for the political aims of one party or even the political majority. The same meaning should apply to the Presidency of the supreme defence Council, entrusted to the Head of State, the composition and functions of which, however, are not indicated by the Constitution. Law No. 624/1950 configures the supreme defence Council as a coordinating organ, including specific members of government (namely the Prime Minister, with the role of Vice-President, the Ministers of Foreign Affairs, the Interior, Defence, Economy and Finance, and Economic Development) and the head of the general defence staff: a Presidential Decree (No. 251/1990) regulates its functions.

Finally, during his term of office, President Cossiga raised the problem of a more accurate definition of competences and procedures of the Armed Forces in the event of emergency, but legislative rules on this point are still lacking (*see* General Introduction, Chapter 2).

§5. Parliamentary Control

530. The Constitution provides that the State of war must be duly deliberated by both Chambers, which must in turn assign the necessary powers to government (Article 78) – although this provision has not as yet been given any specific legislative form – and declared by the President of the Republic (Article 87, paragraph 9).

The more current problems, however, derive from the fact that the deployment of the Armed Forces and recourse to war take place, as a matter of fact, in cases of urgency, outside any formal procedures implying deliberations and declarations of war. The deployment of the Armed Forces in foreign territories generally occurs within the framework of international agreements, previously authorized by Parliament (such as the NATO treaty), but which in turn then envisage decisional and operational procedures that are generally left to the discretion of the executive authority.

The normal practice is for government to obtain the agreement of Parliament, at least ex post facto, as ratification, for all cases where the Armed Forces are deployed outside Italy, or even within Italy for duties not institutionally envisaged by the Constitution, as, for example, when soldiers are deployed to provide extraordinary reinforcement for reasons of public order in particular areas of the country.

Selected Bibliography

Commentaries on the Italian Constitution

Bifulco, R., A. Celotto & M. Olivetti (eds). *Commentario alla Costituzione*. Turin: UTET, 2006.

Branca, G. (ed.). *Commentario alla Costituzione.* Bologna-Rome: Zanichelli, 1981.

Calamandrei, P. & A. Levi (eds). *Commentario sistematico della Costituzione italiana.* Florence: Barbera, 1950.

Clementi, F., L. Cuocolo, F. Rosa & G.E. Vigevani (eds). *La Costituzione italiana. Commento articolo per articolo*, vols I and II. Bologna: il Mulino, 2021.

Crisafulli, V. & L. Paladin (eds). *Commentario breve alla Costituzione italiana.* 2nd edn. edited by S. Bartole & R. Bin. Padua: Cedam, 2008.

Historical Outline of Italian Constitutional Law

Allegretti, U. *Profilo di storia costituzionale italiana: individualismo e assolutismo nello Stato liberale.* Bologna: il Mulino, 1989.

Allegretti, U. *Storia costituzionale italiana. Popolo e istituzioni.* Bologna: il Mulino, 2014.

Bonini, F. *Storia costituzionale della Repubblica.* Rome: La nuova Italia Scientifica, 1993.

Ghisalberti, C. *Storia costituzionale d'Italia: 1848–1948.* Roma-Bari: Laterza, 2000.

Lepre, A. *Storia della prima Repubblica: l'Italia dal 1943 al 1998.* Bologna: il Mulino, 1999.

Paladin, L. *Per una storia costituzionale dell'Italia repubblicana.* Bologna: il Mulino, 2004.

The Features of the Republican Constitution

Barile, P., P. Caretti & F. Margiotta Broglio. *La Costituzione per tutti.* Florence: Sansoni, 1996.

Barile, P., E. Cheli & S. Grassi. *Istituzioni di Diritto Pubblico.* 16th edn. Milan: Wolters Kluwer, 2017.

Bin, R. & G. Pitruzzella. *Diritto costituzionale.* 24th edn. Turin: Giappichelli, 2003.

Caretti, P. & U. De Siervo. *Istituzioni di diritto pubblico.* 5th edn. Turin: Giappichelli, 2023.

Cartabia M. & N. Lupo. *The Constitution of Italy. A Contextual Analysis*. London: Hart Publishing, 2022.

Selected Bibliography

Cheli, E. *La riforma mancata.* Bologna: il Mulino, 2000.
Martines, T. & G. Silvestri. *Diritto costituzionale.* 16th edn. Milan: Giuffrè, 2022.
Neppi Modona G. (ed.). *Stato della Costituzione.* Milan: Il saggiatore, 1998.
Pasquino, G. *La rivoluzione promessa. Lettura della Costituzione italiana.* Milan-Turin: Mondadori, 2011.
Onida, V. 'Costituzione italiana'. In *Digesto Discipline Pubblicistiche,* Turin: UTET, 1990.
Onida, V. *La Costituzione.* Latest edn. edited by M. Cartabia. Bologna: il Mulino, 2023.
Pizzorusso, A. *La Costituzione.* Turin: Einaudi, 1996.

Sources of Law

Bin, R. & G. Pitruzzella. *Le fonti del diritto.* 4th edn. Turin: Giappichelli, 2023.
Cicconetti, S.M. *Le fonti del diritto italiano.* 6th edn. Turin: Giappichelli, 2019.
Crisafulli, V. *Lezioni di diritto costituzionale*, II, 1, *L'ordinamento costituzionale italiano (Le fonti normative).* 6th edn. edited by F. Crisafulli. Padua: Cedam, 1993.
Giocoli Nacci, P. *Appunti sulle fonti normative (dalle lezioni).* Bari: Cacucci, 1992.
Guastini, R. 'Le fonti del diritto. Fondamenti teorici'. In *Trattato di diritto civile e commerciale già diretto da A. Cicu e F. Messineo L. Mengoni e continuato da P. Schlesinger.* Milan: Giuffrè, 2010.
Modugno, F. 'Le fonti del diritto (gerarchia delle)'. In *Enciclopedia del diritto.* Update I., Milan: Giuffrè, 1997.
Modugno, F. *Appunti dalle lezioni sulle Fonti del Diritto.* Turin: Giappichelli, 2005.
Morrone, A. *Fonti normative. Concetti generali, problemi, casi.* Bologna: il Mulino, 2022.
Paladin, L. *Le fonti del diritto italiano.* Bologna: il Mulino, 1996.
Pedrazza Gorlero, M. & S. Catalano. *Le fonti dell'ordine repubblicano.* 2nd edn. Milan: Giuffrè, 2018.
Pedrazza Gorlero, M., & M. Nicolini. 'Le fonti del diritto'. In *Compendio di diritto costituzionale.* 4th edn. edited by M. Pedrazza Gorlero & V. Onida. Milan: Giuffrè, 2018.
Pizzorusso, A. 'Delle fonti del diritto'. In *Commentario del codice civile. Art. 1–9. Disposizioni sulla legge in generale*, edited by A. Scialoja & G. Branca. Bologna-Rome: Zanichelli-Società Editrice del Foro Italiano, 2011.
Politi, F. *Le fonti del diritto nell'ordinamento italiano.* Turin: Giappichelli, 2020.
Ruggeri, A. *Fonti, norme, criteri ordinatori. Lezioni.* 5th edn. Turin: Giappichelli, 2009.
Sorrentino, F. *Le fonti del diritto italiano.* Milan: Wolters Kluwer, 2023.
Spadacini, L. *Decreto-legge e alterazione del quadro costituzionale. Distorsioni del bicameralismo, degenerazioni del sistema delle fonti e inefficacia dei controlli.* Bari: Cacucci, 2022.
Zagrebelsky, G. *Il sistema costituzionale delle fonti del diritto.* Turin: UTET, 1992.

Forms of Direct Democracy and Abrogative Referenda

Amato, G., M. Luciani & M. Volpi (eds). *Referendum.* Rome-Bari: Laterza, 1992.
Ambrosini, G. *Referendum.* Turin: Bollati Boringhieri, 1993.

Barbera, A. & A. Morrone. *La Repubblica dei Referendum.* Bologna: il Mulino, 2003.
Cariola, A. *Referendum abrogativo e giudizio costituzionale.* Milan: Giuffrè, 1994.
Carnevale, P. *Il referendum abrogativo e i limiti alla sua ammissibilità nella giurisprudenza costituzionale.* Padua: Cedam, 1992.
Chiappetti, A. *L'ammissibilità del referendum abrogativo.* Milan: Giuffrè, 1974.
De Marco, E. *Contributo allo studio del referendum nel diritto pubblico italiano.* Padua: Cedam, 1974.
Gabriele, F. 'Referendum'. In *Appendice al Novissimo digesto italiano*, vol. VI. Turin: UTET, 1986.
Lojodice, A. 'Referendum'. In *Enciclopedia giuridica italiana*, vol. XXVI. Rome: Treccani, 1991.
Luciani, M. 'Art. 75'. *Il referendum abrogativo.* In *Commentario alla Costituzione*, edited by G. Branca & A. Pizzorusso. Bologna-Rome: Zanichelli-Il Foro Italiano, 2005.
Pertici, A. *Il giudice delle leggi e il giudizio di ammissibilità del referendum abrogativo.* Turin: Giappichelli, 2010.
Raveraira, M. *Problemi di costituzionalità dell'abrogazione popolare.* Milan: Giuffrè, 1983.
Salerno, G. *Il referendum.* Padua: Cedam, 1992.

Introduction to the Italian System of Government

Balboni E. et al. *La difficile alternanza: il sistema parlamentare italiano alla prova, 1985–1987.* Milan: Giuffrè, 1998.
Crisafulli, V. 'Aspetti problematici del sistema parlamentare vigente in Italia'. In *Jus.* Milan: Vita e Pensiero, 1958. Now in *Stato Popolo Governo.* Milan: Giuffrè, 1985.
D'Andrea, A. (ed.). *Verso l'incerto bipolarismo. Il sistema parlamentare italiano nella transizione, 1987–1999.* Milan: Giuffrè, 1999.
Elia, L. 'Governo (forme di)'. In *Enciclopedia del diritto*, vol. XIX. Milan: Giuffrè, 1970.
Galli, G. *Il bipartitismo imperfetto.* Bologna: il Mulino, 1967.
Mangiameli, S. *La forma di governo parlamentare.* Turin: Giappichelli, 1998.
Onida, V. 'Recenti sviluppi della forma di governo in Italia: prime osservazioni'. In *Quaderni costituzionali.* Bologna: il Mulino, 1981.
Pitruzzella, G. *Forme di governo e trasformazioni della politica.* Rome-Bari: Laterza, 1996.

The President of the Republic

Armaroli, P. *L'elezione del Presidente della Repubblica in Italia.* Padua: Cedam, 1977.
Baldassarre, A. 'Capo dello Stato'. In *Digesto discipline pubblicistiche*, vol. II. Turin: UTET, 1987.
Baldassarre, A. 'Il Capo dello Stato come rappresentante dell'unità nazionale'. In *Lezioni Magistrali di Diritto Costituzionale,* edited by A. Vignudelli, vol. II. Modena: Mucchi, 2012.

Selected Bibliography

Baldassarre, A. & C. Mezzanotte. *Gli uomini del Quirinale. Da De Nicola a Pertini.* Rome-Bari: Laterza, 1985.

Baldassarre, A. & G. Scaccia (eds). *Il Presidente della Repubblica nell'evoluzione della forma di governo* (Atti del convegno di Roma, 26 novembre 2010). Rome: Aracne, 2012.

Barile, P. 'I poteri del Presidente della Repubblica'. In *Rivista trimestrale di diritto pubblico.* Milan: Giuffrè, 1958.

Bin, R. 'Il Presidente Napolitano e la topologia della forma di governo'. In *Quaderni costituzionali.* Bologna: il Mulino, 2013.

Biscaretti di Ruffia, P. 'Le attribuzioni del Presidente della Repubblica'. In *Rivista trimestrale di diritto pubblico.* Milan: Giuffrè, 1963.

Capotosti, P.A. 'Presidente della Repubblica e formazione del Governo'. In *Scritti in onore di E Tosato.* vol. III. Milan: Giuffrè, 1984.

Carlassarre, L. 'Governo, Parlamento, Presidente della Repubblica'. In *Annuario AIC, Atti del XVI convegno annuale della Associazione italiana dei costituzionalisti.* Padua: Cedam, 2002.

Cassese, S., G. Galasso & A. Melloni. *I Presidenti della Repubblica.* Bologna: il Mulino, 2018.

Cheli, E. 'Poteri autonomi del Capo dello Stato e controfirma ministeriale: l'esperienza italiana'. In *Quaderni costitutzionali.* Bologna: il Mulino, 1983.

Chessa, O. *Il Presidente della Repubblica parlamentare. Un'interpretazione della forma di governo italiana.* Naples: Jovene, 2010.

Chinni, D. 'Sulle esternazioni del Presidente della Repubblica al tempo dei new media. Spunti a partire dalla prassi del Presidente Napolitano'. In *Giurisprudenza costituzionale.* Milan: Giuffrè, 2010.

Cuocolo, F. 'Imparzialitá e tutela della Costituzione nell'esercizio dei poteri del Presidente della Repubblica'. In *Rassegna di diritto pubblico.* Naples: Jovene 1959.

D'Andrea, A. 'Questioni metodologiche e qualche rilievo a caldo sulla "Presidenza Napolitano"'. In *Quaderni costituzionali.* Bologna: il Mulino, 2013.

Dimora, F. *Alla ricerca della responsabilità del Capo dello Stato.* Milan: Giuffrè, 1991.

Esposito, C. 'Capo dello Stato'. In *Enciclopedia del diritto*, vol. VI. Milan: Giuffrè, 1960.

Esposito, C. 'Controfirma ministeriale'. In *Enciclopedia del diritto*, vol. X. Milan: Giuffrè, 1962.

Fusaro, C. *Il Presidente della Repubblica.* Bologna: il Mulino, 2003.

Galeotti, S. *Il Presidente della Repubblica garante della Costituzione (la concezione garantistica del Capo dello Stato negli scritti dell'autore dal 1949 ad oggi).* Milan: Giuffrè, 1992.

Galeotti, S. & B. Pezzini. 'Il Presidente della Repubblica nella Costituzione italiana'. In *Digesto discipline pubblicistiche.* Turin: UTET, 1996.

Galliani, D. *Il Capo dello Stato e le leggi*, vols. I–II. Milan: Giuffrè, 2011.

Galliani, D. *I sette anni di Napolitano. Evoluzione politico-costituzionale della Presidenza della Repubblica.* Milan: EGEA, 2012.

Giuffrè F. & I.A. Nicotra. *L'eccezionale 'bis' del Presidente della Repubblica Napolitano.* Turin: Giappichelli, 2014.

Gorlani, M. *Libertà di esternazione e sovraesposizione funzionale del Capo dello Stato. Ricadute recenti sulla forma di governo italiana.* Milan: Giuffrè, 2012.

Grisolia, M.C. *Potere di messaggio ed esternazioni presidenziali.* Milan: Giuffrè, 1986.

Guarino, G. 'Il Presidente della Repubblica italiana'. In *Rivista trimestrale di diritto pubblico*. Milan: Giuffrè, 1951.

Guiglia, G. *L'autorizzazione alla presentazione dei disegni di legge governativi.* Turin: Giappichelli, 1991.

Labriola, S. *Il Presidente della Repubblica.* Padua: Cedam, 1986.

Lippolis, V. & G.M. Salerno. *La presidenza più lunga: I poteri del Capo dello Stato e la Costituzione*. Bologna: il Mulino, 2016.

Luciani, M. & M. Volpi. *Il Presidente della Repubblica.* Bologna: il Mulino, 1997.

Motzo, G. 'Il potere presidenziale di esternazione e di messaggio'. In *Archivio giuridico*. Modena: Mucchi, 1957.

Occhiocupo, N. *Il Segretariato generale della Presidenza della Repubblica.* Milan: Giuffrè, 1973.

Occhiocupo, N. 'Presidenza della Repubblica'. In *Enciclopedia giuridica italiana*, vol. XXIV. Rome: Treccani, 1991.

Onida, V. 'L'ultimo Cossiga: recenti novità nella prassi della Presidenza della Repubblica'. In *Quaderni costituzionali.* Bologna: il Mulino, 1992.

Pace, A. 'Esternazioni presidenziali e forma di governo. Considerazioni critiche'. In *Quaderni costituzionali.* Bologna: il Mulino, 1992.

Paladin, L. 'La funzione presidenziale di controllo'. In *Quaderni costituzionali.* Bologna: il Mulino, 1982.

Paladin, L. 'Presidente della Repubblica'. In *Enciclopedia del diritto*, vol. XXXV. Milan: Giuffrè, 1986.

Rescigno, G.U. 'La responsabilità politica del Presidente della Repubblica. La prassi recente'. In *Studi parlamentari.* Rome: Edistudio, 1980.

Rizza, G. 'Il Capo dello Stato nella forma di governo parlamentare: una rivisitazione'. In *Diritto e società.* Padua: Cedam, 1992.

Rossano, C. 'Presidente della Repubblica (dir. cost.)'. In *Enciclopedia giuridica italiana*, vol. XXIV. Rome: Treccani, 1991.

Ruggeri, A. (ed.). *Evoluzione del sistema politico-istituzionale e ruolo del Presidente della Repubblica* (Atti di un incontro di studio, Messina-Siracusa, 19 e 20 novembre 2010). Turin: Giappichelli, 2011.

Sica, V. *La controfirma.* Naples: Jovene, 1953.

Silvestri, G. (ed.). *La figura e il ruolo del Presidente della Repubblica nel sistema costituzionale italiano* (atti del convegno svoltosi a Messina e Taormina dal 25 al 27 ottobre 1984). Milan: Giuffrè, 1985.

Sperti, A. *La responsabilità del Presidente della Repubblica. Evoluzione e recenti interpretazioni*. Turin: Giappichelli, 2010.

Tebaldi, M. *Il Presidente della Repubblica.* Bologna: il Mulino, 2005.

Valentini, A. *Gli atti del Presidente della Repubblica.* Milan: Giuffrè, 1965.

Ventura, L. (ed.). *Le crisi di governo nell'ordinamento e nell'esperienza costituzionale* (atti di un convegno, Catanzaro 22 e 23 ottobre 1999). Turin: Giappichelli, 2001.

Selected Bibliography

The Structure of Parliament

Parliament in General

Celotto, A. *Diritto parlamentare: casi e materiali.* Bologna: Zanichelli, 2005.
Cicconetti, S.M. *Diritto parlamentare.* 2nd edn. Turin: Giappichelli, 2010.
Di Ciolo, V. & R. Ciaurro. *Il diritto parlamentare nella teoria e nella pratica.* 4th edn. Milan: Giuffrè, 2003.
Dickmann, R. *Il parlamento italiano.* Naples: Jovene, 2011.
Elia, L. *Costituzione, partiti istituzioni.* Bologna: il Mulino, 2009.
Gianniti, L. & N. Lupo. *Corso di diritto parlamentare.* Bologna: il Mulino, 2008.
Labriola, S. (ed.). *Il parlamento repubblicano (1948–1998).* Milan: Giuffrè, 1999.
Mannino, A. *Diritto parlamentare.* Milan: Giuffrè, 2010.
Marongiu, A. 'Parlamento (storia)'. In *Enciclopedia del diritto.* vol. XXXI. Milan: Giuffrè, 1981.
Manzella, A. *Il Parlamento.* 3rd edn. Bologna: il Mulino, 2003.
Martines, T. & G. Silvestri. *Diritto parlamentare.* 2nd edn. Milan: Giuffrè, 2011.
Mastroapaolo, A. & L. Verzichelli. *Il Parlamento: le assemblee legislative nelle democrazie contemporanee.* Rome-Bari: Laterza, 2006.
Mazziotti, M. 'Parlamento (principi generali)'. In *Enciclopedia del diritto*, vol. XXXI. Milan: Giuffrè, 1981.
Mazzoni Honorati, M. *Diritto parlamentare.* 2nd edn. Turin: Giappichelli, 2005.
Tosi, S. & A. Mannino. *Diritto parlamentare.* 3rd edn. Milan: Giuffrè, 1999.
Traversa, S. *Il Parlamento nella Costituzione e nella prassi.* Milan: Giuffrè, 1989.
Ungari, P. *Profilo storico del diritto parlamentare in Italia.* Rome: Bulzoni, 1971.
Violante, L. (ed.). *Il parlamento.* Turin: Einaudi, 2001.

The Bicameral System

Bonfiglio, S. *Il Senato in Italia: riforma del bicameralismo e modelli di rappresentanza.* Rome-Bari: Laterza, 2006.
Cheli, E. 'Unità nazionale e prospettiva federale nelle ipotesi di riforma del bicameralismo italiano'. In *Scritti in onore di Lorenza Carlassare: il diritto costituzionale come regola e limite al potere.* Naples: Jovene, 2009.
Decaro, C. (ed.). *Il bicameralismo in discussione: Regno Unito, Francia, Italia: profili comparati.* Rome: Luiss University Press, 2008.
Manzella, A. & F. Bassanini. *Per far funzionare il Parlamento: quarantaquattro modeste proposte.* Bologna: il Mulino, 2007.
Paladin, L. 'Bicameralismo'. In *Enciclopedia giuridica italiana*, vol. V. Rome: Treccani, 1988.

The Electoral System of the Chambers

Astrid. *La riforma elettorale.* Florence: Passigli, 2007.
Barbera, A. & G. Guzzetta. *Il governo dei cittadini: referendum elettorali e riforma della politica.* Soveria Mannelli (Cz): Rubbettino, 2007.
D. Casanova, *Eguaglianza del voto e sistemi elettorali. I limiti costituzionali alla discrezionalità del legislatore.* Naples: Editoriale Scientifica, 2020.
D'Alimonte, R. & A. Chiaramonte. *Proporzionale ma non solo: le elezioni politiche del 2006.* Bologna: il Mulino, 2007.

D'alimonte, R. & C. Fusaro. *La legislazione elettorale italiana: come migliorarla e perché.* Bologna: il Mulino, 2008.
D'Andrea, A. 'L'insostenibile ragionevolezza della nuova legge elettorale'. In *Quaderni costituzionali.* Bologna: il Mulino, 2006.
De Fiores, C. (ed.). *Rappresentanza politica e legge elettorale.* Turin: Giappichelli, 2007.
Fusaro, C. *Le regole della transizione. La nuova legislazione elettorale italiana.* Bologna: il Mulino, 1995.
Oliviero, M. & M. Volpi. *Sistemi elettorali e democrazie.* Turin: Giappichelli, 2007.
Palici di Suni, E. 'Parità di genere'. In *Digesto delle discipline pubblicistiche*, Turin: UTET, 2008.
Pasquino, G. *Una legge elettorale come si deve.* Bologna: il Mulino, 2006.
Spadacini, L. 'I limiti alla discrezionalità del legislatore in materia elettorale desumibili dalla sentenza della Corte costituzionale n. 1 del 2014'. In *Forum di Quaderni Costituzionali Rassegna.* Bologna: il Mulino, 2013.

Parliamentary Privileges

D'Andrea, A. *Note sull'autorizzazione all'arresto dei membri del Parlamento.* Milan: Giuffrè, 1985.
Giupponi, T.E. *Le immunità della politica.* Turin: Giappichelli, 2005.
Grisolia, M.C. *Immunità parlamentari e Costituzione.* Padua: Cedam, 2000.
Martinelli, C. *Le immunità costituzionali nell'ordinamento italiano e nel diritto comparato: recenti sviluppi e nuove prospettive.* Milan: Giuffrè, 2008
Orlandi, R. & A. Pugiotto. *Immunità politiche e giustizia penale.* Turin: Giappichelli, 2005.
Sciannella, L.G. *Le immunità parlamentari. Profili storici e comparativi.* Turin: Giappichelli, 2010.
Traversa, S. 'Immunità parlamentare'. In *Enciclopedia del diritto*, vol. XX. Milan: Giuffrè, 1970.
Zagrebelsky, G. *Le immunità parlamentari.* Turin: Einaudi, 1979.
Zanon, N. *Il libero mandato parlamentare.* Milan: Giuffrè, 1991.

Standing Orders

D'Andrea, A. *Autonomia costituzionale delle Camere e principio di legalità.* Milan: Giuffrè, 2004.
Floridia, G.G. *Il regolamento parlamentare nel sistema delle fonti.* Milan: Giuffrè, 1996.
Gianfrancesco, E. & N. Lupo. *Le regole del diritto parlamentare nella dialettica tra maggioranza e opposizione.* Rome: Luiss University Press, 2007.
Lippolis, V. 'Regolamenti parlamentari, forma di governo, innovazione istituzionale'. In *Quaderni costituzionali.* Bologna: il Mulino, 2009.
Manetti, M. *La legittimazione del diritto parlamentare.* Milan: Giuffrè, 1990.
Modugno, F. 'Regolamenti parlamentari e autonomia della funzione delle Camere'. In *Scritti in onore di Lorenza Carlassare: il diritto costituzionale come regola e limite al potere*. Naples: Jovene, 2009.
Podetta, M. *Governare le Camere. Tendenze e miti delle riforme regolamentari.* Bari: Cacucci, 2020.

Selected Bibliography

The Organization of the Chambers

Caputo, M. 'Giunta per il regolamento'. In *Rassegna parlamentare*. Naples: Jovene, 2009.

Ciancio, A. *I gruppi parlamentari. Studio intorno a una manifestazione del pluralismo politico.* Milan: Giuffrè, 2008.

Iacometti, M. *I Presidenti di Assemblea parlamentare*. Milan: Giuffrè, 2001.

Longo, F. *Parlamento e politica estera. Il ruolo delle commissioni.* Bologna: il Mulino, 2011.

Malinconico, G. 'La Giunta per le elezioni'. In *Rassegna parlamentare*. Milan: Giuffrè, 2001.

Merlini, S. *Rappresentanza politica, gruppi parlamentari, partiti politici: il contesto italiano,* II. Turin: Giappichelli, 2004.

Rossi, E. (ed.). *Maggioranza e opposizioni nelle procedure parlamentari.* Padua: Cedam, 2004.

Sicardi, S. 'Parlamento (organizzazione e funzionamento)'. In *Digesto discipline pubblicistiche.* Turin: UTET, 1995.

Torre, A. 'Presidente di assemblea parlamentare'. In *Dizionario di diritto pubblico diretto da Sabino Cassese*, vol. V. Milan: Giuffrè, 2006.

Parliament: Its Activities

The Lawmaking Process

Ainis, M. *La legge oscura.* 2nd edn. Bari-Milan: Laterza, 2010.

Albanesi, E. *Pareri parlamentari e limiti della legge*. Milan: Giuffrè, 2010.

Caretti, P. (ed.). *Osservatorio sulle fonti 2008: la legge parlamentare oggi.* Turin: Giappichelli, 2010.

Costanzo, P. (ed.). *La qualità della normazione nella dialettica Governo-Parlamento.* Naples: Jovene, 2011.

Cuocolo, F. 'Legge'. In *Enciclopedia giuridica italiana*, vol. XVIII. Rome: Treccani, 1990.

Di Ciolo, V. *Procedimento legislativo*, in *Enciclopedia del diritto*, vol. XXXV. Milan: Giuffrè, 1986.

Manetti, M. 'Procedimenti, controlli costituzionali e conflitti nella formazione degli atti legislativi'. In *Decisone, conflitti, controlli. Procedure costituzionali e sistema politico*. Naples: Jovene, 2012.

Piccirilli, G. *L'emendamento nel processo di decisione parlamentare.* Padua: Cedam, 2008.

Recchia, G. & R. Dickmann. *Istruttoria parlamentare e qualità della normazione*. Pauda: Cedam, 2002.

Decree-Laws

Concaro, A. *Il sindacato di costituzionalità sul decreto-legge.* Milan: Giuffrè, 2000.

Pitruzzella, G. *La legge di conversione dei decreti legge.* Padua: Cedam, 1989.

Simoncini, A. *Le funzioni del decreto legge.* Milan: Giuffrè, 2003.

Spadacini, L. *Decreto-legge e alterazione del quadro costituzionale. Distorsioni del bicameralismo, degenerazioni del sistema delle fonti e inefficacia dei controlli.* Bari: Cacucci, 2022.

Zaccaria, R. (ed.). *Aspetti problematici nella evoluzione delle fonti normative*. Rome: Camera dei deputati, 2008.

Legislative Decrees

Caretti, P. & A. Ruggeri. *Le deleghe legislative: riflessioni sulla recente esperienza normativa e giurisprudenziale*. Milan: Giuffrè, 2003.
Cervati, A.A. *La delega legislativa*. Milan: Giuffrè, 1972.
De Fiores, C. *Trasformazioni della delega legislativa e crisi delle categorie normative*. Padua: Cedam, 2001.
Eds. *La delega legislativa*. Atti del Seminario svoltosi a Roma, Palazzo della Consulta il 24 ottobre 2008. Milan: Giuffrè, 2009.
Maccabiani, N. *La legge delegata: vincoli costituzionali e discrezionalità del Governo*. Milan: Giuffrè, 2005.
Rossi, E. (ed.). *Le trasformazioni della delega legislativa: contributo all'analisi delle deleghe legislative nella XIV e XV legislatura*. Padua: Cedam, 2009.

Parliamentary Control on the Government's Political Activities

Amato, G. *L'ispezione politica del Parlamento*. Milan: Giuffrè, 1968.
Borrello, R. *Segreti pubblici e poteri giudiziari delle Commissioni d'inchiesta: profili costituzionalistici*. Milan: Giuffrè, 2003.
Manzella, A. *I controlli parlamentari*. Milan: Giuffrè, 1970.
Manzella, A. 'Interrogazione e interpellanza parlamentare'. In *Enciclopedia del diritto*. vol. XXII. Milan: Giuffrè, 1972.
Pace, A. *Il potere di inchiesta delle Assemblee legislative*. Milan: Giuffrè, 1973.

The Executive

Government in General

Associazione Italiana dei Costituzionalisti. *Annuario 2001. Il Governo. Atti del XVI Convegno annuale (Palermo, 8–9–10 novembre 2001)*. Padua: Cedam, 2002.
Bartole, S. 'Governo italiano'. In *Digesto Discipline Pubblicistiche*. vol. VIII, Turin: UTET, 1991.
Biscaretti di Ruffia, P. 'Governo'. In *Novissimo Digesto Italiano*. vol. VII. Turin: UTET, 1961.
Calandra, P. *Il Governo della Repubblica*. Bologna: il Mulino, 2001.
Capotosti, P.A. 'Governo'. In *Enciclopedia giuridica*. vol. XV. Rome: Treccani, 1989.
Catelani, E. *Potere e organizzazione del governo nel contesto degli ordinamenti pluralistici contemporanei*. Pisa: Tipografia Editrice Pisana, 2017.
Cuocolo, F. *Il governo nel vigente ordinamento italiano*. Milan: Giuffrè, 1959.
Eds. 'Il Governo della Repubblica a trent'anni dalla legge n. 400/1988'. In *Osservatoriosullefonti.it*. Special Issue, 2019.
Labriola, S. *Il Governo della Repubblica. Organi e poteri*. 2nd edn. Rimini: Maggioli, 1997.
Merlini, S. & G. Tarli Barbieri. *Il governo parlamentare in Italia*. Turin: Giappichelli, 2017.

Melis, G. 'Prima e dopo la Costituente. Il governo debole'. In *Rivista trimestrale di diritto pubblico*. Milan: Giuffrè, 2018.
Musella, F. (ed.). *Il governo in Italia. Profili costituzionali e dinamiche politiche*. Bologna: il Mulino, 2019.
Niccolai, S. *Il governo*. Rome-Bari: Laterza, 2003.
Pajno, A. & L. Torchia. *La riforma del governo*. Bologna: il Mulino, 2000.
Paladin, L. 'Governo italiano'. In *Enciclopedia del Diritto*, vol. XIX. Milan: Giuffrè, 1970.
Spagna Musso, E. (ed.). *Costituzione e struttura del Governo*, vol. IV. Padua: Cedam, 1979–1988.

The Council of Ministers

Barile, P. 'Consiglio dei Ministri'. In *Enciclopedia Giuridica*, vol. VIII. Rome: Treccani, 1991.
Biscaretti di Ruffia, P. 'Consiglio dei Ministri'. In *Novissimo Digesto Italiano*, vol. IV. Turin: UTET, 1959.
Cuocolo, F. 'Consiglio dei Ministri'. In *Enciclopedia del Diritto*, vol. IX. Milan: Giuffrè, 1961.
Pitruzzella, G., et al. 'Il Consiglio dei Ministri: art. 92–96'. In *Commentario della Costituzione*, edited by G. Branca & A. Pizzorusso. Bologna-Rome: Zanichelli-Il Foro Italiano, 1994.
Ruggeri, A. *Il Consiglio dei ministri nella Costituzione italiana.* Milan: Giuffrè, 1981.

President of the Council of Ministers

Capotosti, P.A. 'Presidente del Consiglio dei Ministri'. In *Enciclopedia del Diritto*, vol. XXXV. Milan: Giuffrè, 1986.
Cassese, S., A. Melloni, & Pajno, A. (eds). *I presidenti e la presidenza del Consiglio dei ministri nell'Italia repubblicana. Storia, politica, istituzioni*. Rome-Bari: Laterza, 2022.
Ciolli, I. '*La questione del vertice di Palazzo Chigi. Il Presidente del Consiglio nella Costituzione repubblicana*'. Naples: Jovene, 2018.
Clementi F. *Il Presidente del Consiglio dei Ministri. Mediatore o decisore?* Bologna: il Mulino, 2023.
Di Andrea, C. (ed.). *Il nuovo ordinamento del Governo in Italia. Introduzione e testi*. Rome: Istituto Poligrafico e Zecca dello Stato, 2002.
Gatta, E. 'Presidenza del Consiglio dei Ministri'. In *Novissimo Digesto Italiano*, vol. XIII. Turin: UTET, 1966.
Labriola, S. 'Presidenza del Consiglio dei Ministri'. In *Enciclopedia del Diritto,* vol. I. Milan: Giuffrè, 1997.
Manzella, A. 'Il Presidente del Governo'. In *Rivistaaic.it*. Rome: Giappichelli, 2021.
Pitruzzella, G. *Il Presidente del Consiglio dei Ministri e l'organizzazione del Governo.* Padua: Cedam, 1986.
Predieri, A. 'Presidente del Consiglio dei Ministri'. In *Enciclopedia Giuridica*, vol. XXIV. Rome: Treccani, 1991.

Razza, A. (ed.). *La Presidenza del Consiglio dei ministri a trent'anni dalla legge n. 400 del 1988: atti del Convegno di studi del 20 febbraio 2018, Roma Università LUISS Guido Carli*. Rome: Presidenza del Consiglio dei Ministri, Dipartimento per l'informazione e l'editoria, 2020.
Rizza, G. *Il Presidente del Consiglio dei Ministri*. Naples: Jovene, 1970.
Rotelli, E. *La Presidenza del Consiglio dei Ministri*. Milan: Giuffrè, 1970.
Severi, F.S. '"Presidenza del Consiglio" (organizzazione amministrativa)'. In *Digesto Discipline Pubblicistiche*, vol. XI. Turin: UTET, 1996.
Tedoldi, L. (ed.). *Il presidente del Consiglio dei ministri dallo Stato liberale all'Unione europea*. Milan: Biblion, 2019.

Ministers

Bertolini, F. 'Ministri e Vice Ministri'. In *Enciclopedia Giuridica*, vol. XVII. Rome: Treccani, 2009.
Carlassare, L. 'Ministeri'. In *Enciclopedia del Diritto*, vol. XXVI. Milan: Giuffrè, 1976.
Cuccodoro, E. *I limiti dell'autonomia ministeriale nel governo parlamentare di partito*. Florence: Noccioli, 1991.
Ciaurro, G.F. 'Ministro'. In *Enciclopedia del Diritto*, vol. XXVI. Milan: Giuffrè, 1976.
Gatta, E. 'Ministeri e Ministri'. In *Novissimo Digesto Italiano*, vol. X. Turin: UTET, 1964.
Sepe, O. 'Ministeri e Ministri'. In *Novissimo Digesto Italiano, Appendice*, vol. V. Turin: UTET, 1984.
Severi, F.S. 'Ministro e Ministeri'. In *Digesto Discipline Pubblicistiche*, vol. IX. Turin: UTET, 1994.
Stipo, M. 'Ministero'. In *Enciclopedia Giuridica*, vol. XX. Rome: Treccani, 1990.
Romanelli Grimaldi, C. 'Ministro'. In *Enciclopedia Giuridica*, vol. XX. Rome: Treccani, 1990.

Under Secretaries of State

Ciaurro, L. 'Sottosegretario di Stato'. In *Enciclopedia del Diritto*, vol. XLIII. Milan: Giuffrè, 1990.
Cuocolo, F. 'Sottosegretari di Stato'. In *Novissimo Digesto Italiano*, vol. XVII. Turin: UTET, 1976.
Cuocolo, F. 'Sottosegretari di Stato'. *Enciclopedia Giuridica*, vol. XXX. Rome: Treccani, 1993.

Government High Commissioners

Biscaretti di Ruffia, P. 'Alto Commissario'. In *Enciclopedia del Diritto*, vol. II. Milan: Giuffrè, 1958.
Rizza, G. 'Commissario e Alto Commissario'. In *Enciclopedia Giuridica*, vol. VII. Rome: Treccani, 1988.
Rizza, G. 'Commissario straordinario'. In *Enciclopedia Giuridica*, vol. VII. Rome: Treccani, 1988.

Selected Bibliography

Interministerial Committees and Committees of Ministers

Bachelet, V. 'Comitati interministeriali'. In *Enciclopedia del Diritto*, vol. VII. Milan: Giuffrè, 1960.

Coduti, D. *I comitati interministeriali tra affermazione e crisi del governo maggioritario*. Naples: Jovene, 2013.

Mattioni, A. 'Comitati interministeriali'. In *Enciclopedia Giuridica*, vol. VI. Rome: Treccani, 1988.

Pizzetti, F. 'Comitati interministeriali'. In *Novissimo Digesto Italiano, Appendice*, vol. II. Turin: UTET, 1981.

Quadri, G. *I Comitati di Ministri.* Milan: Giuffrè, 1997.

Treves, G. 'Comitato interministeriale'. In *Novissimo Digesto Italiano*, vol. III, Turin: UTET, 1959.

The Cabinet Council

Rescigno, G.U. 'Consiglio di Gabinetto'. In *Enciclopedia del Diritto, Aggiornamento*, vol. II. Milan: Giuffrè, 1998.

Government Formation

Armaroli, P. 'Crisi di governo'. In *Enciclopedia giuridica italiana*, vol. X. Rome: Treccani, 1988.

Caravita, B., F. et al. (eds). *La nascita dei Governi della Repubblica. 1946–2021.* Turin: Giappichelli, 2022.

Cavaggion, G. *La formazione del Governo. Aspetti e problemi tra quadro costituzionale e nuove prassi.* Turin: Giappichelli, 2020.

Galizia, M. 'Crisi di gabinetto'. In *Enciclopedia del Diritto*, vol. XI. Milan: Giuffrè, 1962.

Romano, A.A. *La formazione del Governo.* Padua: Cedam, 1977.

The Status and Responsibility of Government Members

Caretti, P. 'Responsabilità politica'. In *Enciclopedia Giuridica*, vol. XXVII. Rome: Treccani, 1991.

Ciancio, A. *Il reato ministeriale.* Milan: Giuffrè, 2000.

Dell'Anno, P. *Il procedimento per i reati ministeriali.* Milan: Giuffrè, 2001.

Di Raimo, G. '*Reati ministeriali e presidenziali*'. In *Enciclopedia del Diritto*, vol. XXXVIII. Milan: Giuffrè, 1987.

Donati, F. *La responsabilità politica dei ministri nella forma di governo italiana.* Turin: Giappichelli, 1997.

Masera, L. *Immunità della politica e diritti fondamentali. I limiti all'irresponsabilità penale dei ministri*. Turin: Giappichelli, 2020.

Rescigno, G.U. 'Responsabilità'. In *Enciclopedia del Diritto*, vol. XXXIX. Milan: Giuffrè, 1988.

Sagone, C. 'Profili ricostruttivi della responsabilità penale dei ministri tra modello astratto e prassi applicativa'. In *Rivistaaic.it*. Rome: Giappichelli 2021.

Scarlato, G. 'Reati ministeriali'. In *Enciclopedia Giuridica*, vol. XXVI. Rome: Treccani, 1991.

Zagrebelsky, G. 'Procedimento e giudizi d'accusa'. In *Enciclopedia del Diritto*, vol. XXXV. Milan: Giuffrè, 1986.

The Government in Parliament: The Relationship of Confidence

Confidence

Galizia, M. *Studi sui rapporti fra Parlamento e Governo*. Milan: Giuffrè, 1972.
Giocoli Nacci, P. *Il rapporto Parlamento-Governo nella consuetudine e nella prassi.* Padua: Cedam, 1995.
Mannino, A. *Indirizzo politico e fiducia nei rapporti tra Governo e Parlamento.* Milan: Giuffrè, 1973.

The No-confidence Motion Against a Single Member of Government

Chiola, C. 'Uno strappo alla Costituzione: la sfiducia al singolo ministro'. In *Giurisprudenza costituzionale.* Milan: Giuffrè, 1986.
Mazzoni Honorati, M.L. 'Sfiducia individuale e responsabilità governativa'. In *Diritto e società.* Padua: Cedam, 1988.
Angiolini, V., et al. 'Sei domande ai costituzionalisti provocate dal "caso Mancuso"'. In *Giurisprudenza costituzionale.* Milan: Giuffrè, 1995.

The Question of Confidence

Rizza, G. 'Questione di fiducia, regolamenti parlamentari e attribuzioni dell'Esecutivo'. In *Diritto e società.* Padua: Cedam, 1991.
Olivetti, M. *La questione di fiducia nel sistema parlamentare italiano.* Milan: Giuffrè, 1996.

The Judicial Power

Bartole, S. *Autonomia e indipendenza dell'ordine giudiziario.* Milan: Giuffrè, 1964.
Bartole, S. 'Materiali per un riesame della posizione del Consiglio Superiore della Magistratura'. In *Scritti in onore di C. Mortati*, IV. Milan: Giuffrè, 1977.
Bartole, S., et al. 'Il Consiglio Superiore della Magistratura'. In *Quaderni costituzionali.* Bologna: il Mulino, 1989.
Biondi, F., 'Ordinamento giudiziario: novità, attese e prospettive'. In *Federalismi.it.* Rome: 2023.
Onida, V. 'Giurisdizione e giudici nella giurisprudenza della Corte costituzionale'. In *Corte costituzionale e sviluppo della forma di governo in Italia*, edited by P. Barile, E. Cheli & S. Grassi. Bologna: il Mulino, 1982.
Cheli, E. *Il giudice delle leggi.* 2nd edn. Bologna: il Mulino, 1999.
Pizzorusso, A. (ed.). *L'ordinamento giudiziario.* Bologna: il Mulino, 1974.
Pizzorusso, A. *L'organizzazione della giustizia in Italia.* Turin: Einaudi, 1982.
Silvestri, A. 'Giudici ordinari, giudici speciali e unità della giurisdizione nella Costituzione italiana'. In *Scritti Giannini*, vol. III. Milan: Giuffrè, 1988.
Romboli, R. & S. Panizza. *Ordinamento giudiziario e forense.* Pisa: Università di Pisa, 2003.
Teresi, F. *Il Consiglio Superiore della Magistratura.* Milan: Giuffrè, 1985.
Verde, G. *L'amministrazione della giustizia fra Ministro e Consiglio Superiore.* Padua: Cedam, 1990.

Vigoriti, V. et al. 'Il giudice e l'organizzazione giudiziaria', In *Quaderni costituzionali*. Bologna: il Mulino, 1983.
Zanon, N. *Pubblico ministero e Costituzione.* Padua: Cedam, 1996.
Zanon, N. & F. Biondi. *Diritto costituzionale dell'ordine giudiziario.* Milan: Giuffrè, 2002.

The Constitutional Court

Cappelletti, M. *Il controllo di costituzionalità delle leggi nel diritto italiano e comparato*. Milan: Giuffrè, 1968.
Cerri, A. *La giustizia costituzionale.* Milan: Giuffrè, 1998.
Crisafulli, V. *Lezioni di diritto costituzionale*, vol. II. Padua: Cedam, 1984.
D'Amico, M. *Parti e processo nella giustizia costituzionale.* Turin: Giappichelli, 1991.
D'Amico, M. & G. D'Elia. *Diritto costituzionale*. Milan: FrancoAngeli, 2012.
Barsotti, V. et al. *Italian Constitutional Justice in Global Context.* New York: Oxford University Press USA, 2015.
Barsotti, V. et al. *Dialogues on Italian Constitutional Justice: A Comparative Perspective*. London-New York-Turin: Routledge-Giappichelli, 2020.
D'Orazio, G. *La genesi della Corte costituzionale*. Milan: Giuffrè, 1981.
Grassi, S. *I conflitti di attribuzione fra Stato e regioni e fra regioni.* Milan: Giuffrè, 1984.
Lamarque, E. *Corte costituzionale e giudici nell'Italia repubblicana. Nuova serie, altri episodi*. Naples: Editoriale Scientifica, 2021.
Mezzanotte, C. *La Corte costituzionale, I, Le ideologie del costituente.* Rome: Veneziana, 1979.
Onida, V. 'L'attuazione della Costituzione fra magistratura e Corte costituzionale'. In *Scritti in onore di C. Mortati*, vol. IV. Milan: Giuffrè, 1977.
Onida, V. & M. D'Amico. *Il giudizio di costituzionalità delle leggi. Materiali di giustizia costituzionale, I, Il giudizio in via incidentale*. Turin: Giappichelli, 1998.
Pisaneschi, A. *I conflitti di attribuzione fra Poteri dello Stato.* Milan: Giuffrè, 1992.
Ruggeri, A. & V. Spadaro. *Lineamenti di giustizia costituzionale.* Turin: Giappichelli, 1998.
Tarchi, R. (ed.). 'Patrimonio costituzionale europeo e tutela dei diritti fondamentali. Il ricorso diretto di costituzionalità'. In *Quaderni del Dipartimento di Diritto Pubblico dell'Università di Pisa.* Turin: Giappichelli, 2012.
Zagrebelsky, G. & V. Marcenò. *Giustizia costituzionale.* Bologna: il Mulino, 2012.

Judicial Control of Administrative Action

Balboni E., *Amministrazione giudiziale*. Padua: Cedam, 1986.
Caringella, F. & M. Protto. *Manuale di diritto processuale amministrativo.* Rome: Dike giuridica, 2012.
Garofoli, R. & G. Ferrari. *Manuale di diritto amministrativo*. 6th. edn, Molfetta: Nel diritto, 2012.
Travi, A. *Lezioni di giustizia amministrativa.* Turin: Giappichelli, 2012.

Selected Bibliography

The Administration in the Constitution

Cerulli Irelli, V. *Lineamenti di diritto amministrativo.* 3rd edn. Turin: Giappichelli, 2012.
Torchia, L. *Il sistema amministrativo italiano.* Bologna: il Mulino, 2009.
Pastori, G. *Scritti scelti*, vols I and II. Naples: Jovene, 2010.

The Budget Process

De Joanna, P. *Parlamento e spesa pubblica.* Bologna: il Mulino, 1993.
Onida, V. *Le leggi di spesa nella Costituzione.* Milan: Giuffrè, 1969.
Pieroni, M. 'Il ciclo dei documenti programmatici di consuntivo'. In *Rivista della Corte dei conti.* Soveria Mannelli (Cz): Rubettino, 2001.

The State and Its Subdivisions

Barbera, A. & F. Bassanini. *I nuovi poteri delle regioni e degli enti locali. Commentario del decreto 616.* Bologna: il Mulino, 1978.
Bartole, S. & F. Mastragostino. *Le Regioni.* Bologna: il Mulino, 1999.
Bartole, S. & P. Giangaspero, *Diritto regionale. Una conversazione.* Bologna: il Mulino 2022.
Berti, G. & C. De Martin. *Le autonomie territoriali: dalla riforma amministrativa alla riforma costituzionale.* Milan: Giuffrè, 2001.
Bin, R. & G. Falcon. *Diritto regionale.* Bologna: il Mulino, 2018.
Bin, R. & F. Ferrari. *Il futuro delle regioni.* Naples: Edizioni scientifiche, 2023.
Caravita, B. *La Costituzione dopo la riforma del titolo V.* Turin: Giappichelli, 2003.
Caretti, P. & G. Tarli Barbieri. *Diritto regionale.* Turin: Giappichelli, 2019.
Carli, M. *Diritto regionale. Le autonomie regionali, speciali e ordinarie.* 3rd edn. Turin: Giappichelli, 2022.
Cavaleri, P. *Diritto regionale.* Padua: Cedam, 2009.
Camerlengo, Q. *Le fonti regionali del diritto in trasformazione.* Milan: Giuffrè, 2000.
Carloni, E. & F. Cortese, *Diritto delle autonomie territoriali.* Padua: Cedam, 2020.
D'Atena, A. *Costituzione e Regioni.* Milan: Giuffrè, 1991.
D'Atena, A. *Diritto regionale.* Turin: Giappichelli, 2019.
Di Maria, R., C. Napoli & A. Pertici, *Diritto delle autonomie locali*, Turin: Giappichelli, 2022.
Ferrara, M. *Verso una fase costituente delle Regioni?* Milan: Giuffrè, 2001.
Falcon, G. et al. *Governi locali, regioni e Stato nel nuovo titolo V della parte II della Costituzione.* In *Le Regioni.* Bologna: il Mulino, 2001.
Giarda, P. *Regioni and federalismo fiscale.* Bologna: il Mulino, 1995.
Groppi, T. & M. Olivetti. *La Repubblica delle autonomie: Regioni ed enti locali nel nuovo titolo V.* 2nd edn. Turin: Giappichelli, 2003.
Martines, T., A. Ruggeri, C. Salazar & A. Morelli. *Lineamenti di diritto regionale.* Milan: Giuffrè, 2022.
Onida, V. 'Il regionalismo in Italia: origini, caratteri, prospettive'. In *Associazione per gli studi e le ricerche parlamentari*, vol. III. Milan: Giuffrè, 1993.
Paladin, L. *Diritto regionale.* Padua: Cedam, 1997.
Pizzetti, F. *Il sistema costituzionale delle autonomie locali.* Milan: Giuffrè, 1979.

Pizzetti, F. *Il nuovo ordinamento italiano tra riforme amministrative e riforme costituzionali.* Turin: Giappichelli, 2002.
Romboli, R. et al. 'Le modifiche al titolo V della parte seconda della Costituzione'. In *Il Foro italiano*. Rome: Il Foro italiano, 2001.
Rotelli, E. *Dal regionalismo alla Regione.* Bologna: il Mulino, 1973.
Ruggeri, G. *Le fonti di diritto regionale: ieri, oggi, domani.* Turin: Giappichelli, 2001.
Tosi, A. 'I nuovi statuti delle Regioni ordinarie: procedimento and limiti'. In *Le Regioni*. Bologna: il Mulino, 2000.
Vandelli L. *Il sistema delle autonomie locali.* 8th. edn. Bologna: Il Mulino, 2021.
Volpi, M. 'Considerazioni di metodo e di merito sulla legge costituzionale n. 1 del 1999'. In *Politica del diritto*. Bologna: il Mulino, 2000.

The Citizenship

Biscottini, G., '*Cittadinanza'*. In *Enciclopedia del diritto*, vol. VI. Milan: Giuffrè, 1960.
Clerici, R. *La cittadinanza.* Milan: Giuffrè, 1993.
Bariatti, S. *La disciplina giuridica della cittadinanza italiana.* Milan: Giuffrè, 1996.
Castorina, E. *Introduzione allo studio della cittadinanza.* Milan: Giuffrè, 1997.
Grosso, E. *Le vie della cittadinanza.* Milan: Giuffrè, 1997.
Cuniberti, M. *La cittadinanza*. Padua: Cedam, 1997.
Nascimbene, B. (ed.). *Diritto degli stranieri*. Padua: Cedam, 2004.

The General Aspects of Fundamental Rights

Angiolini, V. (ed.). *Libertá e giurisprudenza costituzionale.* Turin: Giappichelli, 1992.
Angiolini, V. *Diritti Umani. Sette lezioni.* Turin: Giappichelli, 2012.
Baldassarre, A. *Diritti della persona e valori costituzionali.* Turin: Giappichelli, 1997.
Barile, P. *Il soggetto privato nella costituzione italiana*. Padua: Cedam, 1953.
Barile, P. *Diritti dell'uomo e libertà fondamentali.* Bologna: il Mulino, 1984.
Bobbio, N. *L'Etá dei diritti.* Turin: Einaudi, 1992.
Caretti, P. *I diritti fondamentali*. Turin: Giappichelli, 2002.
Carlassare, L. (ed.). *Le garanzie giurisdizionali dei diritti fondamentali.* Padua: Cedam, 1988.
Grossi, P.F. *I dritti di libertà ad uso di lezioni.* Turin: Giappichelli, 1991.
Lamarque, E. 'The Italian Constitution: A Personalist Constitution'. In *Italian Journal of Public Law*. Naples: Editoriale Scientifica, 2022.
Lombardi, G. *Contributo allo studio dei doveri costituzionali.* Milan: Giuffrè, 1967.
Lombardi, G. *Potere privato e diritti fondamentali*. Milan: Giuffrè, 1970.
Modugno, F. *I nuovi diritti nella giurisprudenza costituzionale.* Turin: Giappichelli, 1995.
Nania, R. & P. Ridola. *I diritti costituzionali*, vols I and II. Turin: Giappichelli, 2001.
Pace, A. *Problematica delle libertà costituzionali, Parte generale*, vol. I. Padua: Cedam, 1990.

Ponthoreau, M.C. *La reconnaissance des droits non écrits par les Cours constitutionnelles italienne et française.* Paris: Economica, 1994.
Ridola, P. *Diritti di libertà e costituzionalismo.* Turin: Giappichelli, 1997.
Romboli, R. (ed.). *La tutela dei diritti fondamentali davanti alle Corti costituzionali.* Turin: Giappichelli, 1994.

Multilevel Protection of Fundamental Rights

Cartabia, M. 'The Many and The Few: Clash of Values or Reasonable Accommodation?'. In *American University International Law Review*. Washington: Washington College of Law Journals & Law Reviews, 2017.
Cartabia, M. 'A Pluralistic Europe of Rights'. In H.W. Micklitz & B. De Witte, *The European Court of Justice and the Autonomy of the Members States*. Cambridge-Antwerp-Portland: Intersentia, 2012.
Cartabia, M. 'The European Court of Human Rights: Judging Non-discrimination'. In *International Journal of Constitutional Law*. Oxford: Oxford University Press, 2011.
Cartabia, M. 'Europe and Rights: Taking Dialogue Seriously'. In *European Constitutional Law Review*. Cambridge: Cambridge University Press, 2009.
Guarnier, T. & E. Lamarque. 'Interpretation in Conformity with EU Law in the Italian Legal System'. In *Effectiveness and Application of EU and EEA Law in National Courts. Principles of Consistent Interpretation*, edited by C.N.K. Franklin. Cambridge: Intersentia, 2018.
Randazzo, B. *Giustizia costituzionale sovranazionale. La Corte europea dei diritti dell'uomo.* Milan: Giuffrè, 2012.
Tega, D. *I diritti in crisi. Tra corti nazionali e Corte europea dei diritti.* Milan: Giuffrè, 2012.

Key Rights Enshrined in the Constitution

Rights of Freedom

Amato, G. 'Libertà'. In *Enciclopedia del diritto*, vol. XXIV. Milan: Giuffrè, 1974.
Baldassarre, A. 'Libertà'. In *Enciclopedia giuridica italiana*, vol. XIX. Rome: Treccani, 1990.
Pace, A. *Problematica delle libertà costituzionali, parte speciale*, vol. II. Padua: Cedam, 1992.

Personal Liberty

Amato, G. *Individuo e autorità nella disciplina della libertà personale.* Milan: Giuffrè, 1967.
Barbera, A. *I principi costituzionali della libertà personale.* Milan: Giuffrè, 1967.
Caretti, P. 'La libertà personale'. In *Trattato di diritto amministrativo*, vol. XII, edited by G. Santaniello. Padua: Cedam, 1990.
Cerri, A. 'Libertà personale'. In *Enciclopedia giuridica italiana*, vol. XIX. Rome: Treccani, 1990.
Elia, L. *Libertà personale e misure di prevenzione.* Milan: Giuffrè, 1962.
Galeotti, S. *La libertà personale.* Milan: Giuffrè, 1953.

Nania, R. *La libertà individuale nell'esperienza costituzionale italiana*. Turin: Giappichelli, 1989.
Pace, A. 'Libertà personale'. In *Enciclopedia del diritto*, vol. XXIV. Milan: Giuffrè, 1974.
Tallin, S. *La privazione della libertà personale. Metamorfosi normative, apporti giurisprudenziali, applicazioni amministrative*. Naples: Editoriale Scientifica, 2018.

Inviolability of Personal Domicile

Barile, P. & E. Cheli. 'Domicilio'. In *Enciclopedia del diritto*, vol. XIII. Milan: Giuffrè, 1964.
Caretti, P. 'Domicilio'. In *Digesto discipline pubblicistiche,* vol. V. Turin: UTET, 1990.
Chiarelli, A. 'Domicilio'. In *Enciclopedia giuridica italiana*, vol. XII. Rome: Treccani, 1989.

Freedom of Movement, Residence, Expatriation and Emigration

D'Amico, G. *La libertà «capovolta». Circolazione e soggiorno nello stato costituzionale*. Naples: Editoriale Scientifica, 2020.
De Siervo, U. 'Soggiorno, circolazione, emigrazione'. In *Novissimo digesto italiano*, vol. XVIII. Turin: UTET, 1970.
Mazziotti, M. 'Circolazione'. In *Enciclopedia del diritto*, vol. VII. Milan: Giuffrè, 1960.
Mazziotti, M. 'Espatrio'. In *Enciclopedia del diritto*, vol. XV. Milan: Giuffrè, 1966.

Freedom of Assembly

Borrello, P. 'Riunione'. In *Enciclopedia del diritto*, vol. XL. Milan: Giuffrè, 1988.

Freedom of Association

Barile, P. 'Associazione'. In *Enciclopedia del diritto*, vol. III. Milan: Giuffrè, 1958.
Bartole, S. *Problemi costituzionali della libertà di associazione*. Milan: Giuffrè, 1970.
Brunelli, G. *Struttura e limiti del diritto di associazione politica*. Milan: Giuffrè, 1991.
De Siervo, U. 'Associazione'. In *Digesto discipline pubblicistiche*, vol. I. Turin: UTET, 1987.
Ridola, P. 'Associazione'. In *Enciclopedia Giuridica italiana*, vol. II. Rome: Treccani, 1988.
Ridola, P. *Democrazia pluralistica e libertà associative*. Milan: Giuffrè, 1987.
Rigano, F. *La libertà assistita*. Padua: Cedam, 1995.

Freedom of Communication

Barile, P. & E. Cheli. 'Corrispondenza'. In *Enciclopedia del diritto*, vol. X. Milan: Giuffrè, 1962.
Caretti, P. 'Corrispondenza'. In *Digesto discipline pubblicistiche*, 4th edn, vol. IV. Turin: UTET, 1989.

Italia, V. *Libertà e segretezza della corrispondenza e delle comunicazioni.* Milan: Giuffrè, 1963.

Freedom of Expression and Freedom of the Arts and Sciences

Barile, P. *La libertà di manifestazione del pensiero.* Milan: Giuffrè, 1975.
Bassini, M. *Internet e libertà di espressione. Prospettive costituzionali e sovranazionali.* Rome: Aracne, 2019.
Caruso, C. *La libertà di espressione in azione. Contributo a una teoria costituzionale del discorso pubblico.* Bologna: Bononia University Press, 2014.
Cerri, A. 'Arte e scienza'. In *Enciclopedia giuridica italiana*, vol. III. Rome: Treccani, 1988.
Chiola, C. *L'informazione nella costituzione.* Padua: Cedam, 1973.
Chiola, C. 'Manifestazione del pensiero'. In *Enciclopedia giuridica italiana*, vol. XIX. Rome: Treccani, 1988.
Cuniberti, M., et al. *Percorsi di diritto dell'informazione.* Turin: Giappichelli, 2003.
Di Giovine, A. *I confini della libertà di manifestazione del pensiero.* Milan: Giuffrè, 1988.
Esposito, C. *La libertà di manifestazione del pensiero nell'ordinamento italiano.* Milan: Giuffrè, 1958.
Fois, S. *Principi costituzionali e libera manifestazione del pensiero.* Milan: Giuffrè, 1957.
Luciani, M. 'La libertà di informazione nella giurisprudenza costituzionale italiana'. In *Politica del diritto.* Bologna: il Mulino, 1989.
Pace, A. *Stampa, giornalismo, radiotelevisione.* Padua: Cedam, 1983.
Pedrazza Gorlero, M. *Giornalismo e costituzione.* Padua: Cedam, 1988.
Pollicino, O. *Judicial Protection of Fundamental Rights on the Internet: A Road Towards Digital Constitutionalism?* Oxford: Hart Publishing, 2021.
Vigevani, G.E., et al. *Diritto dell'informazione e dei media.* Turin: Giappichelli, 2019.
Rimoli, F. *La libertà dell'arte nell'ordinamento italiano.* Padua: Cedam, 1991.

Protection of the Family

Carlotto, I. *La ricerca delle proprie origini nel bilanciamento dei diritti.* Naples: Edizioni Scientifiche Italiane, 2020.
Giuffrè, F. & I. Nicotra. *La famiglia davanti ai suoi giudici.* Naples: Editoriale Scientifica, 2014.
Lamarque, E. *Prima i bambini. Il principio dei best interests of the child nella prospettiva costituzionale.* Milan: FrancoAngeli, 2016.

Social Rights

Balboni E., B. Baroni, A. Mattioni & G. Pastori, *Il sistema integrato dei servizi sociali.* 2nd edn. Milan: Giuffrè, 2007.
Balboni E. (ed.). *Il sistema multilivello dei diritti sociali.* Naples: Jovene, 2008.
Baldassarre, A. 'Diritti sociali'. In *Enciclopedia giuridica italiana*, vol. XI. Rome: Treccani, 1989.
Corso, A. 'I diritti sociali nella Costituzione italiana'. In *Rivista trimestrale di diritto pubblico.* Milan: Giuffrè, 1981.

Longo, E. *Le relazioni giuridiche nel sistema dei diritti sociali. Profili teorici e costituzionali.* Padua: Cedam, 2012.
Luciani, M. 'Sui diritti sociali'. In *Studi in onore di M. Mazziotti*, vol. II. Padua: Cedam, 1995.
Mazziotti, M. 'Diritti sociali'. In *Enciclopedia del diritto*, vol. XII. Milan: Giuffrè, 1964.
Scala, G. & G. Verde. *I diritti sociali dal riconoscimento alla garanzia. Il ruolo della giurisprudenza.* Naples: Editoriale Scientifica, 2013.

Health Safeguards

Anzon, A. 'L'altra faccia del diritto alla salute'. In *Giurisprudenza costituzionale.* Milan: Giuffrè, 1988.
Balduzzi, R. (ed.). *La sanità italiana alla prova del federalismo fiscale.* Bologna: il Mulino, 2012.
Bottari, C. *Principi costituzionali e assistenza sanitaria.* Milan: Giuffrè, 1991.
Lamarque, E. *Le cure palliative nel quadro costituzionale*. In *Rivistaaic.it*. Rome: Giappichelli, 2021.
Luciani, M. 'Il diritto costituzionale alla salute'. In *Diritto e società*. Padua: Cedam, 1980.
Luciani, M. 'Salute'. In *Enciclopedia giuridica italiana.* Rome: Treccani, 1988.

The Rights of Workers

Cerri, A. 'Profili costituzionali del sistema pensionistico'. In *Diritto e società*. Padua: Cedam, 1983.
Fois, S. *Sindacati e sistema politico.* Milan: Giuffrè, 1977.
Nania, R. *Sciopero e sistema costituzionale.* Turin: Giappichelli, 1995.
Villone, M. *Sciopero e solidarietà nella Costituzione italiana.* Naples: Jovene, 1980.

The Protection of Linguistic Minorities

Bartole, S. 'Minoranze nazionali'. In *Novissimo digesto italiano, Appendice*, vol. V. Turin: UTET, 1985.
Pizzorusso, A. *Le minoranze nel diritto pubblico interno.* Milan: Giuffrè, 1967.
Pizzorusso, A. *Minoranze e maggioranze.* Turin: Einaudi, 1993.

Relations Between the State and Religious Denominations

Berlingò, S. 'Fonti del diritto ecclesiastico'. In *Digesto Discipline Pubblicistiche*, vol. VI. Turin: UTET, 1991.
Cardia, C. *Il sistema pattizio.* Bologna: il Mulino, 1985.
Cardia, C. *Stato e confessioni religiose.* Bologna: il Mulino, 1990.
Colajanni, N. 'Stato e confessioni religiose diverse dalla cattolica'. In *Enciclopedia del Diritto*, vol. XLIII. Milan: Giuffrè, 1990.
Colajanni, N. 'Stato e Chiesa cattolica'. In *Enciclopedia del Diritto*, vol. XLIII. Milan: Giuffrè, 1990.
Finocchiaro, M. 'Concordato e Costituzione'. In *Digesto discipline pubblicistiche*, vol. III. Turin: UTET, 1989.
Long, G. 'Intese con le confessioni religiose diverse dalla cattolica'. In *Enciclopedia Giuridica italiana*, vol. XVII. Rome: Treccani, 1993.

Margiotta Broglio, F. 'Chiesa cattolica e organizzazione internazionale'. In *Digesto Discipline Pubblicistiche*, vol. III. Turin: UTET, 1989.
Peyrot. 'Confessioni religiose diverse dalla cattolica'. In *Digesto Discipline Pubblicistiche*, vol. III. Turin: UTET, 1989.
Randazzo, B. *Diversi ed uguali. Le confessioni religiose davanti alla legge.* Milan: Giuffrè, 2008.

The Economic Constitution

Amato, G. *Il governo dell'industria in Italia.* Bologna: il Mulino, 1972.
Amato, G. *Economia, politica e istituzioni in Italia.* Bologna: il Mulino, 1976.
Bachelet, V. *L'attività di coordinamento nell'amministrazione pubblica dell'economia.* Milan: Giuffrè, 1957.
Baldassarre, A. 'Iniziativa economica privata'. In *Enciclopedia del Diritto*, vol. XXI. Milan: Giuffrè, 1971.
Baldassarre A. & A. Cervati (ed.). *Critica dello stato sociale.* Rome-Bari: Laterza, 1982.
Bilancia, P. *Modello economico e quadro costituzionale.* Turin: Giappichelli, 1996.
Bognetti, G. *La Costituzione economica.* Milan: Giuffrè, 1995.
Carabba, M. 'Programmazione economica'. In *Enciclopedia del diritto*, vol. XXXVI. Milan: Giuffrè, 1983.
Carli, G. *Cinquant'anni di vita italiana.* Rome-Bari: Laterza, 1996.
Cassese, S. *La nuova costituzione economica.* Rome-Bari: Laterza, 2021.
Cassetti, L. *La cultura del mercato fra interpretazioni della Costituzione e principi comunitari.* Turin: Giappichelli, 1997.
Cavaleri, P. *Iniziativa economica privata e Costituzione vivente.* Padua: Cedam, 1978.
Eds., *La costituzione economica nel quarantennale della sua approvazione.* Milan: Giuffrè, 1990.
Esposito, C. 'Gli artt. 3, 41 e 43 della Costituzione e le misure legislative in materia economica'. In *Giurisprudenza costituzionale.* Milan: Giuffrè, 1962.
Guarino, G. *Scritti di diritto pubblico dell'economia e di diritto dell'energia*, vols I and II. Milan: Giuffrè, 1962 and 1970.
Luciani, M. *La produzione economica privata nel sistema costituzionale.* Padua: Cedam, 1983.
Luciani, M. 'Economia nel diritto costituzionale'. In *Il Digesto Discipline Pubblicistiche*, 4th edn., vol. V. Turin: UTET, 1990.
Mangiameli, S. *La proprietà privata nella Costituzione.* Milan: Giuffrè, 1986.
Mazziotti, M. *Il diritto al lavoro.* Milan: Giuffrè, 1956.
Pace, A. 'Iniziativa privata e governo pubblico dell'economia'. In *Scritti in onore Tosato*, vol. II. Milan: Giuffrè, 1982.
Predieri, A. 'Collettivizzazione'. In *Enciclopedia del diritto*, vol. VII. Milan: Giuffrè, 1960.
Pugliatti, S. *La proprietà nel nuovo diritto.* Milan: Giuffrè, 1964.
Rodotà, S. *Il terribile diritto.* Bologna: il Mulino, 1981.
Rodotà, S. & G. Marramao. *Trasformazione e crisi del Welfare State.* Bari: De Donato, 1983.

Selected Bibliography

International Relations

Bruno, F. *Il Parlamento italiano e i trattati internazionali*. Milan: Giuffrè, 1997.

Cannizzaro, E. *Trattati internazionali e giudizio di costituzionalità*. Milan: Giuffrè, 1991.

Cannizzaro, E. 'Trattato internazionale (adattamento al)'. In *Enciclopedia del Diritto*, vol. XLIV. Milan: Giuffrè, 1992.

Cannone, A. 'Trattato internazionale (adattamento al)'. In *Enciclopedia del Diritto, Annali*, vol. V. Milan: Giuffrè, 2012.

D'Atena, A. 'Adattamento del diritto interno al diritto internazionale'. In *Enciclopedia Giuridica*, vol. I. Rome: Treccani, 1988.

Fabozzi, C. *L'attuazione dei trattati internazionali mediante ordine di esecuzione*. Milan: Giuffrè, 1961.

Franchini, M. *'I poteri del Governo nella conclusione di accordi internazionali'*. In *Rivista trimestrale di diritto pubblico*. Milan: Giuffrè, 1980.

Labriola, S. 'Ratifica'. *Enciclopedia giuridica italiana*. vol. XXVI. Rome: Treccani, 1991.

La Pergola, A. *Costituzione ed adattamento dell'ordinamento interno al diritto internazionale*. Milan: Giuffrè, 1961.

Lippolis, V. *La Costituzione italiana e la formazione dei trattati internazionali*. Rimini: Maggioli, 1989.

Index

The numbers here refer to paragraph numbers.

Index

Made in United States
Orlando, FL
04 November 2026

90208070R00234